Lecture Notes in Computer Science 5705

Commenced Publication in 1973
Founding and Former Series Editors:
Gerhard Goos, Juris Hartmanis, and Jan van Leeuwen

Alessandro Aldini   Gilles Barthe
Roberto Gorrieri (Eds.)

Foundations of Security Analysis and Design V

FOSAD 2007/2008/2009 Tutorial Lectures

 Springer

Volume Editors

Alessandro Aldini
Università degli Studi di Urbino "Carlo Bo"
Istituto di Scienze e Tecnologie dell'Informazione
Piazza della Repubblica 13, 61029 Urbino, Italy
E-mail: alessandro.aldini@uniurb.it

Gilles Barthe
Universidad Politécnica de Madrid
Facultad de Informatica
Fundación IMDEA Software
Campus Montegancedo, 28660 Boadilla del Monte, Madrid, Spain
E-mail: gilles.barthe@imdea.org

Roberto Gorrieri
Università degli Studi di Bologna
Dipartimento di Scienze dell'Informazione
Mura Anteo Zamboni 7, 40127 Bologna, Italy
E-mail: gorrieri@cs.unibo.it

Library of Congress Control Number: 2009932255

CR Subject Classification (1998): D.4.6, C.2, K.6.5, K.4, D.3, F.3, E.3

LNCS Sublibrary: SL 4 – Security and Cryptology

ISSN   0302-9743
ISBN-10   3-642-03828-X Springer Berlin Heidelberg New York
ISBN-13   978-3-642-03828-0 Springer Berlin Heidelberg New York

springer.com

© Springer-Verlag Berlin Heidelberg 2009
Printed in Germany

Typesetting: Camera-ready by author, data conversion by Scientific Publishing Services, Chennai, India
Printed on acid-free paper   SPIN: 12738250   06/3180   5 4 3 2 1 0

Preface

This book presents a collection of tutorial papers accompanying lectures from the last three editions of the International School on Foundations of Security Analysis and Design (FOSAD).

FOSAD has been one of the foremost educational events established with the goal of disseminating knowledge in the critical area of security in computer systems and networks. The main aim of FOSAD is to offer a good spectrum of current research in foundations of security – ranging from programming languages to analysis of protocols, from cryptographic algorithms to access control policies and trust/identity management – that can be of help for graduate students and young researchers from academia or industry who intend to approach the field. Another objective of FOSAD is to propose panels dedicated to topical open problems and to allow a selected number of participants to give presentations about their ongoing work, in order to favor discussions and novel scientific collaborations.

The topics covered in this book include cryptographic protocol analysis, program and resource certification, identity management and electronic voting, access and authorization control, wireless security, mobile code and communications security.

The opening paper presented by Santiago Escobar, Catherine Meadows, and José Meseguer gives an overview of the Maude-NRL Protocol Analyzer, a tool for the analysis of cryptographic protocols using functions that obey different equational theories. In a proof-carrying code framework, Gilles Barthe and César Kunz present a technique to build, from a certificate of the source program, a certificate for the result of its compilation. The paper by David Chadwick addresses in a survey several different topics concerning federated identity management. Bart Jacobs and Wolter Pieters discuss technical and social aspects of electronic voting systems, by presenting as a case study the system implemented in practice in The Netherlands. The paper by Martín Abadi provides an overview of the role of logic in access control, by covering logical foundations for access control and their applications in languages for security policies. Sebastian Mödersheim and Luca Viganò introduce the open-source fixed-point model checker OFMC for symbolic cryptographic protocol analysis. Rustan Leino, Peter Müller, and Jan Smans describe a verifier for concurrent programs called Chalice, whose methodology centers around permissions and permission transfer. Frédéric Besson, David Cachera, Thomas Jensen and David Pichardie propose a tutorial on building analyzers using the Coq proof assistant. In particular, they propose an interval analysis for the static verification of the absence of array-out-of-bounds accesses. Elvira Albert, Puri Arenas, Samir Genaim, Germán Puebla, and Damiano Zanardini present the COSTA system, a state-of-the-art analyzer that automatically generates precise resource usage information for a large class of Java programs. In the last paper, Javier Lopez, Rodrigo Roman, and Cristina Alcaraz analyze how different requirements of sensor networks can influence the security mechanisms.

We would like to thank all the institutions that have promoted and founded FOSAD in the last few years. In particular, we are grateful to the IFIP Working Group 1.7 on "Theoretical Foundations of Security Analysis and Design," which was established to promote research and education in security-related issues. Among the sponsors, we would like to mention CNR-IIT, Department of the Navy Grant N00014-08-1-1109 issued by Office of Naval Research Global, EU projects SENSORIA and MOBIUS, International Workshop on Views On Designing Complex Architectures (VODCA), and Università di Bologna. Every year, FOSAD is supported by EATCS-IT, EEF, and ERCIM Working Group on Security and Trust Management.

Finally, we also wish to thank the entire staff of the University Residential Centre of Bertinoro for the organizational and administrative support.

June 2009   Alessandro Aldini
                                                                        Gilles Barthe
                                                                     Roberto Gorrieri

Table of Contents

Maude-NPA: Cryptographic Protocol Analysis Modulo Equational Properties

Santiago Escobar[1], Catherine Meadows[2], and José Meseguer[2]

[1] Universidad Politécnica de Valencia, Spain
sescobar@dsic.upv.es
[2] Naval Research Laboratory, Washington, DC, USA
meadows@itd.nrl.navy.mil
[3] University of Illinois at Urbana-Champaign, USA
meseguer@cs.uiuc.edu

Abstract. In this tutorial, we give an overview of the Maude-NRL Protocol Analyzer (Maude-NPA), a tool for the analysis of cryptographic protocols using functions that obey different equational theories. We show the reader how to use Maude-NPA, and how it works, and also give some of the theoretical background behind the tool.

1 Introduction

The Maude-NPA is a tool and inference system for reasoning about the security of cryptographic protocols in which the cryptosystems satisfy different equational properties. The tool handles searches in the unbounded session model, and thus can be used to provide proofs of security as well as to search for attacks. It is the next generation of the NRL Protocol Analyzer [36], a tool that supported limited equational reasoning and was successfully applied to the analysis of many different protocols.

The area of formal analysis of cryptographic protocols has been an active one since the mid 1980's. The idea is to verify protocols that use encryption to guarantee secrecy, and that use authentication of data to ensure security, against an attacker (commonly called the *Dolev-Yao* attacker [17]) who has complete control of the network, and can intercept, alter, and redirect traffic, create new traffic on his/her own, perform all operations available to legitimate participants, and may have access to some subset of the longterm keys of legitimate principals. Whatever approach is taken, the use of formal methods has had a long history, not only for providing formal proofs of security, but also for uncovering bugs and security flaws that in some cases had remained unknown long after the original protocol's publication.

A number of approaches have been taken to the formal verification of cryptographic protocols. One of the most popular is model checking, in which the interaction of the protocol with the attacker is symbolically executed. Indeed, model-checking of secrecy (and later, authentication) in protocols in the bounded-session model (where a *session* is a single execution of a process representing an

A. Aldini, G. Barthe, R. Gorrieri (Eds.): FOSAD 2007/2008/2009, LNCS 5705, pp. 1–50, 2009.

honest principal) has been shown to be decidable [42], and a number of bounded-session model checkers exist. Moreover, a number of unbounded model checkers either make use of abstraction to enforce decidability, or allow for the possibility of non-termination.

The earliest protocol analysis tools, such as the Interrogator [30] and the NRL Protocol Analyzer (NPA) [35], while not strictly speaking model checkers, relied on state exploration, and, in the case of NPA, could be used to verify security properties specified in a temporal logic language. Later, researchers used generic model checkers to analyze protocols, such as FDR [32] and later Murphi [40]. More recently the focus has been on special-purpose model-checkers developed specifically for cryptographic protocol analysis, such as Blanchet's ProVerif [8], the AVISPA tool [3], and Maude-NPA itself [23].

There are a number of possible approaches to take in the modeling of cryptoalgorithms used. In the simplest case, the free algebra model, cryptosystems are assumed to behave like black boxes: an attacker knows nothing about encrypted data unless it has the appropriate key. This is the approach taken, for example, by the above-cited use of Murphi and FDR to analyze cryptographic protocols, and current tools such as SATMC [4] and TA4SP [9] , both used in the AVISPA tool. However, such an approach, although it can work well for protocols based on generic shared key or public key cryptography, runs into problems with algorithms such as Diffie-Hellman or algorithms employing exclusive-or, which rely upon various algebraic properties such as the law of exponentiation of products, associativity-commutativity and cancellation. Without the ability to specify these properties, one needs to rely on approximations of the algorithms that may result in formal proofs of secrecy invalidated by actual attacks that are missed by the analysis (see, e.g., [41, 43, 46]). Thus there has been considerable interest in developing algorithms and tools for protocol analysis in the presence of algebraic theories [1, 7, 10, 11, 12].

Another way in which tools can differ is in the number of sessions. A *session* is defined to be one execution of a protocol role by a single principal. A tool is said to use the *bounded session model* if the user must specify the maximum number of sessions that can be generated in a search. It is said to use the *unbounded session model* if no such restrictions are required.

Secrecy is known to be decidable in the free theory together with the bounded session model [42], and undecidable in the free theory together with the unbounded session model [18]. The same distinction between bounded and unbounded sessions is known to hold for a number of different equational theories of interest, as well as for some authentication-related properties; see for example [10]. Thus, it is no surprise that most tools, whether or not they offer support for different algebraic theories, either operate in the bounded session model, or rely on abstractions that may result in reports of false attacks even when the protocol being analyzed is secure.

Maude-NPA is a model-checker for cryptographic protocol analysis that both allows for the incorporation of different equational theories and operates in the unbounded session model without the use of abstraction. This means that the analysis is *exact*. That is, (i) if an attack exists using the specified algebraic properties, it will be found; (ii) no false attacks will be reported; and (iii) if the tool terminates without finding an attack, this provides a *formal proof* that the protocol is secure for that attack modulo the specified properties. However, it is always possible that the tool will not terminate; although, as explained in Section 7, a number of heuristics are included to drastically reduce the search space and make nontermination less likely. In order to have a steady, incremental approximation of the analysis, the user is also given the option of restricting the number of steps executed by Maude-NPA.

Maude-NPA is a backwards search tool, i.e., it searches backwards from a final insecure state to determine whether or not it is reachable from an initial state. This backwards search is *symbolic*, i.e., it does not start with a *concrete* attack state, but uses instead a symbolic *attack pattern*, i.e., a term with logical variables describing a general attack situation. The backwards search is then performed by *backwards narrowing*. Each backwards narrowing step denotes a state transition, such as a principal sending or receiving a message or the intruder manipulating a message, all in a backwards sense. Each backwards narrowing step takes a symbolic state (i.e., a term with logical variables) and returns a previous symbolic state in the protocol (again a term with logical variables). In performing a backwards narrowing step, the variables of the input term are appropriately instantiated in order to apply the concrete state transition, and the new previous state may contain new variables that are differentiated from any previously used variable to avoid confusion. To appropriately instantiate the input term, narrowing uses *equational unification*. As it is well-known from logic programming and automated deduction (see, e.g., [5]), unification is the process of solving equations $t = t'$. Standard unification solves these equations in a term algebra. Instead, *equational unification* (w.r.t. an equational theory E) solves an equation $t = t'$ in a free algebra for the equations E, that is, *modulo* the equational theory E. In the Maude-NPA, the equational theory E used depends on the protocol, and corresponds to the algebraic properties of the cryptographic functions (e.g. cancellation of encryption and decryption, Diffie-Hellman, or exclusive-or).

Sound techniques for equational unification are paramount to Maude-NPA, and much of the research behind it has concentrated on that. The idea is to develop, not only special–purpose equational unification techniques that can be used for specific theories, but general methods that can be extended to different theories that arise in actual practice. We thus consider a broad class of theories that incorporate those equational axioms commonly appearing in cryptosystems and for which Maude has dedicated unification algorithms [13], such as commutativity (C) or associativity-commutativity (AC) of some function symbols [19]. Our approach is designed to be as extensible as possible to different algebraic theories, and Maude-NPA is designed with this in mind. Maude-NPA has thus both dedicated and generic narrowing-based methods for solving unification problems in such theories [27], which under appropriate checkable conditions yield narrowing-based unification algorithms with a finite number of solutions

[26]. Maude-NPA currently supports a number of algebraic theories, including exclusive-or, cancellation of encryption and decryption (both public and shared key), bounded associativity, and Diffie-Hellman exponentiation. We include examples of several of these in this tutorial; others can be found in the Maude-NPA manual [23] and in our previous papers [19, 21]. Moreover, we continue to explore new generic unification algorithms which we plan to incorporate into Maude-NPA in the future.

Since Maude-NPA allows reasoning in the unbounded session model, and because it allows reasoning about different equational theories (which typically generate many more solutions to unification problems than syntactic unification, leading to bigger state spaces), it is necessary to find ways of pruning the search space in order to prevent infinite or overwhelmingly large search spaces. A key technique for preventing infinite searches is the generation of *formal grammars* describing terms unreachable by the intruder; such formal grammars are described in [20, 36] and in Section 7.7. However, grammars do not prune out all infinite searches, and there is a need for other techniques. Moreover, even when a search space is finite it may still be necessary to reduce it to a manageable size. State space reduction techniques for doing that have been provided in [22], with an empirical average state-space size reduction of 96% (i.e., the average size of the reduced state space is 4% of that of the original one). Furthermore, our often combined techniques are effective in obtaining a *finite* state space for all protocol analyses in many of our experiments.

The rest of this tutorial is organized as follows. Section 2 gives definitions of some of the terminology that is used throughout this tutorial; we have tried to reduce definitions to a minimum and to illustrate each definition by means of examples. Sections 3 and 4 explain the basic mechanics of using Maude-NPA, including writing specifications and formulating queries. It gives the minimum amount of background needed for using the tool. Sections 5 and 6 describe how Maude-NPA actually works. They are intended for two types of readers: first the reader who wants to get better insight into how to use the tool to best advantage, and secondly for the reader who wants to understand the basic concepts behind Maude-NPA, without necessarily using the tool. Section 7, on state space reduction, is somewhat more specialized. It is intended for someone who is interested in the design of crypto protocol analysis tools and wants a more complete picture of the techniques Maude-NPA uses or plans to use, but is not really necessary to read it in order to be able to use the tool. Section 8 concludes the tutorial.

Maude-NPA is publicly available[1], including a user manual and some protocol examples. Maude-NPA is written in Maude, which is a publicly available[2] implementation of rewriting logic. To be more specific, Maude-NPA requires a version of Maude that includes the implementation of order-sorted unification modulo commutativity and associativity–commutativity [13], e.g., version 2.4 or later.

---

[1] At http://maude.cs.uiuc.edu/tools/Maude-NPA
[2] At http://maude.cs.uiuc.edu

2   Preliminaries

We follow the classical notation and terminology from [47] for term rewriting and from [37, 38] for rewriting logic and order-sorted notions. We assume an *order-sorted signature* Σ with a finite poset of sorts $(S, \leq)$ and a finite number of function symbols. For example, consider a signature with sorts Msg, Encryption, Concatenation, Nonce, Fresh, and Name that satisfy the following subsort order between sorts:

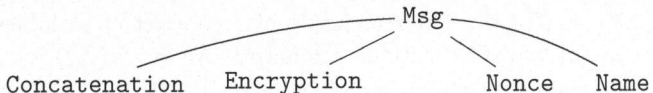

and function symbols pk (for "public" key encryption), sk (for "secret" or "private" key encryption), n (for nonces), and _;_ (for concatenation) that satisfy the following sort declarations[3]:

pk : Name × Msg → Encryption   n : Name × Fresh → Nonce
sk : Name × Msg → Encryption   _;_ : Msg × Msg → Concatenation

We assume an S-sorted family $\mathcal{X} = \{\mathcal{X}_s\}_{s \in S}$ of disjoint variable sets with each $\mathcal{X}_s$ countably infinite. $\mathcal{T}_\Sigma(\mathcal{X})_s$ is the set of terms of sort s, and $\mathcal{T}_{\Sigma,s}$ is the set of ground terms (i.e., without variables) of sort s. We write $\mathcal{T}_\Sigma(\mathcal{X})$ and $\mathcal{T}_\Sigma$ for the corresponding term algebras. We write $Var(t)$ for the set of variables present in a term t.

A term is viewed as a tree labeled with function symbols, where the arity of a symbol coincides with the number of its children in the tree (and the sort declaration for the symbol is satisfied by its children). For example, the term[4] $t = n(a,r) ; (n(b,r') ; n(b,r''))$, where a, b, and c are symbols with arity 0 (called constants) of sort Name and r, r', and r'' are variables of sort Fresh, is a term of sort Concatenation and has the following tree representation

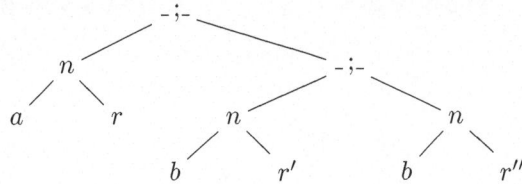

A position p of a term t is described by a string of natural numbers that specifies a path from the root of the term to the desired subterm position. For

---

[3] Note that Maude allows function declarations of symbols with a user-defined syntax, where each underscore denotes the position of one function argument, e.g. "_;_" denotes a symbol ; with two arguments written in an infix notation.

[4] For a Maude term with symbols that contain underscores, a blank space must appear between the subterm corresponding to an underscore and any other part of the term, e.g. "n(a,r) ; n(b,r')".

example, in the term t above, position $p_1 = 1.1$ identifies the subterm a, and positions $p_2 = 2.1.1$ and $p_3 = 2.2.1$ both identify the subterm b, although different occurrences of it. The set of positions of a term t is written $Pos(t)$. The set of non-variable positions of a term t is written $Pos_\Sigma(t)$. The root of a term is Λ. The subterm of t at position p is $t|_p$, and $t[u]_p$ is the result of replacing $t|_p$ by u in t. For example, we have $t|_{p_1} = a$ and $t|_{p_2} = t|_{p_3} = b$.

A *substitution* σ is a sort-preserving mapping from a finite subset of $\mathcal{X}$ to $\mathcal{T}_\Sigma(\mathcal{X})$. The application of substitution σ to term t is denoted $\sigma(t)$. The identity substitution is *id*. Substitutions are naturally extended to homomorphic functions $\sigma : \mathcal{T}_\Sigma(\mathcal{X}) \to \mathcal{T}_\Sigma(\mathcal{X})$. The restriction of σ to a set of variables V is $\sigma|_V$. The composition of two substitutions σ, θ is $(\sigma\theta)(X) = \theta(\sigma(X))$ for $X \in \mathcal{X}$.

A Σ-*equation* is an unoriented pair of terms (t, t'), written $t = t'$, where $t, t' \in \mathcal{T}_\Sigma(\mathcal{X})_\mathsf{s}$ for some sort $\mathsf{s} \in \mathsf{S}$. Given Σ and a set E of Σ-equations such that $\mathcal{T}_{\Sigma,\mathsf{s}} \neq \emptyset$ for every sort s, order-sorted equational logic induces a congruence relation $=_E$ on terms $t, t' \in \mathcal{T}_\Sigma(\mathcal{X})$ (see [38]). Throughout this tutorial we assume that $\mathcal{T}_{\Sigma,\mathsf{s}} \neq \emptyset$ for every sort s. The E-*subsumption* order on terms $\mathcal{T}_\Sigma(\mathcal{X})_\mathsf{s}$, written $t \preccurlyeq_E t'$ (meaning that t' is more general than t), holds if there exists a substitution σ such that $t =_E \sigma(t')$. The order on terms $\mathcal{T}_\Sigma(\mathcal{X})_\mathsf{s}$ is naturally extended to substitutions, i.e., $\sigma \preccurlyeq_E \sigma'$ iff there exists a substitution θ such that $\sigma =_E \sigma'\theta$.

An E-*unifier* for a Σ-equation $t = t'$ is a substitution σ s.t. $\sigma(t) =_E \sigma(t')$. Given two E-unifiers σ_1 and σ_2 for a Σ-equation $t = t'$, σ_2 is more general than σ_1, written $\sigma_1 \preccurlyeq_E \sigma_2$, if there exists τ such that $\sigma_2\tau =_E \sigma_1$, i.e., for each variable X, $(\sigma_2\tau)(X) =_E \sigma_1(X)$. A *complete* set of E-unifiers of an equation $t = t'$, written $CSU_E(t = t')$, is a set of unifiers of $t = t'$ such that for each E-unifier σ of $t = t'$, there exists $\tau \in CSU_E(t = t')$ such that $\sigma \preccurlyeq_E \tau$. We say that $CSU_E(t = t')$ is *finitary* if it contains a finite number of E-unifiers. We say that $CSU_E(t = t')$ is *the set of most general unifiers* if each unifier $\tau \in CSU_E(t = t')$ is maximal among all unifiers of $t = t'$ w.r.t. $\preccurlyeq_E$. For example, consider an infix symbol $\_*\_ : \mathtt{Msg} \times \mathtt{Msg} \to \mathtt{Msg}$ satisfying the following associativity and commutativity (AC) equational properties (where X, Y, Z are variables of sort $\mathtt{Msg}$):

$$X * Y = Y * X \qquad X * (Y * Z) = (X * Y) * Z$$

A complete set of most general AC-unifiers of the two terms $t = X * Y$ and $s = U * V$ (where X, Y, U, V are variables of sort $\mathtt{Msg}$) is

$$
\begin{aligned}
\sigma_1 &= \{\, X \mapsto X', & Y &\mapsto Y', & U &\mapsto X', & V &\mapsto Y' & \} \\
\sigma_2 &= \{\, X \mapsto X', & Y &\mapsto Y', & U &\mapsto Y', & V &\mapsto X' & \} \\
\sigma_3 &= \{\, X \mapsto X', & Y &\mapsto Y' * Y'', & U &\mapsto X' * Y'', & V &\mapsto Y' & \} \\
\sigma_4 &= \{\, X \mapsto X', & Y &\mapsto Y' * Y'', & U &\mapsto Y'', & V &\mapsto X' * Y' & \} \\
\sigma_5 &= \{\, X \mapsto X' * X'', & Y &\mapsto Y', & U &\mapsto X'', & V &\mapsto X' * Y' & \} \\
\sigma_6 &= \{\, X \mapsto X' * X'', & Y &\mapsto Y', & U &\mapsto X'' * Y', & V &\mapsto X' & \} \\
\sigma_7 &= \{\, X \mapsto X' * X'', & Y &\mapsto Y' * Y'', & U &\mapsto X'' * Y'', & V &\mapsto X' * Y' & \}
\end{aligned}
$$

Consider now the exclusive-or symbol $\_ \oplus \_ : \mathtt{Msg} \times \mathtt{Msg} \to \mathtt{Msg}$ and the constant $0 : \mathtt{Msg}$ satisfying the following xor-properties (where X, Y, Z are variables of sort $\mathtt{Msg}$):

$$X \oplus Y = Y \oplus X \qquad\qquad X \oplus X = 0$$
$$X \oplus (Y \oplus Z) = (X \oplus Y) \oplus Z \qquad X \oplus 0 = X$$

A complete set of most general xor-unifiers of the two terms $t = X \oplus Y$ and $s = U \oplus V$ (where X, Y, U, V are variables of sort Msg) is the unique unifier $\theta_1 = \{X \mapsto Y' \oplus U' \oplus V', Y \mapsto Y', U \mapsto U', V \mapsto V'\}$.

3 Protocol Specification in Maude-NPA

In this section, we describe how to specify a protocol and all its relevant items in the Maude-NPA. We postpone until Section 4 the topic of formal protocol analysis in the Maude-NPA.

3.1 Templates and File Organization for Protocol Specification

Protocol specifications are given in a single file (e.g., foo.maude), and consist of three Maude modules, having a fixed format and fixed module names. In the first module, the *syntax* of the protocol is specified, consisting of sorts, subsorts, and operators. The second module specifies the *algebraic properties* of the operators. Note that algebraic properties *cannot be arbitrary* and must satisfy some specific conditions described in Section 6.3. The third module specifies the *actual behavior of the protocol* using a strand-theoretic notation [28]. This third module includes the intruder strands (Dolev-Yao strands) and regular strands describing the behavior of principals. *Attack states*, describing behavior that we want to prove cannot occur, are also specified in this third module, but we postpone their presentation until Section 4.

We give a template for any Maude-NPA specification below. Throughout, lines beginning with three or more dashes (i.e., ---) or three or more asterisks (i.e., ***) are comments that are ignored by Maude. Furthermore, the Maude syntax is almost self-explanatory [14]. The general point is that each syntactic element –e.g. a sort, an operation, an equation, a rule– is declared with an obvious keyword: sort, op, eq, rl, etc., ended by a space and a period.

```
fmod PROTOCOL-EXAMPLE-SYMBOLS is
  protecting DEFINITION-PROTOCOL-RULES .
  ------------------------------------------------------------
  --- Overwrite this module with the syntax of your protocol.
  --- Notes:
  --- * Sorts Msg and Fresh are special and imported
  --- * Every sort must be a subsort of Msg
  --- * No sort can be a supersort of Msg
  --- * Variables of sort Fresh are really fresh
  ---    and no substitution is allowed on them
  --- * Sorts Msg and Public cannot be empty
  ------------------------------------------------------------
endfm
```

```
fmod PROTOCOL-EXAMPLE-ALGEBRAIC is
  protecting PROTOCOL-EXAMPLE-SYMBOLS .
  -----------------------------------------------------------------
  --- Overwrite this module with the algebraic properties
  --- of your protocol.
  --- * Use only equations of the form (eq Lhs = Rhs [nonexec] .)
  --- * Maude attribute owise cannot be used
  --- * There is no order of application between equations
  -----------------------------------------------------------------
endfm

fmod PROTOCOL-SPECIFICATION is
  protecting PROTOCOL-EXAMPLE-SYMBOLS .
  protecting DEFINITION-PROTOCOL-RULES .
  protecting DEFINITION-CONSTRAINTS-INPUT .


  ----------------------------------------------------------
  --- Overwrite this module with the strands
  --- of your protocol and the attack states
  ----------------------------------------------------------

  eq STRANDS-DOLEVYAO =
      --- Add Dolev-Yao intruder strands here. Strands are
      --- properly renamed.
  [nonexec] .

  eq STRANDS-PROTOCOL =
      --- Add protocol strands here. Strands are properly renamed.
  [nonexec] .

  eq ATTACK-STATE(0) =
      --- Add attack state here
      --- More than one attack state can be specified, but each
      --- must be identified by a number (e.g. ATTACK-STATE(1) = ...
      --- ATTACK-STATE(2) = ... etc.)
  [nonexec] .
endfm

--- THE FOLLOWING COMMAND HAS TO BE THE LAST ACTION !!!!

select MAUDE-NPA .
```

In what follows we explain in detail how each of these three modules, comprising a Maude-NPA protocol specification, are specified.

3.2   Specifying the Protocol Syntax

The protocol syntax is specified in the module PROTOCOL-EXAMPLE-SYMBOLS. Note that, since we are using Maude also as the specification language, each declaration has to be ended by a space and a period.

We begin by specifying *sorts*. In general, sorts are used to specify different types of data, that are used for different purposes. We have a special sort called Msg that represents the messages in our protocol. If only keys can be used for encryption, we would want to have a sort Key, and specify that an encryption operator e can only take a term of sort Key as its first argument, which can be specified in Maude as follows:

```
op e : Key Msg -> Msg .
```

Sorts can also be *subsorts* of other sorts. Subsorts allow a more refined distinction of data within a concrete sort. For example, we might have a sort MasterKey which is a subsort of Key. Or two sorts PublicKey and PrivateKey that are subsorts of Key. These two relevant subsort relations can be specified in Maude as follows:

```
subsort MasterKey < Key .
subsorts PublicKey PrivateKey < Key .
```

Most sorts are user-defined. However, there are several special sorts that are automatically imported by any Maude-NPA protocol definition through the DEFINITION-PROTOCOL-RULES module. The user must make sure that certain constraints are satisfied for the sorts and subsorts specified in PROTOCOL-EXAMPLE-SYMBOLS, which are the following:

Msg. Every sort specified in a protocol must be *connected* to the sort Msg, i.e., for every sort S given by the user, and every term t of sort S, there must be a term t' in Msg and a position p in t' such that $t'|_p = t$. Any subsort of Msg is of course directly connected to Msg. No sort defined by the user can be a supersort of Msg. The sort Msg should not be empty, i.e., there should be enough function symbols and constants such that there is at least one ground term (i.e., a term without variables) of sort Msg.

Fresh. The sort Fresh is used to identify terms that must be unique. No sort can be a subsort of Fresh. It is typically used in protocol specifications as an argument of some data that must be unique, such as a nonce, or a session key, e.g., "n(A,r)" or "k(A,B,r)", where r is a variable of sort Fresh. It is not necessary to define symbols of sort Fresh, i.e., the sort Fresh can be empty, since only variables of such sort will be allowed.

Public. The sort Public is used to identify terms that are publicly available, and therefore assumed known by the intruder. No sort can be a supersort of Public. This sort cannot be empty.

To illustrate the definition of sorts, we use the Needham-Schroeder Public Key Protocol (NSPK) as the running example. This protocol uses public key cryptography, and the principals exchange encrypted data consisting of names and nonces. We recall the informal specification of NSPK as follows:

1. $A \to B : pk(B, A; N_A)$
2. $B \to A : pk(A, N_A; N_B)$
3. $A \to B : pk(B, N_B)$

where N_A and N_B are nonces generated by the respective principals.

Thus, we will define sorts to distinguish names, keys, nonces, and encrypted data. This is specified as follows:

```
--- Sort Information
sorts Name Nonce Enc .
subsort Name Nonce Enc < Msg .
subsort Name < Public .
```

The sorts Nonce and Enc are not strictly necessary, but they can make the search more efficient, since Maude-NPA will not attempt to unify terms with incompatible sorts. For example, if in this specification a principal is expecting a term of sort Enc, he/she will not accept a term of sort Nonce; technically because Nonce is not declared as a subsort of Enc. If we are looking for type confusion attacks, we would not want to include these sorts, and instead would declare everything as having sort Msg or Name. See Section 3.3 for details on type confusion attacks.

We can now specify the different operators needed in NSPK. These are pk and sk, for public and private key encryption, the operator n for nonces, designated constants for the names of the principals, and concatenation using the infix operator "_;_".

We begin with the public/private encryption operators.

```
--- Encoding operators for public/private encryption
op pk : Name Msg -> Enc [frozen] .
op sk : Name Msg -> Enc [frozen] .
```

The frozen attribute is technically necessary to tell Maude not to attempt to apply rewrites in arguments of those symbols. The frozen attribute *must be included in all operator declarations in Maude-NPA specifications*, excluding constants. The use of sort Name as an argument of public key encryption may seem odd at first. But it is used because we are implicitly associating a public key with a name when we apply the pk operator, and a private key with a name when we apply the sk operator. A different syntax specifying explicit keys could have been chosen for public/private encryption.

Next we specify some principal names. For NSPK, we have three constants of sort Name, a (for "Alice"), b (for "Bob"), and i (for the "Intruder").

```
--- Principals
op a : -> Name . --- Alice
op b : -> Name . --- Bob
op i : -> Name . --- Intruder
```

These are not all the possible principal names. Since Maude-NPA is an unbounded session tool, the number of possible principals is unbounded. This is achieved by using variables (i.e., variables of sort Name in this specification of NSPK) instead of constants. However, we may have a need to specify constant principal names in a goal state. For example, if we have an initiator and a responder, and we are not interested in the case in which the initiator and the responder are the same, we can prevent that by specifying the names of the initiator and the responder as different constants. Also, we may want to identify the intruder's name by a constant, so that we can cover the case in which principals are talking directly to the intruder.

We now need two more operators, one for nonces, and one for concatenation. The nonce operator is specified as follows.

```
--- Nonce operator
op n : Name Fresh -> Nonce [frozen] .
```

Note that the nonce operator has an argument of sort Fresh to ensure uniqueness. The argument of type Name is not strictly necessary, but it provides a convenient way of identifying which nonces are generated by which principal. This makes searches more efficient, since it allows us to keep track of the originator of a nonce throughout a search.

Finally, we come to the message concatenation operator. In Maude-NPA, we specify concatenation via an infix operator "_;_" defined as follows:

```
--- Concatenation operator
op _;_ : Msg  Msg  -> Msg [gather (e E) frozen] .
```

The Maude operator attribute "gather (e E)" indicates that symbol "_;_" has to be parsed as associated to the left; whereas "gather (E e)" indicates association to the right (see [14, Section 3.9]). Note that this *gather* information is specified *only for parsing purposes*: it does *not* specify an associativity property, although the associativity of an operator is certainly expressible in Maude either as an explicit "equational rule", or as an "equational axiom" as explained in Section 3.4 below. Therefore, _;_ in this NSPK example is just a *free* function symbol, which, when no parenthesis are added, is *parsed* in a left–associative way.

3.3   User-Defined Subsorts of Sort Msg in Protocol Specification

The Maude-NPA tool always assumes that the sort Msg is the top sort, but it allows user-defined subsorts of Msg that can be specified by the user for a more accurate protocol specification and analysis. However, protocol modeling in Maude-NPA should pay careful attention to when and why a subsort of sort Msg can be used, since an overly general specification using sort Msg will negatively affect performance, whereas a too restrictive specification may jeopardize finding some attacks, since some attacks possible in a less restrictive specification may become excluded by using some subsort in the reception of a message.

The two relevant concepts here are: (i) whether a principal can check the sort of a bit string and (ii) whether a principal can check the structure of a term to find out if it matches some given pattern. In general, data received by a principal for which the principal cannot check its structure, but can check its sort, must be represented by a variable of the appropriate sort. For example, if a principal receives a message that he/she expects to be a nonce but he/she cannot check that is has sort Nonce, then such a message will be represented by a variable of sort Msg.

Sometimes, even though we do not assume that type-checking is possible, we may want to use sorts to limit the size of the search space. How this can be done, and the ramifications of doing this, are discussed later in this tutorial.

Therefore, if we are interested in a type confusion attack for a given informal protocol specification, we would like a protocol specification in Mauge-NPA that makes no distinctions on messages, i.e., principals cannot perform type checking of messages (for instance, may not be able to detect whether a string of bits is a nonce) and may not even be able to separate messages into their different components. In this very general case, we are interested in a unsorted protocol, i.e., there will be no extra sorts and every symbol will be of sort Msg. See [21] for an example of a type confusion attack specified in Maude-NPA.

A third relevant concept here is the use of variables of sort Fresh. Every variable of sort Fresh denotes an unguessable message. Those variables of sort Fresh that a principal generates have to be explicitly written in the protocol specification (see Section 3.6). Therefore, every nonce that a principal generates is represented by a message containing a variable of sort Fresh, e.g. $n(A, r)$, with r a variable of sort Fresh. If a principal is expecting this nonce again, it will be represented in the protocol specification by the same term $n(A, r)$, meaning that the principal can check the sort of the message and can also check the structure of the message. This is safe because typically a principal can verify whether two nonces are the same, i.e., whether the sequences of their bits coincide. If a principal is expecting a nonce different from one of his/her nonces, it will be represented in the protocol specification by a variable N of sort Nonce or of sort Msg, depending on the type checking facilities available to the principal.

3.4   Algebraic Properties

There are two types of algebraic properties: (i) *equational axioms*, such as commutativity, or associativity-commutativity, called *axioms*, and (ii) *equational rules*, called *equations*. Equations are specified in the PROTOCOL-EXAMPLE-ALGEBRAIC module, whereas axioms are specified within the operator declarations in the PROTOCOL-EXAMPLE-SYMBOLS module, as illustrated in what follows.

An equation is oriented into a rewrite rule in which the left–hand side of the equation is *reduced* to the right–hand side. In writing equations, one needs to specify the variables involved, and their type. Variables can be specified globally for a module, e.g., "var Z : Msg .", or locally within the expression using it, e.g., a variable A of sort Name in "pk(A:Name,Z)". Several variables of the same sort can be specified together, as "vars X Y Z1 Z2 : Msg .". In NSPK, we use two equations specifying the relationship between public and private key encryption, as follows:

```
var Z : Msg .
var A : Name .


--- Encryption/Decryption Cancellation
eq pk(A,sk(A,Z)) = Z [nonexec] .
eq sk(A,pk(A,Z)) = Z [nonexec] .
```

The `nonexec` attribute is technically necessary to tell Maude not to use an equation or rule within its standard execution, since it will be used only at the Maude-NPA level rather than at the Maude level. The `nonexec` attribute *must be included in all user-defined equation declarations of the protocol.* Furthermore, the Maude attribute `owise` (i.e., otherwise) *cannot be used* in equations, since no order of application is assumed for the algebraic equations.

Since Maude-NPA uses built-in unification algorithms [13] for the case of operators having either no equational axioms, or the commutative (C) or associative-commutative (AC) equational axioms, these are specified not as standard equations but as *axioms* in the operator declarations. For example, suppose that we want to specify exclusive-or. We can specify an infix associative-commutative operator "`<+>`" in the `PROTOCOL-EXAMPLE-SYMBOLS` module as follows:

```
--- XOR operator and equational axioms
op _<+>_ : Msg Msg -> Msg [frozen assoc comm] .
op null : -> Msg .
```

where the *associativity and commutativity* axioms are declared as attributes of the `<+>` operator with the `assoc` and `comm` keywords. Similarly, we could specify an operator that is commutative but not associative with the `comm` keyword alone.[5]

We specify the equational rules for `<+>` in the `PROTOCOL-EXAMPLE-ALGEBRAIC` module as equations declared with the `eq` keyword as follows[6]:

```
vars X Y : Msg .

--- XOR equational rules
eq X <+> X <+> Y = Y [nonexec]   .
eq X <+> X = null [nonexec]   .
eq X <+> null = X [nonexec]   .
```

If we want to include a Diffie-Hellman mechanism, we need two operations. One is exponentiation, and the other is modular multiplication. Since Diffie-Hellman is a commonly used algorithm in cryptographic protocols, we discuss it also here.

We begin by including several new sorts in `PROTOCOL-EXAMPLE-SYMBOLS`: `Gen`, `Exp`, `GenvExp`, and `NeNonceSet`.

---

[5] In Maude, it is possible to specify and operator that is associative but not commutative using the `assoc` keyword, but in the Maude-NPA, symbols having the *assoc* but not the *comm* attribute *should not be specified*. The reason for this is that associative unification is not finitary (see, e.g., [5]) and is not supported in Maude. Various forms of *bounded* associativity with finitary unification are possible, but this is done differently, namely, by specifying bounded associativity with rules, see [21] for details.

[6] Note that the first equational rule, i.e., X <+> X <+> Y = Y, is not essentially needed for the exclusive-or theory, but it is necessary for rewriting purposes to ensure coherence, see Section 6.2.

```
sorts Name Nonce NeNonceSet Gen Exp Key GenvExp Enc Secret .
subsorts Gen Exp < GenvExp .
subsorts Name NeNonceSet GenvExp Enc Secret Key < Msg .
subsort Exp < Key .
subsort Nonce < NeNonceSet .
subsorts Name Gen < Public .
```

We now introduce three new operators. The first, g, is a constant that serves as the Diffie-Hellman *generator* of the multiplicative group. The second is exponentiation, and the third is an associative-commutative multiplication operation on nonces and products of such nonces.

```
op g : -> Gen .
op exp : GenvExp NeNonceSet -> Exp [frozen] .
op _*_ : NeNonceSet NeNonceSet -> NeNonceSet [frozen assoc comm] .
```

We then include the following equational property, to capture the fact that $z^{x^y} = z^{x*y}$:

```
eq exp(exp(W:Gen,Y:NeNonceSet),Z:NeNonceSet)
 = exp(W:Gen, Y:NeNonceSet * Z:NeNonceSet) [nonexec] .
```

There are several things to note about this Diffie-Hellman specification. The first is that, although modular multiplication has a unit and inverses, this is not included in our equational specification. Instead, we have only included the key algebraic rule that is necessary for Diffie-Hellman to work. The second is that we have specified types that will rule out certain kinds of intruder behavior. In actual fact, there is nothing that prevents an intruder from sending an arbitrary string to a principal and passing it off as an exponentiated term. The principal will then exponentiate that term. However, given our definition of the exp operator, only terms of type GenvExp can be exponentiated. This last restriction is necessary in order to ensure that the unification algorithm is finitary; see Section 6.3 for technical details. The omission of units and inverses is not necessary to ensure finitary unification, but rules out behavior of the intruder that is likely to be irrelevant for attacking the protocol, or that is likely to be easily detected (such as the intruder sending an exp(g,0)).

We note that if one is interested in obtaining a proof of security using these restrictive assumptions, one must provide a proof (outside of the tool) that security in the restricted model implies security in the more general model. This could be done along the lines of the proofs in [33, 34, 39].

3.5 Protocol Specification: Intruder Strands

The protocol itself and the intruder capabilities are both specified in the PROTOCOL- SPECIFICATION module. They are specified using strands. A *strand*, first defined in [28], is a sequence of positive and negative messages[7] describing

---

[7] We write $m^{\pm}$ to denote m^+ or m^-, indistinctively. We often write $+(m)$ and $-(m)$ instead of m^+ and m^-, respectively.

a principal executing a protocol, or the intruder performing actions, e.g., the strand for Alice in NSPK is:

$$[\ pk(K_B,\ A; N_A)^+,\ pk(K_A, N_A; Z)^-,\ pk(K_B, Z)^+\ ]$$

where a positive node implies sending, and a negative node implies receiving. However, in our tool each strand is divided into the past and future parts by means of a vertical line. That is, the messages to the left of the vertical line were sent or received in the past, whereas the messages to the right of the line will be sent or received in the future. Also, we keep track of all the variables of sort Fresh generated by a concrete strand; see Section 5.2 for technical details. That is, all the variables $r_1, \ldots, r_j$ of sort Fresh generated by a strand are made explicit right before the strand, as follows:

$$:: r_1, \ldots, r_j :: [\ m_1^{\pm},\ \ldots,\ m_i^{\pm}\ |\ m_{i+1}^{\pm},\ \ldots,\ m_k^{\pm}\ ]$$

Note that there is some difference between the variables of sort Fresh generated in a strand and those appearing in a strand. In the specification of a role, they must coincide, in the sense that all the variables appearing in the description of a principal are generated during an execution (an instance) of such a strand. However, in a given protocol state, a strand may contain many more variables of sort Fresh than those specified at the left of the strand due to the message exchange between the principals.

We begin by specifying all the variables that are used in this module, together with the sorts of these variables. In the NSPK example, these are

```
vars X Y Z : Msg .
vars r r' : Fresh .
vars A B : Name .
vars N N1 N2 : Nonce .
```

After the variables are specified, the next thing to specify is the actions of the intruder, or Dolev-Yao rules [17]. These specify the operations an intruder can perform. Each such action can be specified by an intruder strand consisting of a sequence of negative nodes, followed by a single positive node. If the intruder can (non-deterministically) find more than one term as a result of performing one operation (as in deconcatenation), we specify each of these outcomes by separate strands. For the NSPK protocol, we have four operations: encryption with a public key (pk), decryption with a private key (sk), concatenation (_;_), and deconcatenation.

Encryption with a public key is specified as follows. Note that we use a principal's name to stand for the key. That is why names are of type Name. The intruder can encrypt any message using any public key.

```
:: nil:: [ nil | -(X), +(pk(A,X)), nil ]
```

Encryption with the private key is a little different. The intruder can only apply the sk operator using his own identity. So we specify the rule as follows, assuming that i denotes the name of the intruder:

```
:: nil:: [ nil | -(X), +(sk(i,X)), nil ]
```

Concatenation and deconcatenation are straightforward. If the intruder knows X and Y, he can find $X; Y$. If he knows $X; Y$ he can find both X and Y. Since each intruder strand should have at most one positive node, we need to use three strands to specify these actions:

```
:: nil :: [ nil | -(X), -(Y), +(X ; Y), nil ]
:: nil :: [ nil | -(X ; Y), +(X), nil ]
:: nil :: [ nil | -(X ; Y), +(Y), nil ]
```

The final Dolev-Yao specification looks as follows. Note that our tool requires the use of the constant symbol STRANDS-DOLEVYAO as the repository of all the Dolev-Yao strands, and uses the associative-commutative symbol _&_ as the union operator to form sets of strands. Note, also, that our tool considers that variables are not shared between strands, and thus will appropriately rename them when necessary.

```
eq STRANDS-DOLEVYAO
 = :: nil :: [ nil | -(X), -(Y), +(X ; Y), nil ] &
   :: nil :: [ nil | -(X ; Y), +(X), nil ] &
   :: nil :: [ nil | -(X ; Y), +(Y), nil ] &
   :: nil :: [ nil | -(X), +(sk(i,X)), nil ] &
   :: nil :: [ nil | -(X), +(pk(Ke,X)), nil ]
[nonexec] .
```

Every operation that can be performed by the intruder, and every term that is initially known by the intruder, should have a corresponding intruder strand. For each operation used in the protocol we should consider whether or not the intruder can perform it, and specify a corresponding intruder strand that describes the conditions under which the intruder can perform it.

For example, suppose that the operation requires the use of exclusive-or. If we assume that the intruder can exclusive-or any two terms in its possession, we should represent this by the following strand:

```
:: nil :: [ nil | -(X), -(Y), +(X <+> Y), nil ]
```

If we want to give the intruder the ability to generate his own nonces, we should represent this by the following rule:

```
:: r :: [ nil | +(n(i,r)), nil ]
```

In general, it is a good idea to provide Dolev-Yao strands for all the operations that are defined, unless one is explicitly making the assumption that the intruder can *not* perform the operation. It is also *strongly recommended* that operations not used in the protocol should not be provided with Dolev-Yao strands. This is because the tool will attempt to execute rules associated with these strands, even if they are useless, and this will negatively affect performance.

3.6   Protocol Specification: Protocol Strands

In the Protocol Rules section of a specification we define the messages that are sent and received by the honest principals. We will specify one strand per role. However, since the Maude-NPA analysis supports an arbitrary number of sessions, each strand can be instantiated an arbitrary number of times.

In specifying protocol strands it is important to remember to specify them *from the point of view of the principal executing the role.* For example, in NSPK the initiator A starts out by sending her name and a nonce encrypted with B's public key. She gets back something encrypted with her public key, but all she can tell is that it is her nonce concatenated with some other nonce. She then encrypts that other nonce under B's public key and sends it out.

As explained in Section 3.3, we represent the construction of A's nonce explicitly as n(A,r), where r is a variable of sort Fresh therefore appearing in the header of A's strand, and the extra nonce that she receives is represented by a variable N of sort Nonce. The entire strand for the initiator role is as follows:

```
:: r ::
[ nil | +(pk(B,A ; n(A,r))), -(pk(A,n(A,r) ; N)), +(pk(B, N)), nil ]
```

In the responder strand, the signs of the messages are reversed. Moreover, the messages themselves are represented differently. B starts out by receiving a name and some nonce encrypted under his key. He creates his own nonce, appends the received nonce to it, encrypts it with the key belonging to the name, and sends it out. He gets back his nonce encrypted under his own key. This is specified as follows:

```
:: r ::
[ nil | -(pk(B,A ; N)), +(pk(A, N ; n(B,r))), -(pk(B,n(B,r))), nil ]
```

Note that, as explained in Section 3.3, the point here is to only include things in a strand that a principal executing a strand can actually *verify*. The complete STRANDS-PROTOCOL specification for NSPK is as follows.

```
eq STRANDS-PROTOCOL =
  :: r ::
  [nil | +(pk(B,A ; n(A,r))), -(pk(A,n(A,r) ; N)), +(pk(B, N)), nil]
  &
  :: r ::
  [nil | -(pk(B,A ; N)), +(pk(A, N ; n(B,r))), -(pk(B,n(B,r))), nil]
[nonexec] .
```

As a final note, we remark that, if B received a message Z encrypted under a key he does not know, he would not be able to verify that he received pk(A,Z), because he cannot decrypt the message. So the best we could say here is that A received some term Y of sort Msg.

The complete specification of the Needham-Schroeder shared-key protocol and the Diffie-Hellman protocol can be found in [23].

4 Protocol Analysis

In this section we describe how to analyze a protocol in practice. First, we explain how a protocol state looks like, and how an attack state is specified in the protocol. Then, we explain how the actual protocol analysis is performed. Technical details on how the backwards search is performed are postponed until Section 5.

4.1 Protocol States

In Maude-NPA, each state associated to the protocol execution (i.e., a backwards search) is represented by a term with four different components separated by the symbol || in the following order: (1) the set of current strands, (2) the current intruder knowledge, (3) the sequence of messages encountered so far in the backwards execution, and (4) some auxiliary data.

Strands || Intruder Knowledge || Message Sequence || Auxiliary Data

The first component, the set of current strands, indicates in particular how advanced each strand is in the execution process (by the placement of the bar). The second component contains messages that the intruder already knows (symbol _inI) and messages that the intruder currently doesn't know (symbol _!inI) but will learn in the future. Note that the set of strands and the intruder knowledge *grow along with* the backwards reachability search (see Section 5.2 for technical details) as follows:

- by propagation of the substitutions computed by unification modulo the equational theory,
- by introducing more protocol or intruder strands,
- by introducing more positive knowledge of the intruder (e.g., M inI), and
- by transforming positive knowledge into negative knowledge due to the backwards execution (e.g., M inI → M !inI).

The third component, the sequence of messages, is nil for any attack state at the beginning of the backwards search and records the actual sequence of messages exchanged so far in the backwards search from the attack state. This sequence grows as the backwards search continues and some variables may be instantiated in the backwards search. It gives a complete description of an attack when an initial state is reached but this component is intended for the benefit of the user, and is not actually used in the backward search itself, except just by recording it. Finally, the last component contains information about the search space that the tool creates to help manage[8] its search. It does not provide any information about the attack itself, and is currently only displayed by the tool to help in debugging. More information about this last component can be found in Sections 5 and 7.

---

[8] Indeed, we use the fourth component of a protocol state to store the data related to the Super Lazy Intruder of Section 7.6.

4.2   Initial States

An initial state is the final result of the backwards reachability process and is described as follows:

1. in an initial state, all strands have the bar at the beginning, i.e., all strands are of the form :: $r_1, \ldots, r_j$ :: [$nil \mid m_1^{\pm}, \ldots, m_k^{\pm}$];
2. in an initial state, all the intruder knowledge is negative, i.e., all the items in the intruder knowledge are of the form $(m \, !\mathtt{inI})$.

From an initial state, no further backwards reachability steps are possible, since there is nothing for the intruder to unlearn or to learn due to the following two facts: (i) since all the intruder knowledge is already negative (m !inI), no positive knowledge can be unlearned, and (ii) there is no further reception of messages (no negative node in a strand) that might introduce positive items (m inI) in the intruder knowledge. Note that in an initial state, the third component of a protocol state denotes the concrete message sequence from this initial state to the given attack state.

4.3   Unreachable States

Another interesting concept is that of an *unreachable state*. An unreachable state is a protocol state from which we cannot reach an initial state by further backwards reachability analysis. Interpreted in a forwards way, this of course means that it is an state that can *never* be reached from an initial state by forward execution. Early detection of unreachable states is essential to achieve effective protocol analysis. In Section 7, we describe several techniques for early detection of unreachable states. For instance, consider the following state found by the Maude-NPA for the NSPK:

```
:: nil :: [nil | -(pk(i, b ; n(b, r))), +(b ; n(b, r)), nil] &
:: nil :: [nil | -(n(b, r)), +(pk(b, n(b, r))), nil] &
:: nil :: [nil | -(b ; n(b, r)), +(n(b, r)), nil] &
:: r :: [nil | +(pk(i, b ; n(b, r))), nil] &
:: r :: [nil, -(pk(b, a ; N)), +(pk(a, N ; n(b, r)))
           | -(pk(b, n(b, r))), nil])
||
pk(b, n(b, r)) !inI, pk(i, b ; n(b, r)) !inI, n(b, r) !inI,
(b ; n(b, r)) !inI
||
+(pk(i, b ; n(b, r))), -(pk(i, b ; n(b, r))), +(b ; n(b, r)),
-(b ; n(b, r)), +(n(b, r)), -(n(b, r)), +(pk(b, n(b, r))),
-(pk(b, n(b, r)))
||
nil
```

This state is unreachable, since there are two strands that are generating the same fresh variable r and this is impossible because the fresh data generated by each strand must be unique.

4.4   Attack States

Attack states describe not just single concrete attacks, but *attack patterns* (or if you prefer *attack situations*), which are specified symbolically as terms (with variables) whose instances are the final attack states we are looking for. Given an attack pattern, Maude-NPA tries to either find an instance of the attack pattern or prove that no such instance is possible. We can specify more than one attack state. Thus, we designate each attack state with a natural number.

When specifying an attack state, the user should specify only the first two components of the attack state: (i) a set of strands expected to appear in the attack, and (ii) some positive intruder knowledge. The other two state components should have just the empty symbol nil. Note that the attack state is indeed a term with variables; however, the user does not have to provide the variables denoting "the remaining strands", "the remaining intruder knowledge", and the two variables for the two last state components, since these variables are symbolically inserted by the tool (see Section 7.2 for technical details).

For NSPK, the standard attack is represented as follows:

```
eq ATTACK-STATE(0) =
 :: r ::
 [ nil, -(pk(b,a ; N)), +(pk(a, N ; n(b,r))), -(pk(b,n(b,r))) | nil ]
 || n(b,r) inI
 || nil
 || nil
[nonexec] .
```

where we require the intruder to have learned the nonce generated by Bob. Therefore, we have to include Bob's strand in the attack in order to describe such specific nonce n(b,r).

There are several possibilities to build an attack state by combining what the intruder learned at the attack state and what honest strands are expected to have occurred at the attack state. The most common situation is to include positive intruder facts of the form $(m \ \text{inI})$ and finished strands (i.e., strands that have the bar at the end). Note that an attack state can also contain negative intruder facts of the form $(m \ \text{!inI})$ although this is not common. Partially executed strands of the form

$$:: r_1, \ldots, r_i :: [\ nil, \ m_1^{\pm}, \ \ldots, \ m_i^{\pm} \mid m_{i+1}^{\pm}, \ \ldots, \ m_k^{\pm}, \ nil\ ]$$

are represented in attack states by truncated strands in which only the terms before the bar appear. For instance, a situation in which the intruder learns Bob's nonce without requiring Bob to finish the protocol, is represented as:

```
eq ATTACK-STATE(0) =
  :: r :: [ nil, -(pk(b,a ; N)), +(pk(a, N ; n(b,r))) | nil ]
  || n(b,r) inI
  || nil
  || nil
[nonexec] .
```

The intruder knowledge can also contain *inequalities* (the condition that a term is not equal to some other term), which we can also include in the intruder knowledge component of an attack state. For example, suppose that we want to specify that a responder executes a strand, apparently with an initiator a, but the nonce received is not generated by a. This can be done as follows:

```
eq ATTACK-STATE(0) =
  :: r ::
  [ nil, -(pk(b,a ; N)), +(pk(a, N ; n(b,r))), -(pk(b,n(b,r))) | nil ]
  || N != n(a,r')
  || nil
  || nil
  [nonexec] .
```

where t != s means that for any ground substitution θ applicable to t and s (i.e., $\theta(t)$ and $\theta(s)$ are ground terms), $\theta(t)$ cannot be equal to $\theta(s)$ modulo the equational theory. Note that, since a is a constant and r' is a variable of the special sort Fresh, N != n(a,r') means that N cannot be a term of the form n(a,r').

In summary, we note the following requirements on attack state specifications:

1. Strands in an attack state must have the bar at the end. This also applies to partially executed strands, for which the future messages are discarded.

2. If more than one strand appears in the attack state, they must be separated by the & symbol. If more than one term appears in the intruder knowledge, they must be separated by commas. If no strands appear, or no intruder items appear, the empty symbol should be used, in the strands or intruder knowledge components, respectively.

3. Items that can appear in the intruder knowledge may include not only terms known by the intruder, but also inequality conditions on terms. Terms unknown to the intruder are also possible but are not common in attack states.

4. The last two fields of an attack state must always be nil. These are fields that contain information that is built up in the backwards search, but should be empty in the attack state.

4.5   Attack States with Excluded Patterns: Never Patterns

It is often desirable to exclude certain patterns from transition paths leading to an attack state. For example, one may want to determine whether or not authentication properties have been violated, e.g., whether it is possible for a responder strand to appear without the corresponding initiator strand. For this there is an optional additional field in the attack state containing the never patterns. It is included at the end of the attack state specification.

Here is how we would specify an initiator strand without a corresponding responder in the NSPK protocol[9]:

```
eq ATTACK-STATE(1)
   = :: r ::
     [ nil, -(pk(b,a ; N)), +(pk(a,  N ; n(b,r))), -(pk(b,n(b,r))) | nil ]
     || empty
     || nil
     || nil
     butNeverFoundAny *** for authentication
     (:: r' ::
     [ nil | +(pk(b,a ; N)), -(pk(a,  N ; n(b,r))), +(pk(b,n(b,r))), nil ]
     & S:StrandSet
     || K:IntruderKnowledge
     || M:SMsgList
     || G:GhostList)
[nonexec] .
```

The tool will now look for all paths in which the intruder strand is executed, but the corresponding responder strand is not. That is, when we provide an attack state and some never patterns, a backwards reachability sequence leading to an initial state will not contain any state that matches any of the never patterns, where the place of the bar at each strand appearing in a never pattern is not taken into consideration for matching purposes.

It is also possible to use never patterns to specify negative conditions on terms or strands. Suppose that we want to ask whether it is possible for a responder in the NSPK protocol to execute a session of the protocol, apparently with an initiator, but the nonce received was not the initiator's. This can be done as follows:

```
eq ATTACK-STATE(1)
   = :: r ::
     [ nil, -(pk(b,a ; N)), +(pk(a, N ; n(b,r))),
             -(pk(b,n(b,r))) | nil ]
     || empty
     || nil
     || nil
     butNeverFoundAny
     (  ::: r ::
     [ nil | -(pk(b,a ; n(a,r'))), +(pk(a, n(a,r') ; n(b,r))),
```

---

[9] Note that variable r' in the never pattern is not an error. The regular strand in the attack state is the initiator strand, which generates variable r. The strand in the never pattern is a pattern that must be valid for any responder strand. Any responder strand would generate his variable r'', which would be part of the variable N written in the never pattern if such a pattern is matched. Indeed, note that the variable r written in the never pattern is different by definition from the variable r written in the regular strand, since we are defining an actual strand and a pattern to be matched.

```
                -(pk(b,n(b,r))), nil ] & S:StrandSet
   || K:IntruderKnowledge
   || M:SMsgList
   || G:GhostList )
[nonexec] .
```

It is possible to include more than one never pattern in the specification of an attack state, but then each such pattern must be contained within a pair of parentheses, e.g.,

```
butNeverFoundAny
( ... State 1 ... )
( ... State 2 ... )
```

Never patterns can also be used to cut the down the search space. Suppose, for example, that one finds in the above search that a number of states are encountered in which the intruder encrypts two nonces, but they never seem to provide any useful information. One can reduce the search space by ruling out such intruder behavior with the second never pattern in the following attack state:

```
eq ATTACK-STATE(1)
  = :: r ::
    [ nil, -(pk(b,a ; N)), +(pk(a, N ; n(b,r))),
            -(pk(b,n(b,r))) | nil ]
    || empty
    || nil
    || nil
    butNeverFoundAny
    (:: r' :: [nil | +(pk(b,a ; N)), -(pk(a, N ; n(b,r))),
                      +(pk(b,n(b,r))), nil] & S:StrandSet
    || K:IntruderKnowledge
    || M:SMsgList
    || G:GhostList)
    (:: nil :: [nil | -(N1 ; N2), +(pk(B, N1 ; N2)), nil] & S:StrandSet
    || K:IntruderKnowledge
    || M:SMsgList
    || G:GhostList)
[nonexec] .
```

Note that adding never patterns to reduce the search space, as distinguished from their use for verifying *authentication* properties, means that failure to find an attack does not necessarily imply that the protocol is secure. It simply means that any attack against the security property specified in the attack state must use at least one strand that is specified in the set of never patterns.

There are several things about never patterns that should be noted:

1. The bar in any strand in a never pattern should be at the beginning of the strand. If it is not, the tool does not report any error and places the bar at the beginning.
2. Variables in a never pattern are renamed by the tool to assure that they never appear in the main attack state specification nor in other never patterns.

3. The last two fields in a never pattern must be variables of type SMsgList, and Ghostlist, respectively, as illustrated in the above examples.
4. The first two fields must end in variables of type Strandset and IntruderKnowledge, respectively.
5. More than one never pattern can be used in an attack state. However, each one must be delimited by its own pair of parentheses.

For a good example of the use of never patterns, which makes the Maude-NPA search considerably more efficient without compromising the completeness of the reachability analysis, we refer the reader to the analysis of the Diffie-Hellman protocol in [23].

4.6   Maude-NPA Commands for Attack Search

The commands run, summary, and initials are the tool's commands for attack search. They are invoked by reducing them in Maude, that is, by typing the Maude red command followed by the corresponding Maude-NPA command, followed by a space and a period. To use them we must specify the attack state we are searching for and the number of backwards reachability steps we want to compute. For example, the Maude-NPA command

```
run(0,10)
```

tells Maude-NPA to construct the backwards reachability tree up to depth 10 for the attack state designated with natural number 0. The Maude-NPA run command yields the set of states found at the leaves of the backwards reachability tree of the specified depth that has been generated. When the user is not interested in the current states of the reachability tree, he/she can use the Maude-NPA summary command, which outputs just the number of states found at the leaves of the reachability tree and how many of those are initial states, i.e., solutions for the attack. For instance, when we give the reduce command in Maude with the Maude-NPA command summary(0,2) as shown below for the NSPK example, the tool returns:

```
red summary(0,2) .
result Summary: States>> 4 Solutions>> 0
```

The initial state representing the standard NSPK attack is found in seven steps. That is, if we type

```
red summary(0,7) .
```

the tool outputs:

```
red summary(0,7) .
result Summary: States>> 3 Solutions>> 1
```

A slightly different version of the run command, called initials, outputs only the initial states, instead of all the states at the leaves of the backwards reachability tree. Thus, if we type

```
red initials(0,7) .
```

for the NSPK example, our tool outputs the following initial state[10], which implies that the attack state has been proved reachable and the protocol is insecure:

```
Maude> red initials(0,7) .
result IdSystem: < 1 . 5 . 2 . 7 . 1 . 4 . 3 . 1 > (
:: nil :: [nil | -(pk(i, n(b, #1:Fresh))), +(n(b, #1:Fresh)), nil] &
:: nil :: [nil | -(pk(i, a ; n(a, #0:Fresh))), +(a ; n(a, #0:Fresh)), nil] &
:: nil :: [nil | -(n(b, #1:Fresh)), +(pk(b, n(b, #1:Fresh))), nil] &
:: nil :: [nil | -(a ; n(a, #0:Fresh)), +(pk(b, a ; n(a, #0:Fresh))), nil] &
:: #1:Fresh :: [nil | -(pk(b, a ; n(a, #0:Fresh))),
 +(pk(a, n(a, #0:Fresh) ; n(b, #1:Fresh))), -(pk(b, n(b, #1:Fresh))), nil] &
:: #0:Fresh :: [nil | +(pk(i, a ; n(a, #0:Fresh))),
 -(pk(a, n(a, #0:Fresh) ; n(b, #1:Fresh))), +(pk(i, n(b, #1:Fresh))), nil])
||
pk(a, n(a, #0:Fresh) ; n(b, #1:Fresh)) !inI,
  pk(b, n(b, #1:Fresh)) !inI,
  pk(b, a ; n(a, #0:Fresh)) !inI,
  pk(i, n(b, #1:Fresh)) !inI,
  pk(i, a ; n(a, #0:Fresh)) !inI,
  n(b, #1:Fresh) !inI,
  (a ; n(a, #0:Fresh)) !inI
||
+(pk(i, a ; n(a, #0:Fresh))),
  -(pk(i, a ; n(a, #0:Fresh))),
  +(a ; n(a, #0:Fresh)),
  -(a ; n(a, #0:Fresh)),
  +(pk(b, a ; n(a, #0:Fresh))),
  -(pk(b, a ; n(a, #0:Fresh))),
  +(pk(a, n(a, #0:Fresh) ; n(b, #1:Fresh))),
  -(pk(a, n(a, #0:Fresh) ; n(b, #1:Fresh))),
  +(pk(i, n(b, #1:Fresh))),
  -(pk(i, n(b, #1:Fresh))),
  +(n(b, #1:Fresh)),
  -(n(b, #1:Fresh)),
  +(pk(b, n(b, #1:Fresh))),
  -(pk(b, n(b, #1:Fresh)))
||
nil
```

This corresponds to the following textbook version of the attack:

1. $A \to I : pk(I, A; N_A)$
2. $I_A \to B : pk(B, A; N_A)$
3. $B \to A : pk(A, N_A; N_B)$, intercepted by I;
4. $I \to A : pk(A, N_A; N_B)$
5. $A \to I : pk(I, N_B)$
6. $I_A \to B : pk(B, N_B)$

---

[10] Maude-NPA associates an identifier, e.g. 1.5.2.7.1.4.3.1, to each state generated by the tool. These identifiers are for internal use and are not described here.

It is also possible to generate an unbounded search by specifying the second argument of run, initials, or summary as unbounded. In that case the tool will run until it has shown that all the paths it has found either begin in initial states or in unreachable ones. This check may terminate in finite time, but in some cases may run forever.

We demonstrate this unbounded search with NSPK:

```
red summary(0,unbounded) .
result Summary: States>> 1 Solutions>> 1
```

This tells us, that Maude-NPA terminated with only one attack. If we want to see what that attack looks like, we would instead type

```
red run(0,unbounded) .
```

to get the attack displayed above.

The complete analysis of the Diffie-Hellman protocol can be found in [23], including the initial state proving that the protocol in insecure.

5   How Maude-NPA Works: Backwards Reachability

First, we recall some definitions on rewriting and narrowing in Section 5.1. Then, we explain in Section 5.2 how the backwards reachability analysis works in practice.

5.1   Rewriting and Narrowing

Continuing Section 2, we recall some definitions on term rewriting and illustrate each definition by means of examples.

A *rewrite rule* is an oriented pair of terms (l, r), written $l \rightarrow r$, where $l \notin \mathcal{X}$ and $l, r \in \mathcal{T}_{\Sigma}(\mathcal{X})_s$ for some sort $s \in S$. An *(unconditional) order-sorted rewrite theory* is a triple $\mathcal{R} = (\Sigma, E, R)$ with Σ an order-sorted signature, E a set of Σ-equations, and R a set of rewrite rules. The rewriting relation $\rightarrow_R$ on $\mathcal{T}_{\Sigma}(\mathcal{X})$ is $t \xrightarrow{p}_R t'$ (or $\rightarrow_R$) if $p \in Pos_{\Sigma}(t)$, $l \rightarrow r \in R$, $t|_p = \sigma(l)$, and $t' = t[\sigma(r)]_p$ for some σ. The relation $\rightarrow_{R/E}$ on $\mathcal{T}_{\Sigma}(\mathcal{X})$ is $=_E; \rightarrow_R; =_E$, where $\_;\_$ denotes relation composition. The relation $\rightarrow_{R/E}$ is much harder to implement and the weaker rewrite relation $\rightarrow_{R,E}$ is usually provided, as it happens in Maude. Assuming a finitary and complete matching algorithm modulo the equational theory E, the rewriting relation $\rightarrow_{R,E}$ on $\mathcal{T}_{\Sigma}(\mathcal{X})$ is defined as $t \xrightarrow{p}_{R,E} t'$ (or $\rightarrow_{R,E}$) if $l \rightarrow r \in R$, $t|_p =_E \sigma(l)$, and $t' = t[\sigma(r)]_p$.

Maude supports matching modulo any combination of free, associative, commutative, and associative-commutative, and associative-commutative with identity symbols, so that we in effect can rewrite terms *modulo* any combination of such axioms. Suppose, for example, an unconditional order-sorted rewrite theory $\mathcal{R} = (\Sigma, E, R)$ where Σ contains an infix symbol $+$, E contains the commutativity property for symbol $+$, and R contains a rule of the form $X + 0 = X$. Then we can apply such a rule to the term $0 + 7$ *modulo* commutativity, even though the constant 0 is on the left of the $+$ symbol. That is, the term $0 + 7$ *matches* the left-hand side pattern $X + 0$ *modulo* commutativity, i.e., $0 + 7 =_E (X + 0)\sigma$ where $\sigma = \{X \mapsto 7\}$. We would express this rewrite step modulo commutativity with the arrow notation:

$$0 + 7 \rightarrow_{R,E} 7$$

Likewise, we denote by $\rightarrow^*_{R,E}$ the reflexive-transitive closure of the one-step rewrite relation $\rightarrow_{R,E}$ with the rules R modulo the axioms E. That is, $\rightarrow^*_{R,E}$ corresponds to taking zero, one, or more rewrite steps with the rules R modulo E.

Narrowing generalizes term rewriting by allowing free variables in terms (as in logic programming) and by performing unification instead of matching in order to (non–deterministically) reduce a term. Intuitively, the difference between a rewriting step and a narrowing step is that in both cases we use a rewrite rule $l \rightarrow r$ to rewrite t at a position p in t, but narrowing finds values for the variables in the chosen subject term $t|_p$ before actually performing the rewriting step. The narrowing relation $\leadsto_R$ on $\mathcal{T}_\Sigma(\mathcal{X})$ is $t \overset{p}{\leadsto}_{\sigma,R} t'$ (or $\leadsto_{\sigma,R}$, $\leadsto_R$) if $p \in Pos_\Sigma(t)$, $l \rightarrow r \in R$, $\sigma \in CSU_\emptyset(t|_p = l)$, and $t' = \sigma(t[r]_p)$. Assuming that E has a finitary and complete unification algorithm, the narrowing relation $\leadsto_{R,E}$ on $\mathcal{T}_\Sigma(\mathcal{X})$ is $t \overset{p}{\leadsto}_{\sigma,R,E} t'$ (or $\leadsto_{\sigma,R,E}$, $\leadsto_{R,E}$) if $p \in Pos_\Sigma(t)$, $l \rightarrow r \in R$, $\sigma \in CSU_E(t|_p = l)$, and $t' = \sigma(t[r]_p)$.

Maude supports unification modulo different user-defined theories including any combination of free, commutative, and associative-commutative symbols; see Section 6.3 for the algebraic theories admissible for such equational unification procedure, and Section 6.4 for some examples of admissible theories. Suppose, for example, the same unconditional order-sorted rewrite theory used above for rewriting. Then, we can apply the rule $X + 0 = X$ above to the term $Z + 7$, where X is a variable, *modulo* commutativity. That is, the term $Z + 7$ *unifies* the left-hand side pattern $X + 0$ *modulo* commutativity, i.e., $(Z + 7)\theta =_E (X + 0)\theta$ where $\theta = \{Z \mapsto 0, X \mapsto 7\}$. We would express this narrowing step modulo commutativity with the arrow notation:

$$Z + 7 \leadsto_{\theta,R,E} 7$$

We denote by $\leadsto^*_{\theta,R,E}$ the reflexive-transitive closure of the one-step narrowing relation $\leadsto_{R,E}$ with the rules R modulo the axioms E, where θ is the composition of all the unifiers obtained during the sequence.

In Maude-NPA, narrowing is used at two levels: for backwards reachability analysis from a term with variables (i.e., an attack state), and for equational unification. We postpone until Section 6 how the narrowing-based equational unification is performed in Maude-NPA.

5.2 Backwards Reachability Analysis

Given a protocol $\mathcal{P}$ and an equational theory $E_\mathcal{P}$, Maude-NPA performs backwards narrowing reachability analysis from a state St representing an attack pattern (i.e., a term with variables) using the relation $\leadsto_{R_\mathcal{P}^{-1}, E_\mathcal{P}}$, where the rewrite rules $R_{\mathcal{P}}$ are obtained from the protocol strands $\mathcal{P}$. The rewrite theory $\mathcal{R}_{\mathcal{P}} = (\Sigma, E_{\mathcal{P}}, R_{\mathcal{P}})$ is *topmost*, i.e., there is a sort State such that for each $l \to r \in R_{\mathcal{P}}$, $l, r \in \mathcal{T}_{\Sigma}(\mathcal{X})_{\text{State}}$, $r \notin \mathcal{X}$, and no operator in Σ has State as an argument sort. Intuitively, a topmost rewrite theory describes a specification of a system such that a rewrite or narrowing step can only be performed at the root of each term denoting a state. The fact that $\mathcal{R} = (\Sigma, E_{\mathcal{P}}, R_{\mathcal{P}})$ is a topmost rewrite theory has several advantages:

1. The rewriting relation $\to_{R_{\mathcal{P}}/E_{\mathcal{P}}}$ can be safely simulated by the rewriting relation $\to_{R_{\mathcal{P}}, E_{\mathcal{P}}}$.
2. Similarly, the narrowing relation $\rightsquigarrow_{R_{\mathcal{P}}, E_{\mathcal{P}}}$ achieves the same effect as a more general narrowing relation $\rightsquigarrow_{R_{\mathcal{P}}/E_{\mathcal{P}}}$ (see [48]).
3. We obtain the following *completeness* result between narrowing ($\rightsquigarrow_{R_{\mathcal{P}}, E_{\mathcal{P}}}$) and rewriting ($\to_{R_{\mathcal{P}}/E_{\mathcal{P}}}$):

Theorem 1 (Topmost Completeness). [48] *Let $\mathcal{R} = (\Sigma, E, R)$ be a topmost rewrite theory such that E has a finitary unification algorithm, $t, t' \in \mathcal{T}_{\Sigma}(\mathcal{X})$, and let σ be a substitution such that $\sigma(t) \to^*_{R/E} t'$. Then, there are substitutions θ, τ and a term t'' such that $t \rightsquigarrow^*_{\theta, R, E} t''$, $\sigma(t) =_E \tau(\theta(t))$, and $t' =_E \tau(t'')$.*

A *state* in the protocol execution is a set of Maude-NPA strands unioned together with an associative and commutativity union operator $\_\&\_$ with identity operator empty, along with an additional term describing the intruder knowledge at that point. Note that two extra state components are associated to a Maude-NPA state in Section 4, but they are irrelevant and useful only for user debugging of the protocol, so we omit them in this section and in Section 7.

The *intruder knowledge* is represented as a set of facts unioned together with an associative and commutativity union operator $\_,\_$ with identity operator empty. There are two kinds of intruder facts: positive knowledge facts (the intruder knows m, i.e., $(m \; \text{inI})$), and negative knowledge facts (the intruder does not yet know m but will know it in a future state, i.e., $(m \; !\text{inI})$), where m is a message expression.

Strands communicate between them via a unique shared channel, i.e., by sending messages to the channel and retrieving messages from the channel. However, we do not explicitly represent the channel in our model. Instead, since the intruder is able to learn any message present in the channel, we use the intruder knowledge as the channel. When the intruder observes a message in the channel, then he/she learns it. The intruder has the usual ability to read and redirect traffic, and can also perform operations, e.g., encryption, decryption, concatenation, exclusive or, exponentiation, etc., on messages that it has received. As explained in Section 3, the nature and algebraic properties of such operations depend on the given cryptographic theory $E_{\mathcal{P}}$. Intruder operations are described in terms of the intruder sending messages to itself, which are represented as different strands, one for each action. All intruder and protocol strands are described symbolically, using a mixture of variables and constants, so a single state specification as a term with variables symbolically represents many concrete state instances. There is no restriction on the number of principals, number of sessions, nonces, or time, i.e., no data abstraction or approximation is performed.

The user can make use of a special sort Fresh in the protocol-specific signature Σ for representing fresh unguessable values, e.g., for nonces. The meaning of a variable of sort Fresh is that it will never be instantiated by an E-unifier generated during the backwards reachability analysis. This ensures that if nonces are represented using variables of sort Fresh, they will never be merged and no approximation for nonces is necessary. We make the Fresh variables generated by a strand explicit by writing $(r_1, \ldots, r_k : \text{Fresh}) \, [msg_1^{\pm}, \ldots, msg_n^{\pm}]$, where $r_1, \ldots, r_k$ are all the variables of sort Fresh generated by $msg_1^{\pm}, \ldots, msg_n^{\pm}$. If it does not generate any fresh variable, we add nothing to the strand. As explained in Section 3, the types and algebraic properties of the operators used in messages (cryptographic and otherwise) are described as an equational theory $E_{\mathcal{P}}$.

In principle, the rewrite rules $R_{\mathcal{P}}$ obtained from the protocol strands $\mathcal{P}$ are represented by the following rewrite rules[11]:

$$SS \,\&\, [L \mid M^-, L'] \,\&\, ((M \text{ inI}), IK) \rightarrow SS \,\&\, [L, M^- \mid L'] \,\&\, ((M \text{ inI}), IK) \quad (1)$$

$$SS \,\&\, [L \mid M^+, L'] \,\&\, IK \rightarrow SS \,\&\, [L, M^+ \mid L'] \,\&\, IK \quad (2)$$

$$SS \,\&\, [L \mid M^+, L'] \,\&\, IK \rightarrow SS \,\&\, [L, M^+ \mid L'] \,\&\, ((M \text{ inI}), IK) \quad (3)$$

In a *forward execution* of the protocol strands, Rule (1) synchronizes an input message with a message already learned by the intruder, Rule (2) accepts output messages but the intruder's knowledge is not increased, and Rule (3) accepts output messages and the intruder's knowledge is positively increased. New strands will be added to the state by explicit introduction through dedicated rewrite rules (one for each honest or intruder strand), e.g.

$$SS \,\&\, ((sk(i, M) \text{ inI}), IK) \rightarrow SS \,\&\, [M^- \mid sk(i, M)^+] \,\&\, ((sk(i, M) \text{ inI}), IK)$$

However, we are interested in a *backwards* execution of the protocol from an attack state that contains *positive* facts in the intruder knowledge. Therefore, the rule increasing the intruder knowledge, Rule (3), must make explicit *when* the intruder learned message M:

$$SS \,\&\, [L \mid M^+, L'] \,\&\, ((M \text{ !inI}), IK) \rightarrow SS \,\&\, [L, M^+ \mid L'] \,\&\, ((M \text{ inI}), IK) \quad (4)$$

Note that this is recorded in the previous state by the negative fact (M !inI), which can be paraphrased as: "the intruder does not yet know M, but will learn it in the future".

For the introduction of new additional strands, we simply record when the intruder learned message M in each of the rewrite rules explicitly introducing new strands but, since they are applied backwards, reversing the introduction of the new strand:

---

[11] The top level structure of the state is a multiset of strands formed with the _&_ union operator. The protocol and intruder rewrite rules are "essentially topmost" in that, using an extension variable matching the "remaining strands" they can always rewrite the whole state. Therefore, as explained in [48], completeness results of narrowing for topmost theories also apply to them.

$$\{ \, [\, l_1 \,|\, u^+, \, l_2 \,] \, \& \, \{(u \, !\texttt{inI}), K\} \to \{(u \, \texttt{inI}), K\} \,|\, [\, l_1, \, u^+, \, l_2 \,] \in \mathcal{P}\} \qquad (5)$$

For example, the following Dolev-Yao action:

$$SS \, \& \, [\, M^- \,|\, sk(i, M)^+] \, \& \, ((sk(i, M) \, !\texttt{inI}), IK) \to SS \, \& \, ((sk(i, M) \, \texttt{inI}), IK) \qquad (6)$$

Thus, we can conclude that the set of rewrite rules obtained from the protocol strands that are used for backwards narrowing reachability analysis is $R_{\mathcal{P}} = \{(1), (2), (4)\} \cup (5)$.

For example, consider the the the NSPK attack state:

$$(r : \texttt{Fresh})[\, pk(b, a; N)^-, \; pk(a, N; n(b, r))^+, \; pk(b, n(b, r))^- \,|\, nil \,] \, \& \, (n(b, r) \, \texttt{inI})$$

and the Rule (6). We can apply this rule to our attack state modulo the equational theory for NSPK. That is, the attack term above unifies with the left-hand side of the rule modulo the following cancellation equational rules $E_{\mathcal{P}}$:

$$pk(A, sk(A, Z)) = Z \qquad\qquad sk(A, pk(A, Z)) = Z$$

To be more concrete, the term $n(b, r)$ unifies[12] with the term $sk(i, M)$ modulo the cancellation equational rules yielding the unifier $\theta = \{M \mapsto pk(i, n(b, r))\}$. Therefore, we obtain the following predecessor state using the narrowing relation $\rightsquigarrow_{\theta, R_{\mathcal{P}}^{-1}, E_{\mathcal{P}}}$ from the NSPK attack state:

$$[\, pk(i, n(b, r))^- \,|\, n(b, r)^+ \,] \, \&$$
$$(r : \texttt{Fresh})[\, pk(b, a; N)^-, \; pk(a, N; n(b, r))^+, \; pk(b, n(b, r))^- \,|\, nil \,] \, \& \, (n(b, r) \, !\texttt{inI})$$

In a backwards execution of the protocol using narrowing we start from an attack pattern, i.e., a term with variables, containing: (i) some of the strands of the protocol to be executed backwards, (ii) a variable SS denoting a set of additional strands, (iii) some terms the intruder knows at the attack state, i.e., of the form $(t \, \texttt{inI})$, and (iv) a variable IK denoting a set of additional intruder facts. We then perform narrowing with the rules $R_{\mathcal{P}}$ in reverse to move the bars of the strands to the left until either we find an initial state, or cannot perform any other useful backwards narrowing steps. Note that variables SS and IK will be instantiated by backwards narrowing to additional strands and additional intruder facts, respectively, in order to find an initial state. Indeed, these variables SS and IK are not required for the specification of the attack state as explained in Section 4.4; see Section 7.2 for further technical details.

6   How Maude-NPA Works: Equational Unification

Sound techniques for equational unification are paramount to Maude-NPA, since it performs symbolic reachability analysis *modulo* the equational theory of the

---

[12] This equational unification procedure is also performed by narrowing and is explained in Section 6 below.

protocol. This makes Maude-NPA verification much stronger than verification methods based on a purely syntactic view of the algebra of messages as a term algebra using the standard Dolev-Yao model of perfect cryptography in which no algebraic properties are assumed. Indeed, it is well-known that various protocols that have been proved secure under the standard Dolev-Yao model can be broken by an attacker who exploits the algebraic properties of some cryptographic functions (see, e.g., [41, 43, 46]).

In the standard Dolev-Yao model, symbolic reachability analysis typically takes the form of representing sets of states symbolically as terms with logical variables, and then performing *syntactic unification* with the protocol rules to explore reachable states. This can be done in either a forwards or a backwards fashion. In the Maude-NPA (which can also be used for analyses under the standard Dolev-Yao model when no algebraic properties are specified) symbolic reachability analysis is performed in a *backwards* fashion (as already explained in Section 5), beginning with a symbolic representation of an attack state, and searching for an initial state, which then provides a proof that an attack is possible; or a proof that no such attack is possible if all such search paths fail to reach an initial state.

However, if the Maude-NPA analyzes a protocol for which algebraic properties *have* been specified by an equational theory T, the same symbolic reachability analysis is performed in the same fashion, but now *modulo* T. What this means precisely is that, instead of performing syntactic unification between a term representing symbolically a set of states and the righthand-side (in the backwards reachability case) of a protocol rule, we now perform *equational unification* with the theory T, (also called T-*unification*, or *unification modulo* T) between the same term and the same righthand side of a protocol rule. In what follows we explain several things regarding T-unification in the Maude-NPA:

- In Section 6.1, equational axioms for which the Maude-NPA provides built-in support for equational unification.
- In Section 6.2, narrowing-based equational unification in general, which is however infeasible for Maude-NPA analysis when the number of unifiers generated is infinite.
- In Section 6.3, the most general class of equational theories for which the Maude-NPA can currently support unification by narrowing, with the important requirement of the number of unifier solutions being *finite*. These are called *admissible* theories.
- Some examples of admissible theories in Section 6.4.

6.1   Built-In Support for Unification Modulo Equational Axioms

The Maude-NPA has built-in support for unification modulo certain equational theories T thanks to the underlying Maude infrastructure. Specifically, the Maude-NPA automatically supports unification modulo T for T any order-sorted theory of the form $T = (\Sigma, Ax)$, where Σ is a *signature* declaring sorts, subsorts, and function symbols (as we have already illustrated with examples in

Section 3.2) and Ax is a collection of equational *axioms* where some binary operators f in the signature Σ may have axioms in Ax for either *commutativity* ($f(x,y) = f(y,x)$), or commutativity and *associativity* ($f(x,f(y,z)) = f(f(x,y),z)$). Associativity alone is not supported, because it is well-known that unification problems modulo associativity may have an *infinite* number of unifiers (see, e.g., [5]). As already illustrated in Section 3.4, the way associativity, and/or commutativity axioms are specified in Maude for a function symbol f is not by giving those axioms explicitly, but by declaring f in Maude with the assoc and/or comm attributes. For example a function symbol f of sort S which is associative and commutative is specified in Maude as follows:

```
op f : S S -> S [assoc comm] .
```

6.2   Narrowing-Based Equational Unification and Its Limitations

Of course, many algebraic theories T of interest in protocol analysis fall outside the scope of the above-mentioned class of theories T based on combinations of associativity and/or commutativity axioms, for which the Maude-NPA provides automatic built-in support. Therefore, the burning issue is how to support more general classes of algebraic theories in the Maude-NPA.

In this regard, a very useful, generic method to obtain T-unification algorithms is narrowing [29, 31]. Mathematically, an algebraic theory T is a pair of the form $T = (\Sigma, E \cup Ax)$, where Σ is a signature declaring sorts, subsorts, and function symbols, and where $E \cup Ax$ is a set of *equations*, that we assume is split into a set Ax of equational axioms such as our previous combinations of associativity and/or commutativity axioms, and a set E of oriented equations to be used from left to right as rewrite rules. In Maude, the axioms Ax are declared by means of the assoc and/or comm attributes. Instead, the equations E are declared with the eq keyword as we have illustrated with examples in Section 3.4.

An algebraic theory $T = (\Sigma, E \cup Ax)$ must satisfy the following four requirements:

1. The axioms Ax can declare some binary operators in Σ to be commutative (with the comm attribute), or associative-commutative (with the assoc and comm attributes).
2. The equations E are confluent modulo Ax.
3. The equations E are terminating modulo Ax.
4. The equations E are coherent modulo Ax.

We now explain in detail what these requirements mean. First, the equational theory $T = (\Sigma, E \cup Ax)$ is viewed as an unconditional order-sorted *rewrite theory* $\mathcal{R}_T = (\Sigma, Ax, E)$, so that we perform rewrite steps with the rewrite rules E modulo Ax, i.e., the reduction relation $\to_{E,Ax}$ explained in Section 5.1, where, in the notation $\to_{R,E}$, now $R = E$ and $E = Ax$.

Confluence. The equations E are called *confluent* modulo Ax if and only if for each term t in the theory $T = (\Sigma, E \cup Ax)$, if we can rewrite t with E modulo

Ax in two different ways as: $t \longrightarrow^*_{E,Ax} u$ and $t \longrightarrow^*_{E,Ax} v$, then we can always further rewrite u and v to a common term up to identity modulo Ax. That is, we can always find terms u', v' such that:

- $u \longrightarrow^*_{E,Ax} u'$ and $v \longrightarrow^*_{E,Ax} v'$, and
- $u' =_{Ax} v'$

That is, u' and v' are essentially the same term, in the sense that they are equal modulo the axioms Ax. In the example of Section 5.1, we have, for instance, $0 + 7 =_{Ax} 7 + 0$.

Termination. The equations E are called *terminating* modulo Ax if and only if all rewrite sequences terminate; that is, if and only if we never have an infinite sequence of rewrites

$$t_0 \to_{E,Ax} t_1 \to_{E,Ax} t_2 \ldots t_n \to_{E,Ax} t_{n+1} \ldots$$

Coherence. Rather than explaining the *coherence modulo Ax* notion in general (the precise definition of the general notion can found in [31]), we explain in detail its meaning in the case where it is needed for the Maude-NPA, namely, the case of associative-commutative (AC) symbols. The best way to illustrate the meaning of coherence is by its *absence*. Consider, for example, an exclusive or operator $\oplus$ which has been declared AC. Now consider the equation $X \oplus X = 0$. This equation, if not completed by another equation, is *not* coherent modulo AC. What this means is that there will be term *contexts* in which the equation *should* be applied, but it cannot be applied. Consider, for example, the term $b \oplus (a \oplus b)$. Intuitively, we should be able to apply to it the above equation to simplify it to the term $a \oplus 0$ in one step. However, since we are using the weaker rewrite relation $\to_{E,Ax}$ instead of the stronger but much harder to implement relation $\to_{E/Ax}$, we cannot! The problem is that the equation cannot be applied (even if we match modulo AC) to either the top term $b \oplus (a \oplus b)$ or the subterm $a \oplus b$. We can however make our equation *coherent* modulo AC by adding the extra equation $X \oplus X \oplus Y = 0 \oplus Y$, which, using also the equation $X \oplus 0 = X$, we can slightly simplify to the equation $X \oplus X \oplus Y = Y$. This second variant of our equation will now apply to the term $b \oplus (a \oplus b)$, giving the simplification $b \oplus (a \oplus b) \longrightarrow_{E,Ax} a$. Technically, what coherence means is that the weaker relation $\to_{E,Ax}$ becomes semantically equivalent to the stronger relation $\to_{E/Ax}$.

For the Maude-NPA, coherence is only an issue for AC symbols. And there is always an easy way, given a set E of equations, to make them AC-coherent. The method is as follows. For any symbol f which is AC, and for any equation of the form $f(u,v) = w$ in E, we add also the equation $f(f(u,v), X) = f(w, X)$, where X is a new variable not appearing in u, v, w. In an order-sorted setting, we should give to X *the biggest sort possible*, so that it will apply in all generality. As an additional optimization, note that some equations may already be coherent modulo AC, so that we need not add the extra equation. For example, if the variable X has the biggest possible sort it could have, then the equation $X \oplus$

$0 = X$ is already coherent, since X will match "the rest of the $\oplus$-expression," regardless of how big or complex that expression might be, and of where in the expression a constant 0 occurs. For example, this equation will apply modulo AC to the term $(a\oplus(b\oplus(0\oplus c)))\oplus(c\oplus a)$, with x matching the term $(a\oplus(b\oplus c))\oplus(c\oplus a)$, so that we indeed get a rewrite $(a\oplus(b\oplus(0\oplus c)))\oplus(c\oplus a) \to_{E,Ax} (a\oplus(b\oplus c))\oplus(c\oplus a)$.

Limitations. Although narrowing is a very general method to generate T-unification algorithms, general narrowing has a serious limitation. The problem is that, in general, narrowing with an equational theory $T = (\Sigma, E \cup Ax)$ satisfying requirements (1)–(4) above may yield an *infinite* number of unifiers. Since, for T the algebraic theory of a protocol, T-unification must be performed by the Maude-NPA at each *single step* of symbolic reachability analysis, narrowing is in general not practical as a unification procedure, unless the theory T satisfies the additional requirement that there always exists a *finite* set of unifiers that provide a complete set of solutions; and that such a finite set of solutions can be effectively computed by narrowing. We discuss this extra important requirement in what follows.

6.3   General Requirements for Algebraic Theories

The Maude-NPA's unification technique is based on narrowing and in order to provide a *finite* set of unifiers, five specific requirements must be met by any algebraic theory specifying cryptographic functions that the user provides. If these requirements are not satisfied, Maude-NPA may exhibit non-terminating and/or incomplete behavior, and any completeness claims about the results of the analysis cannot be guaranteed. We call theories that satisfy these criteria *admissible* theories. We show in Section 6.4 how all the examples presented in Section 3.4 are admissible theories.

In the Maude-NPA we call an algebraic theory $T = (\Sigma, E \cup Ax)$ specified by the user for the cryptographic functions of the protocol *admissible* if it satisfies the four requirements specified in Section 6.2 and *strongly right irreducibility*, i.e., the following five requirements:

1. The axioms Ax can declare some binary operators in Σ to be commutative (with the comm attribute), or associative-commutative (with the assoc and comm attributes). No other combinations of axioms are allowed; that is, a function symbol has either no attributes, or only the comm attribute, or only the assoc and comm attributes.[13]
2. The equations E are confluent modulo Ax.
3. The equations E are terminating modulo Ax.
4. The equations E are coherent modulo Ax.
5. The equations E are strongly right irreducible.

---

[13] In future versions of the Maude-NPA we also plan to support operators having the assoc, comm and id attributes, adding an identity axiom. At present, identity axioms in Maude-NPA theories should only be defined by means of equations.

Confluence, termination, and coherence were explained in Section 6.2. We now explain in detail what strongly right irreducibility means. Given a theory $T = (\Sigma, E \cup Ax)$, which we assume satisfies requirements (1)-(4) above, we call the set E of equations *strongly right irreducible* iff for each equation $t = t'$ in E, we cannot further simplify by the equations E modulo Ax either the term t', or any substitution instance $\theta(t')$ where the terms in the substitution θ cannot themselves be further simplified by the equations E modulo Ax. Obvious cases of such righthand-sides t' include:

- a single variable;
- a constant for which no equations exist;
- more generally, a *constructor term*, i.e., a term whose function symbols have no associated equations.

But these are not the only possible cases where strong right irreducibility can be applied. Typing, particularly the use of sorts and subsorts in an order-sorted equational specification, can greatly help in attaining strong right irreducibility. We refer the reader to [19, 21] for two examples of how order-sorted typing helps narrowing-based unification to become finitary. We discuss one of these examples, namely Diffie-Hellman, in the following section.

Finally, let us motivate with an example how this narrowing-based equational unification works. Consider the exclusive-or theory:

$$
\begin{aligned}
X \oplus X \oplus Y &= Y \\
X \oplus X &= 0 \\
X \oplus 0 &= X
\end{aligned}
$$

viewed as the order-sorted rewrite theory $\mathcal{R} = (\Sigma, Ax, E)$ where Ax contains the associativity and commutativity of $\oplus$ and E contains the three equational rules above. Given the equational problem $t \stackrel{?}{=} s$, where $t = X \oplus Y$ and $s = U \oplus V$, we perform narrowing on t with the equations E modulo the axioms Ax. We can apply a renamed version (e.g. $Z \oplus Z \oplus W$) of the first equation to the term $X \oplus Y$. That is, the term $X \oplus Y$ unifies modulo AC with the term $Z \oplus Z \oplus W$ and one of the unifiers is $\sigma = \{X \mapsto W' \oplus Z', Y \mapsto Z', W \mapsto W', Z \mapsto Z'\}$. We express this narrowing step as

$$
X \oplus Y \leadsto_{\sigma, E, Ax} W'
$$

Note that, according to [27], we simply unify the terms W' and $U \oplus V$ modulo AC to finish the equational unification procedure, obtaining $\sigma' = \{X \mapsto (U \oplus V) \oplus Z', Y \mapsto Z'\}$ as an equational unifier of terms t and s modulo the equational theory for exclusive-or. This unifier is not necessarily the only one possible: given an equation $t = t'$, by successive narrowing of t and t' followed by attempts of Ax-unification, other unifiers can be computed. However, since the exclusive or theory satisfies conditions (1)-(5) above, we are guaranteed that there will be a finite complete set of unifiers obtained this way by narrowing.

6.4   Some Examples of Admissible Theories

Since any user of the Maude-NPA should write specifications whose algebraic theories are admissible, i.e., satisfy requirements (1)–(5) in Section 6.3, it may be useful to illustrate how these requirements are met by several examples. This can give a Maude-NPA user a good intuitive feeling for how to specify algebraic theories that the Maude-NPA currently can handle. For this purpose, we revisit the theories already discussed in Section 3.4.

Let us begin with the theory of Encryption/Decryption:

```
var Z : Msg .
var A : Name .

*** Encryption/Decryption Cancellation
eq pk(A,sk(A,Z)) = Z [nonexec] .
eq sk(A,pk(A,Z)) = Z [nonexec] .
```

In this case $Ax = \emptyset$. It is obvious that in this case the equations E *terminate*, since the *size* of a term as a tree (number of nodes) strictly decreases after the application of any of the above two rules, and therefore it is impossible to have an infinite chain of rewrites with the above equations. It is also easy to check that the equations are *confluent*: by the termination of E this can be reduced to checking confluence of critical pairs, which can be easily discharged by automated tools [16], or even by hand. Since $Ax = \emptyset$, coherence is a mute point. The equations are also *strongly right irreducible*, because in both cases they are the variable Z, and any instance of Z by a term that cannot be further simplified by the above equations, obviously cannot be further simplified by hypothesis.

Let us now consider the Exclusive Or Theory:

```
--- XOR operator
op _<+>_ : Msg Msg -> Msg [frozen assoc comm] .
op null : -> Msg .

vars X Y : Msg .

--- XOR equational properties
eq X <+> X <+> Y = Y [nonexec]   .
eq X <+> X = null [nonexec]   .
eq X <+> null = X [nonexec]   .
```

In this case $Ax = AC$. *Termination* modulo AC is again trivial, because the size of a term strictly decreases after applying any of the above equations modulo AC. Because of termination modulo AC, *confluence* modulo AC can be reduced to checking confluence of critical pairs, which can be discharged by standard tools [16]. *Coherence* modulo AC is also easy. As already explained, the first equation has to be added to the second to make it coherent. As also explained above, since the sort Msg is the biggest possible for the exclusive or operator, the variable X in the last equation has the biggest possible sort it can have, and therefore that equation is already coherent, so that there is no need to add an extra equation of the form

```
eq X <+> null <+> Y = X <+> Y [nonexec] .
```

because modulo *AC* such an equation is in fact *an instance* of the third equation (by instantiating X to the term X <+> Y). Finally, *strong right irreducibility* is also obvious, since the righthand sides are either variables, or the constant null, for which no equations exist.

Turning now to the Diffie-Hellman theory we have:

```
sorts Name NeNonceset Nonce Gen  Exp GenvExp Enc .
subsort Name NeNonceset Enc  Exp < Msg .
subsort Nonce < NeNonceset .
subsort Gen Exp < GenvExp .
subsort Name  Gen < Public .

op g : -> Gen [frozen] .
op exp : GenvExp NeNonceSet -> Exp [frozen] .
op _*_ : NeNonceSet NeNonceSet -> NeNonceSet [frozen assoc comm] .

eq exp(exp(W:Gen,Y:NeNonceSet),Z:NeNonceSet)
 = exp(W:Gen, Y:NeNonceSet * Z:NeNonceSet) [nonexec] .
```

Again, this theory is *AC*. *Termination* modulo *AC* is easy to prove by using a polynomial ordering with *AC* polynomial functions (see [47]). For example, we can associate to exp the polynomial $x + y + 1$, and to * the polynomial $x + y$. Then the proof of termination becomes just the polynomial inequality $w + y + z + 2 > w + y + z + 1$. Because of termination modulo *AC*, *confluence* modulo *AC* can be reduced to checking the confluence of critical pairs. Here things become interesting. In an untyped setting, the above equation would have a nontrivial overlap with itself (giving rise to a critical pair), by unifying the lefthand side with the subterm exp(W:Gen,Y:NeNonceSet). However, because of the subsort and operator declarations

```
subsort Gen Exp < GenvExp .
op exp : GenvExp NeNonceSet -> Exp [frozen] .
```

we see that the order-sorted unification of the subterm exp(W:Gen,Y:NeNonceSet) (which has sort Exp) and the lefthand side now *fails*, because the sorts Gen and Exp are mutually exclusive and cannot have any terms in common. Therefore there are no nontrivial critical pairs and the equation is confluent modulo *AC*. *Coherence* modulo *AC* is trivially satisfied, because the top operator of the equation (exp) is not an *AC* operator. As in the case of confluence modulo *AC*, the remaining issue of *strong right irreducibility* becomes particularly interesting in the order-sorted context. Note that in an untyped setting, an instance of the righthand side by applying a substitution whose terms cannot be further simplified *could* itself be simplified. For example, if we consider the untyped righthand side term `exp(W, Y * Z)`, the substitution θ mapping `W` to `exp(Q,X)` and being the identity on `Y` and `Z` is itself irreducible by the equations, but when applied to `exp(W, Y * Z)` makes the corresponding instance reducible by the untyped version of the above equation. However, in the order-sorted setting in which our equation is defined, the equation is indeed strongly right irreducible. This is again because the sorts `Gen` and `Exp` are mutually exclusive and cannot have any terms in common, so that the variable `W:Gen` cannot be instantiated by any term having `exp` as its top operator.

It may perhaps be useful to conclude this section with an example of an algebraic theory that *cannot* be supported in the current version of Maude-NPA. Consider, the extension of the above exclusive or theory in which we add a *homomorphism* operator and the obvious homomorphism equation:

```
op h : Msg -> Msg .

vars X Y : Msg .

eq h(X <+> Y) = h(X) <+> h(Y) [nonexec] .
```

The problem now is that the righthand side `h(X) <+> h(Y)` *fails* to be strongly right-irreducible. For example, the substitution θ mapping `X` to `U <+> V` and `Y` to `Y` is itself irreducible, but produces the instance `h(U <+> V) <+> h(Y)`, which is obviously reducible. Since strong irreducibility is only a *sufficient condition* for narrowing-based equational unification to be finitary, one could in principle hope that this homomorphism example might still have a narrowing-based finitary algorithm[14]. However, the hopes for such a finitary narrowing-based algorithm are dashed to the ground by results in both [15], about the homomorphism theory not having the "finite variant" property, and the variant-based unification methods in [25].

In summary, the main point we wish to emphasize is that the equational theories T for which the current version of Maude-NPA will work properly are order-sorted theories of the form $T = (\Sigma, E \cup Ax)$ satisfying the admissibility requirements (1)–(5). Under assumptions (1)–(5), T-unification problems are always guaranteed to have a finite number of solutions and the Maude-NPA will find them by narrowing.

As a final *caveat*, if the user specifies a theory T where any of the above requirements (1)–(5) fail, besides the lack of completeness that would be caused by

---

[14] The fact that an equational theory T does not have a finitary narrowing-based algorithm does not by itself preclude the existence of a finitary unification algorithm obtained by other methods. In fact, the homomorphic theory we have just described does have a finitary unification algorithm [2]; however this dedicated unification algorithm is not an instance of a generic narrowing-based algorithm. However, as already explained, in the Maude-NPA the theories for which finitary unification is currently supported are either order-sorted theories with built-in axioms of commutativity and associativity-commutativity, or theories modulo such built-in axioms that are confluent, terminating, and coherent modulo Ax, and that are also strongly right irreducible.

the failure of conditions (2)–(4), a likely consequence of failing to meet condition (5) will be that the tool may loop forever trying to solve a unification problem associated with just a single transition step in the symbolic reachability analysis process. However, we are investigating conditions more general than (5) (such as the above-mentioned finite variant property) that will still guarantee that a T-unification problem always has a finite complete set of solutions. Future versions of Maude-NPA will relax condition (5) to allow more general conditions of this kind.

7   State Space Reduction Techniques

In this section, we describe the different state-reduction techniques identifying unproductive backwards narrowing reachability steps. First, let us briefly recall a protocol state in Maude-NPA. A *state* in the protocol execution is a set of Maude-NPA strands unioned together with an associative and commutativity union operator _&_ with identity operator empty, along with an additional term describing the intruder knowledge at that point. The *intruder knowledge* is represented as a set of facts unioned together with an associative and commutativity union operator _,_ with identity operator empty. There are mainly two kinds of intruder facts: positive knowledge facts (m inI), and negative knowledge facts (m !inI). Strands communicate between them via a unique shared channel represented by the intruder knowledge.

There are three reasons for detecting unproductive backwards narrowing reachability steps (i.e., the relation $St \rightsquigarrow_{\sigma, R_\mathcal{P}^{-1}, E_\mathcal{P}} St'$ described in Section 5.2). One is to reduce, if possible, the initially infinite search space to a finite one, as in the use of grammars. Another is to reduce the size of a (possibly finite) search space by eliminating unreachable states early, i.e., before they are eliminated by exhaustive search. This elimination of unreachable states can have an effect far beyond eliminating a single node in the search space, since a single unreachable state may appear multiple times and/or have multiple descendants. Finally, it is also possible to use various partial order reduction techniques that can further shrink the number of states that need to be explored.

7.1   Public Data

The simplest optimization possible is when we are searching for some data that it is considered public using a subsort definition, e.g. "subsort Name < Public". That is, given a state St that contains an expression (t inI) in the intruder knowledge where t is of sort Public, we can remove the expression (t inI) from the intruder knowledge, since the backwards reachability steps taken care of such a (t inI) are trivially leading to an initial state but their inclusion in the message sequence is unnecessary.

7.2   Limiting Dynamic Introduction of New Strands

Our second optimization helps explain why attack states given in Section 5.2 contain a variable SS denoting a set of strands and a variable IK denoting a set of intruder facts, whereas the attack states explained in Section 4.4 do not contain those variables.

As pointed out in Section 5.2, Rules of type (5) allow the dynamic introduction of new strands. However, new strands can also be introduced by unification of a state containing a variable SS denoting a set of strands and one of the Rules (1), (2), and (4), where variables L and L' denoting lists of input/output messages will be introduced by instantiation of SS. The same can happen with new intruder facts of the form $(X \text{ inI})$, where X is a variable. That is, consider a state containing a variable SS denoting a set of strands and a variable IK denoting a set of intruder knowledge, and the Rule (1):

$$SS' \mathbin{\&} [L \mid M^-, L'] \mathbin{\&} ((M \text{ inI}), IK') \rightarrow SS' \mathbin{\&} [L, M^- \mid L'] \mathbin{\&} ((M \text{ inI}), IK')$$

The following backwards narrowing step applying such a rule can be performed from the state above using the unifier $\sigma = \{SS \mapsto SS' \mathbin{\&} [L, M^- \mid L'], IK \mapsto ((M \text{ inI}), IK')\}$

$$SS \mathbin{\&} IK \stackrel{\sigma}{\leadsto}_{R,E} SS' \mathbin{\&} [L \mid M^-, L'] \mathbin{\&} ((M \text{ inI}), IK')$$

but this backwards narrowing step is unproductive, since it is not guided by the information in the attack state. Indeed, the same rule can be applied again using variables SS' and IK' and this can be repeated many times.

In order to avoid a huge number of unproductive narrowing steps, we allow the introduction of new strands and/or new intruder facts only by rule application instead of just by unification. For this, we do two things:

1. we remove any of the following variables from attack states; SS denoting a set of strands, IK denoting a set of intruder facts, and L, L' denoting a set of input/output messages; and
2. we replace Rule (1) by the following Rule (7), since we do no longer have a variable denoting a set of intruder facts that has to be instantiated:

$$SS \mathbin{\&} [L \mid M^-, L'] \mathbin{\&} \{(M \text{ inI}), IK\} \rightarrow SS \mathbin{\&} [L, M^- \mid L'] \mathbin{\&} \{IK\} \qquad (7)$$

Note that in order to replace Rule (1) by Rule (7) we have to assume that the intruder knowledge is a set of intruder facts without repeated elements, i.e., the union operator $\_,\_$ is $ACUI$ (associative-commutative-identity-idempotent). This is completeness-preserving, since it is in line with the restriction in [20] that the intruder learns a term only once; if the intruder needs to use a term twice he must learn it the first time it is needed; if he learns a term and needs to learn it again in the backwards search, the state will be discarded as unreachable. Therefore, the set of rewrite rules used for backwards narrowing is $R_{\mathcal{P}} = \{(7), (2), (4)\} \cup (5)$.

Furthermore, one may imagine that Rule (4) and Rules of type (5) must also be modified in order to remove the (M inI) expression from the intruder knowledge of the right-hand side of each rule. However, this is wrong, since, by keeping the (M inI), we force the backwards application of such rule only when there is indeed a message for the intruder to be learned. This provides some sort of on-demand evaluation of the protocol.

7.3   Partial Order Reduction Giving Priority to Input Messages

The different rewrite rules on which the backwards narrowing search from an attack state is based are in general executed nondeterministically. This is because the order of execution can make a difference as to what subsequent rules can be executed. For example, an intruder cannot receive a term until it is sent by somebody, and that send action within a strand may depend upon other receives in the past. There is one exception, Rule (7) (originally Rule (1)), which, in a backwards search, only moves a negative term appearing right before the bar into the intruder knowledge. The execution of this transition in a backwards search does not disable any other transitions; indeed, it only enables send transitions. Thus, it is safe to execute it at each stage *before* any other transition. For the same reason, if several applications of Rule 7 are possible, it is safe to execute them all at once before any other transition. Requiring all executions of Rule 7 to execute first thus eliminates interleavings of Rule 7 with send and receive transitions, which are equivalent to the case in which Rule 7 executes first. In practice, this typically cuts down in half the search space size.

Similar strategies have been employed by other tools in forward searches. For example, in [45], a strategy is introduced that always executes send transitions first whenever they are enabled. Since a send transition does not depend on any other component of the state in order to take place, it can safely be executed first. The original NPA also used this strategy; it had a receive transition which had the effect of adding new terms to the intruder knowledge, and which always was executed before any other transition once it was enabled.

7.4   Detecting Inconsistent States Early

There are several types of states that are always unreachable or inconsistent. If the Maude-NPA attempts to search beyond them, it will never find an initial state. For this reason, we augment the Maude-NPA search engine to always mark the following types of states as unreachable, and not search beyond them any further:

1. A state St containing two contradictory facts $(t\,\texttt{inI})$ and $(t\,\texttt{!inI})$ for a term t.
2. A state St whose intruder knowledge contains the fact $(t\,\texttt{!inI})$ and a strand of the form $[m_1^{\pm}, \ldots, t^{-}, \ldots, m_{j-1}^{\pm} \mid m_j^{\pm}, \ldots, m_k^{\pm}]$.
3. A state St containing a fact $(t\,\texttt{inI})$ such that t contains a fresh variable r and the strand in St indexed by r, i.e., $(r_1, \ldots, r, \ldots, r_k : \texttt{Fresh})\,[m_1^{\pm}, \ldots, m_{j-1}^{\pm} \mid m_j^{\pm}, \ldots, m_k^{\pm}]$, cannot produce r, i.e., r is not a subterm of any output message in $m_1^{\pm}, \ldots, m_{j-1}^{\pm}$.
4. A state St containing a strand of the form $[m_1^{\pm}, \ldots, t^{-}, \ldots, m_{j-1}^{\pm} \mid m_j^{\pm}, \ldots, m_k^{\pm}]$ for some term t such that t contains a fresh variable r and the strand in St indexed by r cannot produce r.

Note that case 2 will become an instance of case 1 after some backwards narrowing steps, and the same happens with cases 4 and 3. The proof of inconsistency of cases 1 and 3 is obvious.

7.5 Transition Subsumption

Partial order reduction techniques (POR) are common in state exploration techniques due to their simplification properties. However, partial order techniques for narrowing-based state exploration have not been explored in detail, although they may be extremely relevant and even simplify much more than in standard state exploration techniques, based on ground terms rather than terms with variables. For instance, the simple concept of two states being equivalent modulo renaming of variables does not apply to standard state exploration techniques whereas it does apply to narrowing-based state exploration. In [24], Escobar and Meseguer explored narrowing-based state exploration and POR techniques, which may transform an infinite-state system into a finite one. However, the Maude-NPA needs a dedicated POR technique that should combine different previous ideas in order to be applicable to the concrete execution model.

Let us motivate this with an example before giving more technical explanations. Consider again the NSPK attack state:

$$(r : \texttt{Fresh})[\, pk(b, a; N)^-, pk(a, N; n(b, r))^+, pk(b, n(b, r))^- \mid nil \,] \,\&\, (n(b, r) \,\texttt{inI})$$

After a couple of backwards narrowing steps, the Maude-NPA finds the following state:

$$[\, nil \mid n(b, r)^-, pk(b, n(b, r))^+ \,] \,\&$$
$$(r : \texttt{Fresh})[\, pk(b, a; N)^-, pk(a, N; n(b, r))^+ \mid pk(b, n(b, r))^- \,] \,\&$$
$$((pk(b, n(b, r)) \,!\texttt{inI}), (n(b, r) \,\texttt{inI}))$$

which corresponds to the intruder generating (i.e., learning) the message $pk(b, n(b, r))$ from the message $n(b, r)$, which he/she already knows; and the following state

$$(r : \texttt{Fresh})[\, pk(b, a; N)^-, pk(a, N; n(b, r))^+ \mid pk(b, n(b, r))^- \,] \,\&$$
$$(r' : \texttt{Fresh})[pk(b, A'; n(A', r'))^+ \mid pk(A', n(A', r'); n(b, r))^-, pk(b, n(b, r))^+ \,] \,\&$$
$$((pk(b, n(b, r)) \,!\texttt{inI}), (pk(A', n(A', r'); n(b, r)) \,\texttt{inI}), (n(b, r) \,\texttt{inI}))$$

which corresponds to the responder (identified by variable r) talking to an initiator (identified by variable r'). However, this second state is implied by the first state. Intuitively, the elements present in the first state that are relevant for the backwards reachability are both included in the second state, namely the (n(b,r) inI) item and the message $pk(b, a; N)^-$ that will be converted at some point into (pk(b,a;N) inI). Indeed, the unreachability of the following "kernel" state implies the unreachability of both states, although this kernel state is never computed by the Maude-NPA:

$$(r : \texttt{Fresh})[\, pk(b, a; N)^-, pk(a, N; n(b, r))^+ \mid pk(b, n(b, r))^- \,] \,\&\, (n(b, r) \,\texttt{inI})$$

Note that the converse is not true, i.e., the second state does not imply the first one, since it contains one more intruder item relevant for backwards reachability purposes, namely (pk(A',n(A',r');n(b,r)) inI).

In the following, we write $IK^{\in}$ (resp. $IK^{\notin}$) to denote the subset of intruder facts of the form $(t \text{ inI})$ (resp. $(t \text{ !inI})$) appearing in the set of intruder facts IK. We abuse the set-theoretic notation and write $IK_1 \subseteq_{E_{\mathcal{P}}} IK_2$ for IK_1 and IK_2 sets of intruder facts to denote that all the intruder facts of IK_1 appear in IK_2 (modulo $E_{\mathcal{P}}$).

Definition 1. *Given a topmost rewrite theory* $\mathcal{R} = (\Sigma, E_{\mathcal{P}}, R_{\mathcal{P}})$ *representing protocol* $\mathcal{P}$, *and given two non-initial states* $St_1 = SS_1 \& \{IK_1\}$ *and* $St_2 = SS_2 \& \{IK_2\}$, *we write* $St_1 \triangleright St_2$ *(or* $St_2 \triangleleft St_1$*) if* $IK_1^{\in} \subseteq_{E_{\mathcal{P}}} IK_2^{\in}$, *and for each non-initial strand* $[m_1^{\pm}, \ldots, m_{j-1}^{\pm} \mid m_j^{\pm}, \ldots, m_k^{\pm}] \in SS_1$, *there exists* $[m_1^{\pm}, \ldots, m_{j-1}^{\pm} \mid m_j^{\pm}, \ldots, m_k^{\pm}, m_{k+1}^{\pm}, \ldots, m_{k'}^{\pm}] \in SS_2$. *Note that the comparison of the non-initial strand in* SS_1 *with the strands in* SS_2 *is performed modulo* $E_{\mathcal{P}}$.

Definition 2 ($\mathcal{P}$-subsumption relation). *Given a topmost rewrite theory* $\mathcal{R} = (\Sigma, E_{\mathcal{P}}, R_{\mathcal{P}})$ *representing protocol* $\mathcal{P}$ *and two non-initial states* St_1, St_2. *We write* $St_1 \preceq_{\mathcal{P}} St_2$ *and say that* St_1 *is* $\mathcal{P}$*-subsumed by* St_2 *if there is a substitution* θ *s.t.* $St_1 \triangleleft \theta(St_2)$.

This technique is used as follows: we keep all the states of the backwards narrowing-based tree and compare each new leaf of the tree with all the previous states in the tree. If a leaf is $\mathcal{P}$-subsumed by a previously generated node in the tree, we discard such leaf.

7.6   The Super Lazy Intruder

Sometimes terms appear in the intruder knowledge that are trivially learnable by the intruder. These include terms initially available to the intruder (such as names) and variables. In the case of variables, the intruder can substitute any arbitrary term of the same sort as the variable,[15] and so there is no need to try to determine all the ways in which the intruder can do this. For this reason it is safe, at least temporarily, to drop these terms from the state. We will refer to those terms as *lazy intruder* terms. The problem of course, is that later on in the search the variable may become instantiated, in which case the term now becomes relevant to the search. In order to avoid this problem, we take an approach similar to that of the lazy intruder of Basin et al. [6] and extend it to a more general case, that we call the *super-lazy terms*. We note that this use of what we here call the super-lazy intruder was also present in the original NPA.

Super-lazy terms are defined inductively as the union of the set of lazy terms, i.e., variables, with the set of terms that are produced out of other super-lazy terms using operations available to the intruder. That is, $e(K, X)$ is a super-lazy term if the intruder can perform the e operation, and K and X are variables. More precisely, the set of super-lazy intruder terms is defined as follows.

---

[15] This, of course, is subject to the assumption that the intruder can produce at least one term of that sort. But since the intruder is assumed to have access to the network and to all the operations available to an honest principal, this is a safe assumption to make.

Definition 3. *Given a topmost rewrite theory* $\mathcal{R} = (\Sigma, E_{\mathcal{P}}, R_{\mathcal{P}})$ *representing protocol* $\mathcal{P}$, *and a state* St *where* $IK^{\notin}(St) = \{x \mid (x \,!inI) \in St\}$, *its set of super-lazy terms w.r.t.* St *(or simply super-lazy terms) is defined as the union of the following:*

- *the set of variables of sort* Msg *or one of its subsorts,*
- *the set of terms* t *appearing in strands of the form* $[t^+]$, *and*
- *the set of terms of the form* $f(t_1, \ldots, t_n)$ *where* $\{t_1, \ldots, t_n\}$ *are super-lazy intruder terms w.r.t.* St, $\{t_1, \ldots, t_n\} \not\subseteq IK^{\notin}(St)$, *and there is an intruder strand* $[(X_1)^-, \ldots, (X_n)^-, (f(X_1, \ldots, X_n))^+]$ *with* $X_1, \ldots, X_n$ *variables.*

The idea behind the super-lazy intruder is that, given a term made out of lazy intruder terms, such as "$a; e(K, Y)$", where a is a public name and K and Y are variables, the term "$a; e(K, Y)$" is also a (super) lazy intruder term by applying the operations e and $\_;\_$.

Let us first briefly explain how the (super) lazy intruder mechanism works before formally describing it. When we detect a state St with a super lazy term t, we replace the intruder fact $(t \,inI)$ in St by a new expression $ghost(t)$ and keep the modified version of St in the history of states used by the transition subsumption of Section 7.5. If later in the search tree we detect a state St' containing an expression $ghost(t)$ such that t is no longer a super lazy intruder term (or *ghost expression*), then t has been instantiated in an appropriate way and we must reactivate the original state St that introduced the $ghost(t)$ expression (and that precedes St' in the narrowing tree) with the new binding for variables in t applied. That is, we "roll back" and replace the current state St' with an instantiated version of state St.

However, if the substitution θ binding variables in t includes variables of sort Fresh, since they are unique in our model, we have to keep them in the reactivated version of St. Therefore, the strands indexed by these fresh variables must be included in the "rolled back" state, even if they were not there originally. Moreover, they must have the bar at the place it was when the strands were originally introduced. We show below how this is accomplished.

Furthermore, if any of the strands thus introduced have other variables of sort Fresh as subterms, then the strands indexed by those variables must be included too, and so on. Thus, when a state St' properly instantiating a ghost expression $ghost(t)$ is found, the procedure of rolling back to the original state St that gave rise to that ghost expression implies not only applying the bindings for the variables of t to St, but also introducing in St all the strands from St' that produced fresh variables and that either appear in the variables of t or are recursively connected to them.

First, before formally defining the super-lazy intruder technique, we must modify Rules of type 5 introducing new strands:

$$\{\, [\, l_1 \mid u^+] \,\&\, \{(u \,!inI), K\} \rightarrow \{(u \,inI), K\} \text{ s.t. } [l_1, u^+, l_2] \in \mathcal{P}\} \qquad (8)$$

Therefore, the set of rewrite rules used by narrowing in reverse are now $R_{\mathcal{P}} = \{(7), (2), (4)\} \cup (8)$. Note that Rules of type (5) introduce strands $[\, l_1 \mid u^+, l_2\,]$, whereas here Rules of type (8) introduce strands $[l_1 \mid u^+]$. This slight modification allows to safely move the position of the bar back to the place where the strand was introduced.

We extend the intruder knowledge to allow an extra fact $ghost(t)$. Indeed, this corresponds to the fourth component of a Maude-NPA state explained in Section 4. We first describe how to reactivate a state. Given a strand $s = (r_1, \ldots, r_k : \texttt{Fresh})\ [m_1^\pm, \ldots \mid \ldots, m_n^\pm]$, when we want to move the bar to the rightmost position (denoting a final strand), we write $s\gg = (r_1, \ldots, r_k : \texttt{Fresh})\ [m_1^\pm, \ldots, m_n^\pm \mid nil]$.

Definition 4. *Given a state St containing an intruder fact $ghost(t)$ for some term t with variables, we define the set of strands associated to t, denoted $SS_{St}(t)$, as follows: for each strand s in St of the form $(r_1, \ldots, r_k : \texttt{Fresh})\ [m_1^\pm, \ldots \mid \ldots, m_n^\pm]$, if there is $i \in \{1, \ldots, k\}$ s.t. $r_i \in Var(t)$, then $s\gg \in SS_{St}(t)$; or if there is another strand $s' \in SS_{St}(t)$ of the form $(r_1', \ldots, r_{k'}' : \texttt{Fresh})\ [w_1^\pm, \ldots \mid \ldots, w_{n'}^\pm]$, $i \in \{1, \ldots, k\}$, and $j \in \{1, \ldots, n'\}$ s.t. $r_i \in Var(w_j)$, then $s\gg \in SS_{St}(t)$.*

Improving the super lazy intruder. When we detect a state St with a super lazy term t, we may want to analyze whether the variables of t may be eventually instantiated or not before creating a ghost state. Therefore, if for each strand $[m_1^\pm, \ldots, m_{j-1}^\pm \mid m_j^\pm, \ldots, m_k^\pm]$ in St and each $i \in \{1, \ldots, j-1\}$, $Var(t) \cap Var(m_i) = \emptyset$, and for each term $(w\ \texttt{inI})$ in the intruder knowledge, $Var(t) \cap Var(w) = \emptyset$, then we can clearly infer that the variables of t can never be instantiated and adding a ghost to state St is unnecessary.

Interaction with transition subsumption. When a ghost state is reactivated, we see from the above definition that such a reactivated state will be $\mathcal{P}$-subsumed by the original state that raised the ghost expression. Therefore, the transition subsumption of Section 7.5 has to be slightly modified to avoid checking a resuscitated state with its predecessor ghost state, i.e., $St_1 \succeq_\mathcal{P}' St_2$ iff $St_1 \succeq_\mathcal{P} St_2$ and St_2 is *not* a resuscitated version of St_1.

7.7   Grammars

The Maude-NPA's ability to reason effectively about low-level algebraic properties is a result of its combination of symbolic reachability analysis using narrowing modulo equational properties (see Section 6), together with its grammar-based techniques for reducing the size of the search space, as well as other state space reduction techniques explained in this section. Here we briefly explain how grammars work as a state space reduction technique and refer the reader to [20, 35] for further details.

Automatically generated grammars $\langle G_1, \ldots, G_m \rangle$ represent unreachability information (or co-invariants), i.e., typically infinite sets of states unreachable for the intruder. That is, given a message m and an automatically generated grammar G, if $m \in G$, then there is no initial state St_{init} and substitution θ such that

the intruder knowledge of St_{init} contains the fact $\theta(m)$!inI, i.e., the intruder
will never be able to learn message m in the future. These automatically generated grammars are very important in our framework, since in the best case they
can reduce the infinite search space to a finite one, or, at least, can drastically
reduce the search space.

Let us motivate this with the NSPK attack state:

$$(r : \texttt{Fresh})[\, pk(b, a; N)^-, pk(a, N; n(b, r))^+, pk(b, n(b, r))^- \mid nil \,] \,\&\, (n(b, r) \texttt{ inI})$$

After a couple of backwards narrowing steps, the Maude-NPA finds the following
state:

$$[\, nil \mid (n(b, r); M)^-, n(b, r)^+ \,] \,\&$$
$$(r : \texttt{Fresh})[\, pk(b, a; N)^-, pk(a, N; n(b, r))^+ \mid pk(b, n(b, r))^- \,] \,\&$$
$$((n(b, r) \texttt{ !inI}), (pk(b, n(b, r)) \texttt{ inI}), ((n(b, r); M) \texttt{ inI}))$$

which corresponds to the intruder generating (i.e., learning) the message
$n(b, r)$ from a bigger message $(n(b, r); M)$, although the contents of variable
M have not yet been found by the backwards reachability analysis. This process
of adding more and more intruder strands that look for terms $((n(b, r); M); M')$,
$(((n(b, r); M); M'); M'')$, ... can go infinitely. Note that if we carefully check the
strands for the NSPK protocol given in Page 17, we can see that the honest
strands never produce a message of the form "$Nonce\ ;\ Message$" or such a
message is under a public key encryption (and thus he/she cannot get into the
contents), so the previous state is clearly unreachable and can be discarded. The
grammar, which is generated by Maude-NPA, capturing the previous state as
unreachable is as follows:

```
grl M inL => pk(A, M) inL . ;
grl M inL => sk(A, M) inL . ;
grl M inL => (M' ; M) inL . ;
grl M inL => (M ; M') inL . ;
grl M notInI, M notLeq n(i, r) => (i ; M) inL . ;
grl M notInI, M notLeq n(i, r) => (M ; M') inL . ;
grl M notInI, M notLeq n(i, r) => pk(A, B ; M) inL .
```

Intuitively, the last production rule in the grammar above says that any term
of the form $pk(A, B; M)$ cannot be learned by the intruder if it is different
to $pk(A, B; n(i, r))$ (i.e., it does not match such pattern) and the constraint
(M !inI) appears explicitly in the intruder knowledge of the current state being
checked for unreachability. Moreover, any term of any of the following forms:
$pk(A, M)$, $sk(A, M)$, $(M'; M)$, or $(M; M')$ cannot be learned by the intruder if
subterm M is also not learnable by the intruder.

Unlike the grammars used in NPA, described in [35], and the version of Maude-
NPA described in [20], in which initial grammars needed to be specified by the
user, Maude-NPA now generates initial grammars *automatically*. Each initial
grammar consists of a single seed term of the form grl C => $f(X_1, \cdots, X_n)$ inL,

where f is an operator symbol from the protocol specification, the X_i are variables, and C is either empty or consists of the single constraint $(X_i \text{ notInI})$, similar to expression $(X_i \text{ !inI})$ but used in a different context. For instance, the seed term for the grammar above is "grl M notInI => (M ; M') inL". However, Maude-NPA provides features to control such automatically generated grammars, e.g., adding more seed terms; see [23] for further details.

8 Conclusions

In this tutorial, we have given an overview of the Maude-NRL Protocol Analyzer (Maude-NPA). We have explained the basic mechanics of using Maude-NPA, including writing specifications and formulating queries, that gives the minimum amount of background for using the tool. We have also explained how the Maude-NPA actually works at the backwards reachability level and at the equational unification level. Finally, we have described the different state-reduction techniques identifying unproductive backwards narrowing reachability steps. This, we believe, is enough to give a basic understanding of how Maude-NPA works, and also to get started using it.

Maude-NPA is still under development, and we are currently working on a number of ways of extending its applicability and usability, including more sophisticated narrowing-based algorithms, as mentioned in this tutorial, and a graphical user interface [44] that allows a user to examine a Maude-NPA search tree in detail. However, it still remains grounded in the principles described in this tutorial, and we believe the ideas and techniques we have presented here will remain a useful introduction even as it matures.

Acknowledgments

José Meseguer has been partially supported by NSF grants CNS 07-16638 and CNS 08-31064. Santiago Escobar has been partially supported by the EU (FEDER) and the Spanish MEC/MICINN under grant TIN 2007-68093-C02-02, and Generalitat Valenciana GVPRE/2008/113.

References

1. Abadi, M., Cortier, V.: Deciding knowledge in security protocols under equational theories. Theoretical Computer Science 367(1-2), 2–32 (2006)
2. Anantharaman, S., Narendran, P., Rusinowitch, M.: Unification modulo CUI plus distributivity axioms. Journal of Automated Reasoning 33(1), 1–28 (2004)
3. Armando, A., Basin, D., Boichut, Y., Chevalier, Y., Compagna, L., Cuellar, J., Drielsma, P.H., Heám, P.C., Kouchnarenko, O., Mantovani, J., Mödersheim, S., von Oheimb, D., Rusinowitch, M., Santiago, J., Turuani, M., Viganò, L., Vigneron, L.: The AVISPA tool for the automated validation of internet security protocols and applications. In: Etessami, K., Rajamani, S.K. (eds.) CAV 2005. LNCS, vol. 3576, pp. 281–285. Springer, Heidelberg (2005)

4. Armando, A., Compagna, L., Lierler, Y.: SATMC: A SAT-based model checker for security protocols. In: Alferes, J.J., Leite, J. (eds.) JELIA 2004. LNCS, vol. 3229, pp. 730–733. Springer, Heidelberg (2004)
5. Baader, F., Snyder, W.: Unification theory. In: Robinson, J.A., Voronkov, A. (eds.) Handbook of Automated Reasoning, vol. 2, pp. 445–532. Elsevier and MIT Press (2001)
6. Basin, D., Mödersheim, S., Viganò, L.: OFMC: A symbolic model checker for security protocols. International Journal of Information Security 4(3), 181–208 (2005)
7. Baudet, M., Cortier, V., Delaune, S.: YAPA: A generic tool for computing intruder knowledge. In: Treinen, R. (ed.) RTA 2009. LNCS, vol. 5595, pp. 148–163. Springer, Heidelberg (2009)
8. Blanchet, B.: An Efficient Cryptographic Protocol Verifier Based on Prolog Rules. In: 14th IEEE Computer Security Foundations Workshop (CSFW-14), Cape Breton, Nova Scotia, Canada, pp. 82–96. IEEE Computer Society, Los Alamitos (2001)
9. Boichut, Y., Héam, P.-C., Kouchnarenko, O., Oehl, F.: Improvements on the Genet and Klay technique to automatically verify security protocols. In: Proceedings of Automated Verification of Infinite States Systems (AVIS 2004). ENTCS (2004)
10. Bursuc, S., Comon-Lundh, H.: Protocol security and algebraic properties: decision results for a bounded number of sessions. In: Treinen, R. (ed.) RTA 2009. LNCS, vol. 5595, pp. 133–147. Springer, Heidelberg (2009)
11. Chevalier, Y., Rusinowitch, M.: Hierarchical combination of intruder theories. Inf. Comput. 206(2-4), 352–377 (2008)
12. Ciobâcă, Ş., Delaune, S., Kremer, S.: Computing knowledge in security protocols under convergent equational theories. In: Schmidt, R. (ed.) CADE 2009. LNCS (LNAI), vol. 5663, pp. 355–370. Springer, Heidelberg (2009)
13. Clavel, M., Durán, F., Eker, S., Escobar, S., Lincoln, P., Martí-Oliet, N., Meseguer, J., Talcott, C.: Unification and Narrowing in Maude 2.4. In: Treinen, R. (ed.) RTA 2009. LNCS, vol. 5595, pp. 380–390. Springer, Heidelberg (2009)
14. Clavel, M., Durán, F., Eker, S., Lincoln, P., Martí-Oliet, N., Meseguer, J., Talcott, C.: All About Maude - A High-Performance Logical Framework. LNCS, vol. 4350. Springer, Heidelberg (2007)
15. Comon-Lundh, H., Delaune, S.: The finite variant property: How to get rid of some algebraic properties. In: Giesl, J. (ed.) RTA 2005. LNCS, vol. 3467, pp. 294–307. Springer, Heidelberg (2005)
16. Contejean, E., Marché, C.: The CiME system: tutorial and user's manual. Université Paris-Sud, Centre d'Orsay (manuscript)
17. Dolev, D., Yao, A.: On the security of public key protocols. IEEE Transaction on Information Theory 29(2), 198–208 (1983)
18. Durgin, N., Lincoln, P., Mitchell, J., Scedrov, A.: Multiset rewriting and the complexity of bounded security. Journal of Computer Security, 677–722 (2004)
19. Escobar, S., Hendrix, J., Meadows, C., Meseguer, J.: Diffie-Hellman cryptographic reasoning in the Maude-NRL protocol analyzer. In: Proc. 2nd International Workshop on Security and Rewriting Techniques, SecReT 2007 (2007)
20. Escobar, S., Meadows, C., Meseguer, J.: A rewriting-based inference system for the NRL protocol analyzer and its meta-logical properties. Theoretical Compute Science 367(1-2), 162–202 (2006)
21. Escobar, S., Meadows, C., Meseguer, J.: Equational cryptographic reasoning in the Maude-NRL protocol analyzer. In: Proc. 1st International Workshop on Security and Rewriting Techniques (SecReT 2006). ENTCS, vol. 171(4), pp. 23–36. Elsevier, Amsterdam (2007)

22. Escobar, S., Meadows, C., Meseguer, J.: State space reduction in the Maude-NRL Protocol Analyzer. In: Jajodia, S., Lopez, J. (eds.) ESORICS 2008. LNCS, vol. 5283, pp. 548–562. Springer, Heidelberg (2008)

23. Escobar, S., Meadows, C., Meseguer, J.: Maude-NPA, version 1.0. University of Illinois at Urbana-Champaign (March 2009),
http://maude.cs.uiuc.edu/tools/Maude-NPA

24. Escobar, S., Meseguer, J.: Symbolic model checking of infinite-state systems using narrowing. In: Baader, F. (ed.) RTA 2007. LNCS, vol. 4533, pp. 153–168. Springer, Heidelberg (2007)

25. Escobar, S., Meseguer, J., Sasse, R.: Variant narrowing and equational unification. Technical Report UIUCDCS-R-2007-2910, Dept. of Computer Science, University of Illinois at Urbana-Champaign (October 2007)

26. Escobar, S., Meseguer, J., Sasse, R.: Effectively checking the finite variant property. In: Voronkov, A. (ed.) RTA 2008. LNCS, vol. 5117, pp. 79–93. Springer, Heidelberg (2008)

27. Escobar, S., Meseguer, J., Sasse, R.: Variant narrowing and equational unification. In: Rossu, G. (ed.) Proc. 7th. Intl. Workshop on Rewriting Logic and its Applications. ENTCS. Elsevier, Amsterdam (2008) (to appear)

28. Fabrega, F.J.T., Herzog, J., Guttman, J.: Strand Spaces: What Makes a Security Protocol Correct? Journal of Computer Security 7, 191–230 (1999)

29. Hullot, J.-M.: Canonical forms and unification. In: Bibel, W., Kowalski, R. (eds.) CADE 1980. LNCS, vol. 87, pp. 318–334. Springer, Heidelberg (1980)

30. Millen, S.F.J.K., Clark, S.C.: The interrogator: Protocol secuity analysis. IEEE Transactions on Software Engineering, 274–288 (February 1987)

31. Jouannaud, J.-P., Kirchner, C., Kirchner, H.: Incremental construction of unification algorithms in equational theories. In: Díaz, J. (ed.) ICALP 1983. LNCS, vol. 154, pp. 361–373. Springer, Heidelberg (1983)

32. Lowe, G.: Breaking and fixing the Needham-Schroeder public-key protocol using FDR. Software Concepts and Tools 17, 93–102 (1996)

33. Lynch, C., Meadows, C.: On the relative soundness of the free algebra model for public key encryption. In: Workshop on Issues in Theory of Security 2004 (2004)

34. Lynch, C., Meadows, C.: Sound Approximations to Diffie-Hellman Using Rewrite Rules. In: López, J., Qing, S., Okamoto, E. (eds.) ICICS 2004. LNCS, vol. 3269, pp. 262–277. Springer, Heidelberg (2004)

35. Meadows, C.: Language generation and verification in the NRL protocol analyzer. In: Ninth IEEE Computer Security Foundations Workshop, Dromquinna Manor, Kenmare, County Kerry, Ireland, March 10-12, pp. 48–61. IEEE Computer Society, Los Alamitos (1996)

36. Meadows, C.: The NRL protocol analyzer: An overview. Journal of logic programming 26(2), 113–131 (1996)

37. Meseguer, J.: Conditional rewriting logic as a unified model of concurrency. Theoretical Computer Science 96(1), 73–155 (1992)

38. Meseguer, J.: Membership algebra as a logical framework for equational specification. In: Parisi-Presicce, F. (ed.) WADT 1997. LNCS, vol. 1376, pp. 18–61. Springer, Heidelberg (1998)

39. Millen, J.: On the freedom of decryption. Information Processing Letters 86(3) (2003)

40. Mitchell, J., Mitchell, M., Stern, U.: Automated analysis of cryptographic protocols using Murphi. In: IEEE Symposium on Security and Privacy. IEEE Computer Society, Los Alamitos (1997)

41. Paulson, L.C.: The inductive approach to verifying cryptographic protocols. Journal of Computer Security 6(1-2), 85–128 (1998)
42. Rusinowitch, M., Turuani, M.: Protocol insecurity with a finite number of sessions and composed keys is NP-complete. In: 14th IEEE Computer Security Foundations Workshop, pp. 174–190 (2001)
43. Ryan, P.Y.A., Schneider, S.A.: An attack on a recursive authentication protocol. a cautionary tale. Inf. Process. Lett. 65(1), 7–10 (1998)
44. Santiago, S., Talcott, C., Escobar, S., Meadows, C., Meseguer, J.: A graphical user interface for Maude-NPA. Technical Report DSIC-II/02/09, Universidad Politécnica de Valencia (June 2009)
45. Shmatikov, V., Stern, U.: Efficient finite-state analysis for large security protocols. In: 11th Computer Security Foundations Workshop — CSFW-11. IEEE Computer Society Press, Los Alamitos (1998)
46. Stubblebine, S., Meadows, C.: Formal characterization and automated analysis of known-pair and chosen-text attacks. IEEE Journal on Selected Areas in Communications 18(4), 571–581 (2000)
47. TeReSe (ed.): Term Rewriting Systems. Cambridge University Press, Cambridge (2003)
48. Thati, P., Meseguer, J.: Symbolic reachability analysis using narrowing and its application verification of cryptographic protocols. J. Higher-Order and Symbolic Computation 20(1-2), 123–160 (2007)

An Introduction to Certificate Translation[*]

Gilles Barthe and César Kunz

IMDEA Software, Spain

Abstract. In a Proof-Carrying Code scenario, certificate generation remains a challenging problem. Typically, it is implemented as a compiler module that targets low-level executable code. Hence, since automatic, the properties under verification are limited to very simple safety policies. Discharging verification conditions automatically for arbitrarily complex properties is unfeasible. Therefore, it requires the support of tool-based interactive verification, which commonly targets high-level structured code. To connect source code verification and compiled code certification we have proposed a technique to build, from a certificate of the source program, a certificate for the result of its compilation. In this tutorial, we illustrate the principles of this technique, certificate translation, in the context of a certified quicksort algorithm. For each transformation step that defines the compiler, we explain the corresponding transformation of the certificate.

1 Introduction

Certificate translation [2,4] is a general method that reconciles interactive verification of source programs with automated verification of compiled programs, using certificates as a means to convey evidence about program correctness. More precisely, certificate translation offers the possibility of generating certificates for complex properties of compiled programs—with the potential cost of interactive verification of source programs—and thus provides an alternative to certifying compilation, which is used in the context of Proof-Carrying Code [19] to generate automatically certificates that compiled programs respect simple policies.

Certificate translation primarily focuses on the interplay between compilation and program correctness: given a compiler $\|.\|$ from a source language $\mathcal{S}$ to a target language $\mathcal{T}$, and a compiler $\|.\|_{\mathrm{spec}}$ from a specification language $\mathsf{Spec}_{\mathcal{S}}$ for source programs to a specification language $\mathsf{Spec}_{\mathcal{T}}$ for target programs, certificate translation is concerned with the following two intimately related questions:

1. for every program p and specification ϕ, does the correctness of p w.r.t. ϕ entail the correctness of $\|p\|$ w.r.t. $\|\phi\|_{\mathrm{spec}}$?
2. for every program p and specification ϕ, is there a method to transform evidence of the correctness of p w.r.t. ϕ into evidence $\|p\|$ w.r.t. $\|\phi\|_{\mathrm{spec}}$?

Answering these questions requires making precise the notion of program correctness, and to a lesser extent on the notion of evidence. To ensure compatibility

---

[*] Partially funded by the EU project MOBIUS IST-15905.

A. Aldini, G. Barthe, R. Gorrieri (Eds.): FOSAD 2007/2008/2009, LNCS 5705, pp. 51–95, 2009.

with typical Proof-Carrying Code architectures, we base our infrastructure for verifying program correctness on generators of proof obligations (a.k.a. verification conditions) from annotated programs. On the other hand, we do not need to commit to a particular format for certificates, and assume instead the existence of a binary judgment $c : \vdash \phi$ stating that c is a certificate for ϕ, and of a set of operations for making some basic manipulations on certificates.

Thus, a program p satisfies a specification ϕ iff the set of proof obligations $\mathsf{PO}(p, \phi) = \{\phi_1, \ldots, \phi_n\}$ is provable, and evidence that p satisfies ϕ takes the form of a set of certificates $\mathsf{Cert}(p, \phi) = \{c_1, \ldots, c_n\}$ such that $c_1 : \vdash \phi_1$ and $\ldots$ and $c_n : \vdash \phi_n$. Then, the problem tackled by certificate translation is to find a function $\| \ \|_{\mathrm{cert}} : \forall p \ \phi, \ \mathsf{Cert}(p, \phi) \rightarrow \mathsf{Cert}(\|p\|, \|\phi\|_{\mathrm{spec}})$, i.e., a procedure that transforms a set certificates for the source program into a set of certificates for the result of the compilation.

The purpose of this tutorial is to illustrate the principles and effects of certificate translation on the example of the quicksort function. We start from an interactive proof of the quicksort function in a small imperative language with procedures and arrays; the code is given in Figure 1. We assume that the quicksort function is certified to satisfy the specification

$$\{\mathsf{Pre} : 0 \leq \mathsf{start} \leq \mathsf{end} \leq |\mathsf{vec}|\}$$

$$\mathbf{quicksort}(\mathsf{start}, \mathsf{end})$$

$$\{\mathsf{Post} : \forall k. \ \mathsf{start} \leq k < \mathsf{end} \Rightarrow \mathsf{vec}[k] \leq \mathsf{vec}[k+1]\}$$

where vec is a global array variable. That is, if the values held by the parameters start and end are within the bounds of the array vec, after the execution of quicksort, vec holds increasing values in the range [start, end].

```
quicksort(start, end){              partition(start, end){
    if (start < end) {                  pivot = vec[start];
        p = partition(start, end);      i = start;
        quicksort(start, p);            j = end;
        quicksort(p+1, end);            while (i < j) {
    }                                       while (vec[i] ≤ pivot ∧ i < j)
    return;                                     i++;
}                                           while(pivot < vec[j] ∧ i < j)
                                                j--;
                                            if (i < j) swap(i, j);
swap(i, j){                             }
    t = vec[i];                         swap(start, i-1);
    vec[i] = vec[j];                    return i-1;
    vec[j] = t;                     }
    return;
}
```

Fig. 1. Quicksort Algorithm

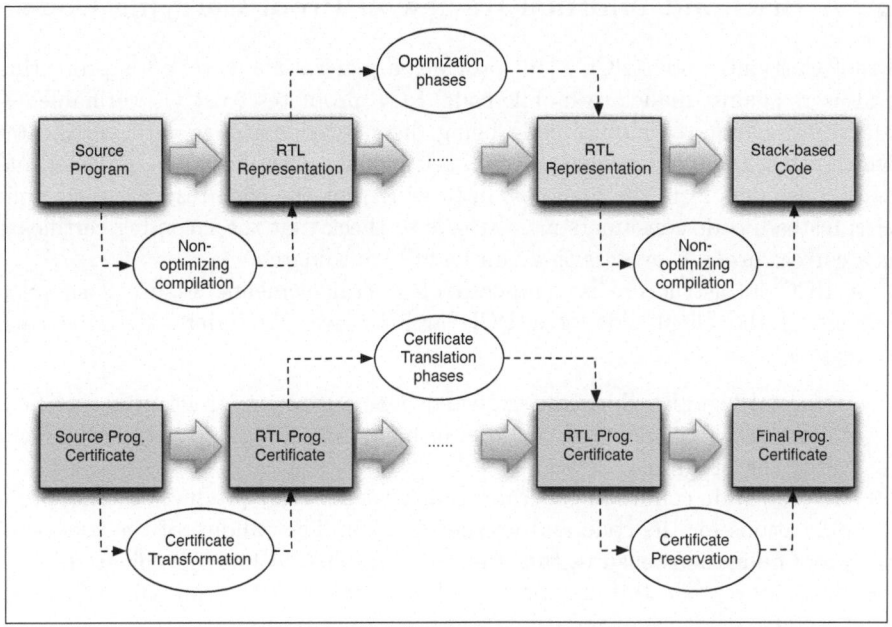

Fig. 2. Overall Compiler and Certificate Translation Phases

The certificate transformation process follows the overall structure of a classical compiler, which operates on the input program in successive and independent transformation steps. For each program compilation step, we transform the specification and the certificates accordingly. An overall scheme of the compiler under consideration can be found in Figure 2, together with the corresponding certificate translation steps. In these transformation steps, the code is gradually transformed towards its final executable representation. First, the high-level structured code is transformed to a low-level intermediate program representation (RTL). In this intermediate representation, the compiler proceeds with successive optimizing transformations. The final step transforms the intermediate representation into stack-based code.

Outline. Section 2 provides an informal review of the principles of Proof Carrying Code. In Section 3, we define the source programming language and a corresponding verification framework. In Section 4, we describe the intermediate RTL program representation. In this setting, a verification framework for RTL is defined, and a short verification example is provided. In Section 5, we deal with certificate transformation along compiler phases, including non-optimizing compilation, loop-induction strength reduction, dead variable elimination loop unrolling, and redundant conditional elimination. In Section 5.8, we show preservation of proof obligations in the generation of the final stack-based code. We conclude in Section 6.

2   A Brief and Informal Review of Proof Carrying Code

Proof Carrying Code (PCC) [16] provides a general framework for protecting end-users against malicious mobile code. PCC promotes trust via verifiable evidence, and requires mobile code being distributed together with certificates which attest its adherence to the end-user policies. Certificates help dispensing code consumers from the high cost of proving that the code respects their policies; instead, code consumers merely have to check that the incoming certificate is a correct proof, a process that can be fully automated.

A PCC infrastructure is composed of several elements. Figure 2 shows a scheme of the client side of a PCC architecture. We briefly describe each component:

- A formal logic in which the expected behavior of the program is specified. Commonly, PCC adopts first-order or higher-order logic to both specify and verify the program.
- A verification condition generator that automatically produces a set of proof obligations for the code and its specification. The validity of the generated proof obligations ensures that the code complies with its specification.
- A formal representation of proofs, a.k.a. certificates, that provides efficiently verifiable evidence of the validity of proof obligations.
- A proof checker that verifies that the certificate does indeed establish the proof obligations.

Proof Carrying Code benefits from a number of distinctive features that make it a very appropriate basis for security architectures for global computers, and in particular for addressing the security issues highlighted above.

Proof Carrying Code is based on verification rather than trust. Indeed, Proof Carrying Code focuses on the behavior of downloaded components rather than on its origins. In particular, it does not require the existence of a global trust infrastructure (although it can be used in combination with cryptographic based trust infrastructures), for a further discussion see [1].

Proof Carrying Code is transparent for end users. While Proof Carrying Code builds upon ideas from program verification, which in its full generality requires interactive proofs, the PCC architecture does not require the code consumers to build proofs. Rather, it requires code consumers to check proofs, which is fully automatic.

Proof Carrying Code is general. The only restriction on the security policy is that it should be expressible in the formal logic, which is often very expressive.

Proof Carrying Code is flexible and configurable. The same architecture can be used for different policies. In particular, the VCGen and the proof checker are independent of the policy, while the certificate generation can in principle be adapted to different safety properties.

Proof Carrying Code does not sacrifice performance to security. PCC technology advocates for static verification, and therefore does not incur in the overhead cost inherent to dynamic techniques based on monitoring.

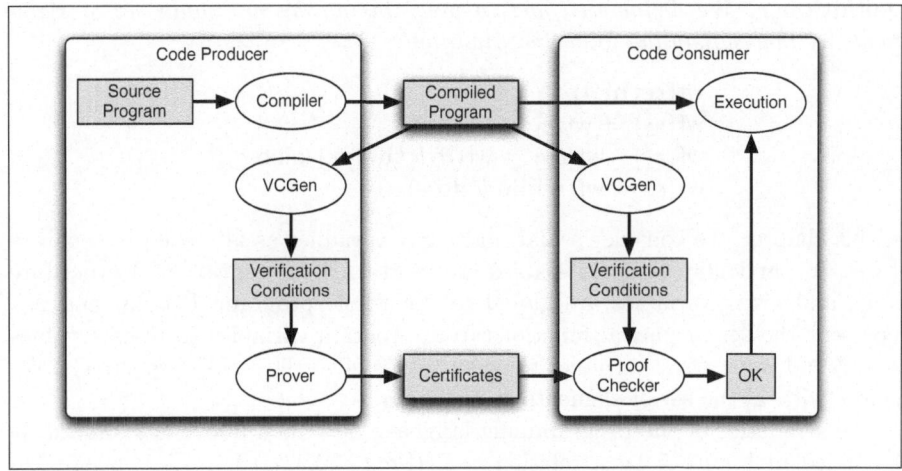

Fig. 3. PCC Scheme - Code Client Side

3   Tool Based Source Code Verification

3.1   Programming Language Setting

In this section, we define the high-level imperative language for writing source programs. A source program is defined as a collection of procedures, each of them consisting of its formal parameters and the statement that defines its body. Expressions and statements are described in Figure 4. $\mathcal{V}$ and $\mathcal{A}$ represent the set of scalar and array variables, respectively. Most of the constructions in the grammar of the figure are standard, $\oplus$ stands for an integer operation and $a[e]$ stands for the integer value stored in the array a at position e. Statements include assignments to array structures, $a[e]:=e$, and procedure invocations of the form $x:=f(e)$. The statement **if** b **then** c stands for **if** b **then** c **else skip**.

For simplicity, we assume source programs to be well-formed, in the sense that every execution path reaches a **return** statement. The following definition formalizes this requirement:

---

integer expressions	$e ::= e \oplus e \mid n \mid x \mid a[e]$
boolean expressions	$b ::= \mathsf{true} \mid \mathsf{false} \mid e \bowtie e \mid b \wedge b \mid \ldots$
statements	$c ::= \mathbf{skip} \mid x:=e \mid a[e]:=e \mid c; c \mid \mathbf{return}\ e$
	$\mid f(e) \mid x:=f(e)$
	$\mid \mathbf{if}\ b\ \mathbf{then}\ c\ \mathbf{else}\ c \mid \mathbf{while}\ b\ \mathbf{do}\ c$

Fig. 4. Source Programs

Definition 1. *We define well-formed programs as the minimum set of statements* wf *that satisfy the following conditions:*

$$wf(\textbf{return})$$
$$wf(c_2) \Rightarrow wf(c_1; c_2)$$
$$wf(c_1) \wedge wf(c_2) \Rightarrow wf(\textbf{if } b \textbf{ then } c_1 \textbf{ else } c_2)$$
$$wf(c) \Rightarrow wf(\textbf{while } b \textbf{ do } c)$$

In this chapter, we consider scalar and array variables as allocated in separate stores. In particular, scalar variables are local to the execution of a procedure body, and array variables are global to the whole program. Let Σ_V and Σ_A represent the set of partial functions from program variables to integer values $V \rightarrow \mathbb{Z}$ and from array variables to array values $A \rightarrow (\mathbb{N} \rightarrow \mathbb{Z})$, respectively. We denote with Σ the set of elements in $\Sigma_V \times \Sigma_A$.

The semantics of the programming language described above is standard. It is defined in Figure 5 by a relation $\Rightarrow \subseteq (\textbf{Prog} \times \Sigma) \times (\Sigma + \Sigma_F)$, where Σ_F denotes the set of final states composed of a final value and a final execution state: $\Sigma_F = \mathbb{Z} \times \Sigma_A$. In the figure, σ represents an element in Σ, and σ_V and σ_A the first and second projection of the pair σ. For a scalar state $\sigma_V \in \Sigma_V$, scalar variable x and $n \in \mathbb{Z}$, $[\sigma_V : x \mapsto n]$ stands for the function that maps x to n, and any other variable y to $\sigma_V y$. For an array state $\sigma_A \in \Sigma_A$, array variable a and $b \in \mathbb{N} \rightarrow \mathbb{Z}$, $[\sigma_A : a \mapsto b]$ stands for the function that maps a to b, and any

$$\frac{}{\langle \textbf{skip}, \sigma \rangle \Rightarrow \sigma} \qquad \frac{[\![e]\!]_\sigma = n \in \mathbb{Z}}{\langle x{:=}e, \sigma \rangle \Rightarrow [\sigma : x \mapsto [\![e]\!]_\sigma]}$$

$$\frac{0 \leq [\![e_1]\!]_\sigma < |a|}{\langle a[e_1]{:=}e_2, \sigma \rangle \Rightarrow [\sigma : a \mapsto [a : [\![e_1]\!]_\sigma \mapsto [\![e_2]\!]_\sigma]]}$$

$$\frac{\langle c_1, \sigma \rangle \Rightarrow \sigma' \qquad \langle c_2, \sigma' \rangle \Rightarrow s}{\langle c_1; c_2, \sigma \rangle \Rightarrow s}$$

$$\frac{\langle c_1, \sigma \rangle \Rightarrow s \qquad s \in \Sigma_F}{\langle c_1; c_2, \sigma \rangle \Rightarrow s} \qquad \frac{[\![e]\!]_\sigma = n \in \mathbb{Z}}{\langle \textbf{return } e, \sigma \rangle \Rightarrow \langle n, \sigma_A \rangle}$$

$$\frac{[\![e]\!]_\sigma = n \in \mathbb{Z} \qquad c \text{ body of } f \qquad \langle c, \langle [x_f \mapsto n], \sigma_A \rangle \rangle \Rightarrow \langle m, \sigma'_A \rangle}{\langle x := f(e), \langle \sigma_V, \sigma_A \rangle \rangle \Rightarrow \langle [\sigma_V : x \mapsto m], \sigma'_A \rangle}$$

$$\frac{\langle c; \textbf{while } b \textbf{ do } c, \sigma \rangle \Rightarrow s}{\langle \textbf{while } b \textbf{ do } c, \sigma \rangle \Rightarrow s} [\![b]\!]_\sigma \qquad \frac{}{\langle \textbf{while } b \textbf{ do } c, \sigma \rangle \Rightarrow \sigma} [\![\neg b]\!]_\sigma$$

$$\frac{\langle c_1, \sigma \rangle \Rightarrow s}{\langle \textbf{if } b \textbf{ then } c_1 \textbf{ else } c_2, \sigma \rangle \Rightarrow s} [\![b]\!]_\sigma \qquad \frac{\langle c_2, \sigma \rangle \Rightarrow s}{\langle \textbf{if } b \textbf{ then } c_1 \textbf{ else } c_2, \sigma \rangle \Rightarrow s} [\![\neg b]\!]_\sigma$$

Fig. 5. Source Program Semantics

other array variable a' to $\sigma_A\, a'$. The expression $[x \mapsto n]$ denotes the function that maps x to n and is undefined for every other variable.

For the integer and boolean expressions e and b, $[\![e]\!]_\sigma$ and $[\![b]\!]_\sigma$ stands for their standard interpretation in the state σ. In the presence of out-of-bounds array accesses, the interpretation function is undefined, and the program execution gets stuck. We denote x_f the formal parameter of a procedure f. Since array variables are considered global to the whole program, x_f is necessarily a scalar variable.

3.2   Verification Setting

Logical verification techniques have been widely studied and used from the early 70's, pioneered by the work of Floyd [11] and Hoare [12]. There is currently a variety of program verification tools, most of them focused on high-level imperative programming languages [7,6,10,15].

One distinctive goal of tool based verification is automating the process as much as possible. In general, a verification tool extracts from a program and its logical specification a set of first-order formulae, namely the verification conditions, that must be discharged in order to prove the program correct. Requiring the verification process to be automatic makes weakest precondition based verification preferable to using Hoare-clauses. In addition, such verification tools feed an automatic theorem prover with the verification conditions. Those verification conditions that fail to be automatically discharged must be proved interactively by the user of the verification tool.

In the rest of this section, we formalize a weakest-precondition based verification method for simple imperative programs, we prove the method sound with respect to the program semantics defined above, and we show the extraction of verification conditions in the example of the quicksort algorithm.

Specification Language. As a specification language we use first-order formulae as defined in Figure 6. Most of the syntactic constructions are standard, except perhaps for the special purpose variable res that refers to the value returned by a procedure, and the scalar and array variables $x^\star$ and $a^\star$ that refer to the initial value of the scalar and array variables x and a, respectively. We let $\mathcal{V}^\star$ and $\mathcal{A}^\star$ stand for the sets of variables $\{x^\star \mid x \in \mathcal{V}\}$ and $\{x^\star \mid x \in \mathcal{A}\}$, respectively.

The validity of an assertion in a particular execution state $\sigma \in \Sigma$ is standard. In particular, an assertion that contains the expression $a[e]$ is invalid in those execution states in which $a[e]$ is not well defined, i.e. in those states in which e is out of the bounds of the array a. We assume a relation $\models$ to denote that an assertion $\varphi \in \mathcal{A}$ is valid when interpreted in the state $\sigma \in \Sigma$, written $\models \sigma : \varphi$.

$$\bar{e} ::= n \mid x \mid x^\star \mid a[\bar{e}] \mid a^\star[\bar{e}] \mid \bar{e} \oplus \bar{e} \mid \text{res}$$
$$\varphi ::= \text{true} \mid \text{false} \mid \bar{e} \bowtie \bar{e} \mid \neg\varphi \mid \varphi \wedge \varphi \mid \varphi \Rightarrow \varphi \mid \forall x.\ \varphi$$

Fig. 6. Specification Language

The specification of a procedure consists of a tuple (Pre, annot, Post), where Pre and Post specify the procedure pre and postcondition. The verification setting only considers partial correctness, i.e., it only ensures the correctness of terminating executions. The partial function annot : $\mathcal{L} \rightharpoonup \mathcal{A}$ maps any program loop at label k to the corresponding loop invariant annot(k). Some restrictions apply to the assertions Pre and Post. Any array variable may appear in the assertion Pre, but the only scalar variables that appear in Pre are the procedure arguments. Similarly, Post can refer to the current and initial value of any array variable, the special return variable res, and the initial values of the procedure arguments. The invariants specified by the partial function annot can refer to the initial and current value of any scalar and array variable, but not to the variable res.

For notational convenience, we associate labels $k \in \mathcal{L}$ to loop statements, denoted $\textbf{while}^k \ b \ \textbf{do} \ c$. In order to be able to extract verification conditions automatically, we require procedure specifications to annotate every program loop, as stated in the following definition.

Definition 2 (Well-annotated Source Program). *A procedure p with specification (Pre, annot, Post) is well-annotated if $k \in \text{dom}(\text{annot})$, for every loop statement $\textbf{while}^k \ b \ \textbf{do} \ c$ in P. A program is well-annotated if all its procedures are well annotated.*

$$\text{WP}(\textbf{skip}, \phi) = \langle \phi, \emptyset \rangle \qquad \text{WP}(\textbf{return} \ e, \phi) = \langle \text{Post}[^e/_{\text{res}}], \emptyset \rangle$$

$$\text{WP}(x := e, \phi) = \langle \phi[^e/_x], \emptyset \rangle$$

$$\text{WP}(a[e_1] := e_2, \phi) = \langle \phi[^{[a:e_1 \mapsto e_2]}/_a], \emptyset \rangle$$

$$\frac{\Phi = \text{Pre}_f[^e/_{x_f}] \wedge \forall \text{res}, V'. \ \text{Post}_f[^{V',V}/_{V,V^*}][^e/_{x_f^*}] \Rightarrow \phi[^{V'}/_V][^{\text{res}}/_x] \qquad V \ \text{array variables modified by} \ f}{\text{WP}(x := f(e), \phi) = \langle \Phi, \emptyset \rangle}$$

$$\frac{\text{WP}(c_1, \phi) = \langle \phi_1, \theta_1 \rangle \qquad \text{WP}(c_2, \phi) = \langle \phi_2, \theta_2 \rangle}{\text{WP}(\textbf{if} \ b \ \textbf{then} \ c_1 \ \textbf{else} \ c_2, \phi) = \langle b \Rightarrow \phi_1 \wedge \neg b \Rightarrow \phi_2, \theta_1 \cup \theta_2 \rangle}$$

$$\frac{\text{WP}(c, \text{annot}(k)) = \langle \phi_1, \theta \rangle \qquad \Phi \doteq \text{annot}(k) \Rightarrow (b \Rightarrow \phi_1) \wedge (\neg b \Rightarrow \phi)}{\text{WP}(\textbf{while}^k \ b \ \textbf{do} \ c, \phi) = \langle \text{annot}(k), \{\Phi\} \cup \theta \rangle}$$

$$\frac{\text{WP}(c_1, \phi_2) = \langle \phi_1, \theta_1 \rangle \qquad \text{WP}(c_2, \phi) = \langle \phi_2, \theta_2 \rangle}{\text{WP}(c_1; c_2, \phi) = \langle \phi_1, \theta_1 \cup \theta_2 \rangle}$$

$$\frac{\langle \phi, \theta \rangle = \text{WP}(c, \text{Post}) \qquad c \ \text{the body of} \ p}{\text{PO}(p) \doteq \{\text{Pre} \Rightarrow \phi[^{\vec{V}}/_{\vec{V}^*}]\} \cup \theta}$$

Fig. 7. Source Code VCgen Rules

In the rest of the chapter, we only consider well-annotated programs.

A VCgen for source programs is defined by the set of proof obligations PO, in terms of the function WP, as shown in Figure 7. In the figure, the expression $\phi[^{\vec{V}}/_{\vec{V}\star}]$ represents the result of substituting in ϕ every array and scalar variable $x^\star$ in $\mathcal{V}^\star$ or $\mathcal{A}^\star$ by x.

One desirable property of a verification framework is its soundness with respect to the program semantics. The following lemma formalizes this result:

Lemma 1 (Source Code VCGen Soundness). *Let the statement c be the body of the procedure p with specification* (Pre, annot, Post). *Let σ represent an initial state that satisfies $\models \sigma :$ Pre, and that every proof obligation in $\mathrm{PO}(p)$ is valid. Then, every reachable final state satisfies the assertion* Post. *Formally, if $\langle c, \sigma \rangle \Rightarrow \langle n, \sigma'_A \rangle$, then $\models \langle [\texttt{res} \mapsto n], \sigma'_A \rangle :$ Post.*

Example 1. To illustrate a verification process of a simple algorithm, consider the procedure **partition** shown in Figure 8. Figure 9, provides the specifications for the running example, including the procedures **quicksort** and **swap**. Every procedure is specified with a pre and postcondition. A partial function annot is defined only for the procedure **partition**, since it is the only one that contains loop statements.

Consider for instance the procedure swap. Since it contains no loops, the VCgen returns a single proof obligation. From the definition of the WP function, the proof obligation we obtain is:

$$\mathsf{inBound}(i) \wedge \mathsf{inBound}(j) \Rightarrow \mathsf{swapped}(i,j)[^{[\mathsf{vec}:j \mapsto t]}/_{\mathsf{vec}}][^{[\mathsf{vec}:i \mapsto \mathsf{vec}[j]]}/_{\mathsf{vec}}][^{\mathsf{vec}[i]}/_t]$$

After computing the set of proof obligations for the whole program, one can see that they are all valid formulae. In the rest of this paper we assume that a certificate is provided for each of these proof obligations.

```
partition(start, end){
    pivot = vec[start];
    i = start;
    j = end;
    while^{[l_a]} (i < j) {
        while^{[l_b]} (vec[i] ≤ pivot ∧ i < j)
            i++;
        while^{[l_c]} (pivot < vec[j] ∧ i < j)
            j--;
        if (i < j) swap(i, j);
    }
    swap(start, i-1);
    return i-1;
}
```

Fig. 8. Quicksort Algorithm - Procedure **partition**

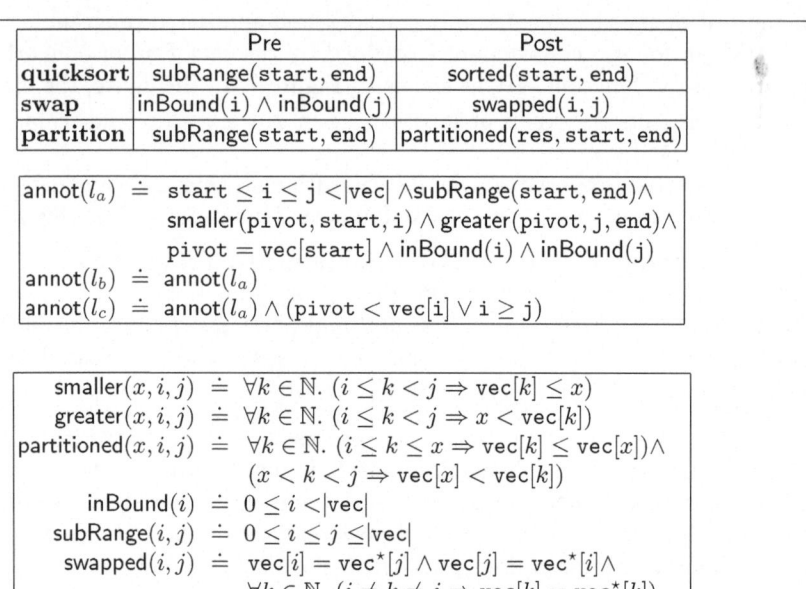

	Pre	Post
quicksort	subRange(start, end)	sorted(start, end)
swap	inBound(i) ∧ inBound(j)	swapped(i, j)
partition	subRange(start, end)	partitioned(res, start, end)

$$\text{annot}(l_a) \doteq \text{ start} \le i \le j < |vec| \wedge \text{subRange(start, end)} \wedge$$
$$\text{smaller(pivot, start, i)} \wedge \text{greater(pivot, j, end)} \wedge$$
$$\text{pivot} = vec[\text{start}] \wedge \text{inBound(i)} \wedge \text{inBound(j)}$$
$$\text{annot}(l_b) \doteq \text{annot}(l_a)$$
$$\text{annot}(l_c) \doteq \text{annot}(l_a) \wedge (\text{pivot} < vec[i] \vee i \ge j)$$

$$\text{smaller}(x, i, j) \doteq \forall k \in \mathbb{N}. \ (i \le k < j \Rightarrow vec[k] \le x)$$
$$\text{greater}(x, i, j) \doteq \forall k \in \mathbb{N}. \ (i \le k < j \Rightarrow x < vec[k])$$
$$\text{partitioned}(x, i, j) \doteq \forall k \in \mathbb{N}. \ (i \le k \le x \Rightarrow vec[k] \le vec[x]) \wedge$$
$$(x < k < j \Rightarrow vec[x] < vec[k])$$
$$\text{inBound}(i) \doteq 0 \le i < |vec|$$
$$\text{subRange}(i, j) \doteq 0 \le i \le j \le |vec|$$
$$\text{swapped}(i, j) \doteq vec[i] = vec^\star[j] \wedge vec[j] = vec^\star[i] \wedge$$
$$\forall k \in \mathbb{N}. \ (i \ne k \ne j \Rightarrow vec[k] = vec^\star[k])$$
$$\text{sorted}(i, j) \doteq \forall k, k'. \ (i \le k \le k' < j \Rightarrow vec[k] \le vec[k'])$$

Fig. 9. Quicksort Algorithm Specification

4   RTL Verification and Certification

4.1   Programming Language Setting

In this section, we provide a definition of an intermediate RTL program representation. Commonly, most of the compiler optimizations are applied after the program is transformed into this RTL representation.

We define the body of an RTL procedure as a directed graph, where nodes represent program points and edges represent the execution of a statement or a conditional jump. The following definition states this formally.

Definition 3. *The body of an* RTL *procedure is defined by a tuple* $\langle \mathcal{N}, \mathcal{E}, G \rangle$, *where* $\mathcal{N} \subseteq \mathcal{L}$ *is a subset of labels that represents the program points, the relation* $\mathcal{E} \subseteq \mathcal{N} \times \mathcal{N}$ *defines the execution flow, and* $G : \mathcal{E} \to (\mathsf{Instr} + \mathsf{B})$ *maps every edge to instructions or boolean expressions, defined in Figure 10. An* RTL *program P is defined as a collection of* RTL *procedures.*

As can be seen in Figure 10, boolean conditions are defined as integer comparisons between two variables. Similarly, instructions involve at most one array access or two program variables. In the figure, e represents an integer expression (one array access or an arithmetic operation between at most two scalar variables).

$$
\begin{array}{rl}
\text{(B)} & b ::= v_1 \bowtie v_2 \mid \neg(v_1 \bowtie v_2) \\
\textbf{(expressions)} & e ::= n \mid v \mid n \oplus v \mid v \oplus v \mid a[v] \\
\textbf{(Instr)}\ ins & ::= \textbf{nop} \mid v := e \mid a[v] := v \\
& \mid \textbf{invoke}\ f\ (\vec{x}) \mid \textbf{return}\ v
\end{array}
$$

Fig. 10. RTL Instructions

For every $l \in \mathcal{N}$, we denote $\mathsf{succ}(l)$ the set of successors of node l, i.e., $\{l' \in \mathcal{N} \mid \langle l, l' \rangle \in \mathcal{E}\}$.

In the rest of the chapter, we use the subscript p to make explicit that the representation $\langle \mathcal{N}_p, \mathcal{E}_p, G_p \rangle$ belongs to a procedure p. We omit, however, the subscript p when it is clear from the context.

In order to define the semantics of RTL programs, we need to define a notion of well-formed code representation.

Definition 4 (Well-formed Program). *A procedure representation* $\langle \mathcal{N}, \mathcal{E}, G \rangle$ *is well-formed if*

- $l_{\mathsf{in}}, l_{\mathsf{out}} \in \mathcal{L}$, *representing the initial and final label, respectively, are in* $\mathcal{N}$. *Furthermore,* $\{l \mid l_{\mathsf{in}} \in \mathsf{succ}(l)\} = \mathsf{succ}(l_{\mathsf{out}}) = \emptyset$.
- *The graph is closed. Formally, for every* $l \in \mathcal{N}$, *we have that* $\mathsf{succ}(l) \subseteq \mathcal{N}$.

A program is well-formed if all its procedures are well-formed.

$$
\dfrac{G_p[\langle l, l_{\mathsf{out}} \rangle] = \textbf{return}\ v}{\langle l, \sigma \rangle \rightsquigarrow_p \langle [\![v]\!]_\sigma, \sigma_\mathcal{A} \rangle}
\qquad
\dfrac{G_p[\langle l, l' \rangle] = \textbf{nop} \qquad \langle l', \sigma \rangle \rightsquigarrow_p s \qquad s \in \Sigma_F}{\langle l, \sigma \rangle \rightsquigarrow_p s}
$$

$$
\dfrac{G_p[\langle l, l' \rangle] = v := \textbf{invoke}\ p'\ x \qquad \langle l_{\mathsf{in}}, \langle [x_{p'} \mapsto [\![x]\!]_\sigma], \sigma_\mathcal{A} \rangle \rangle \rightsquigarrow_{p'} \langle n, \langle \sigma'_\mathcal{V}, \sigma'_\mathcal{A} \rangle \rangle}{\langle l', \langle [\sigma_\mathcal{V} : v \mapsto n], \sigma'_\mathcal{A} \rangle \rightsquigarrow_p s \qquad s \in \Sigma_F}{\langle l, \sigma \rangle \rightsquigarrow_p s}
$$

$$
\dfrac{G_p[\langle l, l' \rangle] = b \qquad b \in \{(v_1 \bowtie v_2), \neg(v_1 \bowtie v_2)\} \qquad [\![b]\!]_\sigma \qquad \langle l', \sigma \rangle \rightsquigarrow_p s \qquad s \in \Sigma_F}{\langle l, \sigma \rangle \rightsquigarrow_p s}
$$

$$
\dfrac{G_p[\langle l, l' \rangle] = v := e \qquad [\![e]\!]_\sigma = n \in \mathbb{Z} \qquad \langle l', \langle [\sigma_\mathcal{V} : v \mapsto n], \sigma_\mathcal{A} \rangle \rangle \rightsquigarrow_p s \qquad s \in \Sigma_F}{\langle l, \langle \sigma_\mathcal{V}, \sigma_\mathcal{A} \rangle \rangle \rightsquigarrow_p s}
$$

$$
\dfrac{G_p[\langle l, l' \rangle] = a[v_1] := v_2}{0 \le [\![v_1]\!]_\sigma < |a| \qquad \langle l', \langle \sigma_\mathcal{V}, [\sigma_\mathcal{A} : a \mapsto [a : [\![v_1]\!]_\sigma \mapsto [\![v_2]\!]_\sigma]] \rangle \rangle \rightsquigarrow_p s \qquad s \in \Sigma_F}{\langle l, \langle \sigma_\mathcal{V}, \sigma_\mathcal{A} \rangle \rangle \rightsquigarrow_p s}
$$

Fig. 11. Semantics of RTL Programs

In the rest of the chapter we consider only well-formed RTL programs. Furthermore, to ensure determinism, we assume that for every node $l \in \mathcal{N}$, only one of
the following situations arise:

- there are exactly two outgoing edges $\langle l, l_t \rangle$ and $\langle l, l_f \rangle$, and they are mapped
  by G to boolean conditions such that $G[\langle l, l_f \rangle] = \neg G[\langle l, l_f \rangle]$, or
- there is a single outgoing edge $\langle l, l' \rangle$, such that $G[\langle l, l' \rangle] \in \mathsf{Instr}$.

The RTL semantics and verification setting consider non-deterministic RTL programs. However, we can restrict our attention to deterministic RTL programs,
since the conditions above are satisfied by the result of compiling a high-level
program into the RTL representation.

Let Σ and Σ_F the set of intermediate and final states defined as in previous
section. The semantics of well-formed RTL programs is defined by a relation
$\leadsto_p : \mathcal{L} \times \Sigma \to \Sigma_F$, where p denotes the procedure under execution.

Example 2. As an example of the intermediate program representation, consider
the RTL graph of the procedure **partition** shown in Figure 15.

4.2 Verification Setting

Specification Language. A specification of an RTL procedure is defined by a
tuple (Pre, annot, Post), where annot maps program labels in $\mathcal{L}$ to intermediate
specifications. The first-order formulae that define the specification follow the
same restrictions as in previous section.

As before, we require every cycle of the control flow graph of the program
to be annotated, so that a full program annotation can be generated from the
partial annotation annot.

Definition 5 (Well-annotated RTL Program). *A procedure with specification* (Pre, annot, Post) *is well-annotated if every loop in the procedure body con-
tains at least one annotation. That is, for every cyclic path* $\langle l_1, l_2 \rangle ... \langle l_k, l_1 \rangle$ *we
require* $\{l_1, \ldots, l_k\} \cap \mathsf{dom}(\mathsf{annot}) \neq \emptyset$. *A program is well-annotated if all its procedures are well-annotated.*

Given a cycle of the directed graph, a first-order formulae annotating one of
its labels can be interpreted as a loop invariant. In fact, as we state later, the
result of compiling a well-annotated program is a well-annotated RTL program,
in which the original loop invariants annotate every cycle of the control-flow
graph.

Notice that the definition of well-annotated code provides an induction prin-
ciple on the set of labels, with $\mathsf{dom}(\mathsf{annot})$ as the set of base cases and $\mathcal{E} \cap (\mathcal{L} \times (\mathcal{L} \setminus \mathsf{dom}(\mathsf{annot})))$ an order relation with no infinite chains.

Example 3. Let (Pre, annot, Post) be the specification for the code in Figure 15.
Due to the presence of a cycle in the graph, at least one of the loop labels must be
annotated. For instance, as in the source program, one may define the invariant

$$\mathsf{wpi}(\mathbf{nop}, \varphi) = \varphi$$

$$\mathsf{wpi}(v := e, \varphi) = \varphi[^e/_v]$$

$$\mathsf{wpi}(a[v_1] := v_2, \varphi) = \varphi[^{[a:v_1 \mapsto v_2]}/_a]$$

$$\mathsf{wpi}(v_1 \bowtie v_2, \varphi) = (v_1 \bowtie v_2) \Rightarrow \varphi$$

$$\mathsf{wpi}(\neg(v_1 \bowtie v_2), \varphi) = \neg(v_1 \bowtie v_2) \Rightarrow \varphi$$

$$\mathsf{wpi}(\mathbf{invoke}\ f\ x, \varphi) = \mathsf{Pre}_f[^x/_{x_f}] \wedge$$
$$\forall_{res,a'} \mathsf{Post}_f[^{a',a}/_{a,a^\star}][^{x_f{}^\star}/_x] \Rightarrow \varphi[^{a'}/_a]$$

$$\mathsf{wpi}(\mathbf{return}\ v, \varphi) = \varphi[^v/_{\mathsf{res}}]$$

$$\mathsf{wp}_p(l) = \begin{cases} \mathsf{Post}_p & \text{if } l = l_{\mathsf{out}} \\ \mathsf{annot}(l) & \text{if } l \in \mathsf{dom}(\mathsf{annot}) \\ \bigwedge_{l' \in \mathsf{succ}(l)} \mathsf{wpi}(G_p[\langle l, l' \rangle], \mathsf{wp}_p(l')) & \text{otherwise} \end{cases}$$

Fig. 12. RTL VCgen rules

at the loop header l as $\mathsf{annot}(l) \doteq y \geq 1 \wedge c * x^y = x^{\star y^\star}$. One can see that this specification is sufficient for the program to be well-annotated.

Given a well-annotated RTL program, a VCgen is defined by extracting a set of proof obligations from each well-annotated procedure p:

$$\mathsf{po}(p) = \{\mathsf{Pre}_p \Rightarrow \mathsf{wp}_p(l_{\mathsf{in}})[^V/_{V^\star}]\} \cup$$
$$\{\mathsf{annot}_p(l) \Rightarrow \bigwedge_{l' \in \mathsf{succ}(l)} \mathsf{wpi}(G_p[\langle l, l' \rangle], \mathsf{wp}_p(l')) \mid l \in \mathsf{dom}(\mathsf{annot}_p)\}$$

where the predicate transformers wpi and wp_p are defined in Figure 12. In the figure, a represents every array variable that may get modified by p. The assertion $\varphi[^{V^\star}/_V]$ stands for the substitution in φ of every array variable $x^\star \in V^\star$ by $x \in V$.

Lemma 2 (VCgen Soundness). *Consider a well-annotated* RTL *program P. Assume that for every procedure p of P, $\mathsf{po}(p)$ is a valid set of proof obligations. Then, for every procedure p, if $\langle l_{\mathsf{in}}, \sigma \rangle \leadsto_p \langle n, \sigma' \rangle$ then $\models [\sigma' : \mathsf{res} \mapsto n] : \mathsf{Post}$.*

4.3   Certificate Infrastructure

In general, a program certificate can be defined as a mathematical object that provides efficiently verifiable evidence of the validity of logical formulae. There are several formal representation of certificates, depending on competing criteria such as ease of generation and transformation, ease of checking, and the size of certificates. One notion of certificate representation are proof scripts, a sequence of logical deduction statements in the language of a proof-assistant. More commonly, certificates are represented as terms of the λ-calculus, as suggested by the Curry-Howard isomorphism [13].

$$\begin{array}{ll}
\mathsf{intro_{true}} & : \ \Gamma \vdash \mathsf{true} \\
\mathsf{axiom}\ A & : \ \Gamma \vdash A \qquad \text{if } A \in \Gamma \\
\mathsf{ring} & : \ \Gamma \vdash n_1 = n_2 \quad \text{if } n_1 = n_2 \text{ is a ring equality} \\[4pt]
\mathsf{intro_\wedge} & : \ \Gamma \vdash A \to \Gamma \vdash B \to \Gamma \vdash A \wedge B \\
\mathsf{elim_{\wedge,l}} & : \ \Gamma \vdash A \wedge B \to \Gamma \vdash A \\
\mathsf{elim_{\wedge,r}} & : \ \Gamma \vdash A \wedge B \to \Gamma \vdash B \\[4pt]
\mathsf{intro_\Rightarrow} & : \ \Gamma; A \vdash B \to \Gamma \vdash A \Rightarrow B \\
\mathsf{elim_\Rightarrow} & : \ \Gamma \vdash A \Rightarrow B \to \Gamma \vdash A \to \Gamma \vdash B \\[4pt]
\mathsf{elim_=} & : \ \Gamma \vdash e_1 = e_2 \to \Gamma \vdash A[^{e_1}\!/_r] \to \Gamma \vdash A[^{e_2}\!/_r] \\[4pt]
\mathsf{weak_\Delta} & : \ \Gamma \vdash A \to \Gamma; \Delta \vdash A \\[4pt]
\mathsf{intro_\forall} & : \ \Gamma \vdash A \to \Gamma \vdash \forall r.A \qquad \text{if } r \text{ is not in } \Gamma \\[4pt]
\mathsf{elim_\forall} & : \ \Gamma \vdash \forall r.A \to \Gamma \vdash A[^e\!/_r] \\[4pt]
\mathsf{intro_\exists} & : \ \Gamma \vdash A[^{e_1}\!/_x] \Rightarrow B[^{e_2}\!/_y] \to \Gamma \vdash \exists x.A \Rightarrow \exists y.B
\end{array}$$

Fig. 13. Proof Algebra

The development of the certificate transformations depends strongly on the representation of certificates. To provide a generic presentation of the proof transformations, we prefer to abstract from the actual implementation of certificates. Instead, we assume a set of operations over proofs, formalized by an abstract proof algebra, shown in Figure 13.

For instance, an actual implementation of these operations in a λ-term representation of certificates would define the $\mathsf{intro_\wedge}$ operation of the proof algebra as the λ-term $\lambda f.\ \lambda g.\ \lambda a.\ \langle fa, ga \rangle$.

5   Certificate Translation

In general, verification conditions are not preserved by program transformations. Consequently, a priori, the certificates that are used to attest the verification of a source program cannot be reused to certify the transformed program. Furthermore, the original specification can become unprovable. In most cases, the transformation of the certificate is closely dependent on the first step of the optimization, in which the compiler gathers static information about the execution of the program. Indeed, in order to preserve the soundness of the specification, several optimizations require that invariants are strengthened with the result of the analysis that justifies the optimization. Intuitively, this comes as a need to propagate, through the invariants, the information returned by the analysis, in order to eventually enforce the preservation of the original semantics. That is the case, for instance, of optimizations that simplify the evaluation of expressions, such as constant propagation, common sub-expression elimination, copy propagation and redundant conditional elimination. In such cases, the transformation of the original certificates entails representing the result of the analysis in the underlying verification logic, and generating a certificate for this specification. A certificate transformation process then integrates this certified analysis result with the original certificate in order to generate a certificate for the optimized program. However, it is not always the case that invariants must be strengthened. Other optimizations, e.g. dead-variable elimination, may require loop invariants to be weakened.

In this section, we study several standard compiler optimizations, applied to our particular running example. Even though some optimizations preserve the verification conditions for our particular example, we give a short explanation of the general technique to transform the certificate. For instance, dead register elimination does not alter verification conditions and thus no certificate translation is needed. In other cases, an ad-hoc transformation may seem more convenient in terms of the final annotation and certificate size, but we prefer to formulate the transformation of the certificate as generally as possible.

5.1   Non-optimizing Compilation

Description. The first compiler transformation translates the high-level representation of the source program into the intermediate RTL representation defined in Section 4. The compilation of a procedure p with body c is defined as $\mathcal{C}_{(l_{in}, l_{out})}(c)$, where the function $\mathcal{C}$ can be found in Figure 14.

The compilation of expressions, $\mathcal{C}^e$, takes a variable v and an expression e and returns a subgraph of RTL instructions that computes the value of the

$$\mathcal{C}^{\mathbf{b}}_{(l, l_t, l_f)}(v_1 \bowtie v_2) = \langle \{l, l_t, l_f\}, \{\langle l, l_t \rangle, \langle l, l_f \rangle\}, G \rangle$$
$$\text{where:} \quad G[\langle l, l_t \rangle] = (v_1 \bowtie v_2)$$
$$G[\langle l, l_f \rangle] = \neg(v_1 \bowtie v_2)$$
$$\mathcal{C}^{\mathbf{b}}_{(l, l_t, l_f)}(e_1 \bowtie e_2) = \mathcal{C}_{(l, l_1)}(v_1 := e_1) \cup \mathcal{C}_{(l_1, l_2)}(v_2 := e_2) \cup \mathcal{C}^{\mathbf{b}}_{(l_2, l_t, l_f)}(v_1 \bowtie v_2)$$
$$\mathcal{C}^{\mathbf{b}}_{(l, l_t, l_f)}(\neg b) = \mathcal{C}^{\mathbf{b}}_{(l, l_f, l_t)}(b)$$
$$\mathcal{C}^{\mathbf{b}}_{(l, l_t, l_f)}(b_1 \wedge b_2) = \mathcal{C}^{\mathbf{b}}_{(l, l'_t, l_f)}(b_1) \cup \mathcal{C}^{\mathbf{b}}_{(l, l_t, l_f)}$$

$$\mathcal{C}_{(l, l')}(v := v_1 \oplus v_2) = \langle \{l, l'\}, \{\langle l, l' \rangle\}, [\langle l, l' \rangle \mapsto v := v_1 \oplus v_2] \rangle$$
$$\mathcal{C}_{(l, l')}(v := a[v']) = \langle \{l, l'\}, \{\langle l, l' \rangle\}, [\langle l, l' \rangle \mapsto v := a[v']] \rangle$$
$$\mathcal{C}_{(l, l')}(v := e_1 \oplus e_2) = \mathcal{C}_{(l, l_1)}(v_1 := e_1) \cup \mathcal{C}_{(l_1, l_2)}(v_2 := e_2) \cup \mathcal{C}_{(l_2, l')}(v := v_1 \oplus v_2)$$
$$\mathcal{C}_{(l, l')}(v := a[e]) = \mathcal{C}_{(l, l'')}(v' := e) \cup \mathcal{C}_{(l'', l')}(v := a[v'])$$

$$\mathcal{C}_{(l, l')}(\mathbf{if}\ b\ \mathbf{then}\ c_1\ \mathbf{else}\ c_2) = \mathcal{C}^{\mathbf{b}}_{(l, l_t, l_f)}(b) \cup \mathcal{C}_{(l_t, l')}(c_1) \cup \mathcal{C}_{(l_f, l')}(c_2)$$
$$\mathcal{C}_{(l, l')}(\mathbf{while}\ b\ \mathbf{do}\ c) = \mathcal{C}^{\mathbf{b}}_{(l, l_t, l')}(b) \cup \mathcal{C}_{(l_t, l)}(c)$$
$$\mathcal{C}_{(l, l')}(v := \mathbf{invoke}\ p(e_1, .., e_k)) = \mathcal{C}(v_1 := e_1) \cup .. \cup \mathcal{C}(v_k := e_k) \cup$$
$$\mathcal{C}(v := \mathbf{invoke}\ f(v_1, .., v_k))$$
$$\mathcal{C}_{(l, l')}(c_1; c_2) = \mathcal{C}_{(l, l'')}(c_1) \cup \mathcal{C}_{(l'', l')}(c_2)$$
$$\mathcal{C}_{(l, l')}(\mathbf{return}\ e) = \mathcal{C}_{l, l''}(v := e) \cup \langle \{l'', l'\}, \{\langle l'', l' \rangle\}, [\langle l'', l' \rangle \mapsto \mathbf{return}\ v] \rangle$$

Fig. 14. Compiler Definition

expression e and stores it on the variable v. In the figure, the union of two graphs $\langle \mathcal{N}_1, \mathcal{E}_1, G_1 \rangle$ and $\langle \mathcal{N}_2, \mathcal{E}_2, G_2 \rangle$ is defined as $\langle \mathcal{N}_1 \cup \mathcal{N}_2, \mathcal{E}_1 \cup \mathcal{E}_2, G_1 \cup G_2 \rangle$. The function $\mathcal{C}^{\mathsf{b}}$ compiles the evaluation of a boolean expression, and takes two additional parameters: the labels l_t and l_f into which the execution must jump depending on whether the boolean condition is satisfied. The function $\mathcal{C}$ takes, in addition to a source statement c, a label that points to the code that must be executed after the execution of c.

Lemma 3. *A well-formed source program is compiled into a well-formed deterministic* RTL *program.*

After this compilation step, we do not need to modify the original procedure specifications:

Definition 6 (Compilation of Specifications). *Let* (Pre, annot, Post) *be a specification for a source level procedure p. We define the specification for the compilation of the procedure p as* (Pre, annot, Post).

Lemma 4. *The result of compiling a well-annotated source program is a well-annotated* RTL *program.*

Transformed Running Example. The code in Figure 15 is the result of compiling the source program procedure partition into an RTL representation.

To simplify the graphical representation, we merge consecutive edges representing assignments into a single edge. The definition of the semantics and the computation of the wp function are easily extended to these edges.

Comparison of Verification Conditions. Consider the first proof obligation of the source version of the procedure partition, i.e. $\mathsf{Pre} \Rightarrow \phi[^{\mathsf{vec}}\!/_{\mathsf{vec}^\star}]$ where $\langle \phi, \xi \rangle = \mathsf{WP}(c, \mathsf{Post})$, for some ξ, and c is the body of the procedure **partition** and Post its postcondition. If we compute the proof obligation we get the following formula:

$$
\begin{aligned}
\mathsf{Pre} \Rightarrow\ & \mathsf{start} + 1 \leq \mathsf{start} + 1 \leq \mathsf{end} < |\mathsf{vec}|\ \wedge \\
& \mathsf{smaller}(\mathsf{vec}[\mathsf{start}], \mathsf{start} + 1, \mathsf{start} + 1) \wedge \\
& \mathsf{greater}(\mathsf{vec}[\mathsf{start}], \mathsf{end}.\mathsf{end}) \wedge \\
& \mathsf{vec}[\mathsf{start}] = \mathsf{vec}[\mathsf{start}] \wedge \\
& \mathsf{inBound}(\mathsf{i}) \wedge \mathsf{inBound}(\mathsf{j})
\end{aligned}
$$

If we unfold the definition of the predicates above we can see that the proof obligation is valid. Computing the corresponding verification condition at the compiled RTL version shows that it is syntactically preserved by non-optimizing compilation.

However, minor transformations of the verification conditions are introduced when considering a fragment of code that evaluates non-trivial conditional expressions. Then, certificates must be adapted accordingly. Consider, for instance, the verification condition related to the loop invariant $\mathsf{annot}(l_b)$. At source level, the VCgen returns the proof obligation $\mathsf{annot}(l_b) \Rightarrow (b \Rightarrow \mathsf{annot}(l_b)[^{\mathsf{i}+1}\!/_{\mathsf{i}}]) \wedge (\neg b \Rightarrow$

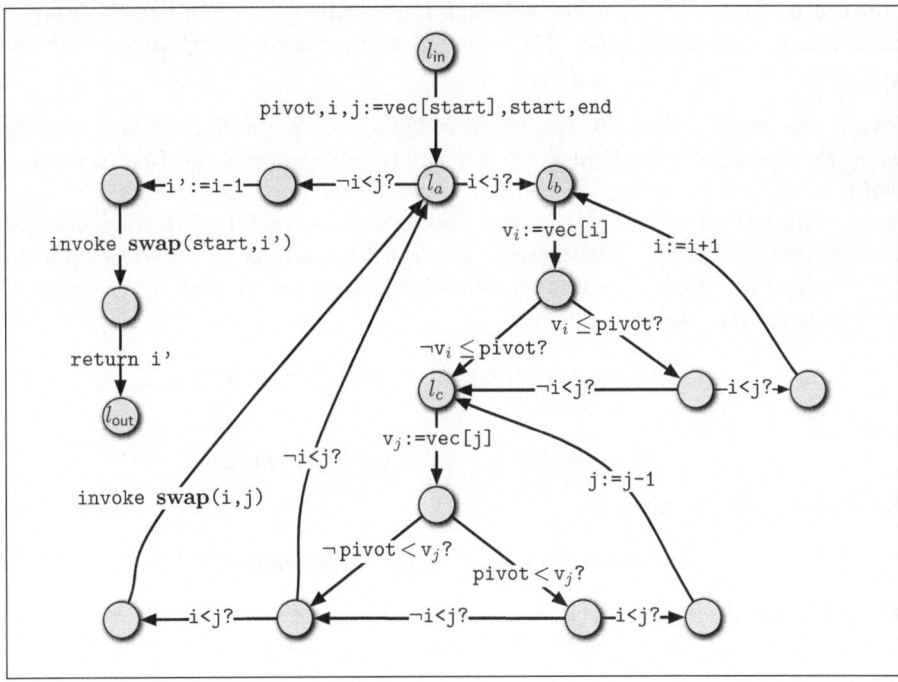

Fig. 15. Intermediate Representation of the procedure `partition`

$\mathsf{annot}(l_c)$), where b stands for $\mathtt{vec[i]} \leq \mathtt{pivot} \wedge \mathtt{i} < \mathtt{j}$. Computing the verification condition at label l_b of the compiled code returns

$$\mathsf{annot}(l_b) \Rightarrow (\mathtt{vec[i]} \leq \mathtt{pivot} \Rightarrow \mathtt{i} < \mathtt{j} \Rightarrow \mathsf{annot}(l_b)[^{i+1}\!/_i]) \wedge$$
$$(\mathtt{vec[i]} \leq \mathtt{pivot} \Rightarrow \neg \mathtt{i} < \mathtt{j} \Rightarrow \mathsf{annot}(l_c)) \wedge$$
$$(\neg \mathtt{vec[i]} \leq \mathtt{pivot} \Rightarrow \mathsf{annot}(l_c))$$

A proof for the verification condition above can be generated from the original one. In the rest of this section we generalize this result to any certified program.

Transformation of the Certificate. The following generic results state that it is possible to reconstruct the original certificates in the presence of non-optimizing compilation.

The first lemma states that the application of the predicate transformer wpi at RTL level *decompiles* the code that results from the compilation of assignments.

Lemma 5. *Let $\langle \mathcal{N}, \mathcal{E}, G \rangle$ be the subgraph that results from computing the assignment $x := e$, i.e. , $\mathcal{C}_{(l,l')}(x := e)$. Then, by structural induction on e, one can proof that $\mathsf{wp}(l)$ is syntactically equal to $\mathsf{wp}(l')[^e\!/_v]$.*

Then, the following lemma states a correspondence between a boolean condition and the code that results from its compilation.

Lemma 6. *Let* $\langle \mathcal{N}, \mathcal{E}, G \rangle$ *be the subgraph that results from compiling the boolean condition* b, *i.e.,* $\mathcal{C}^{\mathbf{b}}_{(l,l_t,l_f)}(b)$. *Then, one can generate a certificate* $c : (b \Rightarrow \mathsf{wp}(l_t)) \wedge (\neg b \Rightarrow \mathsf{wp}(l_f)) \vdash \mathsf{wp}(l)$.

Proof. The proof follows by structural induction on b, *from Lemma 5 and by using the operations on Figure 13. Consider, for instance, the base case, i.e. that* b *is equal to* $v_1 \bowtie v_2$. *Then one can show that* $\mathsf{wp}(l)$ *is syntactically equal to* $(b \Rightarrow \mathsf{wp}(l_t)) \wedge (\neg b \Rightarrow \mathsf{wp}(l_f))$, *and thus* axiom *is a certificate for the goal we want to prove. Consider now the case* $b = b_1 \wedge b_2$ *and thus* $\langle \mathcal{N}, \mathcal{E}, G \rangle$ *is equal to* $\mathcal{C}^{\mathbf{b}}_{l,l'_t,l_f}(b_1) \cup \mathcal{C}^{\mathbf{b}}_{l,l_t,l_f}(b_2)$. *By inductive hypothesis, we know that we can generate a certificate for the goals*

$$c_1 : (b_1 \Rightarrow \mathsf{wp}(l'_t)) \wedge (\neg b_1 \Rightarrow \mathsf{wp}(l_f)) \vdash \mathsf{wp}(l)$$

and

$$c_2 : (b_2 \Rightarrow \mathsf{wp}(l_t)) \wedge (\neg b_2 \Rightarrow \mathsf{wp}(l_f)) \vdash \mathsf{wp}(l'_t)$$

Let φ *stands for the formula*

$$(b_1 \wedge b_2 \Rightarrow \mathsf{wp}(l_t)) \wedge (\neg(b_1 \wedge b_2) \Rightarrow \mathsf{wp}(l_f))$$

The following derivation steps define the certificate c *for the goal we want to prove in this case (we assume* $\neg \varphi$ *is a syntax sugar for* $\varphi \Rightarrow \mathsf{false}$*):*

$$
\begin{aligned}
p_1 &= \mathsf{elim}_{\wedge,r}(\mathsf{axiom}(b_1 \wedge b_2)) : \varphi, b_1, \neg b_2, b_1 \wedge b_2 \vdash b_2 \\
p_2 &= \mathsf{elim}_{\Rightarrow}(\mathsf{axiom}(\neg b_2), p_1) : \varphi, b_1, \neg b_2, b_1 \wedge b_2 \vdash \mathsf{false} \\
p_3 &= \mathsf{intro}_{\Rightarrow}(p_2) : \varphi, b_1, \neg b_2 \vdash \neg(b_1 \wedge b_2) \\
p_4 &= \mathsf{axiom}(\varphi) : \varphi, b_1, \neg b_2 \vdash \varphi \\
p_5 &= \mathsf{elim}_{\wedge,l}(p_4) : \varphi, b_1, \neg b_2 \vdash \neg(b_1 \wedge b_2) \Rightarrow \mathsf{wp}(l_f) \\
p_6 &= \mathsf{elim}_{\Rightarrow}(p_3, p_5) : \varphi, b_1, \neg b_2 \vdash \mathsf{wp}(l_f) \\
p_7 &= \mathsf{intro}_{\Rightarrow}(p_6) : \varphi, b_1 \vdash \neg b_2 \Rightarrow \mathsf{wp}(l_f) \\
p_8 &= \mathsf{intro}_{\wedge}(\mathsf{axiom}(b_1), \mathsf{axiom}(b_2)) : \varphi, b_1, b_2 \vdash b_1 \wedge b_2 \\
p_9 &= \mathsf{elim}_{\wedge,r}(\mathsf{axiom}(\varphi)) : \varphi, b_1, b_2 \vdash b_1 \wedge b_2 \Rightarrow \mathsf{wp}(l_t) \\
p_{10} &= \mathsf{elim}_{\Rightarrow}(p_8, p_9) : \varphi, b_1, b_2 \vdash \mathsf{wp}(l_t) \\
p_{11} &= \mathsf{intro}_{\Rightarrow}(p_{10}) : \varphi, b_1 \vdash b_2 \Rightarrow \mathsf{wp}(l_t) \\
p_{12} &= \mathsf{intro}_{\wedge}(p_7, p_{11}) : \varphi, b_1 \vdash b_2 \Rightarrow \mathsf{wp}(l_t) \wedge \neg b_2 \Rightarrow \mathsf{wp}(l_f) \\
p_{13} &= \mathsf{elim}_{\Rightarrow}(\mathsf{weak}(\mathsf{intro}_{\Rightarrow}(c_2)), p_{12}) : \varphi, b_1 \vdash \mathsf{wp}(l'_t) \\
p_{14} &= \mathsf{intro}_{\Rightarrow}(p_{13}) : \varphi \vdash b_1 \Rightarrow \mathsf{wp}(l'_t) \\
p_{15} &= \mathsf{axiom}(\neg b_1) : \varphi, \neg b_1, b_1 \wedge b_2 \vdash \neg b_1 \\
p_{16} &= \mathsf{elim}_{\wedge,l}(\mathsf{axiom}(b_1 \wedge b_2)) : \varphi, \neg b_1, b_1 \wedge b_2 \vdash b_1 \\
p_{17} &= \mathsf{elim}_{\Rightarrow}(p_{15}, p_{16}) : \varphi, \neg b_1, b_1 \wedge b_2 \vdash \mathsf{false} \\
p_{18} &= \mathsf{intro}_{\Rightarrow}(p_{17}) : \varphi, \neg b_1 \vdash \neg(b_1 \wedge b_2) \\
p_{19} &= \mathsf{elim}_{\wedge,r}(\mathsf{axiom}(\varphi)) : \varphi, \neg b_1 \vdash \neg(b_1 \wedge b_2) \Rightarrow \mathsf{wp}(l_f) \\
p_{20} &= \mathsf{elim}_{\Rightarrow}(p_{18}, p_{19}) : \varphi, \neg b_1 \vdash \mathsf{wp}(l_f) \\
p_{21} &=: \varphi, \neg b_1 \vdash \mathsf{wp}(l_f) \\
p_{22} &= \mathsf{intro}_{\Rightarrow}(p_{21}) : \varphi \vdash \neg b_1 \Rightarrow \mathsf{wp}(l_f) \\
p_{23} &= \mathsf{intro}_{\wedge}(p_{14}, p_{23}) : \varphi \vdash (b_1 \Rightarrow \mathsf{wp}(l'_t)) \wedge (\neg b_1 \Rightarrow \mathsf{wp}(l_f)) \\
c &= \mathsf{elim}_{\Rightarrow}(p_{23}, \mathsf{intro}_{\Rightarrow}(c_1)) : \varphi \vdash \mathsf{wp}(l)
\end{aligned}
$$

Based on these previous results, the following lemma relates the computation of verification conditions between a source program and its RTL representation.

Lemma 7. *Let c be a statement of a procedure p and* (Pre, annot, Post) *its specification. Let $\langle \mathcal{N}, \mathcal{E}, G \rangle$ be defined as $\mathcal{C}_{(l,l')}(c)$, and $(\varphi, \theta) = \mathsf{WP}(c, \mathsf{wp}(l'))$. Then, one can generate, for every program label $l \in \mathcal{N}$, certificates for the goal $\vdash \varphi \Rightarrow \mathsf{wp}(l)$.*

Proof. The proof proceeds by structural induction on the statement c. Consider for instance the case of a conditional statement, i.e., $c = \mathbf{if}\ b\ \mathbf{then}\ c_1\ \mathbf{else}\ c_2$. Then, $\langle \mathcal{N}, \mathcal{E}, G \rangle$ is defined as $\mathcal{C}^{\mathsf{b}}_{l,l_t,l_f}(b) \cup \mathcal{C}_{l_t,l'}(c_1) \cup \mathcal{C}_{l_f,l'}(c_2)$. By I.H., we have the certificates

$$q_1 : \quad \vdash \varphi_1 \Rightarrow \mathsf{wp}(l_t)$$

and

$$q_2 : \quad \vdash \varphi_2 \Rightarrow \mathsf{wp}(l_f)$$

where $\mathsf{WP}(c_1, \mathsf{wp}(l')) = (\varphi_1, \theta_1)$ and $\mathsf{WP}(c_2, \mathsf{wp}(l')) = (\varphi_2, \theta_2)$ for some sets θ_1 and θ_2. By definition we have φ equal to $b \Rightarrow \varphi_1 \wedge \neg b \Rightarrow \varphi_2$. From Lemma 6, we have a certificate $q : b \Rightarrow \mathsf{wp}(l_t) \wedge \neg b \Rightarrow \mathsf{wp}(l_f) \vdash \mathsf{wp}(l)$. The following steps constructs the certificate:

$$
\begin{aligned}
p_1 &= \mathsf{axiom}(b) : \varphi, b \vdash b \\
p_2 &= \mathsf{elim}_{\wedge,l}(\mathsf{axiom}(\varphi)) : \varphi, b \vdash b \Rightarrow \varphi_1 \\
p_3 &= \mathsf{elim}_{\Rightarrow}(p_1, p_2) : \varphi, b \vdash \varphi_1 \\
p_4 &= \mathsf{weak}(q_1) : \varphi, b \vdash \varphi_1 \Rightarrow \mathsf{wp}(l_t) \\
p_5 &= \mathsf{elim}_{\Rightarrow}(p_3, p_4) : \varphi, b \vdash \mathsf{wp}(l_t) \\
p_6 &= \mathsf{intro}_{\Rightarrow}(p_5) : \varphi \vdash b \Rightarrow \mathsf{wp}(l_t) \\
p_7 &= \mathsf{axiom}(\neg b) : \varphi, \neg b \vdash \neg b \\
p_8 &= \mathsf{elim}_{\wedge,r}(\mathsf{axiom}(\varphi)) : \varphi, \neg b \vdash \neg b \Rightarrow \varphi_2 \\
p_9 &= \mathsf{elim}_{\Rightarrow}(p_7, p_8) : \varphi, \neg b \vdash \varphi_2 \\
p_{10} &= \mathsf{weak}(\mathsf{elim}_{\wedge,r}(q_2)) : \varphi, \neg b \vdash \varphi_2 \Rightarrow \mathsf{wp}(l_f) \\
p_{11} &= \mathsf{elim}_{\Rightarrow}(p_9, p_{10}) : \varphi, \neg b \vdash \mathsf{wp}(l_f) \\
p_{12} &= \mathsf{intro}_{\Rightarrow}(p_{11}) : \varphi \vdash \neg b \Rightarrow \mathsf{wp}(l_f) \\
p_{13} &= \mathsf{intro}_{\wedge}(p_6, p_{12}) : \varphi \vdash b \Rightarrow \mathsf{wp}(l_t) \wedge \neg b \Rightarrow \mathsf{wp}(l_f) \\
p_{14} &= \mathsf{elim}_{\Rightarrow}(\mathsf{intro}_{\Rightarrow}(\mathsf{weak}_{\varphi}(q)), p_{13}) : \varphi \vdash \mathsf{wp}(l) \\
p_{15} &= \mathsf{intro}_{\Rightarrow}(p_{14}) : \vdash \varphi \Rightarrow \mathsf{wp}(l)
\end{aligned}
$$

Theorem 1 (Equivalence of Proof Obligations). *Let p be a high-level procedure with specification* (Pre, annot, Post). *Let $\bar{p}$ be an RTL procedure defined as the compilation of p, i.e., $\langle \mathcal{N}, \mathcal{E}, G \rangle$ is equal to $\mathcal{C}_{(l_{in}, l_{out})}(c)$ where c is the body of p. Then, from Lemma 7, one can generate a certificate for the proof obligations in $\mathsf{po}(\hat{p})$ from the original certificate for the proof obligations in $\mathsf{PO}(p)$.*

5.2   Compilation of the Array Representation

Description. One particular difference between high and low level representations is how memory addressing, i.e. array access, is implemented. This compiler

$$\bar{G}[\langle l, l' \rangle] \doteq v' := 4 * v; x := \hat{a}[v'] \qquad \text{if } G[\langle l, l' \rangle] \doteq x := a[v]$$
$$\bar{G}[\langle l, l' \rangle] \doteq v' := 4 * v; \hat{a}[v'] := x \qquad \text{if } G[\langle l, l' \rangle] \doteq a[v] := x$$
$$\bar{G}[e] \doteq G[e] \qquad \text{otherwise}$$

Fig. 16. Compiler Definition

step models abstractly the typical distinction between addressing byte and integer array representations, by multiplying the value used to access an array cell by 4 (assuming an integer value is represented exactly with 4 byte values). Every array a of the source program is then compiled to a corresponding lower-level array $\hat{a}$ such that $|\hat{a}| = 4 * |a|$ and for every integer number n s.t. $0 \leq n < |a|$, we have $\hat{a}[4 * n] = a[n]$. The transformation of an RTL function $\langle \mathcal{N}, \mathcal{E}, G \rangle$ into $\langle \mathcal{N}, \mathcal{E}, \bar{G} \rangle$ is shown in Figure 16. Every assignment that contains an array access is replaced by two consecutive assignments. For simplicity, we abuse notation and do not make explicit the introduction of a fresh intermediate node.

Example 4. The code in Figure 17 is the result of transforming the array representation from the RTL code of Figure 15.

Since every array variable a is compiled into a lower-level array variable $\hat{a}$, we need to modify the original specification accordingly. To that end, we cannot simply substitute the occurrences of a by $\hat{a}$. Instead, we need to define a more complex renaming function. Let θ_a stand for the proposition $\forall i. \ a[i] = \hat{a}[4 * i]$. For every assertion φ, we denote $\alpha_a(\varphi)$ the assertion $\exists a. \ (\varphi \wedge \theta_a)$, i.e. a renaming, in φ, of the array variable a into its corresponding lower-level array variable $\hat{a}$.

Definition 7 (Compilation of Specifications). *Let* (Pre, annot, Post) *be the original specification of a procedure p. We define the specification for the compilation of the procedure p as* $(\alpha_a(\text{Pre}), \alpha_a \circ \text{annot}, \alpha_a(\text{Post}))$.

Comparison of Verification Conditions. Computing the verification condition at label l_2 returns:

$$\text{annot}(l_b) \Rightarrow (\text{vec}[i] \leq \text{pivot} \Rightarrow i < j \Rightarrow \text{annot}(l_b)[^{i+1}\!/_i]) \wedge$$
$$(\text{vec}[i] \leq \text{pivot} \Rightarrow \neg i < j \Rightarrow \text{annot}(l_c)) \wedge$$
$$(\neg \text{vec}[i] \leq \text{pivot} \Rightarrow \text{annot}(l_c))$$

Computing the verification condition at the same label from the transformed program returns:

$$\alpha_{\text{vec}}(\text{annot}(l_b)) \Rightarrow (\hat{\text{vec}}[4 * i] \leq \text{pivot} \Rightarrow i < j \Rightarrow \alpha_{\text{vec}}(\text{annot}(l_b))[^{i+1}\!/_i]) \wedge$$
$$(\hat{\text{vec}}[4 * i] \leq \text{pivot} \Rightarrow \neg i < j \Rightarrow \alpha_{\text{vec}}(\text{annot}(l_c))) \wedge$$
$$(\neg \hat{\text{vec}}[4 * i] \leq \text{pivot} \Rightarrow \alpha_{\text{vec}}(\text{annot}(l_c)))$$

Notice that they are equivalent up to renaming of the array variable vec. Then, it should be clear that one can prove the former from the latter. In the

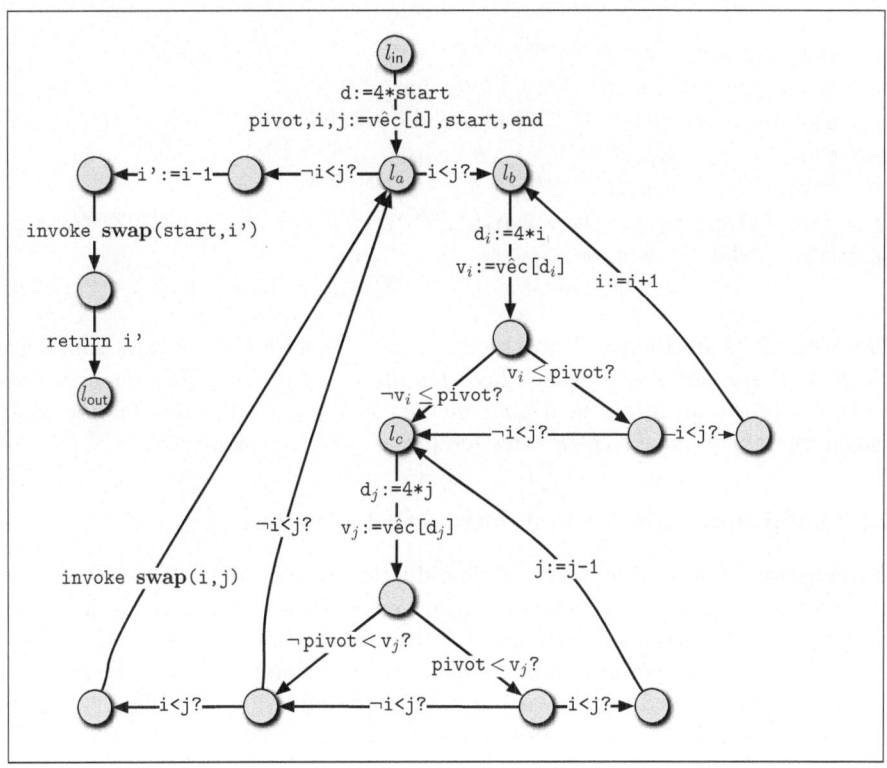

Fig. 17. RTL procedure `partition` after array compilation

rest of this section we show how we can systematically construct certificates for the transformed proof obligations from the original program certificates.

Transformation of the Certificate. The following generic results state that its is possible to reconstruct a certificate for the final code from the original certificate.

Lemma 8. *Let f be the original procedure, and $\bar{f}$ the result of transforming the representation of arrays. Then, one can generate, for every program label $l \in \mathsf{dom}(\mathsf{annot})$, certificates for the goal: $\vdash \alpha_{\mathsf{vec}}(\mathsf{wp}_f(l)) \Rightarrow \mathsf{wp}_{\bar{f}}(l)$.*

Proof. The proof proceeds by the induction principle associated to the definition of well-annotated programs. The base cases, i.e. the labels l such that $l \in \mathsf{dom}(\mathsf{annot})$ or $l = l_{\mathsf{out}}$, arc trivial since by definition $\mathsf{wp}_{\bar{f}}(l) = \alpha_{\mathsf{vec}}(\mathsf{wp}_f(l))$. Consider the case $G_f[\langle l, l' \rangle] = x := a[v]$. Then $\mathsf{wp}_f(l) = \mathsf{wp}_f(l')[^{\mathsf{vec}[v]}/_x]$ and $\mathsf{wp}_{\bar{f}}(l) = \mathsf{wp}_{\bar{f}}(l')[^{\hat{\mathsf{vec}}[4*v]}/_x]$. Let c' stand for the certificate generated as inductive hypothesis, i.e. $c' : \alpha_{\mathsf{vec}}(\mathsf{wp}_f(l)) \vdash \mathsf{wp}_{\bar{f}}(l)$. The following derivation steps construct the certificate we need for this proof case:

$p_1 = \mathsf{elim}_{\wedge,r}(\mathsf{axiom}) : \mathsf{wp}_f(l')[^{\mathsf{vec}[v]}/_x] \wedge \theta \vdash \theta$

$p_2 = \mathsf{elim}_{\wedge,l}(\mathsf{axiom}) : \mathsf{wp}_f(l')[^{\mathsf{vec}[v]}/_x] \wedge \theta \vdash \mathsf{wp}_f(l')[^{a[v]}/_x]$

$p_3 = \mathsf{elim}_{\forall}(p_1) : \mathsf{wp}_f(l')[^{\mathsf{vec}[v]}/_x] \wedge \theta \vdash \mathsf{vec}[v] = \mathsf{v\hat{e}c}[v]$

$p_4 = \mathsf{elim}_{=}(p_3, p_2) : \mathsf{wp}_f(l')[^{\mathsf{vec}[v]}/_x] \wedge \theta \vdash \mathsf{wp}_f(l')[^{\mathsf{v\hat{e}c}[v]}/_x]$

$p_5 = \mathsf{intro}_{\wedge}(p_4, p_1) : \mathsf{wp}_f(l')[^{\mathsf{vec}[v]}/_x] \wedge \theta \vdash \mathsf{wp}_f(l')[^{\mathsf{v\hat{e}c}[v]}/_x] \wedge \theta$

$p_6 = \mathsf{intro}_{\exists}(\mathsf{intro}_{\Rightarrow}(p_5)) :\vdash \exists \mathsf{vec}.\ \mathsf{wp}_f(l')[^{\mathsf{vec}[v]}/_x] \wedge \theta \Rightarrow \exists \mathsf{vec}.\ \mathsf{wp}_f(l')[^{\mathsf{v\hat{e}c}[v]}/_x] \wedge \theta$

$p_7 = \mathsf{intro}_{\Rightarrow}(\mathsf{elim}_{\Rightarrow}(\mathsf{axiom}, \mathsf{weak}(p_6))) :$
$$\vdash \exists \mathsf{vec}.\ \mathsf{wp}_f(l')[^{\mathsf{vec}[v]}/_x] \wedge \theta \Rightarrow \exists \mathsf{vec}.\ \mathsf{wp}_f(l')[^{\mathsf{v\hat{e}c}[v]}/_x] \wedge \theta$$

Theorem 2 (Certificate Translation). *Let p be an* RTL *procedure with specification* (Pre, annot, Post). *Let $\hat{p}$ stand for the result of compiling the array expressions in the procedure p. Then, one can generate certificates for the proof obligations of $\hat{p}$ from the certificates for the original procedure p.*

5.3 Loop Induction Variable Strength Reduction

Description. Loop induction strength reduction is an optimization that reduces the complexity of the arithmetic operations executed inside a loop. Basically, an induction variable of a loop is a variable that is incremented (or decremented) inside the loop by a constant value. A *derived* induction variable of the loop is a variable that is defined as a linear function on an induction variable of the loop. For instance, in the following code fragment:

```
i := 0;
while (i < N) do
    ...
    j := a * i + c
    i := i + 1;
```

the program variable i is a loop induction variable (with an increment of 1), and j is a derived induction variable defined as the linear function $a * i + c$. In the example above, one can see an optimization opportunity if the multiplication operation is replaced by a less costly addition operation. The following code shows an optimized version of the example above:

```
i := 0;
j := c;
while (i < N) do
    ...
    j := j + a
    i := i + 1;
```

It should be clear that the transformation preserves the original semantics.

Transformed Running Example. Consider the optimization of the running example of Figure 15. For convenience in explaining the certificate translation process, we have split the transformation in two independent steps. In the first one, for each derived induction variable j we introduce a corresponding fresh variable j' and a set of assignments to j' in order to make j' hold the same value as j. We require these new assignments to be less costly than those updating j, and that they do not read the value of j.

In the procedure **partition** of the quicksort example, we are interested on reducing the strength of the derived induction variables d_i and d_j, defined as linear functions $4*i$ and $4*j$, respectively. To that end, we introduce assignments immediately after each assignment of i and j. This first transformation step of the procedure **partition** can be found in Figure 18.

In a second transformation step, we take advantage of the fresh variables d_i' and d_j' that has been introduced, replacing in the code the assignments $d_i := 4*i$ and $d_j := 4*j$ by $d_i := d_i'$ and $d_j := d_j'$. The transformation is shown in Figure 19.

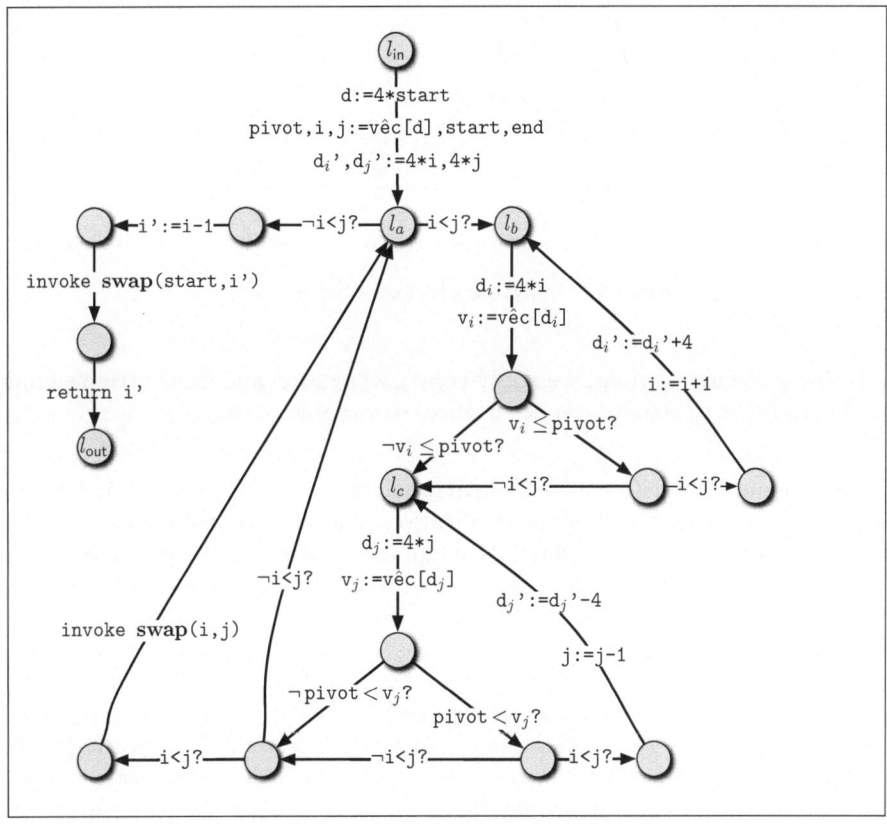

Fig. 18. Strength Reduction - First Step

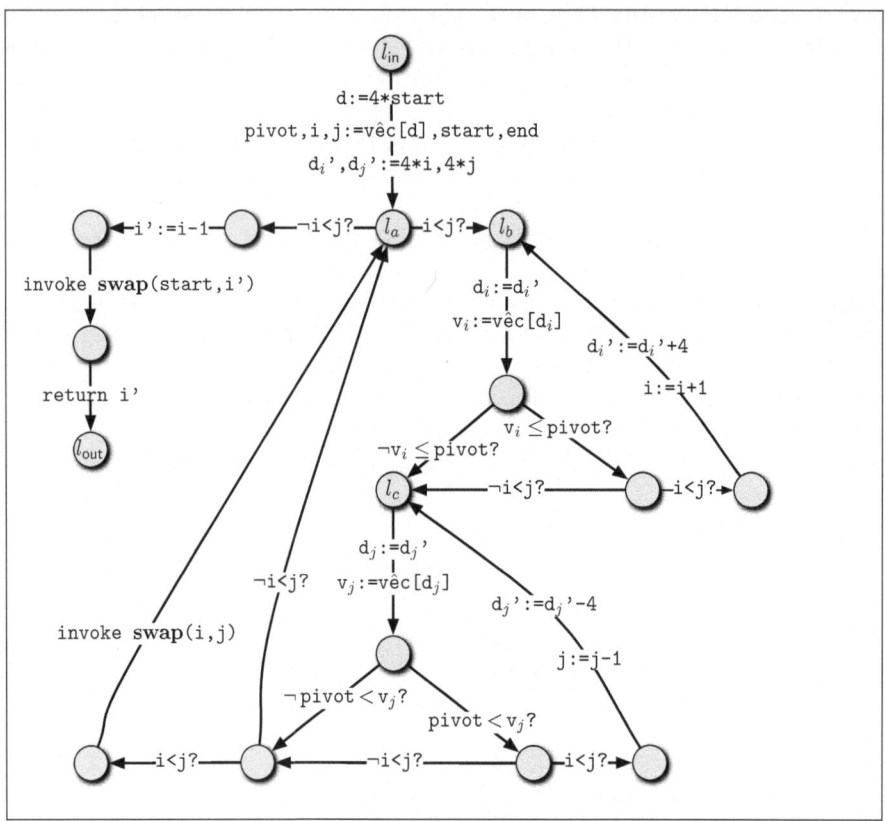

Fig. 19. Strength Reduction - Second Step

In the following sections, we apply copy propagation and dead variable elimination in order to remove the occurrences of variables d_i and d_j.

Comparison of Verification Conditions. One can see that the first transformation step does not alter the verification conditions. Indeed, an affectation of a fresh variable, i.e., a variable that appears neither in the program nor in the specification, does not affect the computation of verification conditions. Formally, from the definition of the function wpi, if x does not occur in φ, then $\mathsf{wpi}(x := e, \varphi) = \varphi$. In addition, one can see that if x does not occur in the program, then it is never introduced by the wpi function. That is, for very φ, if x does not occur in φ nor in ins, then x does not occur in $\mathsf{wpi}(\mathsf{ins}, \varphi)$. Let f and $\bar{f}$ denote the original and transformed procedure, respectively, the argument above implies that $\mathsf{wp}_f(l)$ and $\mathsf{wp}_{\bar{f}}(l)$ coincide syntactically for every label l. Therefore, proof obligations are preserved by this transformation step, and no transformation, neither of the specification nor the certificate, is needed.

However, one can see that certificates cannot be reused after the second transformation step, by simple comparison between the original and transformed program. Consider for instance the case of the verification of a simpler invariant at the loop headers pointed by labels l_b and l_c. Let ϕ stand for the invariant $\forall k \in \mathbb{N}.\ (\mathsf{start} \leq k < \mathsf{i} \Rightarrow \mathsf{v\hat{e}c}[4 * \mathsf{i}] \leq \mathsf{pivot})$, and let $\mathsf{annot}(l_1) = \mathsf{annot}(l_4) = \phi$. Computing the proof obligation for label l_b for the program shown in Figure 18 returns the proof goal:

$$\phi \Rightarrow (\mathsf{v\hat{e}c}[4 * \mathsf{i}] \leq \mathsf{pivot} \Rightarrow \mathsf{i} < \mathsf{j} \Rightarrow \phi[^{\mathsf{i}+1}\!/\!\mathsf{i}])$$

In the other hand, computing the same proof obligation for the program shown in Figure 19 returns

$$\phi \Rightarrow (\mathsf{v\hat{e}c}[\mathsf{d}'_i] \leq \mathsf{pivot} \Rightarrow \mathsf{i} < \mathsf{j} \Rightarrow \phi[^{\mathsf{i}+1}\!/\!\mathsf{i}])$$

which is unprovable unless we assume as hypothesis the result of the analysis, i.e. the condition $d'_i = 4 * i$.

Transformation of the Specification. In order to overcome the transformation of proof obligations, we propose first to strengthen the original specification to incorporate the result of the analysis that justifies the optimization. To simplify the exposition of this procedure, we split it in two steps. To that end, we first represent and certify the result of the static analysis in the underlying verification framework. Then, we merge this certified specification with the original procedure specification.

Consider $(\mathsf{true}, \mathsf{annot}_A, \mathsf{true})$ a procedure specification that represents the results of the analysis. One would like to generate a certificate for the specification $(\mathsf{Pre}, \mathsf{annot} \wedge \mathsf{annot}_A, \mathsf{Post})$ where $\mathsf{annot} \wedge \mathsf{annot}_A$ stands for the partial function such that $(\mathsf{annot} \wedge \mathsf{annot}_A)(l) \doteq \mathsf{annot}(l) \wedge \mathsf{annot}_A(l)$.

After providing a certificate for the specification $(\mathsf{true}, \mathsf{annot}_a, \mathsf{true})$ of the analysis result, we can integrate it with the certificate for the current specification $(\mathsf{Pre}, \mathsf{annot}, \mathsf{Post})$, as follows from the next result:

Lemma 9. *Let $s_1 = (\mathsf{Pre}_1, \mathsf{annot}_1, \mathsf{Post}_1)$ and $s_2 = (\mathsf{Pre}_2, \mathsf{annot}_2, \mathsf{Post}_2)$ be certified specifications of a procedure p. Then, both certificates can be merged to generate a certificate for the specification $s = (\mathsf{Pre}_1 \wedge \mathsf{Pre}_2, \mathsf{annot}_1 \wedge \mathsf{annot}_2, \mathsf{Post}_1 \wedge \mathsf{Post}_2)$.*

Proof. Let wp_{f_1}, wp_{f_2} and wp_f correspond to the weakest-precondition computation with specification s_1, s_2 and s, respectively. One can generate, by the induction principle induced by the definition of well-annotated programs, a certificate for the following goals:

$$\vdash \mathsf{wp}_{f_1}(l) \wedge \mathsf{wp}_{f_2}(l) \Rightarrow \mathsf{wp}_f(l)$$

and

$$\vdash \mathsf{wpi}_{f_1}(l) \wedge \mathsf{wpi}_{f_2}(l) \Rightarrow \mathsf{wpi}_f(l)$$

for every label l. This result follows from a proof of the distributivity of the predicate transformer wp *w.r.t. conjunction. It should be clear, from the definition of* $\text{annot}_1 \wedge \text{annot}_2$, *that this is sufficient to certify the proof obligations corresponding to the result of merging the two specifications.*

Certification of Analysis Results. In the example, for the second transformation step, we implicitly assume that the compiler has run a static analysis that determined that the condition $d_i' = 4 * i$ is valid at program label l_1. And similarly for the condition $d_j' = 4 * j$ at the program label l_4. Therefore, we assume the invariant specification $\text{annot}_A(l)$ defined as $d_i' = 4 * i \wedge d_j' = 4 * j$, for $l \in \{l_a, l_b, l_c\}$. The first goal is to certify the specification $(\text{true}, \text{annot}_A, \text{true})$ in the **partition** procedure. If we compute the verification conditions in order to certify the result of the analysis we get verification goals such as:

$$\text{annot}_A(l_b) \Rightarrow$$
$$(\text{vêc}[4 * i] \leq \text{pivot} \Rightarrow i < j \Rightarrow d_i' + 4 = 4 * (i + 1)) \wedge$$
$$(\text{vêc}[4 * i] \leq \text{pivot} \Rightarrow \neg i < j \Rightarrow \text{annot}_A(l_c)) \wedge$$
$$(\neg \text{vêc}[4 * i] \leq \text{pivot} \Rightarrow \text{annot}_A(l_c))$$

One can see that to prove this goal is enough to perform arithmetic simplification and rewriting of equalities.

Transformation of the Certificate. An essential requirement to translate the certificate is to provide a formal proof that states that predicate transformers of the replaced instructions are consistent with the original ones assuming valid the result of the analysis. More precisely, in the running example, we are interested in providing a formal proof, for every assertion ϕ, of the conditions $\text{wpi}(d_i := 4 * i, \phi) \Rightarrow \text{wpi}(d_i := d_i', \phi)$ and $\text{wpi}(d_j := 4 * j, \phi) \Rightarrow \text{wpi}(d_j := d_j', \phi)$ assuming as hypotheses the conditions $d_i' = 4 * i$ and $d_j' = 4 * j$, respectively. In our setting, this corresponds to an application of the operation $\text{elim}_=$ of the proof algebra. The following result states that this, together with the certificate of the analysis, is sufficient to generate a new certificate corresponding to the transformed program.

Lemma 10. *Let f and $\bar{f}$ stand for the original and transformed program, respectively. Suppose that $(\text{Pre}, \text{annot}, \text{Post})$ is a certified specification for f and that the result of the analysis $(\text{true}, \text{annot}_A, \text{true})$ is certified. Assume, the $\mathcal{N}_f = \mathcal{N}_{\bar{f}}$, $\mathcal{E}_f = \mathcal{E}_{\bar{f}}$ and for every edge $\langle l, l' \rangle \in \mathcal{E}_f$ s.t. $G_f[\langle l, l' \rangle] \neq G_{\bar{f}}[\langle l, l' \rangle]$, and any assertion φ, that we have a certificate* justif *for the following goal:*

$$\vdash \text{wpi}(G[\langle l, l' \rangle], \varphi) \wedge \text{annot}_A(l) \Rightarrow \text{wpi}(G_{\bar{f}}[\langle l, l' \rangle], \varphi)$$

Then, one can generate a certificate for the transformed program $\bar{f}$ with specification $(\text{Pre}, \text{annot} \wedge \text{annot}_A, \text{Post})$.

Proof. Assume for simplicity that annot_A is a total function. From the certificate justif, *and by the induction principle associated to well-annotated programs, one can generate certificates for the following goals:*

$$\vdash \mathsf{wp}_f(l) \wedge \mathsf{annot}_A(l) \Rightarrow \mathsf{wp}_{\bar{f}}(l)$$

and

$$\vdash \mathsf{wpi}(G_f[\langle l, l' \rangle], \mathsf{wp}_f(l')) \wedge \mathsf{annot}_A(l) \Rightarrow \mathsf{wpi}(G_{\bar{f}}[\langle l, l' \rangle], \mathsf{wp}_{\bar{f}}(l'))$$

for every program label l and edge $\langle l, l' \rangle$. Recall that proof obligations have the form $\mathsf{wp}_{\bar{f}}(l) \Rightarrow \bigwedge_{l' \in \mathsf{succ}(l)} \mathsf{wpi}(G_{\bar{f}}[\langle l, l' \rangle], \mathsf{wp}_{\bar{f}}(l'))$, and that $\mathsf{wp}_{\bar{f}}(l) \doteq \mathsf{wp}_f(l) \wedge \mathsf{annot}_A(l)$. It is sufficient then to provide certificates for

$$\vdash \mathsf{wp}_f(l) \Rightarrow \mathsf{wpi}(G_f[\langle l, l' \rangle], \mathsf{wp}_f(l'))$$

and

$$\vdash \mathsf{wp}_A(l) \Rightarrow \mathsf{wpi}(G_f[\langle l, l' \rangle], \mathsf{wp}_A(l'))$$

where $\mathsf{wp}_A(l)$ is computed with the result of the analysis as specification. The certificates required above correspond exactly to the original certificates and the certificates of the result of the analysis.

5.4   Copy Propagation

Description. Copy propagation is a simple compiler optimization that consists in replacing some occurrences of a program variable by a variable that holds the same value. In general, for a sequence of statements of the form

$$x := y\,;\,c_1\,;\,c_2$$

the transformation replaces any occurrence of the variable x by y in c_2, as long as neither x nor y gets modified by one of the instructions in c_1. This is a cleanup transformation, intended to reduce the set of used registers and simplifying the transformed code resulting from a previous optimization. In addition, it is an enabling transformation, that opens the door to further optimization opportunities.

Transformed Running Example. In the previous transformation, we have reduced the operation strength of assignments of the form $d_i := 4 * i$ by a substitution for a copy operation. In principle, there is no reason to preserve both variables d_i and d'_i, nor both of variables d_j and d'_j. We proceed then by substituting the occurrences of the variables d_i and d_j by d'_i and d'_j, respectively, as shown in Figure 20.

Comparison of Verification Conditions. In this particular example, after computing the verification conditions, one can easily see that they are preserved. Hence, no certificate translation is needed in this case.

In general, verification conditions do not coincide after the transformation. However, one can prove that they only differ on some variable renaming. Then, depending on the underlying notion of certificates, it is possible that no transformation is needed at all, or with a minor variable renaming in the representation of the certificate.

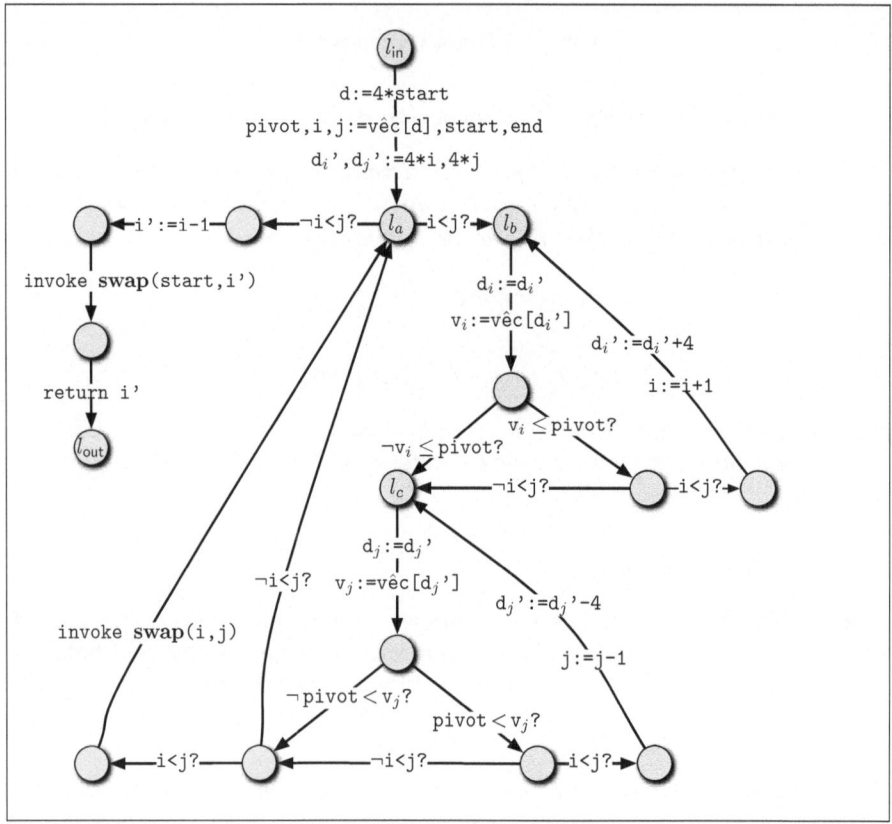

Fig. 20. Copy Propagation Transformation

5.5 Dead Variable Elimination

Description. Dead variable elimination is a compiler transformation that removes assignments to variables that are never used. The occurrence of such assignments are mainly the result of earlier program optimizations. For instance, in the following transformations

$$
\begin{array}{ccccc}
\mathtt{y} := 0 & & \mathtt{y} := 0 & & \mathtt{nop} \\
\mathtt{x} := \mathtt{y} * \mathtt{z} & \longrightarrow & \mathtt{x} := 0 & \longrightarrow & \mathtt{nop} \\
\mathtt{r} := f(\mathtt{x}) & & \mathtt{r} := f(0) & & \mathtt{r} := f(0)
\end{array}
$$

the second sequence of instructions is the result of propagating the constant values held by the variables y and x. Since neither x nor y is used in the rest of the program, the second transformation performs dead variable elimination removing the assignments to x and y.

There are two main improvements as a consequence of dead variable elimination. First, the unnecessary computation of the right hand side expression is removed, reducing execution time and program size. Second, it reduces the number of pseudo-variables that are used, which facilitates register allocation in the last compilation steps.

Commonly, the notion of variable liveness formalizes the situation in which the value of a variable is not needed in the future. We say that a variable is read at a program edge l if it appears at an edge $\langle l, l' \rangle$ in the right hand side of an assignment, as parameter in a function call, in a return statement or in a conditional expression. We say that a variable x is live at a certain program label l if there is a program path from label l to a program point that reads x and in which x is not updated.

Dead variable elimination consists in removing every assignment to a variable that is not live at the following program point.

Transformed Running Example. In the code at the right of Figure 20, the values assigned to the variables d_i and d_j are never used. The transformation,

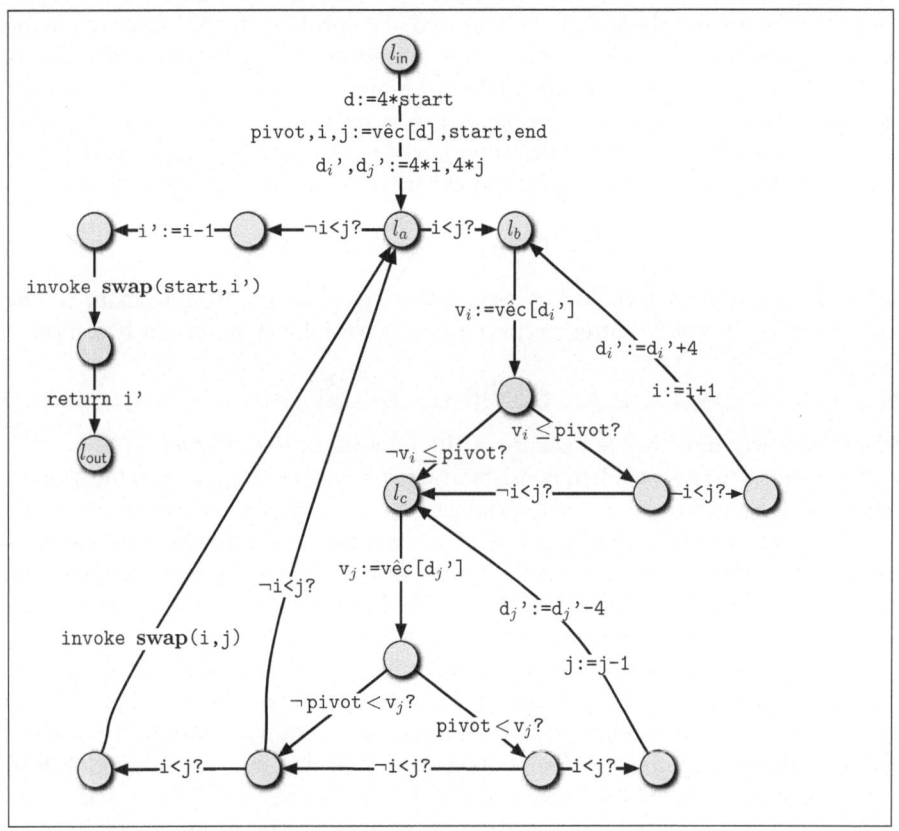

Fig. 21. Dead Variable Elimination

shown in Figure 21, takes the result of the previous optimization and removes the assignments to d_i and d_j.

Comparison of Verification Conditions. As can be seen after computing the verification conditions over the original and transformed program, they are preserved. Hence, there is no need to transform the specification nor the certificates.

However, it is not always the case that verification conditions are preserved. In fact, in general, they can become unprovable due to the occurrence of dead variables in the loop invariants. After some instructions are sliced-out of the program, even though the input/output semantics is preserved, the conditions over dead variables at the intermediate program points may not be satisfied. The following example illustrates this situation:

$$
\begin{array}{ccc}
\texttt{x} := \texttt{z} & & \texttt{nop} \\
\{\texttt{x} = \texttt{z}\} & \longrightarrow & \{\texttt{x} = \texttt{z}\} \\
\texttt{y} := f(\texttt{x}) & & \texttt{y} := f(\texttt{z})
\end{array}
$$

After propagating the variable $\texttt{z}$ to the function call, the assignment $\texttt{x} := \texttt{z}$ is not needed anymore and then it can be removed. The problem is that after removing the assignment to the dead variable, the condition $\texttt{x} = \texttt{z}$ becomes invalid. As a second example, consider the tuple $(\mathsf{true}, \mathsf{annot}, \mathsf{true})$ as a specification for the procedure **partition**, where $\mathsf{annot}(l_a) = \mathsf{annot}(l_b) = \mathsf{annot}(l_c) = \varphi$ and $\varphi \doteq d_i = d_i' \wedge d_i' = 4 * \texttt{i}$. After introduction of logical implication, a fragment of the proof obligation at label l_b for the program before the optimization is:

$$\Gamma \vdash \mathsf{annot}(l_b)[{}^{d_i'+4}\!/_{d_i'}][{}^{i+1}\!/_{\texttt{i}}][{}^{d_i'}\!/_{d_i}]$$

where $\Gamma \doteq \{\mathsf{annot}(l_b), \mathsf{v\hat{e}c}[d_i'] \leq \mathsf{pivot}, \texttt{i} < \texttt{j}\}$. The proof obligation, at the same label l_b, computed after performing dead variable elimination becomes:

$$\Gamma \vdash \mathsf{annot}(l_b)[{}^{d_i'+4}\!/_{d_i'}][{}^{i+1}\!/_{\texttt{i}}]$$

which is clearly unprovable because of the removal of the instruction $d_i := d_i'$.

A solution for this problem consists in weakening the original specification to remove the occurrences of dead variables at the intermediate assertions. More precisely, one can show that it is feasible to quantify existentially the dead variables that occurs at the intermediate annotations, removing dead assignments, and transforming the original certificates. We have developed this method in the context of an abstract interpretation framework [4].

An alternative approach consists in renaming each dead variable that appears in an assertion to its corresponding ghost variable. In this case, assignments to dead variables are not removed but replaced by assignments to ghost variables (namely ghost assignments). Proof obligations coincide up to renaming of dead variables to ghost variables. Since ghost assignments are part of the specification and thus never executed, they can be sliced out by the code client after the verification process and prior to its execution. A more detailed account of this technique can be found in a previous work by Barthe et al. [3].

5.6   Loop Unrolling

Description. Loop unrolling is a compiler transformation that duplicates code by unfolding the execution of a loop body. The transformation does not necessarily improve the code execution performance, it is rather an enabling transformation, i.e., it prepares the code for further compiler opportunities.

There are several variants of this transformation. In this section, we consider a transformation that prefixes a loop with a single sequential execution of its body (under the guard of the loop, in order to preserve the program semantics). Consider for instance a program of the form **while** b **do** c, the result of unrolling the loop in this program is **if** b **then** c; **while** b **do** c. We define the loop unrolling transformation as a particular instance of a more general notion of node duplication, formalized by the following definition:

Definition 8 (Node replication). *A program* $\langle \mathcal{N} \cup \mathcal{N}^+, \mathcal{E}^+, G^+ \rangle$ *is the result of replicating nodes of program* $\langle \mathcal{N}, \mathcal{E}, G \rangle$ *if*

- $\mathcal{N}^+ \subseteq \{l^+ \mid l \in \mathcal{N}\}$;
- *for every* $l_1, l_2 \in \mathcal{N}$, *if* $\langle l_1^+, l_2 \rangle$, $\langle l_1, l_2^+ \rangle$, *or* $\langle l_1^+, l_2^+ \rangle$ *is in* $\mathcal{E}^+$ *then* $\langle l_1, l_2 \rangle$ *is in* $\mathcal{E}$, *i.e., subgraph duplication preserves the structure; and*
- *for every* $l_1, l_2 \in \mathcal{N}$, *if* $e \in \{\langle l_1^+, l_2 \rangle, \langle l_1, l_2^+ \rangle, \langle l_1^+, l_2^+ \rangle\}$ *then* $G^+[e] = G[\langle l_1, l_2 \rangle]$.

Transformed Running Example. Consider the procedure **partition** in the context of the whole running example. Assuming that the procedure **partition** is not called from any program point outside the body of the procedure **quicksort**, we know that the condition i < j always holds just before the execution of the body. Consequently, the loop is executed at least once, for every initial execution state, and one can take advantage of this fact to search for further optimizations. In this section, we unroll one step of the execution of the outer loop statement. In the following section, we optimize the duplicated instance of the loop body.

Figure 22 shows the result of unrolling the outer loop of the procedure **partition**. In the figure, the subgraph corresponding to the loop body is duplicated and placed immediately before the loop header. The evaluation of the loop guard is included in the duplicated code, in order to ensure preservation of the program semantics. Notice that the last duplicated node jumps to the original loop header (i.e., node l_a), instead of jumping backwards to the duplicated evaluation of the guard (i.e., node l'_a), and thus avoiding the re-entrance inside the duplicated code.

Transformation of the Certificate. In general, as one can see, dealing with this transformation is simple since proof obligations are not modified, but duplicated.

Let (Pre, annot, Post) stand for the procedure specification previous to the application of loop unrolling. Consider an invariant specification annot' that extends annot in the set of duplicated labels. That is, annot'(l) = annot(l) for

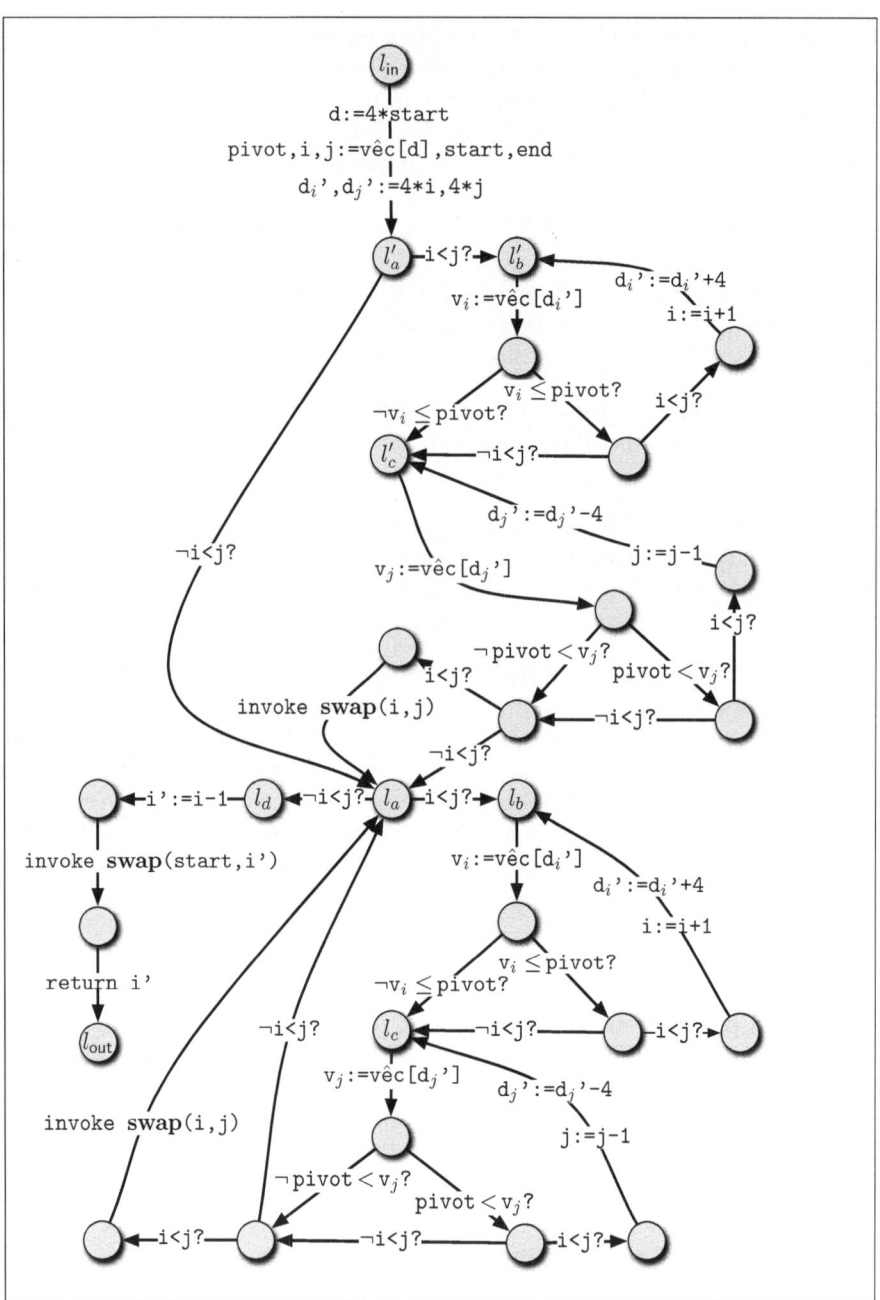

Fig. 22. Loop Unrolling

$l \in \text{dom(annot)}$, and $\text{annot}'(l'_a)$, $\text{annot}'(l'_b)$ and $\text{annot}'(l'_c)$ equal to $\text{annot}(l_a)$, $\text{annot}(l_b)$ and $\text{annot}(l_c)$, respectively.

One can see that the original verification conditions, i.e., those at program points in dom(annot), are not modified. However, new verification conditions are introduced at the annotated program points that are duplicated: l'_a, l'_b ad l'_c. Since the code involved in the computation of the proof obligations at labels l'_b and l'_c preserves the same structure of the original code, then, as one can see, proof obligations are equal to the original proof obligations at l_b and l_c. The proof obligation at label l'_a do not coincide with the original proof obligation at label l_a. The proof obligation at label l_a, after the application of the optimizations is:

$$\vdash \text{annot}(l_a) \Rightarrow (\text{i} < \text{j} \Rightarrow \text{annot}(l_b)) \land (\neg \text{i} < \text{j} \Rightarrow \text{wp}(l_d))$$

If we compute the proof obligation at label l'_a we get

$$\vdash \text{annot}(l'_a) \Rightarrow (\text{i} < \text{j} \Rightarrow \text{annot}(l'_b)) \land (\neg \text{i} < \text{j} \Rightarrow \text{annot}(l_a))$$

which by definition is equal to

$$\vdash \text{annot}(l_a) \Rightarrow (\text{i} < \text{j} \Rightarrow \text{annot}(l_b)) \land (\neg \text{i} < \text{j} \Rightarrow \text{annot}(l_a))$$

Although the new proof obligation at label l'_a is clearly different, it is still trivial to discharge.

The following result generalizes certificate translation after the application of a loop unrolling transformation.

Lemma 11. *Let $p^+ = \langle \mathcal{N} \cup \mathcal{N}^+, \mathcal{E}^+, G^+ \rangle$ be the result of duplicating some of the nodes of the procedure $p = \langle \mathcal{N}, \mathcal{E}, G \rangle$. Let l^+ denote a label in $\mathcal{N}^+$, i.e., a label such that $l \in \mathcal{N}$. Let $\langle \text{Pre}, \text{annot}^+, \text{Post} \rangle$ be the specification of p^+, where $\langle \text{Pre}, \text{annot}, \text{Post} \rangle$ is the specification of p, and annot^+ extends annot to $\mathcal{N}^+$, defining $\text{annot}^+(l^+)$ as $\text{annot}(l)$. Then, one can construct, for $\bar{l} \in \{l, l^+\}$ a certificate for the following goal:*

$$c : \quad \vdash \text{wp}_p(l) \Rightarrow \text{wp}_{p^+}(\bar{l})$$

Since $\text{wp}_p(l)$ coincides with $\text{wp}_{p^+}(\bar{l})$ for every $l \in \text{dom(annot)}$, it follows that one can generate a certificate for the transformed program from the certificate of the goal above and the original certificates.

A more general result is part of a development of certificate translation in the context of an abstract interpretation setting [4].

5.7   Redundant Conditional Elimination

Description. Redundant conditional elimination is a program optimization that removes conditional branching that can be predicted statically. First, an automated analysis gathers information about the program variables along the control flow paths of the program. Then, in the basis of the result of the analysis, a transformation step removes the evaluation of conditional expressions that are inferred to be always valid (or always invalid), and conditional jumps are modified in accordance. In addition, the instructions that become unreachable, and then non-executable, may also be removed. In the following example

$$y := z * z;$$
$$\textbf{while } (x < y) \textbf{ do } c_1;$$
$$\textbf{if } (x < 0) \textbf{ then } c_2;$$

if the statement c_1 does not modify the variable y, the analysis may infer that the condition $x \geq 0$ holds right after the execution of the body of the loop. In that case, we know it is safe to remove the statement **if** $(x < 0)$ **then** c_2, since it will never be executed. In the rest of the section we assume the static analysis is capable of discovering relational properties on the values of program variables.

Transformed Running Example. Consider the code in Figure 22, i.e., after unrolling one execution of the loop body in the running example, executing in the context of the procedure **quicksort**. Notice from Figure 1 that the only invocation of the procedure **partition** is performed with parameters start and end, and under the guard start < end. One would expect thus an inter-procedural analysis to statically infer that the condition $i < j$ always holds at the program point with label l'. Consequently, one of the branches at l'_a is always taken and then it is safe to remove one of the conditional edges. The transformation then removes the branch $\neg(i < j)$ at node l'_a to jump unconditionally to l'_b. The transformed RTL code for the procedure **partition** can be found in Figure 23.

Comparison of Verification Conditions. Inspecting the transformed code in Figure 23, one can see that the proof obligation at label l'_a is the only one that is affected by the transformation. The original proof obligation at label l'_a is

$$\vdash \mathsf{annot}(l'_a) \Rightarrow (i < j \Rightarrow \mathsf{annot}(l'_b)) \land (\neg i < j \Rightarrow \mathsf{annot}(l_a))$$

whereas, after the transformation, the proof obligation becomes

$$\vdash \mathsf{annot}(l'_a) \Rightarrow \mathsf{annot}(l'_b)$$

In this particular example, the new proof obligation can be still discharged, since by definition both $\mathsf{annot}(l'_a)$ and $\mathsf{annot}(l'_b)$ are equal to $\mathsf{annot}(l_a)$. However, that is not generally the case, since $\mathsf{annot}(l'_b)$ may be distinct to $\mathsf{annot}(l_a)$ and thus the condition $i < j$ may be needed as hypothesis to prove the implication $\mathsf{annot}(l_a) \Rightarrow \mathsf{annot}(l'_b)$. In the rest of this section, we generalize certificate transformation in the presence of redundant conditional elimination.

Transformation of the Specification. To deal with this transformation, we proceed by incorporating the result of the analysis as a strengthening of the original invariants. As explained in Section 5.3, this process entails first providing

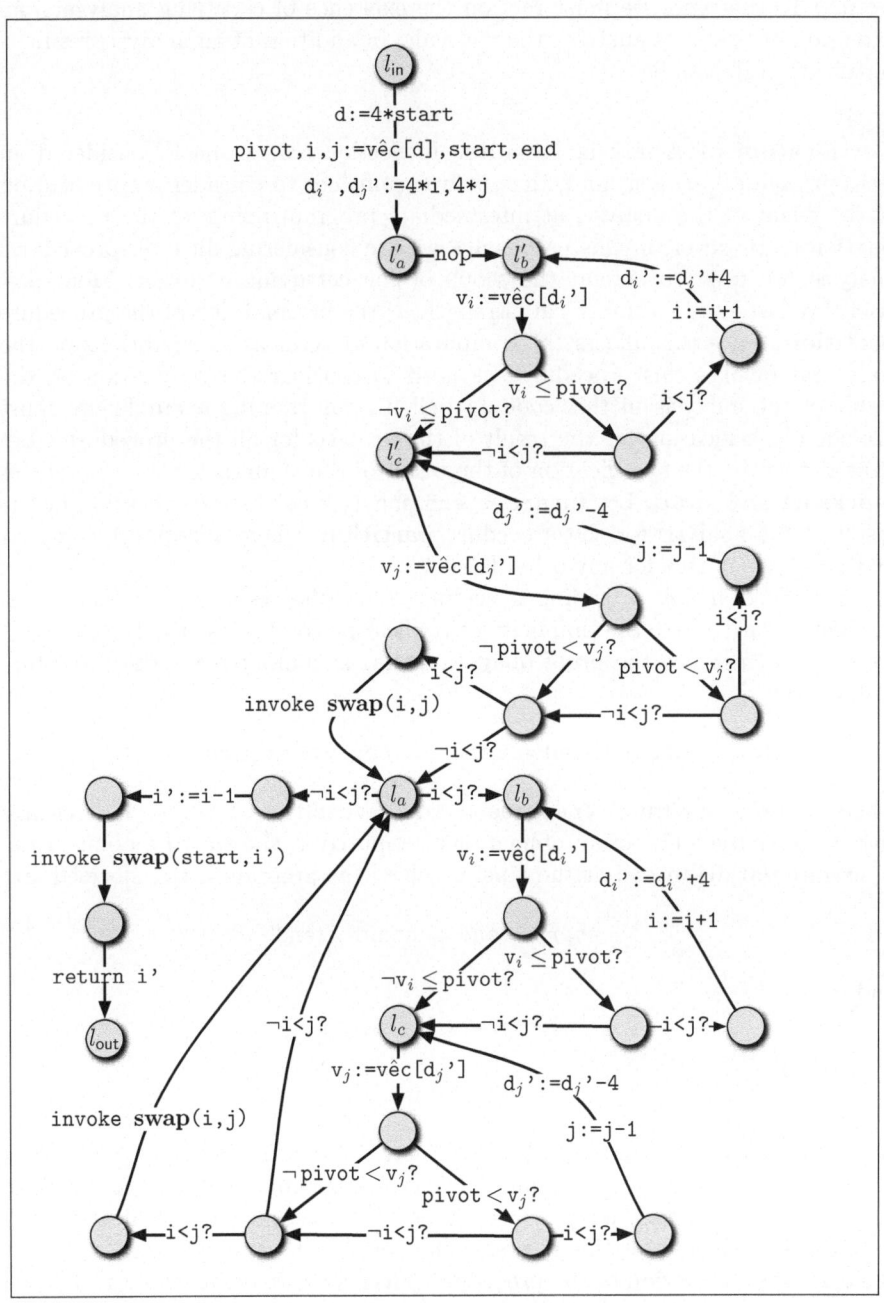

Fig. 23. Redundant Conditional Elimination

a certificate of the result of the analysis represented in the logic of the verification setting. To that end, we must rely on the existence of certifying analyzers, an extension of standard analyses that provide, in addition of an analysis result, a certificate of its validity.

Certification of Analysis Results. In Section 5.3, we have considered an intra-procedural analysis and, thus, it was sufficient to consider a specification of the result of the analysis at intermediate program points of the procedure **partition**. However, in this case, since we are considering an inter-procedural analysis, we need to extend the scope of the certifying analyzer. More precisely, we also need to transform (strengthen) the precondition of the procedure **partition**. Since this affects the computation of verification conditions on the code that invokes this procedure, we need to consider the verification on the result of the analysis in this code as well. In our running example, we must provide a specification for the result of the analysis for all the procedures. Let $(\mathsf{true}, \emptyset, \mathsf{true})$ be the specification of the result of the analysis for the procedures **quicksort** and **swap**. Let $(\mathsf{start} < \mathsf{end}, \mathsf{annot}_a, \mathsf{true})$ the specification of the result of the analysis for the procedure **partition**, where $\mathsf{annot}_a(l'_a) \doteq \mathsf{i} < \mathsf{j}$ and $\mathsf{annot}_a(k) \doteq \mathsf{true}$ for any other label k.

As in Section 5.3, providing a certificate for the result of the analysis is straightforward due to the simplicity of verification conditions. To illustrate this, consider for instance the proof obligation that is computed for the procedure **quicksort**:

$$\mathsf{true} \Rightarrow \mathsf{start} < \mathsf{end} \Rightarrow (\mathsf{start} < \mathsf{end} \wedge \forall \mathsf{res}.(\mathsf{true} \Rightarrow \varphi))$$

where φ stands for $\mathsf{true} \wedge \forall \mathsf{res}(\mathsf{true} \Rightarrow \mathsf{true} \wedge \forall \mathsf{res}(\mathsf{true} \Rightarrow \mathsf{true}))$. It is clearly easy to discharge. The proof obligations computed at the starting point of the procedure **partition** and at the label in which the program is transformed are:

$$\vdash \mathsf{start} < \mathsf{end} \Rightarrow \mathsf{start} < \mathsf{end}$$

and

$$\vdash \mathsf{i} < \mathsf{j} \Rightarrow \mathsf{i} < \mathsf{j} \Rightarrow \mathsf{true}$$

respectively.

Transformation of the Certificate. The transformation of the certificate can be performed by the general technique shown in Section 5.3. Once the result of the analysis is certified, we can incorporate it to the current specification and generate a certificate for this new specification. Let $(\mathsf{Pre}, \mathsf{annot}, \mathsf{Post})$ stand for the current specification of the procedure **partition**, we define the transformed specification as $(\mathsf{Pre} \wedge \mathsf{start} < \mathsf{end}, \mathsf{annot}', \mathsf{Post})$, where $\mathsf{annot}'(l'_a) \doteq \mathsf{annot}(l') \wedge \mathsf{i} < \mathsf{j}$ and $\mathsf{annot}'(k) = \mathsf{annot}(k)$ for any other label k. We know that we can generate a certificate for the extended specification from Lemma 9. Let p and $\hat{p}$ stand for the original and transformed program, and notice that $\mathsf{succ}_{\hat{p}}(l'_a) \subseteq$

$\mathsf{succ}_p(l'_a)$. As in Section 5.3, in order to generate a certificate for the transformed program, we need to provide a formal proof of the following goal:

$$\vdash \bigwedge_{l_i \in \mathsf{succ}_p(l'_a)} \mathsf{wpi}_p(G_p[\langle l'_a, l_i \rangle], \varphi_i) \wedge \mathsf{annot}'(l'_a) \Rightarrow \bigwedge_{l_i \in \mathsf{succ}_{\hat{p}}(l'_a)} \mathsf{wpi}_{\hat{p}}(G_{\hat{p}}[\langle l'_a, l_i \rangle], \varphi_i)$$

for any φ, which in this case is defined as

$$\vdash (\mathtt{i} < \mathtt{j} \Rightarrow \varphi_t) \wedge (\neg \mathtt{i} < \mathtt{j} \Rightarrow \varphi_f) \wedge \mathtt{i} < \mathtt{j} \Rightarrow \varphi_t$$

From Lemma 10, a certificate for the goal above is sufficient to provide a certificate for the transformed program in the general case.

5.8   Stack-Based Code Generation

In this section we consider the last compilation phase, in which the intermediate program representation is transformed into the final interpretable stack-based code. We introduce briefly the programming language, its semantics and the underlying verification framework. We provide a definition of the compiler, that transforms an RTL graph to a sequence of labeled stack-based instructions. Finally, we show that verification conditions are preserved, and thus no transformation of the certificate is needed.

The transformation not only produces a linearized version of an RTL graph, but replaces RTL with stack-based instructions. Stack-based computation relies on instructions that put, remove and modify values stored in the stack. As with RTL programs, a stack-based program is composed of a set of procedures. Each procedure p consists of a set of formal parameters and a list of labeled instructions from the set described in Figure 24. In the figure, *sig* is the signature of the invoked procedure, consisting of a procedure identifier and the number of arguments it takes from the stack. For notational convenience, we let a partial function G_p map program labels to instructions. For every instruction with only one predecessor, we

$$
\begin{aligned}
ins ::= &\ \mathbf{prim} \oplus \\
&\ |\ \mathbf{push}\ n \\
&\ |\ \mathbf{load}\ x \\
&\ |\ \mathbf{store}\ x \\
&\ |\ \mathbf{aload}\ a \\
&\ |\ \mathbf{astore}\ a \\
&\ |\ \mathbf{nop} \\
&\ |\ \mathbf{jmp}\ l \\
&\ |\ \mathbf{cjmp} \bowtie l, l \\
&\ |\ \mathbf{invoke}\ sig \\
&\ |\ \mathbf{return}
\end{aligned}
$$

Fig. 24. Stack-based Instruction Set

$$\frac{G_p[l] = \textbf{return}}{\langle l, n :: \textbf{s}, \sigma \rangle \leadsto_p \langle n, \sigma_A \rangle} \qquad \frac{G_p[l] = \textbf{nop} \quad \langle l+1, \textbf{s}, \sigma \rangle \leadsto_p s \quad s \in \Sigma_F}{\langle l, \textbf{s}, \sigma \rangle \leadsto_p s}$$

$$\frac{G_p[l] = v := \textbf{invoke } q \; k \quad \langle l_{\text{in}}, [], \langle [\vec{x}_q \mapsto \vec{n}], \sigma_A \rangle \rangle \leadsto_q \langle m :: \textbf{s}', \langle \sigma'_V, \sigma'_A \rangle \rangle}{\langle l+1, m :: \textbf{s}, \langle \sigma_V, \sigma'_A \rangle \rangle \leadsto_p s \quad s \in \Sigma_F}{\langle l, \vec{n} :: \textbf{s}, \sigma \rangle \leadsto_p s}$$

$$\frac{G_p[l] = \textbf{jmp } l' \quad \langle l', \textbf{s}, \sigma \rangle \leadsto_p s \quad s \in \Sigma_F}{\langle l, \textbf{s}, \sigma \rangle \leadsto_p s}$$

$$\frac{G_p[l] = \textbf{cjmp} \bowtie l_t, l_f \quad n_1 \bowtie n_2 \quad \langle l_t, \textbf{s}, \sigma \rangle \leadsto_p s \quad s \in \Sigma_F}{\langle l, n_1 :: n_2 :: \textbf{s}, \sigma \rangle \leadsto_p s}$$

$$\frac{G_p[l] = \textbf{cjmp} \bowtie l_t, l_f \quad \neg(n_1 \bowtie n_2) \quad \langle l_f, \textbf{s}, \sigma \rangle \leadsto_p s \quad s \in \Sigma_F}{\langle l, n_1 :: n_2 :: \textbf{s}, \sigma \rangle \leadsto_p s}$$

$$\frac{G_p[l] = \textbf{prim} \oplus \quad \langle l+1, n_1 \oplus n_2 :: \textbf{s}, \sigma \rangle \leadsto_p s \quad s \in \Sigma_F}{\langle l, n_1 :: n_2 :: \textbf{s}, \sigma \rangle \leadsto_p s}$$

$$\frac{G_p[l] = \textbf{push } n \quad \langle l+1, n :: \textbf{s}, \sigma \rangle \leadsto_p s \quad s \in \Sigma_F}{\langle l, \textbf{s}, \sigma \rangle \leadsto_p s}$$

$$\frac{G_p[l] = \textbf{load } x \quad \langle l+1, \sigma_V x :: \textbf{s}, \sigma \rangle \leadsto_p s \quad s \in \Sigma_F}{\langle l, \textbf{s}, \sigma \rangle \leadsto_p s}$$

$$\frac{G_p[l] = \textbf{store } x \quad \langle l+1, \textbf{s}, [\sigma : x \mapsto n] \rangle \leadsto_p s \quad s \in \Sigma_F}{\langle l, n :: \textbf{s}, \sigma \rangle \leadsto_p s}$$

$$\frac{G_p[l] = \textbf{aload } a \quad 0 \le i < |a| \quad \langle l+1, \sigma_A \, a \, i :: \textbf{s}, \sigma \rangle \leadsto_p s \quad s \in \Sigma_F}{\langle l, i :: \textbf{s}, \sigma \rangle \leadsto_p s}$$

$$\frac{G_p[l] = \textbf{astore } a \quad 0 \le i < |a| \quad \langle l+1, \textbf{s}, [\sigma : a \mapsto [a : i \mapsto n]] \rangle \leadsto_p s \quad s \in \Sigma_F}{\langle l, i :: n :: \textbf{s}, \sigma \rangle \leadsto_p s}$$

Fig. 25. Semantics of Stack-based Programs

omit its label. For an instruction at label l with a single successor we let $l+1$ stand for the label of the next instruction. For a label l such that $G[l] = \textbf{cjmp} \bowtie l_t, l_f$, $\text{succ}(l)$ is defined as $\{l_t, l_f\}$, for $G[l] = \textbf{jmp } l'$, $\text{succ}(l) = \{l'\}$ and if $G[l] = \textbf{return}$ then $\text{succ} = \emptyset$. For any other case, $\text{succ}(l) = \{l+1\}$.

A stack-based program is well-formed if the control-flow representation of every procedure is a closed graph. Formally, for every procedure p, and $l \in \text{dom}(G_p)$, we have that $\text{succ}(l) \subseteq \text{dom}(G_p)$. As with RTL programs we assume the existence of an initial label l_{in}. As in previous sections, an execution environment is composed of a global array state in $\Sigma_{\mathcal{A}}$ and a local scalar state in $\Sigma_{\mathcal{V}}$. The semantics of well-formed programs is defined in Figure 25 by a relation $\rightsquigarrow \subseteq \mathcal{L} \times Stack \times \Sigma \rightarrow Stack \times \Sigma$. It differs from the semantics of RTL programs in the computation of expressions, argument passing and value returning.

Verification Setting. The specification language is slightly modified in order to reason about stack expressions. We use the special variable $\mathbf{s}$ to denote the operand stack. The expression $\mathbf{s}[0]$ denotes the top element of the stack $\mathbf{s}$ and the expression $\uparrow \mathbf{s}$ denotes the stack after removing the top element from $\mathbf{s}$. We assume these expressions to be immediately reduced when introduced by variable substitution, according to the rules $(e :: \mathbf{s})[0] = e$ and $\uparrow (e :: \mathbf{s}) = \mathbf{s}$. A specification for a stack-based procedure is a tuple (Pre, annot, Post), where annot is a partial mapping from labels to assertions that may contain stack expressions. Pre and Post do not contain stack expressions.

For the proof obligations to be computable, we require the sequence of instructions to be well-annotated, i.e., that every cycle of the control-flow graph contains at least one annotated label.

From a well-annotated stack-based program a VCgen extracts a set of proof obligations from each of its procedures, by using the functions wp and wpi defined in Figure 26:

$$G[l] = \mathbf{nop} \qquad \mathsf{wpi}(l) = \mathsf{wp}(l+1)$$

$$G[l] = \mathbf{prim} \oplus \qquad \mathsf{wpi}(l) = \mathsf{wp}(l+1)[{}^{\mathbf{s}[0] \oplus \mathbf{s}[1] \, :: \, \uparrow^2 \mathbf{s}}\!/_{\mathbf{s}}]$$

$$G[l] = \mathbf{push} \ n \qquad \mathsf{wpi}(l) = \mathsf{wp}(l+1)[{}^{n \, :: \, \mathbf{s}}\!/_{\mathbf{s}}]$$

$$G[l] = \mathbf{load} \ x \qquad \mathsf{wpi}(l) = \mathsf{wp}(l+1)[{}^{x \, :: \, \mathbf{s}}\!/_{\mathbf{s}}]$$

$$G[l] = \mathbf{store} \ x \qquad \mathsf{wpi}(l) = \mathsf{wp}(l+1)[{}^{\mathbf{s}[0], \uparrow \mathbf{s}}\!/_{x, \mathbf{s}}]$$

$$G[l] = \mathbf{aload} \ x \qquad \mathsf{wpi}(l) = \mathsf{wp}(l+1)[{}^{a[\mathbf{s}[0]] \, :: \, \uparrow \mathbf{s}}\!/_{\mathbf{s}}]$$

$$G[l] = \mathbf{astore} \ x \qquad \mathsf{wpi}(l) = \mathsf{wp}(l+1)[{}^{a:\mathbf{s}[0] \mapsto \uparrow \mathbf{s}[0]], \uparrow^2 \mathbf{s}}\!/_{a, \mathbf{s}}]$$

$$G[l] = \mathbf{jmp} \ l' \qquad \mathsf{wpi}(l) = \mathsf{wp}(l+1)$$

$$G[l] = \mathbf{cjmp} \bowtie l_t, l_f \qquad \mathsf{wpi}(l) = (\mathbf{s}[0] \bowtie \uparrow os[0]) \Rightarrow \mathsf{wp}(l_t)) \wedge$$
$$(\neg(\mathbf{s}[0] \bowtie \uparrow os[0]) \Rightarrow \mathsf{wp}(l_f))$$

$$G[l] = \mathbf{invoke} \ f \ n \qquad \mathsf{wpi}(l) = \mathsf{Pre}[{}^{\mathbf{s}[0], \uparrow \mathbf{s}[0], \dots, \uparrow \mathbf{s}[0]}\!/_{\tilde{x}_f}] \wedge$$
$$\forall_{\mathrm{res}, V'} \mathsf{Post}[{}^{V', V}\!/_{V, V^*}][{}^{x_f{}^*}\!/_x] \Rightarrow \mathsf{wp}(l+1)[{}^{V'}\!/_V]$$

$$G[l] = \mathbf{return} \ v \qquad \mathsf{wpi}(l) = \mathsf{Post}_p[{}^{\mathbf{s}[0]}\!/_{\mathrm{res}}]$$

$$\mathsf{wp}(l) = \begin{cases} \mathsf{annot}(l) & \text{if } l \in \mathrm{dom}(\mathsf{annot}) \\ \mathsf{wpi}(l) & \text{otherwise} \end{cases}$$

Fig. 26. VCgen rules for Stack-based Code

$$\mathsf{po}(p) = \{\mathsf{Pre}_p \Rightarrow \mathsf{wp}_p(l_{\mathsf{in}})[^A\!/\!_{A*}]\}\cup$$
$$\{\mathsf{annot}_p(l) \Rightarrow \mathsf{wpi}_p(l) \mid l \in \mathsf{dom}(\mathsf{annot}_p)\}$$

where A represents the set of array variables that may get modified by p. For simplicity, we overload the predicate transformers wp and wpi to be defined over both **RTL** and stack-based instructions. When a label l has only one successor, this is denoted $l + 1$.

The following result states that the verification framework above is sound with respect to the program semantics.

Lemma 12 (VCgen Soundness). *Consider a well-annotated stack-based program P. Assume that for every procedure p, $\mathsf{po}(p)$ is a valid set of proof obligations. Then, for every procedure p, if $\langle l_{\mathsf{in}}, [], \sigma \rangle \leadsto_p \langle n :: \mathbf{s}, \sigma' \rangle$ then $\models [\sigma' : \mathsf{res} \mapsto n] : \mathsf{Post}$.*

Compilation. In this section, we define a simple compiler that transforms an **RTL** program representation into the stack-based code described above. The transformation can be seen as the last step of a compiler from a simple imperative

$$
\begin{aligned}
\mathcal{C}_l(\langle \mathcal{N}, \mathcal{E}, G \rangle, S) = (\ & \text{if } l \in S \longrightarrow \mathbf{jmp}\ l \\
\Box\ & \text{if } l \notin S \text{ and } G[\langle l, l_t \rangle] = v_1 \bowtie v_2? \longrightarrow \\
& \quad \text{let } (seq_t, S_t) = \mathcal{C}_{l_t}(\langle \mathcal{N}, \mathcal{E}, G \rangle, \{l\} \cup S) \\
& \quad \text{let } (seq_f, S_f) = \mathcal{C}_{l_f}(\langle \mathcal{N}, \mathcal{E}, G \rangle, S_t) \\
& \quad \text{in } (l : \mathbf{load}\ v_2 :: \mathbf{load}\ v_1 :: \mathbf{cjmp}\ \bowtie\ l_t, l_f :: seq_t :: seq_f, S_f) \\
\Box\ & \text{if } l \notin S \text{ and } G[\langle l, l' \rangle] = v := v_1 \oplus v_2 \longrightarrow \\
& \quad \text{let } (seq, S') = \mathcal{C}_{l'}(\langle \mathcal{N}, \mathcal{E}, G \rangle, \{l\} \cup S) \\
& \quad \text{in } (l : \mathbf{load}\ v_2 :: \mathbf{load}\ v_1 :: \mathbf{prim}\ \oplus :: \mathbf{store}\ v :: seq, S') \\
\Box\ & \text{if } l \notin S \text{ and } G[\langle l, l' \rangle] = v := a[v'] \longrightarrow \\
& \quad \text{let } (seq, S') = \mathcal{C}_{l'}(\langle \mathcal{N}, \mathcal{E}, G \rangle, \{l\} \cup S) \\
& \quad \text{in } (l : \mathbf{load}\ v' :: \mathbf{aload}\ a :: \mathbf{store}\ v :: seq, S') \\
\Box\ & \text{if } l \notin S \text{ and } G[\langle l, l' \rangle] = a[v] := v' \longrightarrow \\
& \quad \text{let } (seq, S') = \mathcal{C}_{l'}(\langle \mathcal{N}, \mathcal{E}, G \rangle, \{l\} \cup S) \\
& \quad \text{in } (l : \mathbf{load}\ v' :: \mathbf{load}\ v :: \mathbf{astore}\ a :: seq, S') \\
\Box\ & \text{if } l \notin S \text{ and } G[\langle l, l' \rangle] = \mathbf{invoke}\ f(\vec{x}) \longrightarrow \\
& \quad \text{let } (seq, S') = \mathcal{C}_{l'}(\langle \mathcal{N}, \mathcal{E}, G \rangle, \{l\} \cup S) \\
& \quad \text{in } (l : \mathbf{load}\ x_1 :: .. :: \mathbf{load}\ x_k :: \mathbf{invoke}\ f\ k :: seq, S') \\
\Box\ & \text{if } l \notin S \text{ and } G[\langle l, l' \rangle] = \mathbf{return}\ v \longrightarrow \\
& \quad \text{let } (seq, S') = \mathcal{C}_{l'}(\langle \mathcal{N}, \mathcal{E}, G \rangle, \{l\} \cup S) \\
& \quad \text{in } (l : \mathbf{load}\ v :: \mathbf{return} :: seq, S') \\
\Box\ & \text{if } l \notin S \text{ and } G[\langle l, l' \rangle] = \mathbf{nop} \longrightarrow \\
& \quad \text{let } (seq, S') = \mathcal{C}_{l'}(\langle \mathcal{N}, \mathcal{E}, G \rangle, \{l\} \cup S) \\
& \quad \text{in } (l : \mathbf{nop} :: seq, S') \\
&)
\end{aligned}
$$

Fig. 27. Compiler to Stack-based Code (Excerpt)

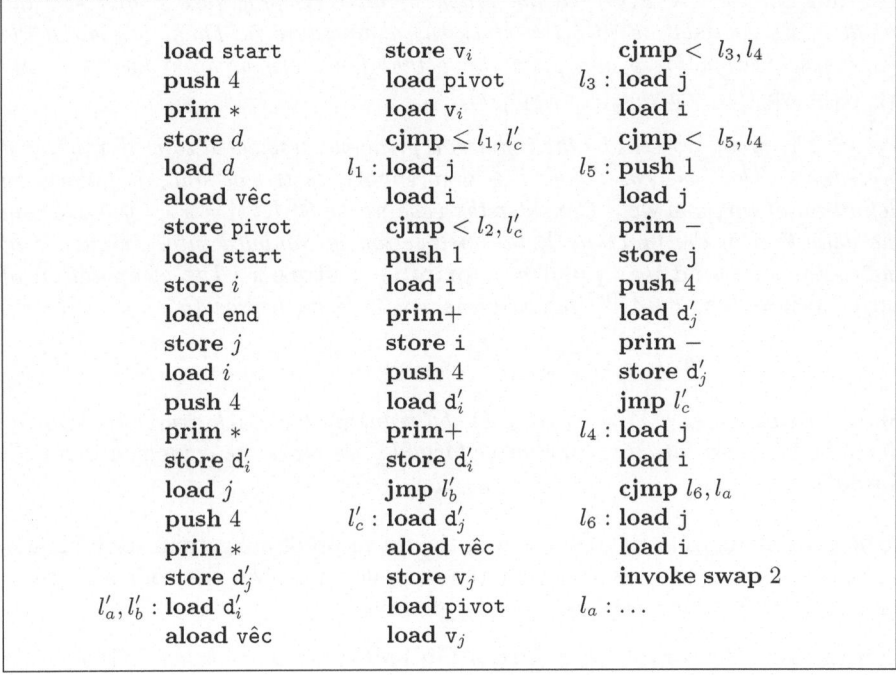

Fig. 28. Stack-based representation of the final code (Excerpt)

language described in Section 3, to the final executable code. The compilation is defined by a function $\mathcal{C}$ that maps an RTL graph into a semantically equivalent sequence of instructions that manipulates the values stored in the execution stack. The definition of this compilation function can be found in Figure 27.

Since the structure of the code is preserved it follows that a well-formed RTL program is compiled into a well-formed stack-based program. Furthermore, if the specification is preserved, a well-annotated RTL program is compiled into a well-annotated stack-based program.

Example 5. Figure 28 shows the result of compiling the RTL representation of Figure 23 into the stack-based representation.

Preservation of Proof Obligations. In this section we formalize the main result of this compilation step: assuming, for the result of the transformation, the same specification as the original code, verification conditions are preserved.

Then, if (Pre, annot, Post) is the specification of an RTL procedure p, we define the specification for the compilation of the procedure p as (Pre, annot, Post). Notice that it follows that intermediate invariants do not refer to stack expressions.

We first prove, in the following lemma, that predicate transformers are preserved by the compiler transformation defined in this section. More precisely, the computation of the wp function coincides at every program point up to the evaluation of stack expressions.

Lemma 13. *Let* $\langle \mathcal{N}, \mathcal{E}, G \rangle$ *be the graph of an* RTL *procedure* p *and* seq *the result of its compilation into the stack-based procedure* $\bar{p}$. *Then, assuming the same specification for* p *and* $\bar{p}$, *we have that for every program label* l *in* $\mathcal{N}$, $\mathsf{wp}_p(l) = \mathsf{wp}_{\bar{p}}(l)$, *and* $\mathsf{wpi}_p(l) = \mathsf{wpi}_{\bar{p}}(l)$.

Proof. *The proof proceeds by the induction principle associated to well-annotated procedures. The base case, e.g.,* $l \in \mathsf{dom}(\mathsf{annot})$, *is trivial since it follows by definition of* wp_p *and* $\mathsf{wp}_{\bar{p}}$. *Consider the case where* $G[\langle l, l' \rangle] \doteq x := y \oplus n$. *From the definition of the function* $\mathcal{C}$, *the instruction is compiled into a sequence of instructions* l : **load** y :: **push** n :: **prim** $\oplus$ :: **store** x. *The computation of* $\mathsf{wp}_p(l)$ *returns* $\mathsf{wp}_p(l+1)[^{y \oplus n}/_x]$, *whereas* $\mathsf{wp}_{\bar{p}}(l)$ *is defined as*

$$\mathsf{wp}_{\bar{p}}(l+1)[^{x,\mathsf{s}}/_{\mathsf{s}[0], \uparrow \mathsf{s}}][^{\mathsf{s}}/_{\mathsf{s}[0] \oplus \mathsf{s}[1]} :: \uparrow^2 \mathsf{s}][^{\mathsf{s}}/_{n \,::\, \mathsf{s}}][^{\mathsf{s}}/_{y \,::\, \mathsf{s}}]$$

Since by I.H. $\mathsf{wp}_p(l+1) = \mathsf{wp}_{\bar{p}}(l+1)$, *by reducing the stack expressions introduced by the substitutions in the latter formula, we prove the coincidence of both formulae.*

Hence, it follows from the definition of the set of proof obligations for RTL and stack-based code, and the fact that the compiler preserves the code structure, that proof obligations are syntactically preserved.

Lemma 14 (Preservation of Proof Obligations). *Let* p *be an* RTL *program and* $\bar{p}$ *the result of its compilation into the stack-based language. Assume* p *is certified w.r.t. the specification* (Pre, annot, Post). *Then,* $\bar{p}$ *is certified w.r.t. the specification* (Pre, annot, Post).

6   Conclusion

Certificate translation is a general method to transform certificates from source programs into certificates of compiled programs. In this tutorial, we have exemplified the underlying mechanisms of certificate translation on a running example. While representative, the example of the quicksort function fails to highlight some important aspects in certificate translation; these are briefly described in the next paragraph. For completeness, we conclude with a brief presentation of existing alternatives to certificate translation. Further discussion and pointers to the literature can be found in [3].

6.1   Other Topics in Certificate Translation

Important issues not covered by this tutorial include:

Certifying analyzers: optimizations that perform arithmetic reasoning require strengthening the loop invariants so that programs remain provable. These strengthened invariants should assert the correctness of the results of the analysis, and should be proved automatically—and weaved together with the original proof of the program. This requires extending standard analyzers into certifying analyzers, that justify analyses upon which the optimizations rely by expressing their results in the logic of the PCC architecture, and produce a certificate of the analysis for each program. The existence of certifying analyzers for transformations such as constant propagation or common subexpression elimination is shown in [2] in the context of a RTL language, and in a more general setting in [4].

Certificate translation in abstract interpretation: It is possible to take a more general approach to certificate translation by embedding the problem in the framework of abstract interpretation [8,9]. One can then give sufficient conditions for transforming a certificate of a program G into a certificate of a program G', where G' is derived from G by a semantically justified program transformation, typically a program optimization. In [4], we provide substantial leverage w.r.t. [2], allowing to consider strongest post-condition calculi as well as weakest precondition calculi as done in this paper, and to some extent concurrent programs.

Hybrid certificates: in order to reduce the verification effort, verification environments increasingly rely on combining static analyses and verification condition generation. The verification condition generator exploits the information of the analysis in two useful ways: on the one hand, verification conditions that originate from spurious edges in the control-flow graph are discarded. This leads to fewer and smaller proof obligations. Furthermore, the verification condition generator adds the results of the analysis as additional assumptions to help prove the verification conditions. In [5], we initiate the study of certificate translation for hybrid verification, and we show preservation of proof obligations between hybrid verification frameworks for source code and a stack-based language similar to that of Section 4.

6.2   Alternatives to Certificate Translation

There are several mechanisms to certify a compiled code from a certificate of the source program:

Certifying compilers: They extend traditional compilers with a mechanism to automatically generate certificates for sufficiently simple safety properties, exploiting the information available about a program during its compilation. Certifying compilation [18] is by design restricted to a specific class of properties and programs— in order to achieve automatic generation of certificates and, thus, to reduce the burden of verification on the code producer side. The counterpart of this approach is that the properties under consideration are restricted to simple properties, namely typing predicates. An early example of certifying compiler is the Touchstone compiler [18], which was intended to explore the feasibility of PCC. This compiler generates, for programs written in a type-safe fragment of C, a formal proof for type-based safety and memory safety of the resulting program in DEC Alpha assembly language. The Touchstone compiler automatically inserts the loops invariants in the resulting program and generates the correctness proofs.

Certified Compilers: The goal of certified compilers is to provide a formal guarantee of its correctness. It is a general result that proves that for every input program the results of the compilation have an equivalent semantics, for a particular definition of equivalence. A notable example of a certified compiler is provided by the CompCert [14] project. CompCert is a compiler, formalized in the Coq proof assistant, from a subset of C into PowerPC assembly code. A formal proof stating the equivalence between the source and the compiled code is formalized in the Coq proof assistant. There are two drawbacks to this approach, from the perspective of certificate translation. First, a formal definition of the compiler can be extremely large and, thus, the certificate of its correctness can be prohibitively expensive to check. Second, one must assume that the source code is available to the code user, in order to be inspected and compared with the compiled code. However, most commonly, one cannot expect code producers to release the corresponding source code.

Translation Validation: Translation validation [20,17] is an alternative technique to formally verifying the correctness of compiler transformations. Instead of providing a full definition of the compiler and proving that it is correct in the sense that any compiled code is observably equivalent to the original one, it certifies correct every run of the compiler. That is, for every particular input program, and each transformation step, the infrastructure compares the semantics of the transformed code to the original semantics. For every transformation step, proof obligations, expressed in first-order logic, stating the semantics equivalence are fed into a prover to be discharged. The main advantage of this approach with respect to the previous one, is that the full definition of the compiler is not needed and, since proofs are specialized to a given particular program, certificates become significantly smaller. However, as with certified compilers, there is also the inconvenience of requiring the availability of the source program.

References

1. Barthe, G., Crégut, P., Grégoire, B., Jensen, T., Pichardie, D.: The MOBIUS proof carrying code infrastructure. In: de Boer, F.S., Bonsangue, M.M., Graf, S., de Roever, W.-P. (eds.) FMCO 2007. LNCS, vol. 5382, pp. 1–24. Springer, Heidelberg (2008)
2. Barthe, G., Grégoire, B., Kunz, C., Rezk, T.: Certificate translation for optimizing compilers. In: Yi, K. (ed.) SAS 2006. LNCS, vol. 4134, pp. 301–317. Springer, Heidelberg (2006)
3. Barthe, G., Grégoire, B., Kunz, C., Rezk, T.: Certificate translation for optimizing compilers. ACM Transactions on Programming Languages and Systems (2009); Extended version of [2]
4. Barthe, G., Kunz, C.: Certificate translation in abstract interpretation. In: Drossopoulou, S. (ed.) ESOP 2008. LNCS, vol. 4960, pp. 368–382. Springer, Heidelberg (2008)
5. Barthe, G., Kunz, C., Pichardie, D., Samborski-Forlese, J.: Preservation of proof obligations for hybrid verification methods. In: Software Engineering and Formal Methods. IEEE Press, Los Alamitos (2008)

6. Burdy, L., Requet, A., Lanet, J.-L.: Java applet correctness: A developer-oriented approach. In: Araki, K., Gnesi, S., Mandrioli, D. (eds.) FME 2003. LNCS, vol. 2805, pp. 422–439. Springer, Heidelberg (2003)
7. Cok, D.R., Kiniry, J.R.: ESC/Java2: Uniting ESC/Java and JML: Progress and issues in building and using esc/java2 and a report on a case study involving the use of esc/java2 to verify portions of an internet voting tally system. In: Barthe, G., Burdy, L., Huisman, M., Lanet, J.-L., Muntean, T. (eds.) CASSIS 2004. LNCS, vol. 3362, pp. 108–128. Springer, Heidelberg (2005)
8. Cousot, P., Cousot, R.: Abstract interpretation: A unified lattice model for static analysis of programs by construction or approximation of fixpoints. In: Principles of Programming Languages, pp. 238–252 (1977)
9. Cousot, P., Cousot, R.: Systematic design of program analysis frameworks. In: Principles of Programming Languages, pp. 269–282 (1979)
10. Darvas, Á., Müller, P.: Formal encoding of JML level 0 specifications in JIVE. Technical report, ETH Zurich, Annual Report of the Chair of Software Engineering (2007)
11. Floyd, R.W.: Assigning meanings to programs. In: Proc. Symp. Appl. Math., vol. 19, pp. 19–31 (1967)
12. Hoare, C.A.R.: An axiomatic basis for computer programming. Communications of the ACM 12(10), 576–580 (1969)
13. Howard, W.A.: The Formulae-As-Types Notion Of Construction. In: Seldin, J.P., Hindley, J.R. (eds.) To H. B. Curry: Essays on Combinatory Logic, Lambda Calculus and Formalism, pp. 479–490. Academic Press, Inc., New York (1980)
14. Leroy, X.: Formal certification of a compiler back-end or: programming a compiler with a proof assistant. In: Morrisett, J.G., Peyton Jones, S.L. (eds.) Principles of Programming Languages, pp. 42–54. ACM Press, New York (2006)
15. Marché, C., Paulin-Mohring, C., Urbain, X.: The Krakatoa tool for certification of Java/JavaCard programs annotated with JML annotations. Journal of Logic and Algebraic Programming 58, 89–106 (2004)
16. Necula, G.C.: Proof-carrying code. In: Principles of Programming Languages, pp. 106–119. ACM Press, New York (1997)
17. Necula, G.C.: Translation validation for an optimizing compiler. ACM SIGPLAN Notices 35(5), 83–94 (2000)
18. Necula, G.C., Lee, P.: The design and implementation of a certifying compiler. In: Programming Languages Design and Implementation, vol. 33, pp. 333–344. ACM Press, New York (1998)
19. Necula, G.C.: Compiling with Proofs. PhD thesis, Carnegie Mellon University, Available as Technical Report CMU-CS-98-154 (October 1998)
20. Pnueli, A., Singerman, E., Siegel, M.: Translation validation. In: Steffen, B. (ed.) TACAS 1998. LNCS, vol. 1384, pp. 151–166. Springer, Heidelberg (1998)

Federated Identity Management

David W. Chadwick

Computing Laboratory, University of Kent, Canterbury, CT2 7NF, UK
d.w.chadwick@kent.ac.uk

Abstract. This paper addresses the topic of federated identity management. It discusses in detail the following topics: what is digital identity, what is identity management, what is federated identity management, Kim Cameron's 7 Laws of Identity, how can we protect the user's privacy in a federated environment, levels of assurance, some past and present federated identity management systems, and some current research in FIM.

Keywords: Identity Management, Shibboleth, CardSpace, Federations.

1 Introduction

What is digital identity? One can find many different variants of this definition on the Internet. Perhaps the most general definition is the one from a new draft ITU-T standard (X.1250) on global identity management [2], which states that identity is the *"Representation of an entity (or group of entities) in the form of one or more information elements which allow the entity(s) to be uniquely recognised within a context to the extent that is necessary (for the relevant applications)."* This definition is so general that it lacks precision of whose identity we are talking about (who or what is an entity?) and what data are we talking about (what is an information element?). Whilst an entity can be any object, in most cases it is personal identity that we are concerned about, so we will restrict this chapter to considering identity management of people rather than of any object. In this context, the information elements are restricted to Personal Indentifying (or Personally Identifiable) Information (PII), which is *"the information pertaining to any living person which makes it possible to identify such individual (including the information capable of identifying a person when combined with other information even if the information does not clearly identify the person)."* [1] We can consider that PII is simply the attributes[1] of a person, such as: their hair colour, sound of their voice, height, name, qualifications, past actions, reputation, medical records, etc. You might think that hair colour is not PII and is not a digital identity as it is too generic, but if we had a rule that stated that ginger haired people are granted a 10% discount at Ginger's hairdressing salon, then hair colour alone would be sufficient identity information to allow a person to be *uniquely recognised within a context to the extent that is necessary (for the relevant applications).* So even something as generic as hair colour can be classed as a digital

---

[1] An attribute is defined in [3] as *"information of a particular type"*.

A. Aldini, G. Barthe, R. Gorrieri (Eds.): FOSAD 2007/2008/2009, LNCS 5705, pp. 96–120, 2009.
© Springer-Verlag Berlin Heidelberg 2009

identity and as PII. To summarise, we can say that a person's (digital) identity comprises a set of attributes, and only a subset of these attributes are necessary to allow the person to be sufficiently recognised within a given context.

So what is identity management? In short it is the whole process of managing a user's identity attributes. Y.2720 [1] has a more comprehensive definition which states that identity management is: *A set of functions and capabilities (e.g. administration, management and maintenance, discovery, communication exchanges, correlation and binding, policy enforcement, authentication and assertions) used for:*

- *Assurance of identity information (e.g., identifiers, credentials, attributes);*
- *assurance of the identity of an entity (e.g., users/subscribers, groups, user devices, organizations, network and service providers, network elements and objects, and virtual objects); and*
- *enabling business and security applications.*

Before proceeding further, we should clarify the difference between an *identifier* and an *Identity*, and an *attribute* and a *credential*. An identifier is usually a series of digits and/or characters that is used to uniquely identify an entity within one domain or system. No two entities (or users) within the same system can have the same identifier. So an identifier is a rather special type of identity attribute, since no two users can share the same identifier, whilst they may have other identity attributes in common, such as hair colour. Furthermore, an identifier is tightly bound to the system or domain in which it is defined; it usually cannot be meaningfully moved between domains, unlike the other identity attributes. Indeed, different domains can use the same identifier to identify different users. An identifier is only one of the identity attributes that comprise that person's digital identity within a system. Different computer systems know different subset's of a person's identity attributes, but each computer system will have its own identifier which uniquely identifies this individual within this system. An individual whose identity is distributed throughout many systems will therefore have multiple identifiers such as: their passport number, login ID, social security number, email address etc., which are each unique within their own domains. Some systems may store the identifiers from remote domains as well as their own. For privacy (and other) reasons, users are typically wary about releasing their identifiers to third parties, since these can uniquely identify them, whereas their other identity attributes, such as age, typically cannot.

An *attribute assertion* is a *claim* made by someone (the asserter) that a particular person possesses a particular attribute. Usually attributes have to be conferred on individuals (or asserted) by authoritative sources. Whilst people may be trusted in some situations to assert some of their identity attributes themselves, for example, their favourite drink, they certainly wont be trusted in all situations to assert all of their identity attributes themselves, for example, their qualifications or criminal record. Thus different authoritative sources are usually responsible for assigning different attributes to individuals. For example, the university that one graduated from is the authoritative source of one's degree attribute. These authoritative sources are also known as attribute authorities (AAs). An identity provider is an attribute authority combined with an authentication service to authenticate its users. An identity provider can authenticate a user and then issue an attribute assertion about the user. Attribute assertions typically have to be digitally signed to ensure their integrity and authenticity. A digitally signed attribute assertion is an *authorization credential*.

Whilst discussing credentials, we need to differentiate between authentic credentials and valid credentials.

- Authentic credentials are ones that have not been tampered with and are received exactly as issued by the issuing authority. Their digital signature is used to prove their authenticity.
- Valid credentials are ones that are trusted for use by the recipient, sometimes called the relying party.

  - Example 1: Monopoly money is authentic if obtained from the Monopoly game pack. It was issued by the makers of the game of Monopoly. Monopoly money is valid for buying houses on Mayfair in the game of Monopoly, but it is not valid for buying groceries in supermarkets such as Tesco's or LIDL.
  - Example 2: My credit card is an authentic credential. I can use it to buy groceries in Tesco, so it is valid there, but I cannot use it in LIDL as they do not accept credit cards. It is not valid there, but it is still authentic.

The difference between an authentic and a valid credential is whether the relying party does or does not trust the issuer of the credential to issue that particular credential.

Authoritative sources may remove attributes as well as assign them. For example, a university may remove a degree from a student, if it was subsequently proved that the student had committed plagiarism in their dissertation. Similarly, in the UK, the General Medical Council (GMC) is the only authoritative source of who is a doctor, and it keeps a register of them. If a doctor commits malpractice, the doctor may be struck off the register by the GMC. Thus in identity management systems, we cannot rely on the individual to assert his various attributes, otherwise he might lie about his various roles, and omit to tell about negative attributes such as the points on his driving license. Similarly we cannot rely on a single identity provider to assert all a user's attributes, but only the attributes they are authoritative for. For example, a credit card company would not normally be trusted to assert someone's degree qualification attribute. Consequently a set of authoritative sources may need to be consulted by service providers before the latter grant users access to their resources. X.1250 defines an authoritative identity provider as "the Identity Provider responsible by law, industry practice, or system implementation" for asserting a particular identity attribute.

This brings us to the topic of federations and federated identity management. A federation is defined in X.1250 as "*an association compromising any number of service providers and identity providers*"[2]. Implicit in this definition is trust. The fact that the various providers have formed an association between themselves means that they must have a certain level of trust between themselves, sufficient to be willing to exchange messages between themselves. When these messages contain the authentication and authorisation credentials of users, allowing users from one system to access resources in a federated system, we have federated identity management (FIM). With FIM, a user can use her credentials (authentication and authorisation) from one or more identity providers to gain access to other sites (service providers) within the federation. FIM brings the following benefits to the various stakeholders:

- it gives users the single sign on (SSO) capability, allowing them to move between the various service providers without having to authenticate or log in again,
- it allows service providers to offload the cost of managing user attributes, passwords and login credentials to trusted identity providers
- it provides scalability, allowing service providers to offer services to a much greater number of users
- it allows identity providers to maintain close relationships with end users and sell them additional services, as well as extract fees from the service providers they support.

In a centralised system, as opposed to a federated system, the user typically presents their identifier and an authentication token (such as a password) to prove that they are entitled to be known by this identifier. The system then associates the user with this identifier and with all the attributes linked to this identifier. The user is then granted access based on these. In a distributed system the user might typically have different identifiers in each local system, so if the user authenticated to one identity provider using his local identifier, this identifier would not be known by and therefore could not be used by the other local systems to grant the user access. Single sign on would not be possible without some sort of federation. When X.509 based PKI systems were first designed, they tried to solve this problem by allocating each user a globally unique identifier (called an X.500 distinguished name) which would be known by all local systems in the distributed system and therefore could be used to grant the user access. Since this global identifier was bound to the user's public key in an X.509 public key certificate, a signature created by the user's private key could be used as an authentication token by each local system.

One of the reasons this X.509 based identity management system failed was the privacy concerns about everyone knowing everyone else's globally unique identifier. The breakthrough came when it was realised that a user's identifier did not need to be globally unique, but could remain local to the system that allocated it. Authorisation to use a remote federated system could be granted based on the user's identity attributes, rather than on the user's identifier. If the identity attributes are provided by trusted authoritative sources, then a service provider can be assured of the identity of the user, even if the user's identifier is unknown (or temporary). This gave birth to early federated identity management systems such as Passport and Athens, and more lately to standardized systems such as Shibboleth [4] and CardSpace [5], which will be described later.

2   The 7 Laws of Identity

After the failure of Microsoft's Passport FIM system (see later), Kim Cameron thought long and hard about what is needed in order to build a successful FIM system. He discussed the issues intently on his blog www.identityblog.com. One of the end results was his 7 Laws of Identity [6] described below. Another was the design and implementation of CardSpace which is now an integral part of Vista and Internet Explorer 7. The seven laws are summarised below.

1.   User Control and Consent

Technical identity systems must only reveal information identifying a user with the user's consent. [6]

The underlying hypothesis here is that users will cease to trust a system that reveals their identity attributes to others, without the users' explicit consent. A user needs to have confidence that any system that is provided with his identity attributes will protect them and respect his wishes for how they should be used.

2.   Minimal Disclosure for a Constrained Use

The solution which discloses the least amount of identifying information and best limits its use is the most stable long term solution. [6]

The underlying hypothesis here is that all systems are vulnerable to attack and the theft (or loss) of the confidential information that they hold. Therefore systems should minimize the PII that they capture and store, and should delete it as soon as the purpose of capture is complete.

3.   Justifiable Parties

Digital identity systems must be designed so the disclosure of identifying information is limited to parties having a necessary and justifiable place in a given identity relationship. [6]

The underlying hypothesis here is that users resent their PII being given to third parties that have no proper role to play in a digital transaction. Thus if a user is posting pictures to his family blog, then he should not need to use a government identity provider, or Microsoft for that matter. This is hypothesized as the primary reason that Microsoft Passport failed to become the identity provider for the Internet.

4.   Directed Identity

A universal identity system must support both "omni-directional" identifiers for use by public entities and "unidirectional" identifiers for use by private entities, thus facilitating discovery while preventing unnecessary release of correlation random identifiers. [6]

The underlying hypothesis here is that users do not want everyone to know their identifiers, they prefer to keep them private, whilst public web sites and commercial organisation do want everyone to know their identifiers and hence be able to contact them. When users establish communications with a public entity such as a service provider, they should be assigned a one-off (or private) identifier that is only for use in this communication (or with this service provider). The use of different identifiers with different service providers will prevent the service providers from colluding together to build global profiles of the user.

5.   Pluralism of Operators and Technologies

A universal identity system must channel and enable the inter-working of multiple identity technologies run by multiple identity providers. [6]

The underlying hypothesis here is that diversity and competition between identity providers is good, and users should be able to switch between pseudonymous identities at will. This necessitates that there is an overarching meta-identity system that uses a common protocol for the transport of identity credentials, whilst supporting an infinite variety in the types of credential technologies that are supported.

6.   Human Integration

The universal identity metasystem must define the human user to be a component of the distributed system integrated through unambiguous human-machine communication mechanisms offering protection against identity attacks. [6]

The underlying hypothesis here is that the vast majority of identity thefts succeed by attacking the link between the PC and the human rather than the links between the PC and the various identity and service providers. The human is the weakest link in the chain and therefore securing this communication link should be an essential component of any identity management system. A second hypothesis is that a well known *ceremony* is needed for this communication, one that will always be used by the user, that the user will become very familiar with, and can therefore immediately determine if and when an attack is taking place. The design of the Identity Selector in CardSpace, described later, is one attempt at making the human-computer link more secure through having a consistent ceremony.

7. Consistent Experience Across Contexts

The unifying identity metasystem must guarantee its users a simple, consistent experience while enabling separation of contexts through multiple operators and technologies. [6]

This law is very closely related to the last law, and is also re-iterating several of the previous laws. It is re-stating that the user needs to have a consistent experience (i.e. ceremony) regardless of the underlying credential technologies that are in use, or the pseudonym that the user chooses to use for any particular transaction. The user should be able to switch between pseudonyms or identities at will. In order for the user to recognize which identity he is using in any given transaction, identities should be "thingyfied" into icons that the user can easily recognize. This naturally leads to the concept of information cards, an electronic representation of the plastic cards we all carry around in our pockets today.

These seven laws of identity are not physical laws that all living things must abide by, like the law of gravity, but they are laws which identity management systems should endeavour to support, and which they break at their peril. The peril in this case is that users are likely to reject any identity management system that does not abide by the seven laws in its implementation. CardSpace has endeavoured to keep them, as we shall see later.

3   Related Issues

3.1   Privacy Protection

As the seven laws of identity management make clear, privacy protection is an important issue that FIM systems should take into account. In many countries there are legal requirement for information systems to protect user privacy. Invariably these all derive from the OECD privacy guidelines [8], which state eight data protection principles. These are:

1. Collection Limitation Principle
There should be limits to the collection of personal data and any such data should be obtained by lawful and fair means and, where appropriate, with the knowledge or consent of the data subject.

2. Data Quality Principle
Personal data should be relevant to the purposes for which they are to be used, and, to the extent necessary for those purposes, should be accurate, complete and kept up-to-date.

3. Purpose Specification Principle
The purposes for which personal data are collected should be specified not later than at the time of data collection and the subsequent use limited to the fulfilment of those purposes or such others as are not incompatible with those purposes and as are specified on each occasion of change of purpose.

4. Use Limitation Principle
Personal data should not be disclosed, made available or otherwise used for purposes other than those specified at the time of collection except with the consent of the data subject or by the authority of law.

5. Security Safeguards Principle
Personal data should be protected by reasonable security safeguards against such risks as loss or unauthorised access, destruction, use, modification or disclosure of data.

6. Openness Principle
There should be a general policy of openness about developments, practices and policies with respect to personal data. Means should be readily available of establishing the existence and nature of personal data, and the main purposes of their use, as well as the identity and usual residence of the data controller.

7. Individual Participation Principle
An individual should have the right:

a) to obtain from a data controller, confirmation of whether or not the data controller has data relating to him;

b) to have communicated to him, data relating to him within a reasonable time, at a charge that is not excessive, in a reasonable manner, and in a form that is readily intelligible to him;

c) to be given reasons if a request made under subparagraphs(a) and (b) is denied, and to be able to challenge such denial; and

d) to challenge data relating to him and, if the challenge is successful to have the data erased, rectified, completed or amended.

8. Accountability Principle
A data controller should be accountable for complying with measures which give effect to the principles stated above. [8]

But how are the above to be implemented in FIM systems and more importantly, can we build FIM systems that automatically safeguard at least some of the above? One method is to separate identity providers (IdPs) from service providers (SPs), and to store identity attributes with the IdPs only and not with the SPs. All modern FIM systems are designed to be capable of this. Then we give the user control over her identity attributes that are held at her various IdPs, and allow her to say which of these may be given which of which SPs. In Shibboleth this is implemented as Attribute Release Policies that can be set by the user (see later) at each IdP. Then we define protocols that do not release the user's identifier from the IdP to the SPs, so that multiple SPs cannot collude together about a specific user. Further if the identifier is randomly generated each time, the SP cannot correlate the multiple sessions of the same user. The OASIS Security Assertion Markup Language (SAML) protocol [7] supports both of these schemes by allowing the IdP to create a new random identifier for the user for each association (this is used by Shibboleth). Alternatively if the user needs to be uniquely identified in order to obtain personalized services, then the IdP can generate a new permanent identifier to identify this user to this specific SP, and use this identifier every time. SAML also supports this, and this is used by Liberty Alliance in its identity management protocols [9]. In this way we prevent the SPs from knowing the real identity of the user of her unique identifier at the IdP. The user is either pseudonymously identified (as in Liberty) or randomly identified (as in Shibboleth). Finally if the IdPs make the attribute assertions which they give to the SP short lived, then we effectively remove the attributes from the possession of the SP at the close of each transaction (or shortly afterwards). Short lived assertions are another feature of the SAML protocol.

3.2 Level of Assurance

Different IdPs will authenticate users in different ways and to different strengths. For example, usernames and passwords are weaker than public-key certificates and private keys. A relying party's *level of assurance* (LOA) that the user is really who it thinks she is depends not only on the electronic authentication method used by the IdP but also on the initial registration process used by the IdP. For example, registering electronically over the Web is much weaker than turning up in person with a passport. Registering over the Web is equivalent to self asserting your identity attributes. So a relying party should rightly give little credence to these identity attributes.

The National Institute of Standards and Technology (NIST) recommends four LOA levels, with level 4 being the strongest and level 1 the weakest. Some SPs may wish to grant a user different access permissions based on the LOA during the current session. For example, if the user authenticates with an LOA of 1, she can read the resource, but with an LOA of 3 she can modify its contents. Limitations of the NIST recommendation are that: the LOA only applies to user authentication, and not to her identity attributes for authorisation, and it is a compound metric that is dependent on both the strength of the registration process and the electronic authentication method being used.

In the latest research being carried out at the University of Kent, we believe it's more useful if the LOA is split into two separate metrics, one for registration of the identity attributes, and one for the authentication method being used in the current session.

Prior to any computer-based authentication, a user must register with a service and provide various credentials to prove her identity. For example, before a new student can register to use the University of Kent's computing services, she must first present her passport and existing qualifications to prove she is entitled to register as a student. We call this the *registration LOA*. Different systems will require different registration documents and have different registration procedures, and will therefore have different registration assurance levels. Any identity attributes that are assigned to the user during registration or afterwards by the IdP, and for which the IdP is the authoritative source, will be given the registration LOA. For example, after successful registration, the University of Kent allocates the student a login ID (her identifier) and associates various attributes with this in its database, for example, degree course, e-mail address, department, tutor, and so on, for which the university is the authoritative source. These will be assigned the registration LOA. Other identity attributes for which the

IdP is not the authoritative source, such as date of birth and name, may be given the same registration LOA value or a lower one depending upon the quality of the documents used at registration time. For example, if the person's name and date of birth were taken from their passport, they would have the same registration LOA as the other identity attributes. If they were asserted by the user without any documentary evidence to support these assertions, they would be given the lowest LOA value. Typically an IdP would not send these attributes to an SP, because it is not authoritative for them.

After registration the IdP will issue the user with authentication credentials, and these will have an associated *authentication LOA*. For example, the University of Kent may offer different authentication mechanisms for student login, such as un/pw with Kerberos, un/pw with Secure Sockets Layer (SSL), one-time passwords via a mobile phone, and so on. The system assigns each of these mechanisms an *authentication LOA* with the proviso that no authentication LOA can be higher than the registration LOA that originally authenticated the user's identity attributes. The reason for this is that the user's identity attributes can never be asserted at a higher assurance level than was carried out during the registration process. Consequently, registering over the web using self assertions must always have the lowest LOA (in NIST this is 1) assigned to both the registration LOA and the authentication LOA. However, if an IdP never asserts any identity attributes to the SP, and merely authenticates the user and presents a uniquely generated identifier to the SP, then the authentication LOA can be set to the strength of the authentication method that is used. The SP can be sure that each time this user contacts it, that it is the same user because the identifier will be the same each time. The SP also has an assurance of this to the value of the authentication LOA. In this scenario, the SP has no idea who the user is, as no identity attributes have been provided, but it does know that it is the same user each time. This is how the early versions of OpenID worked [11], before attribute assertions were added to it. (Note that there is no level of assurance provided by OpenID).

When a user logs in for a session, the authentication service assigns her a *session LOA* equivalent to the authentication LOA of the authentication mechanism she chose to use. Thus the same user may have different session LOAs with the same SP, due to the fact that she used different authentication methods with her IdP in the adjacent sessions.

A new addition to the SAML protocol [10] is adding support for passing the session LOA in each assertion sent from the IdP to the SP. Thus the SP can obtain the level of assurance for the identity attributes that are to be used for authorizing the user in the current session. Note that the SAML specification [10] only allows one LOA value to be passed with an assertion, so all the identity attributes in the assertion must have been registered to that level if they are to be passed.

3   Some Early FIM Systems

3.1   Microsoft's .NET Passport

.NET Passport is an authentication and single sign on system that allows users to access multiple service providers using the same credentials. Each service provider remains in charge of its own authorisation, and may use Passport provided identity attributes to help in this. It works as follows. Users register at a service provider site, but their credentials and profile information are stored centrally by Microsoft at the Passport server. This means that sites must trust Microsoft/Passport to hold the user credentials securely, and to authenticate the users correctly during sign on.

Referring to figure 1 below, the system works as follows:

1. The user browses Site A, a Passport participating site, and clicks the "Sign In" button.

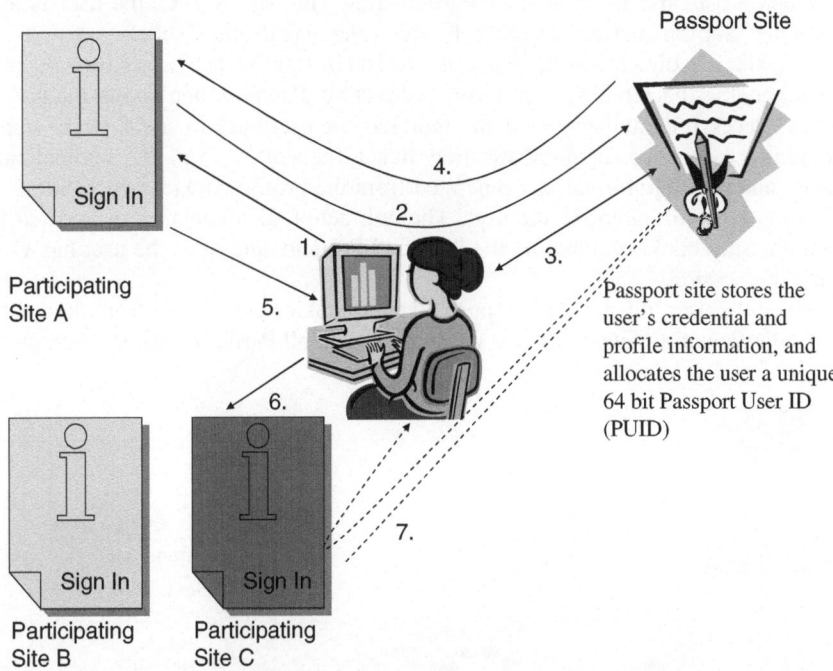

Fig. 1. Message Flows in Passport

2. The user is redirected to a co-branded registration page at the Passport site, which displays the registration fields chosen by Site A. (The minimum number of fields required is two: email address and password.)
3. The user reads and accepts the terms of use (or declines, and the process ends), and submits the registration form containing their profile information. The registration form is sent encrypted to the Passport site via SSL to protect the user's privacy. Next the user can choose whether or not they want to opt in to share their profile information with other Passport-enabled sites or not. They can select any or all of three tick boxes, viz: share email address, share first and last name, share all other profile attributes, which may comprise: Birth Date, Country / Region, First Name, Gender, Last Name, Occupation, Postal Code, Preferred Language, State, and Time Zone. After completing registration, the user is shown a congratulations page and

4. is then redirected back to Site A with their encrypted authentication ticket and profile information attached. The redirect message contains four cookies (a ticket granting cookie containing a secret key, a Participating Sites cookie, an authentication cookie and a profile cookie) which are stored in the user's browser to shortcut future authentication attempts within the lifetime of the cookies. The last three cookies are encrypted with the secret key in the ticket granting cookie, the latter is encrypted with a secret key known only to Passport.

5. Site A decrypts the authentication ticket and profile information and continues the user's registration process, or immediately grants her access to the site.

6. When a user moves to another Participating Site, say Site C, the user is again shown the "Sign In" button as in Step 1, which she may decide to click.

7. If so, she is redirected to the Passport site (as in step 2). The user's browser sends the four cookies back to Passport during redirection. Passport then knows the user has already successfully authenticated and redirects the user back to site C (as in step 4). The redirect contains an authentication ticket (generated from the authentication cookie) and profile information (generated from the profile cookie) which Site C can decrypt and use to authorize the user. The redirection also contains an updated Participating Sites cookie containing the list of all Participating Sites the user has visited during this session.

8. When the user logs out of Passport, all four cookies are deleted from the browser and the Participating Sites cookie is used to clean up all Participating sites computers.

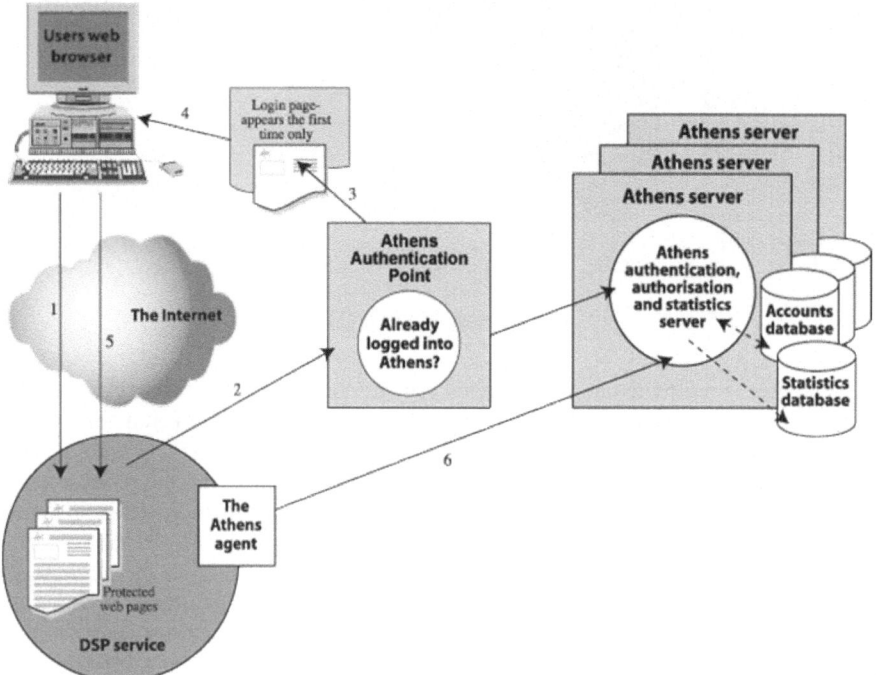

Fig. 2. Message Flows in Athens. © EduServ, 2002.

Passport has been very successful when used between Microsoft owned sites such as MSN and Hotmail. But because all participating sites have to trust Microsoft to hold the identity of the user, and to authenticate the user properly, it fails Kim Camerson's 3rd Law of Justifiable Parties. Why should Microsoft be involved in a transaction between a car hire company and a hotel? It is clearly not appropriate for Microsoft to be involved in all federated communications between different commercial companies. Another failing of Passport is that it does not provide good privacy protection for a user's attributes, since these are made available to Microsoft, and the user does not have fine grained control over how they are released to the affiliated sites (see step 3 above).

3.2 UK Athens

Athens was the de facto standard for secure access management to online services for the UK Education and Health sectors during the late nineties and first decade of two thousand. By 2002, 769 user sites, with over 2 million users, were using Athens to connect to 249 resources at 51 service provider sites such as Elsevier, Wiley, Science Direct, and Oxford University Press. It is therefore one of the most successful federated identity management systems to date.

Athens was originally designed by a team at the University of Bath in a series of JISC-funded projects, and was subsequently made into a commercial service that is owned, developed and operated by EduServ (http://www.eduserv.org.uk). Essentially EduServ is a "trusted third party" identity provider. EduServ operate a large database of over 2 million user IDs and passwords along with authorisation data (which says which sites users can access). The service is replicated to provide a resilient service. Each participating college or university administers its own part of the database to keep their user base up to date. This makes the administration manageable.

Referring to Figure 2 below, Athens works as follows:

· 1.   The user contacts a data service provider (DSP) e.g. Elsevier

2.   The user is re-directed to the Athens Authentication Point (AAP) via an SSL connection

3/4. The AAP displays the login page to the user. The user types in his Athens username and password which is sent encrypted back to the AAP over SSL. If the user is authenticated correctly, the AAP writes an encrypted cookie (with a validity time of 8 hours) back to the browser to enable Single Sign On (see 7 below) and redirects the user back to the DSP.

5.   The redirection message carries an encrypted token to signal the user's successful authentication. This token is symmetrically encrypted with a secret shared between the DSP and the AAP, and it contains the user's Athens username and a short expiry time (60 secs). The user is now authenticated and tries to access various data sources at the DSP, but may not be authorised to access everything.

6.   The DSP web server calls a special Athens Agent plug in software which communicates with the Athens database to see if the user is authorised to access this particular data source. The user is granted or denied access depending upon the reply. The Athens Agent plug-in is provided either as a toolkit (C, Java, Perl implementations all available) for integration into the supplier's system or as pre-packaged modules for Apache and MS IIS.

7. If the user moves to a different DSP, then the user is re-directed to the AAP as in step 2 above. This time however the AAP is sent the cookie by the browser, so the AAP knows the user has been authenticated and does not need to ask him to login again. The user is redirected straight back to the DSP site.

On 1 August 2008, Athens was superseded by Shibboleth as the JISC preferred federated identity management system for UK education. It is now being slowly phased out. Since it appears to have been so successful, why is this? Firstly it uses proprietary protocols and is not easily adaptable to becoming a general federated identity management system. Sites cannot leverage it to set up their own mini-federations. In essence it is a centralised system and suffers from the same trust problems as Passport. Why should all transactions have to be authenticated by the central Athens server? Finally, during the last few years, there have been significant efforts in standardising federated identity management protocols, and the US, Europe and Australia are migrating towards these systems. Consequently the time has come to do the same with Athens.

4 Some Current FIM Systems

4.1 Shibboleth

Shibboleth [4], conceived and developed by the Internet 2 consortium (http://www.internet2.org/), is a system designed to ease the formation of federations and collaborations between organisations. Shibboleth provides a protocol to allow collaborating organisations to more easily authenticate and authorise each other's users. In Shibboleth, authentication is always performed by the user's own organisation – the identity provider – using the organisation's existing authentication scheme. The organisation might use usernames and passwords, or Kerberos, or one time passwords etc. It does not matter, providing the scheme is secure enough for the federating service providers. In this way, the user always uses his existing login credentials and so single sign on is enabled through this. Whilst the current system does not support Levels of Assurance, it clearly will not be difficult to add it, since Shibboleth uses standard SAML protocols.

Authorisation always takes place at the site the user is trying to access – the service provider – using identity attributes of the user provided by the identity provider. A trust relationship exists between the identity and service providers, so that the service provider trusts the identity provider to correctly authenticate the user, and to provide the correct set of attributes for the user. Messages are digitally signed by the identity provider so that the service provider can validate that they are correct and trustworthy. Single sign on is enabled throughout the federation so that if the user contacts a second service provider, the identity provider can immediately send a digitally signed message to the new service provider saying that the user has already been authenticated correctly. Therefore the user does not need to login again.

Importantly, Shibboleth provides strong privacy protection of the user's details. The user's username (identifier) is privacy protected because the user is identified with a different pseudonym, or random identifier, each time he contacts a service provider. Thus the service provider is not able to profile the user's accesses since it has no way of linking together the different identifiers from the different sessions, or of linking an identifier to the actual user. (Note that in the case of abuse of a service provider by a user, the service provider can request the help of the identity provider to identify the abusive user, by scanning its activity logs. However, such breaches of privacy are expected to be exceptional, and only triggered by abuse in the first place.) The user's attributes are privacy protected because both the user and the home site can set Attribute Release Policies (ARPs) that say which attributes can be released to which remote sites. This helps to protect the privacy of the user's attributes, since only the minimum necessary need to be sent to each service provider. It also provides the user with full control and the ability to give consent for the user of his attributes. If a service provider wishes to provide personalized services to the user, then one of the user's identity attributes will need to uniquely identify the user, and be provided in each session. The user will need to agree to this through his ARP.

4.1.1 How Shibboleth Works

Shibboleth is a Web based middleware layer that defines the protocols that are sent between a user's Web browser, his home/identity provider's Web server and the target resource site's Web server. Shibboleth is standard's based, and the current version makes use of the SAML v2 protocol [7] for encoding its messages.

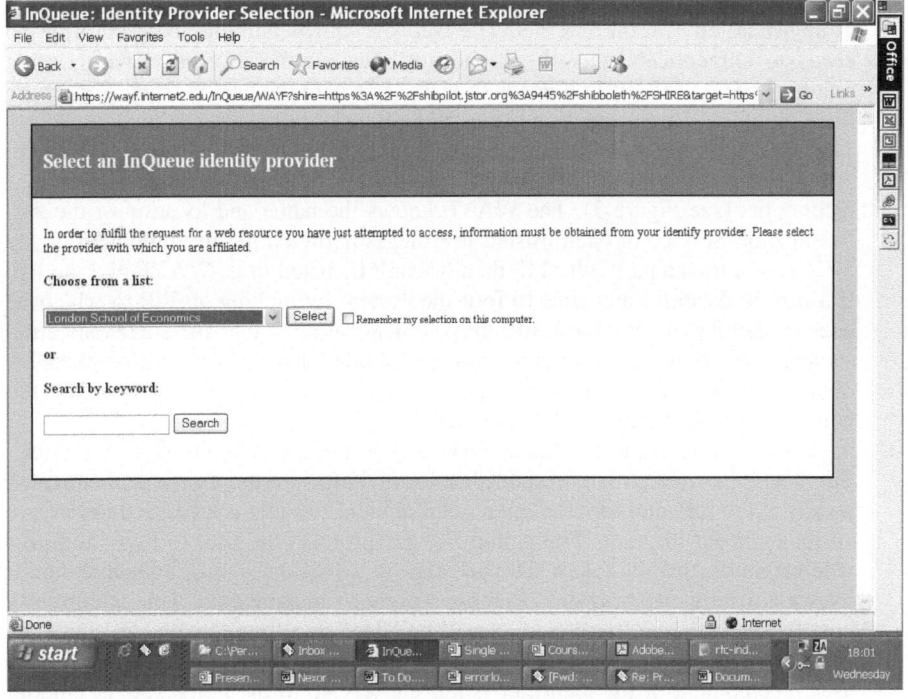

Fig. 3. Screen shot of a typical Shibboleth Where Are You From service

When a user contacts a Shibboleth service provider from their browser, requesting access to a particular URL, Shibboleth single sign on and access control takes place in separate stages as shown in Figures 4 and 5 (although it is possible to combine both stages into a single communication exchange, which is not shown). In a large distributed open environment the authentication stage has a number of complications. Firstly how does the resource site/service provider know where the user's home site/identity provider is in order to redirect the user to the correct authentication service? This is known as the discovery problem. Secondly, how can the SP trust that the authentication statement that is returned is authentic and that the random identifier identifies the current user? A number of different solutions have been attempted to solve the discovery problem. The one used by OpenID [11] is to use globally unique IDs based on DNS names so that the DNS can be used to discover the location of the user's IdP. Another is to pre-configure one or a small number of IdPs into the SP and force the user to use one of these. However, the method currently favoured by Shibboleth is to use a Where Are You From Service which asks the user to pick the site that he or she is from (see Figure 3), from a pre-configured list of all IDPs that the SP trusts. The answer to the second question is provided by the Shibboleth trust model. This requires the sites to establish trust relationships between themselves as part of the process of forming a federation. They do this by exchanging their public key certificates or CA root keys, so that they can validate messages signed by each other.

Referring to Figure 4 below:

1. The user makes a request to a web site. The user can be stationed at his home site, or anywhere else on the Internet. The web site knows nothing about the user, so needs to authenticate and obtain the attributes of the user in order to grant him/her access. The SP first needs to discover where the user is from. This is the function of the Where Are You From (WAYF) service.

2. The Shibboleth SP uses the Http Redirect reply to re-direct the user to its Where Are You From service. This prompts the user to choose his home site from a picking list (see Figure 3). The WAYF knows the name and location of the Authentication Service of each trusted IdP that is participating in Shibboleth. If the SP does not trust a particular IdP then it won't be listed in its WAYF picking list. If a user is deceitful and tries to fool the system by picking an IdP to which he does not belong, he will have difficulty authenticating to that site's authentication service, since he won't have any valid credentials for it. However, if he picks his own home site, he should find authentication is no problem. Consequently the honest user picks his home site, and then

3. the user is re-directed to the Authn Service at his home site by the WAYF service.

4. The Authn Service (AS) is responsible for making sure the user is authenticated locally at the IdP, and for creating a random identifier that can be used to retrieve attributes about the user. The Authn Service prompts the user to login and provide his authentication token. The IdP can use whatever type of authentication it likes e.g. username/password, Kerberos, digital signatures etc. This is currently not relayed to the SP, but the LOA will be added as a future extension. Once the user has authenticated him/her self, the AS produces a random identifier for the user. The content of the identifier is left entirely up to the home site. A random identifier ensures that the user's local identifier remains private to the IdP, and the SP will never know the true identity of the user that is accessing it. Thus Shibboleth automatically provides Privacy Protection of the user's identity.

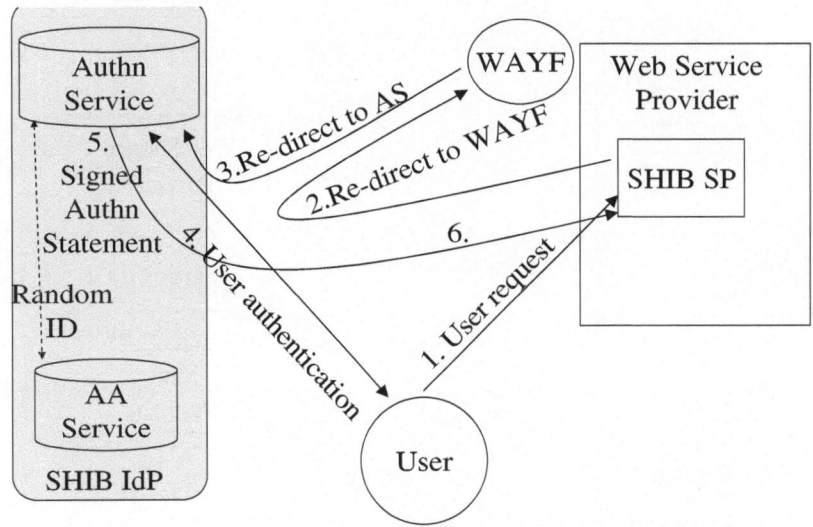

Fig. 4. Authenticating the user in Shibboleth

5. The AS passes the random identifier (in the form of a SAML Authentication statement) back to the user's browser inside an HTML form
6. that POSTS the data back to the destination SHIB SP. This information includes the location of the AA service at which the random identifier will be usable. This message is digitally signed by the AS to prove its authenticity. The SHIB SP must check the signature and the message contents to ensure its validity. The AS ensures that the AA Service knows the new random identifier for the user.
7. Referring to Figure 5 below, the SHIB SP sends a SAML Attribute Query Message to the Attribute Authority (AA) service at the user's IdP. This request needs to be protected i.e. mutually authenticated and have message integrity. SSL with client side authentication is used for this.
8. The AA server returns a SAML Attribute Response Message (ARM) containing a SAML Attribute Statement. This message also needs to be protected by mutual authentication, message integrity and message confidentiality, so SSL is used.
9. Once the ARM is received and validated by the SHIB SP, the embedded attributes are passed to the web service's authorisation code. Shibboleth provides its own simple authorisation code for sites to use, or they can use more sophisticated policy bases systems such as XACML [12] or PERMIS [13].
10. The authorisation code now grants or denies access to the user based on their attributes.

The latest version of the Shibboleth specification has introduced a performance improvement over the original version, by optionally allowing stage one and stage two to be combined together into one message exchange. In this way, the initial request from the SP may ask for both authentication and attribute statements, and the digitally signed SAMLresponse message may optionally contain the user's attributes as well as the authentication assertion.

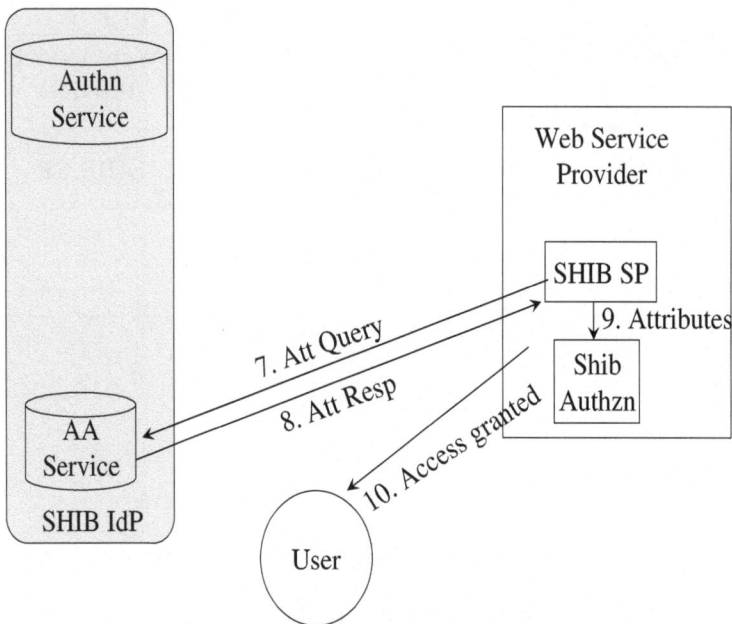

Fig. 5. Authorising the user in Shibboleth

4.1.2 Privacy Protection and Attribute Release Policies in Shibboleth

Shibboleth has four mechanisms to ensure user privacy. Firstly it allows a different pseudonym for the user's identity (the randomly generated identifier) to be returned each time. Secondly it allows the service provider to request specific user attributes to be returned, as opposed to "all", so as to minimise the potential loss of privacy. Thirdly, and most importantly, it requires that the attribute authorities provide some form of control over the release of user attributes to service providers, which they term attribute release policies (ARPs). Both users and administrators should have a say about which attributes can be released. Finally, in order to stop third parties from seeing the attributes as they are transferred over the Internet, the connection between the AA service and the SP should be protected by using SSL/TLS with strong encryption enabled.

A basic ARP rule at the AA consists of the following:

- A destination service provider ID e.g. https://engineering.example.edu/ blackboard/shibboleth-sp
- A list of attribute types (and optionally specific values) that should be re-leased to this SP
- Other optional conditions such as time of day or location of the user etc. as may be implemented by the identity provider (typically none are imple-mented at present, but this allows for more sophisticated privacy controls to be added in the future).

The identity provider can have as many of these rules as it needs for each destination SP. The destination SP ID allows the AA to find the right ARP rules to use when it receives an Attribute Query Message from an SP, since the latter contains the service provider ID as part of the SAML protocol message.

ARPs are specified in XML according to a predefined schema (shibboleth-arp-1.0.xsd). An example ARP is given in Figure 6 below. This ARP consists of 3 rules, one that will release an attribute to any service provider, one that will release an attribute to any service provider within a specific DNS domain, and one that releases a specific attribute value to a specific SP.

The <Target> element of an ARP rule identifies the service provider. It has one child element which is either:

- <Requester> which contains a matching rule (only two are currently defined, regular expression or exact) and an SP ID to match against, or
- <AnyTarget/> which indicates that all SPs match.

The <Target> element is followed by an <Attribute> element which specifies the attributes that can or cannot be released to this target. As shown in the examples, for any particular attribute type, either *any* attribute value can be specified, or a specific value. Each attribute can either be Permitted or Denied from being released. Note that in most cases it is not necessary to Deny an attribute from being released, since it will only be released if it occurs in a Permitted element. However, an administrator (or a user) may want to allow all attribute values to be released except one particular value. In this case, the attribute with *any* values would be Permitted to be released in one ARP rule, and then the specific value would be Denied to be released in another ARP rule.

Each IdP administrator creates the site's ARP and stores it in a file called *arp.site.xml*. This ARP applies to all users for which the AA is answerable.

Each user may also have his/her own ARP and this is stored in a file called *arp.user.<$PRINCIPALNAME>.xml.* in the same directory as the site ARP file. User ARPs can be maintained either by the IdP administrator or by the users themselves, according to the site's local policy. The MAMS project in Australia has produced a user friendly GUI editor for ARPs, called the Shibboleth Attribute Release Policy Editor (ShARPE). This is designed for use by both end users and IdP administrators, and it is distributed as open source software [14].

When an attribute query request is received, the Shibboleth software computes an effective ARP by locating the user's and site's ARPs and extracting from these each rule that matches the SP ID. All the attributes and values that are requested in the query are then compared with the effective ARP, and only those that are permitted to be released are included the response. If the same attribute is simultaneously Permitted in one rule (say in the site's ARP) and Denied in another rule (say in the user's ARP), then it will be denied from being released.

We can see that attribute release policies provide a flexible and powerful tool for preserving the privacy of a user's attributes, and they are one of the strengths of the Shibboleth infrastructure.

```
<?xml version="1.0" encoding="UTF-8"?>
<AttributeReleasePolicy
xmlns:xsi="http://www.w3.org/2001/XMLSchema-instance";
xmlns="urn:mace:shibboleth:arp:1.0"
xsi:schemaLocation="urn:mace:shibboleth:arp:1.0 shibboleth-arp-1.0.xsd">
<Rule>
<!--   This rule will release the edu person affiliation attribute with a value
member@example.edu to any service provider -->
        <Target>
                <AnyTarget/>
        </Target>
        <Attribute name="urn:mace:dir:attribute-def:eduPersonAffiliation">
                <Value release="permit">member@example.edu</Value>
        </Attribute>
</Rule>
<Rule>
<!--   This rule will release the user's edu person principal name attribute to any
example.edu/Shibboleth service provider -->
        <Target>
<Requester     matchFunction="urn:mace:shibboleth:arp:matchFunction:regexMatch">
https://.*\.example\.edu/Shibboleth</Requester>
        </Target>
        <Attribute name="urn:mace:dir:attribute-def:eduPersonPrincipalName">
                <AnyValue release="permit"/>
        </Attribute>
</Rule>
<Rule>
<!--   This rule will release a specific contract value of the edu person entitlement
attribute to the www.external.com/contract.asp service provider -->
        <Target>
<Requester          matchFunction="urn:mace:shibboleth:arp:matchFunction:exactShar"
https://www.external.com/contract.asp</Requester>
        </Target>
        <Attribute name="urn:mace:dir:attribute-def:eduPersonEntitlement">
                <Value release="permit">urn:example:contract:113455</Value>
        </Attribute>
</Rule>
</AttributeReleasePolicy>
```

Fig. 6. An example Attribute Release Policy

4.2 CardSpace

Information Cards are the core component of Microsoft's CardSpace identity management and authorisation system. A good high level overview of CardSpace can be found in [15]. Information Cards are a representation of a person's online digital identity. Information Cards have some excellent features in terms of both usability and security. From a usability perspective, the metaphor that Information Cards use for electronic credentials is the plastic card that everyone is familiar with. These are displayed on the user's desktop so that the user can select the card he wants to use in any transaction (see Figure 7). Cards that are acceptable to the service provider (SP), and hence selectable, appear in full colour, whilst cards that are incompatible with the SP's requirements are greyed out and hence not selectable. Cards can be self generated or managed by an IdP. Self generated cards contain information (attributes) asserted by the user himself, whereas managed cards contain attributes that are asserted by the IdP. Microsoft calls attribute assertions "claims". The fact that the attribute assertions (or claims) of the managed cards do not actually reside on the user's desktop, but are pulled from the IdP on demand, is largely hidden from the user. The only telling feature is that the user has to enter his login credentials with the IdP in order for the claim to be picked up and sent to the SP. This could be seen as a usability disadvantage or inconvenience to users, since the user is distracted from his/her primary task, which is accessing a service provider, into providing authentication credentials to an alternative party, the identity provider. But this is really not that much different to users entering their PINs today in order to activate their plastic cards.

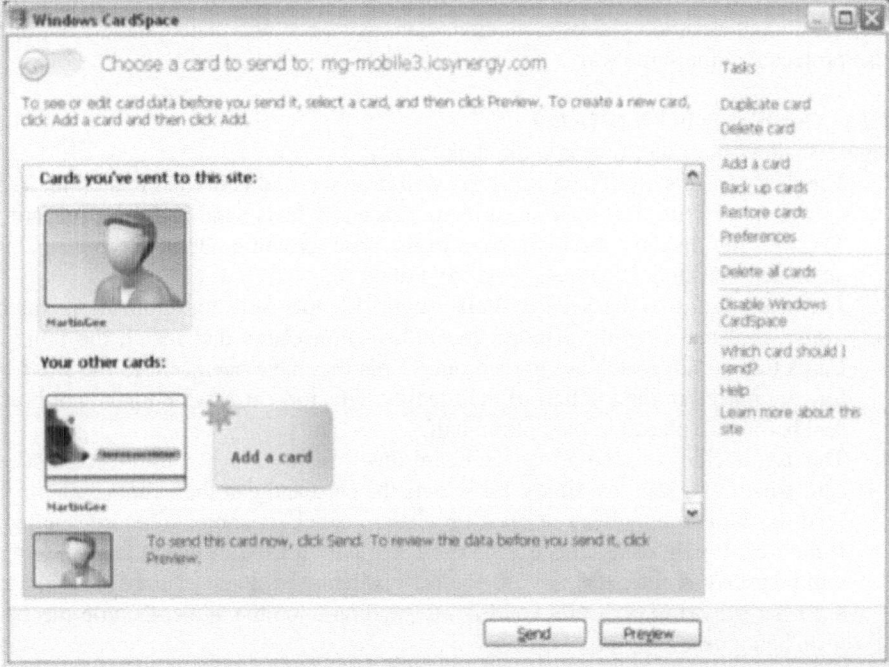

Fig. 7. The CardSpace Identity Selector

From a security and privacy perspective, CardSpace contains some excellent features. It has been designed specifically to conform to Kim Cameron's 7 Laws. Firstly it is resistant to phishing attacks, unlike Shibboleth for example where an SP could redirect users (via its fraudulent WAYF service) to a malicious entity masquerading as the user's identity provider. This is subverting the discovery procedure in order to point to a malicious IdP. In CardSpace the discovery information is stored securely on the user's PCs in the meta-information of their information cards. Phishing can only succeed if the attacker can subvert the user's PC without the user's knowledge, in order to plant subversive information cards in the user's identity selector. Besides the fact that it would be extremely hard to do, the user would most likely recognize this if it did happen. Secondly there is nothing of high value in the user's identity selector that can be stolen by an adversary, since the managed cards don't contain the actual credentials or claims; these are only generated on demand by the IdPs when asked to do so. The credentials/claims are short lived, cryptographically protected, designed to be transferred as quickly as possibly from the IdP to the SP via the user's desktop, and as an additional protection can be encrypted to be read by the SP only. So there is little opportunity for an attacker to steal them whilst in transit. However, some researchers from Germany have already shown that the credentials can be captured and stolen from the user's desktop and then effectively used to masquerade as the user [16]. Fortunately they also show how the vulnerability can be protected against with only a small change to the CardSpace protocols. This requires the SSL channel ID of the connection between the user and the SP, to be included in the credentials sent from the IdP. In this way the credentials cannot be used by any system other than the user's PC. Self asserted claims/credentials can also be stolen in the same way, and also protected in the same way.

4.2.1   CardSpace in More Detail

Figure 8 shows the data flows in more detail.

1. The user contacts a web site using his web browser, and is invited to sign in. The user chooses to use information cards for this and selects Send Information Card.
2. The web site displays the login page to the browser and embeds in this page, as an object, the site's CardSpace Security Policy (see 4.2.2).
3. The browser passes the Security Policy to the Identity Selector application which evaluates it and brightly displays the Information Cards that match the policy. Cards that do not match are greyed out. Cards that have been sent to the site before are placed in the top half of the Identity Selector, cards which have not been sent before are placed in the bottom half.
4. The user decides to send a managed card this time (as opposed to the self issued card which was sent last time). He selects the card and can then choose to either send the card straightaway or click Preview to check its contents before sending. If the card is self issued it could be protected with a PIN, in which case the user will be asked to enter this now. If the card is managed, the user may be asked to enter her password or X.509 key PIN, depending upon the authentication mechanism being used.
5. When the user clicks Send, the Identity Selector fetches the security policy from the IdP (see section 4.2.3) and from this determines the security parameters that are needed in order to request an attribute assertion (claim) for this information card. The card itself says how the user is to be authenticated to the IdP. CardSpace currently supports four authentication mechanisms for managed cards: username and password, KerberosV5 token, X.509 public key certificate and a self-issued token. No authentication is needed for the SIP to issue a self-issued card.

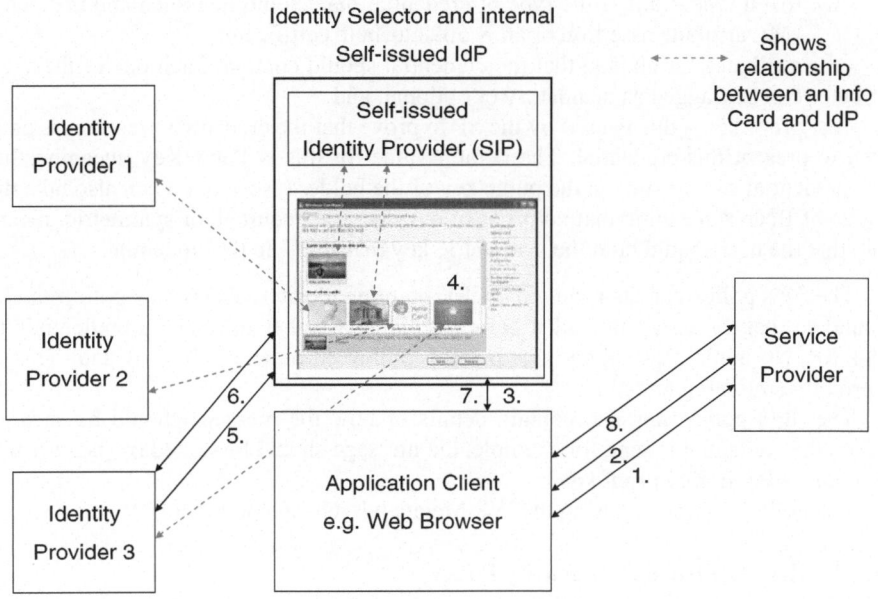

Fig. 8. CardSpace message flows

6. The Identity Selector requests an attribute assertion (claim) from the IdP using the security parameters from the IdP's policy and the credentials specified in the information card. If username-password was specified, the user will have been prompted to provide his password, and this will be encrypted in the request to the IdP. The IdP returns the attribute assertion to the Identity Selector.
7. The Identity Selector returns the attribute assertion/credential to the web browser.
8. The web browser POSTs the credential to the SP (web site).

4.2.2 Service Provider's Security Policy

The SP's policy is an XML document which describes its requirements for the authorization credential that is to be presented. It uses XML elements defined in WS-SecurityPolicy [17] and WS-Trust [19]. Expressing its credential requirements is done through the following policy parameters:

- the issuer – this is the WS-Addressing [18] Endpoint Reference of the Identity Provider who is to issue the credential. This is usually the logical name of the IdP specified as a URI e.g. https://kent.ac.uk/idp. This must match the name of an IdP in one of the information cards stored in the user's Identity Selector. This field can be blank, indicating that any issuer is acceptable to the SP, or it can take the specific value of self-issued (http://schemas.xmlsoap.org/ws/2005/05/identity/issuer/self), meaning that a self issued card is acceptable;

- the token type – this is the type of credential that should be issued and presented e.g. a SAML attribute assertion or an X.509 attribute certificate;
- the attributes (or claims) that the credential should contain. Each one of these attributes can be flagged as mandatory or optional, and
- the proof key – this is used by the SP to prove that the credential presenter is entitled to present this credential. The default value for this is PublicKey, meaning that the credential should contain the pubic key of the holder (user), but it can also take the value of Bearer, meaning that no proof of ownership is required, or symmetric, meaning that the user should hold the symmetric key that is inside the credential.

The SP's policy can also contain a URL pointing to where its privacy policy can be found so that the user can read it before deciding whether to send his credentials to this SP. No automated support for privacy policy enforcement is provided. This is currently a research topic.

The SP's policy can also contain details of how the message should be secured when the credential is sent, for example, the message should be signed by the user if it contains a PublicKey proof key.

The policy is retrieved using the WS-MetadataExchange protocol [20].

4.2.3 Identity Provider's Security Policy

The IdP's policy is used to tell the Identity Selector how it can retrieve a credential from the IdP. The policy is contained within the WSDL that specifies the protocol messages for accessing the IdP's credential issuing web service (called a Security Token Service (STS) in the WS* specifications). The policy contains details of the security that should be applied to the request and response messages, for example whether the XML messages should be digitally signed, or encrypted, or whether security should be performed at the transport level by SSL/TLS. An alternative is that the XML messages are symmetrically encrypted using a short lived session key. The policy will always contain the X.509 public key certificate of the IdP.

4.2.4 Information Card Contents

Information cards are formatted as an XML document, signed by the IdP that issued them. They contain the following fields:

- the logical name of the issuer as a URI. SPs should ensure that the issuer name they use in their policies matches this name,
- an optional image and language dependent friendly name that can be displayed by the Identity Selector to the user,
- a unique reference number for this card (unique to the issuer)
- the issuing and expiry dates of the card,
- a list of Endpoint References, in decreasing order of preference, from where the associated credential can be obtained and the authentication mechanism that is needed to obtain it. If the authentication mechanism is username/password then the card contains the username of the user whose card this is. Each Endpoint Reference also contains the location of the IdP's security policy that controls access to this endpoint.
- the token types that can be issued, e.g. SAML assertion or X.509 attribute certificate,

- the list of attribute types (claim types) that can be issued,
- whether the name of the recipient SP must be provided or not. If this is required, then the issued credential will be encrypted specifically for this SP so that no-one else can read its contents,
- an optional pointer to the privacy policy of the IdP,
- a flag to indicate whether the SP must have been identified by an X.509 public key certificate or not. This prevents the IdP from issuing a confidential credential that could be sent to an unidentified SP.

4.2.5 Limitations of Information Cards

Good as they are, information cards currently have a number of limitations. Firstly they only support 4 authentication mechanisms: username/password, Kerberos V5 ticket, X.509 public key certificate and a self issued token (key pair). Other popular mechanisms such as one time passwords are not supported. Secondly it is not specified how a user collects her information cards for inclusion in her identity selector. This is left up to the individual IdPs to determine. The Identity Selector simply provides an interface for importing Info Cards into it from the local filestore, but how they get to the local filestore is not standardized. However, the biggest limitation of Information Cards is that the user can only select one card to present to a service provider for any given session. In many cases this is insufficient; for example, consider trying to purchase a car road tax license over the Internet. You may need to provide the following credentials: a credit card, a road worthiness certificate for your car, an insurance certificate, and a driving license. Each of these may be issued to you by different authoritative sources (IdPs). The current CardSpace model will only allow you to present one of these credentials to the SP. Research conducted by the University of Kent has devised and implemented a solution to this using a new component called a Linking Service [21]. This allows the user to link his various IdPs together in a privacy preserving manner, by interacting with the Linking Service prior to service provision. It appears to work well with the Shibboleth model as it uses the Shibboleth style of interaction with the user. But it does not employ the CardSpace interface, and integrating this with CardSpace means that the user still only selects one card at service provision time, with the Linking Service providing the remainder. So there is still research to do to design a system which will allow the user to dynamically select several cards at service provision time.

5 Conclusion

This chapter has provided an introduction to the complex topic of federated identity management. FIM is still very much an active research topic and is likely to continue to be so for many years to come. This is because there are so many different issues to consider, some of which are competing or diametrically opposed to each other. Issues include: ease of use, user privacy, strong security, single sign on, total cost of ownership, user profiling and retention of users by service providers, scalability, fine grained access control, personalization of services, and anonymity. Whilst we have not covered all of these issues in this chapter, nevertheless I hope this chapter has been informative and enjoyable to read.

References

1. ITU-T. NGN identity management framework. Recommendation Y.2720
2. ITU-T. Baseline capabilities for enhanced global identity management trust and interoperability. Draft New Recommendation ITU-T X.1250 (X.idmreq) (February 2009)
3. ISO/ITU-T. The Directory: Models ISO 9594-2/ITU-T Rec. X.501 (2009)
4. Bob Morgan, R.L., Cantor, S., Carmody, S., Hoehn, W., Klingenstein, K.: Federated Security: The Shibboleth Approach. Educause Quarterly 27(4) (2004)
5. Nanda, A., Jones, M.B.: Identity Selector Interoperability Profile v1.5. Microsoft Corporation (July 2008), http://download.microsoft.com/download/1/1/a/ 11ac6505-e4c0-4e05-987c-6f1d31855cd2/ Identity_Selector_Interoperability_Profile_V1.5.pdf
6. Cameron, K.: The Laws of Identity (May 2005), http://www.identityblog.com/?p=352/#lawsofiden_topic3
7. OASIS. SAML 2.0 profile of XACMLv2.0. OASIS standard (February 1, 2005)
8. OECD. Guidelines on the Protection of Privacy and Transborder Flows of Personal Data (September 23, 1980)
9. Liberty Alliance Project. Liberty ID-WSF Web Services Framework Overview Version: 2.0, http://www.projectliberty.org/specifications__1
10. OASIS. Level of Assurance Authentication Context Profiles for SAML 2.0 Working Draft 01 (July 1, 2008)
11. OpenID Authentication 2.0 – Final (December 5, 2007), http://openid.net/specs/openid-authentication-2_0.html
12. OASIS. eXtensible Access Control Markup Language (XACML) Version 2.0 OASIS Standard (February 1, 2005)
13. Chadwick, D., Zhao, G., Otenko, S., Laborde, R., Su, L., Nguyen, T.A.: PERMIS: a modular authorization infrastructure. Concurrency And Computation: Practice And Experience 20(11), 1341–1357 (2008)
14. For info about ShARPE, http://www.mams.org.au/confluence/display/SHA/ShARPE , http://www.federation.org.au/twiki/bin/view/Federation/ShARPE
15. Chappell, D.: Introducing Windows CardSpace. MSDN (April 2006), http://msdn.microsoft.com/en-us/library/aa480189.aspx
16. Gajek, S., Schwenk, J., Xuan, C.: On the Insecurity of Microsoft's Identity Metasystem. Technical Report TR-HGI-2008-003, Ruhr-Universitat Bochum (June 2008), http://demo.nds.rub.de/cardspace/GaScXu08_CardSpaceTR.pdf
17. OASIS. WS-SecurityPolicy 1.2, OASIS Standard (July 1, 2007)
18. W3C. Web Services Addressing (WS-Addressing). W3C Member Submission (August 10, 2004)
19. OASIS, WS-Trust 1.3, OASIS Standard (March 19, 2007)
20. BEA Systems, Computer Associates, IBM, Microsoft, SAP, Sun Microsystems, and web Methods. Web Services Metadata Exchange (WS-MetadataExchange) Version 1.1 (August 2006)
21. Chadwick, D.W., Inman, G.: Attribute Aggregation in Federated Identity Management. IEEE Computer, 46–53 (May 2009)

Electronic Voting in the Netherlands: From Early Adoption to Early Abolishment[*]

Bart Jacobs[1] and Wolter Pieters[2]

[1] Digital Security group, Radboud University Nijmegen
bart@cs.ru.nl
[2] Centre for Telematics and Information Technology, University of Twente
w.pieters@utwente.nl

Abstract. This paper discusses how electronic voting was implemented in practice in the Netherlands, which choices were made and how electronic voting was finally abolished. This history is presented in the context of the requirements of the election process, as well as the technical options that are available to increase the reliability and security of electronic voting.

1 Introduction

In information security research, electronic voting is considered a particularly interesting topic. This may be due to a number of reasons. First of all, elections usually have high media coverage, especially if something goes wrong. This makes it easy to explain the societal relevance of the research. Furthermore, electronic voting seems to have a unique combination of security requirements: voters need to be authenticated, results need to be verifiable, but it should *not* be possible to link a vote to a voter.

The secret ballot requirement, in combination with the so-called Australian ballot, listing all candidates on a single sheet, was introduced in many countries in the 19th century (see *e.g.* [28,35]). It is now seen as a cornerstone of election law and international treaties: without the secret ballot, voters could be subject to all kinds of bribery and coercion, for it would be possible to observe the choices they would make in the election. Combined with the demand that results be verifiable, this requires well-designed procedures. It turns out not to be easy to computerise the intuitive ballot box property that what goes in will also come out, unaltered and unlinkably, especially if it is not allowed to reveal the identity of the voter.

Many electronic voting systems that have been deployed worldwide were not especially designed to meet the demand of verifiability. Votes may indeed be stored such that they cannot be traced back to the voter, guaranteeing secrecy of the ballot, but at the same time it is not always possible to judge afterwards if a vote was cast by an eligible voter, or produced by software malfunction or malicious activities. Because they are generally newer and operate over an insecure

---

[*] Version of June 3, 2009, for FOSAD 2008/2009 Tutorial Lectures.

A. Aldini, G. Barthe, R. Gorrieri (Eds.): FOSAD 2007/2008/2009, LNCS 5705, pp. 121–144, 2009.

infrastructure, it may be expected that Internet voting systems involve more efforts to meet verifiability requirements. Whether or not these efforts suffice is a topic of scientific and political debate. As often happens, computerisation of existing procedures leads to a critical reflection on these procedures. This is what we have witnessed over the last decade for voting. The discussion is particularly interesting for voting because of the combination of non-trivial scientific challenges and high societal relevance and interest.

In this paper, we focus on the practical issues involved in electronic voting, both in the context of voting machines at polling stations and in the context of Internet voting. We focus on the situation in the Netherlands because a radical change of position took place there. For electronic voting machines, the Dutch were both early adopters and early abolishers. The machines were introduced on a large scale in the 1990s, and their use was discontinued in 2008 after a short and effective campaign by a pressure group. Meanwhile, experiments with Internet voting had taken place using two completely different systems. While following these developments in a loosely chronological order, many of the issues involved in e-voting will be discussed.

In section 2, we discuss the emergence of electronic voting in the Netherlands, as well as the requirements that are thought to apply to the election process. We also give an overview of techniques that are available to increase the security of electronic voting. In section 3, we describe the controversy that was started by an activist group in 2006. We discuss the issues that were brought up and attempted solutions. In section 4, we describe the Internet voting experiments in the Netherlands. In section 5, we analyse the controversy on electronic voting in terms of trust.

2   Requirements and Techniques

2.1   History of Dutch Elections

The Netherlands are a constitutional monarchy, and have a system of proportional representation for local and national elections. Universal suffrage is in place since 1917 (male) and 1919 (female).

There is no registration procedure. Eligible people received a polling card by mail a couple of weeks before the elections, based on (local) citizen registrations. This polling card was handed in at the polling station. One could be asked to present identification, but the general feeling is that this hardly ever happened. Each polling station had a list of local residents who where expected to vote at that station. The residents names were marked on a list after handing in the polling card (and proceeding to cast a vote), in order to prevent multiple votes by one individual. When voting was limited to the local polling station, one could also vote with a passport instead of a polling card. Now that experiments are being run with voting in any polling station within the municipality, this is not possible anymore, because there is no central voter register for keeping track of who already voted. This has led to some complaints in recent elections by people who lost or forgot their polling cards.

Particularly noteworthy is the liberal policy in the Netherlands for voting by proxy. Since 1928, the option of "stemmen bij volmacht" (voting by proxy) exists: one can authorise other people to cast one's vote. It is meant to be used in case of illness or absence, but this option is not really appreciated elsewhere (see the critical remarks in [27], especially in relation to secrecy of the vote). The possibilities for authorisation have been restricted over time, because, especially in local elections, there had been cases of active vote gathering. By now, each individual is only allowed to have two authorisations. It is not necessary to register a proxy vote; one simply signs the polling card and hands it to the designated proxy.

Since 1983, Dutch citizens living abroad, or having job duties abroad during the elections, are allowed to vote by postal ballot. The postal ballot needs to be accompanied by a signed statement and sent to the election office in The Hague or a special office in the country of residence. Postal voting is not allowed within the country.[1]

The Netherlands were quick to introduce electronic voting. In 1965, a legal provision was put in place to allow the use of machines, including electronic ones, in voting. In the late 1980s, attempts were made to automatise the counting, and the first electronic voting machines appeared. From 1994, the government actively promoted the use of electronic voting machines in elections. Local governments were enthusiastic, mainly about the modern character and administrative efficiency and advantages of these machines: easy, push-button voting, reduction of the number of polling stations, fast delivery of results. Since then, voting machines have been used extensively during elections. Little attention was paid at the time to security and verification possibilities. The main concerns were related to the usability of the machines, especially for elderly people. How the votes were counted and how the result was calculated did not seem to be of much public interest. The introduction of these machines was uncontroversial.

In 1997, regulation on voting machines was established, including an extensive list of requirements that voting machines had to meet ("Regeling voorwaarden en goedkeuring stemmachines"). Demands on the verifiability of the counting, however, largely remained unspecified. Moreover, criteria for software that calculates the results from the totals of the individual machines had not been assessed at all. In 1999, local authorities were even reported to have used self-written software for this purpose [10].

Voting machines in the Netherlands had to be approved by an evaluation institute. Although multiple institutes could be designated in principle, only TNO has been involved in this procedure thus far. Only TNO (the department doing the evaluation now being called BrightSight) was given the source code of the software running on the machines, and the evaluation reports were not public either.

The full requirements specification, consisting of 14 sections, was found as an appendix to the regulation. We quote and translate the items from section 8: Reliability and security of the voting machine. The "normal environmental conditions" referred to are specified elsewhere in the requirements.

---

[1] Source: www.parlement.com, an excellent site on Dutch politics (in Dutch only, alas).

1. The vote stored in the vote memory of the voting machine is the vote cast and confirmed by the voter;
2. A cast vote cannot be lost due to breakdown of the energy supply, failure of one component, "normal" environmental conditions (as specified), normal use, or mistakes in the operation of the voting machine;
3. The read-in lists of candidates are maintained completely in case of breakdown of the energy supply, normal environmental conditions, normal use, or mistakes in the operation of the voting machine;
4. The functions of the voting machine are maintained completely in case of breakdown of the energy supply, normal environmental conditions, normal use, or mistakes in the operation of the voting machine;
5. The storage of the cast votes is made redundant. The vote is stored in such a redundant way in the vote memory, that it can be proved that the failure rate is 10^{-6}. If there is a discrepancy in the redundant storage, the machine will report this to the voter and the voting station;
6. The voting machine is able to avoid or reduce the possibilities for accidental or intended incorrect use as much as is technically feasible in fairness;
7. The way of vote storage does not enable possibilities to derive the choice of individual voters;
8. The voting machine has features which help to avoid erroneous actions during repair, maintenance and checks, for example by mechanical features which preclude assembly in wrong positions or in wrong places;
9. The voting machine may have functions which are not described in the Election Law, the Election Decree, or this appendix, as long as they do not impair the required functionality of the voting machine and are related to the voting procedure.

Note that the possibility of recount or other forms of verification are not mentioned at all. Furthermore, most of the requirements above concern correctness under normal circumstances, and not protection against possible election fraud.

2.2   Nedap Voting Machines/Computers

The most widely used voting machines were produced by the Dutch company Nedap, see Figure 1. These were so-called full-face direct recording electronic voting machines (DRE) with a button for each candidate. Such a Nedap machine contains a Motorola 68000 processor from the 1980s, together with EPROM (2×128KB for the software binary), EEPROM (8KB) and RAM (8KB) memory [13]. It has two simple screens, one for the voter, and one on the election officials' console for enabling the machine. The votes are stored in memory in a redundant manner, in arbitrary order. The system software determining the behaviour of these machines can easily be changed, simply by plugging in different EPROM chips. In this way one can make the machine store votes for one party as votes for another party. One can build this software in such a way that it is practically impossible to detect, see [13] for details.

The verification possibility that these Nedap machines offered is the comparison of the votes per candidate to the votes per party, and to the total number of votes cast. This check, however, is based on votes that have already been processed by the machine. There was no paper trail.

It is interesting to note that this voting equipment has been referred to as a voting *machine*, since its introduction. The word "machine" suggests a single, unchangeable functionality. One of the important points raised by the pressure group against e-voting (see subsection 3.1) is that they should not be called "voting machines" but "voting computers": there is no single unchangeable functionality, because they are proper computers that can be made to do anything. To illustrate this point it was shown [13] that they could be adapted to play chess, or to count fraudulently. Since then it has become almost an ideological issue whether to speak of "voting machines" or of "voting computers" in the Netherlands. Even though we agree that the most appropriate word is "computer", we shall stick to the more common, historical way of referring to them as "machines".

More recently, touch-screen based systems marketed by the former state press Sdu were also used, notably in Amsterdam, see Figure 1.

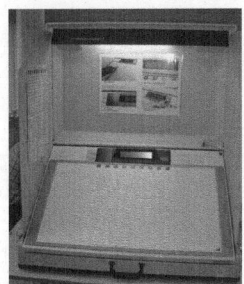

Fig. 1. Voting machines from Nedap (left & middle) and Sdu (right)

2.3 Requirements

In 2007, an official Election Process Advisory Commission was formed, see subsection 3.2 below. It formulated the following requirements for elections, which we quote together with their explanation.

– **Transparency**
  The election process should be organised in such a way that the structure and organisation is clear, so that everyone in principle can understand it. There must be no secrets in the election process: questions must be able to be answered, and the answers must be verifiable.
– **Verifiability**
  The election process should be objectively verifiable. The verification tools may differ, depending on the method of voting that is decided upon.

- **Fairness**
  The election process should operate in a proper manner, and the results must not be capable of being influenced other than by the casting of lawful votes.
- **Eligibility to vote**
  Only persons eligible to vote must be allowed to take part in the election.
- **Free suffrage**
  Every elector must be able to choose how to vote in complete freedom, free from influence.
- **Secret suffrage**
  It must be impossible to connect the identity of a person casting a vote to the vote cast. The process should be organised in such a way that it is impossible to make a voter indicate how he or she voted.
- **Equal suffrage**
  Each voter, given the Dutch election system, must be allowed to cast only one vote in each election, which must be counted precisely once.
- **Accessibility**
  Voters should be enabled as far as possible to participate directly in the election process. If this is impossible, there must be a way of taking part indirectly, i.e. by proxy.

It is widely acknowledged that not all requirements can be guaranteed absolutely, certainly not in combination with each other. For example, paper voting in polling stations is usually judged to provide high guarantees with respect to most of the requirements, but scores quite low on accessibility. Similarly, there are tensions between secrecy on the one hand and authentication and verifiability on the other.

2.4   Techniques

Several techniques are available to realise these requirements (to a certain degree) in electronic voting systems. Some of those have only been the subject of academic analysis, others have been used in real elections. In advanced systems from academia, a distinction can be made (see *e.g.* [16,36]) between protocols based on mix-nets, protocols based on blind signatures and protocols based on homomorphic encryption. These systems have rarely been used in elections though. More practically oriented systems have been based on public key infrastructures, randomised ballots, and hashes. If we do not focus on the electronic possibilities for securing information only, visual cryptography, voter verified paper audit trails and trusted parties can help in achieving security goals.

In order to give an impression of the field, each of these techniques will be described briefly in this subsection. We start with an explanation of the general use of cryptography in voting. For more information we refer to [36] and the references therein.

Cryptography. Key to all secure electronic voting systems is the use of *cryptography*, often abbreviated to "crypto": technology developed in order to protect information by manipulating the information itself. Cryptography can be used to protect the *confidentiality* or *integrity and/or authenticity* of information. The former is realised by *encryption*, the latter by *signing*.

Encryption means scrambling data according to a certain procedure, such that they become unrecognisable. Typically, a (cryptographic) *key* is a parameter in a fixed scrambling method, such as DES or AES. The key is usually just a very big number. A key is also needed for decryption, the recovery of the original data. This key may be the same as or different from the encryption key. The science of designing and analysing encryption schemes is called *cryptology*.

If the same key is used for both encryption and decryption, one speaks about *symmetric* or *secret key* crypto. If different keys are required for encryption and decryption, one calls this *asymmetric* or *public key* crypto. The main advantage of public key crypto is that the problem of establishing a shared key before the transaction is reduced. Instead of having to define a shared secret key for each pair of users, a *certificate* ascribes a *public key* to a person or organisation. This public key can be used to send secret messages to that agent, which only the agent itself can decrypt using its *private key*.

The other way around, the agent can use its *private key* to *sign* messages. The signature can be checked by anyone in order to verify the integrity of the data, using the *public key* in the certificate. The certificate, in its turn, is signed by a higher authority to ensure its authenticity.

Secret-key crypto is generally much faster than public-key crypto. Security-enhanced websites typically use public-key crypto for authentication, based on the site's certificate, during which a *session key* is established. The session key is used in a secret-key scheme for the remainder of the transaction.

It is important to realise that most of these techniques provide *computational* security as opposed to *unconditional* security. This means that security is based on mathematical problems that are *hard* to solve, but not impossible. If one manages to solve the mathematical problem, one can break the confidentiality or integrity of the messages sent. It will take more than a reasonable amount of time to solve them with current computers. If computers get faster, we may start using longer keys to keep new data secure. However, if someone for some reason stored data encrypted using the *old, short* numbers, these may then be easily recovered. So-called 'forward security' is important in voting: even after a very long time it should not be possible to reveal encrypted votes, for instance by brute-force trying.

Future developments, like in quantum computing, may pose more fundamental challenges to these assumptions. If we manage to build real quantum computers, the mathematically hard problems may not be hard for these new machines at all, for instance via Shor's algorithm for integer factorisation. However, new techniques are being developed that use quantum primitives to provide so-called "unconditional" security, which is not dependent on limits of computational power. If these developments are successful, they may have major consequences for e-voting systems (and many other systems as well).

PKI. PKI stands for *Public Key Infrastructure*. Voting systems based on PKI, such as the Estonian system [22], typically use the system of public keys and certificates also applied to for example e-commerce websites. In the Estonian system, the voter encrypts the vote with the election's public key and then signs it with her own private key to prove authenticity. Such systems require each voter to have a certificate and a private key. The private key must be available to the voter in a way that is both secure and easy to use. In the Estonian case, the private key is embedded in a smartcard. Then, voters will need a smartcard plus an installed smartcard reader to be able to vote on their own computer. Due to the limited availability of smartcard readers among voters, PKI-based systems are currently not the best in terms of accessibility.

Blind Signatures. Normally, one signs a message that one knows the contents of. It would be possible to put a signature on a message on carbon paper within a sealed envelope. In this way, I could decide to sign *exactly one* message for each of my friends, after identifying them.

The electronic equivalent of this procedure is called a *blind signature* (see *e.g.* [4]). Blind signatures are useful if we wish to allow voters to choose their own election credentials, *e.g.* a key used to encrypt their vote. They can do this without having to reveal this information to the authorities, through the blinding procedure. They "blind" the information, have it signed, and "unblind" it again. By means of this method, a combination can be achieved of authenticity and anonymity of the vote. Still, the communication channel will need protection, since it is otherwise easy to see from which computer a vote originates.

Mix-nets. When using a ballot box, votes come out in an order different from the order in which they went in. This ensures anonymity of the voters. How to do this electronically? In mix-nets (see *e.g.* [34,1]), encrypted messages are passed on between different authorities, making sure that no-one can derive a relation between the messages going in and the messages coming out. Basically, this is done by having each authority change the order of the votes. The authorities have to prove that the *content* of the messages is still the same after they shuffled them. After the last step, the votes are decrypted. This technique can be used in voting, to make sure that no-one can gain any information from the *order* of the votes, unless *all* of the authorities cooperate. In this way, it is made sure that votes are kept anonymous.

Homomorphic Encryption. Another way to ensure anonymity is to count the votes *while encrypted*. In this way, one calculates a result from the individual votes without revealing the contents of each individual vote. This is exactly what homomorphic encryption achieves (see *e.g.* [7,8,16]). For example, we may *multiply* all the encrypted votes to ensure that if we decrypt the result, this represents the *addition* of the original votes.

Visual Cryptography and Randomised Ballots. Many systems employ a "take-one-destroy-one" principle to ensure security properties. In such a scheme, the vote consists of two parts, which are kept separated, and which do not reveal the vote individually. One example is the visual crypto scheme by [5]. Here, two visual patterns can be combined to a pattern revealing the vote. Prêt-à-Voter by [6] has a similar setup. Here, the voter takes a receipt, but the order of the candidates on the ballot will be destroyed. The order is different on each ballot. The particular order belonging to a ballot can only be recovered through processing by a mix-net, such that each individual vote is kept secret, by separating the vote and the order of the candidates on the ballot. Usability may be a weak factor in these schemes, since voters will have to perform more complicated tasks. Also, voters are prevented from "preparing" their vote at home by finding the name of the candidate on a pre-published candidate list. On the other hand, putting the candidates in different order on each ballot may improve the fairness of the election, because it avoids a possible bias of the voters towards the first-listed candidates [6].

One of the threats to online voting is the possibility of a virus on the voter's computer altering the vote. Randomised ballots may also help to prevent such attacks. Each candidate is then represented by a number, but these numbers are different on each ballot. If the ballot is sent to the voter via traditional mail, and the voter only has to enter a number on a website, it is nearly impossible for the virus to change the voter's choice into one for the party of the virus's choice. This technique was used in the Dutch KOA online voting experiments of 2004 (see Section 4).

Commitments. Some voting systems allow anyone to calculate the result. This can be done by providing before the election a table which can be used to count each possible individual vote. Of course, one cannot put the possible votes themselves in this table, because that would allow people to copy them and send them in as fake votes. However, there are ways to identify some piece of information uniquely (at least with very high probability), without revealing the information itself. Such arrangements are called *commitments*. What can be put in the table instead is for instance a *fingerprint*, a *hash* of each vote.

A hash is a cryptographic operation that assigns to a possibly long document a relatively small sequence of bits. The operation should satisfy the following properties:

- a hash can be efficiently computed from a document;
- it is practically impossible to reconstruct the document from the hash;
- it is practically impossible to find two documents with the same hash.

These properties prevent the reconstruction of valid votes from the table, but when a vote is received it can easily be looked up and counted.

Trusted Parties. Not all security is technical. It is doubtful whether a technically perfect system can be built, and if so, whether it would be practical.

Often, the security of the whole system is based on procedural as well as technical measures. The procedural measures should include a separation and division of responsibilities. In this way, the voter will not have to have full faith in one organisation, but she can be confident that problems can only occur if *all* of the involved organisations cooperate maliciously. The RIES system (section 4) suffers from limited separation of tasks [17].

Still, even in standard public key crypto, we need trusted organisations to sign the certificates that ascribe a public key to a person. Also, in some communication protocols it is assumed that one of the participants is fair. This participant is usually called a trusted third party (TTP). How much trust we should really place in such parties when it comes to voting is a legitimate question.

Voter Verified Paper Audit Trails. A solution to improve the security of electronic voting that has become very popular in the US is the Voter Verified Paper Audit Trail (VVPAT), as proposed by Rebecca Mercuri [23]. This basically means that a voting machine not only stores the vote electronically but also produces a separate print of each vote, which can be used in case a recount is demanded. The print is verified by the voter and then deposited in a ballot box. More than half of the states in the US have now passed legislation making a paper trail mandatory.

Some people argue that a VVPAT does not help much in improving security, because people will have a hard time checking their vote, due to the large number of races on which they have to vote in a single election in the US. It has been suggested to use an audio trail instead [37]. Also, an important question is what to do if in the end the electronic trail and the paper trail differ. Which one has to be preferred? If this question is not properly addressed in advance, VVPAT does not make much sense.

None of these security measures were implemented in the electronic voting machines used in the Netherlands. In the end, this led to major criticism, as we will see in the next section. The Internet voting experiments, which we will address in section 4, did use some.

3   Controversy

3.1   "We Don't Trust Voting Computers"

There have been some isolated incidents and accusations during the history of electronic voting in the Netherlands before 2006. In 1998, it was found that the machines led to a competitive advantage for the numbers 31 of the candidate lists of the parties. Due to space restrictions, these were placed at the top of a second column, next to the candidates heading the lists. Also in 1998, Hans Janmaat, a right-wing maverick, accused the voting machines of deliberately reducing his number of seats.

Criticism of the obscurity of the election procedure when using voting machines has risen after 2000. Main reasons were the secrecy of the source code and the evaluation reports, and the lack of verifiability. Attempts to retrieve the source code of the machines via the Freedom of Information Act failed, because the source code is intellectual property of the producer. But after Ireland judged the Nedap machines they bought unfit for use in the elections,[2] Dutch citizens and politicians started asking questions about the safety and verifiability of such machines. At first, the government responded that everything was OK and not much happened.

In Fall 2006, a chain of events completely changed the e-voting battleground in the Netherlands. A pressure group called "Wij vertrouwen stemcomputers niet" ("We don't trust voting computers") was founded around June by Rop Gonggrijp, who was soon joined by Maurice Wessling. Gonggrijp managed to get hold of a couple of Nedap voting machines, took them apart and reverse-engineered the source code [13]. The results of the analysis were made public in a national television programme on October 4, with the general elections scheduled for November 22 [13]. The first main problem that was illustrated was the easy replacement of the program chips, allowing the attacker to have the machine count incorrectly, or execute any other desired task. Due to the lack of verifiability features, such attacks could go unnoticed: the machine would be able to perform according to its own will. The second main problem shown was the possibility to eavesdrop on the voting machine via a tempest[3] attack. Tempest involves listening to so-called "compromising emanations", *i.e.* radio emission from the device, in this particular case the display. Also, problems were found with the (physical) security of the storage facilities where the machines are kept in between elections.

The tempest attack was particularly successful because there is a special (diacritical) character in the full name of one of the parties. This required the display to switch to a different mode with a different refresh frequency, which could easily be detected.[4] The responsible minister responded to the findings of the activists by having all the EPROM chips containing the software binaries replaced with non-reprogrammable ones (a questionable solution, but the public bought it), seals on all the machines, and having the intelligence agency look into the tempest problem. Tempest expertise is scarce, but typically exists in those circles.

The fix for the diacritical character problem was easy (don't use special characters). With that implemented, the signal emitted from the Nedaps was fairly limited. However, the intelligence agency also looked into the other type of voting machine, the touch-screen based system produced by the former state press Sdu. They found that the tempest issue was much worse there, and someone outside the polling station might be able to reconstruct the whole screen from the signal.

---

[2] http://www.cev.ie/htm/report/first_report.htm, consulted May 28, 2009.

[3] Also written TEMPEST, supposedly being an acronym for Telecommunications Electronics Material Protected from Emanating Spurious Transmission or something similar. For more information, see Chapter 15 of [3].

[4] See the video at http://www.youtube.com/watch?v=B05wPomCjEY

The technical requirements only stated that voting machines should maintain the secrecy of the vote *in storing the vote*, not in casting (see page 124). Nonetheless, the minister suspended the certification for the Sdu machines three weeks before the elections, because the Election Law requires that machines are certified only if the secrecy of the ballot is guaranteed. In the background legal threats from the pressure group played a mayor role. The suspension affected about 10% of the voter population, including Amsterdam. Some districts got spare Nedaps, but others had to use paper ballots, especially because the certification of one of the older Nedap types was suspended later.

There was some discussion about whether eavesdropping on election day was such a realistic scenario that it would justify the suspension. In any case, the pressure group was very happy to have a major event that backed their concerns, even though the focus had shifted from verifiability to secrecy. And the minister was happy to have created an image of a decisive government.

In the beginning of 2007, there was an attempt to re-certify the Sdu machines for the elections for the provinces. However, machines with reduced radio-emission turned out to be unreadable for the colourblind, and Sdu had apparently made mistakes in the machines delivered to the testing agency. In the end, the minister extended the suspension. Sdu demanded a new test in a court case, but the machines failed the test again.

The Ministry of the Interior and Kingdom Relations explained their point of view on the controversy on their website. They stated that apart from the secrecy problem due to the tempest attacks, the security of the machines is acceptable. They argued that in the Dutch proportional system, as opposed to the Anglo-Saxon district-based system, small numbers of votes will not have any major influence on the result. Besides, existing guarantees were thought to be sufficient in order to prevent fraud.[5]

3.2   Two Committees

Another concession of the minister was the initiation of two commissions of independent experts, who would look into, respectively, the past and future of e-voting. The former was the Commission Decision Process Voting Machines[6], the second the Election Process Advisory Commission[7].

In March 2007, the Organization for Security and Co-operation in Europe (OSCE) reported on the Dutch elections [27]. On April 16, the Commission Decision Process Voting Machines published its report [15]. Both reports argued for increased verifiability, by means of a paper trail or equivalent procedure. It was not made clear what kind of (technical) procedures, discussed in the previous section, would count as equivalent.

---

[5] http://www.minbzk.nl/onderwerpen/grondwet_en/verkiezingen_en/
stemmachines, consulted February 13, 2007, not online anymore.

[6] Members: drs. L.M.L.H.A. Hermans and prof. dr. M.J.W. van Twist.

[7] Members: mr. F. Korthals Altes (chairman), prof. mr. J.M. Barendrecht, prof. dr. B.P.F. Jacobs, C. Meesters and M.J.C. van der Wel MBA.

The report of the Commission Decision Process Voting Machines was quite critical about the role of the government in the electronic voting problems. There was too little expertise with the government, and it was too dependent on external parties for the running of elections. The role of TNO as both designer and tester of the machines was questioned. The legal requirements came too late, contained too little security, and did not address the counting software. Also, the government had ignored earlier signals of concern. The government humbly accepted the conclusions, and moved the election process to a more technology-oriented department. There was also an attempt to redraft the requirements.

On September 27, the Election Process Advisory Commission reported on the future of the electoral process in the Netherlands [2]. The report stated that the primary form of voting should be voting in a polling station. Internet voting for the whole population would not be able to guarantee transparency, secrecy and freedom of the vote sufficiently—for the foreseeable future. It was advised to equip polling stations with "ballot printers" and "vote counters" instead of electronic voting machines, providing a paper vote in between the two stages. Ballot printers would only print the voter's choice, which would then be verified by the voter and put in a ballot box. After the close of the polls, the vote counter would scan the votes and calculate the totals.

The American solution of a paper trail was not advised. It was argued that registering the vote twice, electronically and on paper, could lead to different outcomes, depending on which registration would have priority in case of a dispute. Significantly, systems without a paper copy of the vote were not considered as alternatives, for reasons of transparency.

On October 21, 2007, the existing regulation allowing voting machines was withdrawn. A technical expert group was formed to investigate the practical issues involved in the commission's proposal for the new method of voting.

After further research into the tempest issue [20], the option of a ballot printer was judged not to be feasible. A tempest-protected prototype vote printer was built (see Figure 2), with a thick metal shield, but turned out to be too heavy for practical use (almost 100kg). Most importantly, however, the procedures for testing thousands of machines individually for tempest compliance were thought to be way too complicated. Additional measures that are used for tempest protection, like forbidding mobile phones and restricting access to *e.g.* adjacent rooms, turned out to be incompatible with the open nature of elections: you don't want to run them as a high-security military style operation.

Machine counting of manually cast paper votes was not seriously considered: the huge ballots used in the Netherlands are impossible to feed automatically into a machine. Besides, problems in the United Kingdom with this type of e-counting were a reason for the Election Process Advisory Commission not to recommend this option.

On May 16, 2008, the government decided that voting would be on paper for the near future. An experiment with machines similar to the Nedaps for counting by the poll workers only was still proposed. They would then enter the paper votes manually into the machine. Because of the separation between the voter

Fig. 2. A prototype tempest-shielded voteprinter, with touch screen and protected tray for the printed vote

and the entering of the vote in the machine, this would resolve the tempest issue. However, parliament could not be convinced that this would reduce the other security problems involved in electronic voting, and rejected the option.

Thus, in the summer of 2008, the discussion was closed and the Netherlands returned to paper voting, with manual counting of the ballots. Inevitably this will lead to delays in partial results and prognoses on election night—and possibly to a restart of the discussion.

Looking back one must acknowledge that the pressure group has been incredibly effective and has reached its goals in a remarkably short time. It relied on a clear vision, technical skills, bravery, effective use of freedom of information rights, professional communication via their own newsletter and a very informative webpage, frequent and convincing media appearances, and, in the end, threats of legal actions. No politician (or civil servant) likes to have such an adversary.

3.3   The German Constitutional Court

Nedap voting machines were also used in parts of Germany and France. The German Constitutional Court (*Bundesverfassungsgericht*) was asked for a verdict by the Chaos Computer Club (CCC)[8]. On March 3, 2009, the Court ruled

---

[8] There was mutual inspiration, communication and exchange between the German and Dutch campaigns.

that the use of these machines in elections in Germany was unconstitutional because of lack of transparency and verifiability by ordinary citizens. This verdict came too late to have any impact in the Netherlands, but it was received as a confirmation of the decision to abolish voting machines earlier on.

4   Internet Voting

In the Netherlands, several experiments have been performed with voting via the Internet. During the European elections 2004, Dutch citizens living abroad could vote online for the first time. Moreover, elections for two water boards have combined postal ballots with Internet voting in fall 2004, with a total of 120,000 actual online voters. Hence these elections were among the larger ones, worldwide.

Kiezen op Afstand (KOA). The first of the two experiments in the Netherlands was initiated by the Ministry of the Interior and Kingdom Relations. The experiment took place during the European elections in 2004. Participation was intended for expatriates, who only had the option to vote by mail before. This possibility is typically used by 20,000 - 30,000 people, of the about 600,000 potential expat participants. They were given the opportunity to vote via Internet or phone. For this purpose, the KOA system was developed in 2003–2004,[9] and a law regulating the experiment was passed through parliament.

The main setup of the system is as follows [11]. Voters register by ordinary mail, and choose their own access code as password. In return they receive a vote code as "login", together with a list of candidates, each with her own candidate code. There were 1000 different lists in the experiment. Combining login and candidate code, one could then cast a vote.

The system was designed by Logica CMG. However, the government demanded the transfer of the intellectual property rights of the source code with the system. This made it possible to publish the source code after the elections. The source code zip file, published on the website www.ososs.nl, contained all Java code written specifically for the online voting system. Code that was part of general Logica CMG technology was not open source. This meant that it was only possible to inspect the (partial) source, not to compile and run it. A fully open-source version of the system has been developed later by Joe Kiniry and colleagues from Trinity College Dublin [19].

A follow-up trial was conducted in the national elections in 2006. However, the system used was different.

Rijnland Internet Election System. A somewhat more sophisticated system, called RIES, was developed with far less money by the water board of

---

[9] [24], see also http://www.minbzk.nl/persoonsgegeven_en/kiezen_op_afstand, consulted October 11, 2005, not online anymore.

Rijnland[10] together with two companies cooperating under the name TTPI[11], based on earlier work by Robers [33]. A water board (Dutch: hoogheemraadschap or waterschap) is a regional government body for water management. Because the water boards are not bound by the Dutch election law, they are relatively free in their means of voting. Its officials are usually elected via ordinary mail, but voter participation for these elections is typically fairly low. An experiment with election via the Internet has been conducted in the regions Rijnland and Dommel in 2004, with 1 million eligible voters. 120,000 people voted online, but turnout did not increase, against expectation and hope. RIES was also used in the second KOA remote voting experiment during the national elections in 2006, instead of the KOA system from 2004.

The RIES system uses cryptographic operations to protect votes and at the same time offer good transparency, at least in principle. It is possible for voters to verify their vote after the elections, and for independent institutions to do a full recount of the results. The Radboud University Nijmegen did such a recount for all elections in which the system was used, and confirmed the official results [17].

The RIES system uses hashes to publish a pre-election table, see [17,18]. Once the votes have been published, anyone can calculate the result of the election from the pre-election table and the table of received votes. Because of the use of hash functions, the system is relatively simple, offers protection of votes and allows scrutiny of the results. Whereas the hashes of all possible votes are public, it is (or should be) computationally infeasible to deduce valid votes from them without the required voter key.

The system works as follows. First of all, a reference table (see figure 3) is published before the elections, including (anonymously) for each voter the hashes of all possible votes, linking those to the candidates. The original votes are only derivable from a secret key handed to the voter. The confidentiality of these keys is achieved via organisational security measures, in the same way that identification codes for bank cards are handed out. It is possible to compare the number of voters in this table with the number of registered voters.

In the voting phase, voters use their secret to derive a valid vote for their desired candidate. This vote is then submitted to the server via an encrypted connection.

After the elections a document with all received votes is published. This allows for two important verifications: a voter can verify his/her own vote, including the correspondence to the chosen candidate, and anyone can do an independent calculation of the result of the elections, based on this document and the reference table published before the elections. If your vote has been registered wrongly, or not at all, you can detect it. And if the result is incorrect given the received votes, you can detect it as well.[12]

---

[10] http://www.rijnland.net and http://www.rijnlandkiest.nl, consulted May 28, 2009.

[11] http://www.ttpi.nl, consulted May 28, 2009.

[12] Of course, procedures need to be put in place to decide what will happen in case of such a claim.

```
Archive:  01010204.zip
 Length     Date   Time    Name
--------   ----   ----    ----
    2172   08-25-04 09:32   01010204/RT_0.zip
    4017   08-25-04 09:32   01010204/RT_1.zip
    2173   08-25-04 09:32   01010204/RT_2.zip
    1865   08-25-04 09:32   01010204/RT_3.zip
    2789   08-25-04 09:32   01010204/RT_4.zip
    3097   08-25-04 09:32   01010204/RT_5.zip
    2787   08-25-04 09:32   01010204/RT_6.zip
    1559   08-25-04 09:32   01010204/RT_7.zip
    1559   08-25-04 09:32   01010204/RT_8.zip
    2480   08-25-04 09:32   01010204/RT_9.zip
    2784   08-25-04 09:32   01010204/RT_A.zip
    3405   08-25-04 09:32   01010204/RT_B.zip
    2785   08-25-04 09:32   01010204/RT_C.zip
    1867   08-25-04 09:32   01010204/RT_D.zip
    1559   08-25-04 09:32   01010204/RT_E.zip
    3403   08-25-04 09:32   01010204/RT_F.zip
       0   08-25-04 08:51   01010204/
--------                   -------
   40301                   17 files


Archive:  RT_0.zip
 Length     Date   Time    Name
--------   ----   ----    ----
     220   08-25-04 09:31   008AB1E98AEDFBA450A1813DDC153553
     220   08-25-04 09:31   08677B73378E1D59153DE30263A3C47C
     220   08-25-04 09:31   06CAC042AF7D6940DD8A51814E68DFF8
     220   08-25-04 09:31   00FEA51461FBF7B406554EEF2E23554D
     220   08-25-04 09:31   05C02BD8E3863DB24D6C332A17B78EFB
     220   08-25-04 09:32   070C60BFFC06B7355425E6FFADBBED30
     220   08-25-04 09:32   034C37BA687E21477D38A110954207B8
--------                   -------
    1540                   7 files


008AB1E98AEDFBA450A1813DDC153553:

vervangend=0
verstrekt=1
vervallen=0
AC94983743058334B25452E0F63A9C20=0101020401
B0015BAC8ECF766DB67825592DC10957=0101020402
ACE42133255CA8184D18E0293FEF7EE8=0101020403
358AAB0C934757ACCF071A1CD732EDEA=0101020499
```

Fig. 3. Reference table format. The reference table in the figure has been split into 16 parts, which reside in different archive files. Each archive file (*e.g.* RT_0.zip) contains files for different voters, indicated by the hash of the voter's identity. In these files, hashes of possible votes of such a voter are mapped to the corresponding candidates (*e.g.* candidate 0101020401).

The fundamental problem in the RIES system lies in the responsibility of the key generator to destroy the keys immediately after sending them to the voters. Failing to do this may compromise both the secrecy and the authenticity of votes. This allows the organisers, in principle, to vote on behalf of participants[13]. One may wish to improve on this issue by having the voters generate their keys themselves. Here, blind signatures may be useful: the voter can have exactly one key signed by the authorities, without making it public.

Another problem is that the verification procedure might be used to sell votes. If I let someone else verify my vote, he or she could pay me for making the right choice. If I would need a smartcard to verify a vote, this would already be less easy, but this would limit the accessibility and usability of the system.

The water boards intended to use RIES for their combined elections in Fall 2008. This was not a particularly lucky time for the attempt, as the deputy

---

[13] Analogously, bank employees can, in principle, withdraw cash on behalf of clients because also possess PINs.

minister had just abolished the electronic voting machines in polling stations. Parliament demanded an independent evaluation, which was performed by the IT-security company Fox-IT. Internet voting for the water board elections was cancelled after this independent investigation reported additional security problems, such as brute force key search [14] and the possibility of SQL injection attacks [12]. Electronic counting of postal ballots for the water boards was continued, though.

As a result, Internet voting developments in the Netherlands have also come to a halt.

5   Trust in Technology

Trust is a major, but confusing, issue in the discussion on electronic voting [29]. In the following, we briefly investigate the role it played in the controversy in the Netherlands.

Papers discussing trust in electronic voting often seem to be unsure about their definition of trust. In [9], in a section named "*Increasing* trust" [emphasis added], the following sentence is found: "One way to *decrease* the trust voters must place in voting machine software is to let voters physically verify that their intent is recorded correctly." [emphasis added] But was the intent not to *increase* trust? Do we wish to increase and decrease trust at the same time? What is happening here?

Apparently, computing scientists stem from a tradition in which minimising trust is the standard. "In computer security literature in general, the term is used to denote that something must be trusted [...]. That is, something trusted is something that the users are necessarily dependent on." [25] Because we *must* trust certain parts of the system for the whole system to be verifiably correct according to the computing science models, we want to minimise the size of the parts we have to trust, thus minimising trust itself. This desire to minimise is clearly visible in efforts to reduced the so-called Trusted Computing Base (TCB). However, from a psychological perspective, or even a marketing perspective, it is desirable that users trust the *whole* system. Maximising trust seems to lead to more fluent interaction between the user and the system, and is therefore desirable.

To explain these two different types of trust, we consult the German sociologist Niklas Luhmann. Luhmann [21] draws a distinction between *trust* and *confidence*. Both confidence and trust involve the formation of expectations with respect to contingent future events. But there is a difference.

According to Luhmann, trust is always based on assessment of risks, and a decision whether or not to accept those. Confidence differs from trust in the sense that it does not presuppose a situation of risk. Confidence, instead, neglects the possibility of disappointment, not only because this case is rare, but also because there is not really a choice.[14] Examples of confidence that Luhmann gives are expectations about politicians trying to avoid war, and of cars not suddenly breaking down and hitting you. In these cases, you cannot decide for yourself whether or not to take the risk.

When there *is* a choice, trust takes over the function of confidence. Here, the risky situation is evaluated, and a decision is made about whether or not to take the risk: "If you do not consider alternatives [...] you are in a situation of confidence. If you choose one action in preference to others [...], you define the situation as one of trust." [21] If you choose to drive a car by evaluating the risks and accepting them, this is a form of trust. The essential feature of trust as opposed to confidence is the *comparison of alternatives*.

Computing scientists generally try to replace confidence with trust, *i.e.* exchange unconscious dependence on a system for explicit evaluation of the risks, and minimising the parts in which we still have to have confidence. Thus, they wish to minimise confidence and maximise trust (in the terminology of Luhmann). But they do not always state it this way. Philosophers (and social scientists), instead, recognise the positive aspects of confidence, and may evaluate positively people having a relation of assurance with the system without exactly knowing its risks (*i.e.* confidence). This is not meant as a conclusion that holds universally, but rather as an indication of the role of the scientific subcultures in the debates.

Electronic voting systems *may* be seen as alternatives to the existing system. Whether this is indeed the case depends on the situation. If the new technologies are not seen as an alternative, but as an improvement of existing procedures, electronic devices are more attractive, because they are more reliable and thus more easily acquire confidence. In the Netherlands, the pressure group created in their arguments a clear distinction between paper voting on the one hand and electronic voting on the other: they were said to be fundamentally different. If electronic voting is seen as a really different alternative to paper voting, which the pressure group encouraged, people suddenly get the option to decide on a voting system. This invites actively revealing the risks of the different systems, and basing the decision on an analysis of these risks. This means that trust now becomes the dominant form of assurance, as opposed to confidence. This has as a consequence that voting systems are required to be trustworthy rather than reliable only.

By making the distinction between paper voting and e-voting, the pressure group thus created a set of alternatives, requiring a decision, and changing the expectations from reliability to trustworthiness. For now, it seems that no existing voting technology can meet the high demands associated with a comparison with paper voting. Still, the Dutch government indicates that they will follow the technical developments, and most people involved seem to think that the discussion on electronic voting will re-emerge in the next decade. One interesting

---

[14] Some native English speakers have noted that this distinction seems to be counterintuitive. They would rather use the word "trust" for a situation which one has not analysed, and confidence for a more rational form of assurance. In order to avoid confusion in comparison with Luhmann's original text, I will still follow the terminology as introduced there.

question is if socio-technical developments will have made it possible for electronic voting to acquire trust by then. This is especially interesting for Internet voting, since it changes some existing assumptions about the election process.

If it were possible for a technology like Internet voting to acquire trust, this is not merely a technical achievement. New information technologies, like mobile phones, do not merely solve a communication problem. They may profoundly change the experiences and behaviour of citizens [38], and we have indeed seen this in the mobile phone case. With Internet voting, the character of voting as a public ritual is abandoned. Instead, people vote in a private place, with no incentive to abandon their private interests and vote for the "greater good" [32,26]. Even if it is generally not considered acceptable now, future developments may make it possible to link the voting site directly to the sites of political parties, voting advice websites, or discussion fora. It may even become possible to follow the advice of a private organisation and cast this vote directly from their website. This fundamentally changes the place of voting in the democratic process. Also, the fact that the government no longer takes responsibility for the secrecy of the vote may change the importance of the secret ballot. People may vote with their families or friends, and new ways have to be found to prevent undesirable social influence. What, then, is autonomy in voting really? Or in general?

Also, the idea of multi-channel elections, where people can choose the communication medium that most suits them, changes the way we think about equal access in elections. If there is a single channel, like a polling station, some people may live closer than others, but it is generally accepted that this does not constitute an unfair advantage. If people with Internet access can vote from home while others cannot, the acceptability of this inequality is not so trivial. Moreover, the whole system will then be as secure as the least secure channel. Even if fair voters choose the most secure one, unfair voters may take advantage of weaknesses in other channels.

If and when the discussion on electronic voting gets back on the agenda, these issues should be subject to public debate. Otherwise, we may end up in the same situation as with the Dutch voting machines: we did have confidence, but in the end, we had to acknowledge that we failed to address all the issues involved, so that the technology did not deserve our trust.

6   Conclusions

The Netherlands were both an early adopter and an early abolisher of electronic voting. When electronic voting machines were introduced, verifiability was not an issue, and the machines did not include advanced means for verification of votes or results. Questions about the machines were put on the political agenda by a pressure group from 2006. This group also pointed to tempest problems, next to security issues with the integrity of the machines. An alternative voting method was devised by the Election Process Advisory Commission, which consisted of a ballot printer and a vote counter, where only a paper printout of the vote would form the connection between the two stages. However, because of the tempest issue, designing and testing a sufficiently protected ballot printer was judged to be infeasible in any practical election process. Practical issues thus were a major feature in the Dutch electronic voting history.

The experiments with Internet voting showed that fundamental design issues as well as practical details can contribute to the success or failure of Internet voting experiments. The environment may be crucial as well; the demise of the voting machines was not a particularly encouraging event for risking the large-scale elections the water boards had planned.

The success of the pressure group in the Netherlands can be explained in terms of confidence and trust. Whereas the Dutch machines were reliable enough to have confidence, they were not trustworthy enough to survive a critical comparison to the alternative of paper voting.

The big questions, although partially addressed in the Dutch debate, still remain largely unanswered:

1. What are essential requirements in e-voting, and what do they mean?
2. What are the threats?
3. Which techniques should be used to counter them?

Epilogue about the Authors and Their Involvement

Given the broad descriptive character of this article it is appropriate to make the authors' roles and involvement explicit. The second author (WP) has done his PhD work [31] from 2003 to 2007 within the computer security research group at the Radboud University of Nijmegen, where the first author (BJ) holds a professorship. The group has been involved in several evaluation activities with respect to e-voting (KOA, RIES), often together with colleague Engelbert Hubbers, and sometimes on a commercial basis. This resulted in several publications, such as [17,30,18]. Also, the group played a public role in some of the societal discussions around voting in the Netherlands.

The first author was a member of the Commission Decision Process Voting Machines, and was chair of the subsequent more technical commission that studied the tempest issue (see section 3). The second author worked for the Ministry of the Interior from September 2007 until July 2008, on electronic voting and travel documents. Currently he is researching information security at the University of Twente. This text is not based on any non-public information obtained from the authors' work in these commissions or at the Ministry.

References

1. Abe, M.: Universally verifiable mix-net with verification work independent of the number of mix-servers. In: Nyberg, K. (ed.) EUROCRYPT 1998. LNCS, vol. 1403, pp. 437–447. Springer, Heidelberg (1998)
2. Adviesommissie Inrichting Verkiezingsproces. Stemmen met vertrouwen (September 2007), http://www.minbzk.nl/contents/pages/89927/advies.pdf (consulted May 28, 2009)

3. Anderson, R.: Security Engineering. John Wiley & Sons, Chichester (2001), http://www.cl.cam.ac.uk/~rja14/book.html

4. Chaum, D.: Blind signatures for untraceable payments. In: Advances in Cryptology: Proceedings of Crypto 1982, pp. 199–203. Plenum Press (1983)

5. Chaum, D.: Secret-ballot receipts: true voter-verifiable elections. IEEE Security & Privacy 2(1), 38–47 (2004)

6. Chaum, D., Ryan, P.Y.A., Schneider, S.: A practical voter-verifiable election scheme. In: di Vimercati, S.d.C., Syverson, P.F., Gollmann, D. (eds.) ESORICS 2005. LNCS, vol. 3679, pp. 118–139. Springer, Heidelberg (2005)

7. Cramer, R., Franklin, M.K., Schoenmakers, B., Yung, M.: Multi-authority secret-ballot elections with linear work. In: Maurer, U.M. (ed.) EUROCRYPT 1996. LNCS, vol. 1070, pp. 72–83. Springer, Heidelberg (1996)

8. Cramer, R., Gennaro, R., Schoenmakers, B.: A secure and optimally efficient multi-authority election scheme. In: Fumy, W. (ed.) EUROCRYPT 1997. LNCS, vol. 1233, pp. 103–118. Springer, Heidelberg (1997)

9. Evans, D., Paul, N.: Election security: perception and reality. IEEE Security & Privacy 2(1), 24–31 (2004)

10. Het Expertise Centrum, consultants voor overheidsinformatisering. Stand van zaken automatisering rond verkiezingsproces (May 28, 1999)

11. Het Expertise Centrum, consultants voor overheidsinformatisering. Definitierapport kiezen op afstand (September 15, 2000)

12. Gedrojc, B., Hueck, M., Hoogstraten, H., Koek, M., Resink, S.: Rapportage advisering toelaatbaarheid internetstemvoorziening waterschappen. Fox-IT (August 12, 2008), http://www.verkeerenwaterstaat.nl/Images/20081302%20Bijlage%201%20Rappo%rt_tcm195-228336.pdf

13. Gonggrijp, R., Hengeveld, W.-J., Bogk, A., Engling, D., Mehnert, H., Rieger, F., Scheffers, P., Wels, B.: Nedap/Groenendaal ES3B voting computer: a security analysis (October 6, 2006), http://www.wijvertrouwenstemcomputersniet.nl/images/9/91/Es3b-en.pdf (consulted May 28, 2009)

14. Gonggrijp, R., Hengeveld, W.-J., Hotting, E., Schmidt, S., Weidemann, F.: Ries — Rijnland Internet Election System. Very quick scan of published source code and documentation (July 2008), http://www.wijvertrouwenstemcomputersniet.nl/images/7/7f/RIES.pdf (consulted May 28, 2009)

15. Hermans, L.M.L.H.A., van Twist, M.J.W.: Stemmachines: een verweesd dossier. Rapport van de commissie besluitvorming stemmachines (April 2007), http://www.minbzk.nl/contents/pages/86914/rapportstemmachineseenverwees%ddossier.pdf (consulted May 28, 2009)

16. Hirt, M., Sako, K.: Efficient receipt-free voting based on homomorphic encryption. In: Preneel, B. (ed.) EUROCRYPT 2000. LNCS, vol. 1807, pp. 539–556. Springer, Heidelberg (2000)

17. Hubbers, E., Jacobs, B., Pieters, W.: RIES – Internet voting in action. In: Bilof, R. (ed.) Proc. 29th Annual International Computer Software and Applications Conference, COMPSAC 2005, pp. 417–424. IEEE Computer Society, Los Alamitos (2005)

18. Hubbers, E., Jacobs, B., Schoenmakers, B., van Tilborg, H., de Weger, B.: Description and analysis of the RIES internet voting system. Version 1.0 (June 24, 2008), http://www.win.tue.nl/eipsi/images/RIES_descr_anal_v1.0_June_24.pdf

19. Kiniry, J.R., Morkan, A.E., Cochran, D., Fairmichael, F., Chalin, P., Oostdijk, M., Hubbers, E.: The KOA remote voting system: A summary of work to date. In: Montanari, U., Sannella, D., Bruni, R. (eds.) TGC 2006. LNCS, vol. 4661, pp. 244–262. Springer, Heidelberg (2007)

20. Kuhn, M., Friedrichs, G., Aksoy, A., Koch, E., Friedrichs, L.: Tempest specificaties en testmethoden voor elektronische stemapparatuur. Appendix BLG15766 of Kamerstuk 2007-2008, 31200 VII, nr. 64, Tweede Kamer (May 21, 2008)

21. Luhmann, N.: Familiarity, confidence, trust: problems and alternatives. In: Gambetta, D. (ed.) Trust: Making and breaking of cooperative relations. Basil Blackwell, Oxford (1988)

22. Madise, Ü., Vinkel, P., Maaten, E.: Internet voting at the elections of local government councils on October 2005 (2006), http://www.vvk.ee/english/report2006.pdf (consulted November 9, 2007), not online anymore

23. Mercuri, R.T.: A better ballot box? IEEE Spectrum 39(10), 26–50 (2002)

24. Ministerie van Binnenlandse Zaken en Koninkrijksrelaties: Project kiezen op afstand. report BPR2004/U79957 (November 11, 2004), http://www.minbzk.nl/onderwerpen/grondwet-en/verkiezingen-en/kiezen-op-afstand/kamerstukken?ActItmIdt=12800 (consulted May 29, 2009)

25. Nikander, P., Karvonen, K.: Users and trust in cyberspace. In: Christianson, B., Crispo, B., Malcolm, J.A., Roe, M. (eds.) Security Protocols 2000. LNCS, vol. 2133, pp. 24–35. Springer, Heidelberg (2001)

26. Oostveen, A.M., Van den Besselaar, P.: The effects of voting technologies on voting behaviour: Issues of trust and social identity. Social Science Computer Review 23(3), 304–311 (2005)

27. OSCE Office for Democratic Institutions and Human Rights. The Netherlands parliamentary elections 22 November 2006: OSCE/ODIHR election assessment mission report (March 12, 2007), http://www.osce.org/item/23602.html (consulted May 28, 2009)

28. Park, J.H.: England's controversy over the secret ballot. Political Science Quarterly 46(1), 51–86 (1931)

29. Pieters, W.: Acceptance of voting technology: Between confidence and trust. In: Stølen, K., Winsborough, W.H., Martinelli, F., Massacci, F. (eds.) iTrust 2006. LNCS, vol. 3986, pp. 283–297. Springer, Heidelberg (2006)

30. Pieters, W.: What proof do we prefer? variants of verifiability in voting. In: Ryan, P., Anderson, S., Storer, T., Duncan, I., Bryans, J. (eds.) Workshop on e-Voting and e-Government in the UK, Edinburgh, February 27-28, pp. 33–39. e-Science Institute, University of St. Andrews (2006)

31. Pieters, W.: La volonté machinale: understanding the electronic voting controversy. PhD thesis, Radboud University Nijmegen (January 2008)

32. Pieters, W., Becker, M.: Ethics of e-voting: An essay on requirements and values in Internet elections. In: Brey, P., Grodzinsky, F., Introna, L. (eds.) Ethics of New Information Technology: Proc. Sixth International Conference on Computer Ethics: Philosophical Enquiry (CEPE 2005), Enschede, pp. 307–318. Center for Telematics and Information Technology (2005)

33. Robers, H.: Electronic elections employing DES smartcards. Master's thesis (December 1998), http://www.surfnet.nl/bijeenkomsten/ries/robers_scriptie_election.pdf (consulted November 9, 2007), not online anymore

34. Sako, K., Kilian, J.: Receipt-free mix-type voting scheme – a practical solution to the implementation of a voting booth. In: Guillou, L.C., Quisquater, J.-J. (eds.) EUROCRYPT 1995. LNCS, vol. 921, pp. 393–403. Springer, Heidelberg (1995)
35. Saltman, R.G.: The History and Politics of Voting Technology. Palgrave Macmillan, New York (2006)
36. Schoenmakers, B.: Voting schemes. In: Atallah, M., Blanton, M. (eds.) Tools and algorithms for the contruction and analysis of systems. CRC-Press, Boca Raton (to appear, 2009)
37. Selker, T., Goler, J.: Security vulnerabilities and problems with VVPT. Caltech / MIT Voting Technology Project, Working Paper #16 (2004), http://www.vote.caltech.edu/drupal/files/working_paper/vtp_wp16.pdf (consulted May 28, 2009)
38. Verbeek, P.P.C.C.: What things do: Philosophical Reflections on Technology, Agency, and Design. Pennsylvania State University Press (2005)

Logic in Access Control
(Tutorial Notes)

Martín Abadi

Microsoft Research
and
University of California, Santa Cruz

Abstract. Access control is central to security in computer systems. Over the years, there have been many efforts to explain and to improve access control, sometimes with logical ideas and tools. This paper is a partial survey and discussion of the role of logic in access control. It considers logical foundations for access control and their applications, in particular in languages for security policies. It focuses on some specific logics and their properties. It is intended as a written counterpart to a tutorial given at the 2009 International School on Foundations of Security Analysis and Design.

1   Introduction

Access control consists in deciding whether the agent that issues a request should be trusted on this request. For example, the agent may be a process running on behalf of a user, and the request may be a command to read a particular file. In this example, the access control machinery would be charged with deciding whether the read should be permitted. This authorization decision may, in the simplest case, rely on consulting an access control matrix that would map the user's name and the file name to a set of allowed operations [44]. The matrix may be implemented in terms of access control lists (ACLs), attached to objects, or in terms of capabilities, held by principals. Typically, however, the authorization decision is considerably more complex. It may depend, for example, on the user's membership in a group, and on a digitally signed credential that certifies this membership.

Access control is central to security and it is pervasive in computer systems. It appears (with peculiar features and flaws) in many applications, virtual machines, operating systems, and firewalls. Physical protection for facilities and for hardware components are other forms of access control.

Although access control may sometimes seem conceptually straightforward, it is both complex and error-prone in practice. The many mechanisms for access control are often broken or circumvented.

Over the years, there have been many efforts to explain and to improve access control. Some of those efforts have relied on logical ideas and tools. One may hope that logic would provide a simple, solid, and general foundation for access control, as well as methods for designing, implementing, and validating particular access control mechanisms. Indeed, although logic is not a panacea, its applications in research on access control have been substantial and beneficial.

A. Aldini, G. Barthe, R. Gorrieri (Eds.): FOSAD 2007/2008/2009, LNCS 5705, pp. 145–165, 2009.

This paper is a partial survey and discussion of the role of logic in access control. It considers logical formulations of access control and their applications, emphasizing some particular logics and languages for security policies in distributed systems. It does not however aim to be a complete overview. It deliberately neglects several relevant topics that have been the subjects of significant bodies of work. These include:

- Decidability results for problems related to access control (e.g., [36, 49, 51]).
- Logical approaches for authorizing code execution, such as those based on proof-carrying code (e.g., [53, 59]).
- Formal verification of security properties (e.g., [56]).

The next section introduces some logical constructs that have been employed in connection with access control. Section 3 explains, at a high level, some of the choices that need to be made in order to define a logic for access control. Section 4 defines some specific logics. Section 5 briefly discusses non-interference properties. Section 6 considers the relations between various formulas in these logics. Section 7 then describes languages for access control, focusing on the Binder language. Section 8 concludes.

Some of the basic material in this paper is an adaptation and update of a brief survey from 2003 [2]. Other parts summarize recent research papers [3, 4], which contain proofs and additional details.

2   From Matrices to Logics

This section aims to explain, informally, the transition from access control matrices to logics for access control. Subsequent sections define and study these logics more precisely, and also contain further examples.

2.1   From Matrices to Predicates

An access control matrix may be viewed as a description of a ternary relation, which we call may-access. With this interpretation, may-access(p, o, r) would hold whenever the matrix gives principal p the right r on object o. Thus, we may obtain a first logic of access control by representing a global access control matrix with the predicate symbol may-access, in the setting of a predicate calculus.

This trivial logic enables us to state facts such as

$$\text{may-access}(\text{Alice}, \text{Foo.txt}, \text{Rd})$$

(which says that the principal Alice can perform the operation read (Rd) on the object Foo.txt). It also enables us to state rules such as

$$\text{may-access}(p, o, \text{Wr}) \rightarrow \text{may-access}(p, o, \text{Rd})$$

(which makes the Wr right stronger than the Rd right), but perhaps not much else. Therefore, this trivial logic seems of limited direct benefit. However, it suggests more elaborate systems with predicate symbols similar to may-access.

We may reasonably suspect that there is nothing canonical about `may-access`. We may also worry about a proliferation of variants. For instance, thinking about security policies that require separation of duty, we may imagine a predicate symbol `may-jointly-access`, with the intent that `may-jointly-access`(p, q, o, r) would hold if p and q have right r on o when they request r jointly. In addition, we may imagine many useful auxiliary predicates, such as one for expressing that a principal owns an object, and several for grouping principals and objects. We would perhaps be reluctant to develop a logic with the many built-in constructs and axioms that would result.

Nevertheless, rich logics with constructs similar to `may-access` can support a wide range of current models for access control [15, 39, 40]. In addition to primitives for authorization that greatly generalize `may-access`, the logics may include primitives pertaining to groups, roles, object containment, privilege ordering, and perhaps others. In a different direction, such a logic for access control may include a modal operator for reasoning about necessity [21]. There is much room for logical creativity, for better or for worse—richer logics are not automatically more tasteful or more useful.

2.2   Saying Predicates

Several characteristics of computer systems complicate access control. For distributed systems, in particular, these characteristics include size, heterogeneity, the autonomy of system components, and the possibility of component failures (e.g., [30, 43]). These complications have resulted in a substantial line of work. They also suggest the possibility of an important role for logical methods.

In what follows we focus on one logical construct that has often been used in this context, `says` (e.g., [2, 6, 8, 12, 13, 20, 22, 29, 33, 43, 46, 48, 54, 63]). The formula p `says` s represents that principal p makes statement s. This statement may simply be a request for an operation. In more interesting cases, the statement may express that p delegates some of its authority to another principal q, or it may express part of a security policy.

For instance, we may write:

$$p \text{ says may-access}(q, o, r)$$

We may also write the rule:

$$p \text{ says may-access}(q, o, r) \rightarrow (\text{may-access}(p, o, r) \rightarrow \text{may-access}(q, o, r))$$

which states that p may hand off a right r to q. As in these formulas, the use of `says` enables us to consider situations—common in distributed systems—in which there is no global, universally trusted access control policy. Each principal can make its own security-relevant assertions.

In a slightly more substantial and specific example (partly adapted from [28]), we consider a principal `Admin` (an administrator), a user `Bob`, one file `File1`, and the following informal policy:

1. If `Admin` says that `File1` should be deleted, then this must be the case.
2. `Admin` trusts `Bob` to decide whether `File1` should be deleted.

Several different formalizations of these statements are possible. For instance, much as above, we may write:

1. may-access(Admin, File1, Delete)
2. Admin says may-access(Bob, File1, Delete)

Alternatively, letting the proposition symbol deleteFile1 mean that File1 should be deleted, we may write:

1. (Admin says deleteFile1) → deleteFile1
2. Admin says ((Bob says deleteFile1) → deleteFile1)

This second representation allows us to go further, in the following way. Suppose that Bob wants to delete File1. We may represent this statement by

Bob says deleteFile1

We may then expect to conclude that deleteFile1, so File1 should be deleted. Some of the logics described below (in particular, CDD, of Section 4.3) do indeed yield this conclusion. A reference monitor that controls access to File1 and that bases its decisions on such a logic could therefore derive deleteFile1 from the other formulas. Bob and other principals may however help with this proof, providing the whole proof of deleteFile1 or some of its parts; this approach is sometimes called proof-carrying authentication or proof-carrying authorization [8, 9].

Attractively, says abstracts from the details of authentication. When p says s, p may transmit s in a variety of ways:

– on a local channel via a trusted operating system within a computer,
– on a physically secure channel between two machines,
– on a channel secured with shared-key cryptography, or
– in a certificate with a public-key digital signature.

We may assert that p says s even when p does not directly produce s. For example, when p is a user and one of its programs sends s in a message, we may find it convenient and reasonably accurate to state that p says s although p itself may never have even seen s. In this case, p says s means that p has caused s to be said, or that s has been said on p's behalf, or that p supports s. With this interpretation, we may assert that p says s also when p makes a statement s' stronger than s, with the idea that if p supports s' then p must also support s.

If p says s and p speaks for another principal q, then q says s. The "speaks for" relation serves to form chains of responsibility in many important situations [45]. A program may speak for a user, much like a key may speak for its owner, much like a channel may speak for its remote end-point. Therefore, some logics support "speaks for" as a primitive (e.g., [6, 12, 43]) or as a definable construct (e.g., [3, 8]).

Revisiting our example, suppose that instead of having Bob says deleteFile1 directly, Bob hands off his authority to Alice who wants to delete File1. Writing ⇒ for the "speaks for" relation, we may express these statements by:

1. Bob says (Alice ⇒ Bob)
2. Alice says deleteFile1

From these, we may be able to derive `Bob says deleteFile1`, and then to derive `deleteFile1`. Again, some of the logics described below (in particular, CDD) do indeed yield this conclusion. Note that, in this example, `Bob says deleteFile1` does not mean that `Bob` utters the request to delete the file.

3 Defining a Logic (Preliminaries)

Existing logics differ in sometimes subtle but important ways in their syntax, in their axioms and proof rules, and in the intended interpretations of `says` and related constructs. For instance, in some logics `says` requires no special axioms and is treated quite syntactically, like the `cert` construct of Halpern and van der Meyden [34]. Elsewhere, sometimes `says` has axioms familiar from modal logics [38], such as the axiom of closure under consequence:

$$p \text{ says } (s \to s') \to (p \text{ says } s) \to (p \text{ says } s')$$

and the usual necessitation rule according to which the validity of s implies the validity of p says s. Sometimes `says` has additional properties. For instance, early on, Lampson suggested the axiom:

$$s \to (p \text{ says } s)$$

Appel and Felten essentially adopt this axiom (as rule name_i) in their work on proof-carrying authentication [8]. It is stronger than the usual necessitation rule, and should be used with caution (if at all). In a classical-logic context, it can yield unexpected consequences such as:

$$(p \text{ says } s) \to (s \vee (p \text{ says false}))$$

We explore this and related issues in Section 6.

One may imagine that rigorous semantics would clarify the intended interpretations of logical constructs, and that they would also shed some light on the proper choice of syntax, axioms, and proof rules. While semantics have indeed been helpful (for instance, for decidability proofs [6, 28], in relating two definitions of "speaks for" [28], and in establishing some of the results in this paper), so far they provide only limited new insight into notions such as authority and responsibility. Therefore, we tend to use semantics mostly informally or in proofs of metatheorems.

Various high-level desiderata may also influence the choice of syntax, axioms, and proof rules of a logic:

- The logic should be consistent (that is, it should not prove `false`). It should also be sensible in other ways. For instance, if `Alice` and `Bob` are unrelated principals, `Alice says false` should not imply `Bob says false`. This property can be regarded as a non-interference property [5, 29]. (We discuss non-interference in Section 5.)
- Human users should find it easy to write security policies and related assertions, manipulate them, and understand them (e.g., [10]).
- Programs, such as decision procedures, should also be able to manipulate and analyze logical formulas.

These criteria are not fully orthogonal. In particular, one cannot express meaningful security policies in an inconsistent logic. On the other hand, expressiveness often conflicts with algorithmic tractability.

A common approach to addressing these desiderata consists in restricting the forms of logical formulas. In particular, the formulas may be required to be similar to Horn clauses, much as in logic programming. The Binder language of Section 7 can be seen partly as an example of this approach. More general formulas may be allowed for certain purposes (for instance, in theoretical results) but not necessarily used on a day-to-day basis, or entirely disallowed.

4   Some Logics

For concreteness, this section introduces specific logics, more formally. The logics have the same operators and intended applications, but they differ in their axioms and rules. Section 4.1 briefly introduces syntax. Section 4.2 concerns modal treatments of `says`, both intuitionistic and classical. Section 4.3 concerns another logic called CDD. It presents CDD in a self-contained manner, but it also mentions how to view CDD as an extension of the intuitionistic logic of Section 4.2.

4.1   Basic Syntax

The syntax of the logics includes that of propositional logic, second-order quantification over propositions, and the `says` operator. More precisely, formulas are given by the grammar:

$$s ::= \texttt{true} \mid (s \vee s) \mid (s \wedge s) \mid (s \rightarrow s) \mid p \texttt{ says } s \mid X \mid \forall X. s$$

where p ranges over elements of a set $\mathcal{P}$ (intuitively the principals), and X ranges over a set of variables. The variable X is bound in $\forall X. s$, and subject to renaming.

We write `false` for $\forall X. X$. We write $s_1 \equiv s_2$ for $(s_1 \rightarrow s_2) \wedge (s_2 \rightarrow s_1)$. We write $p \Rightarrow q$ as an abbreviation for

$$\forall X. (p \texttt{ says } X \rightarrow q \texttt{ says } X)$$

This formula is our representation of "p speaks for q". We write p `controls` s as an abbreviation for $(p \texttt{ says } s) \rightarrow s$.

4.2   Second-Order Propositional Modal Logics

Our starting point is second-order propositional intuitionistic logic. This logic can be presented as a Hilbert system, with the following axioms:

- `true`
- $s_1 \rightarrow (s_2 \rightarrow s_1)$
- $(s_1 \rightarrow (s_2 \rightarrow s_3)) \rightarrow ((s_1 \rightarrow s_2) \rightarrow (s_1 \rightarrow s_3))$
- $(s_1 \wedge s_2) \rightarrow s_1$
- $(s_1 \wedge s_2) \rightarrow s_2$
- $s_1 \rightarrow s_2 \rightarrow (s_1 \wedge s_2)$
- $s_1 \rightarrow (s_1 \vee s_2)$

- $s_2 \to (s_1 \vee s_2)$
- $(s_1 \to s_3) \to ((s_2 \to s_3) \to ((s_1 \vee s_2) \to s_3))$
- $(\forall X.\, s) \to s[t/X]$
- $(\forall X.\, (s_1 \to s_2)) \to (s_1 \to \forall X.\, s_2)$ where X is not free in s_1

and the rules of modus ponens and universal generalization:

$$\frac{s_1 \qquad s_1 \to s_2}{s_2} \qquad \frac{s}{\forall X.\, s}$$

A classical variant is obtained by adding the axiom of excluded middle:

$$[\textit{Excluded-middle}] \quad \forall X.\, (X \vee (X \to \texttt{false}))$$

Going beyond these standard propositional systems, we axiomatize the operator `says` as a modality, with the axiom of closure under consequence:

$$\forall X, Y.\, ((p \text{ says } (X \to Y)) \to (p \text{ says } X) \to (p \text{ says } Y))$$

and the necessitation rule:

$$\frac{s}{p \text{ says } s}$$

More precisely, `says` is a modality indexed over $\mathcal{P}$: in other words, p `says` is a modality for each $p \in \mathcal{P}$. Thus, we obtain second-order, indexed versions (intuitionistic and classical) of the standard propositional modal logic K [38].

[*Var*] $\Gamma, x : s, \Gamma' \vdash x : s$ [*Unit*] $\Gamma \vdash () : \texttt{true}$

[*Lam*] $\dfrac{\Gamma, x : s_1 \vdash e : s_2}{\Gamma \vdash (\lambda x : s_1.\, e) : (s_1 \to s_2)}$ [*App*] $\dfrac{\Gamma \vdash e : (s_1 \to s_2) \quad \Gamma \vdash e' : s_1}{\Gamma \vdash (e\, e') : s_2}$

[*Pair*] $\dfrac{\Gamma \vdash e_1 : s_1 \quad \Gamma \vdash e_2 : s_2}{\Gamma \vdash \langle e_1, e_2 \rangle : (s_1 \wedge s_2)}$

[*Proj 1*] $\dfrac{\Gamma \vdash e : (s_1 \wedge s_2)}{\Gamma \vdash (\text{proj}_1 e) : s_1}$ [*Proj 2*] $\dfrac{\Gamma \vdash e : (s_1 \wedge s_2)}{\Gamma \vdash (\text{proj}_2 e) : s_2}$

[*Inj 1*] $\dfrac{\Gamma \vdash e : s_1}{\Gamma \vdash (\text{inj}_1 e) : (s_1 \vee s_2)}$ [*Inj 2*] $\dfrac{\Gamma \vdash e : s_2}{\Gamma \vdash (\text{inj}_2 e) : (s_1 \vee s_2)}$

[*Case*] $\dfrac{\Gamma \vdash e : (s_1 \vee s_2) \quad \Gamma, x : s_1 \vdash e_1 : s \quad \Gamma, x : s_2 \vdash e_2 : s}{\Gamma \vdash (\text{case } e \text{ of } \text{inj}_1(x).\, e_1 \mid \text{inj}_2(x).\, e_2) : s}$

[*TLam*] $\dfrac{\Gamma, X \vdash e : s}{\Gamma \vdash (\Lambda X.\, e) : \forall X.\, s}$ [*TApp*] $\dfrac{\Gamma \vdash e : \forall X.\, s}{\Gamma \vdash (et) : s[t/X]}$ (t well-formed in Γ)

[*UnitM*] $\dfrac{\Gamma \vdash e : s}{\Gamma \vdash (\eta_p\, e) : p \text{ says } s}$

[*BindM*] $\dfrac{\Gamma \vdash e : p \text{ says } s \quad \Gamma, x : s \vdash e' : p \text{ says } t}{\Gamma \vdash \text{bind } x = e \text{ in } e' : p \text{ says } t}$

Fig. 1. CDD typing rules

Below, we sometimes refer to the intuitionistic version as "the basic logic", because it is the weakest logic that we use for access control in this paper. Occasionally we emphasize that this logic does not include Excluded-middle, particularly when the inclusion of Excluded-middle would affect the results under consideration.

4.3 CDD

CDD is a formalism related to lax logic and the computational lambda calculus [14, 24, 52]. CDD can be seen both as a type system and as a logic, via the Curry-Howard isomorphism. Figure 1 presents CDD as a set of typing rules, in the style of those of Girard's System F [18, 31]. There, an environment Γ declares a list of distinct type variables and distinct variables with their types (for example, X, $x : X \to$ true, $y : X$). Figure 2 presents CDD as a logical system, with sequent notation. There, an environment Γ is a list of formulas (for example, $X \to$ true, X). When Γ is empty, we may write $\vdash s$, and say that s is a theorem, when $\vdash s$ is derivable by the rules of Figure 2. The rules of Figure 2 are obtained from those of Figure 1 by omitting type-variable declarations and terms.

In the context of access control, CDD arose as a simplified version of the Dependency Core Calculus (DCC) [5], but it is similarly adequate as a logic for access control [3, Section 8]. (CDD is simpler than DCC and a little weaker: for instance, DCC proves $(p \text{ says } q \text{ says } s) \to (q \text{ says } p \text{ says } s)$, and CDD does not.) CDD

$$[Var] \quad \Gamma, s, \Gamma' \vdash s \qquad\qquad [Unit] \quad \Gamma \vdash \text{true}$$

$$[Lam] \quad \frac{\Gamma, s_1 \vdash s_2}{\Gamma \vdash (s_1 \to s_2)} \qquad\qquad [App] \quad \frac{\Gamma \vdash (s_1 \to s_2) \quad \Gamma \vdash s_1}{\Gamma \vdash s_2}$$

$$[Pair] \quad \frac{\Gamma \vdash s_1 \quad \Gamma \vdash s_2}{\Gamma \vdash (s_1 \wedge s_2)}$$

$$[Proj\ 1] \quad \frac{\Gamma \vdash (s_1 \wedge s_2)}{\Gamma \vdash s_1} \qquad\qquad [Proj\ 2] \quad \frac{\Gamma \vdash (s_1 \wedge s_2)}{\Gamma \vdash s_2}$$

$$[Inj\ 1] \quad \frac{\Gamma \vdash s_1}{\Gamma \vdash (s_1 \vee s_2)} \qquad\qquad [Inj\ 2] \quad \frac{\Gamma \vdash s_2}{\Gamma \vdash (s_1 \vee s_2)}$$

$$[Case] \quad \frac{\Gamma \vdash (s_1 \vee s_2) \quad \Gamma, s_1 \vdash s \quad \Gamma, s_2 \vdash s}{\Gamma \vdash s}$$

$$[TLam] \quad \frac{\Gamma \vdash s}{\Gamma \vdash \forall X.\, s} \ (X \text{ not free in } \Gamma) \qquad [TApp] \quad \frac{\Gamma \vdash \forall X.\, s}{\Gamma \vdash s[t/X]}$$

$$[UnitM] \quad \frac{\Gamma \vdash s}{\Gamma \vdash p \text{ says } s}$$

$$[BindM] \quad \frac{\Gamma \vdash p \text{ says } s \quad \Gamma, s \vdash p \text{ says } t}{\Gamma \vdash p \text{ says } t}$$

Fig. 2. CDD logical rules

has been used for language-based authorization [25], and its central rules also appear in other systems for access control, such as Alpaca [46].

While Figure 2 is a complete, stand-alone presentation of CDD, CDD may also be seen as an extension of the intuitionistic logic of Section 4.2. The extension consists in adopting the following two additional axioms, Unit and Bind:

$$[Unit] \quad \forall X. (X \to p \text{ says } X)$$
$$[Bind] \quad \forall X, Y. ((X \to p \text{ says } Y) \to (p \text{ says } X) \to (p \text{ says } Y))$$

These axioms straightforwardly correspond to the rules *UnitM* and *BindM*. It is easy to show that neither of these axioms is derivable in the logic of Section 4.2, neither intuitionistically nor classically.

5   Non-interference

The Dependency Core Calculus (DCC) [3, 5] was not initially designed as a calculus for access control. Rather, it was designed in order to capture the notion of dependency that arises in information-flow control, partial evaluation, slicing, and similar programming-language settings. In those contexts, non-interference results characterize independence properties. Interestingly, non-interference results are also relevant to access control.

A typical non-interference result would imply that if we have a proof e of p says s and it depends on a proof x of q says t, where p and q are unrelated principals, then, from the point of view of e, it does not matter which actual proof we substitute for x. Even more strongly, we should be able to obtain that e can be constructed without x (at least under certain hypotheses on e).

As an example, we show a non-interference result for CDD. For a formula s and principal q, we define the formula $(s)^q$ in Figure 3. Intuitively, $(s)^q$ is a variant of s that corresponds to the situation in which q is completely untrustworthy, so q says t is always true, independently of t. For an environment Γ, we define $(\Gamma)^q$ by applying $(\cdot)^q$ to each formula in Γ. Using these definitions, Theorem 1 aims to show that q's untrustworthiness has a limited effect on other principals:

$$(\text{true})^q = \text{true}$$
$$(s_1 \lor s_2)^q = (s_1)^q \lor (s_2)^q$$
$$(s_1 \land s_2)^q = (s_1)^q \land (s_2)^q$$
$$(s_1 \to s_2)^q = (s_1)^q \to (s_2)^q$$
$$(p \text{ says } s)^q = \begin{cases} \text{true} & \text{if } q = p \\ p \text{ says } (s)^q & \text{otherwise} \end{cases}$$
$$(X)^q = X$$
$$(\forall X. s)^q = \forall X. (s)^q$$

Fig. 3. Definition of $(s)^q$

Theorem 1. *In CDD, for every typing environment Γ, formula s, and principal q, if $\Gamma \vdash e : s$ then there exists e' such that $(\Gamma)^q \vdash e' : (s)^q$.*

As a special case, we derive the following corollary from the theorem:

Corollary 1. *In CDD, for every formula s and principal q, if $\vdash s$ then $\vdash (s)^q$.*

For example, Corollary 1 says that if $q \neq p$, then

$$\vdash (q \text{ says } t) \rightarrow (p \text{ says false})$$

implies

$$\vdash \text{true} \rightarrow (p \text{ says false})$$

and therefore

$$\vdash p \text{ says false}$$

Via a simple translation to System F, we can prove that this judgment is not derivable in CDD, so we conclude that

$$\vdash (q \text{ says } t) \rightarrow (p \text{ says false})$$

is not derivable in CDD either. Thus, no matter what q says, p does not say false.

Such non-interference results are not unique to CDD. Analogous theorems hold for other logics for access control. In fact, one might be inclined to regard with some suspicion a logic for which an analogous theorem does not hold.

6   Relating Axioms

Perhaps because intuitive explanations of says are invariably loose and open-ended, the exact properties that says should satisfy do not seem obvious, as indicated in Section 3. The goal of this section is to explore the formal consequences and the security interpretations of several possible axiomatizations, and thus to help in identifying logics that are sufficiently strong but not inconsistent, degenerate, or otherwise unreasonable.

Some of the axioms that we consider are those of Section 4, which come from modal logic, computational lambda calculus, and other standard formal systems. Other axioms stem from ideas in security, such as delegations of authority and the Principle of Least Privilege [57]. For instance, we consider the hand-off axiom, which says that if p says that q speaks for p, then q does speak for p [43]. We evaluate these axioms in both classical and intuitionistic contexts.

More specifically, we start with the basic axioms of standard modal logic, in particular that says is closed under consequence, together with the necessitation rule. In addition, the axioms that we consider include the following:

1. The hand-off axiom, as described above, and a generalization: if p says that s_1 implies p says s_2, then s_1 does imply p says s_2. In the special case where s_1 is q says s_2, we obtain a hand-off from p to q for s_2.
2. A further axiom that if p can make itself speak for q, then p speaks for q in the first place. This axiom may be seen roughly as a dual to the hand-off axiom.

3. The axiom that s implies p `says` s (Unit). As indicated in Section 3, this axiom is similar to the necessitation rule but stronger. It is also suggested by the computational lambda calculus.

4. The other main axiom from the computational lambda calculus (Bind): if s_1 implies p says s_2, then p says s_1 implies p says s_2.

5. The axiom that if p `says` s then s or p `says` `false`. We call this axiom Escalation, because it means that whenever p `says` s, either s is true or p says anything— possibly statements intuitively "much falser" than s.

6. An axiom suggested by the Principle of Least Privilege, roughly that if a principal is trusted on a statement then it is also trusted on weaker statements.

In short, we obtain the following relations between these axioms:

- In classical logics, the addition of axioms beyond the basic ones from modal logic quickly leads to strong and surprising properties that may not be desired. Bind is equivalent to Escalation, while Unit implies Escalation.

   Pictorially, we have:

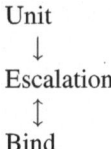

   Some milder, reasonable additions do not lead to Escalation. For instance, we may require the standard axiom C4 from modal logic (if p says p says s then p says s) without obtaining Escalation. Unfortunately, those additions do not always suffice in applications.

- In intuitionistic logics, we have a little more freedom. In particular, CDD (which includes Unit and Bind) does not lead to Escalation.

   Pictorially, we have:

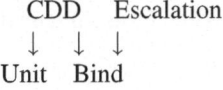

   Many further refinements become possible, in particular because Escalation and Unit are independent intuitionistically.

- The general form of the hand-off axiom (1) is equivalent to Bind.

- Unit implies axiom (2). This axiom is equivalent to Unit if there is a truth-telling principal.

- Finally, Escalation implies axiom (6). Conversely, this axiom and C4 imply Escalation.

Next we elaborate on these relations between the axioms. Sections 6.1 and 6.2 focus on CDD, considering axioms (1), (2), (3), and (4). Section 6.3 focuses on Escalation (axiom (5)). Section 6.4 considers axiom (6).

6.1 C4

As noted in Section 4.3, CDD amounts to adding the axioms Unit and Bind to the basic intuitionistic logic of Section 4.2. We can replace Bind with the simpler C4 when we have Unit. Formally, C4 is:

$$[C4]\quad \forall X.\, (p \text{ says } p \text{ says } X \to p \text{ says } X)$$

We obtain:

Proposition 1. *Starting from the basic logic (without Excluded-middle), we have:*

1. *Bind implies C4;*
2. *Unit and C4 (together) imply Bind;*
3. *C4 does not imply Bind;*
4. *Unit does not imply C4 (and a fortiori not Bind).*

Assuming Excluded-middle, we have:

1. *C4 implies neither Bind nor Unit.;*
2. *Unit implies C4 (and therefore Bind);*
3. *Bind does not imply Unit.*

6.2 Hand-Off

The hand-off axiom is:

$$[\textit{Hand-off}]\quad p \text{ controls } (q \Rightarrow p)$$

In the basic logic, this axiom is not a theorem. Therefore, some examples and applications that require hand-off do not immediately work. For instance, in the example of Section 2, `deleteFile1` does not follow from `Bob says (Alice ⇒ Bob)` and `Alice says deleteFile1`. The axiom or ad hoc assumptions need to be added for those examples and applications (as in [43]). This need may be regarded as a shortcoming of the basic logic.

On the other hand, in CDD we obtain the hand-off axiom as a theorem. A slight generalization of the hand-off axiom is also interesting and also a theorem:

$$[\textit{Generalized-hand-off}]\quad \forall X, Y.\, p \text{ controls } (X \to p \text{ says } Y)$$

Theorem 2. *Starting from the basic logic, Bind is equivalent to Generalized-hand-off.*

Suppose that a principal p is trusted on whether it speaks for another principal q on every statement. In CDD, it follows that p must speak for q in the first place, whether it says so or not. If p does not wish to speak for q, it should reduce its authority, for instance by adopting an appropriate role [43, Section 6.1]. This result might be seen as a reassuring characterization of who can attribute the right to speak for q; it may also be seen as a dual or a limitation of hand-off in the context of CDD.

More precisely, we define:

$$[\textit{Authority-shortcut}]\quad (\forall X.\, p \text{ controls } (p \text{ says } X \to q \text{ says } X)) \to (p \Rightarrow q)$$

We obtain:

Theorem 3. *Starting from the basic logic, Unit implies Authority-shortcut.*

Next we show the proof of this result. Suppose that, for all X,

$$p \text{ controls } (p \text{ says } X \rightarrow q \text{ says } X)$$

and suppose that, for some particular X, we have $p \text{ says } X$. (The following argument is peculiar in that the assumption $p \text{ says } X$ is exploited twice in different ways.) In order to establish that $p \Rightarrow q$, we wish to derive $q \text{ says } X$. Because $p \text{ says } X$, Unit implies $p \text{ says } q \text{ says } X$. (Here we apply Unit under says.) Then by closure under consequence we have $p \text{ says } (p \text{ says } X \rightarrow q \text{ says } X)$. By our assumption that, for all X, $p \text{ controls } (p \text{ says } X \rightarrow q \text{ says } X)$, we obtain $p \text{ says } X \rightarrow q \text{ says } X$. Combining $p \text{ says } X \rightarrow q \text{ says } X$ with $p \text{ says } X$, we obtain $q \text{ says } X$, as desired.

A small variant of the argument shows that Unit also implies:

$$\forall X. \, ((p \text{ controls } (p \text{ says } X \rightarrow q \text{ says } X)) \rightarrow (p \text{ says } X \rightarrow q \text{ says } X))$$

In other words, writing $p \Rightarrow_X q$ for $p \text{ says } X \rightarrow q \text{ says } X$ [45], we have that Unit implies:

$$\forall X. \, ((p \text{ controls } (p \Rightarrow_X q)) \rightarrow (p \Rightarrow_X q))$$

The converse of Theorem 3 is almost true. Suppose that there is a truth-telling principal p, that is, a principal for which

$$\forall X. \, (X \equiv (p \text{ says } X))$$

Applying Authority-shortcut to this principal, we can derive $s \rightarrow (q \text{ says } s)$ by propositional reasoning, for every q and s. In other words, given such a truth-teller, we obtain Unit.

Nevertheless, the converse of Theorem 3 is not quite true. All basic axioms plus rules, plus Authority-shortcut, hold when we interpret $p \text{ says } s$ as true, for every p and s. Unit does not hold under this interpretation.

In addition, Authority-shortcut does not follow from other axioms (such as Bind), even in classical logic. In other words, Authority-shortcut appears to be very close to Unit, and, if one wishes, it can be avoided by dropping Unit.

6.3   Escalation

As indicated above, Escalation is the following axiom:

$$[Escalation] \quad \forall X, Y. \, ((p \text{ says } X) \rightarrow (X \vee (p \text{ says } Y)))$$

Equivalently, Escalation can be formulated as:

$$\forall X. \, ((p \text{ says } X) \rightarrow (X \vee (p \text{ says false})))$$

Escalation embodies a rather degenerate interpretation of says. At the very least, great care is required when Escalation is assumed. For instance, suppose that two principals p

and q are trusted on s, and that we express this as $(p \text{ controls } s) \wedge (q \text{ controls } s)$; with Escalation, if p says q says s then s follows. Formally, we can derive:

$$(p \text{ controls } s) \wedge (q \text{ controls } s) \rightarrow ((p \text{ says } q \text{ says } s) \rightarrow s)$$

This theorem may be surprising. Its effects may however be avoided: p should not say that q says s unless p wishes to say s. As a result, though, the logic loses flexibility and expressiveness.

On the whole, we consider that Escalation is not a desirable property. Unfortunately, it can follow from the combination of properties that may appear desirable in isolation, as we show.

Theorem 4. *Starting from the basic logic (without Excluded-middle),*

1. *Unit and Bind (together) do not imply Escalation (in other words, Escalation is not a theorem of CDD);*
2. *Escalation implies Bind (and therefore C4).*

Assuming Excluded-middle, we have:

1. *Unit implies Escalation (and therefore Bind);*
2. *Escalation (and a fortiori Bind) does not imply Unit;*
3. *Bind implies Escalation;*
4. *C4 does not imply Escalation.*

Going further, in classical logic Unit implies that each principal p is either a perfect truth-teller or says `false`. In the former case, p speaks for any other principal; in the latter case, any other principal speaks for p. Formally, we can derive:

$$(p \Rightarrow q) \vee (q \Rightarrow p)$$

While this conclusion does not represent a logical contradiction, it severely limits the flexibility and expressiveness of the logic: policies can describe only black-and-white situations. This point is a further illustration of the fact that usefulness degrades even before a logic becomes inconsistent.

6.4   Monotonicity of Controls

The monotonicity of controls means that, if a principal controls a formula X, then it controls every weaker formula Y. Formally, we write:

$$[\textit{Control-monotonicity}] \quad \forall X, Y. \left(\begin{array}{c} (X \rightarrow Y) \\ \rightarrow \\ ((p \text{ controls } X) \rightarrow (p \text{ controls } Y)) \end{array} \right)$$

This monotonicity property may seem attractive. In particular, it may make it easier to comply with the Principle of Least Privilege. This principle says [57]:

> Every program and every user of the system should operate using the least set of privileges necessary to complete the job.

The monotonicity of controls implies that, if p wants to convince a reference monitor of Y, and it can convince it of a stronger property X, then p should be able to state Y directly, rather than the stronger property X. For instance, suppose that Y is the statement that q may access a file f_1, and that X is the statement that q may access both f_1 and another file f_2. When p wishes to allow q to access f_1, it should not have to state also that q may access f_2. The monotonicity of controls allows p to say only that q may access f_1.

Nevertheless, the monotonicity of controls has questionable consequences. Starting from the basic logic (without Excluded-middle), Control-monotonicity implies:

$$(p \text{ controls } s_1) \rightarrow (p \text{ says } s_2) \rightarrow (s_1 \vee s_2)$$

Here, the formulas s_1 and s_2 may be completely unrelated. For instance, suppose that p controls whether q may access a file f_1, and p says that q may access another file f_2; curiously, we obtain that q may access f_1 or q may access f_2.

In fact, the monotonicity of controls is equivalent to Escalation in the presence of C4. (Intuitionistically, C4 is strictly required for this equivalence.)

Theorem 5. *Starting from the basic logic (without Excluded-middle), the following are equivalent:*

- *Escalation,*
- *C4 and Control-monotonicity.*

However, neither Control-monotonicity nor C4 implies the other, not even in combination with Unit.

Assuming Excluded-middle, Control-monotonicity is equivalent to Escalation.

The theorems of this section should not be construed as a criticism of the Principle of Least Privilege. Formulations weaker than Control-monotonicity might be viable and less problematic.

7 Languages

The logics described above have had several applications. In particular, a number of research projects have relied on these logics for designing or explaining various languages and systems, such as virtual machines and operating systems (e.g., [7–9, 11, 12, 19, 20, 25, 41, 43, 46, 58, 60]). They have also influenced the languages that are the subject of this section.

7.1 From Logics to Languages

Languages for access control aim to support the practical expression and the enforcement of policies (e.g., [13, 16, 17, 22, 23, 33, 42, 48, 50, 54, 55, 61, 62]). The languages are general and flexible enough for programming a wide range of policies—for example, in file systems and for digital rights management.

Many of these languages are targeted at distributed systems in which cryptography figures prominently. They serve for expressing the assertions contained in cryptographic credentials, such as the association of a principal with a public key, the membership of a principal in a group, or the right of a principal to perform a certain operation at a specified time. They also serve for combining credentials from many sources with policies, and thus for making authorization decisions. More broadly, the languages sometimes aim to support trust management.

Several of these languages rely on concepts and techniques from logic, specifically from logic programming: D1LP [48], SD3 [42], RT [50], Binder [22], Soutei [54], SecPAL [13], and DKAL [33]. Other languages such as SDSI [55], SPKI [23], and XrML 2.0 [62] include related ideas though typically with less generality. Some of these have been influenced by logical work, but they have not been designed or presented as logical systems. We may however view them as logics, at least in a rudimentary sense. They all define systems of notations for describing principals, their statements, authorizations, and sometimes more. The notations come with rules for combining facts and deriving their consequences—for instance, rules for chaining certificates in public-key infrastructures.

Despite substantial progress, one might still question whether the deployment of these sophisticated languages would reduce the number of ways in which access control can be broken or circumvented. Policies in these languages might be difficult to write and to understand—but probably no worse than policies embodied in Perl scripts and the like, which are often the alternative.

7.2   A Look at Binder

Binder is a good representative for this line of work. It shares many of the goals of other languages and several of their features. It has a clean design, based directly on that of logic-programming languages.

Basically, a Binder program is a set of Prolog-style logical rules. Unlike Prolog, Binder does not allow function symbols; in this respect, Binder is close to the Prolog fragment Datalog. Also unlike Prolog, Binder has a notion of context and a distinguished operator says. For instance, in Binder we can write:

```
may-access(p,o,Rd)  :- good(p)
may-access(p,o,Rd)  :- Bob says may-access(p,o,Rd)
```

These clauses can be read as expressing that any principal p may access any object o in read mode (Rd) if p is good or if Bob says that p may do so.

Here only : - and says have built-in meanings. The other constructs (even the predicate symbol may-access) have to be defined or axiomatized. As in Prolog, : - stands for reverse implication ("if"). For instance,

```
may-access(Alice,Foo.txt,Rd)
```

would follow from these clauses and from

```
Bob says may-access(Alice,Foo.txt,Rd)
```

As in previous logical treatments of access control, says serves for representing the statements of principals and their consequences. Thus,

```
Bob says may-access(Alice,Foo.txt,Rd)
```

holds if there is a statement from Bob that contains a representation of the formula

```
may-access(Alice,Foo.txt,Rd)
```

or it can be derived if there is a statement from Bob that contains a representation of the formula

```
may-access(Alice,Foo.txt,Wr)
```

and another one that contains a representation of the clause

```
may-access(p,o,Rd) :- may-access(p,o,Wr)
```

Each formula is relative to a context (a source of statements). In our example, Bob is a context. Another context is implicit: the local context in which the formulas apply. For example,

```
may-access(p,o,Rd) :- Bob says may-access(p,o,Rd)
```

is to be interpreted in the implicit local context, and Bob is the name for another context from which the local context may import statements.

In addition to logic-programming rules, Binder includes a special proof rule for importing clauses a :- a1, ..., an from one context into another. The rule applies only to clauses where the atom a in the head is not of the form q says s. When importing a clause from context p, the rule replaces a with p says a, and replaces ai with p says ai if ai is not of the form q says s, for i = 1..n. For example, when Charlie exports the clauses:

```
may-access(p,o,Rd) :- good(p)
may-access(p,o,Rd) :- Bob says may-access(p,o,Rd)
```

the local context obtains:

```
Charlie says may-access(p,o,Rd) :- Charlie says good(p)
Charlie says may-access(p,o,Rd) :-
    Bob says may-access(p,o,Rd)
```

This proof rule is complicated enough to call for some logical analysis. It can be partly justified by standard modal logic, in particular via the theorem

$$((p \text{ says } s) \land (p \text{ says } s')) \to p \text{ says } (s \land s')$$

and the axiom of closure under consequence. However, more is needed, even for our example. The proof rule can be derived once we add the strong axiom Unit. In fact, a restricted form of Unit suffices:

$$(q \text{ says } s) \to (p \text{ says } q \text{ says } s)$$

Garg has recently studied the logical foundations of Binder and Soutei, considering this restricted form of Unit [26, 27].

Binder does not assume or require that predicate symbols mean the same in every context. For example, Bob might not even know about may-access, and might assert lecteur(Alice,Foo.txt) instead of may-access(Alice,Foo.txt,Rd). In that situation, one may translate explicitly with the clause:

```
may-access(p,o,Rd)  :- Bob says lecteur(p,o)
```

On the other hand, Binder does not provide much built-in support for local name spaces. A closer look reveals that the names of contexts have global meanings. In particular, when `Charlie` exports:

```
may-access(p,o,Rd)  :- Bob says lecteur(p,o)
```

the local context obtains:

```
Charlie says may-access(p,o,Rd)  :-
    Bob says lecteur(p,o)
```

without any provision for the possibility that `Bob` might not be the same locally and for `Charlie`.

Other systems, such as SDSI and SPKI [23, 55], support more elaborate naming mechanisms, with corresponding logical explanations and problems (e.g., [1, 32, 34, 35, 37, 47]). They enable the linking of name spaces, allowing for the possibility that the intended meaning of a name might not be the same in all contexts.

8 Outlook

Logics for access control have been used in a variety of ways, as indicated in this paper. They have played a helpful role in the design and understanding of languages and systems. Nevertheless, they have not replaced traditional mechanisms for access control, nor is there any prospect that they will in the near future. Although logics can be powerful and general, for each specific application there typically exist special-purpose, expedient alternatives. It is questionable whether the proliferation of those alternatives contributes to security. Still, whether logics should be routinely employed for actual access control (at "compile-time" or "run-time", rather than "design-time" or "understanding-time"), and how they should be employed, remains open to debate.

A great deal of caution should be applied in selecting logics for access control, considering both their formal properties and their security implications. In particular, while in a classical setting we may want to stay close to basic modal logic, in an intuitionistic setting we may adopt CDD. This move may be attractive, in particular, because CDD supports the hand-off of authority. Nevertheless, other logics (for instance, with weaker axioms, or with additional operators) may be reasonable choices as well. We do not argue that the use of a particular set of axioms is required for writing good security policies. It is possible that reasonable security policies and other assertions can be formulated in many different systems, with different underlying logics. However, understanding the properties and consequences of these logics is essential for writing appropriate formulas reliably.

Acknowledgments. I am grateful to Andrew Appel, Mike Burrows, William Cook, John DeTreville, Cédric Fournet, Deepak Garg, Butler Lampson, Dave Langworthy, Greg Morrisett, Roger Needham, and Frank Pfenning for discussions and collaborations that contributed to this paper or to its origins.

References

1. Abadi, M.: On SDSI's linked local name spaces. Journal of Computer Security 6(1-2), 3–21 (1998)
2. Abadi, M.: Logic in access control. In: Proceedings of the Eighteenth Annual IEEE Symposium on Logic in Computer Science, pp. 228–233 (2003)
3. Abadi, M.: Access control in a core calculus of dependency. Electronic Notes in Theoretical Computer Science 172, 5–31 (2007); Computation, Meaning, and Logic: Articles dedicated to Gordon Plotkin
4. Abadi, M.: Variations in access control logic. In: van der Meyden, R., van der Torre, L. (eds.) DEON 2008. LNCS, vol. 5076, pp. 96–109. Springer, Heidelberg (2008)
5. Abadi, M., Banerjee, A., Heintze, N., Riecke, J.G.: A core calculus of dependency. In: Proceedings of the 26th ACM Symposium on Principles of Programming Languages, pp. 147–160 (1999)
6. Abadi, M., Burrows, M., Lampson, B., Plotkin, G.: A calculus for access control in distributed systems. ACM Transactions on Programming Languages and Systems 15(4), 706–734 (1993)
7. Abadi, M., Wobber, T.: A logical account of NGSCB. In: de Frutos-Escrig, D., Núñez, M. (eds.) FORTE 2004. LNCS, vol. 3235, pp. 1–12. Springer, Heidelberg (2004)
8. Appel, A.W., Felten, E.W.: Proof-carrying authentication. In: Proceedings of the 6th ACM Conference on Computer and Communications Security, pp. 52–62 (1999)
9. Bauer, L.: Access Control for the Web via Proof-Carrying Authorization. PhD thesis. Princeton University, Princeton (November 2003)
10. Bauer, L., Cranor, L., Reeder, R.W., Reiter, M.K., Vaniea, K.: A user study of policy creation in a flexible access-control system. In: CHI 2008: Conference on Human Factors in Computing Systems, pp. 543–552 (2008)
11. Bauer, L., Garriss, S., McCune, J.M., Reiter, M.K., Rouse, J., Rutenbar, P.: Device-enabled authorization in the grey system. In: Zhou, J., López, J., Deng, R.H., Bao, F. (eds.) ISC 2005. LNCS, vol. 3650, pp. 431–445. Springer, Heidelberg (2005)
12. Bauer, L., Garriss, S., Reiter, M.K.: Distributed proving in access-control systems. In: Proceedings of the 2005 Symposium on Security and Privacy, pp. 81–95 (2005)
13. Becker, M.Y., Fournet, C., Gordon, A.D.: Design and semantics of a decentralized authorization language. In: Proceedings of the 20th IEEE Computer Security Foundations Symposium, pp. 3–15 (2007)
14. Benton, P.N., Bierman, G.M., de Paiva, V.C.V.: Computational types from a logical perspective. Journal of Functional Programming 8(2), 177–193 (1998)
15. Bertino, E., Catania, B., Ferrari, E., Perlasca, P.: A logical framework for reasoning about access control models. ACM Transactions on Information and System Security 6(1), 71–127 (2003)
16. Blaze, M., Feigenbaum, J., Ioannidis, J., Keromytis, A.D.: The KeyNote trust-management system, version 2. IETF RFC 2704 (September 1999)
17. Blaze, M., Feigenbaum, J., Lacy, J.: Decentralized trust management. In: Proceedings 1996 IEEE Symposium on Security and Privacy, pp. 164–173 (1996)
18. Cardelli, L.: Type systems. In: Tucker, A.B. (ed.) The Computer Science and Engineering Handbook, ch. 103, pp. 2208–2236. CRC Press, Boca Raton (1997)
19. Cederquist, J.G., Corin, R., Dekker, M.A.C., Etalle, S., den Hartog, J.I., Lenzini, G.: Audit-based compliance control. Int. J. Inf. Secur. 6(2), 133–151 (2007)
20. Cirillo, A., Jagadeesan, R., Pitcher, C., Riely, J.: Do as I SaY! programmatic access control with explicit identities. In: Proceedings of the 20th IEEE Computer Security Foundations Symposium, pp. 16–30 (2007)

21. Crampton, J., Loizou, G., O'Shea, G.: A logic of access control. The Computer Journal 44(2), 137–149 (2001)
22. DeTreville, J.: Binder, a logic-based security language. In: Proceedings of the 2002 IEEE Symposium on Security and Privacy, pp. 105–113 (2002)
23. Ellison, C., Frantz, B., Lampson, B., Rivest, R., Thomas, B., Ylönen, T.: SPKI certificate theory. IETF RFC 2693 (September 1999)
24. Fairtlough, M., Mendler, M.V.: Propositional lax logic. Information and Computation 137(1), 1–33 (1997)
25. Fournet, C., Gordon, A.D., Maffeis, S.: A type discipline for authorization in distributed systems. In: Proceedings of the 20th IEEE Computer Security Foundations Symposium, pp. 31–45 (2007)
26. Garg, D.: Principal-centric reasoning in constructive authorization logic. Technical Report CMU-CS-09-120, Computer Science Department, Carnegie Mellon University (April 2009)
27. Garg, D.: Proof search in an authorization logic. Technical Report CMU-CS-09-121, Computer Science Department, Carnegie Mellon University (April 2009)
28. Garg, D., Abadi, M.: A modal deconstruction of access control logics. In: Amadio, R.M. (ed.) FOSSACS 2008. LNCS, vol. 4962, pp. 216–230. Springer, Heidelberg (2008)
29. Garg, D., Pfenning, F.: Non-interference in constructive authorization logic. In: Proceedings of the 19th IEEE Computer Security Foundations Workshop, pp. 283–296 (2006)
30. Gasser, M., Goldstein, A., Kaufman, C., Lampson, B.: The Digital Distributed System Security Architecture. In: Proceedings of the 1989 National Computer Security Conference, pp. 305–319 (1989)
31. Girard, J.-Y.: Interprétation Fonctionnelle et Elimination des Coupures de l'Arithmétique d'Ordre Supérieur. Thèse de doctorat d'état, Université Paris VII (June 1972)
32. Grove, A.J., Halpern, J.Y.: Naming and identity in epistemic logics, I: The propositional case. Journal of Logic and Computation 3(4), 345–378 (1993)
33. Gurevich, Y., Neeman, I.: DKAL: Distributed-knowledge authorization language. In: Proceedings of the 21st IEEE Computer Security Foundations Symposium, pp. 149–162 (2008)
34. Halpern, J.Y., van der Meyden, R.: A logic for SDSI's linked local name spaces. Journal of Computer Security 9(1-2), 47–74 (2001)
35. Halpern, J.Y., van der Meyden, R.: A logical reconstruction of SPKI. In: Proceedings of the 14th IEEE Computer Security Foundations Workshop, pp. 59–72 (2001)
36. Harrison, M.A., Ruzzo, W.L., Ullman, J.D.: Protection in operating systems. Communications of the ACM 19(8), 461–471 (1976)
37. Howell, J., Kotz, D.: A formal semantics for SPKI. In: Cuppens, F., Deswarte, Y., Gollmann, D., Waidner, M. (eds.) ESORICS 2000. LNCS, vol. 1895, pp. 140–158. Springer, Heidelberg (2000)
38. Hughes, G.E., Cresswell, M.J.: An Introduction to Modal Logic. Methuen Inc., New York (1968)
39. Jajodia, S., Samarati, P., Subrahmanian, V.S.: A logical language for expressing authorizations. In: Proceedings of the 1997 IEEE Symposium on Security and Privacy, pp. 31–42 (1997)
40. Jajodia, S., Samarati, P., Subrahmanian, V.S., Bertino, E.: A unified framework for enforcing multiple access control policies. In: Proceedings of the ACM SIGMOD International Conference on Management of Data. SIGMOD Record, vol. 26(2), pp. 474–485 (1997)
41. Jia, L., Vaughan, J.A., Mazurak, K., Zhao, J., Zarko, L., Schorr, J., Zdancewic, S.: Aura: A programming language for authorization and audit. In: Proceedings of the 13th ACM SIGPLAN International Conference on Functional Programming, pp. 27–38 (2008)
42. Jim, T.: SD3: A trust management system with certified evaluation. In: Proceedings of the 2001 IEEE Symposium on Security and Privacy, pp. 106–115 (2001)

43. Lampson, B., Abadi, M., Burrows, M., Wobber, E.: Authentication in distributed systems: Theory and practice. ACM Transactions on Computer Systems 10(4), 265–310 (1992)
44. Lampson, B.W.: Protection. In: Proceedings of the 5th Princeton Conference on Information Sciences and Systems, pp. 437–443 (1971)
45. Lampson, B.W.: Computer security in the real world. IEEE Computer 37(6), 37–46 (2004)
46. Lesniewski-Laas, C., Ford, B., Strauss, J., Frans Kaashoek, M., Morris, R.: Alpaca: extensible authorization for distributed services. In: Proceedings of the 14th ACM Conference on Computer and Communications Security, pp. 432–444 (2007)
47. Li, N.: Local names in SPKI/SDSI. In: Proceedings of the 13th IEEE Computer Security Foundations Workshop, July 2000, pp. 2–15 (2000)
48. Li, N., Grosof, B.N., Feigenbaum: Delegation logic: A logic-based approach to distributed authorization. ACM Transactions on Information and System Security 6(1), 128–171 (2003)
49. Li, N., Mitchell, J.C.: DATALOG with constraints: A foundation for trust management languages. In: Dahl, V., Wadler, P. (eds.) PADL 2003. LNCS, vol. 2562, pp. 58–73. Springer, Heidelberg (2002)
50. Li, N., Mitchell, J.C., Winsborough, W.H.: Design of a role-based trust-management framework. In: Proceedings of the 2002 IEEE Symposium on Security and Privacy, pp. 114–130 (2002)
51. Li, N., Mitchell, J.C., Winsborough, W.H.: Beyond proof-of-compliance: security analysis in trust management. J. ACM 52(3), 474–514 (2005)
52. Moggi, E.: Notions of computation and monads. Information and Control 93(1), 55–92 (1991)
53. Necula, G.C.: Proof-carrying code. In: Proceedings of the 24th ACM Symposium on Principles of Programming Languages, pp. 106–119 (1997)
54. Pimlott, A., Kiselyov, O.: Soutei, a logic-based trust-management system. In: Hagiya, M., Wadler, P. (eds.) FLOPS 2006. LNCS, vol. 3945, pp. 130–145. Springer, Heidelberg (2006)
55. Rivest, R.L., Lampson, B.: SDSI — A Simple Distributed Security Infrastructure (1996), http://theory.lcs.mit.edu/~cis/sdsi.html
56. Rushby, J.: Design and verification of secure systems. In: Proceedings of the 8th ACM Symposium on Operating System Principles. ACM Operating Systems Review 15(5), 12–21 (1981)
57. Saltzer, J.H., Schroeder, M.D.: The protection of information in computer system. Proceedings of the IEEE 63(9), 1278–1308 (1975)
58. Vaughan, J.A., Jia, L., Mazurak, K., Zdancewic, S.: Evidence-based audit. In: Proceedings of the 21st IEEE Computer Security Foundations Symposium, pp. 177–191 (2008)
59. Whitehead, N.: A certified distributed security logic for authorizing code. In: Altenkirch, T., McBride, C. (eds.) TYPES 2006. LNCS, vol. 4502, pp. 253–268. Springer, Heidelberg (2007)
60. Wobber, E., Abadi, M., Burrows, M., Lampson, B.: Authentication in the Taos operating system. ACM Transactions on Computer Systems 12(1), 3–32 (1994)
61. eXtensible Access Control Markup Language (XACML) version 1.0. OASIS Standard (2003), http://www.oasis-open.org/committees/xacml/repository/
62. eXtensible Rights Markup Language (XrML) version 2.0, http://www.xrml.org/
63. Zhou, W., Mao, Y., Loo, B.T., Abadi, M.: Unified declarative platform for secure networked information systems. In: Proceedings of the 25th International Conference on Data Engineering, pp. 150–161 (2009)

The Open-Source Fixed-Point Model Checker for Symbolic Analysis of Security Protocols

Sebastian Mödersheim[1] and Luca Viganò[2]

[1] IBM Zurich Research Laboratory, Switzerland
smo@zurich.ibm.com
[2] Department of Computer Science, University of Verona, Italy
luca.vigano@univr.it

Abstract. We introduce the Open-source Fixed-point Model Checker OFMC for symbolic security protocol analysis, which extends the On-the-fly Model Checker (the previous OFMC). The native input language of OFMC is the AVISPA Intermediate Format IF. OFMC also supports AnB, a new Alice-and-Bob-style language that extends previous similar languages with support for algebraic properties of cryptographic operators and with a simple notation for different kinds of channels that can be used both as assumptions and as protocol goals. AnB specifications are automatically translated to IF.

OFMC performs both protocol falsification and bounded session verification by exploring, in a demand-driven way, the transition system resulting from an IF specification. OFMC's effectiveness is due to the integration of a number of symbolic, constraint-based techniques, which are correct and terminating. The two major techniques are the lazy intruder, which is a symbolic representation of the intruder, and constraint differentiation, which is a general search-reduction technique that integrates the lazy intruder with ideas from partial-order reduction. Moreover, OFMC allows one to analyze security protocols with respect to an algebraic theory of the employed cryptographic operators, which can be specified as part of the input. We also sketch the ongoing integration of fixed-point-based techniques for protocol verification for an unbounded number of sessions.

1 Introduction

The automated analysis of security protocols is a field in the intersection of formal methods and IT security that has been intensively studied during the last 20 years, e.g. [1,2,4,5,6,13,15,18,20,21,24,25,27,29,37,43,49,51,53,59,61,62,63]. The Open Source Fixed-point Model Checker OFMC, the successor of the On-the-Fly Model-Checker [12,54,58], is a freely available[1] tool that integrates the most successful techniques of this field. In this paper, we summarize its main modeling and verification techniques, pointing to the corresponding publications where the formal details and proofs can be found.

---

[1] OFMC is available at www.avantssar.eu together with the other back-ends of the AVISPA Tool and of the AVANTSSAR Platform.

A. Aldini, G. Barthe, R. Gorrieri (Eds.): FOSAD 2007/2008/2009, LNCS 5705, pp. 166–194, 2009.
© Springer-Verlag Berlin Heidelberg 2009

The "native" input language of OFMC is the *AVISPA Intermediate Format IF* [7,12,54], which describes a security protocol as an infinite-state transition system using set-rewriting. OFMC also supports a simple and intuitive Alice-and-Bob-style language: *AnB* [56,57]. AnB specifications are automatically translated to IF—this translation defines a formal semantics for AnB in terms of IF. With respect to previous similar languages, AnB supports the specification of protocols that can only be executed correctly when taking the algebraic properties of cryptographic operators into account. For instance, protocols based on the Diffie-Hellman key exchange only make sense in a model where $g^{xy} \approx g^{yx}$.

Moreover, AnB allows one to specify properties of channels used for the transmission of protocol messages, namely authentic, confidential and secure channels [57]. We can specify channels both

- *as assumptions*, i.e. when a protocol relies on channels with particular properties for the transmission of some of its messages, and
- *as goals*, i.e. when a protocol is supposed to establish a certain kind of channel.

This gives rise to an interesting question: given that we have verified that a protocol P_2 provides its goals under the assumption of a particular kind of channel, can we then replace the assumed channel with an arbitrary protocol P_1 that provides such a channel? In general, the answer is negative, while we have proved in [57] that under certain restrictions such a compositionality result is possible. We also have generalized all our results to channels where agents may be identified by pseudonyms rather than by their real names.

OFMC performs both protocol falsification (i.e. detecting attacks) and bounded session verification by exploring, in a demand-driven way, the transition system resulting from an IF specification. OFMC's effectiveness is due to the integration of a number of symbolic, constraint-based techniques, which are correct and terminating. The two major techniques are the

- *lazy intruder* [12], which is a symbolic representation of the intruder, and
- *constraint differentiation* [58], which is a general search-reduction technique that integrates the lazy intruder with ideas from partial-order reduction.

Both techniques significantly reduce the search space associated to a given protocol specification without excluding attacks (or introducing new ones).

Moreover, OFMC allows one to analyze security protocols with respect to an algebraic theory of the employed cryptographic operators, which can be specified as part of the input [11]. We also sketch the ongoing integration of fixed-point-based techniques for protocol verification for an unbounded number of sessions [55].

We proceed as follows. In Section 2, we summarize the input languages AnB and IF, introducing a running example, and describe our standard protocol model in the presence of an active intruder. In Section 3, we introduce the constraint-based analysis techniques, and we then summarize our ongoing work

Protocol : *Authenticated Diffie-Hellman key exchange*
Types :
  Agent A, B;
  Number g, X, Y, Msg;
Knowledge :
  A : A, B, g;
  B : B, g;
Actions :
  $A \bullet\!\!\rightarrow B : \exp(g, X)$
  $B \bullet\!\!\rightarrow A : \exp(g, Y)$
  $A \rightarrow B : \{\!|A, Msg|\!\}_{\exp(\exp(g,X),Y)}$
Goals :
  $A \bullet\!\!\rightarrow\!\!\bullet B : Msg$

Fig. 1. AnB specification of an authenticated Diffie-Hellman key exchange

on integrating over-approximation techniques in Section 4. In Section 5, we report on experimental results and focus on a major example protocol that we have analyzed with OFMC. We conclude, in Section 6, with an outlook on future work.

2   Input Languages and Modeling

In this section, we discuss the specification languages on which OFMC is based and how one can employ them to model security protocols and their properties. We first present AnB (Section 2.1) and then the AVISPA Intermediate Format IF (Section 2.2), to which AnB is internally translated (Section 2.3).

2.1   AnB

A simple and intuitive way to describe security protocols is to use the *Alice and Bob* notation, which describes how messages are exchanged between honest agents acting in the different protocol roles. This popular notation is usually used informally, but there are several formal protocol specification languages based on the Alice and Bob notation, e.g. [7,32,46,49,52,56]. We give an overview of the most advanced one here, called *AnB* [56,57].

The novel features of AnB are its support for protocols that require algebraic properties for the protocol execution, as well as a notion of several types of communication channels that can be used both as assumptions and as goals of a protocol. AnB is one of the specification languages that OFMC accepts as input. The semantics of AnB is formally defined by translation to the more low-level specification language *AVISPA Intermediate Format IF* [7]. IF is more expressive than AnB, but harder to use. It is, however, well suited for formal analysis tools such as OFMC and the other back-ends of the AVISPA Tool [5].

Fig. 1 shows a simple example protocol in AnB; we will use this protocol, which is based on the Diffie-Hellman key exchange, as a running example throughout the paper. An AnB specification comprises of 5 sections. We first state the name of the protocol and then declare the type of each identifier of the protocol specification; this is needed in the translation to IF, although OFMC can optionally ignore the types during analysis so to detect type-flaw attacks. We distinguish two kinds of identifiers, using a naming convention similar to Prolog: identifiers starting with an upper-case letter are called *protocol variables* and are instantiated during the protocol execution, whereas identifiers starting with a lower-case letter represent global constants and functions. Protocol variables of type `Agent` are called *roles*. In our example, we have the roles A and B, which get instantiated by arbitrary agents when executing the protocol. The numbers g, X, and Y are the group and the random exponents used in the Diffie-Hellman key exchange.

The next section of an AnB specification describes the initial knowledge attached to each role. We require that all variables that occur in the initial knowledge section are of type `Agent`. They will later be instantiated arbitrarily with agent names. The initial knowledge is essential for the semantics, as the way honest agents can construct the messages of the protocol depends on it. Variables that do not occur in the initial knowledge of any role represent values that are freshly created by the agent who first uses them.[2] In the example, X and *Msg* are created by A and Y is created by B.

The core of the specification is the list of exchanged messages, which describes the ideal protocol run without interference from the intruder. Every action in the list is of the form $A \to B : M$, meaning that the agent in the role A sends the message M to the agent in the role B. Additionally, we employ the "bullet" ("•") notation from [50] to denote that we have a channel that ensures the identity of the respective end-point. This gives rise to the following four kinds of channels.

- *Insecure channel*: $A \to B : M$ represents an insecure channel from A to B. Insecure channels are controlled by the intruder, i.e. he can read all messages and insert messages under any sender name.
- *Authentic channel*: $A \bullet\!\to B : M$ represents an authentic channel from A to B. This means that B can rely on that fact that A has sent the message M and that A's intention was to send it to B. There is, however, no guarantee of confidentiality, i.e. anybody may see M.
- *Confidential channel*: $A \to\!\bullet B : M$. This means that A can rely on that fact that only B can see the message M. There is, however, no guarantee of authenticity, i.e. anybody could have sent M.
- *Secure Channel*: $A \bullet\!\to\!\bullet B : M$. This is a channel that is both authentic and confidential.

The behavior of channels is described more formally in Section 2.4.

---

[2] As a consequence, all long-term keys in the initial knowledge need to be represented as functions of agent names; for instance, one may use $sk(A, B)$ as the shared key of A and B.

In the running example, A and B generate random values X and Y and exchange the Diffie-Hellman *half keys* $\exp(g, X)$ and $\exp(g, Y)$ over authentic channels; we omit the modulus in our notation for simplicity. The final message is a pair (denoted simply by ",") consisting of A's name and a payload message *Msg* (modeled as a random number). The pair is encrypted symmetrically using the new, agreed-upon Diffie-Hellman key $\exp(\exp(g, X), Y)$, where we use $\{\!| \cdot |\!\}$ to denote symmetric encryption.

Readers unfamiliar with the Diffie-Hellman key exchange may wonder how A can actually construct this key. In fact, this is one of the main problems of previous Alice-and-Bob-style languages: the interpretation of protocols that are based on algebraic properties of the employed cryptographic operators. In AnB, this problem is solved generically with respect to arbitrary algebraic theories.[3] In this example, A knows X, which she generated herself, and $\exp(g, Y)$, which she received from B. She can thus generate $\exp(\exp(g, Y), X)$, which is equal to $\exp(\exp(g, X), Y)$ under the laws of exponentiation. The equations characterizing exponentiation are thus critical, since if we do not take them into account, then the protocol cannot even be "executed": it is unclear what an honest A should do to form the final message of the protocol. We return to this in more detail below. We assume throughout the paper a given algebraic theory defined by a set of equations and we interpret terms in the *quotient algebra* induced by these equations (see [10], for instance): intuitively, two terms are equal, denoted by $s \approx t$, iff this is a consequence of the algebraic equations.

In the final section of an AnB specification, we specify the goals that the protocol is supposed to achieve, in this case the goal that the payload message is transmitted over a secure channel from A to B. We may thus rephrase this protocol and its goal as follows: the Diffie-Hellman key exchange allows us to obtain a secure channel out of authentic channels. We have a similar setup in TLS/SSL, for instance, but we have selected the Diffie-Hellman example for brevity.

2.2   IF

We now give an overview of the AVISPA Intermediate Format IF [7], the "native" language of OFMC, and then sketch how AnB is translated into IF. IF can be considered as a kind of assembly language, because it is a low-level technical language. While it is not simple for human users to specify complex protocols in such a language, it is well-suited for automated tools as it describes the behavior of honest and dishonest agents unambiguously.

An *IF specification* $P = (I, R, G)$ consists of an *initial state I, a set R of rules* that induces a transition relation on states, and a *set G of "attack rules"* (i.e. *goals*) that specify which states count as attack states. The verification question is then whether an attack state is reachable from an initial state: as expected, a protocol is called *safe* when no attack state is reachable from the initial state using the transition relation. The transition system induced by I

---

[3] The implementation currently supports exponentiation and exclusive or.

and R usually has an infinite number of states and the verification question is in general undecidable [35,36].

Terms and States. In IF, we distinguish two kinds of terms. First, we have *message terms* as we have them in AnB, with the same convention that constants start with a lower-case letter and variables with an upper-case letter.[4] On top of that, we have *facts*, which are built using distinguished function symbols and have message terms as arguments. For instance, $\mathsf{iknows}(m)$ denotes the fact that the intruder knows the message m, and $\mathsf{state}_{\mathcal{R}}(m_1, \ldots, m_k)$ is the fact that an agent has reached a local state of its execution that is characterized by the list of messages $m_1, \ldots, m_k$; this list usually consists of the agent's initial knowledge as well as previously sent and received messages. The additional parameter $\mathcal{R}$ represents the protocol role that the agent is playing (we denote all roles with calligraphic letters). Despite the upper-case convention, the role names like $\mathcal{R}$ are constants. Such constants do not appear in the AnB specification, where we have variables like A and B to denote the roles. In IF states, however, these variables will be instantiated with concrete agent names like a and b. In order to specify the role names, we thus need to distinguish in IF between variables that will hold the concrete agent names and constant identifiers for the roles that will not be instantiated. We will later introduce further fact symbols.

An *IF state* is a set of facts, separated by dots ("."). We call a term *ground* when it does not contain variables, and an IF state is ground when all of its terms are. The transition system defined by an IF specification consists of only ground states: the initial state is ground and transitions (as we will define them below) cannot introduce variables. Later on, however, we will also consider symbolic techniques that deal with non-ground states.

Initialization. In general, the security of a protocol should be defined based on an arbitrary number of agents who can execute an arbitrary number of sessions in any role of the protocol in parallel. Often, however, we consider only a fixed, bounded number of sessions, which implies also a bound on the number of agents who can participate. We can specify this directly, by concrete initial local states of honest agents, e.g. writing

$$\mathsf{state}_{\mathcal{A}}(a, 0, id17)$$

to represent an honest agent a playing role $\mathcal{A}$ at the beginning of the protocol execution (step 0), and with a unique identifier (to allow for several parallel sessions). We will later also allow that instead of the constant a, we may have a variable A (of type `Agent`) that can be instantiated by any agent name. This enables us to specify abstractly a number of sessions without enumerating concrete instances.

---

[4] In the concrete syntax of IF, some notation like $\{\!|m|\!\}_k$ is replaced by prefix symbols such as $\mathsf{scrypt}(k, m)$, but, for readability, we will use the pretty notation in this paper anyway.

The initial state also contains the initial knowledge of the intruder in form of iknows(m) facts for every "public" information m such as public keys, public constants, and also usually the names of all agents. Moreover, the intruder should be able to participate in sessions like any other agent, and therefore may have appropriate keys, e.g. public and private keys as well as symmetric keys shared with other agents.

Transition Rules. We consider here IF transition rules of the following form:[5]

$$L \mid EQ =\![V]\!\Rightarrow R$$

where L and R are sets of facts, EQ is a set of equations on terms, and V is a list of variables that do not occur in L or EQ; moreover, R may only contain variables that also occur in L, EQ or V. The semantics of this rule is defined by the state transitions it allows: we can get from a state S to a state S' with this rule iff there is a substitution σ of all rule variables such that

- $L\sigma \subseteq S$,
- $S' = (S \setminus L\sigma) \cup R\sigma$,
- $V\sigma$ are fresh constants (that do not appear in S), and
- all equations of EQ are satisfied under σ.

All equalities between terms/facts are modulo the considered algebra. The conditions on the variables ensure that S' is ground whenever S is.

As an example, consider the rule:

$$\mathsf{iknows}(\{\!|M|\!\}_K).\mathsf{iknows}(K) \Rightarrow \mathsf{iknows}(M).\mathsf{iknows}(\{\!|M|\!\}_K).\mathsf{iknows}(K)\ .$$

This allows the intruder to deduce the plaintext M of a symmetrically encrypted message $\{\!|M|\!\}_K$ whenever he knows the corresponding key K. Observe that the left-hand side facts are repeated on the right-hand side as otherwise the matched instances would get removed during the transition and thus the intruder would "forget" the encrypted message and the key, which, of course, we do not want. As it is safe to assume that the intruder never forgets any message, we allow the simplification that the iknows($\cdot$) facts are *persistent*, i.e. no iknows($\cdot$) fact gets removed during transitions so we do not explicitly need to repeat it on the right-hand side. Thus, we can simplify the previous rule to

$$\mathsf{iknows}(\{\!|M|\!\}_K).\mathsf{iknows}(K) \Rightarrow \mathsf{iknows}(M)\ .$$

Moreover, we can describe the corresponding symmetric encryption rule of the intruder simply as:

$$\mathsf{iknows}(M).\mathsf{iknows}(K) \Rightarrow \{\!|M|\!\}_K\ .$$

---

[5] We have here simplified the form of the rules for the ease of presentation; in [7,54] rules may contain further conditions about the inequality of terms and negative facts, which we do not need for the examples in this paper.

This rule alone produces an infinite state transition system, because the intruder can arbitrarily encrypt messages he knows ad infinitum. It is thus a particular challenge to analyze protocols in the presence of such an infinitary intruder model without excluding attacks. Note that the IF does not prescribe an intruder model—the user may specify any set of such rules—but the analysis techniques we will introduce later constrain the class of intruder models that can be considered.

The IF allows us to specify a wide variety of intruder models by giving a set of intruder deduction rules (in the style of Dolev and Yao [34]) that formalize how he can compose and decompose messages, as in the above example transitions. We slightly generalize standard intruder models in which the intruder acts only under one identity i: in our model, the intruder may have several names that he controls, in the sense that he has the necessary long-term keys to actually work under a particular name. This reflects a large number of situations, like an honest agent who has been compromised and whose long-term keys have been learned by the intruder, or when there are several dishonest agents who all collaborate. This worst case of a collaboration of all dishonest agents is simply modeled by one intruder who acts under different identities. We thus simply assume that dishonest(A) holds for any dishonest agent name A in the initial state (i.e. only for $A = i$ in the classical intruder model). In general, we can allow IF rules that model the compromise of an agent A or the creation of a new dishonest identity A, where we have the predicate dishonest(A) on the right-hand side. We also have a predicate honest(A) and we ensure that for every agent A either honest(A) or dishonest(A) holds.

Goals. We describe the goals of a protocol by *attack states*, i.e. states that violate the goals, which are in turn described by *attack rules*. That is, in IF we describe attack states by means of rules without a right-hand side: a state at which the attack rule can fire is thus an attack state.

We give an example for the common *secrecy* goal. To that end, assume that the transition rules contain the fact secret(M, B) whenever an honest agent A generates a message M that is supposed to be secret with another, not necessarily honest, agent B. Thus, it is an attack if the intruder finds out M but B is honest:

$$\text{secret}(M, B).\text{iknows}(M).\text{honest}(B)$$

We can define other standard goals like *authentication* in a similar way; see [57] for an overview.

2.3   From AnB to IF

The core of the translation from AnB to IF, i.e. the AnB semantics, is to define a "program" for each role of the protocol. This is described in IF by rules of the form

$$\mathsf{state}_{\mathcal{R}}(m_0, \ldots, m_k).\mathsf{iknows}(m_{k+1})$$
$$=\!\!|V|\!\!\Rightarrow$$
$$\mathsf{state}_{\mathcal{R}}(m_0, \ldots, m_{k+2}, V).\mathsf{iknows}(m_{k+2})$$

where m_0 is the initial knowledge of role $\mathcal{R}$, $m_1, \ldots, m_k$ is the sequence of messages that $\mathcal{R}$ has sent and received so far, m_{k+1} is the message that $\mathcal{R}$ receives in this transition, m_{k+2} is the message that $\mathcal{R}$ replies with, and V is the set of fresh variables in m_{k+2}. This rule is applicable whenever an agent playing the role $\mathcal{R}$ is in an appropriate state and receives an appropriate message from the intruder. This reflects an optimization for the case of insecure channels: we can identify intruder and network for insecure channels (that are controlled by the intruder, see [54] for a soundness proof). If[6] we apply the rule, then the agent creates the new variables V and sends the outgoing message m_{k+2} to the "network", and also updates its local state by the received message and the sent one, and by the fresh variables. In the case of the first or the last message of the protocol, the incoming or outgoing message is omitted in the rule.

Example 1. According to this schema, the IF transition rules of A for the AnB example in Fig. 1 are as follows—ignoring the authentic channels for now:

$$\mathsf{state}_A(A, B, g)$$
$$=\!\!|X|\!\!\Rightarrow$$
$$\mathsf{state}_A(A, B, g, \exp(g, X), X).\mathsf{iknows}(\exp(g, X))$$

$$\mathsf{state}_A(A, B, g, \exp(g, X), X).\mathsf{iknows}(\exp(g, Y))$$
$$=\!\!|Msg|\!\!\Rightarrow$$
$$\mathsf{state}_A(\ldots).\mathsf{iknows}(\{\!|A, Msg|\!\}_{\exp(\exp(g,X),Y)})$$

$\square$

This demonstrates the weak points of this naive schema (that reflects the state-of-the art in the previous Alice-and-Bob-style languages): in the second transition, A will accept only messages of the form $\exp(g, Y)$, while in reality, nobody can check this for an unknown Y. In fact, A should accept any incoming message GY here and build the Diffie-Hellman key for the outgoing message as $\exp(GY, X)$. We now sketch how such a translation is computed in general, in particular the appropriate check of incoming messages and the correct construction of outgoing messages.

Two Views. The above example shows that agents are often unable to check that messages have exactly the structure that the protocol demands. To reason about this correctly, our translation from AnB to IF represents all messages from two kinds of *views* m^d, where m is the format that the message is supposed to have according to the protocol (the first view) and d is what is visible to the agent in question (the second view). For the second view, we introduce a new

---

[6] There is nothing that forces us to execute such a rule when it is enabled.

set of variables $\mathcal{X}_1, \mathcal{X}_2, \ldots$; these variables are used to label (parts of) messages of which the agent cannot see the structure. For instance, when in our running example A receives the second message from B, her knowledge looks like this:

$$A^{\mathcal{X}_1}, B^{\mathcal{X}_2}, g^{\mathcal{X}_3}, \exp(g, X)^{\exp(\mathcal{X}_3, \mathcal{X}_4)}, X^{\mathcal{X}_4}, \exp(g, Y)^{\mathcal{X}_5} \; .$$

A can see the structure of the half key $\exp(g, X)$ because she has constructed it herself, while she cannot see the same for $\exp(g, Y)$; here her view is just a variable $\mathcal{X}_5$. We define appropriate deduction rules on such labeled terms so that, in our example, A can generate the full key $\exp(\exp(g, X), Y)$ as follows:

$$\frac{\dfrac{\exp(g, Y)^{\mathcal{X}_5} \quad X^{\mathcal{X}_4}}{\exp(\exp(g, Y), X)^{\exp(\mathcal{X}_5, \mathcal{X}_4)}}}{\exp(\exp(g, X), Y)^{\exp(\mathcal{X}_5, \mathcal{X}_4)}}$$

The root label $\exp(\mathcal{X}_5, \mathcal{X}_4)$ exactly describes how A obtains the key from the components of her knowledge.

More generally, whenever an agent should generate an outgoing message m according to the protocol, the AnB translator checks that m^d can be deduced from the agent's knowledge at that point for some *derivation* d. Then, d is the term of the outgoing message in the IF transition rule that the translator produces.[7] If there is no such derivation, then the translation rejects the protocol as "not executable": the agent cannot generate the outgoing message from its knowledge, which means that there is an error in the AnB specification.

Checking Messages. We now define how agents can check the messages they receive. The idea is to ask whether an agent can derive from its knowledge, in two distinct ways, two terms that are supposed to be the same according to the protocol, i.e. deduce m^{d_1} and m^{d_2} with $d_1 \not\approx d_2$. Each such pair d_1 and d_2 of derivations represents a possible check that the agent can perform on messages, namely constructing the derivations and checking that the results are indeed the same. An example is that an agent receives a hash value $h(m)^{\mathcal{X}_1}$ in some message where it does not know the hashed message m and thus cannot check the structure. Now say that, in a later transition, the agent receives $m^{\mathcal{X}_2}$. He can then check that $\mathcal{X}_1 \approx h(\mathcal{X}_2)$, i.e. that applying the hash function h to the message $\mathcal{X}_2$ gives the same as $\mathcal{X}_1$.

More generally, we integrate such checks into the transition rules of honest agents, e.g. in the hash example we have a transition rule like this:

$$\mathsf{state}_{\mathcal{R}}(\mathcal{X}_1, \ldots).\mathsf{iknows}(\mathcal{X}_2) \mid \mathcal{X}_1 = h(\mathcal{X}_2) \Rightarrow \ldots$$

There are in general infinitely many such possible checks; for instance, in the above example, one may similarly check $h(\mathcal{X}_1) \approx h(h(\mathcal{X}_2))$ and so forth.

---

[7] Indeed, there are usually several different derivations for the same message m; the semantics, however, ensures that they are all equivalent derivations, so the choice of the derivation does not influence the rule meaning as explained in [56].

Moreover, the message deduction problem is in general undecidable. Still, [56] shows that for an example theory that includes exponentiation, exclusive or, and other standard operators, we can decide message deduction and compute a finite sufficient set of checks for a given knowledge. Sufficient here means that the same set of incoming messages are accepted with the reduced finite set of checks. For a more detailed discussion on what an agent can recognize, such as the correct decryption of messages, we refer the reader to [56].

To summarize, the rules for A in our running example look as follows, where, for readability, we use instead of $\mathcal{X}_i$ the more intuitive variables from the AnB specification and replace constants wherever possible:

$$\text{state}_A(A, B, g)$$
$$=\!|X|\!\Rightarrow$$
$$\text{state}_A(A, B, g, \exp(g, X), X).\text{iknows}(\exp(g, X))$$

$$\text{state}_A(A, B, g, \exp(g, X), X).\text{iknows}(GY)$$
$$=\!|Msg|\!\Rightarrow$$
$$\text{state}_A(\ldots).\text{iknows}(\{\!|A, Msg|\!\}_{\exp(GY, X)})$$

2.4   Channels

Much effort has been recently devoted to the composition of protocols, e.g. [3,26,30,31,40,41] to name a few works. We often have vertical composition of protocols, i.e. one protocol is run on top of another. For instance, we may have a banking service that runs over a "secure channel" that is provided by another protocol such as TLS or the authenticated Diffie-Hellman key exchange of our running example. It is desirable not to verify the entire composed system as a whole, but to verify the components individually, for instance, verify that TLS indeed provides a secure channel and that the banking service satisfies its goals when run over a secure channel. This compositional reasoning approach has several advantages over the monolithic verification approach. First, the smaller system components are usually easier to verify. Second, we have a greater reusability of verification results, as we can exchange TLS with any other protocol that provides a secure channel without repeating the analysis of the application protocol. Similarly, we can use TLS for other applications that rely on a secure channel without repeating the analysis of TLS anymore.

Thus, the notion of channel can provide a useful interface for a modular presentation and compositional verification of protocols and services. To that end, we need to define what it means that a protocol *provides* a channel with particular properties as a goal, and what the assumption of such a channel in a protocol means.

Channels as Assumptions. We now sketch our model of channels as assumptions. Actually, we give two models, an abstract and a more concrete one, and then prove them equivalent, so that we can use them interchangeably and the analysis methods can pick the one that suits them best.

The first model is called the *cryptographic channel model CCM*. The idea is that we can realize the channel properties by cryptographic means. We just give the example of authentic channels: we encode an authentic message M from A to B as $\{atag, B, M\}_{inv(ak(A))}$. Here, $\{\cdot\}$ denotes asymmetric encryption, $(ak(A), inv(ak(A)))$ is a dedicated public/private-key pair for realizing authentic channels, and atag is a special tag to distinguish this encoding from other digital signatures. $ak(A)$ is public for every agent A, and the intruder initially knows $inv(ak(A))$ of every dishonest agent A.

The name of the intended recipient is included in the signed part of the message and is thus part of the authenticated information. This does not prevent other agents from reading the message, but makes clear for whom the message is meant.[8] This is just one of many possible ways to ensure authentic channels; one may similarly use MACs, for instance. The encoding of other channels similarly uses cryptography to ensure the channel properties.

To illustrate this encoding, the rules of A in the running example now become:

$$state_A(A, B, ak(A), inv(ak(A)), ak(B), g)$$
$$=\!\lfloor X \rfloor\!\Rightarrow$$
$$state_A(A, B, ak(A), inv(ak(A)), ak(B), g, \exp(g, X), X).$$
$$iknows(\{atag, B, \exp(g, X)\}_{inv(ak(A))})$$

$$state_A(A, B, ak(A), inv(ak(A)), ak(B), g, \exp(g, X), X).$$
$$iknows(\{atag, A, GY\}_{inv(ak(B))})$$
$$=\!\lfloor Msg \rfloor\!\Rightarrow$$
$$state_A(\ldots).iknows(\{\!|A, Msg|\!\}_{\exp(GY, X)})$$

We now present the second model of channels as assumptions, the *Ideal Channel Model ICM*, in which we use special persistent fact symbols for messages on different kinds of channels. The rules of A in our running example, for instance, are expressed as follows:

$$state_A(A, B, g)$$
$$=\!\lfloor X \rfloor\!\Rightarrow$$
$$state_A(A, B, g, \exp(g, X), X).athCh_{A,B}(\exp(g, X))$$

$$state_A(A, B, g, \exp(g, X), X).athCh_{B,A}(GY)$$
$$=\!\lfloor Msg \rfloor\!\Rightarrow$$
$$state_A(\ldots).iknows(\{\!|A, Msg|\!\}_{\exp(GY, X)})$$

$athCh_{A,B}(M)$ represents a message M that was sent by agent A on an authentic channel and meant for agent B. The behavior of the channels with respect to the intruder is then defined by rules such as:

$$iknows(B).iknows(M).dishonest(A) \Rightarrow athCh_{A,B}(M)$$
$$athCh_{A,B}(M) \Rightarrow iknows(M)$$

---

[8] We need this to ensure the correspondence with the standard definition of authentic channels where it counts as an attack if b thinks that a message was sent by a to b while a actually meant to send it to somebody else.

Protocol : *Authentic channel*

Types :

  Agent A', B';

  Number Msg';

  Function pk;

Knowledge :

  A' : $A', B', pk(A'), \mathsf{inv}(pk(A'))$;

  B' : $B', pk(A')$;

Actions :

  $A' \rightarrow B' : \{B', Msg'\}_{\mathsf{inv}(pk(A'))}$

Goals :

  $A' \bullet\!\!\rightarrow B' : Msg'$

Fig. 2. AnB specification of a protocol realizing an authentic channel

The first rule expresses that the intruder can send messages on an authentic channel to any agent B but only under the name of a dishonest agent A.[9] The second rule expresses that the intruder can receive any message on an authentic channel. There are similar rules for the abilities of the intruder on the other kinds of channels.

As shown in [57], the two models are equivalent (under certain conditions). Thus, the CCM is a correct realization of the ICM and we can use both models interchangeably.

Channels as Goals. The goals of a protocol can be specified using the different kinds of channels as in our running example where we have specified the secure transmission of a payload message Msg as a goal. These goal definitions are close to standard ones of security protocols, e.g. [7,48,54]. For authentication goals, we use auxiliary events, as we have done before for secrecy goals. This allows us to express goals in a protocol-independent way.

Compositionality. The study of compositionality with respect to channels has revealed several subtle details about what must be required of a channel (implying, for instance, the inclusion of the intended recipient on an authentic channel).

As an example, consider the protocol in Fig. 2 as a way to realize an authentic channel, as it is assumed in our running example of the authenticated Diffie-Hellman key exchange; $pk(A')$ and $\mathsf{inv}(pk(A'))$ are the public and the private key of A', respectively. We can thus, for instance, implement the first authentic channel of the running example by the protocol of Fig. 2 to obtain the protocol shown in Fig. 3.

---

[9] The intruder knows all agent names by assumption, but we need $\mathsf{iknows}(B)$ on the left-hand side because IF requires all variables that appear on the right-hand side to be already present on the left.

Protocol : *Authenticated Diffie-Hellman key exchange, version 2*

Types :

  Agent A, B;

  Number g, X, Y, Msg;

  Function pk;

Knowledge :

  A : $A, B, g, pk(A), \mathrm{inv}(pk(A))$;

  B : $B, g, pk(A)$;

Actions :

  $A \;\rightarrow\; B : \{B, \exp(g, X)\}_{\mathrm{inv}(pk(A))}$

  $B \;\bullet\!\!\rightarrow\; A : \exp(g, Y)$

  $A \;\rightarrow\; B : \{\!| A, Msg |\!\}_{\exp(\exp(g,X), Y)}$

Goals :

  $A \;\bullet\!\!\rightarrow\!\bullet\; B : Msg$

Fig. 3. AnB specification of the authenticated Diffie-Hellman key exchange, composed with the realization of an authentic channel

In [57], we give suitable definitions and conditions to obtain the desired compositionality results, namely that an assumed channel can be realized by any protocol that provides it as a goal.

Pseudonymous Channels. We have generalized all the above models and results to include channels where agents may alternatively be identified by pseudonyms rather than by their real names. Pseudonymous channels are created by techniques like purpose-built keys (PBK) or TLS without client authentication: we have something similar to a secure channel except that one end is not identified by its real name but by some pseudonym, which is usually related to an unauthenticated public-key; see, e.g., [19,33,42,47]. In the case of authentic channels, this concept has often been referred to as *sender invariance*: the receiver can be sure that several messages come from the same source, whose real identity is not known or not guaranteed. However, there is more to it.

First, pseudonymous channels, both as assumptions and as goals, should not be defined as entirely new concepts unrelated to the previous channels. Rather, we define them as variants of the standard channels discussed above where one (or both) ends are identified by a pseudonym rather than the real name.[10]

Second, the concept of pseudonymous channels is useful to model a number of scenarios. The most common one is probably the above mentioned TLS without client authentication as it is common in the Internet: it is in a sense weaker

---

[10] One may even argue that real names are also just a kind of pseudonym, so there is no difference at all. In our model, the difference between real names and pseudonyms is that we assume that real names uniquely identify agents and do not change over time, while pseudonyms may be arbitrarily created by any agent. As a consequence, every agent (including the intruder) can act under several identities.

Protocol : *Diffie-Hellman key exchange without client authentication*
Types :
  Agent A, B;
  Number g, X, Y, Msg;
Knowledge :
  A : A, B, g;
  B : B, g;
Actions :
  $A \;\rightarrow\; B : \exp(g, X)$
  $B \;\bullet\!\!\rightarrow\; A : \exp(g, Y)$
  $A \;\rightarrow\; B : \{\!|A, Msg|\!\}_{\exp(\exp(g,X),Y)}$
Goals :
  $[A] \;\bullet\!\!\rightarrow\!\!\bullet\; B : Msg$

Fig. 4. AnB specification of the Diffie-Hellman key exchange without client authentication

than a standard secure channel, but (assuming the server's public key is properly authenticated) it is sufficient for submitting a client's password over this channel to achieve full authentication. We thus want to use such a channel both as a goal for protocols like TLS where only one side is authenticated, and as an assumption in high-level protocols that use such a channel for a login, for instance.

In AnB, we write $[A]_\psi$ to denote the identity of an agent A that is not identified by its real name A but by some pseudonym ψ, e.g. we write $[A]_\psi \bullet\!\!\rightarrow B : M$ for an authentic channel. We also allow that the specification of ψ is omitted, and write only $[A] \bullet\!\!\rightarrow B$, when the role uses only one pseudonym in the entire session (which is the case for most protocols). The omitted variant is a short-cut for a pseudonym that A freshly generates when it first uses a pseudonymous channel.

Example 2. The protocol in Fig. 4 establishes a secure channel between an unauthenticated A, which uses its Diffie-Hellman half key $\exp(g, X)$ as a pseudonym, and an authenticated B (just as in the case of TLS). Such a channel is good enough for a login protocol in which a client A transmits her user name and password, and thereby authenticates herself to a server B. □

3   Constraint-Based Model Checking

In the previous section, we have discussed the modeling of protocols and their properties, and thereby set up a challenging task for automated verification. We now discuss how OFMC addresses this challenge.

3.1   The Lazy Intruder

The naive exploration of the search space generated by such a specification including a Dolev-Yao-style intruder is not feasible, due to a large or even infinite number of messages that the intruder can construct and send from a given set of known messages. One of the core ideas in OFMC (and, similarly, in several other approaches, e.g. [1,2,17,18,22,23,25,37,43,53]) is to avoid this naive enumeration by using a symbolic, constraint-based approach, which allows us to significantly reduce the search space without excluding attacks (and without introducing new ones).

Let us illustrate this with an example. Assume that in order to carry out an attack, the intruder needs to send to an honest agent a a message that has the form $\{N\}_{pk(a)}$ for some number N encrypted with a's public key $pk(a)$. This can be satisfied in several different ways. First, the intruder can take any term t that he knows and encrypt it with a's public key and send $\{t\}_{pk(a)}$. Alternatively, he can send instead any message of the form $\{\cdot\}_{pk(a)}$ that he knows (even though he cannot decrypt it). Using constraints, however, we do not explore all these possibilities directly, but rather work with the symbolic term $\{N\}_{pk(a)}$ (i.e. leaving the variable N) and impose the constraint $from(\{\,\{N\}_{pk(a)}\,\}; IK)$ where IK is the set of messages known to the intruder at this point (the current *intruder knowledge*). This constraint means that, whatever N is, the intruder must be able to construct the term $\{N\}_{pk(a)}$ from the knowledge IK. We thus base the protocol analysis on a *constraint satisfaction problem*. This is done in a demand-driven way, i.e. we postpone the substitution of variables as long as possible during search. For this reason, we call the technique the *lazy intruder*.

In general, a constraint has the form

$$from(T; IK)$$

where T and IK are both sets of message terms with variables. The models of such a constraint are those interpretations $\mathcal{I}$ of the variables such that $T^{\mathcal{I}}$ can be generated from $IK^{\mathcal{I}}$ using the rules of the intruder to construct and deconstruct messages.

The lazy intruder technique uses the notion of *simple* constraint, i.e. a constraint in which all terms to be generated are variables. This simple form is always satisfiable as the intruder can always generate some message. The idea is to reduce a given constraint to an equivalent set of simple constraints. Here, "equivalent" refers to the set of models of a constraint, i.e. the satisfying interpretations of the variables. We thus formulate, for a given intruder model, a set of constraint reduction rules that are *correct* (in the sense that they maintain the set of models) and *terminating* (meaning that we arrive, after finitely many steps, at a finite set of simple constraint sets).

The constraint reduction rules of the lazy intruder are of three kinds:

- *generation* rules that describe how the intruder can compose messages from known ones,
- *analysis* rules that describe how he can decompose messages,
- and finally there is a *unification* rule that expresses that the intruder can use unifiable messages from his knowledge to fulfill the constraint.

A set of such rules is given in [12,58], where all the details of the formal constraint reduction are spelled out. Here, we focus only on the main ideas by means of an example.

Example 3. To understand the way the lazy intruder works, let us now consider the non-authenticated Diffie-Hellman key exchange, where the half keys are sent on insecure channels. Consider the following abstract execution trace, where we first ignore the question of whether the intruder can generate any acceptable message and we just use variables for messages sent by the intruder:

1. $a \rightarrow i(b) : \exp(g, x)$
2. $i(b) \rightarrow a : M_1$
3. $a \rightarrow i(b) : \{\!| msg |\!\}_{\exp(M_1, x)}$
   $\mathsf{secret}(msg, b)$

Here, the agent a sends her Diffie-Hellman half key $\exp(g, x)$ to an agent b, but the message is intercepted by the intruder, which we display as $i(b)$.[11] The intruder then replies by sending some message M_1 that a parses as the Diffie-Hellman half key from b. She thus sends the payload message msg symmetrically encrypted with the resulting Diffie-Hellman full key $\exp(M_1, x)$. She also declares the payload as a secret with b. We want now to check whether the intruder can find out this secret, assuming the initial intruder knowledge $IK_0 = \{g\}$. This is formalized by the following constraint set:

$$from(\{M_1\}; IK_1) \quad \text{where } IK_1 = IK_0 \cup \{\exp(g, x)\}$$
$$from(\{msg\}; IK_2) \quad \text{where } IK_2 = IK_1 \cup \{\{\!| msg |\!\}_{\exp(M_1, x)}\}$$

We will now describe only one sequence of reduction steps that leads to the solution of the constraint set, while the actual constraint reduction procedure considers also other reduction sequences, which in this case lead to a dead end (i.e. to unsatisfiable constraints). We follow the path that the intruder successfully decrypts the encrypted message in IK_2. This adds a new constraint that he can indeed generate the key $\exp(M_1, x)$ and we add the cleartext msg to the intruder knowledge IK_2 in the second constraint. The new constraint set after this step of the constraint reduction procedure looks a follows:

$$from(\{M_1\}; IK_1)$$
$$from(\{msg\}; IK_2 \cup \{msg\})$$
$$from(\{\exp(M_1, x)\}; IK_2)$$

Obviously, the second constraint can now be solved (by applying the unification rule) and removed from the constraint set. We next turn to the key-generation constraint. Observe that the intruder cannot directly compose this message as he does not know a's secret value x, but there is a way to compose this term if M_1 has the form $\exp(M_2, M_3)$ for two new variables M_2 and M_3. The resulting form of the key $\exp(\exp(M_2, M_3), x)$ is equivalent to $\exp(\exp(M_2, x), M_3)$ according to the algebraic properties of exponentiation:

$$from(\{\exp(M_2, M_3)\}; IK_1)$$
$$from(\{\exp(\exp(M_2, x), M_3)\}; IK_2)$$

---

[11] Actually, due to our identification of intruder and network for insecure channels, the intruder intercepts *every* message transmitted on such channels.

This latter representation can indeed be composed, i.e. by an application of a generation rule we get:

$$from(\{exp(M_2, M_3)\}; IK_1)$$
$$from(\{exp(M_2, x), M_3\}; IK_2)$$

Now we can unify the term $exp(M_2, x)$ with a's half key, i.e. setting $M_2 = g$ we obtain:

$$from(\{exp(g, M_3)\}; IK_1)$$
$$from(\{M_3\}; IK_2)$$

Finally, since IK_1 contains g we can generate the term in the first constraint, leaving a set of simple constraints:

$$from(\{M_3\}; IK_1)$$
$$from(\{M_3\}; IK_2)$$

Thus, the intruder can perform the attack for any value M_3 that he knows.   □

3.2   Algebraic Reasoning

The above example briefly touched the subject of algebraic reasoning. Now we give an overview of what OFMC supports and how. In fact, as part of the parameters of OFMC, one can specify an algebraic theory that defines the (cryptographic) operators and their algebraic properties.

Finite Theories. To begin with, we allow *finite theories*, i.e. theories under which every term has a finite equivalence class. The exponentiation property that $exp(exp(G, X), Y) \approx exp(exp(G, Y), X)$ is an example, because, intuitively, there are only finitely many re-arrangements of exponents in any term. Note that unification for finite theories is in general already an undecidable problem; thus, we cannot handle such specifications without any restrictions. The approach of OFMC is to limit the number of instantiations of a variable in the form that we had in Example 3. The fact that we only bound the handling of variables (and not the terms that can be substituted) directly ensures that for many theories (like the exponentiation example) the restriction is without loss of generality, i.e. no solutions are excluded. In the example of exponentiation, we have to specify the following hint for OFMC in the theory file:[12]

```
topdec(exp,exp(T1,T2))=
  [T1,T2]
  if T1==exp(Z1,Z2){
    [exp(Z1,T2),Z2]}
```

---

[12] OFMC requires that the specification of the algebraic theory contains such hints in order to guide the analysis procedure. A similar requirement holds also for the cancellation theories discussed below.

This specifies the possible solutions of the unification problem $\exp(\cdot, \cdot) \approx \exp(T_1, T_2)$, i.e. the different ways to compose the term $\exp(T_1, T_2)$ using exp as a top-level symbol. (Composition with other symbols does not yield an exponentiation-term in our algebraic theory.) The first solution is the standard "syntactical" solution, i.e. an exponentiation of the subterms; this is possible for any operator. Second, if (recursively) T_1 can be unified $\exp(Z_1, Z_2)$, then there is also an alternative composition using subterms $\exp(Z_1, T_2)$ and Z_2; this is exactly the case used in the above example. Note that this describes a recursive procedure, as composition/decomposition of the term T_1 may give rise to further such checks for exp-decompositions. In the case that the given term is a variable, this recursion can be repeated arbitrarily, but we bound this in OFMC, however, for the exponentiation case, this bounding is without loss of solutions. More generally, the topdec-specifications, like the one above, give a skeleton for a unification algorithm modulo the described theory. Namely, a recursive structure to find all solutions, and one can either bound the instantiation (sacrificing completeness in general) or leave it unbounded (sacrificing termination).

Cancellation Theories. Many algebraic properties are of the form $\{\!|\{\!|m|\!\}_k|\!\}_k \approx m$, which intuitively expresses that "decryption and encryption cancel each other out". The characteristic is that the right-hand side of each equation is either a subterm of the left-hand side or a constant. This underlying orientation of the rules gives rise to a system of rewrite rules that simplifies given message terms. We interpret these rewrite rules modulo the finite theory we have considered before and require that the resulting rewrite relation is convergent and terminating, so that every term has a unique normal form (modulo the finite theory). When using symbolic terms, however, this implies several potential termination problems. As before, to enforce termination, we consider here a bound on the instantiation of variables, which in many cases is not a restriction. The key idea is to analyze the given intruder knowledge as far as possible using cancellations. Formally, we say that the intruder knowledge is *completely analyzed* iff the normal form of every deducible term is either contained in the intruder knowledge, or can be composed from it (without cancellation). Thus, in a completely analyzed knowledge, we do not need to consider any more analysis steps or cancellation properties, but only composition and unification. In the case of the lazy intruder, due to the variables in the intruder knowledge, this notion is always related to a set of constraints on these variables.

Example 4. As an example, consider IK_2 from Example 3, which is related to the constraint $from(M_1; IK_1)$ due to the variable M_1 in IK_2. This knowledge is not completely analyzed, because the key-term for the encrypted message is derivable, so the intruder can compose the term $\{\!|\{\!|msg|\!\}_{\exp(M_1,x)}|\!\}_{\exp(M_1,x)}$ and thus obtain msg, which cannot be obtained by composition alone (without the cancellation property). After the addition of msg to IK_2, it is completely analyzed. $\qquad\square$

3.3   Symbolic Sessions

Most protocol analysis tools allow the user only to specify a concrete analysis scenario consisting of different protocol sessions executed in parallel, such as "Alice wants to talk to Bob and in parallel to the intruder" (of course, Alice does not know which communication partners are honest and which are not). Such a manual specification is, however, cumbersome, especially since the number of scenarios to analyze for a given number of sessions grows exponentially.

OFMC, in contrast, also allows the user to simply specify the number of sessions that the user wishes to analyze, and covers *all* instantiations of the agents in these sessions. This is not only more convenient but also more efficient, since the enumeration of all scenarios is completely avoided. The trick is to use the lazy intruder technique to instantiate agent names whenever necessary. More precisely, we consider an initial state with variables for all agent names (possibly with constraints like $A \neq B$ or $A \neq i$). The lazy intruder starts with the constraint $from(\{A_1, \ldots, A_n\}; IK_0)$ where A_i are agent names of the initial state and IK_0 is the initial intruder knowledge. We assume that all agent names are public knowledge that the intruder initially knows.[13] This approach reflects that "the intruder chooses the sessions" according to what may help him perform an attack, so instantiation is integrated into the protocol analysis. Since this is done lazily, the names are instantiated only when this matters for an attack. In general, we get attacks with variables for agent names; these attacks thus work for arbitrary agents.

3.4   Constraint Differentiation

The lazy intruder drastically reduces the size of the search tree generated during protocol analysis, providing an effective solution to the problem of the prolific intruder, who can compose and send messages at will. However, the lazy intruder does not address the problem resulting from the large number of interleavings possible due to parallel protocol executions. In standard model-checking approaches for concurrent systems, the interleaving problem is often handled using *partial-order reduction* (*POR*), a technique that reduces the number of interleavings that need to be considered by exploiting independencies between the possible transitions [60]. One might expect that the lazy intruder could be directly combined with partial-order reduction. However, this combination is not effective as the different transitions of the lazy intruder rarely lead to the same (symbolic) successor state and therefore there is practically no independence of transitions that can be exploited by POR.

The *constraint differentiation* technique [58] effectively integrates the lazy intruder and ideas from POR by using independence information from the symbolic transition system when reducing constraints. Constraint differentiation works by introducing a new kind of constraint. However, existing constraint-based methods for the various symbolic intruder approaches [1,2,17,18,22,23,25,37,43,53] do

---

[13] We specify this by a dedicated intruder rule, so we do not need to enumerate this set in the intruder knowledge and can even consider an unbounded number of agents.

not need to be individually updated for constraint differentiation since we have defined our technique in a generic way, namely as a transformation to "differentiate" a given symbolic intruder approach (that already is correct and terminating for a particular intruder model).

We again make use of an example to illustrate the main ideas. Assume that when the agent a receives a message of the form $\{a, X\}_k$, it replies with $\{X\}_{k'}$, for a key k'. Let us call this transition θ_1. Assume further that there is another agent b waiting for a message of the form $\{b, Z\}_{k'}$ to which it replies with $\{Z\}_{k'}$. Let us call this transition θ_2. These two transitions can be performed in either order, although they will produce different constraints: if θ_1 is followed by θ_2, then we have the constraints

$$from(\{\ \{a, X\}_k\ \}; IK)$$
$$from(\{\ \{b, Z\}_{k'}\ \}; IK \cup \{\ \{X\}_{k'}\ \})$$

while if θ_2 is followed by θ_1, then we have

$$from(\{\ \{b, Z\}_{k'}\ \}; IK)$$
$$from(\{\ \{a, X\}_k\ \}; IK \cup \{\ \{Z\}_{k'}\ \})$$

These two sets of constraints represent overlapping but different sets of solutions, due to the different intruder knowledges. The main idea of constraint differentiation is to exploit this overlap by restricting the solutions of one of the constraint sets, say the first one, to the solutions not covered by other one. To that end, we introduce a new kind of constraint that is capable of expressing this difference. For instance, the constraints of the execution "θ_1 followed by θ_2" may in some cases be replaced by the following constraints:

$$from(\{\ \{a, X\}_k\ \}; IK)$$
$$\textit{D-from}(\{\ \{b, Z\}_{k'}\ \}; IK; \{\ \{X\}_{k'}\ \})$$

More generally, we introduce *D-from* constraints of the form

$$\textit{D-from}(T; IK; NIK),$$

where, intuitively, NIK represents new messages that are not in IK; the acronym stands for *new intruder knowledge*. The constraint formalizes that the set of terms T must be generated by the intruder using the knowledge in the set $IK \cup NIK$, but we are only interested in solutions that employ new information in NIK and hence we exclude all solutions of $from(T; IK)$.

Assume now that the key k' cannot be generated from IK. Then the only way to satisfy the *D-from* constraint is to unify $\{X\}_{k'}$ and $\{b, Z\}_{k'}$, i.e. $X \mapsto b, Z$. In particular, the *D-from* constraint forbids using other messages encrypted with k' that occur in IK, if any.

In combination with other constraints, this can rule out the entire interleaving. For instance, if $\{a, n\}_k \in IK$ and from IK we cannot derive any other message encrypted with k, then the only solution allowed by the first constraint is $X = n$. Therefore X and b, Z do not unify and the resulting constraints are unsatisfiable. This shows how constraint differentiation can either limit the possible solutions for one execution order or even rule out a particular execution order.

4   The Fixed-Point Module

In recent years, several techniques and tools have been developed that address the problem of protocol verification with an unbounded number of sessions by employing over-approximation techniques, e.g. [13,15,16,38,39]. Over-approximation means that one considers a model that allows strictly more traces or reachable states than the original model. This can induce attacks that are *false positives*, i.e. attacks that work only in the over-approximated model, but not in the original model. For falsification (i.e. detecting attacks) this is problematic, as the "real" attacks may be buried under false positives. On the other hand, for verification (i.e. trying to prove a protocol correct) over-approximation does make sense: given a precise model and an over-approximation of it, proving that the over-approximation is safe is often much easier than in the original model and, if successful, implies that the original model is safe as well.

We have implemented a prototype of a new module for OFMC that is based on such over-approximation ideas. The result of a verification in this module is a fixed-point of facts that can ever occur in any reachable state, and we thus call it the *fixed-point module*. This module complements the "classical" OFMC: we analyze a protocol first in the classical setting with a bounded number of sessions which may yield an attack. Otherwise, if the protocol is safe for a given number of sessions, then we complete the verification by using the new fixed-point module.

Due to the subtlety of protocol models, it is often not immediate that the considered model is actually an over-approximation of the original model. This is, however, the crucial assumption of the entire approach. Therefore, we have investigated the relationships between several such models in [55]. There, we have shown that for a large class of protocols we indeed have an over-approximation relationship which allows us to conclude that the approach behind the fixed-point module is indeed sound.

We now discuss in more detail two kinds of over-approximation that we use in OFMC's fixed-point module.

4.1   Data Abstraction

A common form of abstraction in many verification tools (not only in protocol verification) is based on the idea of abstract interpretation [28]. We refer to this as *data abstraction*, because we map the infinite set of (fresh) data to finitely many equivalence classes; we then consider the abstract equivalence classes instead of the concrete data.

For instance, in our running example, we can abstract all the exponents that an honest agent a freshly generates in all sessions of the protocol into one that we denote by $exponent(a)$. As a result, if the intruder cannot manipulate any of the half keys, two honest agents a and b will end up with the same key $\exp(\exp(g, exponent(a)), exponent(b))$ in every session.

This technique has an important prerequisite: there may not be any negative comparisons in the rules, e.g. that two half keys must be different, or else the abstract model would not be an over-approximation of the concrete one. This limits the class of protocols that can be handled with such methods, but we can easily check that a given specification meets such conditions.

4.2   Control Abstraction

We also consider another form of over-approximation that was first considered in planning [14] and that makes sense in combination with data abstraction and its assumptions: *control abstraction*. The idea here is that the order in which certain facts are "reached" does often not matter, and we can rather just consider what facts occur in any reachable state, in particular which messages the intruder can ever find out.

The fixed-point that we obtain for the running example under control abstraction represents a situation where the intruder has obtained the half key $\exp(g, exponent(a))$ of each agent a and the exponent $exponent(a)$ of each dishonest agent a. Moreover, he has not obtained the full key $\exp(\exp(g, exponent(a)), exponent(b))$ of any pair of honest agents a and b. Finally, in every local state of an honest agent a that has negotiated a full key for communication with another honest agent b, this full key is $\exp(\exp(g, exponent(a)), exponent(b))$.

This concludes our brief exposition of the fixed-point module of OFMC and we now consider some experimental results.

5   Experimental Results

We have applied OFMC to a large number of industrial-strength protocols including all the protocols in the AVISPA Library [9], which contains about 70 real-world protocols such as SET, IKE v.2, Kerberos in different variants, TLS, and H.530. Detailed experiments with running times and comparisons with other tools can be found in [8,12,54,58].

As a concrete example, we summarize here our analysis of the H.530 protocol [44], a protocol developed by Siemens and proposed as an Internet standard for multimedia communications. We have modeled the protocol in its full complexity and OFMC detected a replay attack serious enough that Siemens revised the protocol [45].

5.1   The H.530 Protocol

The H.530 protocol [44,45] provides mutual authentication and key agreement in mobile roaming scenarios in multimedia communication. H.530 is deployed as follows: a mobile terminal (MT) wants to establish a secure connection and negotiate a Diffie-Hellman key with the gatekeeper (VGK) of a visited domain. As they do not know each other in advance, the authentication is performed using a trusted authentication facility AuF within the home domain of the MT.

Fig. 5 shows the message exchange of H.530 in AnB notation (slightly simplified). There is initially a shared key between the mobile terminal MT and its home server AuF, denoted by $sk(MT, AuF)$, as well as a shared key between the visited gatekeeper VGK and AuF, denoted by $sk(VGK, AuF)$. In the first

1. $MT \rightarrow VGK :\ req(MT, VGK, AuF, \exp(g, X))$
2. $VGK \rightarrow AuF : mac(sk(VGK, AuF), (req(MT, VGK, \exp(g, X)), VGK, ver(X, Y)))$
3. $AuF \rightarrow VGK : mac(sk(VGK, AuF), (VGK, ack(MT, VGK, AuF, X, Y)))$
4. $VGK \rightarrow MT :\ mac(dhk(X, Y), (ack(MT, VGK, AuF, X, Y), \exp(g, Y)))$
5. $MT \rightarrow VGK :\ mac(dhk(X, Y), (MT, VGK))$

$$\begin{aligned}
\text{where} \qquad mac(K, M) &= (M, f(K, M)) \\
dhk(X, Y) &= \exp(\exp(g, X), Y) \\
ver(X, Y) &= xor(\exp(g, X), \exp(g, Y)) \\
req(MT, VGK, AuF, X) &= mac(sk(MT, AuF), (MT, VGK, \exp(g, X))) \\
ack(MT, VGK, AuF, X, Y) &= f(sk(MT, AuF), (VGK, ver(X, Y)))
\end{aligned}$$

Fig. 5. The message exchange of H.530 in AnB notation (slightly simplified)

message, MT sends out a request that contains a fresh Diffie-Hellman half key $\exp(g, X)$. This message, like all the following ones, is "MACed" (Message Authentication Code): a hash value of the message using a *keyed* hash function is added to the message. A keyed hash function is like a normal hash function, but has as an extra parameter a symmetric key, so that only participants who know the key can construct—or check—the hash value.[14]

Since the first message from MT is MACed using the key $sk(MT, AuF)$, the receiver VGK can read the Diffie-Hellman half key and the name of MT (at least what it seems to be), but cannot check the authenticity of the messages. In the second message, VGK forwards this request to AuF, including his own fresh Diffie-Hellman half key $\exp(g, Y)$ which is XOR-ed to the half key from MT.

After having checked that all MACs are "adding up", the AuF answers in the third message with an acknowledgment, which contains both half keys and the name of the participants. As in message 2, we have two nested MACs, the outer one with $sk(VGK, AuF)$ and the inner one with $sk(MT, AuF)$. Observe, however, that this time the inner one is without a copy of the cleartext. That is exactly the weakness of the protocol that we will describe below. The last two messages between MT and VGK are MACed using the new Diffie-Hellman key of MT and VGK, proving that both can construct the key. Note that MT receives the half key from VGK also in cleartext, so that he can build the key to check the hash value used here.

The specification in OFMC took one work-day[15] and after an analysis time of 1.3 seconds, OFMC reported a replay attack, displayed in Fig. 6, which works as

---

[14] Our model of a MAC is based on using a simple implementation using an unkeyed hash function: the key is concatenated together with the message to hash. We do not need to discuss the cryptographic requirements and implications of such an implementation, since in our model the MAC has exactly the properties we want: one can build a MAC iff one knows the key and the MACed message, and one cannot recover from a MAC the MACed message (even if one knows the key).

[15] At the time, OFMC did not support algebraic properties, so a work-around for Diffie-Hellman had to be implemented and XOR was replaced with concatenation.

[Normal session of the protocol (recorded by the intruder)]

$1'$. $i(mt) \rightarrow vgk$: $mt, vgk, auf, \exp(g, z), rand$
$2'$. $vgk \rightarrow i(auf)$: $mac(sk(vgk, auf), (mt, vgk, auf, \exp(g, z), rand, vgk, ver(z, \exp(g, y_2))))$
$3'$. $i(auf) \rightarrow vgk$: $mac(sk(vgk, auf), (vgk, ack(mt, vgk, auf, x, y)))$
$4'$. $vgk \rightarrow i(mt)$: $mac(dhk(z, y2), (ack(mt, vgk, auf, x, y), \exp(g, y2)))$
$5'$. $i(mt) \rightarrow vgk$: $mac(dhk(z, y2), (mt, vgk))$

Fig. 6. An attack on H.530, where *rand* and z are random values created by the intruder, and $y2$ is value created by *vgk* for Y in the second run of the protocol

follows. First the intruder listens to a session between a set of honest agents mt, vgk, and auf. He uses the recorded messages later to "steal" the identity of mt, i.e. to pose as mt towards vgk and negotiate a new Diffie-Hellman key with it. More in detail, in message $1'$, vgk can only see the cleartext part of the message, the intruder can thus insert anything for the keyed hash (denoted by *rand* here). Note that the intruder creates a fresh Diffie-Hellman secret z here. The intruder intercepts message $2'$ from vgk to auf and for the reply $3'$ from auf, he replays the message 3 from the previous session, which is based on the old Diffie-Hellman secrets x and y. Observe that vgk cannot detect this, because these old values are only contained in the ack part of the message, which is a keyed hash using $sk(mt, auf)$. Thus, from vgk's point of view, the auf has just acknowledged the key exchange with mt, namely using the Diffie-Hellman key $dhk(z, y2)$. This key is known to the intruder, since he created z himself and can read $\exp(g, y2)$ for instance from the cleartext part of message $2'$. Therefore, he can complete the attack and vgk believes to share the new Diffie-Hellman key with mt. Due to this attack, Siemens has changed the protocol following our suggestion to include the Diffie-Hellman half keys in the MAC for VGK in message 3 [45].

6   Conclusions

We have presented the main features of the Open-source Fixed-point Model Checker, a state-of-the-art security protocol analysis tool. An ongoing line of work in the context of the AVANTSSAR project is concerned with extending the scope of OFMC towards the security analysis of service-oriented architectures. To that end, we are currently extending the compositional reasoning and abstraction techniques of OFMC.

Acknowledgments

The work presented in this paper was partially supported by the FP7-ICT-2007-1 Project no. 216471, "AVANTSSAR: Automated Validation of Trust and Security of Service-oriented Architectures" and the PRIN'07 project "SOFT". We thank David Basin, Achim Brucker, Paul Hankes Drielsma, and all the members of the projects AVISS, AVISPA and AVANTSSAR for very fruitful discussions.

References

1. Abadi, M., Cortier, V.: Deciding knowledge in security protocols under (many more) equational theories. In: Proceedings of CSFW 2005, pp. 62–76. IEEE Computer Society Press, Los Alamitos (2005)

2. Amadio, R.M., Lugiez, D.: On the reachability problem in cryptographic protocols. In: Palamidessi, C. (ed.) CONCUR 2000. LNCS, vol. 1877, pp. 380–394. Springer, Heidelberg (2000)

3. Andova, S., Cremers, C., Gjøsteen, K., Mauw, S., Mjølsnes, S., Radomirović, S.: A framework for compositional verification of security protocols. Information and Computation 206, 425–459 (2008)

4. Arapinis, M., Delaune, S., Kremer, S.: From one session to many: Dynamic tags for security protocols. In: Cervesato, I., Veith, H., Voronkov, A. (eds.) LPAR 2008. LNCS, vol. 5330, pp. 128–142. Springer, Heidelberg (2008)

5. Armando, A., Basin, D., Boichut, Y., Chevalier, Y., Compagna, L., Cuellar, J., Hankes Drielsma, P., Héam, P.-C., Mantovani, J., Mödersheim, S., von Oheimb, D., Rusinowitch, M., Santiago, J., Turuani, M., Viganò, L., Vigneron, L.: The AVISPA tool for the automated validation of internet security protocols and applications. In: Etessami, K., Rajamani, S.K. (eds.) CAV 2005. LNCS, vol. 3576, pp. 281–285. Springer, Heidelberg (2005)

6. Armando, A., Carbone, R., Compagna, L.: LTL Model Checking for Security Protocols. In: Proceedings of CSF 2007, pp. 385–396. IEEE Computer Society Press, Los Alamitos (2007)

7. AVISPA. Deliverable 2.3: The Intermediate Format (2003), http://www.avispa-project.org

8. AVISPA. Deliverable 7.4: Assessment of the AVISPA Tool v.3 (2005), http://www.avispa-project.org

9. The AVISPA Library of Protocols, http://www.avispa-project.org/library

10. Baader, F., Nipkow, T.: Term Rewriting and All That. Cambridge University Press, Cambridge (1998)

11. Basin, D., Mödersheim, S., Viganò, L.: Algebraic intruder deductions. In: Sutcliffe, G., Voronkov, A. (eds.) LPAR 2005. LNCS (LNAI), vol. 3835, pp. 549–564. Springer, Heidelberg (2005)

12. Basin, D., Mödersheim, S., Viganò, L.: OFMC: A symbolic model checker for security protocols. International Journal of Information Security 4(3), 181–208 (2005)

13. Blanchet, B.: An efficient cryptographic protocol verifier based on prolog rules. In: Proceedings of CSFW 2001, pp. 82–96. IEEE Computer Society Press, Los Alamitos (2001)

14. Blum, A.L., Furst, M.L.: Fast planning through planning graph analysis. Artificial Intelligence 90, 281–300 (1997)

15. Bodei, C., Buchholtz, M., Degano, P., Nielson, F., Riis Nielson, H.: Automatic validation of protocol narration. In: Proceedings of CSFW 2003, pp. 126–140. IEEE Computer Society Press, Los Alamitos (2003)

16. Boichut, Y., Héam, P.-C., Kouchnarenko, O.: Tree automata for detecting attacks on protocols with algebraic cryptographic primitives. In: Proceedings of the INFINITY 2007 Workshop (2007) (to appear in ENTCS)

17. Boreale, M.: Symbolic trace analysis of cryptographic protocols. In: Orejas, F., Spirakis, P.G., van Leeuwen, J. (eds.) ICALP 2001. LNCS, vol. 2076, pp. 667–681. Springer, Heidelberg (2001)

18. Boreale, M., Buscemi, M.G.: A framework for the analysis of security protocols. In: Brim, L., Jančar, P., Křetínský, M., Kucera, A. (eds.) CONCUR 2002. LNCS, vol. 2421, pp. 483–498. Springer, Heidelberg (2002)

19. Bradner, S., Mankin, A., Schiller, J.: A framework for purpose built keys (PBK). Work in Progress (June 2003), Internet Draft: `draft-bradner-pbk-frame-06.txt`

20. Butler, F., Cervesato, I., Jaggard, A., Scedrov, A.: A formal analysis of some properties of Kerberos 5 using MSR. In: Proceedings of CSFW 2002, pp. 175–190. IEEE Computer Society Press, Los Alamitos (2002)

21. Cervesato, I., Durgin, N.A., Lincoln, P.D., Mitchell, J.C., Scedrov, A.: Relating Strands and Multiset Rewriting for Security Protocol Analysis. In: Proceedings of CSFW 2000, pp. 35–51. IEEE Computer Society Press, Los Alamitos (2000)

22. Chevalier, Y., Küsters, R., Rusinowitch, M., Turuani, M.: Deciding the security of protocols with diffie-hellman exponentiation and products in exponents. In: Pandya, P.K., Radhakrishnan, J. (eds.) FSTTCS 2003. LNCS, vol. 2914, pp. 124–135. Springer, Heidelberg (2003)

23. Chevalier, Y., Vigneron, L.: A Tool for Lazy Verification of Security Protocols. In: Proceedings of ASE 2001, pp. 373–376. IEEE Computer Society Press, Los Alamitos (2001)

24. Chevalier, Y., Vigneron, L.: Automated unbounded verification of security protocols. In: Brinksma, E., Larsen, K.G. (eds.) CAV 2002. LNCS, vol. 2404, pp. 324–337. Springer, Heidelberg (2002)

25. Corin, R., Etalle, S.: An improved constraint-based system for the verification of security protocols. In: Hermenegildo, M.V., Puebla, G. (eds.) SAS 2002. LNCS, vol. 2477, pp. 326–341. Springer, Heidelberg (2002)

26. Cortier, V., Delaune, S.: Safely composing security protocols. Formal Methods in System Design 34(1), 1–36 (2009)

27. Cortier, V., Delaune, S., Lafourcade, P.: A survey of algebraic properties used in cryptographic protocols. Journal of Computer Security 14(1), 1–43 (2006)

28. Cousot, P.: Abstract interpretation. Symposium on Models of Programming Languages and Computation. ACM Computing Surveys 28(2), 324–328 (1996)

29. Cremers, C.J.F.: The scyther tool: Verification, falsification, and analysis of security protocols. In: Gupta, A., Malik, S. (eds.) CAV 2008. LNCS, vol. 5123, pp. 414–418. Springer, Heidelberg (2008)

30. Datta, A., Derek, A., Mitchell, J.C., Pavlovic, D.: Secure protocol composition. In: Proceedings of the 2003 ACM workshop on Formal methods in security engineering, pp. 11–23. ACM Press, New York (2003)

31. Delaune, S., Kremer, S., Ryan, M.D.: Composition of password-based protocols. In: Proceedings of CSF 2008, pp. 239–251. IEEE Computer Society Press, Los Alamitos (2008)

32. Denker, G., Millen, J.K., Rueß, H.: The CAPSL Integrated Protocol Environment. Technical Report SRI-CSL-2000-02, SRI International, Menlo Park, CA (2000)

33. Dierks, T., Allen, C.: RFC2246 – The TLS Protocol Version 1 (January 1999)

34. Dolev, D., Yao, A.: On the Security of Public-Key Protocols. IEEE Transactions on Information Theory 2(29) (1983)

35. Durgin, N., Lincoln, P.D., Mitchell, J.C., Scedrov, A.: Undecidability of Bounded Security Protocols. In: Proceedings of the FLOC'99 Workshop on Formal Methods and Security Protocols, FMSP 1999 (1999)

36. Even, S., Goldreich, O.: On the security of multi-party ping pong protocols. In: Proceedings of FOCS 1983, pp. 34–39. IEEE Computer Society Press, Los Alamitos (1983)

37. Fiore, M., Abadi, M.: Computing Symbolic Models for Verifying Cryptographic Protocols. In: Proceedings of CSFW 2001, pp. 160–173. IEEE Computer Society Press, Los Alamitos (2001)

38. Genet, T., Klay, F.: Rewriting for cryptographic protocol verification. In: McAllester, D. (ed.) CADE 2000. LNCS, vol. 1831, pp. 271–290. Springer, Heidelberg (2000)

39. Goubault-Larrecq, J.: A method for automatic cryptographic protocol verification. In: Rolim, J.D.P. (ed.) IPDPS-WS 2000. LNCS, vol. 1800, pp. 977–984. Springer, Heidelberg (2000)

40. Guttman, J.D.: Authentication tests and disjoint encryption: a design method for security protocols. Journal of Computer Security 3–4(12), 409–433 (2004)

41. Guttman, J.D.: Cryptographic protocol composition via the authentication tests. In: de Alfaro, L. (ed.) FOSSACS 2009. LNCS, vol. 5504, pp. 303–317. Springer, Heidelberg (2009)

42. Hankes Drielsma, P., Mödersheim, S., Viganò, L., Basin, D.: Formalizing and analyzing sender invariance. In: Dimitrakos, T., Martinelli, F., Ryan, P.Y.A., Schneider, S. (eds.) FAST 2006. LNCS, vol. 4691, pp. 80–95. Springer, Heidelberg (2007)

43. Huima, A.: Efficient Infinite-State Analysis of Security Protocols. In: Proceedings of the FLOC 1999 Workshop on Formal Methods and Security Protocols, FMSP 1999 (1999)

44. ITU-T Recommendation H.530: Symmetric Security Procedures for H.510 (Mobility for H.323 Multimedia Systems and Services) (2002)

45. ITU-T Recommendation H.530, Corrigendum 1 (2003); Corrected version of [44]

46. Jacquemard, F., Rusinowitch, M., Vigneron, L.: Compiling and verifying security protocols. In: Parigot, M., Voronkov, A. (eds.) LPAR 2000. LNCS, vol. 1955, pp. 131–160. Springer, Heidelberg (2000)

47. Johnson, D., Perkins, C., Arkko, J.: RFC3775 – Mobility Support in IPv6 (June 2004)

48. Lowe, G.: A hierarchy of authentication specifications. In: Proceedings of CSFW 1997, pp. 31–43. IEEE Computer Society Press, Los Alamitos (1997)

49. Lowe, G.: Casper: a Compiler for the Analysis of Security Protocols. Journal of Computer Security 6(1), 53–84 (1998)

50. Maurer, U.M., Schmid, P.E.: A calculus for security bootstrapping in distributed systems. Journal of Computer Security 4(1), 55–80 (1996)

51. Meadows, C.: The NRL Protocol Analyzer: An Overview. Journal of Logic Programming 26(2), 113–131 (1996)

52. Millen, J.K., Muller, F.: Cryptographic protocol generation from CAPSL. Technical Report SRI-CSL-01-07, SRI International (2001)

53. Millen, J.K., Shmatikov, V.: Constraint Solving for Bounded-Process Cryptographic Protocol Analysis. In: Proceedings of CCS 2001, pp. 166–175. ACM Press, New York (2001)

54. Mödersheim, S.: Models and Methods for the Automated Analysis of Security Protocols. PhD Thesis, ETH Zurich (2007)

55. Mödersheim, S.: On the Relationships between Models in Protocol Verification. Information and Computation 206(2-4), 291–311 (2008)

56. Mödersheim, S.: Algebraic Properties in Alice and Bob Notation. In: Proceedings of Ares 2009, pp. 433–440. IEEE Xplore (2009); Extended version: Technical Report RZ3709, IBM Zurich Research Lab (2008), domino.research.ibm.com/library/cyberdig.nsf

57. Mödersheim, S., Viganò, L.: Secure Pseudonymous Channels. In: Proceedings of Esorics 2009 (to appear, 2009); Extended version: Technical Report RZ3724, IBM Zurich Research Lab (2009), domino.research.ibm.com/library/cyberdig.nsf
58. Mödersheim, S., Viganò, L., Basin, D.: Constraint Differentiation: Search-Space Reduction for the Constraint-Based Analysis of Security Protocols. Journal of Computer Security (to appear)
59. Paulson, L.C.: The Inductive Approach to Verifying Cryptographic Protocols. Journal of Computer Security 6(1), 85–128 (1998)
60. Peled, D.: Ten Years of Partial Order Reduction. In: Y. Vardi, M. (ed.) CAV 1998. LNCS, vol. 1427, pp. 17–28. Springer, Heidelberg (1998)
61. Ryan, P., Schneider, S., Goldsmith, M., Lowe, G., Roscoe, B.: Modelling and Analysis of Security Protocols. Addison-Wesley, Reading (2000)
62. The Strand Space Method, http://www.mitre.org/tech/strands/
63. Turuani, M.: The CL-Atse Protocol Analyser. In: Pfenning, F. (ed.) RTA 2006. LNCS, vol. 4098, pp. 277–286. Springer, Heidelberg (2006)

Verification of Concurrent Programs with Chalice

K. Rustan M. Leino[0], Peter Müller[1], and Jan Smans[2]

[0] Microsoft Research, Redmond, WA, USA
leino@microsoft.com
[1] ETH Zurich, Switzerland
peter.mueller@inf.ethz.ch
[2] KU Leuven, Belgium
jan.smans@cs.kuleuven.be

Abstract. A program verifier is a tool that allows developers to prove that their code satisfies its specification for every possible input and every thread schedule. These lecture notes describe a verifier for concurrent programs called Chalice.

Chalice's verification methodology centers around permissions and permission transfer. In particular, a memory location may be accessed by a thread only if that thread has permission to do so. Proper use of permissions allows Chalice to deduce upper bounds on the set of locations modifiable by a method and guarantees the absence of data races for concurrent programs. The lecture notes informally explain how Chalice works through various examples.

0   Introduction

Writing correct sequential programs is *hard*. The correctness of a program typically relies on many implicit assumptions. For example, a developer may assume that a certain variable lies within the bounds of an array, that a parameter is non-null, that a method will not modify the contents of a certain memory location, or that operations on a given data structure follow some particular protocol. However, it is difficult for developers to see whether their assumptions are correct and, as a consequence, it is difficult to write correct programs.

Writing correct concurrent programs is *even harder* because of data races, deadlocks, and potential interference among threads. That is, developers not only need to worry about the assumptions needed for reasoning about sequential programs, but additionally have to make assumptions about the effects of other threads. For example, to avoid data races, programmers need to ensure, at each field access, that other threads will not access the same location concurrently. Similarly, when a lock is acquired, one must determine what memory locations are protected by that lock and whether the acquisition may lead to deadlock.

In this paper, we describe Chalice, a language and program verifier that detects bugs in concurrent programs. More specifically, developers can make the implicit assumptions about their code explicit via annotations, so-called *contracts*. For example, annotations can indicate that a parameter must not be null, that a memory location can safely be accessed by a thread, or that a memory location is protected by a certain lock. The Chalice program verifier analyzes annotated programs and checks that the given annotations are never violated.

A. Aldini, G. Barthe, R. Gorrieri (Eds.): FOSAD 2007/2008/2009, LNCS 5705, pp. 195–222, 2009.

```
class Math {
  method ISqrt(n: int) returns (res: int)
    requires 0 <= n;
    ensures res * res <= n && n < (res+1) * (res+1);
  {
    res := 0;
    while ((res + 1) * (res + 1) <= n)
      invariant res * res <= n;
    {
      res := res + 1;
    }
  }
}
```

Fig. 0. A small sequential program where assumptions have been made explicit via annotations

Let us look at the small sequential program of Fig. 0, to get a feeling for what the annotations look like and how Chalice works. The program consists of a class Math with a single method ISqrt whose goal is to compute and return the positive integer square root of its parameter n. ISqrt's implementation achieves this goal by incrementing the output parameter res until the desired value is reached.

Fig. 0 contains three annotations that explicate assumptions about ISqrt.

First, ISqrt has a *precondition*, starting with the keyword **requires**, which indicates that ISqrt's developer expects callers to supply a non-negative value for n. Chalice checks this assumption at each call site. For example:

```
call x := math.ISqrt(5); // ok
call x := math.ISqrt(-5); // error: unsatisfied precondition 0 <= n
```

Second, ISqrt has a *postcondition*, starting with the keyword **ensures**, which specifies that the output parameter res will contain the integer square root of n on exit of ISqrt. Chalice checks the method's implementation to satisfy this assumption whenever the implementation returns to its caller.

Third, ISqrt's body has a *loop invariant*, starting with the keyword invariant, which declares that every time execution reaches the head of the loop, the square of res is at most n. In general, a loop invariant must hold on entry to the loop and must be preserved by the loop's body. If this is not the case, then Chalice reports an error.

The program of Fig. 0 is sequential and does not use the heap. Therefore, we did not have to worry about data races, deadlocks, or what part of the heap the method modifies. In the remainder of this paper, we describe how Chalice verifies assumptions about complex concurrent programs that use shared mutable state by relying on a system of permissions and permission transfer. Section 1 describes the heart of the Chalice annotation methodology, namely permissions and permission transfer. Section 2 then shows how permissions can be used to determine what locations a method can modify. We discuss fork-join parallelism in Section 3, extend this approach to monitors in Section 4, and show how to avoid deadlocks in Section 5. Data abstraction is handled in Section 6. We show how Chalice verifies a classic example from Owicki and Gries [34] in Section 7 and tackle rely-guarantee reasoning in Section 8. Finally, we conclude in Section 9.

This paper informally describes Chalice through various examples. The goal here is to explain common usage of the annotation style, not to provide a reference manual for the language and program verifier. For more information on how Chalice works internally and on other features not discussed here, we refer the reader to [30].

1 Permissions

Verification in Chalice centers around permissions. Permissions can be held by an *activation record*, that is, a particular invocation of a method. A memory location may be read or written by an activation record only if that activation record has permission to do so. We denote permission to access field f of object o by **acc**(o.f).

Let's look at an illustrative example. Consider the program of Fig. 1. At the start of this program, the stack contains a single activation record for Main that holds no permissions. When a new object is created, the creating activation record gains permission to access the fields of the new object. For example, the first statement of Main gives the activation record permissions to access c.x and c.y. Because of those permissions, the activation record can safely update c.x and read c.y on the next line.

The next statement in Main is a method call: **call** c.Inc(). Execution of a method call starts by pushing a new activation record onto the call stack. Which permissions does the new activation record have initially? The answer to this question can be determined by looking at Inc's precondition, which indicates (0) that the caller must have permission to access **this**.x and (1) that this permission transfers from the caller's activation record to the callee's. In a similar fashion, the postcondition indicates which permissions transfer from the callee back to the caller on exit of Inc. In our example, this annotation returns to callers the permission to access **this**.x. Thus, c.Inc() temporarily borrows the permission to access c.x from Main such that it can read and update this memory location. In other words, the main method loses access to c.x for the duration of the call. It does, however, retain permission to access c.y. The assignment to c.x after the call is safe because Main's activation record once again has access to both c.x and c.y.

The last statement of Main is again a method call. This call consumes the permissions to c.x and c.y: Dispose's precondition causes both permissions to be transferred to the callee, but the postcondition does not return any permissions to the caller.[0] As a consequence, the main method is not allowed to access c's fields after calling Dispose. If Main attempted to update c.x after calling Dispose, Chalice would report the following error: The location c.x might not be writable.

The program of Fig. 1 successfully verifies. That is, Chalice outputs the following message after analyzing Fig. 1. (Boogie is the name of the program verifier Chalice is built on. The seven verified methods correspond to the three methods of class C plus four methods that are generated internally to check the well-formedness of C's contracts.)

---

[0] These permissions are lost forever. Chalice offers a -checkLeaks mode that reports errors when permissions are permanently lost, but we assume the default mode in this paper.

```
class C {
  var x: int; var y: int;

  method Main() {
    var c := new C;
    c.x := 7; var tmp := c.y;
    call c.Inc();
    c.x := c.y + 10;
    call c.Dispose();
  }

  method Inc()
    requires acc(x);
    ensures acc(x);
  { x := x + 1; }

  method Dispose()
    requires acc(x) && acc(y);
    ensures true;
  { }
}
```

Fig. 1. A program that illustrates permissions and permission transfer

Boogie program verifier finished with 7 verified, 0 errors.

However, what happens if we remove the precondition from Inc? Removing this annotation causes the verification of Inc's body to fail, as the activation record then does not have permission to access x. What happens if we leave the precondition in place, but remove Inc's postcondition? Removing this annotation causes the verification of Main's body to fail, as Main then has insufficient permissions to perform the assignment c.x := c.y + 10.

Permissions can neither be duplicated nor forged. Because permissions cannot be duplicated, the stack can never contain permission to access a location more than once.[1] This means that a method with precondition **requires acc**(o.f) && **acc**(o.f) can never be called, since no caller is able to provide permission for accessing o.f twice.

It is important to understand that permissions are purely conceptual. They are needed only for verification, but have no effect during programs execution. Therefore, permissions can be mentioned only inside annotations but not inside method bodies.

As another example, consider the method ISqrt shown in Fig. 2. The major difference between this version and the one of Fig. 0 is the use of the heap. That is, instead of input and output parameters, Fig. 2 computes the integer square root of a field n and stores the result in n itself. A consequence of using a heap cell instead of a parameter is that the pre- and postconditions must require and return permission to access n, respectively. In addition, the loop invariant must demand access to n as well, because the body

---

[1] We relax this rule in Section 3.2 where permissions can be split into fractions.

```
class Math {
  var n: int;

  method ISqrt()
    requires acc(n) && 0 <= n;
    ensures acc(n) && n*n <= old(n) && old(n) < (n+1)*(n+1);
  {
    var N := n;
    n := 0;
    while ((n+1)*(n+1) <= N)
      invariant acc(n) && n*n <= N;
    {
      n := n + 1;
    }
  }
}
```

Fig. 2. A variant of the method ISqrt from Fig. 0 that uses a field instead of parameters

of the loop is verified assuming only the loop condition and the loop invariant—in this regard, each loop iteration is treated as an activation record. If we removed the conjunct **acc**(n) from the loop invariant, then the body would not be allowed to assign to n.

As illustrated by the contract of class Math, annotations typically consist of *access assertions*, which specify the required or guaranteed access permissions, and *pure assertions*, which specify properties of variables. A pure assertion in an annotation may refer to a heap location o.f only if that annotation also contains an access assertion for o.f. Intuitively, one can think of the annotation as reading o.f and, therefore, it must have the permission to do so. Chalice rejects annotations that do not include the appropriate access assertions. For instance, if we omit **acc**(n) from ISqrt's postcondition, Chalice reports the following error:

6.18: Location might not be readable.

The expression **old**(n) in the postcondition of ISqrt represents the value of the field n on entry to the method. In general, **old**(e) is the value that the expression e had in the method pre-state.

In summary, a heap location may be accessed by an activation record only if that activation record has permission to do so. An activation record can gain access to a memory location in one of three ways. First, the activation record can create a new object and thereby gain access to the fields of this new object. Second, a method can demand, via its **requires** annotation, that its caller provide certain permissions. The corresponding permissions are transferred from the caller on entry to the method. Third, an activation record can gain access to a memory location by calling a method that returns permission to access the memory location, as described in its postcondition.

In the next sections, we show why permissions are useful when reasoning about imperative programs. In particular, we demonstrate that one can derive what locations

```
class RockBand {
  var memberCount: int;
  invariant acc(memberCount) && 0 <= memberCount;

  method Init()
    requires acc(memberCount);
    ensures acc(memberCount) && memberCount == 0;
  { memberCount := 0; }

  method AddMembers(howMany: int)
    requires acc(memberCount) && 0 <= howMany;
    ensures acc(memberCount);
    ensures memberCount == old(memberCount) + howMany;
  { memberCount := memberCount + howMany; }
}
```

Fig. 3. The class RockBand. We will explain the meaning of the invariant in Section 4.

a callee can modify from the required permissions (Section 2) and that proper use of permissions prevents data races (Sections 3 and 4).

2 Framing

An important problem in the verification of imperative programs is the *frame problem*: a method contract must not only describe how it affects the program state (typically via pre- and postconditions), but must also make manifest what part of the heap it will definitely not modify. For example, before the call to Inc in the Main method of Fig. 1, c.y and tmp hold the same value. How do we know, only by looking at Inc's contract, that c.Inc() does not assign a new value to c.y?

How can permissions help in solving the frame problem? The answer is that we can deduce an upper bound on the set of locations that can be modified by a method from the permissions that it requires. More specifically, if a callee does not demand access to a memory location to which the caller has access, then that callee cannot modify that location—it did not have the permission initially and it is impossible to forge permissions. For example, the call c.Inc() cannot modify c.y, since Inc requests access only to c.x. Therefore, we can show that c.y still equals tmp after the call.

Let's look at another example. Consider the class RockBand from Fig. 3. RockBand provides methods to initialize a band and to add band members. Init requires access to memberCount and returns this permission to its caller. It also ensures that the value of field memberCount is 0. Similarly, AddMembers requires access to memberCount and additionally requires that a non-negative number is passed for the parameter howMany. The Main method of Fig. 4 shows how permissions solve the frame problem. At program location A, the postcondition of AddMembers holds: Main has regained access to acdc.memberCount and the field holds the value 5. Creating a new object does not affect the values of existing locations; hence, after creating noDoubt, the location acdc.memberCount still holds 5. The next two statements are method invocations

```
class Program {
  method Main() {
    var acdc := new RockBand;
    call acdc.Init();
    call acdc.AddMembers(5); // A

    var noDoubt := new RockBand;
    call noDoubt.Init();
    call noDoubt.AddMembers(4);

    assert acdc.memberCount == 5;
  }
}
```

Fig. 4. A client for RockBand that illustrates how permissions solve the frame problem

whose preconditions do not request permission to access acdc.memberCount. Therefore, the caller never relinquishes its permissions to acdc.memberCount, from which one can conclude that acdc.memberCount is not modified by the two calls; hence, acdc.memberCount does equal 5 when the **assert** statement is reached.

3   Threads

So far we have only considered sequential programs. In this section, we introduce threads, explain how permissions are transferred when threads are forked and joined, and introduce read permissions, which allow several threads to read a location concurrently.

3.0   Creating and Joining Threads

A concurrent program has multiple threads of control. In Chalice, new threads are introduced using explicit **fork** statements. A **fork** statement indicates the method to be used as the starting point of the new thread, and it passes parameters and permissions to this method just as is done for an ordinary method call. For example,

```
fork c.Inc();
```

creates a new thread that will execute the Inc method on object c.

Using the **join** statement, one thread can wait for another to complete. The statement takes as argument a *token*, which uniquely identifies a thread. The **fork** statement creates the token, and allows it to be recorded in a variable:

```
fork tk := c.Inc();
```

For convenience, if the left-hand side of this assignment is not already a local variable, then the **fork** statement implicitly introduces the given identifier as a new local variable of the appropriate type. A thread can be joined only once.[2]

---

[2] Whether or not a token tk is joinable is recorded in the ghost variable tk.joinable, which can be mentioned in program expressions.

The **join** statement arranges for the permissions entailed by the method's postcondition to be transferred to the joining thread. In fact, a **call** statement is nothing but a **fork** immediately followed by a **join**. That is, **call** c.Inc(); will have the same effect as

```
fork tk := c.Inc(); join tk;
```

except possibly for performance differences. Any expression **old**(E) in the method's postcondition refers to the value of expression E at the time of the **fork**.

If the method has output parameters, these are returned at the time of the join. The syntax is

```
join x,y,z := tk;
```

where x, y, and z are local variables that receive the actual output parameters.

3.1 Transferring Permissions to Threads

Because the **fork** statement transfers permissions, the permissions entailed by the preconditions of methods forked concurrently cannot overlap. For example, the Inc method in Fig. 1 lists **acc**(x) in its precondition; therefore, it is not possible to fork two concurrent copies of c.Inc():

```
fork c.Inc();
fork c.Inc();  // error: unsatisfied precondition acc(c.x)
```

Figure 5 shows an example program that uses two concurrent threads to compute the integer square root of two numbers. One thread uses the permission on m0.n and

```
class ParallelMath {
  method TwoSqrts(x: int, y: int) returns (r: int, s: int)
    requires 0 <= x && 0 <= y;
    ensures r*r <= x && x < (r+1)*(r+1);
    ensures s*s <= y && y < (s+1)*(s+1);
  {
    var m0 := new Math { n := x };
    var m1 := new Math { n := y };
    fork tk0 := m0.ISqrt();
    fork tk1 := m1.ISqrt();
    join tk0;
    join tk1;
    r := m0.n;
    s := m1.n;
  }
}
```

Fig. 5. An example program for computing two square roots in parallel. The Math.ISqrt method is defined in Fig. 2.

the other one m1.n, and thus, the two threads operate on disjoint data. An attempt to assign to m0.n just after forking m0.ISqrt() would result in a verification error, since the fork operation transfers the calling thread's permission to m0.n (as indicated by the precondition of Math.ISqrt). However, after joining that thread, which is done by supplying the **join** statement with the token tk0 that resulted from the fork operation, the calling thread regains the permission to m0.n, as indicated by ISqrt's postcondition.

3.2   Read Permissions

In the previous subsection, we showed how to start threads and pass them the permissions to disjoint sets of memory locations. Sometimes, it is desirable to let several

```
class VideoRental {
  var customerId: int;
  var movieId: int;
  var days: int;

  method FrequentRentalPoints() returns (points: int)
    requires rd(customerId) && rd(movieId);
    ensures rd(customerId) && rd(movieId);
  {
    // ...
  }

  method Invoice() returns (dollars: int)
    requires rd(movieId) && rd(days);
    ensures rd(movieId) && rd(days);
  {
    // ...
  }
}

class VideoStore {
  method Charge(vr: VideoRental)
    requires acc(vr.customerId) && acc(vr.movieId) && acc(vr.days);
  {
    fork tk0 := vr.FrequentRentalPoints();
    fork tk1 := vr.Invoice();
    var p: int; var d: int;
    join p := tk0;
    join d := tk1;
    // ...
  }
}
```

Fig. 6. An example that shows the use of **rd** permissions. The two threads created by the Charge method both have read access to movieId, but neither thread can write it.

threads access the same memory location. Such mutual access is harmless as long as no thread updates the memory location. For this reason, for every memory location o.f, Chalice distinguishes between full permission to o.f, written **acc**(o.f), and read permission to o.f, written **rd**(o.f).

We can think of permissions as percentages [6]. Full permission corresponds to 100% of a memory location's permission, whereas a read permission corresponds to an ε of the location's permission, for some infinitesimal ε (that is, some arbitrarily small, yet positive, value ε).

In order for an activation record to write a memory location o.f, it must hold 100% of the permission to o.f, whereas reading o.f can be done with any non-zero amount of permission to o.f. An activation record that holds 100% permission to o.f can transfer any number of ε's of that permission to other activation records and threads; doing so leaves the activation record with less than 100% permission, which means it can no longer write o.f. If the activation record manages to collect back all of the ε's given out, it will once again have 100% access and can then write o.f. Note that while one thread has a read (that is, non-zero) or write (that is, 100%) permission to a location o.f, no other thread can have write permission to o.f, which prevents data races. That is, the sum of the permissions to o.f across the activation records of all threads can never exceed 100%.

As an example, Fig. 6 shows two classes that implement a part of a video store, and in particular a part of the video store's way of charging for video rentals. A video rental indicates a customer and a movie, as well as the duration of the rental, counted in number of days. The method that computes the frequent rental points awarded for this rental requires read access to customerId and movieId, and the method that produces the invoice for the rental requires read access to movieId and days. The Charge method of class VideoStore can therefore compute frequent rental points and produce the invoice concurrently.

The Charge method in Fig. 6 creates one thread for each of the two operations and then just waits for the two threads to finish. This looks symmetric and nice, but it uses more threads than needed. An alternative, which uses a total of only two threads instead of the calling thread plus two worker threads, is the following:

```
fork tk := vr.FrequentRentalPoints();
call d := vr.Invoice();
join p := tk;
```

The **rd** annotation, which specifies ε permissions, is often convenient when indicating read access. If a program gives read access to a location and later wants to regain write access, it must arrange to collect all the ε permissions that were given out. For example, after the two **fork** statements in Fig. 6, the calling thread has $100\% - \varepsilon - \varepsilon$ access to vr.movieId and each of the other threads holds an ε permission. Chalice allows these permissions to be split up in other ways, too, using the **acc**(o.f, n) annotation, which indicates n% of permissions. For example, instead of **rd**(movieId), method FrequentRentalPoints could have said **acc**(movieId,17) and method Invoice could have said **acc**(movieId,31), which would have left the calling thread with 52% after the two **fork** operations. It is sometimes convenient to split the permissions this way (as we shall soon see), but note that 99% permission and ε permission both provide just read access—the difference lies in the ease of writing specifications that give the program the opportunity to assemble back the entire 100% of the permissions. In light of this discussion, **rd**(o.f) can be viewed as a way to write **acc**(o.f, ε).

4 Monitors

The machinery introduced so far allows permission transfer between threads only when threads are forked or joined. However, access to shared data such as a shared buffer requires various threads to obtain and relinquish permissions while the threads are running. Access to shared data is synchronized using *monitors*, which are guarded by mutual-exclusion locks. In Chalice, monitors can hold access permissions, just like activation records. Therefore, a thread can pass permissions to another thread by first storing them in a monitor, which allows the other thread to obtain them from the monitor.

When a thread wants to read the shared memory location, it competes for the mutual-exclusion lock using an **acquire** operation. Upon successful acquisition of the lock, the permissions stored in the monitor are transferred to the acquiring thread. When the thread is done writing, it uses the **release** operation to release the lock and transfer the permissions back into the monitor.

4.0 Monitor Invariants

In Chalice, like in C# and Java, any object can be used as a monitor. Each class has an associated *monitor invariant*, which describes the permissions stored in the monitors associated with the objects of this class. For instance, class RockBand in Fig. 3 declares a monitor invariant that says that the monitor of each RockBand object rb holds 100% permission to rb.memberCount. These permissions are stored in the monitor when no thread holds the lock. The monitor invariant also contains a pure assertion stating that memberCount holds a non-negative value.

4.1 Object Life Cycle

An allocated object in Chalice can be in one of three states: *not-a-monitor*, *available*, and *held*. In the *not-a-monitor* state, which is the state of a newly allocated object, the object cannot be used as a monitor. That is, the **acquire** and **release** operations cannot be applied to the object and the monitor invariant need not hold. The **share** statement associates a monitor with such an object, transitioning the object from the *not-a-monitor* state to the *available* state. In the *available* state, the monitor holds the permissions indicated by the monitor invariant. The **acquire** statement transitions an object from the *available* state to the *held* state, and **release** transitions the object back to *available*.

To illustrate the object life cycle, consider the following code:

```
var rb := new RockBand { memberCount := 0 };
share rb;
// ...
acquire rb;
rb.AddMembers(1);
release rb;
var z := rb.memberCount;   // error: insufficient permission
                           //        to read rb.memberCount
```

The **share** statement makes the object available, checks that the monitor invariant holds, and transfers the permissions entailed by the monitor invariant to rb's monitor. This leaves the calling thread with 0% permission of rb.memberCount. Consequently, the thread cannot access this location.

Upon completion of the **acquire** statement, the monitor's permissions are transferred to the thread. The thread will have full access to rb.memberCount after the **acquire**. In particular, this gives it the permission to perform the method call. In the *available* state, the monitor invariant holds, and thus the monitor invariant can be assumed to hold just after the **acquire** statement.

Like the **share** statement, the **release** statement checks the monitor invariant to hold and then transfers the appropriate permission from the thread to the monitor. In the example, the monitor invariant is known to hold, as can be established from the second postcondition of AddMembers and the fact that the monitor invariant holds upon completion of the **acquire** statement.

The example further shows that rb.memberCount is not readable after the **release**.

5   Deadlock Prevention

To ensure mutual exclusion, the **acquire** operation suspends the execution of the acquiring thread until the requested monitor can be given to that thread. A well-behaved program makes sure that other threads will eventually make such a monitor available. One possible program error is a *deadlock*, which occurs when a set of threads are suspended, each waiting for a monitor that is held by another thread in the set.

5.0   Locking Order

Chalice prevents deadlocks by breaking cycles among acquiring threads. This is done by letting a program associate each monitor with a *locking level* and then checking that the program acquires the monitors in ascending order. The locking levels are values from a set Mu, whose strict partial order is denoted <<. A program specifies the locking level of a monitor using the **share** statement, which takes an optional **between** ... **and** ... clause. Alternatively, a clause **above** ... or **below** ... may be used if only one bound is given. By default, the **share** statement uses **above maxlock**, where **maxlock** denotes the highest monitor currently held by the thread.

For example, consider a program fragment that allocates two objects, a and b, and associates them with monitors:

```
var a := new T;
share a above maxlock;
var b := new T;
share b above a;
```

Here, a is given a locking level above what the thread already holds, and b is given a locking level above that. Acquiring both of these monitors must be done in ascending order, so a thread must first acquire a and then b. An attempt at acquiring them in the opposite order results in the program verifier reporting an error:

```
acquire b;
acquire a;  // error: target lock might not be above maxlock
```

release operations can be done in any order.

The locking level of an object is recorded in a special field called mu. Access to this field is protected by permissions, just as for other fields, but the field cannot be changed by assignment statements.

Figure 7 shows an example program, the famous Dining Philosophers [12], here with 3 philosophers. A philosopher requires two forks to eat,[3] and these are passed as parameters to the Run method. The Run method's precondition specifies the relative locking order required of the parameters. Note the use of **maxlock**, the ordering <<, and the field mu. Since the precondition mentions a.mu and b.mu, the precondition must also require access to these fields; the example does so using two **rd** predicates. The example program avoids deadlocks by assigning forks to philosophers in an asymmetric way, as shown in the parameters passed to Run in the main program's **fork** statements.

5.1 Example: Producer-Consumer

The producer-consumer problem is a classical example that illustrates the need for synchronization in programs with multiple threads and shared data. As an example, consider the program from Figs. 8 and 9. In this program, two worker threads concurrently access a shared buffer. One worker (called the producer) adds items to the buffer, while the other (called the consumer) removes items. To prevent data races, both worker threads must acquire the monitor of the shared buffer before reading or writing its fields.

Let's take a look at the code and the annotations. The first class of Fig. 8 is Buffer. Buffer's monitor invariant indicates that the monitor of a Buffer object b protects the field b.contents. The field contents holds a sequence of integers, which can be of any length; thus, each Buffer object implements an unbounded buffer. The classes Producer and Consumer are similar to each other. Both Produce and Consume require that the given buffer can be acquired, by requiring read access to the buffer's mu field. In the body of a loop, both methods acquire the buffer to gain access to and update the field buff.contents. Note that a loop invariant must be provided which states that buff remains available. Finally, consider the Main method in Fig. 9. After creation of buffer, the main method has permission to access buffer.contents. The

---

[3] These forks denote eating utensils and have no relation to the **fork** statement.

```
class Fork { }

class Philosopher {
  method Run(a: Fork, b: Fork)
    requires rd(a.mu) && rd(b.mu);
    requires maxlock << a.mu && a.mu << b.mu;
  {
    while (true)
      invariant rd(a.mu) && rd(b.mu);
      invariant maxlock << a.mu && a.mu << b.mu;
    {
      // think...
      acquire a;
      acquire b;
      // eat...
      release a;
      release b;
    }
  }
}

class Program {
  method Main() {
    // create forks
    var f0 := new Fork;  share f0;
    var f1 := new Fork;  share f1 above f0.mu;
    var f2 := new Fork;  share f2 above f1.mu;

    // create philosophers
    var aristotle := new Philosopher;
    var plato := new Philosopher;
    var kant := new Philosopher;

    // start eating
    fork aristotle.Run(f0, f1);
    fork plato.Run(f1, f2);
    fork kant.Run(f0, f2);
  }
}
```

Fig. 7. Dining philosophers without deadlocks

share operation consumes this permission and stores it in the monitor, but the thread still has permission to access buffer.mu. The preconditions of Producer.Produce and Consumer.Consume indicate that upon forking the worker threads a fraction (ϵ) of the permission to buffer.mu is passed to the workers. The conjunct **maxlock** << buff.mu is trivially satisfied since a thread initially holds no monitors.

Since we use an unbounded buffer, the producer is always able to add new items to the buffer. However, when the buffer is empty, the consumer is not able to take out an

```
class Buffer {
  var contents: seq<int>;
  invariant acc(contents);
}

class Producer {
  method Produce(buff: Buffer)
    requires rd(buff.mu) && maxlock << buff.mu;
  {
    var x := 0; var y := 1;
    while (true)
      invariant rd(buff.mu) && maxlock << buff.mu;
    {
      lock (buff) {
        buff.contents := buff.contents ++ [x];
        var tmp := x; x := y; y := tmp + x;
      }
    }
  }
}

class Consumer {
  method Consume(buff: Buffer)
    requires rd(buff.mu) && maxlock << buff.mu;
  {
    while (true)
      invariant rd(buff.mu) && maxlock << buff.mu;
    {
      lock (buff) {
        if (0 < |buff.contents|) {
          var x := buff.contents[0];
          buff.contents := buff.contents[1..];
        }
      }
    }
  }
}
```

Fig. 8. A producer and a consumer. A **lock** (c) block is a syntactic shorthand for **acquire** c; *block;* **release** c.

item and has to wait until an item becomes available. In our example, we use busy-waiting to check repeatedly whether the buffer is still empty. A more efficient solution would use condition variables, which allow the consumer to wait until the producer signals the availability of new items. However, condition variables are not yet available in Chalice.

```
class Program {
  method Main() {
    var buffer := new Buffer { contents := [] };
    share buffer;

    var producer := new Producer;
    fork producer.Produce(buffer);

    var consumer := new Consumer;
    fork consumer.Consume(buffer);
  }
}
```

Fig. 9. A client for the producer and consumer of Fig. 8

It is instructive to consider a variation of Consume where, instead of enclosing the assignments by an **if** statement, they are preceded by a loop

```
while (|buff.contents| == 0) { }
```

Such an implementation might fail to make *progress*, because the consumer might acquire the empty buffer and would then enter the loop without releasing the monitor. In that case, the producer could not acquire the monitor to add a new item, the buffer would stay empty, and the consumer would loop forever. Chalice does not prevent livelocks and does not check for termination. So our hypothetical program would verify.

6 Data Abstraction

A method contract specifies which permissions a method requires or returns, together with restrictions on the values of the corresponding locations. For example, the precondition of RockBand.AddMembers from Fig. 3 indicates that AddMembers requires permission to access **this**.memberCount. The method's postcondition ensures that this permission is returned to the callee and that the value of the corresponding location has been increased by howMany. While this specification is correct, it is not implementation independent, since it exposes the internal field memberCount. Exposing the internal representation is problematic for several reasons. First, exposing a class' internals tightly *couples* client code to the implementation. That is, a change to the implementation (for example, one might keep a sequence of band members instead of just an integer) would necessitate a modification of the method contract. Whenever a method contract is changed, the correctness of all its clients must be reverified. Second, if RockBand were an interface,[4] then the field memberCount would not be available and it would be impossible to specify AddMembers.

In this section, we explain how methods can be specified without exposing the class' internal representation. As we have mentioned before, pre- and postconditions consist

---

[4] Interfaces, abstract classes, and subclasses are currently not supported in Chalice.

of a number of pure assertions and a number of access assertions. Pure assertions can be abstracted over via *functions* (see Section 6.0), and both access assertions and pure assertions can be abstracted via *predicates* (see Section 6.1).

6.0 Functions

Functions are a way to abstract over the values of memory locations. More specifically, a function is an abbreviation for an expression with a precondition. For example, consider the new version of the class RockBand in Fig. 10. This class defines a function getMemberCount whose body is an integer expression. The function is defined to yield the value of the field memberCount. getMemberCount's precondition indicates that getMemberCount can be applied only if the caller has permission to read memberCount. Without this precondition, getMemberCount's definition is invalid as reading memberCount requires an access permission. Functions cannot change the program state. In particular, they can neither produce nor consume permissions. For that reason, it is not necessary for functions to explicitly return permissions via postconditions. Instead, a function's caller automatically regains access to all permissions requested by the precondition when the function finishes.

The new version of RockBand does not explicitly dereference memberCount in method contracts, but uses the function getMemberCount instead. A function's meaning (that is, its body) is visible only to the module defining the function. But how can client code outside the module deduce which memory locations affect the function's return value? The answer is that clients can deduce this information from a function's precondition: a function can depend on a memory location o.f only if its precondition

```
class RockBand {
  var memberCount: int;
  invariant acc(memberCount) && 0 <= getMemberCount();

  function getMemberCount(): int
    requires rd(memberCount);
  { memberCount }

  method Init()
    requires acc(memberCount);
    ensures acc(memberCount) && getMemberCount() == 0;
  { memberCount := 0; }

  method AddMembers(howMany: int)
    requires acc(memberCount) && 0 <= howMany;
    ensures acc(memberCount);
    ensures getMemberCount() == old(getMemberCount()) + howMany;
  { memberCount := memberCount + howMany; }
}
```

Fig. 10. The class RockBand from Fig. 3 with a function to abstract over the value of the field memberCount. This version does not abstract over the use of memberCount in access predicates.

demands permission to access o.f. For example, getMemberCount's value depends only on the field memberCount. Therefore, if a client changes some memory locations that do not include memberCount, it can safely assume that this heap update does not affect the result of getMemberCount().

Although RockBand's contracts in Fig. 10 no longer dereference memberCount, the specification is still not implementation independent, since it does not hide what permissions are required by method implementations. In the next subsection, we introduce predicates and demonstrate how they achieve complete implementation independence.

6.1 Predicates

Predicates are a way to abstract over permissions as well as values of memory locations. More specifically, a predicate is an abbreviation for a number of access assertions and a number of pure assertions. For example, the predicate valid in Fig. 11 is a shorthand for the permission to access memberCount and the condition that it holds a non-negative value. That is, the assertion b.valid is equivalent to **acc**(b.memberCount) && 0 <= b.memberCount. In Fig. 11, RockBand's specification uses valid instead of explicitly requesting permission to access memberCount.

Each program point has one of two views of a predicate: the *abstract view* (or, folded view), which is independent of the predicate's definition, and the *concrete view* (or,

```
class RockBand {
  var memberCount: int;
  invariant valid;

  predicate valid
  { acc(memberCount) && 0 <= memberCount }

  function getMemberCount(): int
    requires valid;
  { unfolding valid in memberCount }

  method Init()
    requires acc(this.*);
    ensures valid && getMemberCount() == 0;
  { memberCount := 0; fold valid; }

  method AddMembers(howMany: int)
    requires valid && 0 <= howMany;
    ensures valid;
    ensures getMemberCount() == old(getMemberCount()) + howMany;
  { unfold valid; memberCount := memberCount + howMany; fold valid; }
}
```

Fig. 11. The class RockBand with implementation-independent contracts. The **unfolding** expression in function getMemberCount unfolds the predicate valid before evaluating the nested expression, memberCount. This unfolding is necessary to obtain the permission for this field.

unfolded view), where the predicate has been expanded according to its definition. Contrary to the functions described in the previous subsection, whose definitions are automatically available anywhere inside the module, a program switches between the two views of a predicate via two statements, **fold** and **unfold**. More specifically, **fold** q checks that q's definition holds, consumes the permissions requested by that definition, and returns q. That is, one can think of **fold** valid as an invocation of a method with contract **requires acc**(memberCount) && 0 <= memberCount; **ensures** valid. Vice versa, the statement **unfold** q requires q and returns q's definition. That is, one can think of **unfold** valid as an invocation of a method with contract **requires** valid; **ensures acc**(memberCount) && 0 <= memberCount.

Similarly to pre- and postconditions, predicate definitions must be well-defined. In particular, any dereference o.f in the definition of a predicate must be preceded by an access predicate like **acc**(o.f). This means that a predicate cannot constrain the value of a memory location unless the predicate includes permission to access that location.

Note that the specification of RockBand in Fig. 11 is implementation independent. As a consequence, we can change RockBand's internal representation (within the boundaries set by the method contract) without having to worry about reverifying client code. The conjunct **acc**(**this**.*) in the precondition of Init is a shorthand for requesting access to all fields of **this**, which means that Init does not have to mention what the fields of **this** are.

Chalice provides a number of (command-line) options to reduce annotation overhead. Firstly, the option -autoMagic reduces the size of method contracts, predicates, and invariants by inferring access assertions and other definedness conditions implicit in the explicitly given expressions. For example, this option allows one to write the predicate valid in the class Rockband as follows:

```
predicate valid
{ 0 <= memberCount }
```

In particular, the conjunct **acc**(memberCount) is inferred from the fact that the expression 0 <= memberCount accesses this field. Secondly, the option -defaults instructs Chalice to automatically fold and unfold predicates on entry and exit of methods. For example, all **unfold** and **fold** statements are inferred and can be removed from Fig. 11 if the -defaults option is used. Finally, when Chalice cannot find a particular predicate in the heap, it first tries to automatically close it before reporting an error to the user. This behavior can be activated using -autoFold. When automatic folding is active, Chalice infers the **fold** statements of Fig. 11.

6.2   Example: Aggregate Objects

An aggregate object is an object that uses other objects to represent its internal state. As an example, consider the class Stack in Fig. 12. Stack is implemented in terms of a class List (not shown here). The specification for Stack is idiomatic for aggregate objects. In particular, the valid predicate not only includes permission to access its own fields, but also demands that the representation object be valid.

Note that the specification of Stack is implementation independent, since it does not expose the fact that the class is implemented in terms of a List. A consequence

```
class Stack {
  var contents: List;

  predicate valid
  { acc(contents) && contents.valid }

  function size(): int
    requires valid;
  { unfolding valid in contents.length() }

  method Init()
    requires acc(this.*);
    ensures valid && size() == 0;
  { contents := new List; call contents.Init(); fold valid; }

  method Push(x: int)
    requires valid;
    ensures valid && size() == old(size()) + 1;
  { unfold valid; call contents.Add(x); fold valid; }
}
```

Fig. 12. The class Stack, which exemplifies typical aggregate objects

of implementation independence is that we never have to reverify client code when we change Stack's internal representation.

6.3 Example: Linked Data Structures

Many programs make use of linked data structures, that is, objects whose fields refer to instances of the same class. The class Node of Fig. 13 is an example of such a data structure. Node objects represent binary trees, where left and right refer to the left and right subtree, respectively. Linked data structures are typically specified via recursive predicates. For example, the definition of isTree is defined in terms of itself: o.isTree holds when the thread has permission to access o.value, o.left, and o.right and o.left and o.right are null or valid subtrees. This example illustrates that predicates are useful not only for abstraction, but also for specifying recursive data structures.

The method Sum computes the sum of the values in the trees by recursively calling itself on its subtrees. Note that Sum computes the sum of the left subtree in a different thread. This is just an internal detail of the implementation which is not visible to client code.

7 Example: Owicki-Gries Counter

In 1976, Owicki and Gries [34] proposed an axiomatic approach for verifying properties of concurrent programs. One of the examples they considered is shown in Fig. 14. In the example, a main thread forks two worker threads that both increment a shared

```
class Node {
  var value: int;
  var left: Node; var right: Node;

  predicate isTree {
    acc(value) && acc(left) && acc(right) &&
    (left != null ==> left.isTree) &&
    (right != null ==> right.isTree)
  }

  method Init()
    requires acc(this.*);
    ensures isTree;
  { left := null; right := null; fold isTree; }

  method Sum() returns (total: int)
    requires isTree;
    ensures isTree;
  {
    var tmp: int;

    unfold isTree;
    total := value;
    var tk: token<Node.Sum>;
    if (left != null) { fork tk := left.Sum(); }
    if (right != null) { call tmp := right.Sum(); total := total + tmp; }
    if (left != null) { join tmp := tk; total := total + tmp; }
    fold isTree;
  }
}
```

Fig. 13. A linked tree data structure, illustrating a recursive predicate and a recursive method

counter (in Fig. 14, c.value represents the shared counter). The goal of the example is to prove that the counter's value equals 2 when both worker threads finish. To prove this assertion, Owicki and Gries relied on auxiliary variables. More specifically, each worker thread has a contribution variable that holds the amount added to the shared counter by that thread. The monitor invariant of the shared counter says that the counter's value is the sum of all contributions.

Since both worker threads must be able to compete for and update the counter, OGCounter's monitor (Fig. 14) stores 100% permission for value. However, this implies that no thread has any information about the counter when the monitor is available. In particular, the postconditions of the worker cannot express that the counter has been incremented, since such a specification would require at least read permission for value. We solve this dilemma by introducing two fields c0 and c1 that take the place of the contribution variables in Owicki and Gries's example. The key idea of the Chalice encoding is to store only read permissions (here, 30%) to the contribution variables in

```
class OGCounter {
  var value: int;
  ghost var c0: int; ghost var c1: int; // contribution variables

  invariant acc(value) && acc(c0, 30) && acc(c1, 30) && c0 + c1 == value;

  method Add(b: bool)
    requires rd(mu) && maxlock << mu;
    requires (b ==> acc(c0, 70)) && (!b ==> acc(c1, 70));
    ensures rd(mu);
    ensures b ==> acc(c0, 70) && c0 == old(c0) + 1;
    ensures !b ==> acc(c1, 70) && c1 == old(c1) + 1;
  {
    lock (this) {
      if (b) {
        c0 := c0 + 1;
      } else {
        c1 := c1 + 1;
      }
      value := value + 1;
    }
  }

  method Main() {
    var c := new OGCounter { value := 0, c0 := 0, c1 := 0 };
    share c;

    fork tk0 := c.Add(true);
    fork tk1 := c.Add(false);
    join tk0; join tk1;

    lock (c) {
      assert c.value == 2;
    }
  }
}
```

Fig. 14. A program that uses worker threads to increment a shared counter. The annotations let Chalice prove the **assert** statement in Main. The fields c0 and c1 are auxiliary variables that are needed only to verify the program. Therefore, they are declared as **ghost**, which suggests to the compiler the optimization of omitting them in the executable code.

the monitor. So, each worker can get only a partial permission for the contribution variables by acquiring the monitor. The remainder of the permissions (70%) is transferred from and to the main thread when the worker threads are forked and joined. Because of this read permission, the postcondition of the workers is allowed to contain information about the values of the contribution variables. Together with the last conjunct of the monitor invariant, c0 + c1 == value, this information allows the main thread to determine what the value of the counter is.

Let's turn our attention to the implementation of the Main method. After sharing c, Main no longer has access to c.value. However, it retains 70% permission to the field c.c0 and c.c1. The Main method passes these permissions to two worker threads that each acquires c and increments c.value. By acquiring c, each worker thread gains full access to either c0 or c1 (depending on the value of the parameter b) and can update its value accordingly. Since each worker thread retains 70% after releasing the monitor, it can pass information about its contribution variable to its caller via the postcondition. The main thread gets to assume the postcondition of the worker threads when it joins them, we may deduce that both c.c0 and c.c1 equal 1. When the main thread acquires the counter, it also gets to assume the monitor invariant. In particular, it may assume that c0 + c1 == value and, thus, that the subsequent assertion holds.

8   Rely-Guarantee Reasoning

As explained in the previous section, a thread can keep track of the effect of other threads on shared data structures by using auxiliary variables. However, when the number of threads is not known at compile time, the use of such variables becomes less elegant. For that reason, Chalice provides another way of specifying and restricting the effect of threads on the shared state, namely two-state invariants. A *two-state monitor invariant* can constrain and relate two states, the current state and a previous state referred to using **old** expressions. For example, the monitor invariant of the class Counter of Fig. 15 contains the permission to access x and specifies that its value can only grow.

Like single-state monitor invariants, a two-state monitor invariant must be shown to hold whenever a thread releases a monitor. **old**(e) expressions occurring in the invariant then refer to the value of the expression e at the time the monitor was last acquired. For example, the **release** statement of the method Inc verifies because the new value of x is larger than the value at the time the monitor was acquired. Method Dec on the other hand does not verify, because the monitor invariant does not hold when the monitor is released. Whenever a thread acquires a monitor, the corresponding monitor invariant may be assumed. **old**(e) expressions occurring in the monitor invariant then refer to the value of the expression e at the time the monitor was last shared or released. For example, the assert in the Main method of Fig. 15 verifies because of Counter's two-state invariant. In particular, it follows from the invariant that on entry to the second monitor, x's value is at least tmp0.

A two-state monitor invariant is well-defined only if it is reflexive and transitive. For example, Chalice rejects the following invariant as it is transitive, but not reflexive:

```
invariant acc(x) && old(x) < x;
```

If Chalice did not check well-definedness, the code shown below would verify, although the assert statement fails during the program's execution:

```
var c := new Counter { x := 0 };
share c;
acquire c;
assert 0 < c.x;
```

```
class Counter {
  var x: int;
  invariant acc(x) && old(x) <= x;

  method Main() {
    var c := new Counter; share c;

    fork c.Inc();

    var tmp0: int; var tmp1: int;
    lock (c) { tmp0 := c.x; }
    lock (c) { tmp1 := c.x; }

    assert tmp0 <= tmp1;
  }

  method Inc()
    requires rd(mu) && maxlock << mu;
  { lock (this) { x := x + 1; } }

  method Dec()
    requires rd(mu) && maxlock << mu;
  { lock (this) { x := x - 1; } /* error */ }
}
```

Fig. 15. A class `Counter` illustrating the use of two-state invariants

The two-state monitor invariants described above allow only a limited form of rely-guarantee reasoning [23]. In particular, the conditions that are guaranteed and relied upon are the same for all threads. For information on more advanced forms of rely-guarantee, we refer the interested reader to [10,41,14].

9   Conclusion

In these lecture notes, we explained Chalice from a user's perspective. Readers who are interested in finding out what goes on behind the scenes are encouraged to read our research paper [30]. Further information can be found in the publications that inspired us: Fractional permissions were introduced by Boyland [6], who developed a type system to check concurrent programs for data races. Separation logic [36,35,33,37] used permissions for program verification. Checkers based on symbolic execution for separation logic include jStar [13], VeriFast [22], and Smallfoot [4]. Smans et al. [39] showed how the ideas of separation logic can be incorporated into a traditional verifier based on verification condition generation and first-order theorem proving. The rules for reasoning about monitors were taken from Hoare [19]. Similar approaches are used by Jacobs et al. [21] in the context of Spec# [3], by Cohen et al. [8] in the context of C, and by Gotsman et al. [16] and by Hobor et al. [20] in separation logic. Haack et al. [17,18]

demonstrate how the separation-logic approach can be extended to handle fork/join and reentrant locks. The functions described in Section 6 are similar to pure methods (see, e.g., [28,38]). Chalice's predicates are based on Parkinson's abstract predicates [35], whose use is similar to the valid/state paradigm from ESC/Modula-3 [26,31].

Another model that reuses method contract annotations for concurrency is SCOOP [0]. Other techniques for proving the absence of data races in concurrent programs include model checking [32] and ownership type systems [11,5,9].

Readers who have become excited about automatic verifiers might also want to find out about techniques and tools for sequential programs. Ownership-based verification [29], dynamic frames [24,40,27], and regional logic [1] are interesting techniques for specifying sequential imperative programs, in particular for solving the frame problem. The research community has developed various other program verifiers, including ESC/Java [15], Jahob [42], Spec# [3,2], VCC [8], and Dafny [27]. The Java Modeling Language (JML) [25,7] is the de-facto standard for specifying Java programs.

Chalice demonstrates that permissions can express many concurrency patterns, including concurrent reading, thread-local and shared objects, aggregate objects, linked object structures, and thread collaboration. Other features such as dynamic changes of the locking order are also supported, but not covered in this tutorial. The absence of data races and deadlocks, preservation of monitor invariants, and other interesting properties can be verified automatically. Nevertheless, many concurrency concepts are not yet supported by Chalice; among them are condition variables (like Java's wait-notify mechanism), volatile variables, interlocked operations, and full rely-guarantee reasoning. We hope that the FOSAD summer school, and especially these lecture notes, will encourage readers to address some of these topics. With the pending open-source release of Chalice, they will get the opportunity to experiment with the tool and contribute their solutions.

Acknowledgments. Jan Smans is a research assistant of the Fund for Scientific Research – Flanders (FWO). This research is partially funded by the Interuniversity Attraction Poles Programme Belgian State, Belgian Science Policy. Bart Jacobs showed us how to use permissions to encode the Owicki-Gries counter in Fig. 14.

References

0. Arslan, V., Eugster, P.T., Nienaltowski, P., Vaucouleur, S.: SCOOP – concurrency made easy. In: Kohlas, J., Meyer, B., Schiper, A. (eds.) Dependable Systems: Software, Computing, Networks. LNCS, vol. 4028, pp. 82–102. Springer, Heidelberg (2006)
1. Banerjee, A., Naumann, D.A., Rosenberg, S.: Regional logic for local reasoning about global invariants. In: Vitek, J. (ed.) ECOOP 2008. LNCS, vol. 5142, pp. 387–411. Springer, Heidelberg (2008)
2. Barnett, M., Chang, B.-Y.E., DeLine, R., Jacobs, B., Leino, K.R.M.: Boogie: A modular reusable verifier for object-oriented programs. In: de Boer, F.S., Bonsangue, M.M., Graf, S., de Roever, W.-P. (eds.) FMCO 2005. LNCS, vol. 4111, pp. 364–387. Springer, Heidelberg (2006)
3. Barnett, M., Leino, K.R.M., Schulte, W.: The Spec# programming system: An overview. In: Barthe, G., Burdy, L., Huisman, M., Lanet, J.-L., Muntean, T. (eds.) CASSIS 2004. LNCS, vol. 3362, pp. 49–69. Springer, Heidelberg (2005)

4. Berdine, J., Calcagno, C., O'Hearn, P.W.: Smallfoot: Modular automatic assertion checking with separation logic. In: de Boer, F.S., Bonsangue, M.M., Graf, S., de Roever, W.-P. (eds.) FMCO 2005. LNCS, vol. 4111, pp. 115–137. Springer, Heidelberg (2006)

5. Boyapati, C., Lee, R., Rinard, M.: Ownership types for safe programming: Preventing data races and deadlocks. In: Proceedings of the 2002 ACM SIGPLAN Conference on Object-Oriented Programming Systems, Languages and Applications, OOPSLA 2002, pp. 211–230. ACM, New York (2002)

6. Boyland, J.: Checking interference with fractional permissions. In: Cousot, R. (ed.) SAS 2003. LNCS, vol. 2694, pp. 55–72. Springer, Heidelberg (2003)

7. Burdy, L., Cheon, Y., Cok, D.R., Ernst, M.D., Kiniry, J.R., Leavens, G.T., Leino, K.R.M., Poll, E.: An overview of JML tools and applications. International Journal on Software Tools for Technology Transfer 7(3), 212–232 (2005)

8. Cohen, E., Dahlweid, M., Hillebrand, M., Leinenbach, D., Moskał, M., Santen, T., Schulte, W., Tobies, S.: VCC: A practical system for verifying concurrent C. In: Berghofer, S., Nipkow, T., Urban, C., Wenzel, M. (eds.) TPHOLs 2009. LNCS, vol. 5674, pp. 23–42. Springer, Heidelberg (2009)

9. Cunningham, D., Drossopoulou, S., Eisenbach, S.: Universe types for race safety. In: Proceedings of the 1st Workshop on Verification and Analysis of Multi-threaded Java-like Programs (VAMP), number ICIS-R07021 in Technical Report, pp. 20–51. Radboud University Nijmegen (September 2007)

10. de Roever, W.-P., de Boer, F., Hanneman, U., Hooman, J., Lakhnech, Y., Zwiers, J.: Concurrency Verification. Cambridge University Press, Cambridge (2001)

11. Dietl, W., Drossopoulou, S., Müller, P.: Generic universe types. In: Ernst, E. (ed.) ECOOP 2007. LNCS, vol. 4609, pp. 28–53. Springer, Heidelberg (2007)

12. Dijkstra, E.W.: Hierarchical ordering of sequential processes. Acta Informatica 1, 115–138 (1971)

13. Distefano, D., Parkinson, M.J.: jStar: Towards practical verification of Java. In: Harris, G.E. (ed.) Object-Oriented Programming Systems, Languages and Applications (OOPSLA). SIGPLAN Notices, vol. 37(11), pp. 213–226. ACM, New York (2008)

14. Feng, X.: Local rely-guarantee reasoning. In: Proceedings of the 36th ACM SIGPLAN-SIGACT Symposium on Principles of Programming Languages, POPL 2009, pp. 315–327. ACM, New York (2009)

15. Flanagan, C., Leino, K.R.M., Lillibridge, M., Nelson, G., Saxe, J.B., Stata, R.: Extended static checking for Java. In: Proceedings of the 2002 ACM SIGPLAN Conference on Programming Language Design and Implementation (PLDI), pp. 234–245. ACM, New York (2002)

16. Gotsman, A., Berdine, J., Cook, B., Rinetzky, N., Sagiv, M.: Local reasoning for storable locks and threads. In: Shao, Z. (ed.) APLAS 2007. LNCS, vol. 4807, pp. 19–37. Springer, Heidelberg (2007)

17. Haack, C., Huisman, M., Hurlin, C.: Reasoning about java's reentrant locks. In: Ramalingam, G. (ed.) APLAS 2008. LNCS, vol. 5356, pp. 171–187. Springer, Heidelberg (2008)

18. Haack, C., Hurlin, C.: Separation logic contracts for a Java-like language with fork/Join. In: Meseguer, J., Roşu, G. (eds.) AMAST 2008. LNCS, vol. 5140, pp. 199–215. Springer, Heidelberg (2008)

19. Hoare, C.A.R.: Monitors: An operating system structuring concept. Communications of the ACM 17(10), 549–557 (1974)

20. Hobor, A., Appel, A.W., Nardelli, F.Z.: Oracle semantics for concurrent separation logic. In: Drossopoulou, S. (ed.) ESOP 2008. LNCS, vol. 4960, pp. 353–367. Springer, Heidelberg (2008)

21. Jacobs, B., Leino, K.R.M., Piessens, F., Schulte, W., Smans, J.: A programming model for concurrent object-oriented programs. ACM Transactions on Programming Languages and Systems 31(1) (December 2008)
22. Jacobs, B., Piessens, F.: The VeriFast program verifier. Technical Report CW-520, Department of Computer Science, Katholieke Universiteit Leuven (August 2008)
23. Jones, C.B.: Specification and design of (parallel) programs. In: Proceedings of IFIP 1983, pp. 321–332. North-Holland, Amsterdam (1983)
24. Kassios, I.T.: Dynamic frames: Support for framing, dependencies and sharing without restrictions. In: Misra, J., Nipkow, T., Sekerinski, E. (eds.) FM 2006. LNCS, vol. 4085, pp. 268–283. Springer, Heidelberg (2006)
25. Leavens, G.T., Baker, A.L., Ruby, C.: JML: A notation for detailed design. In: Kilov, H., Rumpe, B., Simmonds, I. (eds.) Behavioral Specifications of Businesses and Systems, pp. 175–188. Kluwer Academic Publishers, Dordrecht (1999)
26. Leino, K.R.M.: Toward Reliable Modular Programs. PhD thesis, California Institute of Technology, Technical Report Caltech-CS-TR-95-03 (1995)
27. Leino, K.R.M.: Specification and verification of object-oriented software. In: Engineering Methods and Tools for Software Safety and Security. NATO Security Through Science Series; Sub-Series D, vol. 22, pp. 231–266. IOS Press, Amsterdam (2009)
28. Leino, K.R.M., Middelkoop, R.: Proving consistency of pure methods and model fields. In: Chechik, M., Wirsing, M. (eds.) FASE 2009. LNCS, vol. 5503, pp. 231–245. Springer, Heidelberg (2009)
29. Leino, K.R.M., Müller, P.: Object invariants in dynamic contexts. In: Odersky, M. (ed.) ECOOP 2004. LNCS, vol. 3086, pp. 491–515. Springer, Heidelberg (2004)
30. Leino, K.R.M., Müller, P.: A basis for verifying multi-threaded programs. In: Castagna, G. (ed.) ESOP 2009. LNCS, vol. 5502, pp. 378–393. Springer, Heidelberg (2009)
31. Leino, K.R.M., Nelson, G.: Data abstraction and information hiding. ACM Transactions on Programming Languages and Systems 24(5), 491–553 (2002)
32. Musuvathi, M., Qadeer, S., Ball, T., Basler, G., Nainar, P.A., Neamtiu, I.: Finding and reproducing Heisenbugs in concurrent programs. In: Draves, R., van Renesse, R. (eds.) 8th USENIX Symposium on Operating Systems Design and Implementation, OSDI 2008, December 2008, pp. 267–280. USENIX Association (2008)
33. O'Hearn, P.W.: Resources, concurrency, and local reasoning. Theoretical Computer Science 375(1-3), 271–307 (2007)
34. Owicki, S., Gries, D.: Verifying properties of parallel programs: An axiomatic approach. Communications of the ACM 19(5), 279–285 (1976)
35. Parkinson, M.J., Bierman, G.M.: Separation logic and abstraction. In: Palsberg, J., Abadi, M. (eds.) Proceedings of the 32nd ACM SIGPLAN-SIGACT Symposium on Principles of Programming Languages, POPL 2005, pp. 247–258. ACM, New York (2005)
36. Parkinson, M.J.: Local Reasoning for Java. PhD thesis. University of Cambridge (2005)
37. Reynolds, J.C.: Separation logic: A logic for shared mutable data structures. In: 17th IEEE Symposium on Logic in Computer Science (LICS 2002), pp. 55–74. IEEE, Los Alamitos (2002)
38. Rudich, A., Darvas, Á., Müller, P.: Checking well-formedness of pure-method specifications. In: Cuellar, J., Maibaum, T., Sere, K. (eds.) FM 2008. LNCS, vol. 5014, pp. 68–83. Springer, Heidelberg (2008)
39. Smans, J., Jacobs, B., Piessens, F.: Implicit dynamic frames: Combining dynamic frames and separation logic. In: Drossopoulou, S. (ed.) ECOOP 2009. LNCS, vol. 5653, pp. 148–172. Springer, Heidelberg (2009)

40. Smans, J., Jacobs, B., Piessens, F., Schulte, W.: An automatic verifier for java-like programs based on dynamic frames. In: Fiadeiro, J.L., Inverardi, P. (eds.) FASE 2008. LNCS, vol. 4961, pp. 261–275. Springer, Heidelberg (2008)
41. Vafeiadis, V., Parkinson, M.: A marriage of rely/Guarantee and separation logic. In: Caires, L., Vasconcelos, V.T. (eds.) CONCUR 2007. LNCS, vol. 4703, pp. 256–271. Springer, Heidelberg (2007)
42. Zee, K., Kuncak, V., Rinard, M.C.: Full functional verification of linked data structures. In: Gupta, R., Amarasinghe, S.P. (eds.) Proceedings of the ACM SIGPLAN 2008 Conference on Programming Language Design and Implementation, pp. 349–361. ACM, New York (2008)

Certified Static Analysis by Abstract Interpretation

Frédéric Besson[1], David Cachera[2,*], Thomas Jensen[3], and David Pichardie[1]

[1] INRIA Rennes, Campus de Beaulieu, 35042 Rennes Cedex, France
[2] ENS Cachan (Bretagne), Campus de Ker Lann, 35170 Bruz, France
[3] CNRS, Campus de Beaulieu, 35042 Rennes Cedex, France

Abstract. A certified static analysis is an analysis whose semantic validity has been formally proved correct with a proof assistant. We propose a tutorial on building a certified static analysis in Coq. We study a simple bytecode language for which we propose an interval analysis that allows to verify statically that no array-out-of-bounds accesses will occur.

1 Introduction

Static program analysis is a fully automatic technique for proving properties about the behaviour of a program without actually executing it. Static analysis is becoming an important part of modern security architectures, as it allows to screen code for potential security vulnerabilities or malicious behaviour before integrating it into a computing platform. A prime example of this is the Java byte code verifier that plays an important role in the Java Virtual Machine security architecture. The byte code verifier ensures by a static analysis that code is well typed and that objects are constructed properly—two properties that when properly verified improve the overall security of the virtual machine. At the same time, it is recognized that static analyzers are complex pieces of software whose integration into the trusted computing base (TCB) may pose problems. Indeed, static analyzers implement sophisticated logics for proving properties about programs and errors in the implementation are possible. Such errors in the implementation may compromise the security of the platform as was the case in some early implementations of the Java type checking mechanism [MF99]. In general, it is desirable to reduce the part of the static analyzer that forms part of the TCB.

The correctness of static analyses can be proved formally by following the theory of abstract interpretation [CC77] that provides a theory for relating two semantic interpretations of the same language. These strong semantic foundations constitute one of the arguments advanced in favor of static program analysis. The implementation of static analyses is usually based on well-understood constraint-solving techniques and iterative fixpoint algorithms. In spite of the nice mathematical theory of program analysis and the solid algorithmic techniques available one problematic issue persists, *viz.*, the *gap* between the analysis that is proved correct on paper and the analyser that actually runs on

---

* Currently delegated as a full time researcher at INRIA, Centre Rennes - Bretagne Atlantique.

A. Aldini, G. Barthe, R. Gorrieri (Eds.): FOSAD 2007/2008/2009, LNCS 5705, pp. 223–257, 2009.

the machine. While this gap might be small for toy languages, it becomes important when it comes to real-life languages for which the implementation and maintenance of program analysis tools become a software engineering task. To eliminate this gap, is possible to merge both the analyser implementation and the soundness proof into the same logic of a proof assistant. This gives raise to the notion of *certified static analysis*, *i.e.* an analysis whose implementation has been formally proved correct using a proof assistant.

Related Work. This tutorial paper follows [CJPR05], where a dataflow analysis for a byte code language has been formalized in Coq. In [CJPS05], the same kind of framework has been applied to a different kind of analysis, namely an analysis certifying the absence of infinite loops in a byte code interprocedural language.

Proving correctness of program analyses is one of the main applications of the theory of abstract interpretation [CC77]. However, most of the existing proofs are pencil-and-paper proofs of analyses (formal specifications) and not mechanised proofs of analysers (implementations of analyses). The only attempt of formalising the theory of abstract interpretation with a proof assistant is that of Monniaux [Mon98] who has built a Coq theory of Galois connections. The Coq proof assistant at this time did not benefit from the current extraction mechanism, which prevented the author from extracting analysers from the specifications. More recently, Bertot has proposed a Coq] formalization of abstract interpretation for a While language [Ber08], based on a weakest precondition calculus. His work however does not consider termination issues. Mechanical proofs about fixpoint iteration using widenings have not been considered by other authors, since widening operators require complex termination proofs. Other existing works only deal with ascending chain condition [KN02, BD04, CGD06, BGL06].

Other approaches use a proof assistant for certifying the correction of static analyses, without developing a framework for a general theory like abstract interpretation. Barthe and al. [BDHdS01] have shown how to formalize Java byte code verification, reasoning on an executable semantics. In [BDJ+01], they automatize the derivation of a certified verifier in a dedicated environment. In another approach, Klein and Nipkow have used Isabelle/HOL to formalize a bytecode verifier [KN02]. In [KN06], they propose a complete formalization of both source language and byte code language semantics, of a non-optimising compiler and of a bytecode verifier, for a Java-like language. The proofs however are not done at the analysis implementation level, and do not offer the same certification level as with a Coq extraction.

Finally, Lee *et al.* [LCH07] have certified the type analysis of a language close to Standard ML in LF and Leroy [Ler06] has certified some of the data flow analyses of a compiler back-end.

Overview. In this work we rely on the Coq proof assistant [Coq09]. Coq is used here as programming language with a very rich type system where full functional correctness of functional programs can be formally established. The program extraction mechanism provides a tool for automatic translation of these programs into a functional language with a simpler type system, namely Ocaml.

The extraction mechanism removes those parts of the lambda-terms that are only concerned with proving properties without actually contributing to the final result. In our context this mechanism allow us to obtain certified Ocaml implementation of static analysis that have been formally proved correct with Coq.

In order to mechanically prove correctness of static analyses we follow the abstract interpretation methodology that provide a rich framework for designing sound static analyses in a methodological way and comparing the precision of static analyses. We are mainly interested here in ensuring correctness of our analyses, rather that systematically design optimal ones. We will then only use a restricted part of the theory in our Coq formalization. Other parts will be presented and used in order to give a formal methodology for static analysis construction, but will not be explicitly defined inside Coq.

The methodology that we present here is generic but we have chosen to develop it in the concrete setting of a Java-like bytecode language for which we propose an interval analysis that allows to verify statically that no array-out-of-bounds accesses will occur.

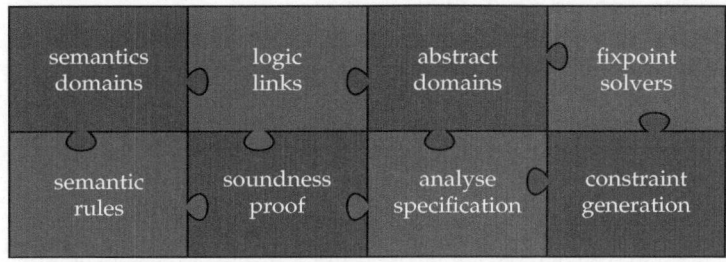

Fig. 1. The main blocks for building a certified static analysis

Building a certified static analysis can be thought as assembling puzzle pieces, as shown in Figure 1, where each piece interacts with its neighbors. The basic components of a static analysis based on abstract interpretation are: (1) a (concrete) semantic domain and (2) semantic rules modelling the program behaviour, (3) an abstract domain allowing the expression of properties on the concrete domain, (4) logic links between abstract and concrete domains, describing how abstract objects represent concrete ones, (5) the specification of the analysis, under the form of constraints between abstract objects, (6) correctness proofs showing that any solution to the analysis specification indeed represents an approximation of the concrete semantics, (7) a way to generate analysis constraints from the program syntax, and (8) a way to compute a solution of the analysis specification.

We will know describe in turn all of these pieces, giving each time most of Coq code used in the development. The whole development is made available on-line at the following url:

http://www.irisa.fr/celtique/pichardie/fosad09/

2   Running Language Example

To illustrate the progress of our methodology, we will develop an interval analysis for a simple byte code language. The analysis is based on existing interval analyses for high-level structured languages [Cou99] but has been extended with an abstract domain of *syntactic expressions* in order to obtain a similar precision at byte code level.

The language we treat is sufficiently general to illustrate the feasibility of our approach and perform experiments on code obtained from compilation of Java source code. We restrict ourselves to programs with only one method manipulating an operand stack, handling integers (with infinite arithmetic) and dynamically allocated arrays. Missing features like method calls, objects or multi-threading could be added to this language, but would require more complex static analyses that are beyond the scope of this tutorial paper.

The syntax of our language is defined in Coq with inductive types.

```
Definition pc := word.
Definition var := word.
Inductive binop := Add | Sub | Mult.
Inductive cmp := Eq | Ne | Gt | Ge.
Inductive instruction :=
    | Nop | Push (n:integer)| Pop | Dup
    | Load (x:var) | Store (x:var) | Binop (op:binop)
    | Newarray | Arraylength | Arrayload | Arraystore
    | Input
    | If (c:cmp) (jump:pc) | Goto (jump:pc).
Definition program := list (pc * instruction).
```

The syntax we use here is similar to Caml's variant types. Type word is kept abstract here but will be made explicit in Section 10. The only requirement we have for the moment is an equality test on objects of this type.

```
Definition eq_word_dec : ∀ w1 w2 : word, {w1=w2}+{w1≠w2} := ...
```

We use here a dependent type: eq_word_dec is a function that takes two arguments (called w1 and w2 here) of type word and returns a *rich* boolean type which explicitly depends on the two arguments of the function. This inductive type contains two constructors. An element of type {w1=w2}+{w1≠w2} is either of the form (Left h) with h a proof of w1=w2, or (Right h) with h a proof of w1≠w2.

The type word is used to model local variable names and program counters. We handle addition, subtraction and multiplication over integers (type binop). Integers can be tested with respect to four kinds of comparisons: equality, disequality, and order (strict or not). The language handles instructions for operand stack manipulation (Pop, Dup), local variable manipulation (Load x, Store x, respectively loading from or storing to memory, to of from the stack) and conditional (If) or unconditional (Goto) jumps. Arrays are dynamically allocated with Newarray, read with Arrayload, written with Arraystore and we can read their length with Arraylength. At last, the instruction Input pushes an arbitrary integer on the operand stack. A program is just an association list between program counters and instructions.

As an example, we give on Figure 2 (first column) the byte code of a program doing a bubble sort. The source version is given on Figure 3. Only program counters that are targets of a jump are displayed.

3   Semantic Domains

The first piece of our puzzle relates to the semantic domain, that is, the runtime structures that are manipulated by the program during execution.

Semantic Domains of the Bytecode Language. Our byte code programs manipulate states of the form (pc, h, s, l) where pc is the control point to be executed next, h is a heap for storing allocated arrays, s is an operand stack, and l is an environment mapping local variables to values. An array is modeled by a dependent pair consisting of the size *length* of the array and a function that for a given index in the range $[0, length - 1]$, returns the value stored at that index. A special error state is used to model execution errors which arise here from indexing an array outside its bounds or allocating an array with a negative size. All this elements are defined with standard enumerate types. Arrays are defined with a record, where the field array_values is a function with a dependent type, taking two arguments: the first one (called i) is an integer and the second one is a proof that i is in the right range.

```
Inductive val : Set := | Num (i:integer)| Ref (l:location).

Inductive var_val : Set := Undef | Def (v:val).
Definition locvar : Set := var → var_val.

Definition opstack : Set := list val.

Record array : Set := {
  array_length : integer;
  array_values : ∀ i:integer, (0 <= i < array_length) → integer
}.

Inductive heap_val : Set :=
  No | Array (a:array).
Definition heap := location → heap_val.

Inductive state : Set :=
| St (i:pc) (s:opstack) (l:locvar) (h:heap)
| Error.
```

Complete Lattice Structure. According to the base postulate of abstract interpretation, the semantic domain for expressing the concrete semantics can be given a complete lattice structure.

0:Ipush 10		$i \in \bot$	$j \in \bot$	$tmp \in \bot$	$n \in \bot$	$t \in \bot$
:Store 4	10	$i \in \bot$	$j \in \bot$	$tmp \in \bot$	$n \in \bot$	$t \in \bot$
:Load 4		$i \in \bot$	$j \in \bot$	$tmp \in \bot$	$n \in [10,10]$	$t \in \bot$
:Newarray	n	$i \in \bot$	$j \in \bot$	$tmp \in \bot$	$n \in [10,10]$	$t \in \bot$
:Store 5	n	$i \in \bot$	$j \in \bot$	$tmp \in \bot$	$n \in [10,10]$	$t \in \bot$
:Ipush 0		$i \in \bot$	$j \in \bot$	$tmp \in \bot$	$n \in [10,10]$	$t \in [10,10]$
:Store 1	0	$i \in \bot$	$j \in \bot$	$tmp \in \bot$	$n \in [10,10]$	$t \in [10,10]$
7:Load 1		$i \in [0,9]$	$j \in [1,9]$	$tmp \in \top$	$n \in [10,10]$	$t \in [10,10]$
:Load 4	i	$i \in [0,9]$	$j \in [1,9]$	$tmp \in \top$	$n \in [10,10]$	$t \in [10,10]$
:Ipush 1	i::n	$i \in [0,9]$	$j \in [1,9]$	$tmp \in \top$	$n \in [10,10]$	$t \in [10,10]$
:Binop Sub	i::n::1	$i \in [0,9]$	$j \in [1,9]$	$tmp \in \top$	$n \in [10,10]$	$t \in [10,10]$
:If Ge 58	i::(Sub n 1)	$i \in [0,9]$	$j \in [1,9]$	$tmp \in \top$	$n \in [10,10]$	$t \in [10,10]$
:Ipush 0		$i \in [0,8]$	$j \in [1,9]$	$tmp \in \top$	$n \in [10,10]$	$t \in [10,10]$
:Store 2	0	$i \in [0,8]$	$j \in [1,9]$	$tmp \in \top$	$n \in [10,10]$	$t \in [10,10]$
14:Load 2		$i \in [0,8]$	$j \in [0,9]$	$tmp \in \top$	$n \in [10,10]$	$t \in [10,10]$
:Load 4	j	$i \in [0,8]$	$j \in [0,9]$	$tmp \in \top$	$n \in [10,10]$	$t \in [10,10]$
:Ipush 1	j::n	$i \in [0,8]$	$j \in [0,9]$	$tmp \in \top$	$n \in [10,10]$	$t \in [10,10]$
:Binop Sub	j::n::1	$i \in [0,8]$	$j \in [0,9]$	$tmp \in \top$	$n \in [10,10]$	$t \in [10,10]$
:Load 1	j::(Sub n 1)	$i \in [0,8]$	$j \in [0,9]$	$tmp \in \top$	$n \in [10,10]$	$t \in [10,10]$
:Binop Sub	j::(Sub n 1)::i	$i \in [0,8]$	$j \in [0,9]$	$tmp \in \top$	$n \in [10,10]$	$t \in [10,10]$
:If Ge 53	j::(Sub (Sub n 1) i)	$i \in [0,8]$	$j \in [0,9]$	$tmp \in \top$	$n \in [10,10]$	$t \in [10,10]$
:Load 5		$i \in [0,8]$	$j \in [0,8]$	$tmp \in \top$	$n \in [10,10]$	$t \in [10,10]$
:Load 2	t	$i \in [0,8]$	$j \in [0,8]$	$tmp \in \top$	$n \in [10,10]$	$t \in [10,10]$
:Ipush 1	t::j	$i \in [0,8]$	$j \in [0,8]$	$tmp \in \top$	$n \in [10,10]$	$t \in [10,10]$
:Binop Add	t::j::1	$i \in [0,8]$	$j \in [0,8]$	$tmp \in \top$	$n \in [10,10]$	$t \in [10,10]$
:Arrayload	t::(Add j 1)	$i \in [0,8]$	$j \in [0,8]$	$tmp \in \top$	$n \in [10,10]$	$t \in [10,10]$
:Load 5	Top	$i \in [0,8]$	$j \in [0,8]$	$tmp \in \top$	$n \in [10,10]$	$t \in [10,10]$
:Load 2	Top::t	$i \in [0,8]$	$j \in [0,8]$	$tmp \in \top$	$n \in [10,10]$	$t \in [10,10]$
:Arrayload	Top::t::j	$i \in [0,8]$	$j \in [0,8]$	$tmp \in \top$	$n \in [10,10]$	$t \in [10,10]$
:If Ge 48	Top::Top	$i \in [0,8]$	$j \in [0,8]$	$tmp \in \top$	$n \in [10,10]$	$t \in [10,10]$
:Load 5		$i \in [0,8]$	$j \in [0,8]$	$tmp \in \top$	$n \in [10,10]$	$t \in [10,10]$
:Load 2	t	$i \in [0,8]$	$j \in [0,8]$	$tmp \in \top$	$n \in [10,10]$	$t \in [10,10]$
:Arrayload	t::j	$i \in [0,8]$	$j \in [0,8]$	$tmp \in \top$	$n \in [10,10]$	$t \in [10,10]$
:Store 3	Top	$i \in [0,8]$	$j \in [0,8]$	$tmp \in \top$	$n \in [10,10]$	$t \in [10,10]$
:Load 5		$i \in [0,8]$	$j \in [0,8]$	$tmp \in \top$	$n \in [10,10]$	$t \in [10,10]$
:Load 2	t	$i \in [0,8]$	$j \in [0,8]$	$tmp \in \top$	$n \in [10,10]$	$t \in [10,10]$
:Load 5	t::j	$i \in [0,8]$	$j \in [0,8]$	$tmp \in \top$	$n \in [10,10]$	$t \in [10,10]$
:Load 2	t::j::t	$i \in [0,8]$	$j \in [0,8]$	$tmp \in \top$	$n \in [10,10]$	$t \in [10,10]$
:Ipush 1	t::j::t::j	$i \in [0,8]$	$j \in [0,8]$	$tmp \in \top$	$n \in [10,10]$	$t \in [10,10]$
:Binop Add	t::j::t::j::1	$i \in [0,8]$	$j \in [0,8]$	$tmp \in \top$	$n \in [10,10]$	$t \in [10,10]$
:Arrayload	t::j::t::(Add j 1)	$i \in [0,8]$	$j \in [0,8]$	$tmp \in \top$	$n \in [10,10]$	$t \in [10,10]$
:Arraystore	t::j::Top	$i \in [0,8]$	$j \in [0,8]$	$tmp \in \top$	$n \in [10,10]$	$t \in [10,10]$
:Load 5		$i \in [0,8]$	$j \in [0,8]$	$tmp \in \top$	$n \in [10,10]$	$t \in [10,10]$
:Load 2	t	$i \in [0,8]$	$j \in [0,8]$	$tmp \in \top$	$n \in [10,10]$	$t \in [10,10]$
:Ipush 1	t::j	$i \in [0,8]$	$j \in [0,8]$	$tmp \in \top$	$n \in [10,10]$	$t \in [10,10]$
:Binop Add	t::j::1	$i \in [0,8]$	$j \in [0,8]$	$tmp \in \top$	$n \in [10,10]$	$t \in [10,10]$
:Load 3	t::(Add j 1)	$i \in [0,8]$	$j \in [0,8]$	$tmp \in \top$	$n \in [10,10]$	$t \in [10,10]$
:Arraystore	t::(Add j 1)::tmp	$i \in [0,8]$	$j \in [0,8]$	$tmp \in \top$	$n \in [10,10]$	$t \in [10,10]$
48:Load 2		$i \in [0,8]$	$j \in [0,8]$	$tmp \in \top$	$n \in [10,10]$	$t \in [10,10]$
:Ipush 1	j	$i \in [0,8]$	$j \in [0,8]$	$tmp \in \top$	$n \in [10,10]$	$t \in [10,10]$
:Binop Add	j::1	$i \in [0,8]$	$j \in [0,8]$	$tmp \in \top$	$n \in [10,10]$	$t \in [10,10]$
:Store 2	(Add j 1)	$i \in [0,8]$	$j \in [0,8]$	$tmp \in \top$	$n \in [10,10]$	$t \in [10,10]$
:Goto 14		$i \in [0,8]$	$j \in [1,9]$	$tmp \in \top$	$n \in [10,10]$	$t \in [10,10]$
53:Load 1		$i \in [0,8]$	$j \in [1,9]$	$tmp \in \top$	$n \in [10,10]$	$t \in [10,10]$
:Ipush 1	i	$i \in [0,8]$	$j \in [1,9]$	$tmp \in \top$	$n \in [10,10]$	$t \in [10,10]$
:Binop Add	i::1	$i \in [0,8]$	$j \in [1,9]$	$tmp \in \top$	$n \in [10,10]$	$t \in [10,10]$
:Store 1	(Add i 1)	$i \in [0,8]$	$j \in [1,9]$	$tmp \in \top$	$n \in [10,10]$	$t \in [10,10]$
:Goto 7		$i \in [1,9]$	$j \in [1,9]$	$tmp \in \top$	$n \in [10,10]$	$t \in [10,10]$
58:		$i \in [9,9]$	$j \in [1,9]$	$tmp \in \top$	$n \in [10,10]$	$t \in [10,10]$

Fig. 2. Byte code for bubble sort

```
class BubbleSort {
    public static void main(String argv ) {
        int i,j,tmp,n;
        n = 10;
        int[] t = new int[n];
        // We omit the initialisation of the array
        for (i=0; i<n-1; i++)
            for (j=0; j<n-1-i; j++)
                if (t[j+1] < t[j])
                    { tmp = t[j]; t[j] = t[j+1]; t[j+1] = tmp; }
    }
}
```

Fig. 3. Source code for buble sort

Definition 1 (Complete lattice). *A complete lattice is a triple* $(A, \sqsubseteq, \bigsqcup)$ *composed of a set* A, *equipped with a partial order* $\sqsubseteq$ *and a least upper bound (lub)* $\bigsqcup$: *for all subset* S *of* A,

- $\forall a \in S,\ a \sqsubseteq \bigsqcup S$
- $\forall b \in A, (\forall a \in S,\ a \sqsubseteq b) \Rightarrow \bigsqcup S \sqsubseteq b$

A complete lattice necessarily has a greatest lower bound (glb) operator $\bigsqcap$. It also necessarily has a greatest element $\top = \bigsqcap \emptyset = \bigsqcup A$, and a least element $\bot = \bigsqcup \emptyset = \bigsqcap A$.

Here, we can consider the set of subsets of state ordered by inclusion as concrete domain. Such a powerset domain $\mathcal{P}(\text{state})$ is given a complete lattice structure $(\mathcal{P}(\text{state}), \subseteq, \cup, \cap)$. Elements of $\mathcal{P}(\text{state})$ are seen as properties on objects of state. The partial order $\subseteq$ thus models the property accuracy: if $P_1 \subseteq P_2$, then P_1 gives more precision, since it describes a smaller set of behaviours.

Complete lattices can be formalised in Coq by means, for example, of a record construct. However, though it remains quite easy to prove general results on complete lattices in Coq, the effective instantiation of such a structure is much more intricate because of the constructive logic used by Coq. For example, if the base set is of an implementable type, the lub will be a function that for any predicate P on the lattice carrier[1] computes the least upper bound of all elements satisfying P. But predicate P is of a logical type that is not necessarily implementable. Still, for the carrier $\mathcal{P}(\text{state})$ the lattice structure can be build in Coq but it is useless for the purpose of our case study. We thus end this section with a simple semantic domain $\mathcal{P}(\text{state})$ without a formal proof that it enjoys a canonical complete lattice structure.

4   Semantic Rules

We still have to formally explain how a program manipulates the elements of the semantic domain during an execution. This is traditionally expressed by means

---

[1] A subset in $\mathcal{P}(A)$ is encoded as a predicate of type $A \rightarrow$ **Prop** in Coq.

of an operational semantics, under the form of a transition relation `-[p]->` between states, parameterized by a program p. The keyword **Inductive** is now used for a different purpose that during the syntax definition. We define here a relation with inductive rules. We rely on the Coq notation system to directly use the notation `-[p]->`. The definition handles one or two rules per instructions in the language. The function `instr_at` is a lookup search in the instruction list in order to find the instruction associated with a given program counter. Function next computes the successor of a program counter. The execution does not progress for ill-typed states, except for arrays out of bound access or allocation of an array with a negative size, that leads to an explicit error state.

```
Inductive step (p:program) : state → state → Prop :=
 | step_nop : ∀ pc h s l,
      instr_at p pc = Some Nop →
      (St pc s l h) -[p]-> (St (next pc) s l h)
 | step_push : ∀ pc h s l n,
      instr_at p pc = Some (Push n) →
      (St pc s l h) -[p]-> (St (next pc) (Num n :: s) l h)
 | step_pop : ∀ pc h s l v,
      instr_at p pc = Some Pop →
      (St pc (v::s) l h) -[p]-> (St (next pc) s l h)
 | step_dup : ∀ pc h s l v,
      instr_at p pc = Some Dup →
      (St pc (v::s) l h) -[p]-> (St (next pc) (v::v::s) l h)
 | step_iload : ∀ pc h s l x v,
      instr_at p pc = Some (Load x) →
      l x = Def v →
      (St pc s l h) -[p]-> (St (next pc) (v::s) l h)
 | step_istore : ∀ pc h s l x v l',
      instr_at p pc = Some (Store x) →
      subst l x v l' →
      (St pc (v :: s) l h) -[p]-> (St (next pc) s l' h)
 | step_binop : ∀ pc h s l v1 v2 b,
      instr_at p pc = Some (Binop b) →
      (St pc (Num v2:: Num v1::s) l h)
           -[p]-> (St (next pc) (Num (binop_sem b v1 v2)::s) l h)
 | step_newarray_1 : ∀ pc h h' s l n loc,
      instr_at p pc = Some Newarray →
      create_new_array h n h' loc →
      (St pc (Num n :: s) l h)
           -[p]-> (St (next pc) (Ref loc :: s) l h')
 | step_newarray_2 : ∀ pc h s l n,
      instr_at p pc = Some Newarray →
      n<0 →
      (St pc (Num n :: s) l h) -[p]-> Error
 | step_arraylength : ∀ pc h a s l loc,
      instr_at p pc = Some Arraylength →
      h loc = Array a →
      (St pc (Ref loc :: s) l h)
```

```
        -[p]-> (St (next pc) (Num a.(array_length) :: s) l h)
| step_arrayload_1 : ∀ pc h a  i s l loc,
    instr_at p pc = Some Arrayload →
    h loc = Array a →
    ∀ hi:(0 <= i < a.(array_length)),
    (St pc (Num i :: Ref loc :: s) l h)
    -[p]-> (St (next pc) (Num (a.(array_values) i hi) :: s) l h)
| step_arrayload_2 : ∀ pc h a  i s l loc,
    instr_at p pc = Some Arrayload →
    h loc = Array a →
    ¬ (0 <= i < a.(array_length)) →
    (St pc (Num i::Ref loc :: s) l h) -[p]-> Error
| step_arraystore_1 : ∀ pc h i s l loc n h',
    instr_at p pc = Some Arraystore →
    heap_update_array h loc i n h' →
    (St pc (Num n :: Num i :: Ref loc :: s) l h)
       -[p]-> (St (next pc) s l h')
| step_arraystore_2 : ∀ pc h i s l loc n a,
    instr_at p pc = Some Arraystore →
    h loc = Array a →
    ¬ (0 <= i < a.(array_length)) →
    (St pc (Num n :: Num i :: Ref loc :: s) l h) -[p]-> Error
| step_goto : ∀ pc jump h s l,
    instr_at p pc = Some (Goto jump) →
    (St pc s l h) -[p]-> (St jump s l h)
| step_if_1 : ∀ pc h s n1 n2 l cmp jump,
    instr_at p pc = Some (If cmp jump) →
    cmp_sem cmp n1 n2 →
    (St pc (Num n2 :: Num n1 :: s) l h) -[p]-> (St jump s l h)
| step_if_2 : ∀ pc h s n1 n2 l cmp jump,
    instr_at p pc = Some (If cmp jump) →
    ¬ cmp_sem cmp n1 n2 →
    (St pc (Num n2 :: Num n1 :: s) l h)
       -[p]-> (St (next pc) s l h)
| step_input : ∀ pc h s l n,
    instr_at p pc = Some Input →
    (St pc s l h) -[p]-> (St (next pc) (Num n :: s) l h)
where "s1_-[_p_]->_s2" := (step p s1 s2).
```

The predicate (subst l s v l') expresses the fact that the set of local variables l' is the update of set l with the value v and for the variable x.

```
Inductive subst : locvar → var → val → locvar → Prop :=
  subst_def : ∀ (env env' : locvar) x n,
    env' x = Def n →
    (∀ y, x ≠ y → env y = env' y) →
    subst env x n env'.
```

The predicate (create_new_array h n' loc) expresses the fact that heap h' results from the allocation of a new array of size n in a heap h at location loc.

```
Inductive create_new_array :
                        heap → integer → heap → location → Prop :=
 create_new_array_def : ∀ h n h' loc a,
    h loc = No →
    (∀ loc', loc' ≠ loc → h loc' = h' loc') →
    h' loc = Array a →
    a.(array_length) = n →
    (∀ i (h:0<=i<a.(array_length)), a.(array_values) i h = 0) →
    create_new_array h n h' loc.
```

The predicate (heap_update_array h loc i n h') expresses the fact that heap h' results from an update of an array at location loc in the heap h. The corresponding array is updated at index i with the value n.

```
Inductive array_subst :
                        array → integer → integer → array → Prop :=
 array_subst_def : ∀ a a' i n,
    ∀ h:(0 <= i < a'.(array_length)),
    a'.(array_length) = a.(array_length) →
    a'.(array_values) i h = n →
    (∀ j,
       i≠j →
       ∀ h:(0 <= j < a.(array_length)),
       ∀ h':(0 <= j < a'.(array_length)),
      a'.(array_values) j h' = a.(array_values) j h) →
    array_subst a i n a'.
Inductive heap_subst :
                        heap → location → heap_val → heap → Prop :=
 heap_subst_def : ∀ h h' loc hv,
    h' loc = hv →
    (∀ loc', loc ≠ loc' → h' loc' = h loc') →
    heap_subst h loc hv h'.
Inductive heap_update_array :
          heap → location → integer → integer → heap → Prop :=
 heap_update_array_def : ∀ h loc i n h' a a',
    h loc = Array a →
    array_subst a i n a' →
    heap_subst h loc (Array a') h' →
    heap_update_array h loc i n h'.
```

The relation cmp_sem gives a semantics to the comparison operators.

```
Definition cmp_sem (cmp:cmp) : integer → integer → Prop :=
  match cmp with
    | Eq ⇒ fun x y ⇒ x=y
    | Ne ⇒ fun x y ⇒ x≠y
    | Gt ⇒ fun x y ⇒ x>y
    | Ge ⇒ fun x y ⇒ x>=y
  end.
```

Semantics of binary operators is given by binop_sem.

```
Definition binop_sem (binop:binop) :
          integer → integer → integer :=
  match binop with
    | Add ⇒ Zplus
    | Sub ⇒ Zminus
    | Mult ⇒ Zmult
  end.
```

We can then define the set of reachable states during the execution of a program.

```
Inductive InitState (p:program) : state → Prop :=
  initState_def :
    InitState p  (St p nil (fun _ ⇒ Undef) (fun _ ⇒ No)).
```

```
Inductive ReachableStates (p:program) : state → Prop :=
    reach_init : ∀ st, InitState p st → ReachableStates p st
  | reach_next : ∀ st1 st2,
      ReachableStates p st1 → st1 -[p]-> st2 →
      ReachableStates p st2.
```

The predicate ReachableStates p (noted $[\![p]\!]$ in mathematical form) is generally given a least fixpoint characterisation

$$[\![p]\!] = lfp(\lambda X.S_0 \cup post_p(X))$$

where S_0 is the set of initial states (called InitState in Coq) and $post$, the operator formally defined by

$$post_p(S) = \{s_2 \mid \exists s_1 \in S,\ s_1 \text{-} [p] \text{->} s_2\}$$

We do not prove here this characterisation in Coq. Instead, the inductive definition we use for ReachableStates gives us for free that:

1. $[\![p]\!]$ contains S_0 (rule reach_init),
2. $[\![p]\!]$ is stable by $post$ (rule reach_next),
3. and this is the least property that satisfies this two conditions (by the intrinsic property of inductive definitions).

This least-postfixpoint characterisation will be sufficient for the rest of the work.

The global objective of the analysis is to prove that all reachable states of a program are safe, *i.e.* are not the error state. More formally, safe is defined by

```
Definition Safe (st:state) : Prop := st ≠ Error.
```

5   Abstract Domains

The concrete semantics is unfortunately not computable. The key idea of abstract interpretation theory is to replace the previous semantic domains by a simpler one, where the computation of the program can be mimicked in a computable way. This new domain is called abstract domain. This simpler version can be seen as a restriction of the set of properties used to express the behaviour of a program. For example, if the concrete domain for a program manipulating integers has the form $\mathcal{P}(\mathbb{Z})$, an abstract domain could contain only the convex parts of $\mathcal{P}(\mathbb{Z})$, that is intervals of integers. Abstract domains are given a lattice structure where the least upper bound represents the disjunction of properties and greatest lower bound represents their conjunction.

Our bytecode analyser will rely on this abstract domain of intervals for abstracting numerical values. We first present this standard domain, before constructing the abstract domains for our byte code language analysis. The link between concrete and abstract domains will be formally explained in Section 7.

Interval Lattice. The set of intervals over integers is naturally equipped with a lattice structure, induced by the usual order on integers, extended to infinite positive and negative values in order to get completeness.

Definition 2 (Interval lattice). *The lattice* $(Int, \sqsubseteq_{Int}, \sqcup_{Int}, \sqcap_{Int})$ *of intervals is defined by*

- *a base set* $Int = \{[a, b] \mid a, b \in \overline{\mathbb{Z}}, a \leq b\} \cup \bot$ *where* $\overline{\mathbb{Z}} = \mathbb{Z} \cup \{-\infty, +\infty\}$,
- *a partial order* $\sqsubseteq_{Int}$ *which is the least relation satisfying the following rules*

$$\frac{I \in Int}{\bot \sqsubseteq_{Int} I} \qquad \frac{c \leq a \quad b \leq d \quad a, b, c, d \in \overline{\mathbb{Z}}}{[a, b] \sqsubseteq_{Int} [c, d]}$$

- *meet and join binary operators, respectively defined by*

$$I \sqcup_{Int} \bot = = I, \ \forall I \in Int$$
$$\bot \sqcup_{Int} I = = I, \ \forall I \in Int$$
$$[a, b] \sqcup_{Int} [c, d] = [\min(a, c), \max(b, d)]$$

$$I \sqcap_{Int} \bot = \bot, \ \forall I \in Int$$
$$\bot \sqcap_{Int} I = \bot, \ \forall I \in Int$$
$$[a, b] \sqcap_{Int} [c, d] = \rho_{Int}([\max(a, c), \min(b, d)])$$

The bottom and top elements are $\bot_{Int} = \bot$ *and* $\top_{Int} = [-\infty, +\infty]$, *respectively.*

This lattice, of infinite width and height, can be depicted as on Figure 4.

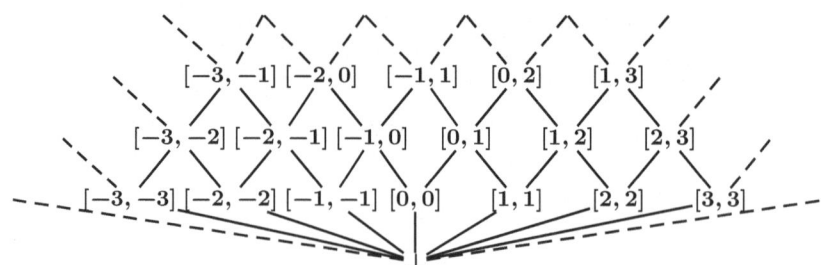

Fig. 4. The lattice of intervals

Abstract Domain of the Bytecode Analysis. The property we want to compute will be attached to each program point of a program. As a consequence, the abstract domain will be of the form

$$pc \rightarrow mem^{\sharp}$$

with $mem^{\sharp}$ a domain that expresses properties on the heap, the local variables and the operand stack. Values are either numerics or references to an array. In the first case we will abstract the corresponding integer with an interval, in the second case we will abstract the size of the array with an interval too. Such an information will be computed for each local variable, and hence the abstract domain of local variables will have the form

$$var \rightarrow Int$$

A naive choice would be to abstract operand stacks with a stack of intervals, in the same spirit as for local variables. Nevertheless, such a choice would have a bad impact on the precision of our analysis. We will discuss this point below. Instead, we will abstract operand stacks by stacks of symbolic expressions. Each symbolic expression represents a relation between the corresponding value of the operand stack and the local variables. The language of expressions is defined by the following inductive type.

```
Inductive expr :=
   Const (n:integer) | Var (x:var) | Bin (bin:binop) (e1 e2:expr).
```

We put a flat lattice structure on expressions, as depicted on Figure 5. For this purpose with the parameterized type `flat` given below.

```
Inductive flat (A:Set) : Set := Top | Base (x:A) | Bot.
```

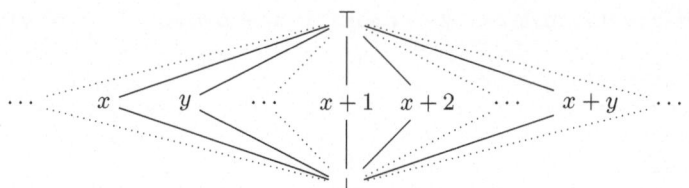

Fig. 5. The lattice of syntactic expressions

Precision Gain of the Symbolic Operand Stack. Representing abstract operands by symbolic expressions has a significant impact on the precision of the analysis, since it allows to preserve the information obtained through the evaluation of conditional expressions. At source level, a test such as `j+i>3` is a constraint over the possible values of `i` and `j` that can be propagated into the branches of a conditional statement. However, at byte code level, before such a conditional the evaluation stack only contains a boolean (encoded by an integer). The explicit constraint between variables i and j is lost because their values have to be pushed onto the stack before they can be compared. Using syntactic expressions to abstract stack contents enables the analysis to reconstruct this information.

A Lattice Library. Building complex lattices in Coq can be done in a modular fashion. A library of Coq functors and modules has thus be developed [Pic08], in order to easily construct complex lattices by composition from simpler ones. The lattice properties are summarized in a Coq module signature named Lattice.

Module Type Lattice.

    Parameter t : **Set**.

    Parameter eq : t → t → **Prop**.
    Parameter eq_refl : ∀ x : t, eq x x.
    Parameter eq_sym : ∀ x y : t, eq x y → eq y x.
    Parameter eq_trans : ∀ x y z : t, eq x y → eq y z → eq x z.
    Parameter eq_dec : ∀ x y : t, {eq x y}+{¬ eq x y}.

    Parameter order : t → t → **Prop**.
    Parameter order_refl : ∀ x y : t, eq x y → order x y.
    Parameter order_antisym :
     ∀ x y : t, order x y → order y x → eq x y.
    Parameter order_trans :
     ∀ x y z : t, order x y → order y z → order x z.
    Parameter order_dec : ∀ x y : t, {order x y}+{¬ order x y}.

    Parameter join : t → t → t.
    Parameter join_bound1 : ∀ x y : t, order x (join x y).
    Parameter join_bound2 : ∀ x y : t, order y (join x y).
    Parameter join_least_upper_bound :
     ∀ x y z : t, order x z → order y z → order (join x y) z.

    Parameter meet : t → t → t.
    Parameter meet_bound1 : ∀ x y : t, order (meet x y) x.
    Parameter meet_bound2 : ∀ x y : t, order (meet x y) y.
    Parameter meet_greatest_lower_bound :
     ∀ x y z : t, order z x → order z y → order z (meet x y).

    Parameter bottom : t.
    Parameter bottom_is_bottom : ∀ x : t, order bottom x.

    Parameter widening : widening_operator eq order bottom.
    Parameter narrowing : narrowing_operator eq order meet.
End Lattice.

Widening and narrowing operators will be described in Section 10.

For our analysis, the base lattices are the interval lattice and the (flat) lattice of syntactic expressions. The functor FlatLattice allows to construct such a structure given a carrier type and an equivalence relation for equality. The other lattices corresponding to semantic subdomains such as local variables or stacks are simply constructed by application of the respective functors for lists, arrays and cartesian product.

```
Module Expr
  Definition t := expr.
  Definition eq (x y : t) : Prop := x=y.

  Lemma eq_refl : ∀ x : t, eq x x.
  Proof. ... Qed.
  Lemma eq_sym : ∀ x y : t, eq x y → eq y x.
  Proof. ... Qed.
  Lemma eq_trans : ∀ x y z : t, eq x y → eq y z → eq x z.
  Proof. ... Qed.
  Lemma eq_dec : ∀ x y : t, {eq x y}+{¬ eq x y}.
  Proof. ... Qed.
End Expr.


Module ExprLat := FlatLattice Expr.
Module LocvarLat := ArrayBinLattice IntervalLat.
Module OpstackLat := ListLattice ExprLat.
Module MemLat := ProdLattice StackLat LocalVarLat.
Module GlobalLat := ArrayBinLattice MemLat.
```

The module ExprLat represents the lattice of symbolic expressions partially ordered according to the Hasse diagram of Figure 5. The module LocvarLat represents the module of functions from word to intervals. Functions are encoded with maps (binary trees). The corresponding partial order is the point-wise extension of the partial order on intervals. The module OpstackLat builds a lattice of lists whose elements live in ExprLat.t. Lists of the same length are ordered point-wise, while lists of different sizes are not comparable. The lattice is extended with two bottom and top extra values (using again the parameterized type flat). MemLat is the product of the two previous lattices. GlobalLat is the final lattice. Again, it is built with the ArrayBinLattice functor of functions.

6   Analysis Specification

The counterpart of the semantics rules is an operational description of the abstract execution of a program. Instead of manipulating concrete properties, this execution manipulates the abstract values that represent only a restricted set of properties. When the transformation of a property does not fit in the restricted set of the abstraction, a conservative alternative must be used instead. For example, the successor function on $\mathcal{P}(\mathbb{Z})$ transforms any property $P \subseteq \mathbb{Z}$ by $\{z + 1 \mid z \in P\}$ but, for the sign abstraction which only represents properties $\mathbb{Z}, \mathbb{Z}^+, \mathbb{Z}^-, \{0\}$ and $\emptyset$, the image of $\{0\}$, $i.e.$ set $\{1\}$, does not fit exactly a particular property and must be over-approximated by $\mathbb{Z}^+$. The set $\mathbb{Z}$ would have been an other sound approximation, but less precise.

For each instruction of the language we have to propose a sound transformation in the abstract domain that mimics the effect of a concrete execution of the instruction in the concrete domain. The word *sound* will be made more formal in the next section.

We specify the analysis under the form of a constraint-based specification. A constraint imposes on a function $X \in pc \to \mathrm{mem}^{\sharp}$ an inequation of the form

$$f(X(i)) \sqsubseteq^{\sharp} X(j)$$

where i,j,f are the three parts of the constraint. Index $i \in pc$ is the source program point, $j \in pc$ the target program point and $f \in \mathrm{mem}^{\sharp} \to \mathrm{mem}^{\sharp}$ the transfer function that must be applied between these two points. The property expressed by a constraint is formalized with a predicate cstr2prop.

```
Record cstr : Set := C
  { source : pc; target : pc; transfer : Mem.t → Mem.t }.

Definition cstr2prop (s:GlobalLat.t) (c:cstr) : Prop :=
  MemLat.order
    (c.(constraint) (GlobalLat.get s c.(source)))
    (GlobalLat.get s c.(target)).
```

Each instruction gives rise to one or two constraints, generated by the function gen_constraint.

```
Definition gen_constraint (i:pc)(ins:instruction) : list cstr :=
  match ins with
    | Nop ⇒ C i (next i) (fun x ⇒ x) ::nil
    | Push n ⇒
        C i (next i)
          (lift0 (fun s l ⇒ (Base (Const n)::s,l))) ::nil
    | Pop ⇒
        C i (next i) (lift1 (fun _ s l ⇒ (s,l))) ::nil
    | Dup ⇒
        C i (next i) (lift1 (fun e s l ⇒ (e::e::s,l))) ::nil
    | Load x ⇒
        C i (next i)
          (lift0 (fun s l ⇒ (Base (Var x)::s,l))) ::nil
    | Store x ⇒
        C i (next i)
          (lift1
            (fun e s l ⇒
              (map (clear_var x) s,ab_store x e l))) ::nil
    | Binop op ⇒
        C i (next i)
          (lift2
            (fun e1 e2 s l ⇒ (ab_binop op e1 e2::s,l))) ::nil
    | Newarray ⇒
        C i (next i) (lift1 (fun e s l ⇒ (e::s,l))) ::nil
    | Arraylength ⇒
        C i (next i) (lift1 (fun e s l ⇒ (e::s,l))) ::nil
```

```
      | Arrayload ⇒
          C i (next i) (lift2 (fun _ _ s l ⇒ (Top::s,l))) ::nil
      | Iastore ⇒
          C i (next i) (lift3 (fun _ _ _ s l ⇒ (s,l))) ::nil
      | Input ⇒
          C i (next i) (lift0 (fun s l ⇒ (Top::s,l))) ::nil
      | If cmp jump ⇒
          C i jump
            (lift2 (fun e2 e1 s l ⇒ (s,ab_cmp cmp e1 e2 l))) ::
          C i (next i)
            (lift2
               (fun e2 e1 s l ⇒ (s,ab_cmp (neg_cmp cmp) e2 e1 l))) ::
          nil
      | Goto jump ⇒
          C i jump (fun x ⇒ x) ::nil
  end.
```

The lift0, lift1, lift2, lift3, functions are used here to simplify the presentation. Each of them is dedicated to symbolic stacks with at least 0, 1, 2 or 3 elements on top of them.

Definition lift1
```
    (f:ExprLat.t → list ExprLat.t → LocvarLat.t →
                              list ExprLat.t*LocvarLat.t)
    (m:MemLat.t) : MemLat.t :=
  let (s,l) := m in
    match s with
      | Top ⇒ m
      | Base (e::s) ⇒ let (s',l') := f e s l  in (Base s',l')
      | _ ⇒ (Bot,LocvarLat.bottom)
    end.
```

These functions allow to factorize many cases of the constraint generation. For example, without lift1, the branch of instruction Dup would be the following.

```
      | Dup ⇒
          C i (next i) (fun (m:Mem.t) ⇒
                          let (s',l) := m in
                            match s' with
                            | Top ⇒ (Top,l)
                            | Base (e::s) ⇒ (Base (e::e::s),l)
                            | _ ⇒ (Bot,LocvarLat.bottom)
                          end)
```

We now informally describe each instruction. The Nop instruction does not modify the memory and we generate hence a constraint with an identity transfer function. The Push n instruction modifies only the abstract operand stack and pushes the symbol Const n on its top. The Dup instruction duplicates the expression on top of the abstract operand stack. The Load x pushes the symbol Var x on top of the abstract operand stack. The Store x modifies both the abstract operand stack and the abstract local variables. First, the abstract operand is cleaned up: every symbolic expression which contains x is replaced by Top, thanks to the operator (clear_var x). This is necessary, because after the execution of this instruction, such expressions will refer to the old value of x. The abstract local variables are updated with the operator ab_store defined below.

```
Definition ab_store (x:var) (e:flat expr) (l:LocvarLat.t) :
  LocvarLat.t :=
  match e with
    | Bot ⇒ LocvarLat.bottom
    | Base e ⇒ AbEnv.assign x e l
    | Top ⇒ AbEnv.forget x l
  end.
```

In the first case we propagate the bottom information. In the second case, we use an abstract assignment of the expression e in the abstract local variables. In the last case we need to forget the information currently known about the variable x. All operators that are specific to the abstraction of variables by intervals are gathered in a module AbEnv. We will not detail them in this document.

The Binop instruction modifies the abstract operand stack with the right symbolic expression.

```
Definition ab_binop (op:binop) (e1 e2:flat expr) : flat expr :=
  match e1, e2 with
    | Bot, _ | _, Bot ⇒ Bot
    | Top, _ | _, Top ⇒ Top
    | Base e1, Base e2 ⇒ Base (Bin op e1 e2)
  end.
```

Newarray and Arraylength do not really modify the abstract operand stack because a location has the same abstraction as the length of the corresponding array. For instruction Arrayload, the content of an array is always represented by Top since our abstraction does not allow us to track more acutely the content of arrays. Updating an array does not modify its length, hence the Arraystore instruction keeps the queue of the operand stack and the local variables in their previous state. The exact value pushed on top of the operand stack by the instruction Input is unknown. We hence push Top on top of the abstract operand stack. The If instruction needs to generate two constraints, one for each potential branch. In each case the abstract local variables are updated according to the fact that the test has been satisfied or not. This operation relies on the operator AbEnv.assert on abstract local variables.

```
Definition ab_cmp (cmp:cmp) (e1 e2:flat expr)
                   (l:LocvarLat.t) : LocvarLat.t :=
  match e1, e2 with
    | Bot, _ | _, Bot ⇒ LocvarLat.bottom
    | Top, _ | _, Top ⇒ l
    | Base e1, Base e2 ⇒ AbEnv.assert cmp e1 e2 l
  end.
```

```
Definition neg_cmp (cmp:cmp) : sem.cmp :=
  match cmp with
    | Eq ⇒ Ne | Ne ⇒ Eq | Ge ⇒ Gt | Gt ⇒ Ge
  end.
```

The Goto instruction is straightforward.

At last, an analysis result is specified as an element of the global lattice that satisfies all the constraints imposed by all the instructions of the program (w1 represents the first program counter of a program).

```
Definition Spec (p:program) (s:GlobalLat.t) : Prop :=
  MemLat.order (Base nil,LocvarLat.bottom) (GlobalLat.get s w1) ∧
  ∀ pc instr,
    instr_at p pc = Some instr →
      ∀ c, In c (gen_constraint pc instr) → cstr2prop s c.
```

Figure 2 gives an example of analysis result that fulfills all the constraints of the bubble sort program. In this Figure, we note c instead of (Const c), x instead of (Var x) and (op e1 e2) instead of (Bin op e1 e2). An empty operand stack is not represented. We note ⊤ the interval $[-\infty, +\infty]$.

7   Logical Link between Concrete and Abstract Domains

We have now to establish a formal link between the concrete and abstract domains. We first give a semantics to the expression language. Note that the abstraction of references by the length of the array they points-to is visible here since a same expression may evaluate both to a numerical value and a reference or the corresponding size.

```
Inductive sem_expr (h:heap) (l:locvar) : expr → val → Prop :=
| sem_expr_const : ∀ n, sem_expr h l (Const n) (Num n)
| sem_expr_var : ∀ x v, l x = Def v → sem_expr h l (Var x) v
| sem_expr_bin : ∀ op e1 e2 n1 n2,
  sem_expr h l e1 (Num n1) →
  sem_expr h l e2 (Num n2) →
  sem_expr h l (Bin op e1 e2) (Num (binop_sem op n1 n2))
| sem_expr_ref : ∀ e a loc,
  h loc = Array a →
  sem_expr h l e (Num a.(array_length)) →
  sem_expr h l e (Ref loc)
| sem_expr_length : ∀ e a loc,
  h loc = Array a →
  sem_expr h l e (Ref loc) →
  sem_expr h l e (Num a.(array_length)).
```

We then link each abstract domain $A^\sharp$ with its concrete counterpart A by means of a *concretization* function $\gamma \in A^\sharp \to \mathcal{P}(A)$ that maps each abstract element to a property in the concrete domain. Since subsets are encoded as predicates in the logic of Coq, γ functions can be defined with inductive relations.

Note that it is sometimes necessary to parameterize some of the relations with the heap or the local variables.

We first give the concretization function for syntactic expressions, that is directly derived from their semantics.

Definition gamma_expr
        (e:ExprLat.t) (h:heap) (l:locvar) (v:val) : **Prop** :=
  match e **with**
    | Top ⇒ True
    | Base e ⇒ sem_expr h l e v
    | Bot ⇒ False
  end.

The concretization function for lists of expressions is an intermediate function used for defining concretization of stacks.

Inductive gamma_list (h:heap) (l:locvar) :
                        list ExprLat.t → list val → **Prop** :=
  | gamma_list_nil : gamma_list h l nil nil
  | gamma_list_cons : ∀ e L v q,
      gamma_expr e h l v → gamma_list h l L q →
      gamma_list h l (e::L) (v::q).

Definition gamma_opstack
      (S:OpstackLat.t) (h:heap) (l:locvar) (s:opstack) : **Prop** :=
  match S **with**
    | Top ⇒ True
    | Base ab_s ⇒ gamma_list h l ab_s s
    | Bot ⇒ False
  end.

Concretization of numerical values or references uses the interval concretization function, and is extended to environments. get denotes here the operator on maps that allow to retrieve the value associated with a key.

Inductive gamma_val (i:IntervalLat.t) (h:heap) : val → **Prop** :=
  | gamma_val_num : ∀ n,
      IntervalAbstraction.gamma i n →
      gamma_val i h (Num n)
  | gamma_val_ref : ∀ a loc,
      h loc = Array a →
      IntervalAbstraction.gamma i a.(array_length) →
      gamma_val i h (Ref loc).

Definition gamma_locvar
            (L:LocvarLatt.t) (h:heap) (l:locvar) : **Prop** :=
  ∀ x v, l x = Def v → gamma_val (LocvarLat.get L x) h v.

Definition gamma_mem :
                  MemLat.t → heap → locvar → opstack → **Prop** :=
  fun M h l s ⇒
    let (S,L) := M **in**

```
match S with
    | Top ⇒ True
    | Base _ ⇒ gamma_opstack S h l s ∧ gamma_locvar L h l
    | Bot ⇒ False
end.
```

We finally define the concretization function for the whole program as follows.

```
Definition gamma (p:program) (F:GlobalLat.t) : state → Prop :=
  fun st ⇒
    match st with
      | St i s l h ⇒ gamma_mem (GlobalLat.get F i) h l s
      | _ ⇒ True
    end.
```

A natural property required on concretization functions is monotony, *i.e*, if $\sqsubseteq^\sharp$ is the partial order relation on abstract domain $A^\sharp$, a concretization function $\gamma \in A^\sharp \to \mathcal{P}(A)$ must satisfy

$$\forall a_1^\sharp, a_2^\sharp \in A^\sharp, \ a_1^\sharp \sqsubseteq^\sharp a_2^\sharp \ \Rightarrow \ \gamma(a_1^\sharp) \subseteq \gamma(a_2^\sharp)$$

This property is indeed natural, since it expresses the fact that the abstract partial order is related to logical implication in the concrete domain. For our bytecode analysis, each concretization function for each semantic sub-domain is monotone, as expressed by the following lemmas (proofs are omitted here).

```
Lemma gamma_expr_monotone : ∀ e1 e2 h l v,
  gamma_expr e1 h l v → ExprLat.order e1 e2 →
  gamma_expr e2 h l v.
Lemma gamma_opstack_monotone : ∀ S1 S2 h l s,
  gamma_opstack S1 h l s → OpstackLat.order S1 S2 →
  gamma_opstack S2 h l s.
Lemma gamma_val_monotone : ∀ V1 V2 h v,
  gamma_val V1 h v → IntervalLat.order V1 V2 →
  gamma_val V2 h v.
Lemma gamma_locvar_monotone : ∀ L1 L2 h l,
  gamma_locvar L1 h l → LocvarLat.order L1 L2 →
  gamma_locvar L2 h l.
Lemma gamma_mem_monotone : ∀ M1 M2 h l s,
  gamma_mem M1 h l s → MemLat.order M1 M2 →
  gamma_mem M2 h l s.
Lemma gamma_global_monotone : ∀ p F1 F2 st,
  gamma p F1 st → GlobalLat.order F1 F2 →
  gamma p F2 st.
```

The Standard Abstract Interpretation Framework. The presentation order we have chosen from now is not exactly the *official way* since we have presented the analysis specification before the logical interpretation of abstract domains. The theory of abstract interpretation proposes a different way for presenting the construction of static analyses. Abstracting the semantics of a program consists in restricting the set of properties used to express its behaviour.

The notion of abstraction is naturally represented by a subset of all possible properties. For instance, the sign abstraction is composed of the five properties $\mathbb{Z}, \mathbb{Z}^+, \mathbb{Z}^-, \{0\}$ and $\emptyset$ which all belong to $\mathcal{P}(\mathbb{Z})$.

The question that naturally arises is: what is a good abstraction?, *i.e.*, what are the best choices for defining the set of abstract properties? The "reasonable hypothesis" proposed by Patrick and Radhia Cousot in their seminal paper [CC79] is that for any property P, the set of all correct approximations of P must have a least element. In addition, abstract properties are defined as elements of a distinct lattice, instead of being a subset of the set of concrete properties. This gives birth to the notion of a Galois connection.

Definition 3. *Galois connection Let* $(L_1, \sqsubseteq_1, \bigsqcup_1, \bigsqcap_1)$ *and* $(L_2, \sqsubseteq_2, \bigsqcup_2, \bigsqcap_2)$ *be two complete lattices. A pair of functions* $\alpha \in L_1 \to L_2$ *and* $\gamma \in L_2 \to L_1$ *is a* Galois connection *if*

$$\forall x_1 \in L_1, \forall x_2 \in L_2, \ \alpha(x_1) \sqsubseteq_1 x_2 \iff x_1 \sqsubseteq_2 \gamma(x_2)$$

In that case, we use the following notation.

$$\left(L_1, \sqsubseteq_1, \bigsqcup_1, \bigsqcap_1\right) \xrightleftharpoons[\alpha]{\gamma} \left(L_2, \sqsubseteq_2, \bigsqcup_2, \bigsqcap_2\right)$$

Given such a Galois connection, the following properties hold [CC92a].

- α and γ are monotonic functions
- α is a union morphism: $\forall S \subseteq L_1, \ \gamma\left(\bigsqcup_1 S\right) = \bigsqcap_2 \alpha(S)$
- γ is an intersection morphism: $\forall S \subseteq L_2, \ \gamma\left(\bigsqcap_2 S\right) = \bigsqcap_1 \gamma(S)$

Conversely, if $(L_1, \sqsubseteq_1, \bigsqcup_1, \bigsqcap_1)$ and $(L_2, \sqsubseteq_2, \bigsqcup_2, \bigsqcap_2)$ are two complete lattices, and if $\gamma \in L_2 \to L_1$ is an intersection morphism, then there exists a unique function $\alpha \in L_1 \to L_2$ such that (α, γ) is a Galois connection between L_1 et L_2. α is defined by $\alpha(x) = \bigsqcap_2 \{ y \mid x \sqsubseteq_2 \gamma(y) \}$.

From now on, we will assume that our concrete and abstract semantics are expressed in two lattices A and $A^\sharp$, respectively, in relation with a Galois connection:

$$\left(A, \sqsubseteq, \bigsqcup, \bigsqcap\right) \xrightleftharpoons[\alpha]{\gamma} \left(A^\sharp, \sqsubseteq^\sharp, \bigsqcup^\sharp, \bigsqcap^\sharp\right)$$

Given a concrete semantics $[\![P]\!] \in A$ of a program P, the approximated behaviour of P will be computed by an abstract semantics $[\![P]\!] \in A^\sharp$. The abstraction will be correct iff $[\![P]\!] \sqsubseteq \gamma([\![P]\!]^\sharp)$, or equivalently $\alpha([\![P]\!]) \sqsubseteq^\sharp [\![P]\!]^\sharp$. $\alpha([\![P]\!])$ thus represents the best abstract semantics we can get with this choice of (α, γ). Fortunately, the theory of abstract interpretation gives more details on how we can construct $[\![P]\!]^\sharp$. The idea is to follow the structure of $[\![P]\!]$. If $[\![P]\!]$ is expressed as a composition of functions, $[\![P]\!]^\sharp$ will be a composition of abstract functions: this is the principle of abstract evaluation, that we briefly develop now.

Let us consider a function $f \in A \to A$. A concrete computation in A is represented by a couple $(a, f(a))$ with $a \in A$. We have to define a function $f^\sharp \in A^\sharp \to A^\sharp$ that correctly approximates all concrete computations. Formally, we can state the following definition.

Definition 4 (Correct function approximation). *Function* $f^\sharp \in A^\sharp \to A^\sharp$
is a   correct approximation of $f \in A \to A$ *if*

$$\forall a \in A, a^\sharp \in A^\sharp, \alpha(a) \sqsubseteq^\sharp a^\sharp \Rightarrow \alpha(f(a)) \sqsubseteq^\sharp f^\sharp(a^\sharp)$$

If the concrete or the abstract function is monotone, we can give the following equivalent correcteness criteria.

Theorem 1. *If* $f \in A \to A$ *or* $f^\sharp \in A^\sharp \to A^\sharp$ *is monotonic, the following assertions are equivalent:*

(i) $f^\sharp$ *is a correct approximation of* f,
(ii) $\alpha \circ f \mathrel{\dot{\sqsubseteq}}^\sharp f^\sharp \circ \alpha$
(ii) $\alpha \circ f \circ \gamma \mathrel{\dot{\sqsubseteq}}^\sharp f^\sharp$
(iv) $f \circ \gamma \mathrel{\dot{\sqsubseteq}}^\sharp \gamma \circ f^\sharp$

where $\mathrel{\dot{\sqsubseteq}}$ *is the point-wise order between functions.*

Abstract interpretation provides a characterisation of correct abstractions of the concrete semantics, but also tackles an optimality issue. The case where $f^\sharp = \alpha \circ f \circ \gamma$ indeed gives an optimal approximation for $f^\sharp$. However, this is rather a specification than an implementation, since function α is rarely computable. Using an abstraction function α thus requires providing proofs that a given subset of concrete states respect a intensionally defined property. On the other hand, we are mainly interested here in ensuring correctness of our analyses, rather that systematically design optimal ones. We thus only retain concretization functions in our framework, requiring that these functions are monotone, which is one condition of the minimalist framework proposed by P. and R. Cousot [CC92b].

8   Soundness Proof

The analysis specification must be proved sound with respect to the concrete operational semantics and the logical interpretation of the abstract domain previously defined. The main component of this proof is a *subject reduction* theorem. This theorem intuitively expresses the fact that progression of one step in the concrete operational semantics preserves the correctness w.r.t the concretization function, provided that the abstract state respects the locally generated constraints.

```
Lemma step_correct : ∀ p F i ins h l s s2,
  instr_at p i = Some ins →
  (∀ c, In c (gen_constraint i ins) → cstr2prop F c) →
  (St i s l h) -[p]-> s2 →
  wf_state (St i s l h) →
  gamma p F (St i s l h) →
  gamma p F s2.
```

Here `wf_state` represents a well-formedness property on reachable states. We have to prove that it is a semantic invariant.

```
Inductive wf_val (h:heap) : val → Prop :=
| wf_val_num : ∀ n, wf_val h (Num n)
| wf_val_ref : ∀ a loc, h loc = Array a → wf_val h (Ref loc).

Definition wf_state (st:state) : Prop :=
  match st with
    | St pc s l h ⇒ (∀ x v, l x = Def v → wf_val h v)
                                ∧ (∀ v, In v s → wf_val h v)
    | Error ⇒ True
  end.

Lemma wf_state_invariant_step : ∀ p st1 st2,
   st1 -[p]-> st2 → wf_state st1 → wf_state st2.
```

In order to prove the subject reduction lemma, we proceed by a case study on (St i s l h) -[p]->s2. For each semantic step towards a state st2 of the form (St i2 s2 l2 h2), we have to prove a result of the form

$$\text{gamma\_mem (GlobalLat.get F i2) h2 l2 s2.}$$

To achieve this, we choose among the constraints associated with the current instruction the one which has i2 as target. Using the monotony of gamma_mem, there remains to show

$$\text{gamma\_mem (transf (GlobalLat.get F i)) h2 l2 s2}$$

where f is the transfer function of the chosen constraint. Combined with the hypothesis gamma_mem (GlobalLat.get F i) h l s, we thus have recovered the standard criterion

$$f \circ \gamma \subseteq \gamma \circ f^{\sharp}$$

Thanks to the subject reduction lemma, we can establish that any solution of the constraint-based specification is a correct approximation of the set of reachable sets.

```
Lemma spec_correct : ∀ p F,
   Spec p F → ∀ st, ReachableStates p st → gamma p F st.
```

The proof is based on the induction principle associated with ReachableStates which generate two sufficient properties to be proved.

```
∀ p F, Spec p F, ∀ st, InitState st → gamma p F st          (1)

∀ p F, Spec p F, ∀ st1 st2,
    ReachableStates st1 → st1 -[p]-> st2 →                  (2)
    gamma p F st1 → gamma p F st2
```

The first property is proved thanks to the constraint on (GlobalLat.get F w1). The second property is easily proved with the subject reduction lemma and the proof of invariance of wf_state.

9   Constraint Generation

It remains to collect all the constraints of a program in order to generate an equation system. This part is generic: it does not depend on the constraints chosen for each instruction. It is then adaptable for many static analyses on our bytecode language.

```
Fixpoint collect_all_cstr (gen:pc → instruction → list cstr)
                          (l:list (pc*instruction)) : list cstr :=
  match l with
  | nil ⇒ nil
  | (i,ins)::q ⇒ (gen i ins)++(collect_all_cstr f q)
  end.
```

The collected list of constraints is then turned into a global operator on the global lattice.

```
Definition global_fun (l:list cstr) : GlobalLat.t → GlobalLat.t
:= fun s ⇒
fold_left
  (fun s' c ⇒
    GlobalLat.modify s' c.(target)
      (MemLat.join (c.(constraint) (GlobalLat.get s c.(source))))
  )
  l
  (GlobalLat.modify
      GlobalLat.bottom w1 (fun _ ⇒ (Base nil,LocvarLat.bottom))).
```

We rely here on the operator `modify` of the maps library which updates a map. More precisely, `modify m x f` return a new map equal to `m`, except for the key `x` which is associated to the value (`f (get m x)`).

We end this part by proving that any post-fixpoint of the operator

```
        global_fun (collect_all_cstr gen_constraint p)
```

is a solution of the constraint-based specification.

```
Lemma global_fun_correct : ∀ p s,
  GlobalLat.order
    (global_fun (collect_all_cstr gen_constraint p) s) s →
  Spec p s.
```

10   Fixpoint Computations

The semantics of a program can often be expressed as the least fixpoint of a monotone operator. The abstract semantics mimics this situation, and approximate the concrete fixpoint by an abstract one. The classical setting of complete lattices provides fundamental results, that we briefly recall and illustrate with the example of the interval lattice, before addressing the particularities of this issue in constructive logic.

Classical Results. The Knaster-Tarski theorem states that in any complete lattice, there exists a smallest fixpoint for any monotone function. This theorem ensures that this smallest fixpoint coincides with the smallest post-fixpoint (see Figure 6(a)), however it does not say anything on the method that could be followed to compute such a fixpoint. If the function is continuous, the Kleene theorem provides a more effective characterisation by providing a computation method: iterating the function from the smallest element of the lattice indeed reaches the smallest fixpoint, *if the iteration terminates* (see Figure 6(b)). The most simple criterion ensuring termination is the *ascending chain condition* (ACC), that forbids existence of infinite strictly increasing chains. Unfortunately, this condition is quite strong, and does not admit constructive proofs in general, even for lattices as simple as $\{\bot, \top\}$ [Pic05].

Instead of computing a least (post-)fixpoint of a monotone function, we can accomodate ourselves with an over-approximation, keeping correction in mind, but loosing optimality. This decision is generally taken when the lattice does

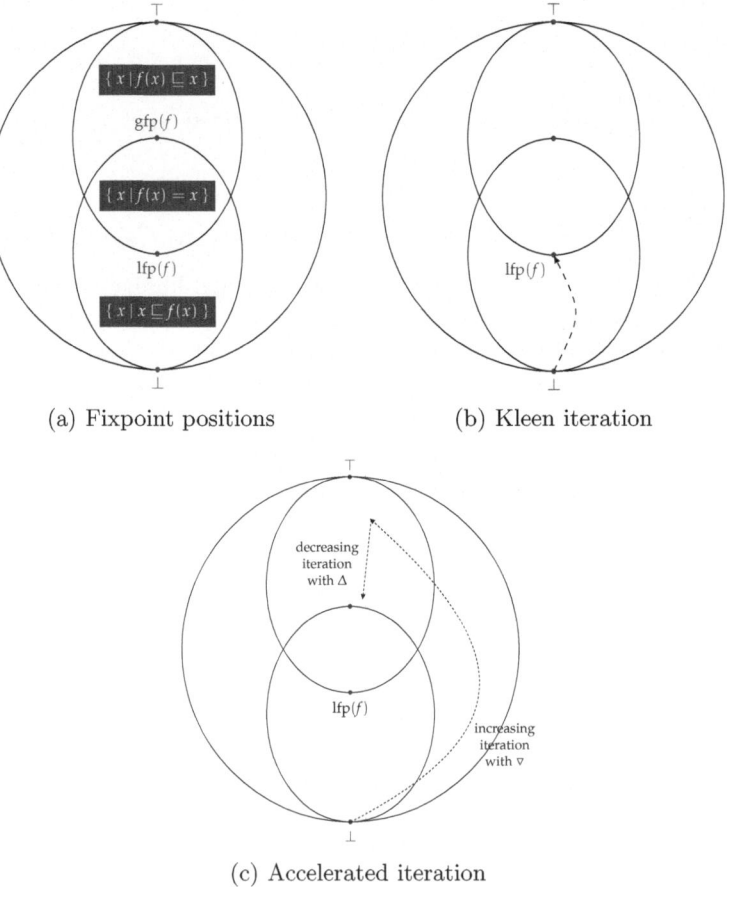

(a) Fixpoint positions   (b) Kleen iteration

(c) Accelerated iteration

Fig. 6. Fixpoint positions in a complete lattice

not respect the ACC property, or when the iteration chain would be too long to allow an acceptable computation time.

The solution proposed by P. and R. Cousot consists in accelerating the ascending iteration, thus reaching a post-fixpoint, but not necessarily the least one. It is done by using a binary *widening* operator, that extrapolates both of its arguments. Intuitively, at the n-th iteration, the n-th iterate of the function is compared to the preceeding value, in order to detect the beginning of a possible infinite or very long chain. If this is the case, we skip to a point farther up in the iteration. If the binary operator fulfills the requirements of a widening operator (see [CC92a] for details), then this modified iteration is guaranteed to converge to a post-fixpoint in finite time (see Figure 6(c)).

When a post-fixpoint is reached, a new descending iteration starting from this point allows to improve the approximation. The termination issue is similar to that of the ascending iteration, and a *narrowing* operator can be used to accelerate and ensure convergence.

Interval Lattice Example. The interval lattice obviously does not fulfill the ascending chain condition. For instance, $\perp_{Int} \sqsubseteq_{Int} [0,0] \sqsubseteq_{Int} [0,1] \sqsubseteq_{Int} [0,2] \sqsubseteq_{Int} \cdots \sqsubseteq_{Int} [0,n] \sqsubseteq_{Int} \cdots$ is an infinite increasing chain. We will thus define a widening operator ∇_{Int}. In the infinite chain above, we would like to replace interval $[0,n]$ by $[0,+\infty]$ after a finite (preferably small) number of iterations. We would like for instance that $[0,1]\nabla_{Int}[0,2] = +\infty$. The general definition of ∇_{Int} is as follows.

$$[a,b]\nabla_{Int}[a',b'] = [\text{if } a' < a \text{ then } -\infty \text{ else } a,$$
$$\text{if } b' > b \text{ then } +\infty \text{ else } b]$$
$$\perp_{Int}\nabla_{Int}[a,b] = [a,b]$$
$$I\nabla_{Int}\perp_{Int} = I$$

As an example, let us take a program composed of one single loop decrementing a counter x, starting from value 100 and stopping when x reaches 0, which control flow graph and abstract semantics are displayed on Figure 7. The abstract semantics is written as a set of inequations, where X_i denotes the abstract value of variable x at program point i.

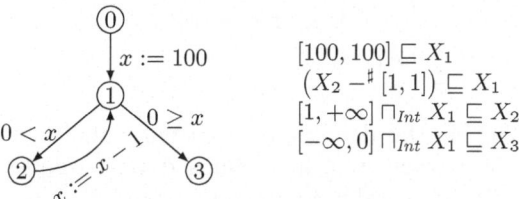

Fig. 7. A program and the specification of its abstract semantics

We now want to compute the result of the analysis, *i.e.* a solution to this set of inequations. Equivalently, we are looking for a post-fixpoint of the fonction F constructed as the composition of elementary functions $F_{i,j} : X \mapsto X[j \mapsto X_j \sqcup_{Int} f(X_i)]$ for each constraint of the form $f(X_i) \sqsubseteq X_j$. We then have to choose an iteration strategy for evaluating these elementary functions. We take for instance a round-robin scheme, computing X_1, X_2 and X_3 in turn and iterating over the three equations defining these variables. We thus compute the successive iterates of the following sequences.

$$
\begin{aligned}
X_1^0 &= \bot & X_1^{n+1} &= [100, 100] \sqcup_{Int} \left(X_2^n -^\sharp [1, 1]\right) \\
X_2^0 &= \bot & X_2^{n+1} &= [1, +\infty] \sqcap_{Int} X_1^{n+1} \\
X_3^0 &= \bot & X_3^{n+1} &= [-\infty, 0] \sqcap_{Int} X_1^{n+1}
\end{aligned}
$$

The result of this computation is given below.

Iteration	0	1	2	3	4		100	101
X_1	$\bot$	$[100, 100]$	$[99, 100]$	$[98, 100]$	$[97, 100]$	$\cdots$	$[1, 100]$	$[0, 100]$
X_2	$\bot$	$[100, 100]$	$[99, 100]$	$[98, 100]$	$[97, 100]$	$\cdots$	$[1, 100]$	$[1, 100]$
X_3	$\bot$	$\bot$	$\bot$	$\bot$	$\bot$	$\cdots$	$\bot$	$[0, 0]$

Even if on this example the iteration converges in finite time, the length of the iteration sequence depends on the concrete value of the loop bound. If we now introduce widening operations at each control point, we get the following equations

$$
\begin{aligned}
X_1^0 &= \bot & X_1^{n+1} &= X_1^n \nabla_{Int} \left([100, 100] \sqcup_{Int} \left(X_2^n -^\sharp [1, 1]\right)\right) \\
X_2^0 &= \bot & X_2^{n+1} &= X_2^n \nabla_{Int} \left([1, +\infty] \sqcap_{Int} X_1^{n+1}\right) \\
X_3^0 &= \bot & X_3^{n+1} &= X_3^n \nabla_{Int} \left([-\infty, 0] \sqcap_{Int} X_1^{n+1}\right)
\end{aligned}
$$

resulting in a much shorter iteration sequence.

Iteration	0	1	2
X_1	$\bot$	$[100, 100]$	$[-\infty, 100]$
X_2	$\bot$	$[100, 100]$	$[-\infty, 100]$
X_3	$\bot$	$\bot$	$[-\infty, 0]$

As explained above, a subsequent iteration using a narrowing operator can be used to refine the post-fixpoint computed by the widening iteration sequence. The general definition of the narrowing operator we use for intervals is as follows.

$$
\begin{aligned}
[a, b] \Delta_{Int} [c, d] &= [\text{if } a = -\infty \text{ then } c \text{ else } a \; ; \; \text{if } b = +\infty \text{ then } d \text{ else } b] \\
I \; \Delta_{Int} \bot_{Int} &= \bot_{Int} \\
\bot_{Int} \Delta_{Int} \; I \; &= \bot_{Int}
\end{aligned}
$$

The intuition behind this definition is that only infinite bounds, that may have been too widely extrapolated, are refined down to finite ones. In practice, a few iterations already notably improve the result that has been obtained after widening. If we come back to our previous example and introduce a narrowing operation for each control point, starting from the already computed result we get convergence after only 2 steps, once again with a round-robin strategy.

$$Y_1^0 = X_1^2 \qquad Y_1^{n+1} = Y_1^n \Delta_{Int} \left([100, 100] \sqcup_{Int} \left(Y_2^n -^\sharp [1, 1]\right)\right)$$
$$Y_2^0 = X_2^2 \qquad Y_2^{n+1} = Y_2^n \Delta_{Int} \left([1, +\infty] \sqcap_{Int} Y_1^{n+1}\right)$$
$$Y_3^0 = X_3^2 \qquad Y_3^{n+1} = Y_3^n \Delta_{Int} \left([-\infty, 0] \sqcap_{Int} Y_1^{n+1}\right)$$

Iteration	0	1	2
Y_1	$[-\infty, 100]$	$[-\infty, 100]$	$[0, 100]$
Y_2	$[-\infty, 100]$	$[1, 100]$	$[1, 100]$
Y_3	$[-\infty, 0]$	$[-\infty, 0]$	$[0, 0]$

Besides the introduction of widening operators, the order in which equations are selected in the fixpoint computation has a noteworthy influence on the convergence speed of the iteration and on the precision of final result. On the other hand, widening operators induce strong over-approximations and must be used as less as possible. A balanced solution consists in introducing widening operations only at a subset of the control points, and selecting an appropriate iteration order. If we start from the following equation system

$$\begin{cases} X_1 = f_1(X_1, \dots, X_n) \\ \vdots \\ X_n = f_n(X_1, \dots, X_n) \end{cases}$$

it is sufficient (and more precise) to use ∇_{Int} (and Δ_{Int}) for a selection of indices W such that each dependence cycle in the control flow graph of the system goes through at least one point in W.

$$\forall k = 1..n, \ X_k^{i+1} = \begin{array}{ll} X_k^i \nabla_{Int} f_k(X_1^i, \dots, X_n^i) & \text{if } k \in W \\ f_k(X_1^i, \dots, X_n^i) & \text{otherwise} \end{array}$$

Constructivity Issues. The classical definition of ACC, as well as those of widening or narrowing operators, are not well suited to constructive proofs, even if it is possible to give a constructive proof of the Knaster-Tarski theorem for complete lattices. In order to implement fixpoint computations in Coq, it is possible to modify the definitions of ACC, widening and narrowing, using the notion of well-founded relation. Note that these definitions are equivalent to the initial ones.

Widening and Narrowing in the Lattice Library. The above definitions are included in a Coq module signature Lattice described in Section 5. The difficulty consists in effectively constructing complex abstract domains. Defining widening and narrowing operators can indeed be tricky, since they have to be accompagnied by their termination proof. The functors provided by the Coq library alleviate this problem, since for each functor such as ListLattice or ArrayBinLattice, a proof of termination for widening and narrowing operators is directly constructed from the termination proofs included in the lattice arguments of the functor. One important technical point concerns the domain of key that is used in functor `ArrayBinLattice`. As we have seen before, keys has of type word. In order to prove termination of point-wise widening on functions we need to consider a finite number of keys. We hence define word as a *finite* type.

Definition word : **Set** := {p:positive | inf_log_bool p 32 = true}.

Such a type reads as follow: an element of type word is a couple (p,h) such that p inhabits the type positive of binary numbers and h is a proof that p as at most 32 bits. It ensures we have only a finite number of keys in our maps.

This modular construction allows us to construct a generic post-fixpoint solver based on widening/narrowing iterations. It takes the form of module functor that, given a lattice module L, implements a function pfp that computes a post-fixpoint of any operator on L.t.

Module PostFixPointSolver (L:Lattice).
   Definition pfp (f : L.t → L.t) :   { x:L.t | L.order (f x) x }
    (* ... omitted ... *)
End PostFixPointSolver.

We use this functor on the lattice module `GlobalLat` in order to find a post-fixpoint of the operator build in the last Section. Combined with the lemmas `spec_correct` of Section 8 and `global_fun_correct` of Section 9 we obtain a certified analyzer of type

```
analyzer : ∀ p:program,
    { F:GlobalLat.t | ∀ st, ReachableStates p st → gamma p F st}
```

11   Abstract Checking

The combination of all the previous parts has allowed us to obtain a provably safe over-approximation of the reachable states. We will now use this approximation to check if a program is safe.

Given an abstract domain $\left(A^{\sharp}, \sqsubseteq^{\sharp}, \sqcup^{\sharp}, \sqcap^{\sharp}\right)$ we provide an abstract safety check function $check^{\sharp} \in A^{\sharp} \to bool$ that checks, in the abstract world, if a given safety property is satisfied. For a given program, if the abstract check succeeds then the program should be safe. It is does not succeed, we can not conclude anything because of the over-approximation.

For our case study, our safety property, for a program p has been defined as:

$$\forall \; st, \; ReachableStates \; p \; st \to Safe \; st$$

We first introduce an intermediate safety property `PreSafe`, using a characterization of states that definitively lead to error states.

```
Inductive pre_state_error (p:program) : state → Prop :=
| no_pre_state_error_newarray : ∀ pc n s l h,
  instr_at p pc = Some Newarray →
  n<0 →
  pre_state_error p (St pc (Num n :: s) l h)
```

```
| no_pre_state_error_iaload : ∀ pc loc s l h i a,
  instr_at p pc = Some Arrayload →
  h loc = Array a →
  ¬ (0 <= i < array_length a) →
  pre_state_error p (St pc (Num i::Ref loc :: s) l h)
| pre_state_error_iastore : ∀ pc loc s l h i n a,
  instr_at p pc = Some Arraystore →
  h loc = Array a →
  ¬ (0 <= i < array_length a →
  pre_state_error p (St pc (Num n :: Num i :: Ref loc :: s) l h).
```

Definition PreSafe (p:program) (st:state) : **Prop** :=
  ¬ pre_state_error p st.

Any successor of a *pre-safe* state is safe.

Lemma pre_safe_implies_safe_step : ∀ p,
  ∀ st1 st2, PreSafe p st1 → st1 -[p]-> st2 → Safe st2.

As a consequence, it is sufficient to check if all reachable states satisfy the PreSafe property.

Lemma pre_safe_implies_safe_reach : ∀ p,
  (∀ pc st, ReachableStates p st → PreSafe p st) →
  ∀ st, ReachableStates p st → Safe st.

For all instruction that may lead to the error state, the abstract checker verifies if the inferred abstract property enforces the PreSafe property.

Definition check_instr
  (F:GlobalLat.t) (i:pc) (ins:instruction) : bool :=
  match ins **with**
    | Newarray ⇒
    match GlobalLattice.get F i **with**
      | (Top,_) ⇒ false
      | (Base (Top::_),L) ⇒ false
      | (Base (Base e::_),L) ⇒ Interval.check_ge L e (Const 0)
      | _ ⇒ true
    end
  | Arrayload ⇒
    match GlobalLat.get F i **with**
      | (Top,_)
      | (Base (Top::_::_),_)
      | (Base (_::Top::_),_) ⇒ false
      | (Base (Base e_i::Base e_a::_),L) ⇒
        Interval.check_ge L e_i (Const 0)
          && Interval.check_gt L e_a e_i
      | _ ⇒ true
    end
  | Arraystore ⇒
    match GlobalLattice.get F i **with**
      | (Top,_)
```
```

```
          | (Base (_::Top::_::_),_)
          | (Base (_::_::Top::_),_) ⇒ false
          | (Base (_::Base e_i::Base e_a::_),L) ⇒
            Interval.check_ge e_i (Const 0)
              && Interval.check_gt e_a e_i
          | _ ⇒ true
      end
    | _ ⇒ true
  end.
```

```
Fixpoint check (l:program) (F:GlobalLattice.t) : bool :=
  match l with
    | nil ⇒ true
    | (pc,ins)::q ⇒
      if check_instr F pc ins then check q F else false
  end.
```

The function Interval.check_ge (resp. Interval.check_gt) checks if an expression is greater (resp. strictly greater) than an other one in an abstract set of local variables (here denoted by L).

We then prove the soundness of the check function with respect to the PreSafe property.

```
Lemma check_true_implies_PreSafe : ∀ p F,
  (∀ st, ReachableStates p st → gamma p F st) →
  check p F = true →
  ∀ st, ReachableStates p st → PreSafe st.
```

Combined with the previous result pre_safe_implies_safe_reach, this gives us the final soundness property:

```
Lemma check_true_implies_PreSafe : ∀ p F,
  (∀ st, ReachableStates p st → gamma p F st) →
  check p F = true →
  ∀ st, ReachableStates p st → Safe st.
```

12   Conclusions

We can conclude our development by defining a verifier that runs the analyzer and then makes an abstract check on it. To vary a little our Coq style we will perform a proof-as-programing construction that is permitted by the Curry-Howard correspondence underlying the Coq system.

```
Definition verifier (p:program) :
  { b:bool | b = true → ∀ st, ReachableStates p st → Safe st}.
Proof.
  intros p.
  destruct (analyzer p) as [F h].
  exists (check p F).
  exact (check_true_implies_PreSafe p F h).
Defined.
```

This reads as follow:

- First we state that we want to construct a function `verifier` that takes a program p as argument and returns a dependent pair `(b,h)` such that if the boolean b is equal to `true` then the program p is safe;
- We then start an interactive proof in order to progressively prove this type is inhabited. What we have to prove is mainly a statement like:

$$\forall \; p, \; \exists \; b, \; b = \text{true} \rightarrow \forall \; st, \; \texttt{ReachableStates} \; p \; st \rightarrow \texttt{Safe} \; st$$

- We first introduce p in our context and then destruct the result of `analyzer p` as a pair `(F,h)`. By typing of `analyzer`, the term F has type `GlobalLat.t` and h has type $\forall \; st, \; \texttt{ReachableStates} \; p \; st \; \rightarrow \texttt{gamma} \; p \; F \; st$;
- The first part of the result by giving the boolean value `(check p F)`;
- The Coq system now ask us to fill the last missing part and prove

$$\texttt{check} \; p \; F = \text{true} \rightarrow \forall \; st, \; \texttt{ReachableStates} \; p \; st \rightarrow \texttt{Safe} \; st$$

  i.e. give a term of the corresponding type;
- We conclude using the term `(check_true_implies_PreSafe p F h)` which is exactly of the right type.

This last function and the rest of the development can be automatically extracted into a Ocaml program. We obtain for example the following Ocaml code for for the `verifier` function.

```
let verifier p = check p (analyzer p)
```

Note that all the logical elements have been discarded. When launched on our bubble sort program, the extracted analyser computes the result given in Figure 2 and successfully apply all the abstract checks.

The results presented in this tutorial papers demonstrates how to construct a non-trivial, provably correct abstract interpreter inside the Coq. Using the extraction mechanism we can extract a certified array-bound verifier and bridges the gap that often exists between a paper-specification of an analysis and the analyser that is actually implemented. Thanks to the general methodology we follow and the lattice library we provide, our approach is applicable to a large variety of program analyses for different language paradigms.

Acknowledgments. This work is supported by the Integrated Project MOBIUS, within the Global Computing II initiative.

References

[BD04]   Barthe, G., Dufay, G.: A tool-assisted framework for certified byte-code verification. In: Wermelinger, M., Margaria-Steffen, T. (eds.) FASE 2004. LNCS, vol. 2984, pp. 99–113. Springer, Heidelberg (2004)

[BDHdS01]   Barthe, G., Dufay, G., Huisman, M., de Sousa, S.M.: Jakarta: A toolset for reasoning about javaCard. In: Attali, S., Jensen, T. (eds.) E-smart 2001. LNCS, vol. 2140, pp. 2–18. Springer, Heidelberg (2001)

[BDJ+01]   Barthe, G., Dufay, G., Jakubiec, L., Serpette, B.P., de Sousa, S.M.: A formal executable semantics of the javaCard platform. In: Sands, D. (ed.) ESOP 2001. LNCS, vol. 2028, pp. 302–319. Springer, Heidelberg (2001)

[Ber08]   Bertot, Y.: Structural abstract interpretation, a formal study using Coq. In: LERNET Summer School. LNCS. Springer, Heidelberg (2008)

[BGL06]   Bertot, Y., Grégoire, B., Leroy, X.: A structured approach to proving compiler optimizations based on dataflow analysis. In: Filliâtre, J.-C., Paulin-Mohring, C., Werner, B. (eds.) TYPES 2004. LNCS, vol. 3839, pp. 66–81. Springer, Heidelberg (2006)

[CC77]   Cousot, P., Cousot, R.: Abstract interpretation: a unified lattice model for static analysis of programs by construction or approximation of fixpoints. In: Proc. of POPL 1977, pp. 238–252. ACM Press, New York (1977)

[CC79]   Cousot, P., Cousot, R.: Systematic design of program analysis frameworks. In: Proc. of POPL 1979, pp. 269–282. ACM Press, New York (1979)

[CC92a]   Cousot, P., Cousot, R.: Abstract interpretation and application to logic programs. Journal of Logic Programming 13(2-3), 103–179 (1992)

[CC92b]   Cousot, P., Cousot, R.: Abstract interpretation frameworks. Journal of Logic and Computation 2(4), 511–547 (1992)

[CGD06]   Coupet-Grimal, S., Delobel, W.: A uniform and certified approach for two static analyses. In: Filliâtre, J.-C., Paulin-Mohring, C., Werner, B. (eds.) TYPES 2004. LNCS, vol. 3839, pp. 115–137. Springer, Heidelberg (2006)

[CJPR05]   Cachera, D., Jensen, T., Pichardie, D., Rusu, V.: Extracting a data flow analyser in constructive logic. Theoretical Computer Science 342(1), 56–78 (2005)

[CJPS05]   Cachera, D., Jensen, T., Pichardie, D., Schneider, G.: Certified Memory Usage Analysis. In: Fitzgerald, J.S., Hayes, I.J., Tarlecki, A. (eds.) FM 2005. LNCS, vol. 3582, pp. 91–106. Springer, Heidelberg (2005)

[Coq09]   Coq development team. The Coq proof assistant reference manual V8.2. Technical report, INRIA, France (2009),
            http://coq.inria.fr/doc/main.html

[Cou99]   Cousot, P.: The calculational design of a generic abstract interpreter. In: Broy, M., Steinbrüggen, R. (eds.) Calculational System Design. NATO ASI Series F. IOS Press, Amsterdam (1999)

[KN02]   Klein, G., Nipkow, T.: Verified Bytecode Verifiers. Theoretical Computer Science 298(3), 583–626 (2002)

[KN06]   Klein, G., Nipkow, T.: A machine-checked model for a Java-like language, virtual machine and compiler. ACM Transactions on Programming Languages and Systems 28(4), 619–695 (2006)

[LCH07]   Lee, D.K., Crary, K., Harper, R.: Towards a mechanized metatheory of standard ml. In: Proc. of POPL 2007, pp. 173–184. ACM Press, New York (2007)

[Ler06]   Leroy, X.: Formal certification of a compiler back-end or: programming a compiler with a proof assistant. In: Proc. of POPL 2006, pp. 42–54. ACM Press, New York (2006)

[MF99]   McGraw, G., Felten, E.W.: Securing Java: getting down to business with mobile code. John Wiley & Sons, Inc., Chichester (1999)

[Mon98]   Monniaux, D.: Réalisation mécanisée d'interpréteurs abstraits. Rapport de DEA, Université Paris VII (1998) (in french)

[Pic05]   Pichardie, D.: Interprétation abstraite en logique intuitionniste: extraction d'analyseurs Java certifiés. PhD thesis, Université Rennes 1 (2005) (in french)

[Pic08]   Pichardie, D.: Building certified static analysers by modular construction of well-founded lattices. In: Proc. of FICS 2008. Electronic Notes in Theoretical Computer Science, vol. 212, pp. 225–239 (2008)

Resource Usage Analysis and Its Application to Resource Certification

Elvira Albert[1], Puri Arenas[1], Samir Genaim[2],
Germán Puebla[2], and Damiano Zanardini[2]

[1] DSIC, Complutense University of Madrid, E-28040 Madrid, Spain
[2] CLIP, Technical University of Madrid, E-28660 Boadilla del Monte, Madrid, Spain

Abstract. *Resource usage* is one of the most important characteristics
of programs. Automatically generated information about resource usage
can be used in multiple ways, both during program development and
deployment. In this paper we discuss and present examples on how such
information is obtained in COSTA, a state of the art static analysis system. COSTA obtains safe symbolic upper bounds on the resource usage
of a large class of general-purpose programs written in a mainstream programming language such as Java (bytecode). We also discuss the application of resource-usage information for *code certification*, whereby code
not guaranteed to run within certain user-specified bounds is rejected.

1 Introduction

One of the most important characteristics of a program is the amount of resources that its execution will require, i.e., its *resource usage*. Typical examples
of resources include execution time, memory watermark, amount of data transmitted over the net, etc. Resource usage information has many applications, both
during program development and deployment. Therefore, automated ways of estimating resource usage are quite useful and the general area of resource usage
analysis (or resource analysis for short) has received considerable attention.

Statically estimating the resource usage of realistic programs is far from
trivial. Thus, in the current practice, safe resource usage guarantees are only
available for critical applications with strong resource usage constraints. These
include real-time applications, which are required to execute within a certain
maximum amount of time. Such applications are the subject of *Worst Case Execution Time Analysis* (WCET analysis for short), which is a quite active research
area. See e.g. [23]. Unfortunately, WCET analysis for mainstream hardware and
software is extremely complicated. On the hardware side, modern computer architectures have multiple memory levels and internal pipelining which make it
rather difficult to predict the execution time of machine instructions. On the
software side, accurately estimating the number of times each program loop
and recursion will execute is a rather complex problem. In order to ease the
situation, on the hardware side, real-time applications often run on embedded

A. Aldini, G. Barthe, R. Gorrieri (Eds.): FOSAD 2007/2008/2009, LNCS 5705, pp. 258–288, 2009.

systems whose timing behaviour is much more predictable. On the software side, real-time applications are programmed in restricted versions of general languages such as Real-Time Java or are designed and implemented using special languages such as Hume [27] and Timber [1], which are rooted in functional programming and have tool support for performing WCET analysis. Similarly, when strong memory usage limitations are in place, the programming constructs allowed are often very restricted, disallowing recursion or, as in the case of JavaCard, even strongly discouraging the use of dynamic memory allocation after the initialization phase of the applet.

In this paper we discuss the main techniques used in COSTA [5], a static analysis system which allows obtaining safe symbolic upper bounds on the resource usage of Java bytecode (JBC for short). COSTA follows the classical approach to static resource analysis proposed in Wegbreit's seminal work [57] and which consists of two phases. First, given a program and a cost model, the analysis produces *cost relations* (CRs for short). Second, the systems tries to obtain *closed-form upper-bounds* for them. The results are *symbolic* in the sense that they do not refer to concrete, platform dependent, resources such as execution time, but rather they provide platform-independent information. This has the advantage that the results are applicable to any implementation of the Java Virtual Machine (JVM) on any particular hardware. It also has the disadvantage that the information cannot refer to platform specific resources such as run-time. The fact that the analysis handles JBC represents that, at least in principle, it can deal with general-purpose programs written in a mainstream programming language such as Java and potentially other languages compiled to JBC. The upper bounds computed by COSTA can then be compared against user-provided resource usage specifications. This allows automatically rejecting code not guaranteed to execute within the specified resources.

Note that, unlike COSTA, previous resource analyses based on Wegbreit's approach have been formulated on, less widely used, declarative programming languages [57,35,44,22]. There are very few approaches for imperative programming languages [25] and, unlike COSTA, they are formulated at the *source code* level and they do not follow Wegbreit's approach. However, analyzing compile code has wider applicability, since it is quite often the case with Java applications that the *code consumer* has access to the bytecode, often bundled in *jar* files, but no access to the source code, as usual for commercial software and in mobile code. In the context of *mobile code*, programming languages which are compiled to *bytecode* and executed on a *virtual machine* are widely used nowadays. This is the approach used by Java bytecode and .NET. Mobile code was the motivation for the concept of *Proof-Carrying Code* [41]: in order for the mobile code to be verifiable by the user, security properties (including resource usage limitations) must refer to the code available to the user, i.e., the bytecode, so that it is possible to check the provided proof and verify that the program satisfies the requirements (e.g., that the code does not require more than a certain amount of memory, or that it executes in less than a certain amount of time).

Among all possible applications of resource analysis, in this work we describe its application to *resource certification*, whereby programs are coupled with information about their resource usage. This information allows deciding whether the resources used by the program execution are acceptable or not *before* running the program. Note that resource usage can be considered a security property of untrusted mobile code, possibly in the context of proof-carrying code. Programs whose resource usage is not certified are potentially harmful, since their execution may require more resources than we are willing to spend or they may even have monetary cost by executing *billable events* such as sending text messages or making http connections on a mobile phone. In fact, mobile devices is one of the settings where resource certification is more important, because of the limited computing power typically available on mobile devices.

The rest of the paper is structured as follows. In Section 2 object-oriented bytecode, in the style of Java bytecode, is briefly described. This is required to understand the different examples in the paper, which show how resource analysis of a bytecode program is performed. Then, in Section 3, we describe, by means of examples, how to obtain CRs from a program and a cost model, whereas in Section 4 we illustrate how to obtain closed-form upper-bounds for CRs. Section 5 describes the application of resource analysis to resource certification. In Section 6 we present an overview on the existing large body of work on resource analysis. Finally, the conclusions and some venues for future work are discussed in Section 7.

2   The Context: Object-Oriented Bytecode

In order to simplify the formalization of our analysis, a simple object-oriented bytecode language is considered, which roughly corresponds to a representative subset of sequential Java bytecode. We refer to it as *simple bytecode*. For short, unless we explicitly mention *Java* bytecode, all references to bytecode in the rest of the paper correspond to our simple bytecode. Simple bytecode is able to handle integers and object creation and manipulation. For simplicity, simple bytecode does not include advanced features of Java bytecode, such as exceptions, interfaces, static methods and fields, access control (e.g., the use of public, protected and private modifiers) and primitive types besides integers and references. Anyway, such features can be easily handled in this framework, as done in the implementation of the COSTA system.

A bytecode program consists of a set of *classes* C, partially ordered with respect to the *subclass* relation. Each class $c \in C$ contains information about the class it extends, and the fields and methods it declares. Subclasses inherit all the fields and methods of the class they extend. Each method comes with a *signature* m which consists of the class where it is defined, its name and its type. For simplicity, all methods are supposed to return a value. There cannot be two methods with the same signature. The bytecode associated to a method m is a sequence $\langle b_1, \ldots, b_n \rangle$ where each b_i is a bytecode instruction. Local variables of a k-ary method are denoted by $\langle l_0, \ldots, l_n \rangle$ with $n \geq k-1$. In contrast to Java

public static int binarySearch(int[ ] t, int v, int l, int u) {
    int m;
    while (l <= u) {
        m = (l + u) / 2;
        if (t[m] == v) return m;
        if (t[m] > v) u = m - 1;
        else l = m + 1;
    }
    return -1;
}
	0 : load 2
	1 : load 3
	2 : ifgt 31
	3 : load 2
	4 : load 3
	5 : add
	6 : push 2
	7 : div
	8 : store 4
	9 : load 0
	10 : load 4
	11 : aload
	12 : load 1
	13 : ifneq 16
	14 : load 4
	15 : return
		16 : load 0
		17 : load 4
		18 : aload
		19 : load 1
		20 : ifleq 26
		21 : load 4
		22 : push 1
		23 : isub
		24 : store 3
		25 : goto 0
		26 : load 4
		27 : push 1
		28 : add
		29 : store 2
		30 : goto 0
		31 : push −1
		32 : return

Fig. 1. A Java source (left) with its corresponding bytecode (right)

source, in bytecode the *this* reference of instance (i.e., non-static) methods is passed explicitly as the first argument of the method, i.e., l_0 and $\langle l_1, \ldots, l_k \rangle$ correspond to the k formal parameters, and the remaining $\langle l_{k+1}, \ldots, l_n \rangle$ are the local variables declared in the method. For static k-ary methods $\langle l_0, \ldots, l_{k-1} \rangle$ are used for the formal parameters and $\langle l_k, \ldots, l_n \rangle$ for the local variables declared in the method. Similarly, each field f has a unique signature which consists of the class where it is declared, its name and its type . A class cannot declare two fields with the same name. The following instructions are included:

$$bcInstr ::= \quad \text{load } i \mid \text{store } i \mid \text{push } n \mid \text{pop} \mid \text{dup} \mid \text{add} \mid \text{sub} \mid \text{div}$$
$$\mid \text{iflt } j \mid \text{ifgt } j \mid \text{ifleq } j \mid \text{ifeq } j \mid \text{ifneq } j \mid \text{ifnull } j \mid \text{goto } j$$
$$\mid \text{new } c \mid \text{getfield } f \mid \text{putfield } f$$
$$\mid \text{newarray } d \mid \text{aload} \mid \text{astore} \mid \text{arraylength}$$
$$\mid \text{invokevirtual } m \mid \text{invokenonvirtual } m \mid \text{return}$$

Similarly to Java bytecode, simple bytecode is a stack-based language. The instructions in the first row manipulate the *operand stack*. The second row contains *jump* instructions. Instructions in the third row manipulate *objects* and their fields, while the fourth row works on *arrays*. The last row contains instructions dealing with *method invocation*. As regards notation, i is an integer which corresponds to a local variable index, n is an integer or null, j is an integer which corresponds to an index in the bytecode sequence, $c \in C$, m is a method signature, and f is a field signature.

We assume an operational semantics which is a subset of the JVM specification [37]. The execution environment of a bytecode program consists of a *heap* h and a stack A of *activation records*. Each activation record contains a program counter, a local operand stack, and local variables. The heap contains all objects and arrays allocated during the execution of the program. Each method invocation generates a new activation record according to its signature. Different activation records do not share information, but may contain references to the same objects in the heap.

Example 1. (running example) Figure 1 depicts the bytecode and a possible Java source (only shown for clarity of the presentation) of our running example. The Java program implements the binary search of an element v in a sorted array t. Variables I and u represent two indexes in the array t. If there exists a position I≤m≤u such that t[m] is equal to v, then m is returned as result. Otherwise the method returns −1. The table of local variables is indexed from 0 to 4 and it contains the values of t, v, I, u and m respectively.

The first three instructions check the negation of the loop condition. If the check succeeds, i.e., the loop condition does not hold, then the body of the loop is not executed and the control goes to instruction 31, where the constant −1 is returned as the result (instruction 32) of the method. Otherwise the value of (I+u)/2 is stored in m in instructions 3–8. Then, instructions 9–13 check whether t[m]! =v holds. It the check fails, meaning that t[m]==v, then instruction 14 is executed, where variable m is pushed on the stack and returned as result in 15. Otherwise, the execution jumps to line 16, where the second if is checked (instructions 16,...,20). If t[m]>v then instructions 21,...,24 store the value of m−1 in u and at instruction 25 the control goes back to the beginning of the loop, i.e., instruction 0. Otherwise, the value of m+1 (instructions 26,...30) is assigned to I and, similarly, control returns to instruction 0.   □

3   Cost Analysis: From Bytecode to Cost Relations

This section describes how a bytecode program is analyzed in order to produce a *cost relation system* (CRS) which describes its resource consumption. The analysis consists of a number of steps: (1) the *control flow graph* of the program is computed, and afterwards (2) the program is transformed into a *rule-based representation* which facilitates the subsequent steps of the analysis without losing information about the resource consumption; (3) size analysis and abstract compilation are used to generate size relations which describe how the size of data changes during program execution; (4) the chosen cost model is applied to each instruction in order to obtain an expression which represents its cost; (5) finally, a cost relation system is obtained by joining the information gathered in the previous steps.

3.1   Control Flow Graph

The *control flow graph* of a program allows statically considering all possible paths which might be taken at runtime, which is essential information for studying its cost. Unlike structured languages such as Java, bytecode features *unstructured* control flow, due to conditional and unconditional *jumps*. Reasoning about unstructured programs is more complicated for both human-made and automatic analysis. Moreover, the control flow is made even more difficult to deal with by *virtual method invocation* and the need to handle *exceptions*. Each node of a control flow graph contains a (maximal) sequence of *non-branching* instructions, which are guaranteed to be executed sequentially. This amounts

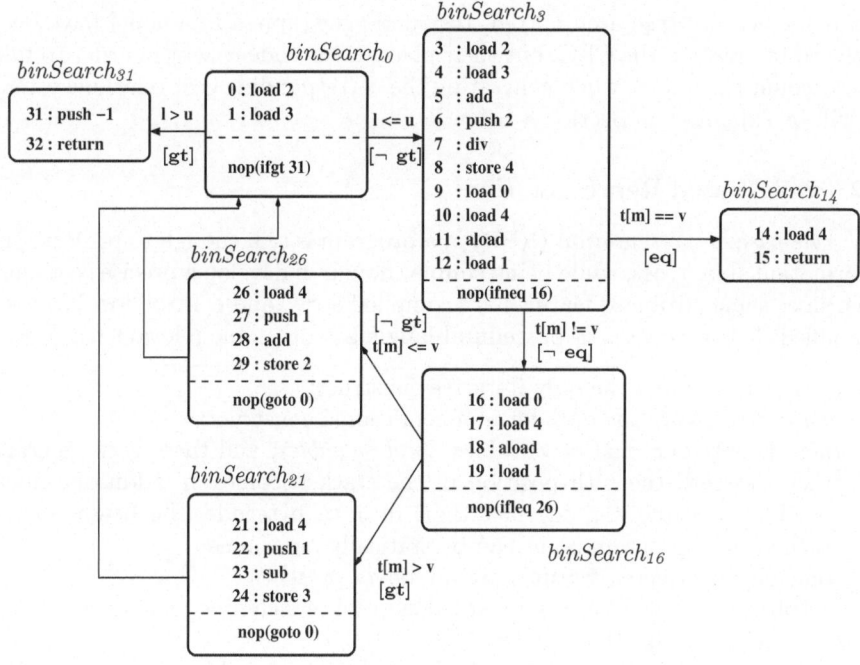

Fig. 2. The control flow graph of the running example

to saying that execution always starts at the beginning of the sequence, and the instructions in the sequence are executed one after the other until the end, without executing any other piece of code in the meanwhile.

The CFG can be built using standard techniques [2], suitably extended in order to deal with virtual method invocation. For this, it is essential to perform *class analysis* (see e.g. [51] and its references) which allows statically obtaining a safe approximation of the set of classes to which an object variable may belong to at runtime. Consider, for example, an object o, and suppose class analysis determines that a set C contains all classes to which o may belong at a given program point which contains a call of the form $o.m()$. Then, such call is translated into a set of calls $o.m_c$, one for every class $c \in C$ where m is defined. This is obtained by adding new *dispatch blocks*, containing calls invoke($c.m$) to each implementation of m. Access to such blocks is guarded by mutually exclusive conditions on the runtime class of o.

Figure 2 shows the CFG of the running example. The graph contains 7 nodes, each composed of non-branching instructions which are always executed sequentially. All nodes end either in a return instruction (as in $binSearch_{31}$ and $binSearch_{14}$), or in an instruction labeled with nop(), which indicates a conditional or unconditional jump in the original bytecode. Edges corresponding to conditional jumps are marked with a guard (which appears in brackets in the figure; for clarity, conditions in the original Java program are also shown without brackets) representing the condition under which the edge can be traversed.

Guards which are *true* are omitted. Instructions wrapped in a nop() have been replaced by edges in the CFG, but their place in the code is kept in order to take into account their costs when generating the corresponding cost relation system, as will be explained in Section 4 below.

3.2   Rule-Based Representation

The *rule-based representation* (RBR) of a program is rich enough to preserve the information about cost, while being simple enough to develop a precise cost analysis, since some advanced features are compiled away, and control flow has been simplified. It is a *structured* procedural language with some relevant features:

1. *recursion* becomes the only iterative construct;
2. *guarded rules* are the only form of conditional construct;
3. there is only one kind of variables: *local variables*; and there is no operand stack (instead, the k-th position in the stack becomes an additional local variable s_k, exploiting the fact that, in Java bytecode, the height of the stack at each program point can be statically determined);
4. some object-oriented features are no longer present:
   - objects can be basically regarded as records including an additional field which contains their type;
   - the behaviour due to dynamic dispatch is compiled into *dispatch blocks*;
   - the language deals with the rest of object-oriented features by supporting object creation, field manipulation and arrays;
5. methods are represented as collections of related blocks, and executing a method is equivalent to executing the entry block of its representation.

These design choices help to make the generation of cost relation systems feasible, and consistent with the program structure. The rule-based representation of a program consists of a set of (global) procedures, one for each node in the CFG. Each procedure consists of one or more rules. A rule for a procedure p with k input arguments $\bar{x}$ and a (single) output argument y takes the form $p(\bar{x}, y) \leftarrow g, body$ where $p(\bar{x}, y)$ is the *head*, g is a *guard* expressing a boolean condition, and *body* is (a suitable representation of) the instructions which are contained in the node.

A guard can be either *true*, any linear condition about the value of variables (e.g., $x + y > 10$), or a type check type(x, c). Every (non-branching) instruction in the body is represented in a more readable (and closer to source code) syntax than the original bytecode (Figure 3). E.g., the instruction load i which loads the i-th local variable l_i into a new topmost stack variable s_{t+1} is written as $s_{t+1} := l_i$ (remember that variables named s_k originate from the k-th position in the stack but they are actually local variables in the RBR). Moreover, add is translated to $s_{t-1} := s_{t-1} + s_t$, where t is the current height of the stack in the original program, and putfield f is turned into $s_t.f := s_t$. As in the control flow graph, branching instructions such as jumps and calls (which have become edges in the CFG, but may still be relevant to the resource consumption) are wrapped into a nop(_) construct, meaning that they are not executed in the

b_j	$comp(b_j)$		b_j	$comp(b_j)$
load i	$s_{t+1} := l_i$		$\neg$ eq	$s_{t-1} \neq s_t$
store i	$l_i := s_t$		$\neg$ null	$s_t \neq$ null
push n	$s_{t+1} := n$		type(n,c)	type(s_{t-n}, c)
pop	$nop(pop)$		new c	$s_{t+1} :=$ new c
dup	$s_{t+1} := s_t$		getfield $f.$	$s_t := s_t.f$
add	$s_{t-1} := s_{t-1} + s_t$		putfield $f.$	$s_{t-1}.f := s_t$
sub	$s_{t-1} := s_{t-1} - s_t$		newarray c	$s_t :=$ newarray(c, s_t)
lt	$s_{t-1} < s_t$		aload	$s_{t-1} := s_{t-1}[s_t]$
gt	$s_{t-1} > s_t$		astore	$s_{t-2}[s_{t-1}] := s_t$
eq	$s_{t-1} = s_t$		arraylength	$s_t :=$ arraylength(s_t)
null	$s_t =$ null		invoke m	$m(s_{t-n}, \ldots, s_t, s_{t-n})$
$\neg$ lt	$s_{t-1} \geq s_t$		return	$out := s_t$
$\neg$ gt	$s_{t-1} \leq s_t$		nop(b)	nop(b)

Fig. 3. Compiling bytecode instructions (as they appear in the CFG) to rule-based instructions (t stands for the height of the stack before the instruction)

RBR, but will be taken into account in the following steps of the analysis. RBR programs are restricted to *strict determinism*, i.e., the guards for all rules for the same procedure are pairwise mutually exclusive, and the disjunction of all such guards is always true.

A CFG can be translated into a rule-based program by building a rule for every node of the graph, which executes its sequential bytecode, and calls the rules corresponding to its successors in the CFG. Figure 4 shows the rule-based program for the CFG of Figure 2. The RBR for the *binSearch* method has an *entry procedure* which simply initializes all local variables and calls $binSearch_0$. In turn, the body of $binSearch_0$ loads l and u (corresponding to l and u), and calls its *continuation* $binSearch_0^c$, that decides which block will be executed next, depending on the comparison between s_1 and s_2 (note that the guards of the continuation rules are mutually exclusive). Procedures which are not continuations are named after the corresponding nodes in the CFG. Note that rules $binSearch_{26}$ and $binSearch_{21}$ contain a call to $binSearch_0$, which is in fact the loop condition.

An *operational semantics* can be given for the rule-based representation, which mimics the bytecode one. In particular, executing an RBR program still needs a *heap* and a *stack* of activation records. The main difference between the two semantics lies in the granularity of procedures: every method in the bytecode program has been partitioned into a set of procedures. In spite of this, it can be proven that any rule-based program is *cost-equivalent* to the bytecode program it comes from. Intuitively, cost-equivalence means that no information about the resource consumption is lost. The main cost-equivalence result states that the execution from cost-equivalent input configurations for a bytecode program and its RBR leads to (1) non-termination in both cases; or (2) cost-equivalent output configurations.

$binSearch(t, v, l, u, r) \leftarrow init\_vars(m), binSearch_0(t, v, l, u, m, r)$
$binSearch_0(t, v, l, u, m, r) \leftarrow$
  $s_1 := l, s_2 := u, \mathsf{nop}(if\_icmpgt\ 31), binSearch_0^c(t, v, l, u, m, s_1, s_2, r).$
$binSearch_0^c(t, v, l, u, m, s_1, s_2, r) \leftarrow s_1 > s_2, binSearch_{31}(t, v, l, u, m, r).$
$binSearch_0^c(t, v, l, u, m, s_1, s_2, r) \leftarrow s_1 \le s_2, binSearch_3(t, v, l, u, m, r).$
$binSearch_{31}(t, v, l, u, m, r) \leftarrow s_1 := -1, r := s_1.$
$binSearch_3(t, v, l, u, m, r) \leftarrow$
  $s_1 := l, s_2 := u, s_1 := s_1 + s_2, s_2 := 2, s_1 := s_1/s_2, m := s_1, s_1 := t, s_2 := m,$
  $s_1 := s_1[s_2], s_2 := v, \mathsf{nop}(if\_icmpne\ 16), binSearch_3^c(t, v, l, u, m, s_1, s_2, r).$
$binSearch_3^c(t, v, l, u, m, s_1, s_2, r) \leftarrow s_1 = s_2, binSearch_{14}(t, v, l, u, m, r).$
$binSearch_3^c(t, v, l, u, m, s_1, s_2, r) \leftarrow s_1 \ne s_2, binSearch_{16}(t, v, l, u, m, r).$
$binSearch_{14}(t, v, l, u, m, r) \leftarrow s_1 := m, r := s_1.$
$binSearch_{16}(t, v, l, u, m, r) \leftarrow$
  $s_1 := t, s_2 := m, s_1 := s_1[s_2], s_2 := v,$
  $\mathsf{nop}(if\_icmple\ 26), binSearch_{16}^c(t, v, l, u, m, s_1, s_2, r).$
$binSearch_{16}^c(t, v, l, u, m, s_1, s_2, r) \leftarrow s_1 \le s_2, binSearch_{26}(t, v, l, u, m, r).$
$binSearch_{16}^c(t, v, l, u, m, s_1, s_2, r) \leftarrow s_1 > s_2, binSearch_{21}(t, v, l, u, m, r).$
$binSearch_{26}(t, v, l, u, m, r) \leftarrow$
  $s_1 := m, s_2 := 1, s_1 := s_1 + s_2, v := s_1, \mathsf{nop}(goto\ 0), binSearch_0(t, v, l, u, m, r).$
$binSearch_{21}(t, v, l, u, m, r) \leftarrow$
  $s_1 := m, s_2 := 1, s_1 := s_1 - s_2, u := s_1, \mathsf{nop}(goto\ 0), binSearch_0(t, v, l, u, m, r).$

Fig. 4. RBR of the example (guards which are *true* are omitted)

3.3   Cost Relations

Given a program P (without loss of generality, it is supposed here that P has
already been translated into its RBR form) and a cost model $\mathcal{M}$, the classical
approach to cost analysis [57] consists in generating a set of *recurrence relations*
(RRs) which capture the cost (w.r.t. $\mathcal{M}$) of running P on some input. As usual
in this area, data structures are replaced by their *sizes* in the recurrence relations. From rule-based programs it is possible to obtain *cost relations* (CRs), an
extended form of recurrence relations, which approximate the cost of running
the corresponding programs. In the presented approach, each rule in the RBR
program results in an equation in the CRS. Figure 5 shows the cost relation
system (i.e., a system of cost relations) for the running example, where it is easy
to see in the rule names the correspondence with the rule-based representation.
In these equations, variables are in fact constraint variables which correspond to
the sizes of those of the RBR. The right-hand side of an equation consists of an
expression e which gives the cost of executing the body of the rule, and, for simplicity of the subsequent presentation, a linear constraint φ which denotes the
effect of the body on the variables. An important point to note is that, there are
some cases where the simplification above may be incorrect. We opt by keeping
this simplification in the presentation, though not in the implementation, because problems are rare and otherwise the presentation gets more complicated.
In more detail, input-output size relations cannot always be merged together in

$$
\begin{array}{lll}
(1)\ binSearch(t,v,l,u) & = binSearch_0(t,v,l,u,0) & \\
(2)\ binSearch_0(t,v,l,u,m) & = 3 + binSearch_0^c(t,v,l,u,m,s_1,s_2) & \{s_1{=}l,s_2{=}u\} \\
(3)\ binSearch_0^c(t,v,l,u,m,s_1,s_2) & = binSearch_{31}(t,v,l,u,m) & \{s_1{>}s_2\} \\
(4)\ binSearch_0^c(t,v,l,u,m,s_1,s_2) & = binSearch_3(t,v,l,u,m) & \{s_1{\leq}s_2\} \\
(5)\ binSearch_{31}(t,v,l,u,m) & = 2 & \\
(6)\ binSearch_3(t,v,l,u,m) & = 11 + binSearch_3^c(t,v,l,u,m',s_1,s_2) & \\
& \qquad \left\{ s_2{=}v, m' \in \left[\frac{l+u}{2} - \frac{1}{2}, \frac{l+u}{2} \right] \right\} & \\
(7)\ binSearch_3^c(t,v,l,u,m,s_1,s_2) & = binSearch_{16}(t,v,l,u,m) & \\
(8)\ binSearch_3^c(t,v,l,u,m,s_1,s_2) & = binSearch_{14}(t,v,l,u,m) & \\
(9)\ binSearch_{16}(t,v,l,u,m) & = 5 + binSearch_{16}^c(t,v,l,u,m,s_1,s_2) & \{s_2{=}v\} \\
(10)\ binSearch_{14}(t,v,l,u,m) & = 2 & \\
(11)\ binSearch_{16}^c(t,v,l,u,m,s_1,s_2) & = binSearch_{26}(t,v,l,u,m) & \\
(12)\ binSearch_{16}^c(t,v,l,u,m,s_1,s_2) & = binSearch_{21}(t,v,l,u,m) & \\
(13)\ binSearch_{26}(t,v,l,u,m) & = 5 + binSearch_0(t,v,l',u,m) & \{l'{=}m{+}1\} \\
(14)\ binSearch_{21}(t,v,l,u,m) & = 5 + binSearch_0(t,v,l,u',m) & \{u'{=}m{-}1\}
\end{array}
$$

Fig. 5. CRS of the running example

φ. Constraints which originate from input-output relations of procedures called in the body of the rule cannot be taken into account until after the corresponding calls. This is because, by merging them, we can no longer distinguish finite failures from infinite failures. For instance, this happens when we have a procedure, say p, which never terminates. The input-output relation for p is represented with the constraint *false*, indicating that there are no successful executions for p. Any equation which has a call to p will have $\varphi = false$. If, by mistake, we take this *false* as a finite failure, we would incorrectly discard (part of) this equation as unreachable, when in reality execution never returns from this equation. In our running example, this phenomenon does not happen since even after adding constraints originating from input-output relations, no φ becomes *false*.

Finally, note also that the output variable of the rule does not appear in the equation, as explained below. The generation of a cost equation for a given RBR rule goes through the following steps.

Size Measures. A *size measure* is chosen to represent and manipulate information relevant to cost, and a variable is abstracted to its *size* w.r.t. such measure. For example, (1) an array may be abstracted to its length, since this can typically give information about the cost of traversing it in a loop; or (2) an object can be abstracted to the longest path reachable from it (in this case, the size measure is well-known and is called *path-length* [52]) in order to describe the cost of traversing data structures such as trees or linked lists. The choice of a size measure, in particular for heap structures, heavily depends on the program to be analyzed, and is intended to represent the maximum amount of relevant information. E.g., in cost and termination analysis, the measure used to abstract a piece of data or a data structure should give information about the behavior of a loop whose exit condition depends, as in the examples above, on the data.

Abstract Compilation. In the presented setting, one important issue is to capture relations between the size of a variable at different program points. For example, in analyzing $x := x + 1$, the interest usually lies in the relation "the value of x *after* is equal to 1 plus the value of x *before*".

In this steps of the cost analysis, instructions are replaced by *linear constraints* which approximate the relation between states (and, typically, between different program points) w.r.t. the chosen size measure. For instance, $s_1 := o$ is replaced by $s_1 = o$, meaning that, after the assignment, the size of s_1 at the current program point is equal to the size of o. As another example, $x :=$ new c can be replaced, using the path-length measure, by $x = 1$, meaning that the maximal path reachable from x after the object creation has length 1.

Importantly, the use of path-length as a size measure for reference requires extra information in order to obtain precise and sound results in the abstract compilation of instructions involving references:

(a) *sharing* information [48] is required in order to know whether two references may point to a common region of the heap; and
(b) *non-cyclicity* information [46] is required to guarantee that, at some specific program point, a reference points to a non-cyclic data structure, i.e., that the length of its longest path (therefore, the number of iteration on a typical traversing loop) is guaranteed to be finite.

A slightly more complicated example where non-cyclicity information is used is represented by a field access $x := y.f$: in this case

- no linear constraint can be inferred if f is a non-reference field;
- if y is detected as non-cyclic, then the size of x after the assignment can be guaranteed to be *strictly less* than the size of y before (since the data structure pointed by x is now a sub-structure of the one pointed by y);
- if y may be cyclic, then the size of x can only be taken to be *not greater* than the size of y (thus basically forbidding to find useful results on x and y in the following steps, as explained in Section 4).

The result of this *abstract compilation* is an *abstract program* which can be used to approximate the values of variables w.r.t. the given size measure.

Input-Output Size Relations. As mathematical relations, CRs cannot have output variables: instead, they should receive a set of input parameters and return a number which represents the cost of the associated computation. This step of the analysis is meant to transform the abstract program in order to remove output variables from it. The basic idea relies on computing abstract *input-output (size) relations* in terms of linear constraints, and using them to propagate the effect of calling a procedure. Concretely, input-output size relations of the form $p(\bar{x}, y) \to \varphi$ are inferred, where φ is a constraint describing the relation between the sizes of the input $\bar{x}$ and the output y upon exit from p. This information is needed since the output of one call may be input to another call. Interestingly, input-output relations can be seen also as a denotational semantics for the abstract programs previously obtained. Sound input-output size relations can be obtained by taking abstract rules generated by abstract compilation, and combine them via a fixpoint computation [13], using abstract interpretation techniques [20] in order to avoid infinite computations.

Example 2. Consider the following RBR rules

$$incr(this, i, out) \leftarrow incr_1(this, i, out)$$
$$incr_1(this, i, out) \leftarrow s_1 := i, \ s_2 := 2, \ s_1 := s_1 + s_2, \ out := s_1$$

which basically come from the method

```
int incr(int i) { return i+2; }
```

All variables relevant to the computation are integers, so that abstract compilation abstracts every variable into itself (due to the choice of the size measure for numeric variables), and the abstract program looks like (constraints $\{s_1 = 0, s_2 = 0, out = 0\}$ describe the initial values of variables)

$$incr(this, i, out) \leftarrow incr_1(this, i, out)$$
$$incr_1(this, i, out) \leftarrow \{s_1 = 0, s_2 = 0, out = 0\} \mid$$
$$s_1' = i, \ s_2' = 2, \ s_1'' = s_1' + s_2', \ out' = s_1''$$

By combining the constraints through the bodies, it can be inferred that the output value of *out* is 2 plus the input value of i, which, in the end, is represented by the input-output size relation

$$incr(this, i, out) \leftarrow \{out = i + 2\}$$

$\square$

Cost Models. Resource usage analysis is a clear example of a program analysis where the focus is not only on the input-output behavior (i.e., *what* a program computes), but also on the history of the computation (i.e., *how* the computation is performed). Since the history of a computation can be normally extracted by its trace, it is natural to describe resource usage in terms of execution traces.

The notion of a *cost model* for bytecode programs formally describes how the resource consumption of a program can be calculated, given a resource of interest. It basically defines how to measure the resource consumption, i.e., the cost, associated to each execution step and, by extension, to an entire trace.

In the present setting, a cost model can be viewed as a function from a bytecode instruction, and dynamic information (local variables, stack, and heap) to a real number. Such number is the amount of resources which is consumed when executing the current step in the given configuration. Example 3 below introduces some interesting cost models which will be used in the next sections.

Example 3. The *instructions* cost model, denoted $\mathcal{M}_{inst}$, counts the number of bytecode instructions executed by giving a constant cost 1 to the execution of any instruction in any configuration: it basically measures the length of a trace.

The *heap* cost model, $\mathcal{M}_{heap}$, is used for estimating the amount of memory allocated by the program for dynamically storing objects and arrays (i.e., its heap consumption): it assigns to any instruction the amount of memory which it allocates in the current configuration. For instance, newarray *int* (resp., newarray *c*) allocates $v * size(int)$ (resp., $v * size(ref)$) bytes in the heap, where v denotes the length of the array (currently stored on the top of the stack), and $size(int)$ (resp., $size(ref)$) is the size of an integer (resp., a reference) as a memory area.   □

Generation of Cost Relation Systems. Cost relation in a CRS are generated by using the abstract rules to build the constraints, and the original rule together with the selected cost model to generate *cost expressions* representing the cost of the bytecodes w.r.t. the model. Consider the cost relations identified by equations (6), (7) and (8) in the CRS of the running example (Figure 5), reproduced here for more clarity.

$$(6) \qquad binSearch_3(t, v, l, u, m) = 11 + binSearch_3^c(t, v, l, u, m', s_1, s_2)$$
$$\left\{ s_2 = v, m' \in \left[\tfrac{l+u}{2} - \tfrac{1}{2}, \tfrac{l+u}{2} \right] \right\}$$
$$(7) \quad binSearch_3^c(t, v, l, u, m, s_1, s_2) = binSearch_{16}(t, v, l, u, m)$$
$$(8) \quad binSearch_3^c(t, v, l, u, m, s_1, s_2) = binSearch_{14}(t, v, l, u, m)$$

This excerpt shows that the inferred cost of executing $binSearch_3$ amounts to 11 plus the cost of executing $binSearch_3^c$. In turn, the cost of $binSearch_3^c$ can be either the cost of $binSearch_{16}$ or the cost of $binSearch_{14}$. In this case, cost expressions (as 11 in (6), or 0, left implicit in (7) and (8)) are simply constant values, which correspond to the number of executed instructions, since the cost model $\mathcal{M}_{inst}$ has been chosen. That is, eleven instruction are executed in $binSearch_3$ before calling $binSearch_3^c$, while no instructions are executed before calling $binSearch_{16}$ or $binSearch_{14}$ from $binSearch_3^c$. The constraints which appear at the end of some equations (as in (6); see also the complete CR for more examples) will be used in the following section. CRs extend recurrence relations in the sense that they allow to handle advanced features such as *non-determinism* (see for instance equations (7) and (8)) *constraints*, and *multiple arguments*, which arise in the cost analysis of realistic programs.

4   From Cost Relations to Closed-Form Upper Bounds

Though cost relations (CRs) are simpler than the programs they originate from, since all variables have integer type, in several respects they are not *as static as* one would expect from the result of a static analysis. First, cost relations are recursive, so that one may need to iterate for computing their value on a concrete input. Second, even for deterministic programs, it is well known that the loss of precision introduced by the size abstraction may result in cost relations which are non-deterministic. This happens in the above example in the loop inside binarySearch: since the array t is abstracted to its length, the contents of the array are lost in the abstraction. In particular, the value of t[m] is unknown in the CR. Hence, the pairs of Equations 7–8 and 11–12 end up having the same guards and the evaluation of this CR turns out to be non-deterministic. In order to find the worst-case cost, one would need to compute and compare many results. In some cases, the number of results may even be infinite. For both reasons, it is clear that it is interesting to compute *closed-form* upper bounds for the cost relation, whenever this is possible, i.e., upper bounds which are in non-recursive form. For example, the goal is to infer that the cost of calling $binSearch(t, v, l, u)$ is $24 * \lceil\log_2(\mathsf{nat}(u - l) + 1)\rceil + 40$, where $\mathsf{nat}(a) = max(a, 0)$.

Since CRs are syntactically quite close to *Recurrence Relations* (*RRs* for short), in most resource analysis frameworks, it has been assumed that cost relations can be easily converted into *RRs*. This has led to the belief that it is possible to use existing *Computer Algebra Systems* (CAS for short) for finding closed forms of the relations generated by resource analysis. As it will be shown, cost relations are far from *RRs*, and using CAS to obtain closed-form upper bounds is, in general, not practical, and requires a considerable amount of human intervention in many phases.

The main idea in the approach used in the COSTA system is to view CRSs as *programs*, and then use semantic-based static-analysis and program-transformations techniques in order to infer closed-form upper bounds [8]. We first explain the basic ideas on small examples, then we explain how they can be extended to the general case.

4.1   Bounds on the Number of Applications of Equations

The first dimension of the problem of obtaining closed-form upper bounds is to bound the number of recursive calls in each relation, which directly affects the number of times an equation can be applied. Consider, for example, the following cost relation:

$$C(n) = 3 \qquad \{n \leq 0\}$$
$$C(n) = 9 + C(n') \quad \{n > 0, n' < n\}$$

An evaluation of an initial call $C(v)$, where v is an integer value works as follows: if $v \leq 0$ then we apply the first equation and we accumulate 3 units to the cost, and if $v > 0$ then we apply the second equation, which in turn accumulates 9 units to the cost plus the cost of the recursive call $C(v')$ where v' is an integer number such that $v' < v$ (which corresponds to the constraint $n' < n$). Clearly, if I_r and I_b are, respectively, upper bounds on the *number of applications* of the recursive and base-case equations, then $9 * I_r + 3 * I_b$ is an upper bound on the corresponding cost. In the above example, in each recursive call the argument of C decreases at least by 1 (since $n' < n$), and therefore the maximum number of applications of the second equation is $I_r = n_0$, where n_0 corresponds to the (initial) input value, and $I_b = 1$, since the base-case equation is applied only once. Note that when n_0 is negative, we do not make any recursive call, therefore in order to capture these cases we define $I_r = \mathsf{nat}(n_0)$ where $\mathsf{nat}(a) = max(a, 0)$. Putting everything together we obtain that an upper bound for the call $C(n_0)$ is $9 * \mathsf{nat}(n_0) + 3$.

The above example demonstrates that inferring how the values of arguments change during evaluation plays an important role in bounding the number of application of each equation. This change might come in different forms, for example if we change the second equation in the above CR to

$$C(n) = 8 + C(n') \quad \{n > 0, n' \leq \tfrac{n}{2}\}$$

then C's argument decreases by at least half in each recursive call, and therefore the maximum number of application of the recursive equation is $I_r = \lceil \log_2(\mathsf{nat}(n_0) + 1) \rceil$ which in turn implies that the upper bound would be $8 * \lceil \log_2(\mathsf{nat}(n_0) + 1) \rceil + 3$.

Another important factor that affects the number of applications of the different equations is the number of recursive calls in a single equation. For example, assuming that the recursive equation in the above CR is of the form

$$C(n) = 7 + C(n') + C(n'') \quad \{n > 0, n' < n, n'' < n\}$$

then the recursive equation would be applied in the worst-case $I_r = 2^{\mathsf{nat}(n_0)} - 1$ times, because each call generates 2 recursive calls, and in each call the argument decreases at least by 1. Note that $2^{\mathsf{nat}(n_0)} - 1$ corresponds to the number of internal nodes which a complete binary tree of height $\mathsf{nat}(n_0)$ has. In addition, unlike the above examples, the base-case equation would be applied in the worst-case $I_b = 2^{\mathsf{nat}(n_0)}$ times, and therefore the upper bound would be $7 * (2^{\mathsf{nat}(n_0)} - 1) + 3 * 2^{\mathsf{nat}(n_0)}$.

In general, a CR does not include only two equations as above. It may include several base cases and/or several recursive equations. In addition, equations are not necessarily mutually exclusive, which means that at each evaluation step there are several equations that can be applied. For example, if all three recursive equations that we have seen above are defined in the same CR, then the upper bound would be $max([7, 8, 9]) * (2^{\mathsf{nat}(n_0)} - 1) + 3 * 2^{\mathsf{nat}(n_0)}$. Note that the worst-case for the cost of each application is determined by the first equation, which contributes the largest cost, i.e., 9. The worst case for the number of applications of the recursive case is determined by the third equation, which has two recursive calls.

As we explained at the beginning, the problem of bounding the number of applications of each equation is related to bounding the number of consecutive recursive calls, which has been extensively studied in the context of termination analysis. Automatic termination analyzers usually prove that an upper bound of the consecutive recursive calls exists by proving that there exists a function f from the loop's arguments to a *well-founded* partial order, such that f decreases in any two consecutive calls. This, in turn, guarantees the absence of infinite traces, and therefore termination. These functions are usually called *ranking functions*. If instead of proving that such function exists we actually compute one, then we can use it as the upper bound on the number of consecutive calls, which in turn can be used to bound the number of applications.

4.2   Bounds on the Cost of Equations

In the above examples, in each application the corresponding equation contributes a constant number of cost units. This is not the case in general. For example, it is common to have a CR of the following form:

$$C(n) = 3 \qquad\qquad\qquad \{n \leq 0\}$$
$$C(n) = \mathsf{nat}(n + 2)^2 + C(n') \quad \{n > 0, n' \leq \tfrac{n}{2}\}$$

where in the second equation we accumulate a non-constant, i.e., $\mathsf{nat}(n + 2)^2$, number of units in each application. In equations with a non-constant direct cost expression, a closed-form upper bound can be obtained by considering the worst-case (the maximum) value that the expression can be evaluated to, multiplied by the number of applications of the corresponding equation. For example, in the above equation, the maximum value that the expression $(n+2)$ can be evaluated to is $(n_0 + 2)$, and therefore we would produce the upper bound $\mathsf{nat}(n_0 + 2)^2 * \lceil \log_2(\mathsf{nat}(n_0) + 1) \rceil + 3$.

In order to infer the maximum value of non-constant expressions automatically, we first infer *invariants* (linear relations) between the equation's variables and the values which such variables had at the initial call, and then *maximize* the expression w.r.t. these values. For the above example we would infer the relation $\{n_0 \geq n > 0\}$, from which we can see that the maximum value for n is n_0. This in turn implies that $(n_0 + 2)$ is the maximum value of $(n + 2)$ and therefore $\mathsf{nat}(n_0 + 2)^2$ is the maximum value for $\mathsf{nat}(n + 2)^2$. Again, if several recursive equations are involved, we should combine them all using the *max* operator on the corresponding expressions, as we have done above.

4.3   The General Case

In all the above examples, a single relation was involved and all recursions were direct. We refer to such CRs as *stand-alone* CRs. This is not the case in general. Instead, in most cases, CRSs consist of several CRs with complex call graphs. In order to cope with this, we first transform the given CRS into a structured form with only direct recursions, and incrementally apply the above techniques. We do so by first applying *Partial Evaluation* [32], a well-known program transformation technique, to each of the strongly connected components (SCC) in the corresponding call graph. By applying partial evaluation starting from a cover point of the SCC, it is guaranteed that get rid of mutual recursion. After partial evaluation, there must be at least one stand-alone CR (does not call any other CR), therefore we can apply the techniques described above in order to solve all these stand-alone CRs. Substituting the results in their calling contexts results in more stand-alone CRs that can in turn be solved using the above techniques again. This process is repeated until there are no more CRs left.

4.4   Obtaining an Upper Bound for the Running Example

The CRS for the running example, shown in Figure 5, contains multiple relations and includes non-direct recursion, which avoids obtaining a closed-form upper bound in a compositional way. As explained above, the first step is to transform the CRS into an equivalent one where we have only direct recursion. The CRS depicted in Figure 5 has 2 SCCs: the first SCC only has Equation 1, and it is not recursive; the second SCC contains Equations 2–14 and corresponds to the loop in *binSearch* and is therefore recursive. After applying partial evaluation to the recursive SCC we obtain the following transformed CRS:

(1) $binSearch(t, v, l, u) = loop(t, v, l, u, 0)$
(2) $loop_b(t, v, l, u, m) = 5$ $\qquad\qquad\qquad \{l > u\}$
(3) $loop_b(t, v, l, u, m) = 16$ $\qquad\qquad\qquad \{l \leq u\}$
(4) $loop_b(t, v, l, u, m) = 24 + loop_b(t, v, l', u, m')$
$$\{l \leq u, m' \in [\tfrac{l+u}{2} - \tfrac{1}{2}, \tfrac{l+u}{2}], l' = m' + 1\}$$
(5) $loop_b(t, v, l, u, m) = 24 + loop(t, v, l, u', m')$
$$\{l \leq u, m' \in [\tfrac{l+u}{2} - \tfrac{1}{2}, \tfrac{l+u}{2}], u' = m' - 1\}$$

The recursive SCC has been transformed into Equations 2–5 above. Note that Equations 3–5 have the same guard ($l \leq u$), which results in a non-deterministic CR. The reason for this is that Equation 3 corresponds to the case where $t[m] ==$ v, Equation 4 to the case where $t[m] > v$ and Equation 5 to the case where $t[m] < v$. However, the value of $t[m]$ is not observable at the cost relation level and even though the original program is deterministic, its associated CRS is not.

Solving the above CRS starts by solving the stand-alone CR which consists in Equations 2–5. Note that Equations 2–3 are the base-cases and 4–5 are the recursive ones. Examining the recursive equations and their attached constraints, we can automatically infer that the difference between the values of u and l decreases logarithmically at each recursive call and, in particular, we can provide $I_r = \lceil \log_2(\mathsf{nat}(u_0 - l_0) + 1) \rceil + 1$ as an upper bound for the number of applications of the recursive equation. The base-case equations are applied only once. Therefore the closed-form upper bound is:

$$loop_b(t_0, v_0, l_0, u_0, m_0) = 24 * (\lceil \log_2(\mathsf{nat}(u_0 - l_0) + 1) \rceil + 1) + 16$$

This closed form can then be substituted in Equation 1 and after some simplification we obtain the following closed-form upper bound for *binSearch*:

$$binSearch(t_0, v_0, l_0, u_0) = 24 * \lceil \log_2(\mathsf{nat}(u_0 - l_0) + 1) \rceil + 40$$

In order to illustrate the use of invariants and the maximization of cost expressions, let us now assume that the method *binSearch* is used in another method as follows:

```
public static int m(int[ ] t){
    int c=0;
    int u=t.length;
    for (int i=0; i<u;i++)
        if (binarySearch(t,i,i,u) != -1 ) c++;
    return c;
}
```

and that we are interested in inferring closed-form upper bounds for m. We first build the CRS that corresponds to m. For brevity, we show the CRS after partial evaluation:

(1) $m(t)$ $\qquad\quad = 9 + loop_m(t, c, u, i)$ $\qquad\qquad\qquad\qquad$ $\{i{=}0, u{=}t, c{=}0\}$
(2) $loop_m(t, c, u, i) = 3$ $\qquad\qquad\qquad\qquad\qquad\qquad\qquad$ $\{i{\geq}u\}$
(3) $loop_m(t, c, u, i) = 12 + binSearch(t, i, i, u) + loop_m(t, c, u, i')$ $\{i{<}u, i'{=}i{+}1\}$
(4) $loop_m(t, c, u, i) = 13 + binSearch(t, i, i, u) + loop_m(t, c', u, i')$ $\{i{<}u, i'{=}i{+}1, c'{=}c{+}1\}$

First we solve the CR $loop_m$ (Equations 2–4). We start by substituting the close-form upper bound of $binSearch_m$ in the corresponding calls and we obtain the following stand-alone CR

$loop_m(t, c, u, i) = 3$ $\qquad\qquad\qquad\qquad\qquad\qquad\qquad\qquad\qquad$ $\{i{\geq}u\}$
$loop_m(t, c, u, i) = 24 * \lceil \log_2(\mathsf{nat}(u - i) + 1) \rceil + 52 + loop_m(t, c, u, i')$ $\{i{<}u, i'{=}i{+}1\}$
$loop_m(t, c, u, i) = 24 * \lceil \log_2(\mathsf{nat}(u - i) + 1) \rceil + 53 + loop_m(t, c', u, i')$ $\{i{<}u, i'{=}i{+}1, c'{=}c{+}1\}$

Examining the recursive equations and their attached constraints we automatically infer that the maximum number of applications of the recursive equations is $\mathsf{nat}(u_0 - i_0)$, since i increases by one until it reaches u (which does not change). Now, in order to infer the closed-form upper bound we need to approximate the maximum values that $\log_2(\mathsf{nat}(u - i) + 1)$ can be evaluated to. This happens when $u - i$ is maximal. This occurs for the maximal values of u and the minimal values of i. Since the invariant that we infer includes $i \geq i_0$ and $u \leq u_0$, we can conclude that $u_0 - i_0$ is the maximum value to which $u - i$ can be evaluated. Therefore the closed-form upper bound for $loop_m$ is:

$$loop_m(t_0, c_0, u_0, i_0) = \mathsf{nat}(u_0 - i_0) * (24 * \lceil \log_2(\mathsf{nat}(u_0 - i_0) + 1) \rceil + 53) + 3$$

Substituting this upper bound in the first equation results in a non-recursive CR which consists in a single equation:

$$m(t) = 9 + \mathsf{nat}(u - i) * (24 * \lceil \log_2(\mathsf{nat}(u - i) + 1) \rceil + 53) + 3 \; \{i{=}0, u{=}t, c{=}0\}$$

and since in this context we have $i = 0$ and $u = t$, we can conclude with the following closed-form upper bound for m:

$$m(t) = 24 * \mathsf{nat}(t) * \lceil \log_2(\mathsf{nat}(t) + 1) \rceil + 53 * \mathsf{nat}(t) + 12$$

5   Application to Resource Certification

In order to motivate the interest of *resource usage certification* or (resource certification for short), we will start by describing *mobile code*. Nowadays, the use of mobile code is widespread. It includes, for example running applets and/or plug-ins downloaded from the net in a web browser or a mobile phone. The current approach to security of mobile code is a combination of static verification of certain properties, which guarantees a certain level of security, with dynamic checking, which supervises all operations which are still potentially unsecure after the static verification. For example, in the Java Virtual Machine, mobile code is subject to *bytecode verification* before being executed, while operations such as array indexing are checked at runtime. Bytecode verification, if successful, provides a number of guarantees on the program, such as being well typed, with jumps to existing instructions, etc. Note that if the bytecode verification process fails, the program is discarded.

Ideally, one would like to extend this model in order to include more sophisticated *security policies* in the static verification part. In particular, and as already sketched in Section 1, the purpose of resource certification is to consider resource usage bounds as security policies. This means that prior to executing a program, it must be guaranteed that the program satisfies a given resource usage policy. This problem can be formulated in two ways. One is to have an automatic system which given a program and a resource usage policy answers *yes* only if it succeeds to prove that the program satisfies the policy. Alternatively, we can split this process in two steps: first, an automatic system obtains an upper bound on the resource usage of the program and second, another automatic system, which in what follows we refer to as *comparator*, checks whether the computed upper bound is smaller than or equal to the resource usage policy for any possible input value. We advocate for the second alternative because we believe it is more flexible: we first use COSTA on the code producer side to infer upper bounds which are independent of any resource policy and consumer, and then, on the code consumer side we check whether the upper bound abides by the policy.

5.1 An Example of Resource Certification

We illustrate through a simple example the fundamental intuition behind resource certification. Let us assume a resource usage policy for method m in Figure 1 that imposes a resource usage policy, which we call *policy*, on the number of instructions executed of:

$$policy = 60 * [\mathsf{nat}(t)]^2 + 120 * \mathsf{nat}(t) + 13$$

COSTA infers the upper bound $ub = 24 * \mathsf{nat}(t) * \lceil \log_2(\mathsf{nat}(t)+1) \rceil + 53 * \mathsf{nat}(t) + 12$. The code will be acceptable, provided that *policy* is guaranteed, i.e., $ub \leq policy$, which happens to be the case in our example and that the comparator succeeds to prove it.

Developing a comparator which handles closed-forms that involve logarithmic, exponential, polynomial expressions, etc. is far from trivial. Based on the ideas in [26], we are currently implementing in COSTA the basics of such comparator, but it is still subject of ongoing work.

Also, though in some contexts, especially when considering memory usage, non-asymptotic policies are to be expected, sometimes it is more reasonable that the policy is asymptotic. In COSTA, policies are currently non-asymptotic and handling of asymptotic policies is also subject of ongoing work. Coming back to our previous example, this would result in a new *policy'* s.t. $policy' = [\mathsf{nat}(t)]^2$. The comparator should again be able to prove that *policy'* is satisfied by method m.

5.2   Scenarios for Resource Certification

Within the alternative we propose, in which code certification is performed in two steps, there are several *scenarios* one could imagine. We now describe three different ones.

The Consumer-Based Scenario. In this first scenario, it is the sole responsibility of the mobile code consumer to both obtain an upper bound and to compare such upper bound with the policy. This scenario is simple, since it does not involve any further actor, but it is inefficient, since the mobile code has to be certified separately for every consumer. Also, it may be unfeasible on devices with limited computing power, such as mobile phones.

The Server-Based Scenario. In this second scenario, there is an additional actor which acts as the server of the mobile code. Such server not only distributes the mobile code. It also computes once and for all an upper bound for it. Assuming that this server is trusted by the code consumer, the consumer downloads a bundle which contains both the code and its upper bound. In order to guarantee that the bundle is actually produced by the trusted server, the bundle is signed using standard *Public Key Infrastructure* (PKI) techniques. Then, the code consumer, using the public key of the server, checks that the bundle is correct and uses the provided upper bound. Similarly, the comparison phase could also either be outsourced to trusted servers and be accessed using PKI or be performed locally.

The PCC-Based Scenario. In this final scenario, the situation is somewhat intermediate between the two other extremes. The main advantage of the pcc-based scenario w.r.t. the server-based one is that in the pcc-scenario the server does not need to be trusted by the code consumer. Unlike the simpler notion of PKI (which merely guarantees that the code has been produced or approved by the signing entity, such as a program, person, or organization), now the pcc server provides an unsigned bundle which contains the code, an upper bound, and some *verifiable evidence*[1] about the upper bound being correct. Then, the code consumer has to have an automatic (and efficient) system for verifying that the provided upper bound is actually valid for the code, by using the provided evidence.

As it is well know from the proof-carrying code [41] theory, the main advantage of this scenario is that the evidence only needs to be generated once and the verification process which occurs at the consumer side should be much more efficient than computing the upper bounds from scratch. Essentially, the hard work is shifted from the code consumer to the code producer (i.e., the programmer and/or the compiler), which now has to not only produce the code, but also an upper bound and the verifiable evidence which must be bundled with it.

---

[1] In the original PCC framework, this *evidence* was called *certificate*. We prefer avoiding the use of such terminology since it is already rather overloaded.

In the case of COSTA, a PCC-based scenario can obtained by using ideas from Abstraction-Carrying Code [7] (ACC), which proposes to use abstract interpretation as enabling technology for PCC. The main idea in ACC is to use, at the producer's side, a fixed point-based static analyzer, in order to automatically infer an abstract model (or simply *abstraction*) of the mobile code which can then be used to prove that this code is secure w.r.t. the given policy in a straightforward way. A simple, easy-to-trust (analysis) verifier at the consumer's side could verify the validity of the information on the mobile code. This verifier could be indeed a specialized abstract interpreter whose key characteristic is that it does not need to iterate in order to reach a fixed point (in contrast to standard analyzers). Furthermore, as the process of inferring the abstraction is fully automatic, the analyzer itself could be used at the consumer side, as discussed in the consumer-based scenario above.

We are currently working on building a PCC infrastructure for COSTA by following the principles of ACC. Since the analyzer computes several abstractions of the program (size relations, invariants, ranking functions, etc.) in order to be able to compute an upper bound, the evidence should in principle contain the fixed points of multiple analyses. However, depending on the analysis times and the amount of space required to store its result, for some analyses it may be more efficient to recompute things on the consumer side than to verify the evidence provided by the server. Thus, there are still important practical decisions regarding which analyses results to include in the evidence and which to recompute on the consumer.

In our opinion, regardless of which of the three scenarios are put into practice, generalized use of resource certification will not be a reality until there are fully automatic resource analyzers available which are capable of computing accurate upper bounds for real-life applications. This is the requirement which COSTA aims at solving. Once this is sufficiently solved, the rest of the infrastructure will be in place relatively easily.

6   Related Work

In this section, we review related work by focusing first in existing tools developed for the analysis and transformation of Java bytecode in Section 6.1. Then, in Section 6.2, we give a brief overview of the features that resource analyses have on the different programming paradigms and the most interesting aspects of each of them. Later, in Section 6.3, we compare our system for obtaining closed-form upper bounds with existing solvers. Finally, in Section 6.5, we summarize the work on certification of the resource consumption of programs.

6.1   Tools for Analysis of Java Bytecode

Analysis of Java bytecode is currently an active research area with a number of analysis and transformation tools available. Especially relevant are the analyses developed on the Soot framework [54] and the Julia generic analyzer [50]. Soot is a framework for the development of optimizations and analyses for Java byte-code which already includes points-to, purity, and dynamic data structure analyses, among others. The most similar part between these systems and COSTA is the transformation of the bytecode into an intermediate (procedural) representation. Indeed, intermediate representations are common practice to develop analysis and transformations on JBC. Of relevant importance is BoogiePL [36] as well. The main differences with our RBR are: (1) they do not provide a uniform treatment of all kinds of loops by means of recursion, (2) they do not perform the loop extraction transformation we propose, which is important for compositionality in resource analysis; and (3) the intermediate representation called Shimple in Soot performs SSA, but neither Shimple nor BoogiePL convert stack variables into local variables as COSTA does. In our representation, in one pass, we can eliminate almost all variables which originate from stack variables, which results in a more efficient subsequent size analysis. The Julia Java bytecode analyzer [50] provides a generic analysis engine for which sharing, class, non-nullness, information flow, escape, constancy, and static initialisation analyses have been integrated. Neither Julia nor Soot include a resource analysis, though Julia also contains implementations of some of the pieces (in particular the class, nullity, sharing, and cyclicity analyses) which are required in the size analysis component.

6.2   Resource Analysis for Different Programming Paradigms

Focusing on resource analysis, important effort has been devoted to extend Weg-breit's framework [57] to different languages and programming paradigms. The main objective in this task is to define a resource analysis framework in which it is possible to generate CRS from the programs in the corresponding language. As mentioned in Section 1, most of the extensions to Wegbreit's framework have taken place in the context of high-level declarative languages, whose recursive structure simplifies the process of generating cost relations. In general, these analyses consider languages without a mutable heap, and they do not deal with objects and exceptions as in our case. We are not aware of any work, apart from ours, that applies Wegbreit's framework to imperative languages. Below we review several frameworks defined for the corresponding declarative programming paradigms.

Cost Analysis in Functional Programming. Early work on resource analysis [57,35,44] was developed for a first order subset of Lisp. Rosendahl [44] presented a system based on transforming a program into a step-counting version which was then analyzed by relying on abstract interpretation. The result of such analysis was expressed as a CRS which was then attempted to be transformed into a closed form by relying on a series of source-to-source transformations. Theoretical advances for analyzing lazy functional languages were made by [56] and [15]. They used projections and demand analysis to model a call-by-need reduction strategy of typed lambda calculus. Still in the context of functional languages, the technique of cost counting programs mentioned above [44,35] was extended in [47] to higher-order programs. Recent work [33] describes a complexity analysis for programs extracted from proofs carried out with the Coq proof assistant. The generated CRSs are solved in this case by relying on MAPLE. Again, the first transformational part is not required and size analysis does not have to deal with object-oriented features. An automatic complexity analysis for computing upper bounds on the time complexity of higher-order Nuprl programs is presented in [14]. The analysis derives recursive cost equations which are passed to Mathematica. In general, in functional programming, resource analysis focuses on dealing with higher-order functions and lazy evaluation.

Cost Analysis in Logic Programming. One of the first resource analysis frameworks [22] was developed in the context of logic programming. In this setting, resource analysis needs to consider peculiar features of logic languages, such as approximating the number of solutions (due to non-deterministic computations), type and mode inference, and non-failure information. The CASLOG system [22] was designed to solve CRSs for logic program and it is currently used in the CiaoPP system [28]. As in functional programming, obtaining CRSs is simplified by the fact that they already start from a recursive programming language where recursion is the only form of iteration. Also, size analysis in logic programming differs from ours as it does not support object-oriented features. The resource analysis integrated in the CiaoPP system includes a resource analysis [40] based on a size analysis for logic programs and hence differs fundamentally from ours.

6.3   Systems for Computing Closed-Form Upper-Bounds

There are two main ways of viewing CRSs which lead to different mechanisms for finding closed-form upper-bounds. We call the first view *algebraic* and the second view *transformational*. The algebraic one is based on regarding CRSs as *recurrence relations*. This view was the first one to be proposed and it is the one which is advocated for in a larger number of works. It allows reusing the large existing body of work in solving recurrence relations. Within this view, two alternatives have been used in previous analyzers. One alternative consists in implementing restricted recurrence solvers based on standard mathematical techniques within the analyzer, as done in e.g. [57,22]. The other alternative, motivated by the availability of powerful *computer algebra systems* (CASs for short) such as Mathematica, MAXIMA, MAPLE, etc., consists in connecting the analyzer with an external solver, as proposed in [56,47,14,6,38].

The transformational view consists in regarding CRSs as (functional) programs. In this view, closed-form upper-bounds are produced by applying (general-purpose) program transformation techniques on the CRS [44] until a non-recursive program is obtained. The transformational view was first proposed in the ACE system [35], which contained a large number of program transformation rules aimed at obtaining non-recursive representations. It was also used by Rosendahl in [44], who later in [45] provided a series of program transformation techniques based on super-compilation [53] which were able to obtain closed-forms for some classes of programs.

The need for improved mechanisms for automatically obtaining closed-form upper-bounds was already pointed out in Hickey and Cohen [29]. A significant work in this direction is PURRS [10], which has been the first system to provide, in a fully automatic way, non-asymptotic closed-form upper and lower bounds for a wide class of recurrences. Unfortunately, and unlike our proposal, it also requires CRSs to be deterministic. The problem with all the approaches mentioned above is that, though they can be successfully applied for obtaining closed-forms for CRSs generated from simple programs, they do not fulfill the initial expectations in that they are not of general applicability to CRSs generated from real programs.

The main motivation for developing the solver [8] that we use in COSTA was our own experience in trying to apply the algebraic approach on the CRSs generated by [6]. We argue that automatically converting CRSs into the format accepted by CASs is unfeasible. Furthermore, even in those cases where CASs can be used, the solutions obtained are so complicated that they become useless for most practical purposes. In contrast, our approach can produce correct and comparatively simple results even in the presence of non-determinism.

6.4   Other Approaches to Cost Analysis

In the imperative programming paradigm, most of the work has been done by the real-time and embedded systems community. It has mainly focused on real-time aspects, with major inroads made in WCET analysis, see e.g. [23], which is technically different from our resource analysis, the main similarity being the need to infer upper bounds on the number of iterations of loops.

There exist other approaches to resource analysis which are not based on Wegbreit's framework. These include analyses based on type-and-effect systems [11,49,55]. Type-and-effect systems [42] are a well-known technique for automatic program analysis. They main difference w.r.t. abstract interpretation approaches like ours is that they avoid having the implementation of specialised inference engines that may be required by abstract interpretation and they simplify the construction of the soundness proofs through analogy with similar and well-understood proofs for the underlying type system. The latest work by [49] uses a type-and-effect system based on Hindley-Milner types to expose constraints on sized types [31] for higher order, recursive functional programs, to provide improved quality of resource analysis. Apart from the underlying differences between the considered languages, in contrast to our proposal, this approach to resource analysis is restricted to linear upper bounds. Besides, the language does not support recursion and the analysis is restricted to a cost model that counts the number of steps. The analysis presented in [11] proposes an extension of the λ-calculus to ensure that resources are correctly used. They also rely on a type-and-effect system to over approximate the set of histories of events (i.e., the usage of resources) that a program can generate at runtime. A model-checking technique then validates such approximations. In essence, this work is focused on the enforcement of resource usage policies, but their techniques cannot be used to generate upper bounds on the resource usage as our method does.

There is also work which studies the relationship between syntactical constructions of programming languages and their computational complexity [34,12]. These analyses are developed on simple imperative languages which are far from our bytecode and, in contrast to our work, they cannot be used to compute non-asymptotic upper bounds.

The work in [39] shows how to apply sub-interpretation (firstly used in first order functional programming to deal with computational complexity) to object-oriented programs without recursion in order to provide upper bounds on their stack usage. This approach is restricted to polynomial bounds and to the particular resource of stack usage.

More recent work develops resource analyses to estimate the memory consumption. In particular, [16] describes a technique for Java-like languages which computes symbolic polynomial approximations of the amount of memory required by a program. The work by [19] studies the memory consumption (including both heap space and stack usage) of low-level programs which are similar to our bytecode programs. In both cases, the analyses are less general than ours, both in the kind of properties they can estimate (specific to memory consumption) and in the kind of upper bounds that they can generate (polynomial bounds).

The SPEED system [25,24] is able to automatically compute symbolic complexity bounds of procedures written in C/C++. The basic idea of their methodology is to instrument monitor variables to count the number of loop iterations and then statically compute an upper bound on these counter variables in terms of programming inputs using invariant generation tools. They allow the user the possibility of defining some quantitative functions over abstract data-structures to avoid the need of shape analysis. Besides, SPEED performs some program transformations to improve the precision of the analysis when inferring bounds on certain types of loops. Some of these ideas could be applied in order to improve our framework.

6.5   Resource Usage Certification

As already mentioned in Section 5, resource usage certification [21,9,30,18,43] proposes the use of security properties involving resource requirements, i.e., that the untrusted code adheres to specific bounds on resource consumption. Related work in the context of Java bytecode includes the work in the MRG project [9], which can be considered complementary to ours. MRG focuses on building a proof-carrying code [41] architecture for ensuring that bytecode programs are free from run-time violations of resource bounds. The cost model which has been used to develop the analysis is heap consumption, since applications to be deployed on devices with a limited amount of memory, such as smartcards, should be rejected if they require more memory than that available. The framework is restricted to polynomial bounds and to the above cost model, while our resource analysis can infer a wider set of bounds (including exponential, algorithmic, etc.) and it is parametric with respect to the cost model. More related work is the one proposed by [17], where a resource usage analysis is presented. Again, this work focuses on one particular notion of cost, memory consumption, and it aims at verifying that the program executes in bounded memory by making sure that the program does not create new objects inside loops, but it does not infer resource usage bounds. The analysis has been certified by proving its correctness using the Coq proof assistant. Compared to previous work, our system shows, for the first time, that it is possible to automatically generate resource bounds guarantees, not restricted to polynomial bounds, for a realistic mobile language.

7   Conclusions and Future Perspectives

In this paper we have illustrated, by means of examples, how the COSTA system performs resource analysis. The analysis is done in two steps. First, *cost relation systems* are generated for an input bytecode w.r.t. a *cost model*. Such relations provide useful approximations of the resource usage of the program w.r.t. the considered cost model, in terms of the size of the input arguments, and provided an accurate *size analysis* is used to establish relationships between arguments. Second, *closed-form upper bounds* for the cost relation systems are obtained. This is possible provided that *ranking functions* are found for all loops which affect the cost and that accurate *invariants* are obtained. To the best of our knowledge, COSTA is the first system to perform fully automatic resource analysis of object-oriented bytecode and we believe that COSTA opens the door to the application of *resource usage analysis* in the context of general purpose applications written in mainstream programming languages.

Though the efficiency and robustness of the system can be considerably improved, COSTA can already deal with a relatively large class of JBC programs, and gives reasonable results in terms of precision and efficiency for different cost models: the number of executed bytecode instructions, heap consumption, and number of calls to user-specified methods. We plan to distribute the system as free software soon. Currently, it can be tried out through a web interface available from the COSTA web site: http://costa.ls.fi.upm.es.

The system can deal with most features of JBC. However, non-sequential code, dynamic class loading and reflection are not supported. Java API methods used by programs are analyzed much in the same way as user code, since their bytecode is available to the analyzer. As for native code, i.e., methods not implemented in Java, calls to native methods are shown in upper bounds as symbolic constants, since the code for those methods is not written in Java and COSTA cannot analyze them. This could be further improved by providing assertions which describe the cost of the native method for the different cost models and (optionally) a safe approximation of their input-output behavior, but it is not supported.

In addition to the web interface, COSTA has a command-line interface and an Eclipse plugin which make interaction with the analyzer quite straightforward, even during program development. The different interfaces allow customizing the behaviour of COSTA by modifying the value of several options, including:

1. whether the code of Java API classes should also be analyzed or not;
2. whether auxiliary analyses (sign, nullity, slicing, constant propagation) should be included, thus possibly improving both precision and performance;
3. whether input-output size relations have to be computed (Section 3.3);
4. if exceptions, either explicitly thrown in the code or resulting from semantic violations, have to be taken into account;
5. which cost model has to be considered.

Also, although not discussed in this paper, COSTA also performs termination analysis of Java bytecode programs (see [3]). When COSTA fails to find an upper bound for a program, sometimes it may be useful to try and find out whether the program is guaranteed to terminate. Maybe COSTA fails because the program contains a bug and loops unexpectedly with a non-zero cost associated to each iteration of the loop. In that case, there exist no upper bound for the program and there is no way that COSTA can find an upper bound. Although COSTA results are safe, they are obviously incomplete, since finding an upper bound is an undecidable problem. This means that there are programs for which it is possible to find an upper bound, but COSTA fails to find one.

As regards future work, there are plenty of ways in which both the theoretical foundations and the practical implementation can be improved in order to handle a larger class of programs, and obtain improvements both in terms of efficiency and accuracy. On the foundations side, progress in the area of object-oriented languages of any of the analyses used by the system will be potentially applicable to COSTA. For example, one of the most challenging problems is to account for loops and recursion where the number of iterations depends on *numeric fields*. Here, an approach working in all cases might not be practical; however, heuristics may allow us to account for special, simple but quite common cases which can significantly enlarge the class of analyzable programs. A first step in this direction, in the context of termination analysis, has been taken in [4]. On the implementation side, currently, COSTA handles bytecode programs for Java SE 1.4.2.13 and Java ME. The reason for this is that Java SE 1.4.2.13 is the version of Java taken as starting point for Java ME and, in particular, for MIDP. The latter is the profile used by mobile phone applications, i.e., *midlets*, which are the main target in the MOBIUS project. However, there is no fundamental reason for not supporting more recent versions of Java and we plan to extend COSTA to also handle Java 5 and 6 soon.

Acknowledgments

This work was funded in part by the Information Society Technologies program of the European Commission, Future and Emerging Technologies under the IST-15905 *MOBIUS* and IST-231620 *HATS* projects, by the Spanish Ministry of Education (MEC) under the TIN-2005-09207 *MERIT*, TIN-2008-05624 *DOVES* and HI2008-0153 (Acción Integrada) projects, and the Madrid Regional Government under the S-0505/TIC/0407 *PROMESAS* project.

References

1. The Timber Language, http://www.timber-lang.org
2. Aho, A.V., Sethi, R., Ullman, J.D.: Compilers – Principles, Techniques and Tools. Addison-Wesley, Reading (1986)
3. Albert, E., Arenas, P., Codish, M., Genaim, S., Puebla, G., Zanardini, D.: Termination analysis of java bytecode. In: Barthe, G., de Boer, F.S. (eds.) FMOODS 2008. LNCS, vol. 5051, pp. 2–18. Springer, Heidelberg (2008)
4. Albert, E., Arenas, P., Genaim, S., Puebla, G.: Dealing with numeric fields in termination analysis of java-like languages. In: Huisman, M. (ed.) 10th Workshop on Formal Techniques for Java-like Programs (July 2008)
5. Albert, E., Arenas, P., Genaim, S., Puebla, G., Zanardini, D.: The COSTA System web site, http://costa.ls.fi.upm.es
6. Albert, E., Arenas, P., Genaim, S., Puebla, G., Zanardini, D.: Cost analysis of java bytecode. In: De Nicola, R. (ed.) ESOP 2007. LNCS, vol. 4421, pp. 157–172. Springer, Heidelberg (2007)
7. Albert, E., Puebla, G., Hermenegildo, M.: Abstraction-Carrying Code: A Model for Mobile Code Safety. New Generation Computing 26(2), 171–204 (2008)
8. Albert, E., Arenas, P., Genaim, S., Puebla, G.: Automatic inference of upper bounds for recurrence relations in cost analysis. In: Alpuente, M., Vidal, G. (eds.) SAS 2008. LNCS, vol. 5079, pp. 221–237. Springer, Heidelberg (2008)
9. Aspinall, D., Gilmore, S., Hofmann, M.O., Sannella, D., Stark, I.: Mobile resource guarantees for smart devices. In: Barthe, G., Burdy, L., Huisman, M., Lanet, J.-L., Muntean, T. (eds.) CASSIS 2004. LNCS, vol. 3362, pp. 1–26. Springer, Heidelberg (2005)
10. Bagnara, R., Pescetti, A., Zaccagnini, A., Zaffanella, E.: PURRS: Towards computer algebra support for fully automatic worst-case complexity analysis. Technical report (2005) arXiv:cs/0512056, http://arxiv.org/
11. Bartoletti, M., Degano, P., Ferrari, G.-L., Zunino, R.: Types and effects for resource usage analysis. In: Seidl, H. (ed.) FOSSACS 2007. LNCS, vol. 4423, pp. 32–47. Springer, Heidelberg (2007)
12. Ben-Amram, A.M., Jones, N.D., Kristiansen, L.: Linear, polynomial or exponential? Complexity inference in polynomial time. In: Beckmann, A., Dimitracopoulos, C., Löwe, B. (eds.) CiE 2008. LNCS, vol. 5028, pp. 67–76. Springer, Heidelberg (2008)
13. Benoy, F., King, A.: Inferring Argument Size Relationships with CLP(R). In: Gallagher, J.P. (ed.) LOPSTR 1996. LNCS, vol. 1207, pp. 204–223. Springer, Heidelberg (1997)
14. Benzinger, R.: Automated Higher-Order Complexity Analysis. Theor. Comput. Sci. 318(1-2) (2004)
15. Bjerner, B., Holmstrom, S.: A Compositional Approach to Time Analysis of First Order Lazy Functional Programs. In: Proc. ACM Functional Programming Languages and Computer Architecture, pp. 157–165. ACM Press, New York (1989)
16. Braberman, V., Fernández, F., Garbervetsky, D., Yovine, S.: Parametric Prediction of Heap Memory Requirements. In: Proceedings of the International Symposium on Memory management (ISMM). ACM, New York (2008)
17. Cachera, D., Jensen, T., Pichardie, D., Schneider, G.: Certified memory usage analysis. In: Fitzgerald, J.S., Hayes, I.J., Tarlecki, A. (eds.) FM 2005. LNCS, vol. 3582, pp. 91–106. Springer, Heidelberg (2005)

18. Chander, A., Espinosa, D., Islam, N., Lee, P., Necula, G.C.: Enforcing resource bounds via static verification of dynamic checks. In: Sagiv, M. (ed.) ESOP 2005. LNCS, vol. 3444, pp. 311–325. Springer, Heidelberg (2005)
19. Chin, W.-N., Nguyen, H.H., Popeea, C., Qin, S.: Analysing Memory Resource Bounds for Low-Level Programs. In: Proceedings of the International Symposium on Memory management (ISMM). ACM, New York (2008)
20. Cousot, P., Cousot, R.: Abstract Interpretation: a Unified Lattice Model for Static Analysis of Programs by Construction or Approximation of Fixpoints. In: Fourth ACM Symposium on Principles of Programming Languages, pp. 238–252 (1977)
21. Crary, K., Weirich, S.: Resource Bound Certification. In: POPL 2000, pp. 184–198. ACM Press, New York (2000)
22. Debray, S.K., Lin, N.W.: Cost Analysis of Logic Programs. ACM Transactions on Programming Languages and Systems 15(5), 826–875 (1993)
23. Eisinger, J., Polian, I., Becker, B., Metzner, A., Thesing, S., Wilhelm, R.: Automatic identification of timing anomalies for cycle-accurate worst-case execution time analysis. In: Proceedings of IEEE Workshop on Design & Diagnostics of Electronic Circuits & Systems (DDECS), pp. 15–20. IEEE Computer Society, Los Alamitos (2006)
24. Gulavani, B.S., Gulwani, S.: A numerical abstract domain based on *expression abstraction* and *max operator* with application in timing analysis. In: Gupta, A., Malik, S. (eds.) CAV 2008. LNCS, vol. 5123, pp. 370–384. Springer, Heidelberg (2008)
25. Gulwani, S., Mehra, K.K., Chilimbi, T.M.: Speed: precise and efficient static estimation of program computational complexity. In: POPL, pp. 127–139. ACM, New York (2009)
26. Gulwani, S., Tiwari, A.: An abstract domain for analyzing heap-manipulating low-level software. In: Damm, W., Hermanns, H. (eds.) CAV 2007. LNCS, vol. 4590, pp. 379–392. Springer, Heidelberg (2007)
27. Hammond, K., Michaelson, G.J.: Hume: A domain-specific language for real-time embedded systems. In: Pfenning, F., Smaragdakis, Y. (eds.) GPCE 2003. LNCS, vol. 2830, pp. 37–56. Springer, Heidelberg (2003)
28. Hermenegildo, M., Puebla, G., Bueno, F., López-García, P.: Integrated Program Debugging, Verification, and Optimization Using Abstract Interpretation (and The Ciao System Preprocessor). Science of Computer Programming 58(1-2), 115–140 (2005)
29. Hickey, T., Cohen, J.: Automating program analysis. J. ACM 35(1) (1988)
30. Hofmann, M., Jost, S.: Static prediction of heap space usage for first-order functional programs. In: POPL (2003)
31. Hughes, J., Pareto, L., Sabry, A.: Proving the correctness of reactive systems using sized types. In: POPL, pp. 410–423 (1996)
32. Jones, N.D., Gomard, C.K., Sestoft, P.: Partial Evaluation and Automatic Program Generation. Prentice Hall, New York (1993)
33. Jouannaud, J., Xu, W.: Automatic Complexity Analysis for Programs Extracted from Coq Proof. ENTCS (2006)
34. Kristiansen, L., Jones, N.D.: The flow of data and the complexity of algorithms. In: Cooper, S.B., Löwe, B., Torenvliet, L. (eds.) CiE 2005. LNCS, vol. 3526, pp. 263–274. Springer, Heidelberg (2005)
35. Le Metayer, D.: ACE: An Automatic Complexity Evaluator. ACM Transactions on Programming Languages and Systems 10(2), 248–266 (1988)
36. Lehner, H., Müller, P.: Formal translation of bytecode into BoogiePL. In: Bytecode 2007. ENTCS, pp. 35–50. Elsevier, Amsterdam (2007)

37. Lindholm, T., Yellin, F.: The Java Virtual Machine Specification. Addison-Wesley, Reading (1996)
38. Luca, B., Andrei, S., Anderson, H., Khoo, S.-C.: Program transformation by solving recurrences. In: PEPM 2006: Proceedings of the 2006 ACM SIGPLAN symposium on Partial evaluation and semantics-based program manipulation, pp. 121–129. ACM, New York (2006)
39. Marion, J.-Y., Pèchoux, R.: Resource control of object-oriented programs. In: International LICS affiliated Workshop on Logic and Computational Complexity (LCC 2007), Wroclaw, Poland (2007)
40. Navas, J., Mera, E., López-García, P., Hermenegildo, M.V.: User-definable resource bounds analysis for logic programs. In: Dahl, V., Niemelä, I. (eds.) ICLP 2007. LNCS, vol. 4670, pp. 348–363. Springer, Heidelberg (2007)
41. Necula, G.: Proof-Carrying Code. In: Proc. of ACM Symposium on Principles of programming languages (POPL), pp. 106–119. ACM Press, New York (1997)
42. Nielson, F., Nielson, H.R., Hankin, C.: Principles of Program Analysis, 2nd edn. Springer, Heidelberg (2005)
43. Niggl, K.-H., Wunderlich, H.: Certifying Polynomial Time and Linear/Polynomial Space for Imperative Programs. SIAM J. Comput. 35(5), 1122–1147 (2006)
44. Rosendahl, M.: Automatic Complexity Analysis. In: Proc. ACM Conference on Functional Programming Languages and Computer Architecture, pp. 144–156. ACM, New York (1989)
45. Rosendahl, M.: Simple Driving Techniques. In: Mogensen, T.Æ., Schmidt, D.A., Sudborough, I.H. (eds.) The Essence of Computation. LNCS, vol. 2566, pp. 404–419. Springer, Heidelberg (2002)
46. Rossignoli, S., Spoto, F.: Detecting non-cyclicity by abstract compilation into boolean functions. In: Emerson, E.A., Namjoshi, K.S. (eds.) VMCAI 2006. LNCS, vol. 3855, pp. 95–110. Springer, Heidelberg (2005)
47. Sands, D.: A naïve time analysis and its theory of cost equivalence. J. Log. Comput. 5(4) (1995)
48. Secci, S., Spoto, F.: Pair-sharing analysis of object-oriented programs. In: Hankin, C., Siveroni, I. (eds.) SAS 2005. LNCS, vol. 3672, pp. 320–335. Springer, Heidelberg (2005)
49. Simões, H.R., Hammond, K., Florido, M., Vasconcelos, P.B.: Using intersection types for cost-analysis of higher-order polymorphic functional programs. In: Altenkirch, T., McBride, C. (eds.) TYPES 2006. LNCS, vol. 4502, pp. 221–236. Springer, Heidelberg (2007)
50. Spoto, F.: JULIA: A Generic Static Analyser for the Java Bytecode. In: Proc. of the 7th Workshop on Formal Techniques for Java-like Programs, FTfJP 2005, Glasgow, Scotland (July 2005)
51. Spoto, F., Jensen, T.: Class analyses as abstract interpretations of trace semantics. ACM Trans. Program. Lang. Syst. 25(5), 578–630 (2003)
52. Spoto, F., Hill, P.M., Payet, E.: Path-length analysis of object-oriented programs. In: Proc. International Workshop on Emerging Applications of Abstract Interpretation (EAAI). Electronic Notes in Theoretical Computer Science. Elsevier, Amsterdam (2006)
53. Turchin, V.F.: The concept of a supercompiler. ACM Transactions on Programming Languages and Systems 8(3), 292–325 (1986)

54. Vallee-Rai, R., Hendren, L., Sundaresan, V., Lam, P., Gagnon, E., Co, P.: Soot - a Java optimization framework. In: Proc. of Conference of the Centre for Advanced Studies on Collaborative Research (CASCON), pp. 125–135 (1999)
55. Vasconcelos, P.B., Hammond, K.: Inferring cost equations for recursive, polymorphic and higher-order functional programs. In: Trinder, P., Michaelson, G.J., Peña, R. (eds.) IFL 2003. LNCS, vol. 3145, pp. 86–101. Springer, Heidelberg (2004)
56. Wadler, P.: Strictness analysis aids time analysis. In: Proc. ACM Symposium on Principles of Programming Languages (POPL), pp. 119–132. ACM Press, New York (1988)
57. Wegbreit, B.: Mechanical Program Analysis. Comm. of the ACM 18(9) (1975)

Analysis of Security Threats, Requirements, Technologies and Standards in Wireless Sensor Networks

Javier Lopez, Rodrigo Roman, and Cristina Alcaraz

Computer Science Department
University of Malaga, Spain
{jlm,roman,alcaraz}@lcc.uma.es

Abstract. As sensor networks are more and more being implemented in real world settings, it is necessary to analyze how the different requirements of these real-world applications can influence the security mechanisms. This paper offers both an overview and an analysis of the relationship between the different security threats, requirements, applications, and security technologies. Besides, it also overviews some of the existing sensor network standards, analyzing their security mechanisms.

1 Introduction

Wireless sensor networks, or WSN, have evolved in the past years from a promising research field to a useful technology applicable to real-world scenarios (e.g. industrial monitoring in critical infrastructures [1]). Research on security for sensor networks have advanced as well, showing promising results such as efficient implementations of public key cryptography algorithms and lightweight self-healing mechanisms. Still there is one particular aspect of sensor network security that is commonly neglected or overlooked: the relationship between the security requirements, the features of the application and its context, and the security mechanisms. Indeed, the context and the requirements of a specific application have a great influence on the security mechanisms that should be used to protect the network. Besides, new standards for WSN are being developed, but there are some security aspects that seem to be overlooked as these standards focus mainly on securing the communications between nodes.

The purpose of this paper is twofold. Our first objective is to provide an analysis of the relationship between requirements, applications, and security mechanisms. Therefore, we will review the different security attacks that target WSN, and will explain the different security requirements that a sensor network application should fulfil in order to protect itself from those attacks. Afterwards, we will indicate explicitly how the different technologies, applications and network structures influence over the selection and provisioning of the security services. Finally, we will overview the state of the art of the security mechanisms for sensor networks, pointing out already available solutions and open issues. As for our second objective, we aim to describe the existing sensor network standards

A. Aldini, G. Barthe, R. Gorrieri (Eds.): FOSAD 2007/2008/2009, LNCS 5705, pp. 289–338, 2009.

and their security mechanisms. Consequently, we will provide an overview of these different standards, focusing on their security capabilities. Later, we will analyze not only how these standards compare with each other, but also if they offer support for implementing the previously mentioned security mechanisms.

2 Overview of Wireless Sensor Networks

The ability to perceive the physical world is not inherent to the nature of computer systems: they are tightly tied to the realm of the abstract. The existence of sensor hardware tries to build a bridge between the abstract world and the physical world. These sensors are devices that can measure a physical quantity (e.g. temperature, humidity) and convert it into a digital signal. Using these sensors, computer systems ranging from the simplest washing machine to the Large Hadron Collider (a particle accelerator located at the European Organization for Nuclear Research (CERN) [2]) can acquire and process information coming from the physical world. This ability to "feel" the world is usually embedded in the design of a computer system, e.g. sensors in a washing machine are integrated within the system from the initial design. However, it would be particularly interesting to make this ability available as an off-the-shelf component. As a result, any computer system, regardless of its design, could be able to perceive the physical world. Such is the task of Wireless Sensor Networks, or WSN.

The structure of a wireless sensor network can be seen in Figure 1. A wireless sensor network is composed by two types of devices: sensor nodes, and base stations. The sensor nodes, also known as motes or simply nodes, are small and constrained devices that have the ability to "feel", "think", "talk", and "subsist". They can "feel", because they can sense the physical features of their surrounding (e.g. temperature, humidity, radiation, vibration) using hardware sensors. They can "think", because although they are highly constrained in both computational power and memory, they are capable of processing information on their own. They can "talk", because they are equipped with wireless transceivers, and can collaborate towards a common goal. Finally, they can "subsist" because

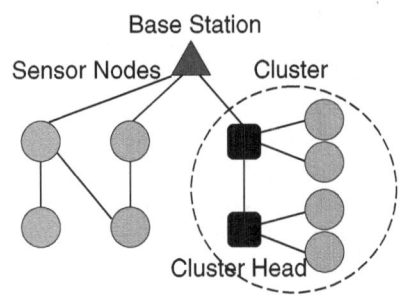

Fig. 1. An overview of the architecture of WSN

they are in most cases powered by batteries, and can survive in their deployment field for more than a year if their internal operations are optimized.

Regarding the base station, it is a more powerful device that usually behaves as an interface between the services provided by the sensor nodes (the "data acquisition network") and the users of the network (the "data dissemination network"). Normally, the base station collects all the information coming from the sensor nodes and stores it for later use. Also, it can issue control orders to the sensor nodes in order to change their behaviour. While it would seem that wireless sensor networks are highly dependent of the existence of this base station, the architecture of the network is not centralized. Sensor nodes can operate in a decentralized fashion, managing themselves without accessing to the base station.

A powerful simile that can be used to illustrate the structure of wireless sensor networks is to consider them as "living beings". The sensor nodes behaves as "cells", since they all belong to the same body (WSN), are usually loaded with the same "DNA" (program), and cooperate unselfishly towards a common goal. On the other hand, the base station could be considered as the "brain", since it receives and processes all the physical information coming from the "cells", and can also send control information to them. Note that, in terms of communications, the "cells" also behave as "nerves", since they transmit (wirelessly) the information sensed by other "cells" to the "brain".

The services offered by wireless sensor networks can be classified into four major categories: monitoring, alerting, provisioning of information "on-demand", and actuating. As for the first case, sensor nodes can continuously monitor certain features of their surroundings (e.g. measuring the ambient noise level) and timely send such information to the base station. Secondly, sensor nodes can check whether certain physical circumstances (e.g. a fire) are occurring, alerting the users of the system when an alarm is triggered. In the third case, the network can be queried about the actual levels of a certain feature, providing information "on-demand". Finally, sensor nodes can be able to change the behaviour of an external system (e.g. an irrigation system) according to the actual state of the context (e.g. humidity of the soil)[1]. Due to the computational capabilities of the sensor nodes, it is possible to reprogram the network during its lifetime, or even use it as a distributed computing platform under specific circumstances.

Finally, wireless sensor networks can be organized in a completely distributed way (flat configuration), but they can also implement levels of hierarchy (hierarchical configurations). In flat configurations, all the nodes contribute in the decision-making process and participate in the internal protocols, like routing. Conversely, in hierarchical configurations the network is divided into clusters or group of nodes. Inside a cluster all organizational decisions, like data aggregation, are made by a single entity called cluster head. It should be noticed that it is also possible to have a combination of the two previous configurations into the same network; for instance, to avoid situations where the "spinal cord" of the network - the cluster heads - fail and the information must be routed to the base station.

---

[1] These type of sensor networks are also known as Wireless Sensor and Actuator Networks (WSAN).

Aside from their structure, services, and organization, there are some features that help to define what a wireless sensor networks is: specificity, autonomy, self-configurability, long lifetime, deployment location, and mobility. The embedded intelligence of sensor nodes allow them to perform various tasks, but their services, protocols and architectures are highly dependent on the functionality of the network, due to their inherent constraints. Also, unlike other more capable devices such as PDAs, there is no human user directly controlling the sensor node: motes are usually accessed through other motes or through the base station. In fact, sensor nodes can set up their services and function properly in situations where there is no central control available. Due to this autonomy, sensor nodes need to self-configure and maintain themselves during the lifetime of the network. Precisely, a wireless sensor network can function for long periods of time, ranging from several days to one or two years. Regarding the network deployment, sensor nodes are usually deployed near the physical source of the events, and the exact deployment location of these sensor nodes is usually not known in advance. Finally, sensor nodes are usually not mobile, although there might be scenarios where some sensor nodes or even the base station need to move (e.g. tracking a target).

3   Security Aspects of Wireless Sensor Networks

In any environment, either physical or logical, there exists the need of maintaining someone or something safe, away from harm. This is the role of security. On any computer-related environment, security can be considered as a non-functional requirement that maintains the overall system usable and reliable, protecting the information and information systems. In fact, in wireless sensor networks, security is of paramount importance: the network must be adequately protected against malicious threats that can affect its functionality. Due to the role of sensor networks as a "sensory system", any disturbance in a sensor network may have consequences in the real world. However, sensor networks are especially vulnerable against external and internal attacks due to their peculiar characteristics.

- The devices of the network (i.e. sensor nodes) are constrained in terms of computational capabilities, memory, communication bandwidth, and battery power. As a result, it is challenging to implement and use the cryptographic algorithms and protocols required for the creation of security services.
- In most cases, it is easy to physically access sensor nodes: they must be located near the physical source of the events. Since nodes are not tamper-resistant due to cost constraints, any human user or machine can reprogram them or simply destroy them.
- Any internal or external device can access to the information exchange because the communication channel is public. Besides, attacking the availability of the wireless channel is not a complex task.

– It is a difficult task to monitor and control the actual state of the elements of the network due to the inherent distributed nature of sensor networks. Any failure in any of its elements may remain unnoticed, or the actual cause of the malfunction may not be known. Besides, a sensor network can be attacked at any point.

3.1   Security Threats

Due to their previously shown inherent vulnerabilities, sensor networks have to face multiple passive and active attacks that may easily hinder its functionality and nullify the benefits of using its services. Passive attacks are able to retrieve data from the network, but do not influence over its behaviour. On the other hand, active attacks directly hinder the provisioning of services. The different threats that target sensor networks will be detailed in the following paragraphs, and they can be categorized as follows:

– *Common Attacks.* As the wireless medium is used as the main transmission channel in WSN, it is easily subject to various types of attacks, either passive (eavesdropping) or active (data injection).
– *Denial of Service Attacks* (DoS). These attacks prevent any part of WSN from functioning correctly or in a timely manner. Such attacks can target the communication channel (e.g. jamming) or the life of the nodes themselves (e.g. power exhaustion).
– *Node Compromise.* An embedded device is considered being compromised when an attacker, through various means, gains control or access to the node itself after it is being deployed. These attacks are usually utilized as a foundation for more powerful, damaging attacks.
– *Side-channel Attacks.* An adversary can monitor certain physical properties of the nodes, such as electromagnetic emanation, whenever it performs a cryptographic operation. If the recorded physical values are influenced by the secret key, then the adversary can extract information about that key.
– *Impersonation Attacks.* A malicious sensor node can create multiple fake identities (sybil attack), and also can create duplicates with the same identity (replication attack). These types of attacks are also the initial step which enables the attacker to conduct a wide range of malicious attacks.
– *Protocol-specific Attacks.* Some essential protocols used in WSN, such as routing, aggregation, and time synchronization, are targeted by specific attacks that aim to influence the internal services of the network.

By using the so-called *common attacks class*, a malicious adversary uses a device that does not belong to the sensor network in order to access to the contents of the communication channel. The simplest instance of common attack is eavesdropping. It can be defined as the interception of information or data by an unintended party. Due to the broadcast nature of the communication channel, any adversary (using a mote or a more powerful device such as a PDA) can sniff out packets at a particular frequency, obtaining confidential information about the state of the network and the physical parameters sensed by the nodes. As the eavesdropping attack has an inherent passive nature, it does not directly influence over the behaviour of the network.

However, the acquired information from passive attacks can be used to perform active attacks. The effects of active attacks are far more destructive: adversaries can create fake events or hide problematic situations, and can even introduce bogus control information. One of these active attacks is message modification, where an adversary intercepts and modifies the packets' content meant for the base station or intermediate nodes. Another active attack is message replay. In this attack, the adversary reuses valid transaction messages or packets' content with malicious intent. The adversary performs a replay attack by first intercepting a valid critical transaction data packet and then re-transmitting at a later time. Lastly, attackers can use message injection to fabricate and send out false data into the network, maybe masquerading as one of the nodes.

One special class of active attack, known as *Denial of Service (DoS)*, deserves a category of its own. In this kind of attack, the objective of the malicious adversary is simple: to avoid the provisioning of services. As these services are published by the sensor nodes through a wireless channel, the most basic DoS attacks can target the nodes themselves (power exhaustion attack) or the communication channel (jamming attack). In the power exhaustion attack, an attacker imposes a particularly complex task to a sensor node in order to deplete its battery life. Sensor nodes usually have a limited supply of energy, thus this attack is particularly dangerous. Besides, as sensor nodes have limited computational power, this attack can also slow down their reaction time. An example of an expensive operation is the verification of a cryptographic signature using public key cryptography. An attacker can take advantage of the complexity of this operation by repeatedly sending fake signatures to force the receiver to check their correctness. Power exhaustion attacks are not limited to only CPU attacks: an attacker can target the MAC protocol of the WSN, effectively preventing nodes from entering their duty/sleep cycle an wasting their batteries [4].

Jamming is the primary physical layer DoS attack against WSN. In a jamming attack, the attacker constantly emits radio frequency signals that do not follow an underlying MAC protocol, thus any member of the network in the affected area will not be able to send or receive any packet. The energy requirements of this attack are very high, as the attacker must flood the communication channel with noise. There are some optimizations to the basic jamming attack, such as the random jamming, where the attacker alternates between sleep and jamming to save energy, or the reactive jamming, where the jam signal is transmitted only when the attacker senses traffic [3]. Finally, another clever optimization that reduces the energy consumption of the attacker is to target MAC protocols on the link layer [4][5], e.g. by jamming only request-to-send (RTS) packets. As a side note, it should be mentioned that DoS attacks can be performed by using some of the attacks explained in other categories [6], although those attacks are usually more complex and can be used to disrupt other functional elements of the network (e.g. the authenticity of the physical/control data).

Most of the previously shown attacks can be performed by outsiders: attackers that do not have access to the network elements and services. However, if an attacker have access to the network as one of its elements, i.e. as an insider, it is possible to perform attacks that are more subtle and devastating. The first step to become an insider is to compromise a node, usually by performing *node compromise attacks*. A sensor node can be considered compromised when an attacker, through various means, can either read or modify its internal memory. The ultimate goal of this attack is, in most cases, to obtain the secret keys stored within a trusted node in order to infiltrate a mole inside the network. Attacks that can lead to a node compromise are invasive or non-invasive. In an invasive attack, the attacker physically breaks into the hardware by modifying its hardware structure (e.g. using focused ion beam, or drilling a hole in the storage media). On the other hand, in non-invasive attacks the data is taken from the hardware device without any form of structural modification done to the device itself. Invasive attacks usually fall under the category of side channel attacks, as these attacks obtain confidential data directly from the chips of the nodes.

Regarding non-invasive attacks, they usually take advantage of the hardware interfaces of the nodes. One example is the JTAG interface [8]. This interface enables accessing and controlling of the signal levels on the processor chip, and is also used for debugging purposes. Through the use of an AVR ICE JTAG programming tool, an attacker can dump all the information from the program flash, the EEPROM and also the SRAM. As a result, the attacker can replicate the functionality of the node to facilitate the integration of the malicious node. While most of these non-invasive attacks simply aim to obtain information from the node, there exist more advanced attacks that are capable of injecting code inside a working sensor node. For example, it is possible to exploit the serial bootstrap loader (BSL) of certain models of the Texas Instruments MSP430 low-power microcontrollers with the aim of extracting or replacing the firmware [9]. Even more, it is possible to inject malicious code remotely in AVR-based nodes by exploiting buffer overflow vulnerabilities [10].

In order to compromise a node, it is also possible to attack its hardware through *side-channel attacks*. The main objective of side channel attacks is to obtain confidential data stored within the node. Most attackers focus on obtaining security credentials such as secret keys, since these credentials will provide the attacker with a powerful tool capable of crafting more powerful attacks. Side channel attacks can be classified in the following categories: passive vs. active and non-invasive vs. semi-invasive vs. invasive. Passive attacks extract information from the device merely by observing physical properties of the devices, while active attacks involve the manipulation (tampering) of the device itself. In contrast, non-invasive attacks do not manipulate the device substantially, while semi-invasive attacks depackage the device but do not make direct electrical contact with the chip's surface, and invasive attacks have practically no limits to the measures which can be taken to extract the information of the device (e.g. probing station, focused ion beam). Note that not all semi-invasive or invasive attacks are active attacks: passive semi-invasive attacks may try to just read sensitive data from memory components, and passive invasive attacks can use a probe station to sense valuable data signals.

Specific examples of side-channel attacks are power analysis attacks, electromagnetic attacks, and timing attacks [7]. In power analysis attacks, the adversary studies the power consumption of the devices, focusing mainly on the energy used by cryptographic operations. For performing these attacks, it is possible to either use single power traces to look for distinguishing features (Simple power analysis, SPA) or use larger numbers of power traces alongside with powerful statistical methods (Differential power analysis, DPA). Electromagnetic attacks (or EM attacks) are similar to power analysis attacks, since they also analyze power traces with simple (SEMA) and differential (DEMA) methods. However, they derive the power traces from electromagnetic emanations, collected by EM probes. Beyond simple and differential analysis, EM attacks can employ more advanced techniques, such as adding spatial information to the measurement data, or analysing the frequency domain rather than the time domain. Finally, as the execution time of cryptographic algorithms often shows slight differences dependent on the input of the algorithm, timing attacks exploits the variance in execution time for different branches in the cryptosystem.

Once an attacker becomes an insider, it is easier to perform *impersonation attacks*. For this particular class of attack, the goal of the adversary is to make the victim believe that it is communicating with an impersonated entity. As a result, a malicious node will interact with other nodes as one trusted member, but at the same time it can manipulate the internal behaviour of the network whenever the adversary needs it. Impersonation attacks can either replicate and insert duplicate nodes back into selected regions of the network (node replication attack or clone attack) or use multiple identities to deceive other sensor nodes (sybil attack). In node replication attacks, the attacker only needs to subvert one node in order to create an army of clones following his orders. These clones can not only manipulate the internal operations of the network, but also exert a strong influence over those processes that require of a majority vote. As for sybil attacks, a sybil node can either fabricate new identities or steal them from legitimate nodes [11]. Sybil nodes can be able to execute powerful attacks, disrupting several of the functions that may be conducted on a WSN including data aggregation, voting, routing and fair resource allocation.

Beyond impersonation, an insider can perform *protocol-specific attacks*, attacking those "core" protocols needed by the network such as routing protocols, aggregation protocols, and time synchronization protocols. Attacks against routing protocols in a WSN fall into one of the following categories [12]: corruption of the internal control information such as the routing tables (Spoofed Routing Information), selective forwarding of the packets that traverse a malicious node depending on some criteria (Selective Forwarding), creation of a 'wormhole' that captures the information at one location and replays them in another location either unchanged (Wormhole attack) or tampered (Sinkhole attack), creation of false control packets during the deployment of the network (HELLO

Flood Attack), and creation of false acknowledge information (Acknowledgment Spoofing).

Data aggregation protocols combine information coming from the same area in order to reduce the overall communication overhead. As these protocols need to use routing protocols in order to fuse information and forward it to the base station, every attack that target the routing infrastructure can also be used to hinder the aggregation process. Most of these attacks try to discard data, either selectively or indiscriminately. Though losing data is a problematic situation for the network, this is not the primary type of attack against aggregation: most attacks focus on falsifying information. If an aggregator node is being controlled by an adversary, it can easily ignore the data received from its neighbours and create false reports. Moreover, trusted aggregators can still receive false data from faulty nodes or from nodes being controlled by an adversary.

Regarding time synchronization, it is needed because as the time obtained from clocks of different nodes may differ due to different starting times (offset), inaccurate quartz crystals (skew), or ambient influence (drift), it is necessary to synchronize these clocks in order to maintain a global notion of time [13]. Most time synchronization protocols rely on two neighbouring nodes adjusting their local clocks by means of sender-receiver (mutual synchronization) and receiver-receiver (beacon signals) protocols. In these scenarios, the main objective of an attacker is to deceive other nodes into thinking that an incorrect time is accurate. Besides internal attacks, where the attacker can outrightly lie about the value of its internal clock, an attacker can use the following external attacks: manipulation of the contents of the negotiation messages through message forging and replay, and delaying the messages exchanged in the negotiation process by means of a pulse-delay attack.

3.2   Security Requirements

As we have previously seen, sensor networks are vulnerable to external and internal attacks. The effects of those attacks in the network are not trivial, since they can render the services of the network useless. It is clear that there is the need of using security mechanisms either to prevent the attacks from influencing over the functionality of the network or to minimize the adverse effects of such attacks. By using the security mechanisms, it can be possible to enforce in sensor networks the following security properties:

– *Confidentiality*. This property tries to fulfil the following principle: A given message must not be understood by anyone other than the desired recipients. While confidentiality is an important security property, it may be not mandatory in certain scenarios where the data is public by itself (i.e. the temperature of a street) and no other information can be derived from it. However, there are particular situations and scenarios where the physical data obtained by the network can be deemed as sensitive, and should not be read by external entities. Data can be considered sensitive due to its inherent nature (e.g. patient data such as temperature), the nature of the context (e.g. a private household, a military setting), or the nature of the sensed entities (e.g. a protected animal like a panda). Besides, certain control data exchanged by the nodes, such as security credentials and secret keys, must be hidden from unauthorized entities.

– *Integrity*. This property states that the data produced and consumed by the sensor network must not be maliciously altered. Unlike confidentiality, integrity is, in most cases, a mandatory property. The wireless channel can be accessed by anyone, thus any peer (outsiders and insiders) can manipulate the contents of the messages that traverse the network. Even more, data loss or damage may occur due to the harsh communication environment, and in the worst case the network will accept corrupted data. As the main objective of a sensor network is to provide services to its users, the sensor network will fail in its purpose if the reliability of those services can not assured due to inconsistencies in the information.

– *Authentication*. Informally, data authentication allows a receiver to verify that the data is really sent by the claimed sender. This security property is quite important in sensor networks. In fact, without authentication the barrier between external and internal members of the network would not exist, as any outsider could claim that it is a registered member of the network. Moreover, even existing network members could easily pose as their neighbours. This situation would encourage many problematic situations, such as adversaries forging the whole packet stream by injecting additional packets, and nodes accepting false administrative tasks (e.g. network reprogramming).

– *Authorization*. As for this property, it states that only authorized entities (sensor nodes and base station) can be able to perform certain operations in the network (e.g. information providing, controlling the system). Since a sensor network can be considered as one single entity, where all nodes perform the same tasks and acknowledge the role of the base station as manager and supervisor, it could be supposed that any authenticated device is inherently authorized to perform its tasks. Nevertheless, there might be situations (e.g. when nodes actuate over physical systems) where some members of the network need to have a proper authorization in order to perform certain tasks. Is in these situations where authorization must be taken into account.

– *Availability*. The users of a sensor network must be capable of accessing its services whenever they need them. As a result, the different hardware and software elements of the network must be robust enough to be able to provide services even in the presence of malicious entities or adverse situations. Nevertheless, this property is related not only to the protection of the services, but also to the security mechanisms themselves: all protection mechanisms should be as energy efficient as possible in order not to quickly drain the batteries of the nodes.

– *Freshness*. Sensor networks are very data-centric: they exist due to the physical data they have to collect from an environment. One important property that arises from this fact is freshness: the data produced by the sensor network must be recent. Consequently, the messages of the network should aim to reduce the network delay to the smallest possible value, even in unfavourable situations where the network is under attack. While in some networks is admissible to have a certain delay, in certain scenarios the information must be received as soon as possible (e.g. alerts in nuclear power plants). Freshness is not only linked to delay but also linked to forgery: if an adversary success on replaying an old message inside the network, the data not only will be useless, but also harmful (e.g. it may inform of a non-existent alarm).

— *Forward and Backward Secrecy.* As new sensor nodes can be deployed whenever other sensor nodes fails, there are two properties that need to be considered: forward secrecy, where a sensor should not be able to read any future messages after it leaves the network, and backward secrecy, where a joining sensor should not be able to read any previously transmitted message. These properties may not be important in certain scenarios, where there is no need to hide the contents of the network from old nodes and new nodes authorized to perform the same tasks as their partners. However there are other scenarios where these properties must be taken into account, such as in networks with nodes that must be authorized to perform certain tasks.

— *Self-Organization.* One specific property related to the autonomous nature of sensor networks is self-organization: sensor nodes must be independent and flexible enough to autonomously react against problematic situations, organizing and healing themselves. These problematic situations can be caused either by external or internal attackers trying to influence over the behaviour of the elements of the system or by extraordinary circumstances in the environment or in the network itself. This is an essential property to the functioning of a sensor network and optimal resource use during its lifetime. It is desirable that all possible problems that may occur can be detected and prevented without any margin of error. However, as the previous statement may not be realistic, nodes should be able to at least adapt their activities to assure the continuity of the services.

— *Auditing.* The elements of a sensor network must be able to store any significant events that occur inside the network. This property is necessary due to the autonomous nature of the nodes. As users do not operate the sensor nodes directly, but through the base station, they may not be able to know about the existence of a certain event unless the nodes store it. Besides, if the whole sensor network fails, auditing information can be used to analyze the behaviour of the system prior to the failure. This property is also closely related to self-organization: in order to adjust their behaviour, sensor nodes must be able to know the state of their surroundings. Note that the inherent memory constraints of sensor nodes complicate the task of storing audit data.

— *Non-repudiation.* While non-repudiation is not considered in the existing literature as an important security property for most sensor networks, it may be necessary to at least consider its applicability in certain contexts where sensor nodes monitor critical components, as acknowledging the reception and processing of serious alarms is of key importance. This property is

described as follows: a node cannot deny sending a message it has previously
sent. Note that non-repudiation can also consider repudiation of receipt,
where the recipient tries to deny the reception of the message. For achieving
non-repudiation, it is necessary to produce certain 'evidence' in case a dispute arises. Using the evidence, it is possible to prove that a device of the
network performed a task.

- *Privacy and Anonymity.* These security properties are very important in
those scenarios where the location and identities of the base station and
the nodes that generated information should be hidden or protected. For
example, any network that monitors endangered species should provide no
clues on their physical location. Also, in a battlefield, it would be important
to not be able to distinguish whether a certain signals belongs to a soldier
or a vehicle. In contrast, there are situations where this property should not
be enforced: in an earthquake rescue situation locating the source nodes (if
the nodes are worn by, for example, dogs) is an absolute must. Note that
this property can transcend beyond the technological dimension and affect
its social environment, since sensor networks could be used as a surveillance
tool to collect data about the behaviour of human beings.

4   The Influence of Technologies and Applications in Security

Although it would seem that every security property needs to be completely
enforced in order to have an entirely secure sensor network, it is usually not the
case [15][16][17]. The role of security is to protect the network against the existing
threats that may affect it, and not all sensor networks are equally affected by
all threats. As a result, it is necessary to analyze how a specific sensor network
could be affected by possible attackers, and if its elements are suitable enough to
implement the security countermeasures that are needed. In this section we will
review the different technologies associated to sensor networks and the context
of the applications, and how these technologies and applications influence over
the selection of the security mechanisms.

4.1   Technologies: Hardware and Software

A sensor node is typically made up of four basic components: sensing unit,
transceiver, processor unit, and power unit, as seen in Figure 2. The sensing unit
consists of an array of sensors that can measure the physical characteristics of
its environment, like temperature, light, vibration, and others. The processing
unit is, in most cases, a microcontroller, which can be considered as a highly
constrained computer that contains the memory and interfaces required to create
simple applications. The transceiver is able to send and receive messages through
a wireless channel. Finally, the power unit provides the energy required by all
components, and such energy may come from either a battery or renewable
sources. Most nodes have additional components, such as LEDs and buttons,

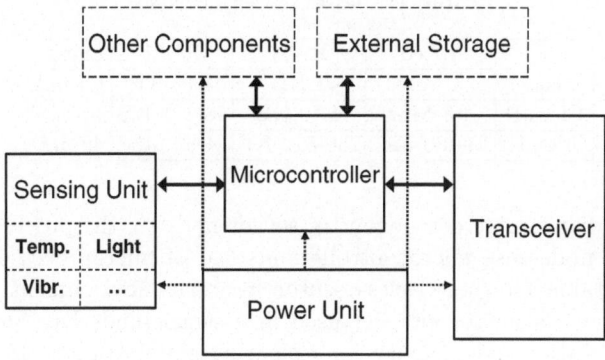

Fig. 2. HW Elements of a Sensor Node

which are used as user interfaces. There can be also other components depending on the needs of the application, like external data storage (e.g. flash memory), location devices (e.g. GPS chips), or cryptographic chips [18].

One of the most important components in a sensor node is the transceiver (i.e. transmitter-receiver). As one of the foundations of the sensor network paradigm is distributed collaboration through wireless communication, it is necessary for the sensor nodes to be able to "converse" with other nodes. Most sensor nodes have a limited energy supply, thus transceivers have to offer an adequate balance between a low data rate (e.g. between 19.2 Kbps and 250 Kbps) and a small energy consumption in low-voltage environments (i.e. around 3V), allowing the node to live for an extended period of time. For most environments, Radio frequency (RF) communication is ideal because it is not limited by line of sight and current technology allows implementation of low-power radio transceivers [18].

As for the evolution of transceivers used in sensor nodes, the first prototype platforms tended to use transceivers that conformed to proprietary standards or to no standards at all. Most of these early transceivers used narrowband communication, which typically operate at lower frequencies (433Mhz - 915Mhz) and provide low data rates (10 Kbps - 76.8 Kbps), but have less power consumption and faster wakeup times. After the appearance in 2003 of the IEEE 802.15.4 standard [78] for low-rate wireless personal area networks (PANs), most sensor nodes started to use transceivers that complied with this standard. This standard uses wideband communication (faster, more robust, more power-demanding), operating in the 2.4 Ghz frequency band with a maximum (theoretical) throughput of 250 Kbps. Other mote platforms chose to integrate transceivers that implemented the Bluetooth standard. While this standard is widely adopted in mobile phones and other electronic devices, its power consumption is significantly higher than the IEEE 802.15.4 standard. Notice that, in all cases, the energy consumption of the transceiver is far greater than the energy consumption of the microcontroller, thus sensor nodes are encouraged to do as much in-network processing as possible [14].

Table 1. Classes of Sensor Nodes

	Speed	RAM	ROM	Energy
Class I	4 Mhz	1 KB	4-16 KB	1.5 mA
Class II	4-8 Mhz	4-10 KB	48-128 KB	2-8 mA
Class III	13-180 Mhz	256-512 KB	4-32 MB	40 mA

Another indispensable component in sensor nodes is the processor unit. Actually, sensor nodes use microcontrollers instead of microprocessors. They are especially suitable for the wireless sensor networks environment due to their cost-effectiveness: a microcontroller used in a sensor node has enough computational capabilities and memory for executing simple tasks while consuming as less energy as possible. The selection of a microcontroller depends on what services has to provide to the node in terms of energy consumption, instruction memory and RAM memory, storage, speed, and external IO ports. It is possible to classify the microcontrollers used in sensor nodes intro three types, as seen in table 1. The most constrained class of sensor nodes (class I) is very limited and its elements barely support the "de-facto" standard operating system for sensor nodes, TinyOS [19], while the most powerful sensor nodes (class III) have PDA-like capabilities and can host complex operating systems or Java-based virtual machines. Finally, there are devices that are resource-constrained but powerful enough to hold complex applications (class II). This is the most common type of device for sensor nodes, and there are many microcontrollers that fall into this category.

As of 2009, one open question that remains is how these constrained microcontrollers will evolve. Since 2004, the technical specifications of class II nodes range from 4 KB of RAM and 48 KB of instruction memory to 16 KB of RAM and 128 KB of instruction memory. It has been hinted (cf. [20]) that future versions of these nodes will achieve around 16 KB of RAM and 256 KB of instruction memory. It should be noted that the CPU speed and the amount of memory available to the node are not the only factors that must be taken into account when selecting a microcontroller: other factors include a low active current, a wide operating voltage range, a 16-bit sleep timer, fast wakeup from sleep, and the existence of direct memory access (DMA) channels that can operate while the CPU sleeps [20]. Class III nodes are not linked to these requirements: they already provide the computer horsepower required by more complex applications at the expense of higher energy consumption, reduced lifetime, and higher costs.

One of the components of sensor nodes that deserve an analysis of its own is the power unit. This subsystem supplies power to the node, allowing it to survive for weeks, months or even years without any maintenance. Most class II sensor nodes are powered by AA batteries, while class III sensor nodes are usually powered by high energy density batteries (e.g. based on lithium-ion chemistry). As nodes will stop functioning once the battery voltage drops below the recommended operation voltage range of the node and its components, the protocols and services of a sensor network have to take energy consumption into consideration.

It is also possible to harvest energy from the environment to power the electronic circuits of a node. The main sources of ambient energy considered suitable for use with WSNs are solar (generated by sunlight or artificial light), mechanical (generated by the movements of objects) and thermal energy (generated by temperature differences between two objects) [21]. Although there are many challenges in the design of energy harvesters for sensor nodes, such as reducing the size of the harvesters while storing the energy in an efficient way, the state of the art is advanced enough to offer off-the-shelf components that can provide some power to the nodes [22]. Besides, there are also commercial nodes like eKo [23] that use renewable energy (i.e. solar energy). Note that in most cases ambient energy is used only to recharge the batteries of a node, but there are also some research lines that pursue the implementation of long-lived sensor networks that rely only on harvested energy in order to operate [21].

Security Analysis. The different hardware components used in a sensor node have a great influence on both the nature and the capabilities of the different security primitives and security protocols that can be used in a sensor network. For transceivers, the main influence factors are bandwidth, energy consumption, and channel error rate. The speed of the wireless channel will influence on the completion time of the security protocols, and also will determine the overhead produced by any security mechanism that protects the confidentiality, integrity, and authentication of messages. As for the energy consumption, if the transceiver spends too much energy on sending and receiving messages, it is necessary to reduce both the message size and the number of steps of the security protocols. Moreover, the reliability of the wireless channel will affect the design of the security protocols, as they must be robust against failures in the communication.

A specific example of the influence of the transceiver in the security protocols can be found in underwater environments [24]. Here, it is unpractical to use radio frequency transceivers, because of the severe attenuation factor presented by water. It is then necessary to use specific underwater acoustic modems, which have different features than RF transceivers: they are highly unreliable, their bandwidth is very limited, and sending or receiving one bit of information carries a high energy penalty. A table comparing radio transceivers and acoustic modems can be found at table 2. Due to these differences, certain CPU-intensive identity-based key establishment protocols such as Sakai, Ohgishi and Kasahara (SOK) are more optimal than other public key-based protocols like Elliptic Curve

Table 2. Analysis of the energy consumption of acoustic modems

	MICA2	MICAz	UWM2000	UWM4000
Working range	150 m	100 m	1500 m	4000 m
Throughput	19.2 Kbit/s	250 Kbit/s	9600 bit/s	4800 bit/s
Tx. consumption	81mW	52.2mW	4000 mW	7000 mW
Rx. consumption	30mW	59.1mW	800 mW	800 mW
μJ per bit (Tx)	4.12 μJ	0.204 μJ	416.66 μJ	1458.33 μJ
μJ per bit (Rx)	16.8 μJ	16.8 μJ	83.33 μJ	166.66 μJ

Menezes-Qu-Vanstone (ECMQV). The reason is simple: in this underwater environment, where the energy consumption and the channel error rate of the channel are very high, the number of messages exchanged in a security protocol should be reduced to a minimum. Identity-based protocols need to exchange only one message: the ID of the node is used as its public key.

The processor unit (its memory and CPU power) also has an influence over the security mechanisms and protocols. The amount of memory available to the node dictates how many mechanisms, both security-related and application-related, can be included inside it. In sensor nodes with limited memory, it is necessary to achieve a balance between the different components. If the application is too complex, there will be little room for security mechanisms. Conversely, if the security mechanisms occupy too much space, it will be very difficult to implement the application logic. Besides, it should be necessary to optimize the use of the security primitives. For example, by using a symmetric cryptography algorithm like AES, it is possible to obtain message authentication codes through the CMAC mode of operation. On the other hand, nodes with more available memory can implement more security mechanisms if needed. Memory is also important for holding important security data such as credentials. Precisely, the low amount of memory available to the nodes is one of the reasons that have made the field of key management systems one of the most active fields of sensor networking research [25].

The CPU power of the microprocessor dictates how much time is needed to execute a security primitive. If the microcontroller is too slow, any security protocol that is based on complex security primitives won't be practical for specific situations. For example, in scenarios where sensor nodes are mobile, two nodes that meet for a short period of time will need to use a fast protocol to perform a handshake and exchange information. However, those nodes won't be able to communicate successfully if they use protocols based on CPU-intensive primitives such as identity-based encryption and signatures. Note that there are other lightweight primitives (such as stream ciphers [28]) that do not require of a fast microcontroller, or applications with low bandwidth requirements where the overhead imposed by the security primitives is negligible. On these cases, there is no need to have a class III microcontroller where a class II microcontroller can provide the necessary services.

As for the power unit, the energy contained within the battery dictates how many operations can be performed before the sensor node disappears from the network. As a result, the lifetime of the network will be increased if energy-consuming operations, such as certain security primitives and protocols, are scarcely used. However, it can be possible to use batteries with higher capacities. For example, D cells have a typical capacity of 12000mAh, while AA cells have a typical capacity of 2400mAh [2]. As a result, for typical class II sensor nodes, the lifetime of the network will increase by a factor of 5. In scenarios where the size of the sensor nodes is not a problem and applications can benefit from expensive security operations, it is possible to use high capacity batteries. Note that

---

[2] Note that D cell batteries are approximately 5 times bigger than AA batteries.

the opposite also holds: in certain scenarios it is mandatory to use batteries of lower capacity, mainly due to size requirements. Here, the execution of complex security primitives and protocols must be severely limited.

4.2 Applications

The evolution of sensor networks into a generic wireless "sensing layer" for computer systems has opened a wide range of application possibilities. These kind of networks can not be considered as the "panacea" for all the sensing needs of computer systems, since they are not especially suitable for very complex applications (such as the Large Hadron Collider [29]) or applications with hard Quality of Service (QoS) requirements. Nevertheless, there are many applications that can take advantage of the inherent characteristics of WSN (survivability, independence, reactivity, low cost, easy to maintain). According to Culler et. al. [30], those applications can be classified into the following categories:

- *Monitoring space.* The sensor network simply monitors the physical features of a certain environment. This category includes applications such as environmental and habitat monitoring, precision agriculture, indoor climate control, surveillance, treaty verification, and intelligent alarms.
- *Monitoring things.* The sensor network controls the status of a physical entity. This category includes applications such as structural monitoring, ecophysiology, condition-based equipment maintenance, medical diagnostics, and urban terrain mapping.
- *Monitoring interactions.* The sensor network monitors the interactions of things (both inanimate and animate) with each other and the encompassing space. This category includes applications such as wildlife habitats, disaster management, critical (information) infrastructure systems, emergency response, asset tracking, healthcare, and manufacturing process flow.

While all the application areas presented in the previous classification are mere ideas of where wireless sensor networks could be applied, the research community has already proven the usefulness of wireless sensor networks in real-world settings. Some examples of prototypes and research areas include: Monitoring of ageing infrastructures, critical (information) infrastructures, surveillance, detecting equipment vibration, control of vineyards, water quality analysis, control of glacier behaviour, monitoring of an active volcano, habitat monitoring, firefighters assistance, monitoring of assisted-living residents, healthcare, smart environments, checking availability of washing machines, and optimization of HVAC systems. In fact, wireless sensor networks have already jumped from the research laboratories to the commercial world, with applications such as precision agriculture, pipeline and freighter monitoring, management of critical infrastructures, and many others.

The characteristics of the applications and their context have a great influence on the structure and the elements of a sensor network. This is quite normal, as the requirements of an application will dictate how software and hardware elements should work in order to achieve the desired functionality. Examples of these influencing factors are lifetime, complexity, size, mobility, network deployment, and environment. Short-lived networks can provide its services without taking energy consumption as a primary factor in the design of the network. Complex applications may need of powerful sensor nodes that can handle the required standards and services. Smaller networks usually do not have scalability problems, while big networks need to consider not only scalability but also other issues like maintaining and monitoring the overall structure. If some devices are mobile, the network needs of specific mobility-aware protocols that can handle neighbourhoods where nodes and base stations appear and disappear. If the deployment location of nodes is known in advance, it is possible to preload information within the nodes that will optimize the behaviour of the internal protocols (e.g. provide default routing tables that can be used to offer the services of the network as soon as possible). Finally, in harsh environments it is necessary to include extra mechanisms (e.g. more redundancy) in order to preserve the reliability and robustness of the network.

Security Analysis. The aforementioned examples are only a small subset of the influence that the characteristics of the applications have on sensor networks. In fact, security is also influenced by the characteristics of the applications and their context. As a first step, it is necessary to obtain the security requirements of the application and to quantify the risks and consequences of a failure in the network security. Starting from this point, it is possible to know not only what security mechanisms are needed, but also the actual importance of every mechanism. However, this is not enough. There are different approaches for implementing the security mechanisms (cf. [25] for examples in Key Management Systems), but not all approaches can be optimally applied to a certain scenario. It is therefore necessary to choose the implementations of the security mechanisms that are more suitable for the context of a specific application.

An example of application requirement analysis and risk assessment for sensor networks can be found in [26]. This paper provides an analysis of the security requirements of sensor networks that monitors large suspension bridges and underground tunnels, and it shows how the importance of the security mechanisms can be derived from the application and security requirements. For example, the existence of node actuators is not considered in both scenarios, as operators can cross-check the sensor readings with other clues. Therefore, there is no need to include actuator-related security mechanisms. On the other hand, the integrity of the sensed data is very important for both applications, as false positives can force maintenance operators to waste time trying to locate and repair non-existent faults. Finally, some requirements like confidentiality and availability do not have the same importance. In the suspension bridge scenario, sensor readings are not expected to show anything extraordinary or embarrassing, and it is expected that the bridges will not depend exclusively on the sensor readings. In contrast, the information from underground tunnels should be accessed only by the operators before anyone else, and any issue that affects the availability of the sensor readings will hinder the operator capabilities of reacting in real time to possible problems.

As for the suitability of the security mechanisms, an application designer must select those security algorithms and protocols that provide advantageous properties for the application. Therefore, it is necessary to discover those properties (e.g. low memory footprint, scalability, high energy consumption), and link them afterwards to the different application requirements. The protocols and algorithms that fulfil most requirements will be considered as suitable for the application. An example of this type of analysis can be found in the area of Key Management Systems (KMS) [27]. The following list details the different properties of KMS, and explicitly shows how the application requirements directly influence over choosing a certain security mechanism:

- Memory Footprint (ROM and RAM used for the protocol). The importance of this property will be linked to the complexity of the application. If the application is complex, a KMS with a high memory footprint will not be useful in most cases.
- Communication Overhead (Number of messages exchanged between peers). The following scenarios require of KMS with a small communication overhead: scenarios where the communication channel is unreliable or prone to errors, scenarios where the network must advertise itself as less as possible.
- Processing Speed (Computational cost of the protocol). The processing speed is a critical property whenever it is crucial to set up a secure channel between two previously unknown nodes as fast as possible.
- Network Bootstrapping (Confidentiality of the bootstrap process). For applications where the deployment environment is secure enough, confidentiality is not an issue. Problems may arise whenever the deployment area is public or when the information managed by the sensor nodes is important.
- Network Resilience (Resistance against stolen credentials). The need for network resilience increases as the chances of a node being subverted by an adversary becomes higher.
- Global Connectivity (Existence of a "key path" between any node of the network). This is, in most cases, an essential property, because in many scenarios all nodes are equally important for providing the network services.
- Local Connectivity (Existence of a shared secret between neighbour nodes). This will assure that most nodes will be able to set up a pairwise key with their neighborhood with a negligible overhead.
- Node Connectivity (Existence of a shared secret between nodes regardless of their location). This is indispensable in scenarios where nodes are mobile, as they will need to open a secure channel with any node in their vicinity.
- Scalability (Support for big networks). In applications that require of a large number of nodes, KMS should be scalable.
- Extensibility (Capability of adding new nodes). This property is important for those scenarios that have dangerous external conditions, or that have to provide certain services for long periods of time.
- Energy (Optimization of the energy usage). There are some scenarios (short-lived networks) where saving energy is not crucial.

4.3 Network Type and Context

One remarkable effect of the influence of the applications is the configuration of the network architecture and its context. In fact, the "Wireless Sensor Networks" concept can be seen as a generic term that encompasses many different types of sensing architectures. The most "classic" WSN architecture is known as terrestrial sensor networks, where sensor nodes are distributed over a reasonably-sized geographical area, and use the air as a transmission medium. Examples of applications that use these terrestrial sensor networks are healthcare monitoring and precision agriculture systems. However, there are other types of sensor networks, which are especially suitable for different classes of applications. Every one of these networks has a particular name and some inherent features that differentiate them from other types of WSN.

There are some factors that can determine the existence of new types of sensor networks. One of these factors is the physical location of the network. Sensor nodes can be deployed underwater (underwater sensor networks or UWSN) or underground (underground sensor networks or WUSN), although there are also very small networks that are located on, near, or within a human body (body sensor networks or BSN). Another factor is the content of the network: while most sensor networks provide only physical information of the environment, other networks manage more complex information like video and audio streams (multimedia sensor networks or MWSN). Finally, there are some WSN that have either an unorthodox structure or specific goals: some networks do not require the permanent existence of a base station (unattended sensor networks or USN), while other networks collaborate in a heterogeneous environment similar to an Ad-hoc network (embedded peer to peer systems or EP2P).

One of the most important WSN paradigms whose features are completely influenced by the location of the nodes is known as underwater sensor networks, or UWSN. In these networks, sensor nodes are deployed below the ocean surface. These sensors can be used to measure seismic activity in order to provide tsunami warnings (disaster prevention), to detect the location of underwater oilfields (undersea explorations), and to monitor sea-based structures such as oil platforms and undersea cables (structural monitoring), amongst other things [31]. It would seem that the only difference between underwater and terrestrial sensor networks is the water that surrounds the nodes. However, this particular situation imposes additional constraints to the network [32]. For example, underwater sensor nodes must use an acoustic communication channel in order to exchange information wirelessly. This channel has a limited capacity, and the energy consumption and the propagation delay of the channel are very high. Sensor nodes are also especially prone to failure, due to specific underwater threats such as fishing trawlers, underwater life, failure of waterproofing, or mere corrosion. Moreover, underwater nodes are equipped with a limited battery that cannot be recharged due to their location.

There are other special features of UWSN that must be taken into account: cost, coverage, hardware capabilities, and mobility. Unlike terrestrial sensor networks, the deployment of underwater sensor nodes is more costly, due to the complex components of the nodes (e.g. water-proof housing, acoustic modems) and the equipment that must be used to deploy the nodes (e.g. ships). As the deployment of underwater sensor nodes is usually sparser, and because sensor nodes can move due to anchor drift or other external effects, the coverage of the network is reduced. However, the capabilities of underwater sensor nodes are usually greater: they have more memory to perform data caching in case of intermittent connections, and they also have a battery with a higher capacity due to the cost of using the communication channel and the complexity of replacing a drained battery. Finally, some UWSN can have mobile underwater robots that either support an existing architecture of fixed nodes or collaborate on their own to monitor chemical leaks and other biological phenomena.

A paradigm that is structurally similar to underwater sensor networks is wireless underground sensor networks (WUSN) [33]. In these types of networks, sensor nodes are buried or deployed in a cave or mine, monitoring the state of the soil or the air quality of an underground environment. The major design challenges of this paradigm are the communication channel, topology planning, power conservation, and environmental threats. As electromagnetic (EM) waves encounter a high attenuation in soil, it is necessary to optimize factors such as the packet size [34] and the location of the nodes in order to achieve reasonable connectivity. Besides, some sensor nodes may not be located close to the surface, thus battery replacement may not be a viable option. Moreover, the node can be affected by various threats, such as wildlife and environmental extremes. Note that WUSN do not have some of the constraints that affect its underwater counterpart: network deployment is easier and cheaper, sensor nodes are usually not mobile, and there exist scavenging opportunities for WUSN devices (such as seismic vibration and thermal gradients).

While most UWSN and WUSN consider that their nodes are distributed over a reasonably-sized geographical area, there is one specific paradigm where the network is located within a very small area: body sensor networks, or BSN [35]. The reason is simple: In these BSN nodes are located on, near, or within a human body. Such nodes monitor the physical state of its wearer, offering real-time measurements that can be integrated in complex healthcare scenarios such as telemedicine. These networks are simpler than other sensor networks, as there are a limited number of sensor nodes surrounding the patient. Besides, the architecture of the network is inherently hierarchical, where all data is, in most cases, directly retrieved and managed by a central device known as body area aggregator. Nodes are only affected by a limited number of physical threats, as they are worn by a human user. Moreover, these nodes and their batteries (excluding nodes located within the body of the patient) can be easily replaced in case of hardware problems or energy depletion.

Nevertheless, BSN have some particular challenges that must be considered. Different devices (e.g. blood pressure and electrocardiography (ECG) sensors) have different energy, QoS and bandwidth requirements, thus it is necessary to prioritize certain traffic according to the state of the network and the patient. However, communication is hindered by factors such as body shadowing (body absorption of RF energy) and movement. In fact, device and service heterogeneity suggest the coexistence of diverse communication technologies, such as inductive coupling, in-body RF-communication, and Ultra-Wideband [36]. Another factor that must be taken into account is the size of the nodes: as nodes must be small, unobtrusive, and ergonomic, the capacity of the batteries of certain BSN devices will be extremely limited due to size restrictions. Besides, it is not possible to use protocols that take advantage of the redundancy of the network due to the low number of nodes. Finally, the QoS requirements of BSN applications are very high, as the devices are managing physical data from a human being: the failure of one device could threaten life.

Location is not the only important factor that determines the existence of new types of sensor networks: content is another of those factors. An example of content-oriented sensor networks is the multimedia sensor networks paradigm, or MWSN. In these networks [37], the devices are able to retrieve, process, and distribute video and audio streams, still images, and scalar sensor data, through the use of embedded cameras. These specific sensor networks can be used to enhance and complement existing surveillance systems (surveillance), to monitor car traffic and to analyze accident scenes (traffic monitoring), to monitor the behaviour of elderly people, and so on. The main characteristics of this type of WSN are the specific bandwidth and QoS requirements of the applications, as well as the need of including cross-layer optimizations and in-network processing of raw data. Actually, even for low-resolution images, it is suggested that class II nodes are more energy-consuming than class III nodes, mainly due to the time needed to perform operations in the image stream. Besides, it is necessary to analyze the tradeoffs between physical layer protocols that provide high data rates (e.g. IEEE 802.11) and protocols that do not have a high bandwidth but are lightweight in terms of energy consumption (e.g. IEEE 802.15.4). There are many other specific challenges in this kind of networks, such as achieving a balance between reliability and congestion control, describe optional routing metrics, and inter-media synchronization.

As for the WSN that have an unorthodox structure or specific goals, we can mention the unattended sensor networks (USN) and embedded peer-to-peer systems (EP2P). The main characteristic of USN is the location of the base station [38]. Base stations are not present at all times in the network, and only appear near the network whenever there is data to retrieve. As a result, sensor nodes must store the physical information retrieved from the environment within themselves or in collector nodes. These nodes should have enough storage to store this temporal physical information. In fact, data should be moved or replicated in order to assure its survivability against possible attackers. Moreover, it is not possible to perform any kind of self-healing or self-management protocol that depends on the participation of the base station, as the base station is not always present. Since nodes have to proactively collaborate with each other in order to store the data and maintain the integrity of the network, it is necessary to support a communication model where nodes can open a channel with any other node in the network.

Finally, in the EP2P paradigm [39], sensor nodes and other devices collaborate in the processing and management of information in a P2P fashion. This paradigm has some resemblance with the unattended sensor networks paradigm: all nodes need to collaborate in order to perform a particular service. However, there are some crucial differences between these paradigms. For instance, a base station can be constantly available, and PDA-like devices can act as both temporal base stations and data retrieval devices due to the network heterogeneity. Besides, the network is more dynamic: its elements can enter the system and exit in an independent way. As a result, connections and disconnections may happen in an unpredictable and frequent manner, causing frequent reorganizations. From all the paradigms that are described in this section, this paradigm is the one that is more similar to an Ad Hoc network.

Security Analysis. All the inherent features of the previously mentioned types of sensor networks not only have influence on the importance of the security requirements and the characteristics of the security mechanisms, but also limits the number of security mechanisms that could be used to protect the network.

Regarding the security requirements, their importance can be strengthened (i.e. the property must be enforced no matter how) by the features of the network. For example, the self-organization property is crucial for the survivability of unattended sensor networks: the network is truly decentralized, and if there is a problem within it, there is neither base station that can be notified nor users that can provide feedback about the incident. Also, availability and freshness are essential for body sensor networks, because there are human lives at risk if the physiological data is not received on time. Other examples include forward and backward secrecy in embedded P2P systems (due to the dynamic nature of the network) and auditing for underwater sensor networks (as it is very difficult to physically reach the nodes after their deployment). Note that the characteristics of an application also have an influence over the security requirements (e.g. authorization is crucial whenever various users try to directly access the contents of the nodes). However, the influence that exerts the type of sensor network (UWSN, BSN, ...) remains constant, regardless of the nature of the application.

The features of the network will also help to dictate what security algorithms and protocols are more suitable for a certain context. For example, protocols with poor scalability are surprisingly suitable for body sensor networks, because the network size is small and most, if not all interactions with the external world are performed through a centralized device. Also, it is necessary to use mobility-aware protocols in embedded P2P systems and in certain types of underwater sensor networks due to their dynamic nature. There are more examples: unattended sensor networks will greatly benefit from protocols that can test whether a certain node has been subverted or not (i.e. code attestation protocols), and both underwater and multimedia sensor networks can be able to use computationally-intensive primitives if needed due to the extra power of their sensor nodes.

Note that the sensor network type also limits the kind of security mechanisms that can be used to protect the network. One of the most clear examples is underwater sensor networks, whose security protocols must send as few packets as possible due to the high cost of sending and receiving messages through the acoustic modem. Another clear example is the unattended sensor network, which is not able to incorporate any security mechanism that depend on the existence of a base station. Multimedia sensor networks also have to take care with the overhead imposed by the cryptographic primitives, as it needs to reduce the latency while sending video and audio streams. Finally, body sensor networks need to severely limit the use of energy-consuming primitives and protocols due to the size of its batteries, and embedded P2P systems cannot depend on key management systems that do not provide node connectivity.

5   Overview of Existing Security Mechanisms

5.1   Security Primitives

Most security protocols and mechanisms need of cryptographic primitives in order to integrate the security properties into their operations. These cryptographic primitives are Symmetric Key Cryptography (SKC), Public Key Cryptography (PKC), and Hash functions [40]. Symmetric Key Cryptography (SKC) can provide confidentiality and integrity to the communication channel, and require that both the origin and destination share the same security credential (i.e. secret key), which is utilized for both encryption and decryption. As a result, any third-party that does not have such secret key cannot access the information exchange. Public Key Cryptography (PKC), also known as asymmetric cryptography, is useful for secure broadcasting and authentication purposes. It requires of two keys: a key called secret key, which has to be kept private, and another key named public key, which is publicly known. Any operation done with the private key can only be reversed with the public key, and vice versa. As for (cryptographic) hash functions, they are used to create "digital fingerprints" of data. This property can be used to build other cryptographic primitives like the Message Authentication Code (MAC), which provides authenticity and integrity in the messages. These primitives alone are not enough to protect a system, since they just provide the confidentiality, integrity, authentication, and non-repudiation properties. Nevertheless, without these primitives, it would be nearly impossible to create secure and functional protocols.

The development of optimal implementations of security primitives for sensor nodes is a very advanced research field, with solutions that can be easily used in new sensor deployments. In the area of Symmetric Key Cryptography, There are two types of primitives: Block Ciphers and Stream Ciphers. Block Ciphers are more flexible and powerful, while Stream Ciphers are simpler and faster. One of the most important block ciphers is the Advanced Encryption Standard or AES, which is the encryption standard used by all U.S. government organizations for the protection of sensitive information. While this encryption primitive is not one of the fastest primitives, it is usable in sensor nodes: one of the most optimized software implementation of AES-128 achieves an encryption speed of 286.35 Kbps, a RAM requirement of 260 bytes, and a code size of 5160 bytes running on a 8 Mhz Texas Instruments' MSP430 microcontroller with no operative system [41]. There are even other block ciphers that, when implemented on software, offer an adequate balance between resource consumption and security. For example, the Skipjack cipher is slightly less secure than AES-128 due to its key size (80 bits), but some implementations have achieved a reasonably low encryption overhead per byte (25 μs) and a low memory overhead (code size of 2600 bytes).

Regarding stream ciphers, one of the most known ciphers is RC4, which is very simple and has an impressive speed. Although it is possible to implement it in a sensor node with just 428 bytes of code size [42], its inherent weaknesses (which are mostly concentrated on the initialization phase [43]) make advisable the use of other stream ciphers in new applications. Precisely, the eSTREAM project (organized by the EU ECRYPT network [28]) aimed to identify new stream ciphers that could be used even in constrained devices. Some of the ciphers of the resulting portfolio provide good results [44] in sensor nodes: the Salsa 20/12 algorithm requires 1412 bytes of code size in AVR platforms and it provides a throughput of 43700 bytes per second, and the Sosemanuk algorithm requires more memory (9092 bytes of code size in AVR platforms) but provides a higher throughput (67660 bytes per second)[3].

Public Key Cryptography was considered to be unattainable for sensor node platforms, but that assumption was shattered a long time ago. The approach that made PKC possible and usable in sensor nodes was Elliptic Curve Cryptography (ECC), which is based on the algebraic structure of elliptic curves over finite fields. ECC has smaller requirements both in computation and memory storage, due to its small key sizes and its simpler primitives. One of the most known software implementations of ECC, TinyECC [45], implements ECC-based signature generation and verification (ECDSA), encryption and decryption (ECIES), and key agreement (ECDH). Note that the computational and memory requirements of these algorithms are not small (e.g. ECDSA requires 19308 ROM and 1510 RAM for the MICAz, generating a signature in 2s. and verifying it in 2.43s), although the implementation of these primitives is constantly evolving and improving [46].

In fact, the improvements on the implementations of ECC primitives have allowed the existence of more complex PKC primitives in sensor nodes, such as identity-based cryptography (IBC). In IBC systems, only the identity of the sensors must be exchanged, and as a result there is no need to send either public keys or certificates. This saves energy as there is less data to be sent through the communication channel, although IBC is also very costly in terms of memory and CPU usage. One of the most optimal implementation of pairings executes the $\eta_T(P,Q)$ pairing on 1.71 seconds, requiring 4.17 KB of RAM and 23.66 KB of code size running on a 8 Mhz Texas Instruments' MSP430 microcontroller [47]. While it would seem that this primitive is not useful in sensor nodes, there may be certain contexts where it could be useful, such as underwater sensor networks (cf. Section 4.3).

---

[3] Note that, in the reference paper [44], the throughput of AES-128 is 43671 bytes per second.

As for hash functions, some standards like SHA-1 can be easily included in sensor nodes: an unoptimized implementation needs of 122 μs for digesting one byte [48]. Note that, as practical collision attacks can be found against SHA-1 [49], NIST is currently working on the selection of a new hash standard [50]. The work on this new standard is focused on PC-like platforms, although performance on embedded systems will not be overlooked. As a result, it is possible that new hash functions applicable to sensor nodes will appear soon. Nevertheless, it is not necessary to use hash functions to assure the integrity of a message if special modes of operation (such as CMAC) are used, although they require of specific block ciphers that could implement that functionality.

5.2   Key Management and Secure Channels

All devices that want to open a secure channel with other nodes must share some security credentials, i.e. secret keys. Key management systems (KMS) aim to solve the problem of creating, distributing, and maintaining those secret keys. The design of a KMS for sensor networks is not a trivial task, though: it is not advisable to rely on centralized entities due to the distributed and self-configurable nature of the network. Also, the existing constraints of sensor nodes (memory, computational capabilities) may discourage the use of resource-intensive algorithms for most scenarios. Finally, there are other factors, such as the potential size of the network, the connectivity of its nodes, the energy spent in the key setup processes, etc, that influence over the design of a KMS as well.

Due to their importance, the Key Management Systems for Wireless Sensor Networks have received increasing attention on the scientific literature, spanning many different types of protocols [25]. In fact, since one of the most important link-layer standards in sensor networks, IEEE 802.15.4, does not specify how secret keys should be exchanged, it is essential to utilize one of these protocols. These protocols can be classified into four major frameworks. Although the major purpose of all these frameworks is to bootstrap the secret keys that are needed by the link layer, their underlying mechanisms and design goals are different.

– *"Key Pool" Framework*. This is one of the first and most important KMS frameworks. The basic scheme behind this framework is quite simple [51]: the network designer creates a "key pool", a large set of precalculated secret keys, and before the network deployment every node in the network is assigned with a unique "key chain", i.e. a small subset of keys from the "key pool" (Key pre-distribution phase). After the deployment, the nodes can interchange the identification numbers of the keys from their "key chains", trying to find a common shared secret key (shared-key discovery phase). If two nodes do not share any key, they will try to find a "key path" between them in order to negotiate a pairwise key (path-key establishment phase). The major design goal of the protocols that belong to this framework is to assure a limited secure connectivity between nodes, regardless of the size of the network.

- *Mathematical Framework.* Certain KMS protocols use mathematical concepts (Linear Algebra, Combinatorics, and Algebraic Geometry) for calculating the pairwise keys of the nodes. The foundation of the Linear Algebra schemes is the Blom scheme [52]. In this scheme, every node i can calculate the pairwise key it shares with another node j by solving $A(i) \cdot G(j)$, whereas G is a public Vandermonde matrix and A is calculated using a symmetric random secret matrix D. On the field of Combinatorics, the Generalized Quadrangle and Symmetric Design models [53] are the most important. Using Generalized Quadrangles $GQ(s,t)$ or Finite Projective Planes $FPP(q)$, a network designer can construct a "key chain" of size $s + 1$ or $q + 1$, respectively. Finally, on the field of Algebraic Geometry, the basic primitive is the Bivariate Polynomial [54]. By using a bivariate polynomial f, every node A in the network is able to obtain a pairwise key with another node y by solving $f(A, y)$. All these protocols allow the creation of pairwise keys between nodes without major communication overhead. On the other hand, these designs are often difficult to apply, and they are not very scalable.
- *Negotiation Framework.* All protocols that generate their keys through mutual agreement, negotiating keys with their closer neighbours just after the deployment of the network, can be considered part of this framework. They are usually applied under the assumption that there is little or no treat against the integrity of the network in its first moments of life [55]. Nevertheless, it is possible to use other mechanisms and protocols (such as the Guy Fawkes protocol [56]) in order to assure the authenticity of the peers in any step of the network deployment. Other protocols that can be included inside this framework are those protocols that organize the network into dynamic or static clusters [57].
- *Public Key Framework.* Most of the previous frameworks rely only on Symmetric Key Cryptography. However, Public Key Cryptography can also be used to securely bootstrap the pairwise key of two nodes over a public communication channel. In these protocols, two nodes just need to interchange their public keys and some information (through protocols such as ECDH and ECMQV) to effectively create their pairwise secret keys. While constrained sensor nodes can be able to use PKC through Elliptic Curve Cryptography, the amount of memory required for the implementation and the time and energy needed to complete the negotiation is, in most cases, substantially higher than other KMS frameworks. However, PKC-based KMS usually have better properties than the systems of other frameworks.

As for the actual state of the art, every one of these frameworks contains many different protocols, and these protocols can implement specific optimizations (e.g. use of deployment knowledge, optimize the message exchange, tweak the behaviour of the protocols, combine protocols from different frameworks) in order to improve their features and be more useful for certain contexts. In fact, there exists certain methods that are able to select the most adequate KMS for a certain context by using the application requirements as an input [27]. By using these tools, it is possible to conclude that the actual state of the art for KMS in sensor networks is good enough for protecting certain applications. However, there are some issues that remain to be solved, such as the creation of protocols with better resilience (resistance against stolen credentials) and extensibility (capability of adding new nodes) properties.

One interesting detail is that, for most applications, simple KMS protocols such the basic polynomial-based and Blom schemes provide most of the properties needed by the applications. The reason is simple: most real-world applications have a number of nodes ranging from 50 to 1000. And for this size, simpler protocols are good enough. Another interesting point is the use of PKC. For every single situation PKC seems to be the ideal protocol, and in fact PKC-based protocols such as EDH and ECMQV provide good properties like excellent resilience and extensibility. Nevertheless, there might be situations where simpler KMS protocols can provide the properties needed by the applications.

5.3   Network Core Protocols

When speaking about "core" protocols, we refer to those network protocols that a sensor network needs in order to function properly. These protocols are: routing (transmitting a packet from one sensor node to another sensor node), data aggregation (briefing many sensor readings into one single piece of data), and time synchronization (synchronizing the clocks of the network). The behaviour and the properties of these protocols are highly dependent on the characteristics of the sensor network application where they are running, because they must be adapted to the requirements of the scenario. As a result, there are many core protocols from where an application designer can choose the most optimal for his/her scenario.

One of the factors that should be considered by every one of these protocols is security. Due to the vulnerable nature of sensor networks, the core protocols should be able to withstand attacks from malicious adversaries, either external or internal. However, it is very difficult to define security mechanisms that could be seamlessly adapted to every type of protocol. They must be prepared to analyze their internal processes in order to detect failure or misbehaviour, and to react to these events in order to maintain the functionality of the network.

Routing is one of the most important protocols of sensor networks. As sensor networks have an inherent distributed nature, the nodes must be able to forward the information to those devices that need it. Many, if not most sensor network protocols depend on the availability of a routing infrastructure. Its importance makes it a potential target for attackers: most of the attacks presented in section 3.1 can be crafted to hinder the routing processes. As there are many types of routing strategies (e.g. flat routing, data-centric routing, hierarchical routing, location-based routing), it is necessary to find suitable security approaches for every strategy that take into account their specific properties. Nevertheless, it can be possible to define certain generic countermeasures that can provide some security properties to all strategies.

Some of the existing countermeasures against routing protocol attacks are analyzed by both existing surveys [58] and by drafts of routing standards for sensor networks like ROLL (Routing over Low power and Lossy Networks) [59]. Attackers trying to manipulate the routing discovery mechanisms (using HELLO flood and acknowledgement spoofing attacks) transmit their packets with a higher transmission power. Therefore, nodes can defend themselves by verifying that the link is truly bidirectional, using extra protection mechanisms such as one-time keys if needed. An adversary can also try to overload a sensor node with irrelevant messages, as the lifetime of sensor networks is highly tied to the number of exchanged messages. Nodes can lessen the effects of this attack by introducing traffic quotas if the network seems overloaded.

There are also some countermeasures that defend against more complex attacks, such as selective forwarding, sinkholes, and wormholes. Selective forwarding attacks can be mitigated by using multipath routing, either by sending replicated packets through different paths or by choosing a different path for every packet that is being sent. Sinkholes and wormholes can be detected by estimating the distance between neighbours, as neighbours joined through a wormhole will be physically distant from each other. Other solutions for the wormhole problem include using the base station to identify distortions in the distribution of the number of neighbours, use packet leashes (e.g. timestamps included within the packet) to detect if the sender is further away than the nodes' communication range, or performing various distance-bounding protocols. Note that all these protection techniques could be further improved, although routing protocols may use other protection mechanisms included within the node to detect and react against possible problems (e.g. using an intrusion detection system to sense a possible selective forwarder). Moreover, it can be possible to take advantage in the specific features of the context to implement extra protection mechanisms. For example, if the nodes were aware of their physical location, the detection of attacks such as sinkholes and wormholes could be done in an easier way.

There is a specific case of routing that must be considered separately due to its importance: authenticated broadcast. Not only it is important to avoid a malicious flooding that would drain the energy of battery-dependant nodes, but also it is essential to assure that the received data comes from its intended source and is not manipulated. In nodes with enough resources, it is possible to use public key cryptography to apply a digital signature scheme to the broadcasted message. Another solution can use one-way hash chains (a collections of values where c_{n-1} is a one-way function of the next value c_n) in conjunction with symmetric-based message authentication codes (MAC) to "sign" a broadcasted message. Knowing cn in advance, nodes cannot "sign" messages that use c_{n-1} because they do now know it, but after receiving c_{n-1}, they can verify its validity by using c_n (as $H(c_{i+1}) = c_i$). There are many mechanisms that take advantage of this particular property of hash chains, such as μTesla and its variants, and the protocols that use one-way signatures.

Aggregation may not be mandatory for all sensor networks, but it provides a very useful service: the combination of data coming from nodes deployed at the same area. This is very important for most sensor network contexts, as it is necessary to optimize the usage of the communication channel. The aggregation process is closely related to the routing service, since aggregation capabilities are usually embedded inside routing protocols. There are also different strategies for aggregating data: routing-driven algorithms (opportunistic aggregation), coding-driven algorithms (compression at the source), and fusion-driven algorithms (full-fledged aggregation along the routing path). Both this heterogeneity and the dependence on the routing protocols add an extra complexity to the development of protection mechanisms, although some of the mechanisms that were used to protect the routing protocols can also be used to protect the aggregation messages. Nevertheless, there are specific aggregation attacks, targeting the data sources and the aggregation nodes, which must be lessened somehow [60][61].

One simple countermeasure to limit the effect of a compromised node trying to inject false data is to improve the resilience of the aggregation functions, as some functions (e.g. minimum, maximum, sum, average) are more insecure than others. The redundancy of some networks can be also used as a tool to detect fake or faulty readings that are too deviated from the average of the neighbourhood (e.g. due to the physical properties of heat, a node cannot sense that the environment is extremely hot when its neighbours located in the same area feel much colder values). While detecting problematic data is important, the main challenge of secure data aggregation is to detect a misbehaving aggregator. One solution is to use interactive proofs, where the user can verify that the aggregated data provided by the aggregator is a good approximation of the true value. Another solution uses witnesses, that is, redundant sensor nodes that aggregate the data and create a proof (e.g. a MAC) of the validity of the aggregation value.

If the network aims to provide end-to-end confidentiality, that is, to make the data known only by the original server and the receiver, it is necessary to use specific mechanisms such as homomorphic encryption. This primitive aims to perform specific algebraic operations in the ciphertext without decrypting it. Some aggregation protocols implement this feature by using elliptic curves for the sake of efficiency, as homomorphic encryption is expensive for sensor nodes in terms of computational resources. However, these protocols can only work with specific query-based aggregation functions such as sum and average. End-to-end aggregation, and aggregation in general, is an open field with research issues such as aggregation in dynamic environments, detection of compromised nodes injecting fake data, design of efficient homomorphic cryptography able to work with all types of functions, development of multilayer hierarchical data aggregation protocols, and so on.

Time synchronization does not provide any direct functionality to the users, but it is extremely important for the consistency of the network. It is essential not only to know when certain data was retrieved, but also to know the exact sequence in which events such as alarms occurred. Therefore, all nodes must have a similar time stored in their internal clocks regardless of hardware problems such as offset, skew and drift problems. Both sender-receiver and receiver-receiver time synchronization protocols (cf. Section 3.1) need of two nodes exchanging timing information. As a result, it is possible to use a secure communication channel in order to avoid attacks (e.g. message replay) perpetrated by outsider attackers. However, insider attackers have more chances to break these protocols by providing a fake time [62].

A simple protection against malicious insiders is to use delay thresholds. The typical drift rate of the nodes is not very high (clocks of sensor nodes usually accumulate several seconds of drift error per day), thus it is possible to specify the maximum amount of time offsets they will tolerate. Another method uses statistic techniques such as GESD (generalized extreme studentized deviate) to identify messages coming from compromised nodes. Note that these techniques only limit the effect of attacks, although some fine-tuned algorithms can decrease the threshold to very low values. A logical evolution is to have more than one partner for performing the clock synchronization. As for the time aggregation strategy, some protocols use the median (instead of the mean) to calculate the clock drift, sacrificing the ability to improve precision through multiple independent observations in order to have a high protection against malicious nodes.

While these protection mechanisms are focused on assuring the security of the information exchange between two nodes, it is also necessary to protect protocols that broadcast synchronization information in order to adjust the clocks of all the nodes in the network. This can be possible by using mechanisms such as secure synchronization trees [63]. Besides, other mechanisms even provide support for group synchronization, and are able to deal with inconsistent behaviour from a subset of nodes in the group [64]. The precision of the most advanced protection mechanisms is quite good, as they restrict the maximum impact of the attacker on the synchronization precision to under a few microseconds. Note, however, that most of these protocols have been tested in terrestrial sensor networks, with no experimental results on radio unfriendly environments. Still, some applications simply require the clocks of their nodes to be loosely synchronized.

5.4   Self-healing and Self-management Protocols

All protocols, regardless of their design and functionality, should be aware of their environment: which nodes are on a certain neighbourhood, whether a node seems to be alive or dead, the actual state of the communication channel, and so on. Therefore, it is essential to have certain self-awareness mechanisms that provide this information (e.g. whether a certain node has disappeared from a neighbourhood) to the protocols of the sensor node. This information is also vital for allowing the existence of self-healing mechanisms, as a sensor node that does not know its own situation and the situation of its environment cannot react to possible events that may influence its functionality. By knowing the context where it is located and the situation of its surroundings and its neighbourhood, a sensor node can be able to tweak its functionality to be more robust and work in a more optimal way.

Besides, those self-healing mechanisms can facilitate the creation of security services such as intrusion detection systems and trust management systems. By using intrusion detection systems, it is possible to know if a certain node is suspicious of misbehaviour or malicious. This knowledge can be used by any of the protocols of the network to ignore any interactions with these malicious entities. As for trust management systems, they can indicate if a certain node can be trusted for a particular task (e.g. route a packet to the base station), improving the overall intelligence of the protocols of the network.

An intrusion detection system (IDS) for WSN must have certain specific capabilities in order to be useful and functional [65][66]: audit data management (works with very application-specific partial audit data), simplicity (IDS should not take much resources from the nodes), secure cooperation (no node should be completely trusted in cooperative algorithms), full network coverage (all the elements of the network must be considered as potential entry points), support for extensibility (distinguish the incorporation of new nodes from other attacks), flexibility (possibility to include new detection mechanisms), and robustness (the system should be able to withstand an attack against itself). There are many challenges that must be considered in order to create a IDS that fulfils these features, such as the development of efficient detection mechanisms, the definition of a IDS architecture, the location of the detection entities (i.e. IDS clients), and so on.

There already exist various lightweight detection mechanisms that can detect anomalous events in the network, like jamming, malfunctioning sensors, node subversion, and time-related attacks (e.g. delay). Besides, although there is still room for improvement, the research community has also developed other detection mechanisms that analyze the state of sensor-specific protocols and derive the existence of an attack. For example, sinkhole attacks can be detected by using anomaly detection techniques, and some specific aggregation attacks can be detected with more accuracy if integrated with other IDS mechanisms. All these alerts can be processed by the base station, which can derive the identity of the nodes performing the attacks or distinguish errors and network failures from attacks.

As for the architecture of the IDS client, there is a "de-facto" agreement on its basic elements: a local packet monitoring entity that receives the packets from the neighbourhood, a statistics module that stores the information derived from the packets, a local detection engine that detects the existence of the different attacks, an alert database that stores information about possible attacks, and a cooperative detection engine that collaborate with agents located within the neighbourhood. In fact, in order to achieve full network coverage, all nodes should have a IDS client installed. Note that it has been proved in real world settings that this architecture is lightweight enough to work in class II nodes, although it is possible to further optimize this distribution by running the detection mechanisms at regular intervals and by selecting (manually or statistically) the nodes that will be in charge of monitoring the messages coming from the neighbourhood.

Regarding trust, it aids the members of a WSN (trustors) to deal with uncertainty about the future actions of other participants (trustees): nodes with high trust values are expected to provide the services they have been asked for. Most of the existing work on trust management systems for sensor nodes has focused on solving specific problems, that is, on developing trust solutions that only solve one problem in particular [68][69]. Reputation ('What is generally said or believed about an entity') is often used as one of the inputs for calculating the trust values. Most systems represent it through a Bayesian formulation, more specifically, a beta reputation system (a,b), where a denotes good behaviour and b denotes bad behaviour. A common optimization in trust management systems for sensor networks is to make use of clusters to calculate and store the trust of the network entities. Other systems consider the use of extra parameters such as risk and entropy.

One important point that must be considered when developing a trust management system for WSN is how it should be influenced by the inherent features of sensor networks. In fact, it is possible to link those features with the state of the art in order to obtain a set of "best practices" that any trust management system for WSN should take into account. Note that existing trust protocols do not consider all these principles at the same time, although they fulfil some of them. These "best practices" are described as follows:

– Considering Trust and Reputation. A trust management system for WSN should have the following two elements: A reputation manager (to store the behaviour of nodes) and a trust manager (to calculate the trust values using reputation as one of its inputs). By not calculating the trust directly from the behaviour of a node, it is possible to better handle aspects such as the evolution of the node, aging, etc.
– Trust and the Base Station. The base stations should be able to participate on the trust management process. A base station can use the information produced by the sensor network to observe and analyze the behaviour of its nodes, storing their reputation and making global trust decisions.
– Information Gathering. The events that occur during the lifetime of a WSN can be used as inputs for a trust management system, as they model the behaviour of a certain sensor node. Besides, the reputation information about other nodes should be distributed, as neglecting the use of such second-hand information may result on decisions that are not fully consistent with the actual state of the network.
– Initial Values. At the beginning of the lifetime of the WSN, all its nodes must have a good reputation and be equally trusted. Nodes are usually programmed in a controlled environment, and at the very beginning any malicious adversary had neither the time nor the chance to influence or subvert a node.

- Granularity. A node needs to maintain separate opinions about the existing actions of their peers, thus it needs a different set of reputation values. Besides, different trust values should also exist: A specific trust value (e.g. routing) cannot be used in most cases to deduce what the peer could do in a different task (e.g. sensing).
- Updating and Aging. The internal state of the trust management system must be updated with information received during the lifetime of the network. Regarding aging, in the updating process trust entities should use aging mechanisms as a way to incorporate new information in a smooth way. Besides, different events should not have the same impact on the reputation of a node, and the evolution of the reputation and trust values should not be ignored.
- Risk and Importance. Two factors that should influence over the calculation of the trust values are the risk of the interaction between the trustor and the trustee, and the importance of the reputation value and that specific interaction. Risk and importance also should have influence when selecting a threshold.

5.5   Privacy and Anonymity in Sensor Networks

As mentioned in the overview of the security requirements, there are certain scenarios where the privacy of the elements of the network needs to be taken into account. There are basically three types of threats against privacy [67]: content, location, and identity. If an adversary can determine the meaning of a communication exchange because of the existence of a message and the context and timing of the situation, there is a content privacy threat. If the adversary is able to infer the physical location of a communication entity or to approximate the relative distance to that entity, there is a location privacy threat. And if an adversary is able to deduce the identities of the nodes involved in a communication, there is an identity privacy threat. It should be noted that these privacy threats are closely linked with the anonymity property. However, privacy techniques may also aim for unobservability (messages cannot be distinguished from random noise), whereas anonymity do not try to hide the existence of a certain event but just tries to make it undistinguishable from events of the same kind.

Existing privacy-preserving solutions for WSN can be classified in data privacy protection, which aims to protect the privacy of the data content, and context privacy protection, which aims to protect contextual information such as location and timing [70]. For data protection, there are mechanisms that try to preserve the privacy of data from malicious adversaries during the aggregation process. One idea is to add specially crafted noise to the raw data sensed by the WSN, thus the aggregator will not be able to know the individual raw data items but can obtain precise aggregated values. There are other approaches that protect aggregation privacy, such as slicing original data into pieces in order to recombine the randomly, and forcing the aggregator to obtain only an accurate estimate of the histogram of the data distribution instead of raw data. Other data protection mechanisms try to protect the privacy of queries, as it is possible to infer some information from the existence of these queries (e.g. a patient staying at home being monitored by a BSN). One possible solution is to fuzzy the target region of the query according to pre-defined transformation functions.

For context privacy protection, existing techniques focus on protecting the location of nodes and the timing of the generation of the data. On the field of location privacy, it is possible to attain perfect unobservability by constantly sending bogus data, thus an attacker will not be able to discover the existence of traffic coming from a real target (i.e. the location of pandas or elephants). As this technique is quite energy-consuming, it is necessary to create more optimal mechanisms, although there is some preliminary work on this matter based on random routing techniques. Note that these mechanisms protect the location of a node, but not the location of a base station. For protecting the base station, it is necessary to thwart local attackers by hiding the parent-child relationship between nodes, while global attackers may require of more complex mechanisms. The techniques that aim to protect temporal privacy are actually simpler, based on random delays. Certainly, there is a need to make a tradeoff between the protection of timing privacy, the efficiency of buffer space, and the maximum delay allowed.

5.6   Software-Based Protection and Testing

By reviewing the different attacks presented in section 3.1, it can be deduced that one of the most dangerous class of attacks that an adversary can perform is node compromise. Whenever a node is compromised there is no immediate effect in the network, but starting from that point an external attacker becomes an internal attacker, and the amount and scope of the attacks it can be able to perform is simply devastating. Therefore, one of the priorities for protecting a sensor network should be to incorporate hardware and software mechanisms that either delay or avoid these compromise attacks. There are some hardware strategies that may protect the nodes against attackers with limited resources, such as deactivating the JTAG debugging interface and randomizing the password to access the bootstrap loader in certain microprocessors [9]. Unfortunately, most sensor nodes do not have any kind of tamper resistant package, and any attacker with enough resources will surely success on retrieving information directly from the nodes.

Fortunately, there exist some software-based techniques that can check if a node has been subverted or replicated by an adversary. Remote Attestation is one of these tools [71], where any node (verifier) can send a challenge to another node (target). As nodes are "cells" that are usually loaded with the same code, the challenge usually consist on a "pseudorandom memory traversal", where the target needs to randomly access and store some positions of its own memory. If the target has the same code as the verifier, it should provide a correct answer to the challenge within acceptable time bounds. There are some enhancements that improve the reliability of this basic scheme: the challenge routine can be obfuscated or use a keyed hash, and some important state information such as the program counter can be included as part of the verification process.

Another remote identification method is radio fingerprinting. This technique make use of the Received Signal Strength Indicator (RSSI) values and the Link Quality Indicator (LQI) values of radio signals. These values can be used for estimating the distance between a pair of nodes, thus they can be used to detect certain types of attacks (e.g. HELLO floods). However, it can be possible to extract an unique fingerprint from these values due to the physical characterization of the signal. As a result, one node can identify the sender of a message analyzing its RSSI and LQI values [72]. The actual state of the art is very promising, as the identification method yields no false negatives and the false positives rate is small (1.05%). It is also possible to improve the signal capturing method by using extra hardware [73]. In this HW solution, sensor nodes can be recognized from large distances (up to 40 m indoors) with a high accuracy (achieving a Equal Error Rate (EER) of 0.24%.)

5.7   Other Protocols and Mechanisms

Beyond the "core" protocols and the information retrieval mechanisms of sensor networks, there are other services and protocols that can be useful to improve the functionality of the network. For example, it is possible to upload new code to the motes through the wireless channel. This way, there is no need to physically obtain every node in the network in order to reprogram it. It is also possible to include small virtual machines inside the motes, greatly enhancing the ability of the base station to issue orders to the network. Another interesting service is group management: in certain WSN the nodes must group themselves in dynamic clusters that try to solve a particular problem. Not surprisingly, all these services and protocols need to be protected against possible external and internal attacks.

Regarding code dissemination, it is necessary to protect the code fragments that traverse the WSN. Signing all fragments is a valid solution, but it imposes a considerable overhead over the sensor nodes. Therefore, there are many techniques that try to simplify the process (using hash chains, hash trees, and others) while providing protection against attacks such as Denial of Service due to battery exhaustion. As for group management, the basic mechanisms that need to be provided are group key management and cluster head election. Note that there are many challenges to solve in these areas: forward and backward secrecy properties should be provided in the maintenance of group keys and node revocation processes, and the election of a cluster head should not be affected by the presence of malicious adversaries.

Furthermore, there are plenty of security mechanisms for sensor networks that need to be further investigated. For example, random number generation is an important primitive for sensor nodes, as many cryptographic primitives depend on it. The creation of a pseudorandom number generator for WSN that complies with certain quality metrics is still underdeveloped. Other mechanisms are related to authorization, as the base station may delegate some of its privileges to other devices in order to perform maintenance and management tasks "on-site". At last, other aspects of the security in WSN that are in need of more research are: the relationship between the security and the QoS requirements of the network, methodologies such as attacks trees applied to WSN in order to quantify their risks, development of secure location algorithms, analysis of name and addressing vulnerabilities, creation of secure architectures and middlewares that use cross-layer optimizations, distributed computing, data redundancy and survivability, mechanisms for the protection of the MAC layer, and so on.

6   Existing Standards and Their Security Mechanisms

Since Wireless Sensor Networks are being demanded for industrial control and automation applications, diverse international organizations have joined efforts to standardize their communications. One of the first consortiums was the Zig-Bee Alliance [75], which produced the following ZigBee standards: 2004, 2006 and 2007/PRO. Previous releases of ZigBee Alliance were thought for home automation environments; however, and due to the critical nature of diverse systems, last versions contemplate diverse and specific services to improve the monitoring of complex systems, industrial systems and critical infrastructures [74]. After ZigBee, other standards that try to address the needs of industrial and automation systems have been developed. Examples of these standards are WirelessHart [76] and ISA100.11a [77], as shown in Figure 3. The remainder of this section will study these communication standards for WSN, focusing on their network architectures and their security mechanisms.

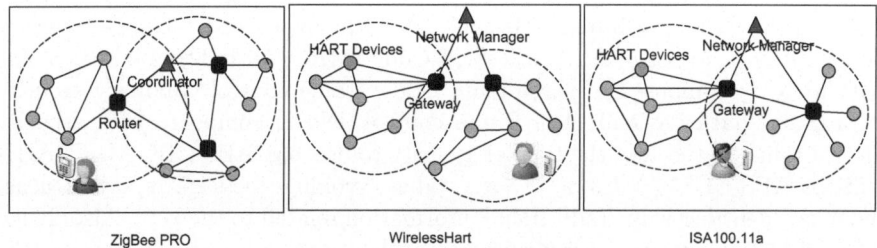

ZigBee PRO   WirelessHart   ISA100.11a

Fig. 3. WSN Standards

6.1   IEEE 802.15.4-2006

Most of the wireless communication standards applicable to WSN are based on the IEEE 802.15.4-2006 standard [78], that specifies the physical (PHY) and Media Access Control layer (MAC) layers of a Wireless Personal Area Network (WPAN). The PHY layer is in charge of activating the transmission radio to send/receive packets through the most suitable radio frequency (RF), protecting the channel from other unauthenticated devices and managing signal functions. In contrast, the MAC layer is in charge of generating beacons (frames for synchronizing the clock of all the networks devices belonging to a same network) and providing association services.

This standard also offers diverse mechanisms for secure deployment, network and device discovery, energy control (through low-duty cycles, i.e., cycles where a device can be in a sleeping state), and RF channel change to control interferences and noise in the communication channels. Such mechanisms work over networks based on a star and peer-to-peer topology with low complexity and transmission rate. Furthermore, it can operate in the following unlicensed frequency bands: 2.4GHz (worldwide use) using up to sixteen channels at 250Kbps, 868-868.8MHz (Europe) using one channel at 20/100/250Kbps, and 902-928MHz (North America) using up to thirty channels at 40/250Kbps.

Noise control is performed by using the Direct Sequence Spread Spectrum (DSSS) method. This method is responsible for modulating the information before its transmission using a lower spectral power density in order to assure an interference reduction in the frequency channels. The standard also defines three types of modulations that preserve the DSSS approach: Binary Phase Shift Keying (BPSK), Offset Quadrature Phase Shift Keying (O-QPSK) and Parallel Sequence Spread Spectrum (PSSS). Regarding interferences, they are controlled through the CSMA-CA (Carrier-Sense Multiple-Access with Collision Avoidance) collision control protocol, which listens to the medium before starting a transmission. If the medium is being used by another network device, then the node must wait a random time again. Another way of controlling the interferences is to use Guarantee Time Slots (GTS) protocol with centralized medium access times.

From a security standpoint, this standard provides HW support for AES-128 (Advanced Encryption Standard with key length of 128 bits) to assure confidentiality in the messages. Integrity is achieved with the use of a Message Integrity Code (MIC) or Message Authentication Code (MAC) with 32/64/128bits. The MIC/MAC is composed of three main fields: frame control, auxiliary security control and data payload. The frame control field is composed of a security control value (it specifies the type of security to use, e.g. AES-CBC-MAC, AES-CTR or AES-CCM), a frame counter value (avoiding message replay attacks) and a key identifier value (additional information related to the key). Also, IEEE 802.15.4-2006 allows network devices to authenticate any message received by using an Access Control List (ACL). This list includes the address of trustworthy neighbours, a key with 128bits length, a last initial vector (IV), a replay counter (making sure the freshness of the messages) and a security policy, as for instance AES-CTR. In case where a device is not included on the list, the message will have to be refused or go through another authentication mechanism.

6.2   ZigBee 2006, 2007 and PRO

The ZigBee standard, created by the ZigBee alliance, is a wireless communication standard for constrained devices. At present, there are three versions of the standard: ZigBee-2006, ZigBee-2007 (it is also known as ZigBee) and ZigBee PRO (Zigbee-2004 is considered as an obsolete release). These three ZigBee versions have certain features in common. For example, they are capable of supporting mesh networks using different types of network devices: i) coordinator, ii) routers to help end-points to transmit data to the coordinator, and iii) end-points - sensor nodes. Generally, the coordinator behaves like a trust center, which is able to manage the deployment, maintenance and control processes on the network. A mesh network simplifies the coexistence with other communication systems, such as Bluetooth or WiFi. Furthermore, this topology provides communication reliability since alternatives paths can be dynamically chosen through the Ad Hoc On Demand Distance Vector Routing (AODV) protocol.

Regarding the stack architecture of ZigBee, it is based on four main layers: PHY, MAC, NWK (Network) and APS (Application) layers. This last layer also includes two important sub-layers: ZDO (ZigBee Device Object) and Application Framework. Basically, the two lowest layers (PHY and MAC layers) are specified by the IEEE 802.15.4 standard. The NWK layer is in charge of packet routing, network and security management, and joining/rejoining management. The APS layer defines the application domains, and provides data transmission, security and binding (matching of compatible devices such as switches and lamps) to the endpoints. The APS layer must also keep a table that stores the nodes or clusters deployed on the whole network. The ZDO sub-layer is the responsible for the local and over-the-air management on the network, security management, and node and service discovery. Lastly, the Application Framework sub-layer allows to add new applications to the network.

ZigBee 2006, 2007 and PRO are being applied to diverse commercial systems, consumer applications and industrial systems. Table 3 represents a summary about the services and mechanisms provided by these three standards. Particularly, ZigBee-2007 and Zigbee provide self-forming and self-configurable mesh and cluster tree networks with 31,101 nodes. These specifications offers diverse application services and mechanisms, such as device and service discovery, acknowledge service, fragmentation and reassembly of packets, a PAN ID conflict

Table 3. A brief comparative of the ZigBee specifications

Feature Set	ZigBee 2006	ZigBee 2007	ZigBee PRO
Mesh networks	✓	✓	✓
Cluster tree networks	✓	✓	
Many-to-one networks			✓
Scalability	✓	✓	✓
Commissioning cluster		✓	✓
Fragmentation and reassembly		✓	✓
Frequency agility		✓	✓
Source routing			✓
Symmetric link			✓
Stochastic addressing			✓
Multicasting			✓
Broadcasting	✓	✓	✓
Security standard mode	✓	✓	✓
Security high mode			✓
Application context	Residential	Residential	Commercial

resolution mechanism, a commissioning cluster to configure the devices based on additional information related to the network or the nodes, and a RF channel change service with the frequency agility method.

With respect to security, ZigBee supports symmetric keys with AES-128, providing authentication and confidentiality at NWK and APS levels through a transversal security service provider layer. The security mode utilized in this case is officially known as "Standard Security" mode and is compatible with residential security of ZigBee-2006. In this mode, it is considered that "all nodes on the network trust each other" and the coordinator is the trust center responsible for managing, distributing and updating the symmetric keys on the whole network. In addition, the standard mode manages two important keys: link key, which is shared between two network devices and used for the confidentiality at the APS layer, and network key, which is shared by all the nodes on the network and is used for the confidentiality at the NWK layer. The network key can be obtained through two ways: either transmitting it without protection from coordinator or encrypting it with the link key, which must be previously preconfigured in the new device. Note that updates of the network key are frequently broadcasted by the coordinator.

In contrast, ZigBee PRO, included in the ZigBee-2007 specification, was designed for large mesh and many-to-one networks with a maximum of 65,540 nodes. At present, this standard shares some services with ZigBee-2007, such as frequency agility, commissioning cluster or fragmentation. However, other and new attractive services are only offered by ZigBee PRO, such as multicasting, symmetric link, source routing or stochastic addressing. The multicasting service allows a network device to transmit packets to many devices at the same time. The symmetric link is a method able to choose a path with better link quality. The source routing allows gateway to return traffic to a source node, embedding the path from the source node to the gateway into packet header. Moreover, this mechanism assures an entry reduction in the routing tables and minimizes the broadcast traffic in the network. The stochastic addressing consists of randomly assigning an address to the new network devices. In case where such address is in conflict with another one in the network, a conflict resolution mechanism is automatically activated along with the IEEE MAC physical addresses.

As regards security in ZigBee PRO, it offers a "High Security" mode with better protection levels than the standard mode. Basically, this introduces a new key, known as master key. Such key is preconfigured in the new devices in order to generate the link key by means of a Symmetric-Key-Key-Exchange (SKKE) algorithm. At the moment that the link key is generated, the network key is transmitted encrypted with it. The network key is frequently updated in a unicast mode and protected with the link key by the coordinator. This set of security keys assures that any application under ZigBee PRO is robust enough to face threatening situations. Moreover, it is considered a suitable standard for the control of critical and complex systems, as for example an energy generation/distribution plant.

6.3   WirelessHart™

Nowadays, the vast majority of industrial leaders are demanding state of the art technologies and infrastructures so that the control processes can take advantages of new and attractive control services. In fact, their installations are continually changing in order to provide reliability, security, and an improved system functionality. In fact, one of the most demanded technologies is wireless communication, since it provides the same advantages than a wired infrastructure but with a low installation and maintenance cost. However, the integration of multiple wireless technologies at the same critical system supposes to take into consideration several important issues. Predominantly, interoperability among wireless communication systems (Bluetooth (IEEE 802.15.1), RFID, Wireless Sensor Networks (using IEEE 802.15.4), WiMAX (IEEE 802.16), WiFi (IEEE 802.11), etc.), compatibility with existing hardware and software components, security, and reliability in the communications. All of these requirements were recently considered by HART [76] to define a specific protocol as part of the HART Field Communication Protocol Revision 7. This new protocol, known as WirelessHart, has as goal to provide industrial solutions through wireless mesh networks composed of node groups.

The WirelessHart network architecture is based on four essential components: i) a gateway, ii) a network manager, iii) the sensor nodes, and iv) the existing industrial devices or equipments (such as a Remote Unit Terminal, RTU). The network manager is considered as a trusted node in the whole network, and it could be integrated in the gateway. Generally, this device possesses enough resources to manage the routing tables, the synchronization schedule, the network configuration and the security. In fact, the network manager updates the routing tables and the communication schedule as new nodes join the network. The tables are based on information associated to a routing graph with redundant paths for each node. On the other hand, the gateway is the interface between the WSN world and the control system, as for example the control center of a SCADA (Supervisory Control and Data Acquisition) system [79]. Such interface should be able to interpret any type of protocol, as may be: Modbus/TCP [80], DNP3 [81] or IEC-104 [82].

With respect to the stack of WirelessHart, the PHY layer is based on the IEEE 802.15.4-2006 whereas the MAC layer is exclusive. Its MAC layer uses the TDMA (Time Division Multiple Access) protocol for collision control with a fixed time-slot (i.e., 10 ms). In addition, the concept of superframe is introduced in order to group a sequence of time-slots whose value starts with an absolution slot number (ASN) equal zero. Such superframes are periodically repeated by time periods. On the other hand, WirelessHart controls the noise and interferences in the communication channel by applying frequency hopping and blacklisting methods. The frequency hopping method allows network devices to change of RF channel. The blacklisting method consists of including on a blacklist those RF channels with interferences or noise.

In terms of enforcing security, it provides protection at both NWK-level and MAC-level, managing four types of security keys: public key, network key, join key and session key. The public key and the join key have to be preconfigured in every new network device in order to generate the MIC of the MAC layer and NWK layer, respectively. This process will allow any device to be later authenticated in the network manager. Whenever a new node is authenticated by the network manager, it will receive the session key and the network key. The session key is a unique key between two network devices to encrypt any interchanged messages, while network key is shared by all network devices to generate the MIC of the MAC layer. The MIC is generated with CCM* (counter with CBC-MAC) using the AES-128 algorithm. For its generation is necessary to include a 128-bit key whose value will depend on node state (a new node-public key or an old node - network key), a nounce of 13 bytes and the message header without encryption.

WirelessHart also offers other very suitable services for critical environment, such as: energy management, a diagnostic mechanism (embedding the path to follow into the message header) or message priority management. This last service identifies four priority levels and classified by: commands, measurements, normal messages and alarms (which includes both the event occurred and the alarm).

6.4   ISA100.11a

ISA100.11 release one is an open standard approved by the ISA100 Standards Committee in April 2009 [77]. This standard is focused on providing diverse control services at automation and control systems. In fact, its main goal is to assure interoperability with other communication systems, compatibility with existing hardware and software systems, energy conservation, reliability and security. Moreover, the standard contemplates a set of functions and operations for the monitoring of non-critical and critical systems, among them the industrial and control systems (e.g. a SCADA system). Furthermore, this first version offers specific functions for supervisory control, detection of anomalous situation and alerting in mesh and star networks.

The ISA100.11a architecture is focused on the OSI model, where the lowest layers (PHY and MAC layers) use the IEEE 802.15.4-2006 standard operating in the 2.4GHz frequency band. The Data Link Layer (DLL) layer implements the TDMA protocol and several functions to provide frequency hopping and mesh routing. On the other hand, the NWK layer is in charge of offering functions of inter-networking routing (i.e., mesh to mesh routing), such as addressing, routing, quality of service (QoS) and management functions. The transport layer includes a set of functions to transmit data between network devices in a reliable way, incorporating mechanisms such as flow control, reliable / unacknowledged service, enhanced-secure / basic-secure service, fragmentation and reassembly, and so on. Finally, the application layer include services that guarantee interoperability among diverse communication technologies and infrastructures with very low latencies. Moreover, This layer also provides a native protocol and a tunneling protocol. The native protocol is composed of specific functions that manage the bandwidth and energy of the network, while the tunneling protocol allows interoperability with other standards such as Modbus, Profibus [83],

Fieldbus [84], etc. Regarding the security services, these are extended throughout the whole stack and are based on the security offered by IEEE 802.15.4-2006 with symmetrical and asymmetrical keys, configuration, operation and maintenance.

6.5   Discussion

Table 4 presents a brief summary and comparative among the different wireless communication standards. It is possible to observe that the three standards follow common objectives, such as: interoperability with other communication systems, scalability, energy saving, communication reliability, compatibility with existing industrial devices, and security. Precisely, all the standards protect the communication channel against external attackers, and provide some mechanisms to refresh the keys used in the network.

Still, there are some WSN-specific aspects that are not considered by the current standards. This does not mean that the standards have neglected security in their design. Most standards include protection against jamming and Denial of Service attacks through the use of frequency hopping techniques. Also, all protocols provide secure communication channels, assuring the confidentiality, integrity, and authentication of data. As a result, it can be possible to avoid or mitigate the effects of attacks perpetrated by malicious outsiders. However, it is fairly easy to include a malicious node inside the network by using node compromise attacks (cf. section 3.1). As a result, the protocols used by these standards can be attacked by malicious insiders, effectively hindering the provisioning of services. It should be noted that sensor nodes working on industrial environments may have tamper-resistant packages due to the criticality of the environment.

As insider attacks can affect the functionality of the network, the core protocols defined by the standards should incorporate some lightweight security mechanisms in order to be robust against attacks. Besides, these standards should provide support for self-healing and intrusion detection mechanisms. Note that some standards, like WirelessHART, already provide support for self-healing.

Table 4. A brief comparative among wireless communication standards

Feature Set	ZigBee PRO	WirelessHART	ISA100.11a
Mesh networks	✓	✓	✓
Many-to-one networks	✓	✓	
Star networks			✓
Scalability	✓	✓	✓
RF channel change	✓	✓	✓
High security	✓	✓	✓
Noise/interference control	✓	✓	✓
Priority management		✓	✓
Energy saving	✓	✓	✓
Interoperability with other systems	✓	✓	✓
Application context	Commercial	Industrial	Industrial

However, these mechanisms are oriented to apply corrections in the event of routing faults such as nodes disappearing from the network, not to react against attacks such as blackholes. Another challenge is the use of Public Key Cryptography: all standards use symmetric cryptography to establish the security infrastructure of the network, and the properties of PKC (e.g. network resilience, authenticated broadcasts) could be very useful for an industrial environment. Finally, all these standards have been only tested in terrestrial sensor networks, and may not work correctly or efficiently in other network types such as underwater sensor networks and body sensor networks. Nevertheless, this is comprehensible, as these standards aim to provide a specific service for terrestrial environments.

6.6   Addendum: 6LoWPAN and the Internet

6LoWPAN is an open standard for low power WPANs under IPv6 [85], whose name comes from the working group on the Internet area of IETF (Internet Engineering Task Force). This working group was established in 2004 to address the challenges of enabling wireless IPv6 communication over the IEEE 802.15.4-2006 standard with low-power radio network devices and with limited resources. At present, this standard is considered a suitable element to introduce the concept "Internet of Things" [86].

The 6LoWPAN stack architecture is slightly similar to the OSI model, although its session and presentation layer are not explicitly used. The two lowest layers are based on the IEEE 802.15.4-2006 standard, where the PHY layer transmits packets with a payload of 127 bytes and an offered load of 250Kbps. Likewise, the MAC layer provides diverse services to guarantee single-hop communication links between network devices using the CSMA/CA protocol. On the other hand, the NWK layer is the responsible for providing internetworking capabilities, addressing IPv6, network management with SNMP (Simple Network Management Protocol) and security services. Furthermore, the NWK layer has integrated a special sub-layer for routing, known as Adaptation layer. This sub-layer provides a set of services and functions, such as: TCP/IP header compression, fragmentation and reassembly, network device discovery, multicasting and routing. In fact, besides ROLL [59], there are several routing protocols defined, such as LOAD (6LoWPAN Ad hoc Routing Protocol), DYMO Low (Dynamic MANET On-demand) or Hi-Low.

Therefore, 6LoWPAN offers essential services for routing in the personal area network (PAN) space, providing packet routing between the IPv6 domain and the PAN domain, IP adaptation and interoperability, addressing schemes and address management, device and service discovery, and security considering set-up, deployment and maintenance. As for security, 6LoWPAN depends on the security offered by IEEE 802.15.4 with AES-128, and it lacks of strong security mechanisms. However, even if 6LoWPAN were able to provide a stronger foundation for security, there are plenty of previously unidentified security challenges when integrating WSN and the Internet. Those challenges must be taken into account by both sides. Some of the challenges include: communication security, device and user authentication, availability, accountability, WSN-specific optimizations, and robustness against attacks [87]. Note that these challenges are mostly protocol-independent: future IP extensions of protocols like ZigBee should also take these challenges into account.

7   Conclusions

As sensor networks become increasingly used in real-world settings, it is necessary to provide efficient and usable security mechanisms that could protect the network against attacks. While it is possible to deploy a secure sensor network for certain applications, there are some challenges that need to be considered. However, one of those challenges is not related to the technology but to the network designers and users: they must become aware of the existing connections between the context of the application, its security requirements, and the security mechanisms. The purpose of this paper was to raise the awareness on this particular subject, and to show how existing standards should also consider this factor and the specific needs of sensor networks, such as support for self-healing mechanisms that can mitigate the effect of internal attacks.

Acknowledgements

This work has been partially supported by the ARES CONSOLIDER project (CSD2007-00004) and the CRISIS project (TIN2006-09242). The third author was funded by the Ministry of Education and Science of Spain under the "Programa Nacional de Formacion de Profesorado Universitario".

References

1. Petersen, S., Carlsen, S.: Wireless Sensor Networks: Introduction to Installation and Integration on an Offshore Oil & Gas Platform. In: Proceedings of the 19th Australian Conference on Software Engineering (ASWEC 2008), Perth, Australia (March 2008)
2. European Organization for Nuclear Research (CERN). LHC - The Large Hadron Collider, http://lhc.web.cern.ch (retrieved on June 2009)
3. Xu, W., Trappe, W., Zhang, Y., Wood, T.: The Feasibility of Launching and Detecting Jamming Attacks in Wireless Networks. In: Proceedings of the 6th ACM international symposium on Mobile ad hoc networking and computing (MobiHoc 2005), pp. 46–57. Urbana-Champaign, USA (2005)
4. Raymond, D.R., Marchany, R.C., Brownfield, M.I., Midkiff, S.F.: Effects of Denial-of-Sleep Attacks on Wireless Sensor Network MAC Protocols. IEEE Transactions on Vehicular Technology 58(1), 367–380 (2009)
5. Law, Y.W., Palaniswami, M., Van Hoesel, L., Doumen, J., Hartel, P., Havinga, P.: Energy-Efficient Link-Layer Jamming Attacks against Wireless Sensor Network MAC Protocols. ACM Transactions on Sensor Networks 5(1), 6:1–6:38 (2009)
6. Raymond, D.R., Midkiff, S.F.: Denial-of-Service in Wireless Sensor Networks: Attacks and Defenses. IEEE Pervasive Computing 7(1), 74–81 (2008)

7. Pongaliur, K., Abraham, Z., Liu, A.X., Xiao, L., Kempel, L.: Securing Sensor Nodes Against Side Channel Attacks. In: Proceedings of the 11th IEEE High Assurance Systems Engineering Symposium (HASE 2008), Nanjing, China, December 2008, pp. 353–361 (2008)

8. Becher, A., Benenson, Z., Dornseif, M.: Tampering with motes: Real-world physical attacks on wireless sensor networks. In: Clark, J.A., Paige, R.F., Polack, F.A.C., Brooke, P.J. (eds.) SPC 2006. LNCS, vol. 3934, pp. 104–118. Springer, Heidelberg (2006)

9. Goodspeed, T.: Wireless Sensor Networks as an Asset and a Liability. In: Proceedings of the SOURCE Conference, Boston, USA (March 2009)

10. Francillon, A., Castelluccia, C.: Code Injection Attacks on Harvard-Architecture Devices. In: Proceedings of the 15th ACM conference on Computer and communications security (CCS 2008), Alexandria, USA, October 2008, pp. 15–26 (2008)

11. Newsome, J., Shi, E., Song, D., Perrig, A.: The Sybil Attack in Sensor Networks: Analysis & Defenses. In: Proceedings of the IEEE 3rd International Workshop on Information Processing in Sensor Networks (IPSN 2004), Berkeley, USA, April 2004, pp. 259–268 (2004)

12. Karlof, C., Wagner, D.: Secure Routing in Wireless Sensor Networks: Attacks and Countermeasure. Ad-Hoc Networks 1(2-3), 293–315 (2003)

13. Manzo, M., Roosta, T., Sastry, S.: Time Synchronization Attacks in Sensor Networks. In: Proceedings of the 3rd ACM Workshop on Security of Ad Hoc and Sensor Networks (SASN 2005), Alexandria, USA, November 2005, pp. 107–116 (2005)

14. Shnayder, V., Hempstead, M., Chen, B., Allen, G.W., Welsh, M.: Simulating the Power Consumption of Large-Scale Sensor Network Applications. In: Proceedings of the 2nd International Conference on Embedded Networked Sensor Systems (SenSys 2004), Baltimore, USA, August 2004, pp. 188–200 (2004)

15. Sabbah, E., Majeed, A., Kang, K.-D., Liu, K., Abu-Ghazaleh, N.: An Application-driven Perspective on Wireless Sensor Network Security. In: Proceedings of the 2nd ACM International Workshop on Quality of Service & Security for Wireless and Mobile Networks, Torremolinos, Spain, pp. 1–8 (2006)

16. Ransom, S., Pfisterer, D., Fischer, S.: Comprehensible Security Synthesis for Wireless Sensor Networks. In: Proceedings of the 3rd international Workshop on Middleware for Sensor Networks, Leuven, Belgium, pp. 19–24 (2008)

17. Roman, R.: Application-driven Security in Wireless Sensor Networks. Ph.D. Thesis, University of Malaga (June 2008)

18. Healy, M., Newe, T., Lewis, E.: Wireless Sensor Node Hardware: A Review. In: Proceedings of IEEE SENSORS 2008, Lecce, Italy, October 2008, pp. 621–624 (2008)

19. Levis, P., Madden, S., Polastre, J., Szewczyk, R., Whitehouse, K., Woo, A., Gay, D., Hill, J., Welsh, M., Brewer, E., Culler, D.: TinyOS: An Operating System for Sensor Networks. In: On Ambient Intelligence. Springer, Heidelberg (2005)

20. Dutta, P., Taneja, J., Jeong, J., Jiang, X., Culler, D.: A Building Block Approach to Sensornet Systems. In: Proceedings of the Sixth ACM Conference on Embedded Networked Sensor Systems (SenSys 2008), Raleigh, USA, November 2008, pp. 267–280 (2008)

21. Seah, W.K.G., Eu, Z.A., Tan, H.-P.: Wireless Sensor Networks Powered by Ambient Energy Harvesting (WSN-HEAP) - Survey and Challenges. In: Proceedings of CTIF Wireless VITAE 2009, Aalborg, Denmark (May 2009)

22. Penella, M.T., Gasulla, M.: A Review of Commercial Energy Harvesters for Autonomous Sensors. In: Proceedings of IEEE Instrumentation and Measurement Technology Conference Proceedings (IMTC 2007), Warsaw, Poland, May 2007, pp. 1–5 (2007)

23. Crossbow Technology, Inc. eKo Pro Precision Agriculture, http://www.xbow.com/eko/ (retrieved on June 2009)

24. Galindo, D., Roman, R., Lopez, J.: A Killer Application for Pairings: Authenticated Key Establishment in Underwater Wireless Sensor Networks. In: Franklin, M.K., Hui, L.C.K., Wong, D.S. (eds.) CANS 2008. LNCS, vol. 5339, pp. 120–132. Springer, Heidelberg (2008)

25. Camtepe, S.A., Yener, B.: Key Management in Wireless Sensor Networks. In: On Wireless Sensor Network Security. IOS Press, Amsterdam (2008)

26. Stajano, F., Cvrcek, D., Lewis, M.: Steel, Cast Iron and Concrete: Security Engineering for Real World Wireless Sensor Networks. In: Bellovin, S.M., Gennaro, R., Keromytis, A.D., Yung, M. (eds.) ACNS 2008. LNCS, vol. 5037, pp. 460–478. Springer, Heidelberg (2008)

27. Alcaraz, C., Roman, R.: Applying Key Infrastructures for Sensor Networks in CIP/CIIP Scenarios. In: López, J. (ed.) CRITIS 2006. LNCS, vol. 4347, pp. 166–178. Springer, Heidelberg (2006)

28. ECRYPT Network of Excellence. eSTREAM, the ECRYPT Stream Cipher Project, http://www.ecrypt.eu.org/stream/ (retrieved on June 2009)

29. European Organization for Nuclear Research (CERN). LHC - The Large Hadron Collider, http://lhc.web.cern.ch (retrieved on June 2009)

30. Culler, D., Estrin, D., Srivastava, M.: Overview of Sensor Networks. IEEE Computer 37(8), 41–49 (2004)

31. Akyildiz, I., Pompili, D., Melodia, T.: Underwater acoustic sensor networks: Research challenges. Ad Hoc Networks Jounal (Elsevier) 3(3), 257–279 (2005)

32. Heidemann, J., Wei, Y., Wills, J., Syed, A., Yuan, L.: Research Challenges and Applications for Underwater Sensor Networking. In: Proceedings of the IEEE Wireless Communications and Networking Conference (WCNC 2006), Las Vegas, USA, April 2006, vol. 1, pp. 228–235 (2006)

33. Akyildiz, I.F., Stuntebeck, E.P.: Wireless Underground Sensor Networks: Research Challenges. Ad Hoc Networks Journal 4(6), 669–686 (2006)

34. Vuran, M.C., Akyildiz, I.F.: Cross-layer Packet Size Optimization for Wireless Terrestrial, Underwater, and Underground Sensor Networks. In: Proceedings of the 27th IEEE Conference on Computer Communications (INFOCOM 2008), Phoenix, USA, April 2008, pp. 226–230 (2008)

35. Hanson, M.A., Powell, H.C., Barth, A.T., Ringgenberg, K., Calhoun, B.H., Aylor, J.H., Lach, J.: Body Area Sensor Networks: Challenges and Opportunities. IEEE Computer 42(1), 58–65 (2009)

36. Ullah, S., Higgin, H., Siddiqui, M.A., Kwak, K.S.: A Study of Implanted and Wearable Body Sensor Networks. In: Nguyen, N.T., Jo, G.-S., Howlett, R.J., Jain, L.C. (eds.) KES-AMSTA 2008. LNCS, vol. 4953, pp. 464–473. Springer, Heidelberg (2008)

37. Akyildiz, I.F., Melodia, T., Chowdhury, K.R.: Wireless multimedia sensor networks: A survey. IEEE Wireless Communications 14(6), 32–39 (2007)

38. Di Pietro, R., Mancini, L.V., Spognardi, A., Soriente, C., Tsudik, G.: Catch Me (If You Can): Data Survival in Unattended Sensor Networks. In: Proceedings of the 6th Annual IEEE International Conference on Pervasive Computing and Communications (PerCom 2008), Hong Kong, China, March 2008, pp. 185–194 (2008)

39. Albano, M., Brogi, A., Popescu, R., Diaz, M., Dianes, J.A.: Towards Secure Middleware for Embedded Peer-to-Peer Systems: Objectives & Requirements. In: Proceedings of the 2nd Workshop on Requirements and Solutions for Pervasive Software Infrastructures (RSPSI 2007), Innsbruck, Austria, September 2007, pp. 1–6 (2007)
40. Roman, R., Alcaraz, C., Sklavos, N.: On the Hardware Implementation Efficiency of Cryptographic Primitives. In: On Wireless Sensor Network Security. IOS Press, Amsterdam, ISBN: 978-1-58603-813-7
41. Didla, S., Ault, A., Bagchi, S.: Optimizing AES for Embedded Devices and Wireless Sensor Networks. In: Proceedings of the 4th International Conference on Testbeds and Research Infrastructures for the Development of Networks & Communities (TRIDENTCOM 2008), Innsbruck, Austria (March 2008)
42. Jun Choi, K., Song, J.-I.: Investigation of Feasible Cryptographic Algorithms for Wireless Sensor Network. In: Proceedings of the 8th International Conference on Advanced Communication Technology (ICACT 2006), Phoenix Park, Korea (February 2006)
43. Mantin, I.: Analysis of the Stream Cipher RC4. Master's Thesis, Weizmann Institute of Science (2001)
44. Meiser, G., Eisenbarth, T., Lemke-Rust, K., Paar, C.: Efficient Implementation of eSTREAM Ciphers on 8-bit AVR Microcontrollers. In: Proceedings of the International Symposium on Industrial Embedded Systems (SIES 2008), Montpellier, France, June 2008, pp. 58–66 (2008)
45. Liu, A., Ning, P.: TinyECC: A Configurable Library for Elliptic Curve Cryptography in Wireless Sensor Networks. In: Proceedings of the 7th International Conference on Information Processing in Sensor Networks (IPSN 2008), SPOTS Track, St. Louis, USA, April 2008, pp. 245–256 (2008)
46. Seo, S.C., Han, D.-G., Kim, H.C., Hong, S.: TinyECCK: Efficient Elliptic Curve Cryptography Implementation over $GF(2^m)$ on 8-bit MICAz Mote. IEICE Transactions on Info and Systems E91-D(5), 1338–1347 (2008)
47. Szczechowiak, P., Kargl, A., Scott, M., Collier, M.: On the Application of Pairing based Cryptography to Wireless Sensor Networks. In: Proceedings of the 2nd ACM conference on Wireless Network Security (WiSec 2009), Zurich, Switzerland, March 2009, pp. 1–12 (2009)
48. Ganesan, P., Venugopalan, R., Peddabachagari, P., Dean, A., Mueller, F., Sichitiu, M.: Analyzing and Modeling Encryption Overhead for Sensor Network Nodes. In: Proceedings of the 2nd ACM International Conference on Wireless Sensor Networks and Applications (WSNA 2003), San Diego, USA, September 2003, pp. 151–159 (2003)
49. Wang, X.: Recent Progress on SHA-1. Rump Session, Crypto 2005 (2005)
50. NIST hash function competition, http://www.nist.gov/hash-competition (retrieved on June 2009)
51. Eschenauer, L., Gligor, V.D.: A Key-management Scheme for Distributed Sensor Networks. In: Proceedings of the 9th ACM conference on Computer and communications security (CCS 2002), Washington, DC, USA, November 2002, pp. 41–47 (2002)
52. Du, W., Deng, J., Han, Y.S., Varshney, P., Katz, J., Khalili, A.: A Pairwise Key Predistribution Scheme for Wireless Sensor Networks. ACM Transactions on Information and System Security (TISSEC) 8(2), 228–258 (2005)
53. Camtepe, S.A., Yener, B.: Combinatorial Design of Key Distribution Mechanisms for Wireless Sensor Networks. IEEE/ACM Transactions on Networking 15(2), 346–358 (2007)

54. Liu, D., Ning, P., Li, R.: Establishing Pairwise Keys in Distributed Sensor Networks. ACM Transactions on Information and System Security 8(1), 41–77 (2005)
55. Anderson, R.J., Chan, H., Perrig, A.: Key Infection: Smart Trust for Smart Dust. In: Proceedings of the 12th IEEE International Conference on Network Protocols (ICNP 2004), Berlin, Germany, October 2004, pp. 206–215 (2004)
56. Seshadri, A., Luk, M., Perrig, A.: SAKE: Software attestation for key establishment in sensor networks. In: Nikoletseas, S.E., Chlebus, B.S., Johnson, D.B., Krishnamachari, B. (eds.) DCOSS 2008. LNCS, vol. 5067, pp. 372–385. Springer, Heidelberg (2008)
57. Panja, B., Madria, S., Bhargava, B.: Energy and Communication Efficient Group Key Management Protocol for Hierarchical Sensor Networks. In: Proceedings of the IEEE International Conference on Sensor Networks, Ubiquitous, and Trustworthy Computing (SUTC 2006), Taichung, Taiwan (June 2006)
58. Acs, G., Buttyan, L.: Secure Routing in Wireless Sensor Networks. In: On Wireless Sensor Network Security. IOS Press, Amsterdam, ISBN: 978-1-58603-813-7
59. Routing Over Low power and Lossy networks (ROLL) Working Group. Internet Engineering Task Force (IETF),
    http://www.ietf.org/html.charters/roll-charter.html (retrieved on June 2009)
60. Alzaid, H., Foo, E., Nieto, J.G.: Secure Data Aggregation in Wireless Sensor Network: a Survey. In: Proceedings of the Australasian Information Security Conference 2008: Conferences in Research and Practice in Information Technology (CRPIT), Wollongong, NSW, Australia, March 2008, pp. 93–105 (2008)
61. Ozdemir, S., Xiao, Y.: Secure data aggregation in wireless sensor networks: A comprehensive overview. Computer Networks (Elsevier) (2009) Article in press, http://dx.doi.org/10.1016/j.comnet.2009.02.023
62. Boukerche, A., Turgut, D.: Secure time synchronization protocols for wireless sensor networks. IEEE Wireless Communications 14(5), 64–69 (2007)
63. Yang, Y., Sun, Y.: Securing Time-synchronization Protocols in Sensor Networks: Attack Detection and Self-healing. In: Proceedings of the IEEE 2008 Global Telecommunications Conference (GLOBECOM 2008), New Orleans, USA, November-December 2008, pp. 1–6 (2008)
64. Ganeriwal, S., Popper, C., Capkun, S., Srivastava, M.B.: Secure Time Synchronization in Sensor Networks. ACM Transactions on Information and System Security (TISSEC) 11(4) (July 2008)
65. Giannetsos, T., Krontiris, I., Dimitriou, T., Freiling, F.C.: Intrusion Detection in Wireless Sensor Networks. In: On Security in RFID and Sensor Networks. Auerbach Publications, CRC Press (2009) ISBN: 978-1420068-399
66. Roman, R., Lopez, J., Gritzalis, S.: Situation Awareness Mechanisms for Wireless Sensor Networks. IEEE Communications Magazine 46(4), 102–107 (2008)
67. Ozturk, C., Zhang, Y., Trappe, W., Ott, M.: Source-Location Privacy for Networks of Energy-Constrained Sensors. In: Proceedings of the 2004 IEEE Workshop on Software Technologies for Future Embedded and Ubiquitous Systems (WSTFEUS 2004), Vienna, Austria (May 2004)
68. Aivaloglou, E., Gritzalis, S., Skianis, C.: Trust establishment in sensor networks: Behaviour-based, certificate-based and a combinational approach. International Journal System of Systems Engineering 1(1/2), 128–148 (2008)
69. Roman, R., Fernandez-Gago, M.C., Lopez, J., Chen, H.-H.: Trust and Reputation Systems for Wireless Sensor Networks. In: On Security and Privacy in Mobile and Wireless Networking. Troubador Publishing Ltd. (2009) ISBN: 978-1905886-906

70. Na, L., Zhang, N., Das, S.K., Thuraisingham, B.: Privacy Preservation in Wireless Sensor Networks: A State-of-the-art Survey. Ad Hoc Networks (Elsevier) (2009) Article in press, http://dx.doi.org/10.1016/j.adhoc.2009.04.009
71. Yasinsac, A.: Remote Attestation - Identification. On Wireless Sensor Network Security. IOS Press, Amsterdam, ISBN: 978-1-58603-813-7
72. Sang, L., Arora, A.: Spatial Signatures for Lightweight Security in Wireless Sensor Networks. In: Proceedings of the 27th IEEE Conference on Computer Communications (INFOCOM 2008), Phoenix, USA, April 2008, pp. 2137–2145 (2008)
73. Danev, B., Capkun, S.: Physical-layer Identification of Wireless Sensor Nodes. Technical Reports 604, ETH Zürich, System Security Group D-INFK (August 2008)
74. Peerenboom, J.P., Fisher, R.E.: Analyzing Cross-Sector Interdependencies. In: Proceedings of the 40th Annual Hawaii International Conference on System Sciences (HICSS 2007), Hawaii, USA, pp. 112–119 (2007)
75. ZigBee Alliance, http://www.zigbee.org/ (retrieved on June 2009)
76. HART Communication, http://www.hartcomm2.org (retrieved on June 2009)
77. ISA100.11a, Wireless Systems for Industrial Automation: Process Control and Related Applications, http://www.isa.org/isa100 (retrieved on June 2009)
78. IEEE Standard, 802.15.4-2006. Wireless medium access control and physical layer specifications for low-rate wireless personal area networks (2006) ISBN 0-7381-4997-7
79. Alcaraz, C., Fernandez, G., Roman, R., Balastegui, A., Lopez, J.: Secure Management of SCADA Networks. New Trends in Network Management, Cepis UP-GRADE 9(6), 22–28 (2008)
80. Modbus-IDA. The Architecture for Distributed Automation, http://www.modbus.org (retrieved on June 2009)
81. DNP3. DNP Users Group, http://www.dnp.org (retrieved on June 2009)
82. IEC 60870-5-104, International Electrotechnical Commission, http://www.iec.ch/ (retrieved on June 2009)
83. PI Profibus - Profinet, http://www.profibus.com (retrieved on June 2009)
84. Fieldbus Foundation, http://www.fieldbus.org (retrieved on June 2009)
85. Montenegro, G., Kushalnagar, N., Hui, J., Culler, D.: RFC 4944: Transmission of IPv6 Packets over IEEE 802.15.4 Networks. Request for Comments (September 2007)
86. International Telecommunication Union. The Internet of Things. ITU Internet Reports (2005)
87. Roman, R., Lopez, J.: Integrating Wireless Sensor Networks and the Internet: A Security Analysis. Internet Research 19(2), 246–259 (2009)

Author Index